Fifth Edition

THE MIND AND HEART OF THE NEGOTIATOR

Leigh L. Thompson
Kellogg School of Management
Northwestern University

PEARSON

Boston Columbus Indianapolis New York San Francisco Upper Saddle River
Amsterdam Cape Town Dubai London Madrid Milan Munich Paris Montréal Toronto
Delhi Mexico City São Paulo Sydney Hong Kong Seoul Singapore Taipei Tokyo

Editorial Director: Sally Yagan
Acquisitions Editor: Brian Mickelson
Director of Editorial Services: Ashley Santora
Editorial Assistant: Carter Anderson
Director of Marketing: Maggie Moylan
Senior Marketing Manager: Nikki Ayana Jones
Marketing Assistant: Ian Gold
Senior Managing Editor: Judy Leale
Supervisor/Sr. Production Project Manager: Lynn Savino Wendel
Senior Operations Supervisor: Arnold Vila
Operations Specialist: Cathleen Petersen
Creative Director: Jayne Conte
Cover Designer: Bruce Kenselaar
Cover Illustration/Photo: Robert Weeks
Full-Service Project Management and Composition: Integra
Printer/Binder: Courier
Cover Printer: Courier
Text Font: 10/12 Times Ten Roman

Library of Congress Cataloging-in-Publication Data

Thompson, Leigh L.
  The mind and heart of the negotiator / Leigh L. Thompson. — 5th ed.
    p. cm.
  ISBN-13: 978-0-13-254386-6
  ISBN-10: 0-13-254386-9
  1. Negotiation in business.   2. Negotiation.   I. Title.
  HD58.6.T478 2012
  658.4′052—dc22

                                        2011014992

10 9 8

ISBN 10:   0-13-254386-9
ISBN 13: 978-0-13-254386-6

To the loves of my life:
Bob, Sam, Ray, and Anna

BRIEF CONTENTS

PART I **Essentials of Negotiation** **1**

Chapter 1 Negotiation: The Mind and The Heart 1
Chapter 2 Preparation: What to Do Before Negotiation 12
Chapter 3 Distributive Negotiation: Slicing the Pie 38
Chapter 4 Win-Win Negotiation: Expanding the Pie 69

PART II **Advanced Negotiation Skills** **92**

Chapter 5 Developing a Negotiating Style 92
Chapter 6 Establishing Trust and Building a Relationship 125
Chapter 7 Power, Persuasion, and Ethics 153
Chapter 8 Creativity and Problem Solving in Negotiations 179

PART III **Applications and Special Scenarios** **215**

Chapter 9 Multiple Parties, Coalitions, and Teams 215
Chapter 10 Cross-Cultural Negotiation 252
Chapter 11 Tacit Negotiations and Social Dilemmas 285
Chapter 12 Negotiating Via Information Technology 312

APPENDICES

Appendix 1 Are You a Rational Person? Check Yourself 329
Appendix 2 Nonverbal Communication and Lie Detection 351
Appendix 3 Third-Party Intervention 361
Appendix 4 Negotiating a Job Offer 370

CONTENTS

Preface   xvii
Overview   xix

Part I   Essentials of Negotiation   1

Chapter 1   NEGOTIATION: THE MIND AND THE HEART   1

Negotiation: Definition and Scope   2

Negotiation as a Core Management Competency   3

Dynamic Nature of Business   3

Interdependence   3

Economic Forces   4

Information Technology   4

Globalization   4

Most People Are Ineffective Negotiators   5

Negotiation Traps   5

Why People Are Ineffective Negotiators   6

Egocentrism   6

Confirmation Bias   6

Satisficing   7

Self-Reinforcing Incompetence   7

Debunking Negotiation Myths   8

Myth 1: Negotiations Are Fixed-Sum   8

Myth 2: You Need to Be Either Tough or Soft   8

Myth 3: Good Negotiators Are Born   8

Myth 4: Life Experience Is a Great Teacher   9

Myth 5: Good Negotiators Take Risks   9

Myth 6: Good Negotiators Rely on Intuition   9

Learning Objectives   10

The Mind and Heart   11

Chapter 2   PREPARATION: WHAT TO DO BEFORE NEGOTIATION   12

Self-Assessment   13

What Do I Want?   14

What Is My Alternative to Reaching Agreement in This Situation?   15

Determine Your Reservation Point   16

Be Aware of Focal Points   19

Beware of Sunk Costs   19

Do Not Confuse the Target Point with Your Reservation Point   19

Identify the Issues in the Negotiation   19

Identify the Alternatives for Each Issue   20

Identify Equivalent Multi-Issue Proposals   20

Assess Your Risk Propensity   20

Endowment Effects   23

Am I Going to Regret This?   24

Violations of the Sure Thing Principle   25

Do I Have an Appropriate Level of Confidence?   26

Sizing Up the Other Party   26

Who Are the Other Parties?   27

Are the Parties Monolithic?   27

Counterparties' Interests and Position   27

Counterparties' BATNAs   27

Situation Assessment   28

Is the Negotiation One Shot, Long Term, or Repetitive?   28

Do the Negotiations Involve Scarce Resources, Ideologies, or Both?   28

Is the Negotiation One of Necessity or Opportunity?   29

Is the Negotiation a Transaction or Dispute Situation?   30

Are Linkage Effects Present?   30

Is Agreement Required?   30

Is It Legal to Negotiate?   31

Is Ratification Required?   32

Are Time Constraints or Other Time-Related Costs Involved?   32

Are Contracts Official or Unofficial?   34

Where Do the Negotiations Take Place?   34

Are Negotiations Public or Private?   34

Is Third-Party Intervention a Possibility?   35

What Conventions Guide the Process of Negotiation (Such as Who Makes the First Offer)?   35

Do Negotiations Involve More Than One Offer?   35

Do Negotiators Communicate Explicitly or Tacitly?   36

Is There a Power Differential Between Parties?   36

Is Precedent Important?   36

Conclusion   36

Chapter 3 DISTRIBUTIVE NEGOTIATION: SLICING THE PIE   38

The Bargaining Zone   39

Bargaining Surplus   41

Negotiator's Surplus   41

Pie-Slicing Strategies   42

Strategy 1: Assess Your BATNA and Improve It   43

Strategy 2: Determine Your Reservation Point, but Do Not Reveal It   43

Strategy 3: Research the Other Party's BATNA and Estimate Their Reservation Point   44

Strategy 4: Set High Aspirations (Be Realistic but Optimistic)   44

Strategy 5: Make the First Offer (If You Are Prepared)   46

Strategy 6: Immediately Reanchor if the Other Party Opens First   47

Strategy 7: Plan Your Concessions   47

Strategy 8: Support Your Offer with Facts   49

Strategy 9: Appeal to Norms of Fairness   49

Strategy 10: Do Not Fall for the "Even Split" Ploy   50

The Most Commonly Asked Questions   50

Should I Reveal My Reservation Point?   50

Should I Lie About My Reservation Point?   50

Should I Try to Manipulate the Counterparty's Reservation Point?   52

Should I Make a "Final Offer" or Commit to a Position?   52

Saving Face   52

The Power of Fairness   53

Multiple Methods of Fair Division   54

Situation-Specific Rules of Fairness   54

Social Comparison   56

The Equity Principle   58

Restoring Equity   59

Procedural Justice   60

Fairness in Relationships   62

Egocentrism   62

Wise Pie-Slicing   66

Consistency   67

Simplicity   67

Effectiveness   67

Justifiability   67

Consensus   67

Generalizability   67

Satisfaction   68

Conclusion   68

Chapter 4   WIN-WIN NEGOTIATION: EXPANDING THE PIE   69

What Is Win-Win Negotiation?   70

Telltale Signs Of Win-Win Potential   70

Does the Negotiation Contain More Than One Issue?   70

Can Other Issues Be Brought In?   71

Can Side Deals Be Made?   71

Do Parties Have Different Preferences Across Negotiation Issues?   71

A Pyramid Model   72

Most Common Pie-Expanding Errors   73

False Conflict   73

Fixed-Pie Perception   74

Strategies That Do Not Really Work   75

Commitment to Reaching a Win-Win Deal   75

Compromise   75

Focusing on a Long-Term Relationship   75

Adopting a Cooperative Orientation   75

Taking Extra Time to Negotiate   75

Effective Pie-Expanding Strategies   76

Perspective-Taking   76

Ask Questions About Interests and Priorities   77

Provide Information About Your Interests and Priorities   79

Unbundle the Issues   81

Make Package Deals, Not Single-Issue Offers   81

Make Multiple Offers of Equivalent Value Simultaneously   82

Structure Contingency Contracts by Capitalizing on Differences   85

Presettlement Settlements (PreSS)   87

Search for Postsettlement Settlements   87

A Strategic Framework for Reaching Integrative Agreements   88

Resource Assessment   88

Assessment of Differences   89

Offers and Trade-Offs   90

Acceptance/Rejection Decision   90

Prolonging Negotiation and Renegotiation   90

Do Not Forget About Claiming   90

Conclusion   91

Part II   Advanced Negotiation Skills   92

Chapter 5   DEVELOPING A NEGOTIATING STYLE   92

Motivational Orientation   94

Assessing Your Motivational Style   95

Strategic Issues Concerning Motivational Style   98

Interests, Rights, and Power Model of Disputing   102

Assessing Your Approach   104

Strategic Issues Concerning Approaches   108

Emotions and Emotional Knowledge   114

Emotions and Moods   114

Expressed Versus Felt Emotion   115

Genuine Versus Strategic Emotion   116

Negative Emotion   118

Emotional Intelligence   119

Positive Emotion   120

Emotional Intelligence and Negotiated Outcomes   121

Strategic Advice for Dealing with Emotions at the Table   122

Conclusion   124

Chapter 6   ESTABLISHING TRUST AND BUILDING A RELATIONSHIP   125

The People Side of Win-Win   126

Trust as the Bedrock of Relationships   128

Three Types of Trust in Relationships   128

Building Trust: Rational and Deliberate Mechanisms   131

Building Trust: Psychological Strategies   134

What Leads to Mistrust?   138

Repairing Broken Trust   139

Reputation   142

Relationships in Negotiation   143

Negotiating with Friends   145

Negotiating with Businesspeople   148

When in Business with Friends and Family   150

Conclusion   151

Chapter 7 POWER, PERSUASION, AND ETHICS   153

Your BATNA Is Your Most Important Source of Power in Negotiation   154

Sources of Power   155

Analyzing Your Power   155

Persuasion Tactics   156

Two Routes to Persuasion   156

Central Route Persuasion Tactics   156

Peripheral Route Persuasion Tactics   160

The Effects of Power on Those Who Hold Power   168

The Effects of Power on Those with Less Power   168

Negotiation Ethics   169

Lying   169

Other Questionable Negotiation Strategies   171

Sins of Omission and Commission   172

Costs of Lying   175

Under What Conditions Do People Engage in Deception?   175

Psychological Bias and Unethical Behavior   175

Conclusion   178

Chapter 8 CREATIVITY AND PROBLEM SOLVING IN NEGOTIATIONS   179

Creativity in Negotiation   180

Test Your Own Creativity   180

What Is Your Mental Model of Negotiation?   180

Haggling   180

Cost-Benefit Analysis   184

Game Playing   184

Partnership   185

Problem Solving   185

Creative Negotiation Agreements   185

Fractionating Problems into Solvable Parts   185

Finding Differences: Issue Alignment and Realignment   186

Expanding the Pie   186

Bridging   187

Cost Cutting   187

Nonspecific Compensation   188

Structuring Contingencies   188

Threats to Effective Problem Solving and Creativity   191

The Inert Knowledge Problem   191

Availability Heuristic   193

Representativeness   194

Anchoring and Adjustment   195

Unwarranted Causation   195

Belief Perseverance   196

Illusory Correlation   196

Just World   197

Hindsight Bias   197

Functional Fixedness   197

Set Effect   198

Selective Attention   199

Overconfidence   199

The Limits of Short-Term Memory   200

Creative Negotiation Strategies   200

Analogical Training   200

Feedback   201

Counter-Factual Reflection   202

Incubation   202

Rational Problem-Solving Model   204

Fluency, Flexibility, and Originality   205

Brainstorming   205

Convergent Versus Divergent Thinking   206

Deductive Reasoning   207

Inductive Reasoning   207

Flow   209

Conclusion   210

Part III Applications and Special Scenarios   215

Chapter 9 MULTIPLE PARTIES, COALITIONS, AND TEAMS   215

Analyzing Multiparty Negotiations   216

Multiparty Negotiations   217

Key Challenges of Multiparty Negotiations   217

Key Strategies for Multiparty Negotiations   224

Coalitions   226

Key Challenges of Coalitions   226

Strategies for Maximizing Coalitional Effectiveness   231

Principal-Agent Negotiations   231

Disadvantages of Agents   233

Strategies for Working Effectively with Agents   235

Constituent Relationships   236

Challenges for Constituent Relationships   237

Strategies for Improving Constituent Relationships   239

Team Negotiation   240

Challenges That Face Negotiating Teams   241

Strategies for Improving Team Negotiations   242

Intergroup Negotiation   244

Challenges of Intergroup Negotiations   244

Strategies for Optimizing Intergroup Negotiations   246

Conclusion   249

Chapter 10   CROSS-CULTURAL NEGOTIATION   252

Learning About Cultures   253

Defining Culture   253

Culture as an Iceberg   254

Cultural Values and Negotiation Norms   255

Individualism Versus Collectivism   256

Egalitarianism Versus Hierarchy   265

Direct Versus Indirect Communications   268

Key Challenges of Intercultural Negotiation   271

Expanding the Pie   271

Dividing the Pie   271

Sacred Values and Taboo Trade-Offs   272

Biased Punctuation of Conflict   274

Ethnocentrism   275

Affiliation Bias   275

Faulty Perceptions of Conciliation and Coercion   276

Naïve Realism   277

Predictors of Success in Intercultural Interactions   278

Advice for Cross-Cultural Negotiations   279

Anticipate Differences in Strategy and Tactics That May Cause Misunderstandings   280

Analyze Cultural Differences to Identify Differences in Values That Expand the Pie   280

Recognize That the Other Party May Not Share Your View of What Constitutes Power   280

Avoid Attribution Errors   280

Find Out How to Show Respect in the Other Culture   281

Find Out How Time Is Perceived in the Other Culture   282

Know Your Options for Change   282

Conclusion   283

Chapter 11 TACIT NEGOTIATIONS AND SOCIAL DILEMMAS   285

Business as a Social Dilemma   287

The Prisoner's Dilemma   287

Cooperation and Defection as Unilateral Choices   288

Rational Analysis   289

Psychological Analysis of Why Tit-for-Tat Is Effective   291

Social Dilemmas   295

The Tragedy of the Commons   297

Types of Social Dilemmas   298

How to Build Cooperation in Social Dilemmas   301

How to Encourage Cooperation in Social Dilemmas When Parties Should Not Collude   307

Escalation of Commitment   308

Avoiding the Escalation of Commitment in Negotiations   310

Conclusion   311

Chapter 12 NEGOTIATING VIA INFORMATION TECHNOLOGY   312

Place-Time Model of Social Interaction   313

Face-to-Face Communication   314

Same Time, Different Place   316

Different Time, Same Place   317

Different Place, Different Time   317

Information Technology and Its Effects on Social Behavior   322

Trust   322

Status and Power: The "Weak Get Strong" Effect   322

Social Networks   324

Risk Taking   324

Rapport and Social Norms   325

Paranoia   325

Strategies for Enhancing Technology-Mediated Negotiations   326

Initial Face-to-Face Experience   326

One-Day Videoconference/Teleconference   327

Schmoozing   327

Humor   328

Conclusion   328

Appendix 1 ARE YOU A RATIONAL PERSON? CHECK YOURSELF   329

Why Is It Important to Be Rational?   329

Individual Decision Making   330

Riskless Choice   330

Decision Making Under Uncertainty   332

Risky Choice   332

Summing Up: Individual Decision Making   345

Game Theoretic Rationality   345

Nash Bargaining Theory   346

Appendix 2 NONVERBAL COMMUNICATION AND LIE DETECTION   351

What Are We Looking for in Nonverbal Communication?   351

Are Women More "Nonverbally Gifted" Than Men?   352

Dominance   353

Personal Charisma   354

Detecting Deception   355

Direct Methods   357

Indirect Methods   357

How Motivation and Temptation Affect Lying and Deception   359

Deception and Secrecy Can Create a Life of Their Own   360

Appendix 3 THIRD-PARTY INTERVENTION   361

Common Third-Party Roles   361

Mediation   361

Arbitration   362

Mediation-Arbitration   363

Arbitration-Mediation   363

Key Choice Points in Third-Party Intervention   **363**

Outcome Versus Process Control   363

Formal Versus Informal   364

Invited Versus Uninvited   364

Interpersonal Versus Intergroup   364

Content Versus Process Orientation   364

Facilitation, Formulation, or Manipulation   364

Disputant Preferences   365

Mediators and Gender   365

Challenges Facing Third Parties   **365**

Meeting Disputants' Expectations   365

Increasing the Likelihood That Parties Reach an Agreement
if a Positive Bargaining Zone Exists   366

Promoting a Pareto-Efficient Outcome   366

Promoting Outcomes That Are Perceived as Fair in the Eyes of
Disputants   366

Improving the Relationship Between Parties   366

Empowering Parties in the Negotiation Process   366

Debiasing Negotiators   367

Maintaining Neutrality   368

Strategies for Enhancing Effectiveness of Third-Party Intervention   **369**

Accept Your Share of Responsibility   369

Test Your Own Position   369

Role-Play a Third Party in Your Own Dispute   369

Training in Win-Win Negotiation   369

Appendix 4   NEGOTIATING A JOB OFFER   370

Preparation   370

Step 1: Figure Out What You Really Want   370

Step 2: Do Your Homework   370

Step 3: Determine Your BATNA and Your Aspiration
Point   370

Step 4: Research the Employer's BATNA   372

Step 5: Determine the Issue Mix   372

Step 6: Prepare Several Scenarios   372

Step 7: Consider Getting a "Coach"   372

In Vivo: During the Negotiation Itself   373

Think About the Best Way to Position and Present Your Opening
Offer   373

Assume the Offer Is Negotiable   373

Immediately Reanchor the Interviewer by Reviewing Your Needs and Your Rationale   374

Reveal Neither Your BATNA nor Your Reservation Point   375

Rehearse and Practice   375

Imagine You Are Negotiating on Behalf of Someone Else (Not Just Yourself)   375

Comparables and Benchmarks   376

Post-Offer: You Have the Offer, Now What?   376

Do Not Immediately Agree to the Offer   376

Get the Offer in Writing   376

Be Enthusiastic and Gracious   377

Assess the Interviewer's Power to Negotiate with You   377

State Exactly What Needs to Be Done for You to Agree   377

Do Not Negotiate If You Are Not or Could Not Be Interested   377

Exploding Offers   377

Do Not Try to Create a Bidding War   378

Know When to Stop Pushing   378

Use a Rational Strategy for Choosing Among Job Offers   378

Name Index   379

Subject Index   397

Note: Every effort has been made to provide accurate and current Internet information in this book. However, the Internet and information posted on it are constantly changing, so it is inevitable that some of the Internet addresses listed in this textbook will change.

PREFACE

This book is dedicated to negotiators who want to improve their ability to negotiate—whether in multimillion-dollar business deals or personal interactions. It is possible for most people to dramatically improve their ability to negotiate. You can improve your monetary returns and feel better about yourself and the people with whom you deal. New to this edition is an integration of theory, scientific research, and practical examples. Moreover, the practical examples—selected from hundreds of real-world negotiations involving people from several organizations and many different cultures—illustrate effective, as well as ineffective, negotiation skills.

Here is what you can expect when you read this book:

- *Illustrative case studies.* I include multiple examples and actual cases of negotiating in managerial and executive contexts. Each chapter opens with a case study or actual business situation (from business, government, world affairs, community, and personal life). New to this edition, are more than 122 updated examples from the business world.
- *Real-life negotiations.* Furthermore, many of the points in the chapters are supplemented with illustrations and examples drawn from actual negotiations, both contemporary and historical. I do not use these examples to *prove* a theory; rather, I use them to *illustrate* how many of the concepts in the book are borne out in real-world situations. New to this edition are updated opening chapter vignettes derived from current business, political, and global events that illustrate real world negotiations.
- *Skills-based approach.* In this edition I provide practical take-away points for the manager and the executive. A good example is Chapter 4 on integrative negotiation. A series of hands-on principles that have been proven to increase the value of negotiated deals is provided.
- *Self-insight.* I include several ways that negotiators can test their own intuition and approach. For example, Chapter 5 gives negotiators an opportunity to assess their "instinctive" bargaining style and provides suggestions for how to further develop their bargaining repertoire. Moreover, Chapter 10 provides a deep look at cultural differences in negotiation so that the negotiator can better understand his or her own cultural style and that of others.
- *Advanced bargaining skills.* The second and third sections of the book deal with complex yet commonly occurring negotiating situations, such as negotiating with agents, mediation and arbitration, negotiating via e-mail and conference calls, negotiating with competitor companies, and, of course, negotiating cross-culturally. These sections have been revised in this edition.
- *Scientific Research.* New to this edition are the groundbreaking results of more than 100 new scientific articles on negotiation.

I benefit greatly from the advice, comments, and critiques given to me by my students and colleagues, and I hope their advice keeps coming so that I am able to improve upon the book even further. The research and ideas in this book come from an invaluable set of scholars in the fields of social psychology, organizational behavior, sociology, negotiation, and cognitive psychology. My research, thinking, and writing have been inspired in important ways by the following people: Wendi Adair, Cameron Anderson, Evan Apfelbaum, Linda Babcock, Chris Bauman, Max Bazerman, Kristin Behfar, Terry Boles, Jeanne Brett, Susan Brodt, Karen Cates, Hoon-Seok Choi,

Taya Cohen, Susan Crotty, Jeanne Egmon, Hal Ersner-Hershfield, Gary Fine, Craig Fox, Adam Galinsky, Wendi Gardner, Dedre Gentner, Robert Gibbons, Kevin Gibson, James Gillespie, Rich Gonzalez, Deborah Gruenfeld, Reid Hastie, Andy Hoffman, Elizabeth Howard, Peter Kim, Shirli Kopelman, Rod Kramer, Laura Kray, Terri Kurtzburg, Geoffrey Leonardelli, John Levine, Allan Lind, George Loewenstein, Jeff Loewenstein, Brian Lucas, Deepak Malhotra, Beta Mannix, Kathleen McGinn, Vicki Medvec, Tanya Menon, Dave Messick, Terry Mitchell, Don Moore, Michael Morris, Keith Murnighan, Janice Nadler, Maggie Neale, Kathy Phillips, Robin Pinkley, Erika Richardson, Ashleigh Rosette, Nancy Rothbard, Edward Smith, Marwan Sinaceur, Harris Sondak, Roderick Swaab, Tom Tyler, Leaf Van Boven, Kimberly Wade-Benzoni, Laurie Weingart, and Judith White. Throughout the text of *The Mind and Heart of the Negotiator,* I use the pronoun "we" because so much of my thinking has been influenced and shaped by this set of eminent scholars.

The revision of this book would not have been possible without the dedication, organization, and editorial skills of Joel Erickson, Larissa Tripp, and Neerali Shah, who created the layout, organized hundreds of drafts, mastered the figures, and researched many case studies for this book.

In this book, I talk about the "power of the situation" and how strongly the environment shapes our behavior. The Kellogg School of Management is one of the most supportive, dynamic environments I have ever had the pleasure to be a part of. In particular, Dean Sally Blount strongly supports research, teaching, and intellectual leadership as well as pedagogical leadership. I am particularly indebted to my wonderful visionary colleague, Jeanne Brett, who created the Dispute Resolution Research Center (DRRC) at Kellogg in 1986, and to the Hewlett Foundation for their generous support of the DRRC.

This book is very much a team effort of the people I have mentioned here, whose talents are diverse, broad, and extraordinarily impressive. I am deeply indebted to my colleagues and my students, and I feel grateful that they have touched my life and this book.

OVERVIEW

This book is divided into three major sections. The first section deals with the essentials of negotiation—the key principles and groundwork for effective negotiation. Chapter 2 leads the manager through effective preparation strategies for negotiation. Chapter 3 discusses distributive negotiation skills, or how to optimally allocate resources in ways that are favorable to one's self—a process called "slicing the pie." Chapter 4 is the integral chapter of the book; it focuses on "win-win" negotiation or, more formally, integrative negotiation. This creative part of negotiation involves expanding the pie of resources in ways that provide more gains to go around.

The second section of the book deals with advanced and expert negotiation skills. Chapter 5 focuses on assessing and developing your negotiation style. This chapter invites readers to honestly appraise their own negotiation style in terms of three dimensions: motivation, approach, and emotion. The negotiator can accurately assess his or her own style and its limitations and learn to assess the styles adopted by other negotiators. Chapter 6 focuses on establishing trust and building relationships. This chapter examines business and personal relationships and how trust is developed, broken, and repaired. Chapter 7 discusses power, persuasion, and influence tactics. This chapter looks at the topic of persuasion and influence as it occurs across the bargaining table and also deals with the important issue of ethics in negotiation. In Chapter 8, the focus is on problem solving and creativity. This chapter provides strategies for learning how to think out of the box and provides techniques for using creativity and imagination in negotiation.

The third section deals with special scenarios in negotiation. Chapter 9 examines the complexities of negotiating with multiple parties, such as conflicting incentives, coalitions, voting rules, and how to leverage one's own bargaining position when negotiating with multiple parties. Chapter 10 focuses on cross-cultural negotiation, which addresses the key cultural values and negotiation norms across a variety of nationalities, along with some advice for cross-cultural negotiations. Chapter 11 deals with dilemmas, or situations in which negotiators make choices in a mixed-motive context, where cooperation involves building trust with the other party and competition involves an attempt to increase one's own share of resources. This chapter examines the nature of social dilemmas and how to negotiate successfully within various types of dilemmas. Chapter 12 focuses on information technology and its impact on negotiation and uses a place-time model of social interaction to examine the challenges and opportunities of negotiation as it occurs in this technological age.

Four appendices provide a variety of additional material: Appendix 1 invites readers to examine the rationality of their negotiation beliefs and preferences; Appendix 2 provides a short course on lie detection and nonverbal communication; Appendix 3 reviews the essentials of third-party intervention; and Appendix 4 provides tips and a checklist for negotiating a job offer.

FACULTY RESOURCES

Instructor Resource Center

At http://www.pearsonhighered.com/educator, instructors can access a variety of print, media, and presentation resources available with this text in downloadable, digital format.

Once you register, you will not have additional forms to fill out, or multiple usernames and passwords to remember to access new titles and/or editions. As a registered faculty member, you can log in directly to download resource files, and receive immediate access and instructions for installing Course Management content to your campus server.

Our dedicated Technical Support team is ready to assist instructors with questions about the media supplements that accompany this text. Visit http://247pearsoned.custhelp.com for answers to frequently asked questions and toll-free user support phone numbers.

To download the supplements available with this text, including an Instructor's Manual, Power Point presentation, and Test Item File, please visit http://www.pearsonhighered.com/educator.

ABOUT THE AUTHOR

Leigh L. Thompson joined the Kellogg School of Management in 1995. She is the J. Jay Gerber Distinguished Professor of Dispute Resolution and Organizations. She directs the Leading High Impact Teams executive program and the Kellogg Team and Group Research Center and co-directs the Negotiation Strategies for Managers program. An active scholar and researcher, she has published over 100 research articles and chapters and has authored 10 books, including: *Making the Team* (4th edition), *Creativity in Organizations, Shared Knowledge in Organizations, Negotiation: Theory and Research, The Social Psychology of Organizational Behavior: Essential Reading, Organizational Behavior Today, The Truth about Negotiation*, and *Conflict in Organizational Teams*. Thompson has worked with private and public organizations in the United States, Latin America, Canada, Europe, and the Middle East. Her teaching style combines experiential learning with theory-driven best practices. For more information about Leigh Thompson's teaching and research, please visit leighthompson.com.

Part I: Essentials of Negotiation

C H A P T E R

1

Negotiation: The Mind and the Heart

The deal was dead. Most people could not imagine turning down a multibillion-dollar acquisition offer. However, that is exactly what Chicago-based Groupon Inc. did in late 2010. Google had offered Groupon $6 billion. Venture capitalist, Paul Kedrosky, bemoaned, "I would have taken that $6 billion in a heartbeat. I would have been knocking over random strangers to accept it." Google's interest in Groupon was to tap into Groupon's massive human network of sales employees and their relationships with small businesses. What was Groupon's best alternative to accepting the Google offer? Well, Groupon had many potential suitors, including Yahoo!, who previously offered $3 billion, and Groupon confidently believed that it still had lots of room to grow (at the time, Groupon did roughly $2 billion in sales and kept half, making $1 billion in revenue). However, the rejection of Google's offer came at the risk of Groupon's venture bankers. Accel Partners, Battery Ventures, Digital Sky Technologies, and New Enterprise Associations had invested a combined $169.8 million in Groupon. What was Google's best alternative to a negotiated agreement with Groupon? Either try to buy something or make it themselves. In this sense, by turning down Google's offer, Groupon set the stage for the creation of another competitor in their marketplace. According to some business analysts, Groupon created a monster: *"I hope they realize that they could have had $6 billion or decide to do battle with a Goliath of the internet world…"* Others speculated that Groupon could defend its turf and further lodge its brand in consumer minds and even add another zero to their Miracle-Gro valuation.[1]

---

[1] Groupon turns down Google: What just happened here? (2010, December 4). *Seeking Alpha.* Seekingalpha.com; Stone, B., & MacMillan, D. (2010, December 12–19). Groupon's $6 Billion snub. *Bloomberg Businessweek*, p. 6–7.

Negotiations like the one between Google and Groupon often involve a complex mix of strategy, signaling, and of course, the personalities of the negotiators. Whereas most of us are not negotiating giant corporate deals, one thing that business scholars and business-people are in complete agreement on is that everyone negotiates nearly every day. *Getting to Yes* begins by stating, "Like it or not, you are a negotiator…. Everyone negotiates something every day."[2] Similarly, Lax and Sebenius, in *The Manager as Negotiator,* state that "Negotiating is a way of life for managers…when managers deal with their superiors, boards of directors, even legisla-tors."[3] G. Richard Shell, who wrote *Bargaining for Advantage,* asserts, "All of us negotiate many times a day."[4] Herb Cohen, author of *You Can Negotiate Anything,* dramatically suggests that "your world is a giant negotiation table." One business article on negotiation warns, "However much you think negotiation is part of your life, you're underestimating."[5]

Negotiation is your key communication and influence tool inside and outside the company. Anytime you cannot achieve your objectives (whether an acquisition or a dinner date) without the cooperation of others, you are negotiating. We provide dramatic (and disturbing) evidence in this chapter that most people do not live up to their negotiating potential. The good news is that you can do something about it.

The sole purpose of this book is to improve your ability to negotiate. We do this through an integration of scientific studies of negotiation and real business cases. And, in case you are wondering, it is not all common sense. Science drives the best practices covered in this book. We focus on business negotiations, and understanding business negotiations helps people to be more effective negotiators in their personal lives.[6]

In this book, we focus on three major negotiation skills: (a) creating value, (b) claiming value, and (c) building trust. By the end of this book, you will have a mind-set or mental model[7] that will allow you to know what to do and say in virtually every negotiation situation. You can prepare effectively for negotiations and enjoy the peace of mind that comes from having a game plan. Things may not always go according to plan, but your mental model will allow you to perform effectively and most important, to learn from your experiences. Indeed, people who view negotiation as a challenge are more successful in reaching high-quality deals than people who view negotiation as threatening.[8]

NEGOTIATION: DEFINITION AND SCOPE

Negotiation is an interpersonal decision-making process necessary whenever we cannot achieve our objectives single-handedly. Negotiations include one-on-one business meetings, but also multiparty, multicompany, and multinational relationships. Whether simple or complex, negotiations boil down to people, communication, and influence. Even the most complex of business deals can be analyzed as a system of one-on-one relationships.

---

[2] Fisher, R., & Ury, W. (1981). *Getting to yes* (p. xviii). Boston: Houghton Mifflin.
[3] Lax, D. A., & Sebenius, J. K. (1986). *The manager as negotiator* (p. 6). New York: Free Press.
[4] Shell, G. R. (1999). *Bargaining for advantage: Negotiation strategies for reasonable people* (p. 76). New York: Viking.
[5] Walker, R. (2003, August). Take it or leave it: The only guide to negotiating you will ever need. *Inc., 25*(8) 75–82.
[6] Gentner, D., Loewenstein, J., & Thompson, L. (2003). Learning and transfer: A general role for analogical encoding. *Journal of Educational Psychology, 95*(2), 393–408.
[7] Van Boven, L., & Thompson, L. (2003). A look into the mind of the negotiator: Mental models in negotiation. *Group Processes & Intergroup Relations, 6*(4), 387–404.
[8] O'Connor, K. M., Arnold, J. A., & Maurizio, A. M., (2010). The prospect of negotiating: Stress, cognitive appraisal and performance. *Journal of Experimental Social Psychology, 46*(5), 729–735.

People negotiate in their personal life (e.g., with their spouses, children, schoolteachers, neighbors), as well as in their business life. Thus, the scope of negotiation ranges from one-on-one to highly complex multiparty and multinational deals. In the business world, people negotiate on multiple levels: within departmental or business units, between departments, between companies, and even across industries. For this reason, managers must understand enough about negotiations to be effective negotiating within, between, up, and across all of these organizational environments.[9]

NEGOTIATION AS A CORE MANAGEMENT COMPETENCY

Negotiation skills are increasingly important for managers. Key reasons for the importance of negotiation skills include (a) the dynamic nature of business, (b) interdependence, (c) economic forces, (d) information technology, and (e) globalization.

Dynamic Nature of Business

Most people do not stay in the same job that they take upon graduating from college or receiving their MBA degree. Sixty percent of younger workers said it is not very likely or not likely at all that they will stay with their current employers for the remainder of their working life; 6 in 10 employed Millennials reported switching careers at least once; 40% expect to stay at their current position for 2 years or less.[10] The dynamic, changing nature of business means that people must renegotiate their existence in organizations throughout their careers. The advent of decentralized business structures and the absence of hierarchical decision making provide opportunities for managers, but they also pose some daunting challenges. People must continually create possibilities, integrate their interests with others, and recognize the inevitability of competition both within and between companies. Managers must be in a near-constant mode of negotiating opportunities. Negotiation comes into play when people participate in important meetings, get new assignments, lead a team, participate in a reorganization process, and set priorities for their work unit. Negotiation should be second nature to the business manager, but often it is not.

Interdependence

The increasing interdependence of people within organizations, both laterally and hierarchically, implies that people need to know how to integrate their interests and work across business units and functional areas. In November of 2010, a long and winding negotiation stretching back more than three decades was resolved when the Beatles and Apple Computer reached a deal that put the entire Beatles catalogue of albums and singles on the iTunes music site. Apple Computer and the Beatles had been fighting on and off since 1978, when the Beatles accused Apple of infringing on the trademark of their Apple Records. While that dispute was settled when the Beatles licensed the Apple name to the computer company, they fought through the years over Apple's music synthesizer and iTunes' apple logo. Apple owned 90% of the online music market, but lacked the Beatles, one of the few bands that had managed to consistently draw huge profits from CD sales after the online digital music revolution. In 2007, the Beatles hired Jeff Jones as the chief executive of their Apple Corps. Unlike his predecessor who was a childhood friend of Paul

---

[9] Thompson, L., Wang, J., & Gunia, B. C. (2010). Negotiation. *Annual Review of Psychology, 61*(1), 491–515.
[10] Thurman, R. (2010, July 21). 36 facts about generation Y in the workplace & beyond. *Brazen Careerist.* Brazencareerist.com

McCartney and George Harrison, Jones—an American executive with Sony/BMG—had no such sentimental ties. The nature of their relationship was purely business and defined a new era of deal-making for the company. Once the deal was struck, the previously competitive relationship changed to a cooperative one. In their first week on iTunes, over 2 million Beatles songs were purchased.[11]

The increasing degree of specialization and expertise in the business world indicates that people are more and more dependent on others. However, others do not always have similar incentive structures, so managers must know how to promote their own interests while simultaneously creating joint value for their organizations. This balance of cooperation and competition requires negotiation.

Economic Forces

The unemployment rate in January 2011 was 9.0%, with about 13.9 million persons unemployed.[12] That was down slightly from the 15.3 million unemployed in November of 2009, the highest number of unemployed Americans since the Bureau of Labor Statistics began tracking the nation's unemployment in 1948.[13] Economic pressures and forces such as these mean that negotiators need to know how to operate in uncertain and ambiguous environments. Focusing on minimizing losses may loom larger than focusing on profits.

Information Technology

Information technology also provides special opportunities and challenges for negotiators. Information technology has created a culture of 24/7 availability. With technology that makes it possible to communicate with people anywhere in the world, managers are expected to negotiate at a moment's notice. Computer technology, for example, extends a company's obligations and capacity to add value to its customers. Among elected officials, staff members, and other in the United States House of Representatives there were 9,140 Blackberry users in 2010. It has become not only necessary, but vital, for elected representatives and staff members to be connected at all times to constituents, fellow representatives, and business partners.[14]

Globalization

Most managers must effectively cross cultural boundaries to do their jobs. Setting aside obvious language and currency issues, globalization presents challenges in terms of different norms of communication. For example, InfoPrint, a combination of IBM's printing systems division with the huge Japanese company Ricoh, requires a great deal of cross-cultural adaptability. For Sandra Zoratti, the head of global solutions at InfoPrint, it's often been a learning experience. From the start, she found Japanese executives very subdued. "I'm Italian, so I talk with my hands and get enthused about what I'm saying. Once, when I gave a presentation in my usual

---

[11] Moore, H. (2010, November 16). Apple and the Beatles: A long and winding road. *New York Times.* Nytimes.com
[12] United States Department of Labor Bureau of Labor Statistics. (2011, January). *The Employment Situation.* Bls.gov/news
[13] United States Department of Labor, Bureau of Labor Statistics. (2011). *Employment status of the civilian population by sex and age.* Bls.gov
[14] Rosenwald, M. S. (2010, June 20). iPhone insurgency stirs where Blackberry rules. *The Washington Post*, p. A01.

style, it got so little response from my audience that I really thought I blew it," she said. "But two weeks later, they gave my proposal the go-ahead. It turned out they did get what I was saying; they just didn't show it at the time." The two companies hold cultural training for all employees. That includes an interactive blog called Culture Jam, where employees from both companies can ask questions and receive feedback.[15] Managers need to develop negotiation skills that can be successfully employed with people of different nationalities, backgrounds, and personalities. Consequently, negotiators who have developed a bargaining style that works only within a narrow subset of the business world will suffer unless they can broaden their negotiation skills to effectively work with different people across functional units, industries, and cultures.[16] It is a challenge to develop negotiation skills general enough to be used across different contexts, groups, and continents but specialized enough to provide meaningful behavioral strategies in a given situation.

MOST PEOPLE ARE INEFFECTIVE NEGOTIATORS

On the question of whether people are effective negotiators, managers and scholars often disagree. Many people regard themselves to be effective at negotiation. However, these same people believe most of their colleagues are distinctly ineffective at the negotiation table. Most people often fall extremely short of their potential at the negotiation table, judging from their performance in realistic business negotiation simulations.[17] Numerous business executives describe their negotiations as win-win only to discover that they left hundreds of thousands of dollars on the table. Fewer than 4% of managers reach win-win outcomes when put to the test,[18] and the incidence of outright lose-lose outcomes is 20%.[19] Even on issues on which negotiators are in perfect agreement, they fail to realize it 50% of the time.[20] Moreover, we make the point several times throughout this book that effective negotiation is not just about money—it is equally about relationships and trust.

NEGOTIATION TRAPS

In our research, we have observed and documented four major shortcomings in negotiation:

1. *Leaving money on the table* (also known as "lose-lose" negotiation) occurs when negotiators fail to recognize and capitalize on their win-win potential.
2. *Settling for too little* (also known as "the winner's curse") occurs when negotiators make too-large concessions, resulting in a too-small share of the bargaining pie.
3. *Walking away from the table* occurs when negotiators reject terms offered by the other party that are demonstrably better than any other option available to them. (Sometimes this shortcoming is traceable to hubris or pride; other times it results from gross miscalculation.)

[15] Fisher, A. (2009, November 16). Flourishing in a merger of two cultures. *Crain's New York Business*, p. 35.
[16] Bazerman, M. H., & Neale, M. A. (1992). *Negotiating rationally*. New York: Free Press.
[17] Neale, M. A., & Bazerman, M. H. (1991). *Cognition and rationality in negotiation*. New York: Free Press; Thompson, L., & Hrebec, D. (1996). Lose-lose agreements in interdependent decision making. *Psychological Bulletin, 120*(3), 396–409; Loewenstein, J., Thompson, L., & Gentner, D. (2003). Analogical learning in negotiation teams: Comparing cases promotes learning and transfer. *Academy of Management Learning and Education, 2*(2), 119–127.
[18] Nadler, J., Thompson, L., & van Boven, L. (2003). Learning negotiation skills: Four models of knowledge creation and transfer. *Management Science, 49*(4), 529–540.
[19] Thompson & Hrebec, "Lose-lose agreements."
[20] Ibid.

4. *Settling for terms that are worse than your best alternative* (also known as the "agreement bias") occurs when negotiators feel obligated to reach agreement even when the settlement terms are not as good as their other alternatives.

This book teaches you how to avoid these errors, create value in negotiation, get your share of the bargaining pie, reach agreement when it is profitable to do so, and quickly recognize when agreement is not a viable option in a negotiation.

WHY PEOPLE ARE INEFFECTIVE NEGOTIATORS

The dramatic instances of lose-lose outcomes, the winner's curse, walking away from the table, and the agreement bias raise the question of why people are not more effective at the bargaining table. Because negotiation is so important for personal and business success, it is rather surprising that most people do not negotiate very well. Stated starkly, it just does not make sense that people would be so poor at a skill that is so important for their personal and business life. The reason is not due to a lack of motivation or intelligence on the part of negotiators. The problem is rooted in four fundamental biases: egocentrism, confirmatory information processing, satisficing, and self-reinforcing incompetence.

Egocentrism

Egocentrism is the tendency for people to view their experiences in a way that is flattering or fulfilling for them. Two-thirds of MBA students rank their decision-making abilities as above average.[21] In one investigation, people who were self-absorbed in terms of reflecting upon their own values were more likely to exhibit decision-making biases, such as the confirmation bias. In contrast, people who had taken time to focus on values that were not important to them were more likely to focus on valid threats and assess correlations more accurately in data.[22] The National Safety Council estimates that 1 in 4 crashes on the highway involve cell phone use—either dialing, talking or texting—and as many as 10,000 deaths can be attributed to one of the activities. Yet, drivers overestimate their own abilities to multitask. According to David Strayer, the director of the University of Utah Applied Cognition Lab, "We have a tendency to overrate our own abilities. We think we are better than average drivers and we think we are better than average multi-taskers."[23]

Confirmation Bias

Confirmation bias is the tendency of people to see what they want to see when appraising their own performance. The confirmation bias leads individuals to selectively seek information that confirms what they believe is true. Whereas the confirmation bias may seem perfectly harmless, it results in a myopic view of reality and can hinder learning. Three weeks into the 2010 BP Deepwater Horizon oil disaster, the former chief executive of BP, Tony Hayward, downplayed the looming environmental disaster despite mounting evidence to the contrary. Hayward claimed the

---

[21] Diekmann, K., & Galinsky, A. (2006). Overconfident, underprepared: Why you may not be ready to negotiate. *Negotiation, 7,* 6–9.

[22] Munro, G. D., & Stanbury, J. A. (2009). The dark side of self-affirmation: Confirmation bias and illusory correlation in response to threatening information. *Personality and Social Psychology Bulletin, 35*(9), 1143–1153.

[23] Walter, L. (2010, June 1). Why we need to hang up on our distracted driving addiction. *EHS Today.* Ehstoday.com

spill in Gulf of Mexico was "relatively tiny" compared with the "very big ocean." Oil continued to leak at a rapid rate for nearly two months until the well was finally capped, and the total amount of oil poured into the Gulf surpassed the 1989 Exxon Valdez disaster as the largest spill in US history.[24]

Satisficing

A third reason why people often fall short in negotiation is the human tendency to satisfice.[25] According to Nobel Laureate Herb Simon, **satisficing** is the opposite of **optimizing**. In a negotiation situation, it is important to optimize one's strategies by setting high aspirations and attempting to achieve as much as possible; in contrast, when people satisfice, they settle for something less than they could otherwise have. Over the long run, satisficing (or the acceptance of mediocrity) can be detrimental to both individuals and companies, especially when a variety of effective negotiation strategies and skills can be cheaply employed to dramatically increase profit. (We discuss these strategies in detail in the next three chapters.)

Self-Reinforcing Incompetence

To achieve and maintain effectiveness in the business world, people must have insight into their limitations. The same is true for negotiation. However, most people are "blissfully unaware of their own incompetence."[26] Moreover, it creates a cycle in which the lack of skill deprives them not only of the ability to produce correct responses but also of the expertise necessary to surmise that they are not producing them. As a case in point, Dunning and colleagues examined the question of whether students taking a test had insight into their performance.[27] The students were grouped into quartiles based on their performance. The lowest-performing quartile greatly overestimated their performance on the test. Even though they were actually in the 12th percentile, they estimated themselves to be in the 60th percentile.[28] This example is not an isolated case, according to Dunning. People overestimate their percentile ranking relative to others by as much as 40 to 50 points. A study of CEOs' merger and acquisition decisions revealed that CEOs develop overconfidence through a self-attribution bias when making deals. CEOs overly attribute their influence when deals are successful. This leads CEOs to make more deals that are not successful.[29] A better business plan would involve judging each deal on its own merits, rather than simply using the past to justify the present decision. Moreover, the problem cannot be attributed to a lack of incentives. The overestimation pattern even appears after people are promised significant financial rewards for accurate assessments of their performance.[30]

---

[24] Webb, T. (2010, May 14). BP boss admits job on the line over Gulf oil spill. *The Guardian,* p.1.

[25] Simon, H. A. (1955). A behavioral model of rational choice. *Quarterly Journal of Economics, 69,* 99–118.

[26] Dunning, D., Johnson, K., Ehrlinger, J., & Kruger, J. (2003).Why people fail to recognize their own incompetence. *Current Directions in Psychological Science, 12*(3), 83–87.

[27] Kruger, J., & Dunning, D. (1999). Unskilled and unaware of it: How difficulties in recognizing one's own incompetence lead to inflated self-assessments. *Journal of Personality and Social Psychology, 77*(6), 1121–1134.

[28] Ehrlinger, J., Johnson, K., Banner, M., Dunning, D., & Kruger, J. (2008). Why the unskilled are unaware: Further explorations of (absent) self-insight among the incompetent. *Organizational Behavior and Human Decision Processes, 105*(1), 98–121.

[29] Billet, M. T., & Qian, Y. (2008). Are overconfident CEOs born or made? Evidence of self-attribution bias from frequent acquirers. *Management of Science, 54*(6), 1037–1051.

[30] Ehrlinger, Johnson, Banner, Dunning, & Kruger, "Why the unskilled are unaware."

Related to the principle of self-reinforcing incompetence is the fact that people are reluc- tant to change their behavior and experiment with new courses of action because of the risks associated with experimentation. In short, the fear of losing keeps people from experimenting with change. Negotiators instead rationalize their behavior in a self-perpetuating fashion. The fear of making mistakes may result in a manager's inability to improve his or her negotiation skills. In this book, we remove the risk of experimentation by providing several exercises and clear demonstrations of how changing one's behavior can lead to better negotiation outcomes. We invite managers to be active learners in terms of understanding their own values when it comes to negotiation.

DEBUNKING NEGOTIATION MYTHS

When we delve into managers' theories and beliefs about negotiation, we are often startled to find that they operate with faulty beliefs. Before we start on our journey toward developing a more effective negotiation strategy, we need to dispel several faulty assumptions and myths about negotiation. These myths hamper people's ability to learn effective negotiation skills and, in some cases, reinforce poor negotiation skills. In this section, we expose six of the most preva- lent myths about negotiation behavior.

Myth 1: Negotiations Are Fixed-Sum

Probably the most common myth is that most negotiations are fixed-sum, or fixed-pie, in nature, such that whatever is good for one person must ipso facto be bad for the other party. The truth is that most negotiations are not purely fixed-sum; in fact, most negotiations are variable-sum in nature, meaning that if parties work together, they can create more joint value than if they are purely combative. However, effective negotiators also realize that they cannot be purely trusting because any value that is created must ultimately be claimed by someone at the table. Our approach to negotiation is based on Walton and McKersie's conceptualization that negotiation is a mixed-motive enterprise, such that parties have incentives to cooperate as well as compete.[31]

Myth 2: You Need to Be Either Tough or Soft

The fixed-sum myth gives rise to a myopic view of the strategic choices that negotiators have. Most negotiators believe they must choose between either behaving in a tough (and sometimes punitive fashion) or being "reasonable" to the point of soft and concessionary. We disagree. The truly effective negotiator is neither tough as nails nor soft as pudding but, rather, princi- pled.[32] Effective negotiators follow an "enlightened" view of negotiation and correctly recognize that to achieve their own outcomes they must work effectively with the other party (and hence, cooperate) but must also leverage their own power and strengths.

Myth 3: Good Negotiators Are Born

A pervasive belief is that effective negotiation skills are something that people are born with, not something that can be readily learned. This notion is false because most excellent negotiators are

---

[31] Walton, R. E., & McKersie, R. B. (1965). *A behavioral theory of labor relations*. New York: McGraw-Hill.
[32] Bazerman & Neale, *Negotiating rationally*; Fisher & Ury, *'Getting to yes.'*

self-made. In fact, naturally gifted negotiators are rare. We tend to hear their stories, but we must remember that their stories are selective, meaning that it is always possible for someone to have a lucky day or a fortunate experience. This myth is often perpetuated by the tendency for people to judge negotiation skills by their car-dealership experiences. Purchasing a car is certainly an important and common type of negotiation, but it is not the best context by which to judge your negotiation skills. The most important negotiations are those that we engage in every day with our colleagues, supervisors, coworkers, and business associates. These relationships provide a much better index of one's negotiation effectiveness. In short, effective negotiation requires practice and feedback. The problem is that most of us do not get an opportunity to develop effective negotiation skills in a disciplined fashion; rather, most of us learn by doing. Experience is helpful but not sufficient.

Myth 4: Life Experience Is a Great Teacher

It is only partly true that experience can improve negotiation skills; in fact, experience in the absence of feedback is largely ineffective in improving negotiation skills.[33] Casual experience as an effective teacher has three strikes against it. First, in the absence of feedback, it is nearly impossible to improve performance. For example, can you imagine trying to learn mathematics without ever doing homework or taking tests? Without diagnostic feedback, it is very difficult to learn from experience.

The second problem is that our memories tend to be selective, meaning that people are more likely to remember their successes and forget their failures or shortcomings. This tendency is, of course, comforting to our ego but it does not improve our ability to negotiate.

In addition, experience improves our confidence, but not necessarily our accuracy. People with more experience grow more confident, but the accuracy of their judgment and the effectiveness of their behavior do not increase in a commensurate fashion. Overconfidence can be dangerous because it may lead people to take unwise risks.

Myth 5: Good Negotiators Take Risks

A pervasive myth is that effective negotiation necessitates taking risks and gambles. In negotiation, this approach may mean saying things like "This is my final offer" or "Take it or leave it" or using threats and bluffs. This is what we call a "tough" style of negotiation. Tough negotiators are rarely effective; however, we tend to be impressed by the tough negotiator. In this book, we teach negotiators how to evaluate risk, how to determine the appropriate time to make a final offer, and, more important, how to make excellent decisions in the face of the uncertainty of negotiation.

Myth 6: Good Negotiators Rely on Intuition

An interesting exercise is to ask managers and anyone else who negotiates to describe their approach to negotiating. Many seasoned negotiators believe that their negotiation style involves a lot of "gut feeling," or intuition. We believe that intuition does not serve people

---

[33] Loewenstein, Thompson, & Gentner, "Analogical learning in negotiation"; Nadler, Thompson, & van Boven, "Learning negotiation skills"; Thompson, L., & DeHarpport, T. (1994). Social judgment, feedback, and interpersonal learning in negotiation. *Organizational Behavior and Human Decision Processes, 58*(3), 327–345; Thompson, L., Loewenstein, J., & Gentner, D. (2000). Avoiding missed opportunities in managerial life: Analogical training more powerful than case-based training. *Organizational Behavior and Human Decision Processes, 82*(1), 60–75.

well. Effective negotiation involves deliberate thought and preparation and is quite systematic. The goal of this book is to help managers effectively prepare for negotiation, become more self-aware of their own strengths and shortcomings, and develop strategies that are proactive (i.e., they anticipate the reactions of their opponent) rather than reactive (i.e., they are dependent upon the actions and reactions of their opponent). Thus, excellent negotiators do not rely on intuition; rather, they are deliberate planners. As a general rule, don't rely on your intuition unless you are an expert.

LEARNING OBJECTIVES

This book promises three things: First (and most important), reading this book will *improve your ability to negotiate successfully.* You and your company will be richer, and you will experience fewer sleepless nights because you will have a solid framework and excellent tool-box for successful negotiation. However, in making this promise, we must also issue a warning: Successful negotiation skills do not come through passive learning. Rather, you will need to actively challenge yourself. We can think of no better way to engage in this challenge than to supplement this book with classroom experiences in negotiation in which managers can test their negotiation skills, receive timely feedback, and repeatedly refine their negotiation strategies. Moreover, within the classroom, data suggest that students who take the course for a grade will be more effective than students who take the course pass-fail.[34]

Second, we provide you with a *general strategy for successful negotiation.* Take a look at the table of contents. Notice the distinct absence of chapter titles such as "Negotiating in the Pharmaceutical Industry" or "Real Estate Negotiations" or "High-Tech Negotiations." We don't believe that negotiations in the pharmaceutical world require a fundamentally different set of skills from negotiations in the insurance industry or the software industry. Rather, we believe that negotiation skills are transferable across situations. In making this statement, we do not mean to imply that all negotiation situations are identical. This assumption is patently false because negotiation situations differ dramatically across cultures and industries. However, certain key negotiation principles are essential in all these different contexts. The skills in this book are effective across a wide range of situations, ranging from complex, multiparty, multicultural deals to one-on-one personal exchanges.

In addition, this book offers *an enlightened model of negotiation.* Being a successful negotiator does not depend on your opponent's lack of familiarity with a book such as this one or lack of training in negotiation. In fact, it would be ideal if your key clients and customers knew about these strategies. This approach follows what we call a *fraternal twin model,* which assumes that the other person you are negotiating with is every bit as motivated, intelligent, and prepared as you are. Thus, the negotiating strategies and techniques outlined in this book do not rely on "outsmarting" or tricking the other party; rather, they teach you to focus on simultaneously expanding the pie of resources and ensuring the resources are allocated in a manner that is favorable to you.

In summary, our model of learning is based on a three-phase cycle: experiential learning, feedback, and learning new strategies and skills.

---

[34] Craver, C. B. (1998). The impact of a pass/fail option on negotiation course performance. *Journal of Legal Education, 48*(2), 176–186.

THE MIND AND HEART

Across the sections of this book, we focus on the *mind* of the negotiator as it involves the development of deliberate, rational, and thoughtful strategies for negotiation. We also focus on the *heart* of the negotiator, because ultimately we care about relationships and trust. We base all our teachings and best practices on scientific research in the areas of economics and psychology, reflecting the idea that the bottom line *and* our relationships are both important.[35] Even through a sustained recession, in which the U.S. national unemployment rate hovered around 10%, many people reported that unemployment, even though painful, had actually improved them in some ways, by being less reliant on materialism, using free time for volunteering, becoming more sensitive to the suffering of others, and reevaluating career choices for their next jobs.[36]

---

[35] Bazerman, M. H., Curhan, J. R., Moore, D. A., & Valley, K. L. (2000). Negotiation. *Annual Review of Psychology, 51,* 279–314.

[36] Peck, D. (2010, March). How a new jobless era will transform America. *The Atlantic.*

Preparation: What to Do Before Negotiation

Jane Boon is a mystery shopper. She is hired to pretend to shop for luxury watches, negotiate on price, and then evaluate the negotiation experience. Many companies hire mystery shoppers to find out if their front-line customer service representatives and sales associates are indeed complying with corporate guidelines. Mystery shoppers are highly prepared when it comes to negotiation. How prepared? During a five hour training session, a group of 10 mystery shoppers engage in intensive role-play training with a sales trainer. The sales trainer teaches the sales associates how to close at the *highest* possible price. Mystery shoppers are trying to get the lowest possible price. The mystery shoppers also learn the etiquette of luxury buying. First, it is key to realize that unlike shopping for used cars, luxury watch negotiation is civilized and friendly. Being rude and aggressive does not work when you are buying a $20,000 timepiece. Thus, Jane is coached to be gentle, patient, and likeable. Jane is trained to use some well-rehearsed sentences when bargaining the price down, including, "Is there something more you can do for me?" and "can you offer any price assistance?" and "This isn't what I was thinking about: is there any further consideration you can offer?" By using these phrases in her first assignment, Jane reduced the price of a Cartier Tank Française watch from $28,200 to $21,500. Another technique is to ask to speak to a higher authority: "I'm a bit embarrassed, but I have a hang up about paying more than $20,000 for a watch. Would your boss consider $19,900." That line worked.[1]

---

[1] Boon, J. (2010, December 9). The watchword in watches: Negotiate. *Bloomberg Businessweek.* Businessweek.com

A s the opening example in this chapter illustrates, preparation is the key to successful negotiation. The work that you do prior to negotiation pays off substantially when you finally find yourself seated at the table. The 80–20 rule applies to negotiation: About 80% of your effort should go toward preparation; 20% should be the actual work involved in the negotiation. Most people clearly realize that preparation is important, yet they do not prepare in an effective fashion. Faulty preparation is not due to lack of motivation; rather, it has its roots in negotiators' faulty perceptions about negotiation.

We noted in Chapter 1 that most negotiators operate under the **fixed-pie** perception.[2] Negotiators who have fixed-pie perceptions usually adopt one of three mindsets when preparing for negotiation:

1. They resign themselves to capitulating to the other side (*soft bargaining*).
2. They prepare themselves for attack (*hard bargaining*).
3. They *compromise* in an attempt to reach a midpoint between their opposing demands (often regarded to be a win-win negotiation, when in fact, it is not).

Depending on what the other party decides to do in the negotiation, fixed-pie perceptions can lead to a battle of wills (e.g., if both parties are in attack mode), mutual compromise (e.g., if both parties are soft), or a combination of attack and capitulation. The common assumption among all three approaches is that concessions are necessary by one or both parties to reach an agreement. The fixed-pie perception is almost *always* wrong; thus, choosing between capitulation, attack, and compromise is not an effective approach to negotiation.

A more accurate model of negotiation is to approach it as a mixed-motive decision-making enterprise. As a **mixed-motive enterprise**, negotiation involves both cooperation and competition. In this chapter, we review the essentials of effective preparation, whether it be with a next-door neighbor, a corporate executive officer, or someone from a different culture. Effective preparation encompasses three general abilities:

1. Self-assessment
2. Assessment of the other party
3. Assessment of the situation

We systematically review each of these abilities and the skills they require. For each, we pose questions that a negotiator should ask himself or herself when preparing for negotiation.

SELF-ASSESSMENT

The most important questions a negotiator needs to ask of himself or herself at the outset of negotiation are "What do I want?" and "What are my alternatives?" Many people do not think carefully about what they want before entering negotiations. The second question defines a negotiator's power in the negotiation and influences the ultimate outcome of the negotiation. We now take up these questions in more detail.

---

[2] Thompson, L., & Hastie, R. (1990). Social perception in negotiation. *Organizational Behavior and Human Decision Processes, 47*(1), 98–123.

What Do I Want?

In any negotiation scenario, a negotiator needs to determine what would constitute an ideal outcome. This ideal is known as a **target** or **aspiration** (sometimes called a **target point** or **aspiration point**). Identifying a target or aspiration may sound straightforward enough, but three major problems often arise:

1. The **underaspiring negotiator** sets his or her target or aspirations too low. The under-aspiring negotiator opens the negotiation by requesting something that is immediately granted, resulting in a regrettable state of affairs known as the **winner's curse**.[3] The winner's curse occurs when a negotiator makes an offer that is immediately accepted by the other party. The largest real-estate deal in history—a $5.4 billion whopper—went bust in 2010 when New York companies Tishman Speyer Properties and Black Rock Realty surrendered two Manhattan housing complexes, totaling 11,000 units that they had purchased four years previous. The investors based their inflated price tag on projected rather than actual rentals, and failed to account for a downturn in the housing market when agreeing to the high purchase price. Observers to the failed deal noted the tendency of auctions to be won by the people who are the most delusionally overoptimistic, a clear sign of the winner's curse.[4] The immediate acceptance of one's offer by an opponent signals that a negotiator did not ask for enough. Another example is that of an army sergeant returning from a tour of duty in the Gulf War. Recently engaged, the sergeant wanted to bring back a beautiful gold necklace for his bride-to-be. When he entered the jewelry store in Saudi Arabia, he knew enough not to offer full price for the gold necklace, so he offered exactly half of the marked price. The shopkeeper was overjoyed, immediately accepted the offer and even included the matching earrings and bracelet! The sergeant's key mistake: His initial offer was too generous because he had not adequately prepared. The winner's curse is nearly impossible to remedy: In a series of experiments, negotiators were given different parameters, full feedback, and several counterexamples in an attempt to counteract the winner's curse, but none was effective in eliminating the faulty behavior.[5]

2. The **overaspiring negotiator** or **positional negotiator** is too "tough"; he or she sets the target point too high and refuses to make any concessions. When Wisconsin Republican Governor Scott Walker refused $800 million in federal grants to establish high-speed rail networks linking Milwaukee and Madison, many thought he was crazy. Walker and Republican Governor John Kasich of Ohio instead wrote to United States Transportation Secretary Ray LaHood asking that they be allowed to repurpose the funds—which both had previously criticized as federal largesse. LaHood's response to Walker was "no" before he pulled the funds from the states. Almost immediately, Illinois, New York, California and North Carolina put in requests for the $1.8 billion given up by Wisconsin and Ohio citing the importance of transportation and new jobs

---

[3] Akerlof, G. (1970). The market for lemons: Quality uncertainty and the market mechanism. *Quarterly Journal of Economics, 84,* 488–500; Neale, M. A., & Bazerman, M. H. (1991). *Cognition and rationality in negotiation.* New York: Free Press.
[4] Allan, N. (2010, January 25). America's most expensive real estate deal goes bust. *The Atlantic Wire.* Theatlanticwire.com
[5] Grosskopf, B., Bereby-Meyer, Y., & Bazerman, M. (2007). On the robustness of the winner's curse phenomenon. *Theory and Decision, 63*(4), 398–418.

in a bad economy.[6] The other problem with positional bargaining, like that displayed by Walker, is that it reinforces egocentrism. Indeed, people quickly develop ownership of the arguments and positions they make, and these positions become part of people's self-concept, making any opposition an ego threat.[7] Ego-defensive behavior triggers competitive communication, retaliatory behavior, negative perceptions of the counter-party, and attitude polarization.

3. The **grass-is-greener negotiator** does not know what he or she really wants—only that he or she wants what the other party does not want to give—and does not want what the other party is willing to offer. This type of negotiation behavior is also known as **reactive devaluation**.[8] For example, in a survey of opinions regarding possible arms reductions by the United States and the Soviet Union, respondents were asked to evaluate the terms of a nuclear disarmament proposal, a proposal that was either allegedly taken by the United States, Soviet Union, or a neutral third party.[9] In all cases, the proposal was identical; however, reactions to it depended upon who allegedly initiated it. The terms were seen as unfavorable to the United States when the Soviets were the initiators, even though the same terms appeared moderately favorable when attributed to a neutral third party and quite favorable when attributed to the United States.[10]

What Is My Alternative to Reaching Agreement in This Situation?

A negotiator needs to determine his or her best alternative to a negotiated agreement or **BATNA** (**B**est **A**lternative **T**o a **N**egotiated **A**greement).[11] Negotiators should be willing to accept any set of terms superior to their BATNA and reject outcomes that are worse than their BATNA. Surprising as it may seem, negotiators often fail on both counts.

BATNAS AND REALITY A BATNA is not something that a negotiator wishes for; rather, it is determined by objective reality. A common problem we have seen in our training of MBA students and executives is that negotiators are reluctant to acknowledge their actual BATNAs, and they fall prey to wishful thinking and unrealistic optimism.

YOUR BATNA IS TIME SENSITIVE Your BATNA—once properly identified—is time sensitive. At any point in time, your BATNA is either improving or deteriorating as a result of market forces, environmental and situational conditions. Thus, negotiators should constantly attempt to improve their BATNAs. One strategy for improving BATNAs is to follow Bazerman and Neale's "falling in love" rule, which means not falling in love with one house, one job, or one set of circumstances, but instead, identifying two or three options of interest.[12] By following this

---

[6] Schaper, D. (2010, November 12). Not so fast: Future for high-speed rail uncertain. *National PublicRadio.* Npr.org

[7] De Dreu, C. K. W., & Van Knippenberg, D. (2005). The possessive self as a barrier to conflict resolution: Effects of mere ownership, process accountability, and self-concept clarity on competitive cognitions and behavior. *Journal of Personality and Social Psychology, 89*(3), 345–357.

[8] Ross, L., & Stillinger, C. (1991). Barriers to conflict resolution. *Negotiation Journal, 7*(4), 389–404; Curhan, J. R., Neale, M. A., Ross, L., & Rosencranz-Engelmann, J. (2008). Relational accommodation in negotiation: Effects of egalitarianism and gender on economic efficiency and relational capital. *Organizational Behavior and Human Decision Processes, 107*(2), 192–205.

[9] Ross & Stillinger, "Barriers to conflict resolution."

[10] Oskamp, S. (1965). Attitudes toward U.S. and Russian actions: A double standard. *Psychological Reports, 16,* 43–46.

[11] Fisher, R., & Ury, W. (1981). *Getting to yes.* Boston: Houghton Mifflin.

[12] Bazerman, M. H., Neale, M. (1992). *Negotiating rationally.* New York: Free Press.

strategy, the negotiator has a readily available set of alternatives that represent viable options should the current alternative come at too high a price or be eliminated. The "falling in love" rule is difficult to follow because most people set their sights on one target job, house, or set of terms and exclude all others. Many negotiators are reluctant to recognize their BATNAs and confuse them with their aspiration point.

Greek Prime Minister George Papandreou understood the time-sensitive nature of BATNAs. At the height of the 2010 financial meltdown, Greece appeared to have a weak BATNA. If Greece did not cooperate with the European Union and slash its budget deficit, it would lose the confidence of investors and default on foreign debts. However, because European countries such as Germany and France were huge lenders to Greece, they *also* had much to lose if the Greek economy collapsed. The BATNAs in this case were best described as a "teetering domino." Papandreou used this time-sensitive information to secure a $39 billion bailout from the International Monetary Fund, despite the country's debt crisis.[13]

DO NOT LET THE OTHER PARTY MANIPULATE YOUR BATNA   The other party has an incentive to minimize the quality of your BATNA and, thus, will be motivated to provide negative information vis-à-vis your BATNA.

If you have not properly prepared, you might be particularly influenced by such persuasive appeals. However, your BATNA should not change as a result of the other party's persuasion techniques. Your BATNA should only change as a result of objective facts and evidence.

In a negotiation, the person who stands to gain most by changing our mind should be the least persuasive. Thus, it is important to develop a BATNA before commencing negotiations and to stick to it during the course of negotiations. It is helpful to write your BATNA in ink on a piece of paper and put it in your pocket before negotiating. If you feel tempted to settle for less than your BATNA, it may be a good time to pull out the paper, call a halt to the negotiation process, and engage in an objective reassessment.

Determine Your Reservation Point

Consider an MBA student negotiating her employment terms. In this case, the MBA student has a $90,000 job offer from company A, plus some stock options, moving expenses, and a signing bonus. The student is interested in getting an offer from company B. Thus, company A is her BATNA. The question the student should ask herself is, "What does company B need to offer me so that I feel it is as attractive as the offer made by company A?" The answer to this question represents her reservation point, which includes all things relevant to the job offer, such as salary, stock options, moving expenses, and signing bonus, as well as quality of life and feelings about the city to which she will move. A reservation point, then, is a *quantification* of a negotiator's BATNA with respect to other alternatives.

A negotiator's reservation point has the most direct influence on his or her final outcome. When three types of information—market price, reservation price, and aspiration—were made available to negotiators, only reservation prices drove final outcomes.[14]

---

[13] Davis, B. (2010, May 10). IMF approves Greek bailout, urges against debt default. *The Wall Street Journal.* Wsj.com
[14] Blount-White, S., Valley, K., Bazerman, M., Neale, M., & Peck, S. (1994). Alternative models of price behavior in dyadic negotiations: Market prices, reservation prices, and negotiator aspirations. *Organizational Behavior and Human Decision Processes, 57*(3), 430–447.

Failure to assess reservation points can lead to two unfortunate outcomes. In some instances, negotiators may agree to an outcome that is worse than their BATNA. In our example, the student could agree to a set of employment terms at company B that are actually worse for her than what company A is offering. A second problem is that negotiators may often reject an offer that is better than their BATNA. For example, the MBA student may reject an offer from company B that is actually more attractive than the offer from company A. Although this example may seem implausible, the incidence of agreeing to something worse than one's BATNA and rejecting an offer better than one's BATNA is quite high. To avoid both of these errors, we suggest that the negotiator follow the steps outlined in Exhibit 2-1.

EXHIBIT 2-1

Developing a Reservation Point

Step 1:	**Brainstorm Your Alternatives.** Imagine that you want to sell your house. You have already determined your target point—in this case, $275,000. That is the easy part. The real question is, "What is the lowest offer you will accept for your home?" This step involves thinking about what you will do in the event that you do not get an offer of $275,000 for your house. Perhaps you reduce the list price by $10,000 (or more), perhaps you stay in the house, or you may consider renting. You should consider as many alternatives as possible. The only restriction is that the alternatives must be feasible—that is, realistic. This requirement involves research on your part.
Step 2:	**Evaluate Each Alternative.** In this step, you should order the various alternatives identified in step 1 in terms of their relative attractiveness, or value, to you. If an alternative has an uncertain outcome, such as reducing the list price, you should determine the probability a buyer will make an offer at that price. For example, suppose that you reduce the list price to $265,000. You assess the probability of a buyer making an offer of $265,000 for your house to be 70%, based on recent home sale prices in the area. Your reservation price is based on research, not hope. The best, most valuable, alternative should be selected to represent your BATNA.
Step 3:	**Attempt to Improve Your BATNA.** Your bargaining position can be strengthened substantially to the extent that you have an attractive, viable BATNA. Unfortunately, this step is the one that many negotiators fail to develop fully. To improve your BATNA in this case, you might contact a rental company and develop your rental options, or you may make some improvements that have high return on investment (e.g., new paint). Of course, your most attractive BATNA is to have an offer in hand on your house.
Step 4:	**Determine Your Reservation Price.** Once you have determined your most attractive BATNA, it is then time to identify your reservation price—the least amount of money you would accept for your home at the present time. Once again, it is *not* advisable to make a guess. Your assessment *must* be based on facts. For example, you assess the probability of getting an offer on your house of $265,000 (or higher) to be 60%, based upon recent home sales in your area. Suppose that you assess the probability that you will get an offer of $250,000 or higher to be 95%, based upon recent sales activity in your area. You think there is a 5% chance that you will not get an offer

(continued)

of $250,000 and will rent your house. You can use this information to assess your expected probabilities of selling your house:

Reduce the price of your home to $265,000
$$P_{sale} = 60\%$$
Reduce the price of your home to $250,000
$$P_{sale} = 35\%$$
Rent the house
$$P_{rent} = 5\%$$

The probabilities represent the chances that you think your house will sell at a particular price or will have to be rented. Thus, you think that if the list price of your house is reduced to $265,000, it is 60% likely that you will receive an offer of that amount within 6 weeks. If you reduce the price of your home to $250,000, you are 95% certain that you will get an offer. (Note that we write this probability as 35% because it includes the 60% probability of receiving an offer of $265,000.) Finally, you think you have only a 5% chance of getting an offer of $250,000 or more in the next 6 weeks and that you will have to rent your house—a value you assess to be worth only $100,000 to you at the present time.

Note that in our calculation, the probabilities always sum to exactly 100%, meaning we have considered all possible events occurring. No alternative is left to chance.

An overall value for each of these "risky" alternatives is assessed by multiplying the value of each option by its probability of occurrence:

Value of reducing price to $265,000
$$= \$265,000 \times 0.6 = \$159,000$$
Value of reducing price to $250,000
$$= \$250,000 \times 0.35 = \$87,500$$
Value of renting the house
$$= \$100,000 \times 0.05 = \$5,000$$

As a final step, we add all the values of the alternatives to arrive at an overall evaluation:

$$= 0.6(\$265,000) + 0.35(\$250,000) + 0.05(\$100,000)$$
$$= \$159,000 + \$87,500 + \$5,000 = \$251,500$$

This value is your reservation price. It means that you would never settle for anything less than $251,500 in the next 6 weeks.[*] It also means that if a buyer were to make you an offer right now of $251,000, you would seriously consider it because it is very close to your reservation price. Obviously, you want to get a lot more than $251,500, but you are prepared to go as low as this amount at the present time.

The offers you receive in the next 6 weeks can change your reservation point. Suppose a buyer offers to pay $260,000 for the house next week. It would be your reservation point by which to evaluate all subsequent offers.

---

[*] After 6 weeks, you may reduce the price of your home to $250,000.

Be Aware of Focal Points

Negotiators who make the mistake of not developing a reservation point before they negotiate often focus on an arbitrary value that masquerades as a reservation price. Such arbitrary points are focal points. **Focal points**, like anchors, are salient numbers, figures, or values that appear to be valid but have no basis in fact. A good example of the arbitrariness of focal points is provided by an investigation in which people were asked for the last four digits of their Social Security number.[15] They were then asked whether the number of physicians in Manhattan was larger or smaller than the number formed by those last four digits. Finally, they were asked to estimate how many physicians were located in Manhattan. Despite the fact that it was obvious to everyone that Social Security digits are random and, therefore, could not possibly be related to the number of doctors in Manhattan, a strong correlation emerged between the digits and people's estimates.

Beware of Sunk Costs

Sunk costs are just what they sound like—money you have invested that is, for all practical purposes, gone. Economic theory asserts that only future costs and benefits should affect decisions. However, people have a hard time forgetting the past, and they often try to recoup sunk costs. One type of sunk cost is the purchase price that home sellers paid for their house. Sellers and buyers in a simulated real estate negotiation were given the same Multiple Listing Service (MLS) sheet describing a house. However, negotiators were given different information about their previous purchase price.[16] Buyers offered significantly higher amounts for a condominium with larger sunk costs, indicating that the seller's sunk costs influenced the buyer's behavior. Moreover, sellers' BATNAs were significantly lower when they had low, as opposed to high, sunk costs. Final settlements were significantly lower in the low (as opposed to high) sunk cost situations. Thus, sunk costs not only influence our own behavior but the behavior of the counterparty.

Do Not Confuse the Target Point with Your Reservation Point

Negotiators often make the mistake of using their target point as their reservation point. This can result in one of two undesirable outcomes. The negotiator who lacks a well-formed reservation point risks agreeing to a settlement that is worse than what he or she could do by following another course of action. In another case, the negotiator may walk away from a potentially profitable deal. For example, many home sellers reject early offers that are superior to their reservation point, only to be forced to accept an offer of less value at some later point in time.

Identify the Issues in the Negotiation

It is a grave mistake to focus on a single issue in a negotiation because single-issue negotiations are purely fixed-sum. By identifying other issues, negotiators can create integrative potential.

---

[15] Lovallo, D., & Kahneman, D. (2003). Delusions of success: How optimism undermines executives' decisions. *Harvard Business Review, 81*(7), 56–63.

[16] Diekmann, K. A., Tenbrunsel, A. E., Shah, P. P., Schroth, H. A., & Bazerman, M. H. (1996). The descriptive and prescriptive use of previous purchase price in negotiations. *Organizational Behavior and Human Decision Processes, 66*(2), 179–191.

Negotiators should take time to brainstorm how a single-issue negotiation may be segmented into multiple issues or they should attempt to add issues.[17]

Identify the Alternatives for Each Issue

Once the negotiator has identified the issues to be negotiated, it is a good idea to identify several alternatives within each issue. For example, in a job negotiation, all of the following have a range: salary, vacation days, and so on. Negotiators can formalize the issues and alternatives by creating a matrix in which the issues are located along the columns and the alternatives specified along the rows.

Identify Equivalent Multi-Issue Proposals

The next step of preparation is to determine a variety of different combinations of the issues that all achieve the target or aspiration point. For example, an MBA student might identify salary, signing bonus, and vacation days as key issues in a job negotiation. The student might then take the step of identifying highly attractive packages that she could present as opening offers in the negotiation. For example, a starting salary of $90,000, three weeks of vacation per year, and a signing bonus of $10,000 might be subjectively equivalent to a starting salary of $100,000, 10 days of vacation per year, and a signing bonus of $12,000. By identifying multiple-issue packages, negotiators expand their options. *The most important aspect of identifying packages of offers is that the packages should all be of equivalent value or attractiveness to oneself.* This requires that negotiators ask themselves some important questions about what they value and what is attractive to them. (As a first step, consult Appendix 1, which helps prepare a negotiator to identify packages of equivalent value by testing the negotiator's rationality.)

We strongly discourage negotiators from stating a range (e.g., a salary range). By stating a range, the negotiator gives up important bargaining ground and moves too close to his or her BATNA. This is known as a *premature concession.* By stating a range ("I would be interested in a salary between $90,000 and $100,000"), a negotiator has already made a concession (implicitly agreeing to a salary of $90,000). Another benefit of identifying packages of offers is that the negotiator does not give the counterparty the impression that he or she is *positional* (won't budge on any issue).[18] By identifying multiple issues and multiple alternatives within each issue, a negotiator is more likely to achieve his or her target.

Assess Your Risk Propensity

Suppose you are offered a choice between the following two options:

> Option A: Receiving a cashier's check for $5,000
>
> Option B: Playing a game that offers a 50% chance of winning a $10,000 cashier's check and a 50% chance of winning nothing

When presented with a choice between a sure thing and a gamble of equivalent value, most people choose option A, the sure thing. Note that the expected value of each choice is $5,000,

---

[17] Lax, D. A., & Sebenius, J. K. (1986). *The manager as negotiator.* New York: Free Press.
[18] Fisher, Ury, & Patton, *Getting to yes.*

which would mean that negotiators should be indifferent (or risk-neutral) between the two. However, the strong preference for option A over B reflects a fundamental principle of negotiator behavior: **risk-aversion**.

Now, imagine yourself facing the following unenviable choice:

Option C: Losing $5,000 because of an unexpected expense

Option D: Playing a game that offers a 50% chance of losing nothing and a 50% chance of losing $10,000

Most people find it difficult to choose between options C and D because both choices are undesirable. However, when forced to make a decision, the majority of negotiators choose option D, even though the expected value of C and D is exactly the same: $5,000. Option D represents the "risky" alternative. The dominant choice of D over C reflects a fundamental principle of human psychology: risk-seeking behavior in the face of loss.

Thus, most people are risk-seeking when it comes to losses, and risk-averse when it comes to gains. A **reference point** defines what a person considers to be a gain or a loss. Thus, rather than weighing a course of action by its impact on total wealth, people generally "frame" outcomes as either "gains" or "losses" relative to some arbitrary reference point.[19]

What are the implications for negotiation? Negotiators should consider the differential impact of three sources of risk in any negotiation: strategic risk, BATNA risk, and contractual risk.[20]

STRATEGIC RISK **Strategic risk** refers to the riskiness of the tactics that negotiators use at the bargaining table. Negotiators often choose between extremely cooperative tactics (such as information sharing and brainstorming) and, at the other extreme, competitive tactics (such as threats and demands). A classic example was the risk that AOL's David Colburn took when negotiating with Microsoft to get the AOL icon on the Microsoft Windows start page—valuable real estate on the computer desktop because it gave AOL access to untold millions of Microsoft customers who might sign up for the online service.[21] It would mean that AOL would not have to send free disks to get people to sign up because the software would already be installed on the computer. During the negotiation, Colburn threatened to use the browser of Microsoft's archenemy—Netscape—if Microsoft did not agree to put the AOL icon on the Windows start page. Microsoft agreed. Consider also the risk taken by Sotheby's when selling the Mark Rothko painting *White Center*. Sotheby's promised owner David Rockefeller that the painting would sell for at least $46 million. (The previous record for a Rothko painting was just $22 million, and Sotheby's would have to pay the difference if the painting didn't sell for the record price it promised.) But Sotheby's knew that the potential payoff would be enormous. It would not only receive a commission from the buyer but also would get a cut of 20% of every dollar over the $46 million price. When auction time came, an anonymous bidder bought the 1950 abstract painting for $72.8 million, granting Sotheby's an estimated take of $11.6 million.[22]

---

[19] Kahneman, D., & Tversky, A. (1979). Prospect theory: An analysis of decision under risk. *Econometrica, 47*(2), 263–291.
[20] Bottom, W. P. (1998). Negotiator risk: Sources of uncertainty and the impact of reference points on negotiated agreements. *Organizational Behavior and Human Decision Processes, 76*(2), 89–112.
[21] Klein, A. (2003, June 15). Lord of the flies. *Washington Post*, p. W06.
[22] The art of the art deal. (2007, June 11). *Bloomberg Businessweek*. Businessweek.com

Negotiators who have recently experienced a string of failures are more likely to adopt a "loss frame" and feel less "in control" in a negotiation; conversely, negotiators who have experienced a recent string of successes feel greater control.[23] Consequently, loss-framed negotiators are reluctant to reveal information that could be used to exploit them; instead, they prefer to manage risk by delaying outcomes.

BATNA   Many people's BATNAs are uncertain because potential alternatives arrive sequentially. For example, consider a student who has several interviews scheduled over the next 10 weeks but no actual offers. The student's BATNA is an estimate about the likelihood of actually receiving an offer. Consider this example of a car dealer's uncertain BATNA: "A car dealer who decides not to make the one last concession needed to close a deal is rarely doing so because an alternative buyer in the next room is waiting to buy the same car at a higher price. The seller must make a conjecture about the likelihood that a more attractive offer will be made in the near future. Rejecting an offer entails a risk that the car will remain on the lot indefinitely, costing the dealer money, with no better offer forthcoming" (p. 94).[24]

Under most circumstances, we might expect negotiators who are in a "gain frame" to be more risk-averse (and therefore, more concessionary) than negotiators who hold a "loss frame" (who might hold out). This gain-loss basis can be a potential problem in negotiation because negotiators can be "framed." To see how, consider the following example: Negotiators who are instructed to "minimize their losses" make fewer concessions, reach fewer agreements, and perceive settlements to be less fair compared to those who are told to "maximize their gains."[25] In short, the negotiators who are told to "minimize their losses" adopt more risky bargaining strategies (just as the majority of people choose option D over C in our previous example), preferring to hold out for a better, but more risky, settlement. In contrast, those who are told to "maximize their gains" are more inclined to accept the sure thing (just as most people choose option A over B in our example). Negotiators who view the glass as "half full" are more inclined to reach agreement, whereas negotiators who view the glass as "half empty" are more likely to use threats and exercise their BATNAs. If one negotiator has a negative frame and the other has a positive frame, the negotiator with the negative frame reaps a greater share of the resources.[26] In price negotiations, buyers and prevention-focused people prefer *vigilant* strategies, whereas sellers and promotion-focused people prefer *eager* strategies.[27] When there is a match between a negotiator's role (buyer, seller) and their strategy, the negotiator is more demanding in the situation. A negotiator's BATNA acts as an important reference point from which other outcomes are evaluated. Outcomes and alternatives that fall short of one's BATNA

[23] Kray, L. J., Paddock, L., & Galinksy, A. D. (2008). The effect of past performance on expected control and risk attitudes in integrative negotiations. *Negotiation and Conflict Management Research, 1*(2), 161–178.

[24] Bottom, "Negotiator risk."

[25] Bazerman, M. H., Magliozzi, T., & Neale, M. A. (1985). Integrative bargaining in a competitive market. *Organizational Behavior and Human Decision Processes, 35*(3), 294–313; Neale, M. A., & Northcraft, G. (1986). Experts, amateurs, and refrigerators: Comparing expert and amateur negotiators in a novel task. *Organizational Behavior and Human Decision Processes, 38,* 305–317; Neale, M. A., Huber, V. L., & Northcraft, G. B. (1987). The framing of negotiations: Contextual versus task frames. *Organizational Behavior and Human Decision Processes, 39*(2), 228–241; Neale & Bazerman, *Cognition and rationality in negotiation.*

[26] Bottom, W. P., & Studt, A. (1993). Framing effects and the distributive aspect of integrative bargaining. *Organizational Behavior and Human Decision Processes, 56*(3), 459–474.

[27] Appelt, K. C., & Higgins, E. T. (2010). My way: How strategic preferences vary by negotiator role and regulatory focus. *Journal of Experimental Social Psychology, 46*(6), 1138–1142.

are viewed as losses; outcomes that exceed a negotiator's reservation point or BATNA are viewed as gains. The more risk-averse the negotiator, the more likely it is that she or he will make greater concessions.[28] Thus, given BATNAs of equal expected value, the more risk-averse negotiator will be in a weaker bargaining position.[29]

CONTRACTUAL RISK **Contractual risk** refers to the risk associated with the willingness of the other party to honor its terms.[30] For example, signing a peace treaty with one's adversaries may lead to genuine peace, or it may lead to a military disadvantage if the other side fails to honor the agreement. One example of contractual risk comes from the business world: In 1995, when NBC Sports outbid Fox Sports by a whopping $700 million for the broadcast rights to the 2010 and 2012 Olympic Games, it was largely seen as a deft move of prime-time dominance for 17 nights for two years, even as the bid price stunned many. But after NBC lost $223 million on the 2010 Vancouver Winter Games because of the global recession and the steep price it paid for them, the network faced even greater losses on the 2012 Olympics in London considering its record $1.18 billion rights fee for those games. Bob Wright, the chairman and chief executive of NBC Universal said that the economic projections that justified a bid could be undone by a bad economy several years later—which is exactly what took place at the time of the Vancouver games. "I don't think anybody at this stage thinks they have to have the Olympics to survive, or that the Olympics will change their business model in a significant way to take a big business risk," said Wright, after the losses from the Vancouver games were clear.[31] Clearly, NBC expected a much better payoff when they signed the original agreement to acquire control of the televised games.

How does such contractual risk affect negotiator behavior? Under contractual risk, negotiators with negative frames (risk-seeking) are more likely to reach integrative agreements than those with positive frames (risk-averse). The reason is that attaining a high aspiration entails some creative risk. Thus, if integrative negotiation outcomes involve "sure things," positive frames are more effective; however, if the integrative outcomes require negotiators to "roll the dice," negative frames are more effective. In negotiations involving contractual risk, negotiators with a "loss frame" are more cooperative and more likely to settle than those with a "gain frame."[32] Further, "loss frame" negotiators create more integrative agreements.

Endowment Effects

The value of an object should be about the same, whether we are a buyer or a seller. (*Note:* Buyers and sellers might want to adopt different *bargaining positions* for the object, but their *private valuations* for the object should not differ as a consequence of who has possession of it.) However, negotiators' **reference points** may lead buyers and sellers to have different valuations for objects. Someone who possesses an object has a reference point that reflects his or her current endowment. When someone who owns an object considers selling it, he or she may view the

---

[28] Neale, M. A., & Bazerman, M. H. (1985). The effects of framing and negotiator overconfidence on bargainer behavior. *Academy of Management Journal, 28,* 34–49.
[29] Crawford, V. P., & Sobel, J. (1982). Strategic information transmission. *Econometrica, 50,* 1431–1451.
[30] Bottom, "Negotiator risk."
[31] Sandomir, R. (2010, December 28). In NBC's shadow, Comcast ponders an Olympic plunge. *New York Times,* p. B8.
[32] Bottom, "Negotiator risk."

situation as a loss. The difference between what sellers demand and what buyers are willing to pay is a manifestation of loss-aversion, coupled with the rapid adaptation of the reference point. Therefore, sellers demand more than buyers are willing to pay.

One example comes from a class of MBA students who were "endowed" with coffee mugs worth $6, as charged by the university bookstore.[33] The students who were not given a coffee mug were told they had the opportunity to buy a mug from a student who owned one, if the student who owned the mug valued it less. The buyers' willingness to pay for the mug and the sellers' willingness to sell the mug were inferred from a series of choices (e.g., "receive $9.75" versus "receive mug," "receive $9.50 versus a mug," etc.). Basic rationality predicts that about half of the buyers will value the mug more than the seller and therefore trade will occur; similarly, about half of the sellers will value the mug more than the buyer and trade will not occur. The reference point effect, however, predicts that because of the loss-aversion behavior engendered by the seller's loss frame, trade will occur less than expected. Indeed, although 11 trades were expected, on average, only 4 took place. Sellers demanded in excess of $8 to part with their mugs; prospective buyers were only willing to pay list price.[34]

If sellers are risk-seeking by virtue of their endowment, how can it be that horses, cars, furniture, companies, and land are bought and sold every day? The endowment effect operates only when the seller regards himself or herself to be the owner of the object. If a seller expects to sell goods for a profit and views the goods as currency (for example, when MBA students are endowed with tokens rather than coffee mugs), the endowment effect does not occur. Endowment effects prevent negotiators from reaching agreement in negotiations; however, by changing the sequencing proposals so that the first one is conceived as a loss and the second as a gain, the endowment effect may be mitigated.[35]

Am I Going to Regret This?

What determines whether we feel we did the right thing (e.g., took the right job, married the right person) or we feel regret? An important component in determining whether a person experiences regret is counterfactual thinking.[36] **Counterfactual thinking**, or thinking about what might have been but did not occur, may be a reference point for the psychological evaluation of actual outcomes. In negotiation, immediate acceptance of a first offer by the counterparty often means a better outcome for the proposing negotiator; however, the outcome is distinctly less satisfying.[37] One of the benefits of having a first offer accepted is that it can improve preparation. Negotiators whose first offer is accepted by the counterparty are more likely to prepare longer for a subsequent negotiation; it also makes negotiators reluctant to make the first offer again.[38]

---

[33] Kahneman, D., Knetsch, J. L., & Thaler, R. H. (1990). Experimental tests of the endowment effect and the Coase theorem. *Journal of Political Economy, 98*(6), 1325–1348.
[34] Ibid.
[35] Galin, A. (2009) Proposal sequence and the endowment effect in negotiations. *International Journal of Conflict Management, 20*(3), 212–227.
[36] Gilovich, T. D., & Medvec, V. H. (1994). The temporal pattern to the experience of regret. *Journal of Personality and Social Psychology, 67*(3), 357–365.
[37] Galinsky, A. D., Seiden, V., Kim, P. H., & Medvec, V. H. (2002). The dissatisfaction of having your first offer accepted: The role of counterfactual thinking in negotiations. *Personality and Social Psychology Bulletin, 28*(2), 271–283.
[38] Ibid.

Consider feelings of regret experienced by athletes in the Olympic games.[39] Although silver medalists should feel happier than bronze medalists because their performance is objectively superior, counterfactual reasoning might produce greater feelings of regret and disappointment in silver medalists than in bronze. Specifically, the bronze medalist's reference point is that of not placing at all, so winning a medal represents a gain. In contrast, the silver medalist views himself or herself as having just missed the gold. With the gold medal as the referent, the silver medalist feels a loss. Indeed, videotapes of medalists' reactions (with the audio portion turned off) reveal that bronze medalists are perceived to be happier than silver medalists.[40] Further, silver medalists report experiencing greater feelings of regret than do bronze medalists.

Violations of the Sure Thing Principle

Imagine you face a decision between going to graduate school X on the East Coast or graduate school Y on the West Coast. You must make your decision before you find out whether your start-up company has received funding from a venture capitalist. In the event you get the funding, the East Coast provides access to many more of your potential customers. In the event that funding does not come through, by going to the East Coast you would be closer to your family, who could help you with finances. This sounds pretty straightforward so far: School X is your dominant choice no matter what the venture capitalist does. In other words, you have chosen school X regardless of whether you get funding. Making a decision between X and Y should not be hard—or should it?

When faced with uncertainty about some event occurring (such as whether your company will be funded), people are often reluctant to make decisions and will even pay money to delay decisions until the uncertain event is known. This is paradoxical because no matter what happens, people choose to do the same thing.[41] Consider a situation in which a student has just taken a tough and exhausting qualifying examination.[42] The student has the option of buying a very attractive 5-day Hawaiian vacation package. The results of the exam will not be available for a week, but the student must decide whether to buy the vacation package now. Alternatively, she can pay a nonrefundable fee to retain the right to buy the vacation package at the same price on the day after the exam results are posted. When presented with these three choices, most respondents (61%) choose to pay a nonrefundable fee to delay the decision. Two other versions of the scenario are then presented to different groups of participants. In one version, the student passed the exam, and in the other version, the student failed. In both of these situations, respondents overwhelmingly preferred to go on the vacation. Thus, even though we decide to go on the vacation no matter what the results of the exam, we are willing to pay money to delay making this decision.

This behavior violates one of the basic axioms of the rational theory of decision making under uncertainty: the **sure thing principle**.[43] According to the sure thing principle, if alternative X is preferred to Y in the condition that some event, A, occurs, and if X is also preferred to Y

---

[39] Medvec, V. H., Madey, S. F., & Gilovich, T. (1995). When less is more: Counterfactual thinking and satisfaction among Olympic medalists. *Journal of Personality and Social Psychology, 69*(4), 603–610.

[40] Ibid.

[41] Tversky, A., & Shafir, E. (1992). The disjunction effect in choice under uncertainty. *Psychological Science, 3*(5), 305–309.

[42] Shafir, E. (1994). Uncertainty and the difficulty of thinking through disjunctions. *Cognition, 50,* 403–430.

[43] Savage, L. J. (1954). *The foundations of statistics.* New York: Wiley.

in the condition that some event, A, does not occur, then X should be preferred to Y, even when it is not known whether A will occur.

Why would people pay a fee to a consultant or intermediary to delay the decision when they would make the same choice either way? Violations of the sure thing principle are rooted in the *reasons* people use to make their decisions. In the Hawaii example, people have different reasons for going to Hawaii for each possible event. If they pass the exam, the vacation is a celebration or reward; if they fail the exam, the vacation is an opportunity to recuperate. When the decision maker does not know whether he or she has passed the exam, he or she may lack a clear reason for going to Hawaii. In the presence of uncertainty, people may be reluctant to think through the implications of each outcome and, as a result, they violate the sure thing principle.

Do I Have an Appropriate Level of Confidence?

How accurate are people in judging probability? Judgments of likelihood for certain types of events are often more optimistic than is warranted. The **overconfidence effect** refers to unwarranted levels of confidence in people's judgment of their abilities and the likelihood of positive events and underestimates the likelihood of negative events. For example, in negotiations involving third-party dispute resolution, negotiators on each side believe the neutral third party will adjudicate in their favor.[44] Obviously, a decision favoring both parties cannot happen. Similarly, in final-offer arbitration, wherein parties each submit their final bid to a third party who then makes a binding decision between the two proposals, negotiators consistently overestimate the probability that the neutral arbitrator will choose their own offer.[45] Obviously, the probability is only 50% that a final offer will be accepted; nevertheless, both parties' estimates typically sum to a number greater than 100%. When we find ourselves to be highly confident of a particular outcome occurring (whether it be our opponent caving in to us, a senior manager supporting our decision, etc.), it is important to examine why. On the other hand, overconfidence about the value of the other party's BATNA might serve the negotiator well. Negotiators who are too optimistic (i.e., they think their counterpart will concede more than he or she really can) have a distinct bargaining advantage.[46]

SIZING UP THE OTHER PARTY

Once the negotiator has thought about his or her own BATNA, reservation point, target point, and interests, it is time to think about the other party (or parties).

---

[44] Farber, H. S., & Bazerman, M. H. (1986). The general basis of arbitrator behavior: An empirical analysis of conventional and final offer arbitration. *Econometrica, 54,* 1503–1528; Farber, H. S., & Bazerman, M. H. (1989). Divergent expectations as a cause of disagreement in bargaining: Evidence from a comparison of arbitration schemes. *Quarterly Journal of Economics, 104,* 99–120; Farber, H. S. (1981). Splitting the difference in interest arbitration. *Industrial and Labor Relations Review, 35,* 70–77.

[45] Neale, M. A., & Bazerman, M. H. (1983). The role of perspective taking ability in negotiating under different forms of arbitration. *Industrial and Labor Relations Review, 36,* 378–388; Bazerman, M. H., & Neale, M. A. (1982). Improving negotiation effectiveness under final offer arbitration: The role of selection and training. *Journal of Applied Psychology, 67*(5), 543–548.

[46] Bottom, W. P., & Paese, P. W. (1999). Judgment accuracy and the asymmetric cost of errors in distributive bargaining. *Group Decision and Negotiation, 8,* 349–364.

Who Are the Other Parties?

A **party** is a person (or group of people with common interests) who acts in accord with his or her preferences. Parties are readily identified when they are physically present, but often the most important parties are not present at the negotiation table. Such parties are known as the **hidden table**.[47] When more parties are involved in the negotiations, the situation becomes a team or multiparty negotiation, and the dynamics change considerably. A variety of issues crop up as more parties enter the bargaining room. For example, with more than two parties, coalitions may develop, and teams of negotiators may form. Team and multiparty negotiations are so important that we devote an entire chapter to them in this book (Chapter 9). Sometimes, it is obvious who the other parties are, and they have a legitimate place at the table. However, in other situations, the other parties may not be obvious at all, and their legitimacy at the table may be questionable.

Are the Parties Monolithic?[48]

Monolithic refers to whether parties on the same side of the table are in agreement with one another concerning their interests in the negotiation. Frequently, the parties are composed of people who are on the same side but have differing values, beliefs, and preferences.

Counterparties' Interests and Position

A negotiator should do as much research and homework as possible to determine the counterparties' interests in the negotiation. For example, which issues are most important to the other party? What alternatives are most preferable to the other party? As a case in point, Rich Gee was well into negotiations with a potential employer when he asked for a flexible travel schedule, one that would limit the number of business trips required of him. The surprised interviewer asked why. Although what was most important for Mr. Gee was more time at home with his wife and kids, he knew he needed to support his request by considering the employer's interests. He outlined several ways in which cutting travel could save time and money for the company. In his interview, he suggested teleconferencing with clients and meeting vendors at a halfway point, thereby eliminating the need to stay overnight. Impressed by Mr. Gee's ideas, the interviewer offered him the job.[49]

Counterparties' BATNAs

Probably the most important piece of information a negotiator can have in a negotiation is the BATNA of the other party. Although, it is unlikely the counterparty will reveal his or her BATNA, most negotiators severely under-research their counterparty's BATNA. For example, when purchasing cars, most people have access to a wealth of information about dealers' costs;

---

[47] Friedman, R. (1992). The culture of mediation: Private understandings in the context of public conflict. In D. Kolb and J. Bartunek (Eds.), *Hidden conflict: Uncovering behind-the-scenes disputes* (pp. 143–164). Beverly Hills, CA: Sage.

[48] This question is raised by Raiffa (1982) in his seminal book *The art and science of negotiation,* Cambridge, MA: Belknap.

[49] Shellenbarger, S. (2007, July 12). The job less traveled: Workers seek relief from business trips. *The Wall Street Journal,* p. B5.

however, they do not access this information prior to negotiating with car salespersons. This lack of information, of course, limits their ability to effectively negotiate. Similarly, many people do not adequately utilize real estate agents when purchasing houses. Real estate agents can provide valuable information about the market and the history of a house—all of which can be informative when trying to determine the counterparty's BATNA. The other party's aspiration point will be quite clear; however, the negotiator who determines only the other party's aspiration point, but not their BATNA, is in a severely disadvantageous negotiation position because the counterparty's aspiration may act as an anchor in the negotiation process.

SITUATION ASSESSMENT

Is the Negotiation One Shot, Long Term, or Repetitive?[50]

In a **one-shot negotiation**, a transaction occurs, and no future ramifications accrue to the parties. One of the few situations that has been identified as a truly one-shot negotiation is the interaction that occurs between customers and wait staff at interstate roadside diners—neither party will likely ever see one another again. (Incidentally, economists are baffled as to why diners leave tips—because tipping is usually a mechanism used in long-term relationships.)

However, most negotiation situations are not one-shot situations. Most people negotiate in the context of social networks, and reputation information is carried through those social networks. Repetitive negotiations are situations in which negotiators must renegotiate terms on some regular basis (e.g., unions and their management). The link between reputation and behavior is stronger for people who are more well-known in communities.[51] In long-term and **repetitive negotiations**, negotiators must consider how their relationship evolves and how trust is maintained over time. One of the most important long-term relationships is the employment negotiation. Because people want to negotiate economically attractive deals but not sour long-term relationships, job negotiations are generally regarded to be uncomfortable. This topic is so important that we devote an entire chapter to trust and relationships (Chapter 6) and a separate appendix on negotiating a job offer.

Do the Negotiations Involve Scarce Resources, Ideologies, or Both?

The two major types of conflict are consensus conflict and scarce resource competition.[52] **Consensus conflict** occurs when one person's opinions, ideas, or beliefs are incompatible with those of another, and the two seek to reach an agreement of opinion. For example, jurors' beliefs may differ about whether a defendant is innocent or guilty; two managers may disagree about whether someone has project management skills; two people may argue over whether gun

---

[50] Raffia, H. (1982). *The art and science of negotiation*. Harvard University Press, Cambridge, MA.

[51] Anderson, C., & Shirako, A. (2008). Are individuals' reputations related to their history of behavior? *Journal of Personality and Social Psychology, 94*(2), 320–333.

[52] Aubert, V. (1963). Competition and dissensus: Two types of conflict and conflict resolution. *Conflict Resolution, 7*, 26–42; Druckman, D., & Zechmeister, K. (1973). Conflict of interest and value dissensus: Propositions on the sociology of conflict. *Human Relations, 26*, 449–466; Kelley, H. H., & Thibaut, J. (1969). Group problem solving. In G. Lindzey & E. Aronson (Eds.), *Handbook of social psychology* (pp. 1–101). Reading, MA: Addison-Wesley; Thompson, L., & Gonzalez, R. (1997). Environmental disputes: Competition for scarce resources and clashing of values. In M. Bazerman, D. Messick, A. Tenbrunsel, & K. Wade-Benzoni (Eds.), *Environment, ethics, and behavior* (pp. 75–104). San Francisco: New Lexington Press.

ownership should be controlled. Consensus conflict is about ideology and fundamental beliefs and, as you might imagine, is difficult to resolve because it involves values and morals. Indeed negotiating over "values" is more difficult than negotiating over "interests," and people are less likely to reach integrative agreements when values are at stake.[53]

Scarce resource competition exists when people vie for limited resources. For example, when business partners are in conflict concerning how to divide responsibilities and profits, each may feel he or she deserves more than the other feels is appropriate.

Many conflict situations involve not only scarce resources but ideologies. People who are in conflict about interests (e.g., money and resources) are more likely to make value-added trade-offs and reach win-win outcomes than are people in conflict about values or beliefs.[54] For example, the Israeli-Palestinian conflict involves the allocation of land (a scarce resource) but stems from fundamentally different religious beliefs and ideologies. When negotiations involve such "sacred issues," more impasses, lower joint profits, and more negative perceptions of the counterparty result; however, this is only true when both parties believe they have attractive BATNAs[55] (see also the discussion of sacred issues in Chapter 10).

Is the Negotiation One of Necessity or Opportunity?

In many cases, we must negotiate; in other situations, negotiations are more of a luxury or opportunity. As an example, consider a couple selling their home because they have been transferred to a different location. They must negotiate a contract on the residence. Even if they have an attractive BATNA, they eventually must negotiate with someone to achieve their needs. In contrast, a person who is interested in enhancing her salary and benefits might want to improve her employment situation. No pressing need to negotiate exists; rather, negotiation is initiated for opportunistic reasons. Consider how the private equity firm Blackstone Group—which owns the Hilton Hotel chain—avoided a negotiation of *necessity* (settling a year-long contract dispute with Hilton workers) but focused on a negotiation of *opportunity* (owing the government about $320 million in the federal bailout program but persuaded the government to accept just $142 million in repayment). The failure to offer proposals to workers in light of the federal monies received led to a short and hostile strike by Hilton workers, which received heavy coverage in the media.[56]

Many people avoid negotiations of opportunity because they feel they lack skills. Indeed, having confidence in oneself as a negotiator is important for success.[57] Some people are comfortable with negotiations, to the point that they are always involved in them.

[53] Harinck, F., & De Dreu, C. K. W. (2004). Negotiating interests or values and reaching integrative agreements: The importance of time pressure and temporary impasses. *European Journal of Social Psychology, 34,* 595–611.

[54] Harinck, F., De Dreu, C. K. W., & Van Vianen, A. E. M. (2000). The impact of conflict issues on fixed-pie perceptions, problem-solving, and integrative outcomes in negotiation. *Organizational Behavior and Human Decision Processes, 81*(2), 329–358.

[55] Tenbrunsel, A. E., Wade-Benzoni, K. A., Tost, L. P., Medvec, V. H., Thompson, L., & Bazerman, M. H. (2009). The reality and myth of sacred issues in ideologically-based negotiations. *Negotiation and Conflict Management Research, 2*(3), 263–284.

[56] Wernau, J. & Byne, J. (2010, October 18). Hilton Chicago hotel workers in last day of strike. *Chicago Tribune.* Chicagobreakingnews.com

[57] Sullivan, B. A., O'Connor, K. M., & Burris, E. R. (2003). How negotiation-related self-efficacy affects tactics and outcomes. Paper presented at the Academy of Management Annual Meeting, Seattle, WA.

Is the Negotiation a Transaction or Dispute Situation?

In a typical negotiation, parties come together to exchange resource, such as when a buyer sees greater value in a seller's goods than the seller wants for them, and an exchange takes place (money is paid for goods or services). In other situations, negotiations take place because a claim has been made by one party and has been rejected by the other party. This is a dispute.[58] In 2010, Cablevision and Fox parent News Corp. were embroiled in a rate dispute that led to a blackout of the Major League Baseball playoffs and the World Series. Cablevision claimed that News Corp. was asking for an extra $80 million per year to access 12 Fox channels, more than doubling the annual rate to $150 million. Cablevision demanded that Fox enter into binding arbitration. Fox in turn blamed Cablevision Systems Corp. for the dispute. The media giants came to an agreement when Cablevision agreed to pay what it termed an "unfair price."[59]

The difference between transactions and disputes concerns the alternatives to mutual settlement. In an exchange situation, parties simply resort to their BATNAs; in a dispute, negotiators often go to court.

Are Linkage Effects Present?[60]

Linkage effects refer to the fact that some negotiations affect other negotiations. One example is in the case of law and setting precedent. Resolutions in one situation have implications for other situations. For example, in 2010, Dr. Pepper Snapple and the union representing 300 workers at the Mott's apple juice plant in New York, settled a 16-week strike that included wage freezes but not the pay cuts for workers that the company had sought. Labor unions feared that if Dr Pepper Snapple were able to push through substantial cuts in wages and benefits, it would cause other profitable companies to do the same.[61] Often direct linkages will occur when a multinational firm has operations in several countries and a decision made in one country carries over to other countries. Sometimes, indirect linkage effects occur, such as when a decision made at the negotiation table affects some interest group in a fashion that no one anticipates fully. A key reason why mergers are often unsuccessful is that companies do not think about linkage effects with current employees. In most merger scenarios, employees of the purchased company are given little information about the turn of events until well after the deal is settled. Rumors fly about what's going on, and employees are left in limbo, bitter about changes, and worried about their jobs and colleagues. Human resource specialists should be involved in the negotiation process to make the linkages for the employees smoother.

Is Agreement Required?[62]

In many negotiation situations, reaching agreement is a matter of preference. For example, in a salary negotiation a person might be willing to decline an offer from one company and either stay with the current company, start his or her own company, or delay negotiations indefinitely. However, in other situations, reaching agreement is not just the only course of action—it is required. For example, on August 17, 1981, when more than 85% of the nation's 17,500 air traffic controllers

[58] Ury, W. L., Brett, J. M., & Goldberg, S. B. (1988). *Getting disputes resolved: Designing systems to cut the costs of conflict.* San Francisco: Jossey-Bass.
[59] Fox, cablevision reach agreement. (2010, October 30). Newark Star Ledger, Nj.com; Associated Press. (2010, October 16). Fox, Cablevision suspend dispute negotiations. *CBS News.* Cbsnews.com
[60] Raiffa, *The art and science of negotiation.*
[61] Greenhouse, S. (2010, September 14). Ending strike, Mott's plant union accepts deal. *New York Times,* p. B6.
[62] Raiffa, *The art and science of negotiation.*

went on strike for better working conditions and improved wages, President Ronald Reagan told the controllers to return to work or the government would assume the striking controllers had quit. By the end of that week, more than 5,000 Professional Air Traffic Controllers Organization (PATCO) members received dismissal notices from the FAA. Reagan stated that Congress had passed a law in 1947 forbidding strikes by government employees, including a nonstrike oath that each air controller must sign upon hiring. Another example: The Taylor Law bars public employees from striking. This legislation affected the negotiations between New York governor George Pataki and the 14 bargaining units representing 190,000 state employees. Negotiations can be automatically extended under the Taylor Law if no new agreement is reached at the time of expiration.[63]

Is It Legal to Negotiate?

In the United States, it is illegal to negotiate the sale of human organs. In September 1999, the online auction house eBay had to retract a seller's posted auction for a human kidney.[64] The bidding went up to $5.7 million before eBay called off the auction. (For another story about controversial organ negotiation in the United States see Exhibit 2-2; Is It Legal to Negotiate?) Sometimes, no specific laws govern what can or cannot be negotiated; rather, individuals rely on strong cultural norms that are highly situation specific. For example, most people in the United States do not negotiate

EXHIBIT 2-2

Is It Legal to Negotiate?

When Mississippi Gov. Haley Barbour agreed to free two imprisoned sisters if one donated a kidney to another, it triggered a legal and an ethical debate. Barbour suspended the life sentences of Jamie and Gladys Scott, who were convicted of a 1993 robbery that their attorney said netted $11. After 16 years in prison, Jamie Scott, 36, was on daily dialysis, which cost the state about $200,000 a year. Barbour agreed to release her because of her medical condition, but her sister's release order stated one of the conditions she must meet is to donate a kidney. Gladys Scott volunteered to donate in her petition for early release. The case stumped experts such as Arthur Caplan, director of the Center for Bioethics at the University of Pennsylvania, who had studied transplants and their legal and ethical ramifications for about 25 years. "It is against the law to buy and sell organs or to force people to give them up," Kaplan said. "When you volunteer to give a kidney, you're usually free and clear to change your mind right up to the last minute. When you put a condition on it that you could go back to prison, that's a pretty powerful incentive." Dr. Michael Shapiro, chief of organ transplants at Hackensack University Medical Center in New Jersey and chairman of the ethics committee at the United Network for Organ Sharing, said the transplant should not be linked to her release. "The simple answer to that is you can't pay someone for a kidney," Shapiro said, adding that the sisters' situation could be construed as trading of value—in this case freedom—for an organ.

Source: Based on Associated Press. (2010, December 30). Kidney donation is sister's key out of prison.

---

[63] Grondahl, P. (2003, March 2). Different worlds, same side of bargaining table. *Times Union,* p. B1.
[64] Harmon, A. (1999, September 3). Auction for a kidney pops up on eBay's site. *The New York Times,* p. A13.

the price of fruit at major grocery stores, but they do it freely in farmer's markets, such as the Pike Place Market in Seattle, Washington. But farmer's markets are not the only place to haggle. Most home electronic stores will negotiate, as will stores that sell large, durable goods. When it comes to financial aid packages, families have more options than they realize. Financial aid officers have some latitude in how they award financial aid, and special family circumstances are often taken into consideration. When a student receives multiple admissions, parents have been known to tell one college about the financial aid package being offered by the other in hopes of the school bettering that offer.[65]

Is Ratification Required?[66]

Ratification refers to whether a party to the negotiation table must have a contract approved by some other body or group. For example, a corporate recruiter may need to have the salary and employment packages offered to recruits ratified by the company's human resources group or the CEO. In some circumstances, negotiators may tell the other side that ratification is required when it is not.

Are Time Constraints or Other Time-Related Costs Involved?[67]

Virtually all negotiations have some time-related costs. Although the negotiator who desperately needs an agreement, or for whom the passage of time is extremely costly, is likely to be at a disadvantage, more time pressure is not necessarily bad.[68] *Final deadlines* are distinct from *time-related costs*.[69] Two negotiators may face radically different time-related costs, but a deadline for one is a deadline for the other. The shortest final deadline is the only one that counts, and if they don't have a deal by that point, the two negotiators must exercise their BATNAs.

TIME PRESSURE AND DEADLINES   A final deadline is a fixed point in time that ends the negotiations. The rate of concessions made by negotiators increases as negotiators approach final deadlines.[70] Negotiators believe that final deadlines (i.e., time pressure) are a strategic weakness, so they avoid revealing their deadlines for fear their "weakness" will be exploited by the counterparty.[71] However, because deadlines restrict the length of the negotiation for all parties, they place all parties under pressure. One person's final deadline is also the other's final deadline.[72] When peace talks were held in Qatar in late 2010 aimed at ending seven years of civil war between Sudan and Darfur rebels, 11 days of negotiations without an agreement prompted frustrated Sudanese President Omar al-Bashir to suddenly announce that his delegation would leave the talks if agreement wasn't reached in the next day.[73] When negotiators keep their deadlines secret, the result is that they rush to get a deal before the deadline, whereas their opponents, who expect longer negotiations, concede at a more leisurely pace.[74] (For another example of strategic use of deadlines at AOL, see Exhibit 2-3.)

[65] Cohen, S. (2010, October 9). Paying for college (When you haven't saved enough) [Web log post]. *Forbes*. Blogs.forbes.com
[66] Raiffa, *The art and science of negotiation*.
[67] Ibid.
[68] Stuhlmacher, A. F., Gillespie, T. L., & Champagne, M. V. (1998). The impact of time pressure in negotiation: A meta-analysis. *International Journal of Conflict Management, 9*(2), 97–116.
[69] Moore, D. A. (2004). The unexpected benefits of final deadlines in negotiation. *Journal of Experimental Social Psychology, 40,* 121–127.
[70] Lim, S. G., & Murnighan, J. K. (1994). Phases, deadlines, and the bargaining process. *Organizational Behavior and Human Decision Processes, 58,* 153–171.
[71] Moore, "The unexpected benefits."
[72] Roth A. E., Murnighan, J. K., & Schoumaker, F. (1988). The deadline effect in bargaining: Some experimental evidence. *American Economic Review, 78*(4), 806–823.
[73] Sudan delegation to leave Darfur peace talks. (2010 December 31). *Cnn.* Cnn.com
[74] Moore, "The unexpected benefits."

EXHIBIT 2-3

Strategic Deadline Pressure

AOL used its knowledge of time pressure and deadlines in a strategic fashion. Its strategy of creating an "insane deadline" would always begin with a delicate courtship and that would end in an ultimatum that would cause the client to acquiesce. AOL would begin negotiations as a "slow waltz" between AOL and a prospective client, involving wooing and talk about how great the client's business was, how great it would be if the two sides worked together, how wonderful it would be if the client bought ads on AOL. Naturally, AOL wouldn't mention it was going through precisely the same process with multiple partners. Weeks would go by and then AOL would suddenly demand immediate action. Abruptly, deal makers would draw up a contract, slam it on the table, and order the prospective client to sign it within 24 hours, or else AOL would take the offer to another party, which happened to be waiting to hear from AOL. What's more, the contracts would always be of mammoth size—impossible to penetrate within the time constraints. Moreover, AOL executives forced deal makers of other companies to sit around for hours in a so-called waiting game, just to signal to them that they were not important.

Source: Based on Klein, A. (2003, June 15). Lord of the flies. *Washington Post,* p. W06.

The reason why negotiators so often incorrectly predict the consequences of final deadlines in negotiation has to do with the more general psychological tendency to focus egocentrically on the self when making comparisons or predictions.[75] Negotiators focus on the deadline's effect on themselves more than its effect on their negotiating partners. The same tendency leads people to predict they will be above average on simple tasks and below average on difficult tasks.[76]

TIME-RELATED COSTS   Setting a final deadline on the negotiations can be helpful, especially if the passage of time is particularly costly to you.[77] When the National Hockey League set a firm and final deadline of December 31, 2010 for the Phoenix Coyotes to find deep-pocketed local ownership or face certain franchise relocation, it set in motion a furious series of events that culminated in a new arena lease and approval of a new ownership group with only weeks to spare.[78]

TIME HORIZON   Another time-related question concerns what Okhuysen and colleagues refer to as the **time horizon**—the amount of time between the negotiation and the consequences or realization of negotiated agreements.[79] Greater temporal distance increases the incidence of profitable win-win

---

[75] Moore, D. A., & Kim, T. G. (2003). Myopic social prediction and the solo comparison effect. *Journal of Personality and Social Psychology, 85*(6), 1121–1135.

[76] Kruger, J. (1999). Lake Wobegon be gone! The "below-average effect" and the egocentric nature of comparative ability judgments. *Journal of Personality and Social Psychology, 77*(2), 221–232; Windschitl, P. D., Kruger, J., & Simms, E. N. (2003). The influence of egocentrism and focalism on people's optimism in competitions: When what affects us equally affects me more. *Journal of Personality and Social Psychology, 85*(3), 389–408.

[77] Moore, "The unexpected benefits."

[78] Associated Press. (2010 December 15). Phoenix suburb approves Coyotes arena lease. Sportingnews.com

[79] Okhuysen, G., Galinsky, A. D., & Uptigrove, T. A. (2003). Saving the worst for last: The effect of time horizon on the efficiency of negotiating benefits and burdens. *Organizational Behavior and Human Decision Processes, 91*(2), 269–279.

behavior, including negotiators' preference for multi-issue (as opposed to single-issue proposals), and value-added trade-off.[80] The longer the temporal distance between the act of negotiation and the consequences of negotiated agreements, the better the agreement.[81] The reason is that parties are less contentious because the realization is in the distance. Moreover, this time benefit is particularly pronounced in the cases where negotiations concern "burdens" as opposed to "benefits," because time gives people opportunity to discount the effects of burdens.

Are Contracts Official or Unofficial?

Many negotiation situations, such as the purchase of a house or a job offer, involve official contracts that legally obligate parties to follow through with stated promises. However, in several negotiation situations of equal or greater importance, negotiations are conducted through a handshake or other forms of informal agreements. Considerable cultural variation surrounds the terms of what social symbols constitute agreement (handshakes versus taking tea together), as well as which situations are treated officially or unofficially. Awkwardness can result when one party approaches the situation from a formal stance and the other treats it informally. Obviously, ill will can result when implicit contracts are broken. (We take up the topic of broken trust in Chapter 6.)

Where Do the Negotiations Take Place?

Common wisdom holds that it is to one's advantage to negotiate on one's own turf, as opposed to that of the other side. So important is this perception that great preparation and expense are undertaken to find neutral ground for important negotiations. For example, for the summit between former president Ronald Reagan and Soviet leader Mikhail Gorbachev, the site was carefully selected. The two met at the Chateau Fleur d'Eau in Geneva, Switzerland. Similarly, the multiparty Irish talks were stalled in 1991 when conflict broke out concerning where the next set of talks would be held. The Unionists, who agreed to talk directly to Irish government ministers about the future of Northern Ireland, were anxious to avoid any impression of going "cap in hand" to Dublin and, therefore, wanted the talks held in London, the capital to which they were determined to remain connected. In contrast, the Social Democratic and Labor Party, which represented the majority of Catholic moderates in the province, preferred that the talks be held in Dublin, the capital to which they felt a strong allegiance.[82] When Israeli and Palestinian leaders held peace talks in conjunction with United States officials in 2010, rounds of talks were strategically held in locations symbolically powerful to each side. The first talks were held at the White House. Then, the parties moved on to Egypt where successful peace talks had previously been held. Also, Egypt has a peace treaty with Israel. And finally, a third round of talks was held in Jerusalem, which both sides hoped to claim as a capital. Palestinian President Mahmoud Abbas was hosted in Israeli Prime Minister Benjamin Netanyahu's private residence.[83]

Are Negotiations Public or Private?[84]

In many areas, the negotiation dance takes place in the public eye. In other negotiation situations, negotiations occur privately. In contrast, one of the unique aspects of sports negotiations is that

---

[80] Henderson, M. D., Trope, Y., & Carnevale, P. J. (2006). Negotiation from a near and distant time perspective. *Journal of Personality and Social Psychology, 91*(4), 712–729.

[81] Okhuysen, Galinsky, & Uptigrove, "Saving the worst for last."

[82] Lewthwaite, G. A. (1991, May 7). Northern Ireland talks deadlock over location. *Baltimore Sun*, p. 5A.

[83] Duryea, B. (2010 September 17). Peace talks promising…maybe. *St. Petersburg Times*, p. 2A.

[84] Raiffa, *The art and science of negotiation.*

they take place in a fishbowl, with fans and the media observing every move at the bargaining table.[85] This kind of attention can lead to a media circus, with owners and players projecting their opinions on issues and events:

> The dickering back and forth makes for entertaining theater, but is a hindrance to the rational settlement of differences. It is customary, therefore, for both owners and players to be advised by their leaders to hold their tongues. NBA owners were made subject to fines of $1 million by the league for popping off in the media. (p. 7)

In some negotiations, political actors make public commitments not to negotiate with adversaries whom they label as being "beneath diplomacy," such as terrorists. Such public commitments are sometimes made even as they are being broken.[86] When a negotiator denounces an adversary, this increases motivation to reach a negotiated settlement if negotiations are undertaken.

Is Third-Party Intervention a Possibility?[87]

In many negotiation situations, third-party intervention is commonplace (and even expected). The mere presence of third parties may escalate the tension in negotiation situations, if the initial parties egocentrically believe that third parties will favor their own position. In other situations, it is less common (and perhaps a sign of personal failure) to involve third parties. (Third-party intervention is so important that we devote Appendix 3 to it in this book.)

What Conventions Guide the Process of Negotiation (Such as Who Makes the First Offer)?

In many negotiations, people have complete freedom of process. However, in other negotiations, strong conventions and norms dictate how the process of negotiation unfolds. For example, when people buy or sell houses in the United States, the first offer is typically made by a prospective buyer and all offers are formalized in writing. However, marked differences characterize the process across the country, with some home negotiations conducted via spoken word and some via official contract.

Do Negotiations Involve More Than One Offer?

In some situations, parties banter offers back and forth several times before a mutually agreeable deal is struck. In other situations, this type of dealing is considered unacceptable. In the real estate world, for example, buyers and sellers expect to negotiate. These same people, however, would not dream of negotiating in an upscale department store.

As another example, many employers now expect that job candidates will attempt to negotiate what is initially offered to them, but extensive haggling is not acceptable for many. Consider what happened to Jay Kaplan, real estate entrepreneur.[88] He traveled through the southeastern United States for eight consecutive days and met with five different owners, trying to purchase apartment buildings and shopping centers. Each meeting was a marathon session, with offers and counteroffers, lasting until dawn before an agreement was made. By the eighth day, with one meeting left, Kaplan

---

[85] Staudohar, P. D. (1999). Labor relations in basketball: The lockout of 1998–99. *Monthly Labor Review, 122*(4), 3–9.
[86] Browne, J., & Dickson, E. S. (2010). We don't talk to terrorists: On the rhetoric and practice of secret negotiations. *Journal of Conflict Resolution, 54*(3), 379–407.
[87] Raiffa, *The art and science of negotiation.*
[88] Kaplan, J. (1994, January 9). Single-offer tactic can be costly. *Arizona Republic,* p. E6.

was tired and decided to use a single-offer strategy. After asking for some aspirin and putting on his most exhausted face, Kaplan said to the other party, "You're asking $4.3 million for your property. I want to buy it for $3.7 million. Let's save ourselves the trouble of a long negotiation. I'm going to make you only one offer. It will be my best shot, and it will be a fair one. If you're a reasonable man, I'm sure you'll accept it." The strategy backfired. Kaplan then offered the other party $4.025 million, and the other party rejected it. They haggled for four hours until they agreed on $4.275. The opponent later told Kaplan there was no way he was going to accept the first offer made—no matter what it was.

Turning points are the events that occur either outside or inside negotiation talks that alter its course. Crises, as opposed to breakthroughs, produce more movements in negotiations with high trust and low power parties.[89]

Do Negotiators Communicate Explicitly or Tacitly?

In a typical buyer–seller negotiation or employment negotiation, negotiators communicate explicitly with one another. However, in other situations, communication is not explicit but tacit, and people communicate through their actions. This issue is so important that we devote an entire chapter to it (Chapter 11, in a discussion of social dilemmas).

Is There a Power Differential Between Parties?

Technically, negotiation occurs between people who are interdependent, meaning the actions of one party affect those of the other party, and vice versa. If one person has complete authority over another and is not affected by the actions of others, then negotiation cannot occur. However, it is often the case that low-power people can affect the outcomes of high-power others. For example, a CEO has more power than a middle-level manager in the company, but the manager can undoubtedly affect the welfare of the company and the CEO. The presence or absence of a power differential between negotiating parties can strongly affect the nature of negotiations. This topic is so important that we devote an entire chapter to power and influence in this book (Chapter 7).

Is Precedent Important?

In many negotiation situations, precedent is important, not only in anchoring negotiations on a particular point of reference but also in defining the range of alternatives. In a sense, the negotiator fears that making a decision in one case will set him or her up for future negotiations. Precedent can also encourage negotiation agreements. For example, in a simulated Israeli versus Palestinian negotiation, negotiators who were told that previous dyads were successful in reaching agreement were more likely to accept deals than those who were merely "urged" to reach agreement.[90]

CONCLUSION

Effective preparation is a strategic advantage at the bargaining table. We outlined three general areas of preparation: the self, the other party, and the context or situation. In terms of personal preparation, the negotiator who has identified a personal BATNA and set a reservation price and a target point is in a much better position to achieve the desired objectives. The negotiator who

---

[89] Druckman, D., Olekalns, M., & Smith, P. L. (2009). Interpretive filters: Social cognition and the impact of turning points in negotiation. *Negotiation Journal, 25*(1), 13–40.

[90] Liberman, V., Anderson, N. R., & Ross, L. (2010). Achieving difficult agreements: Effects of positive expectations on negotiation processes and outcomes. *Journal of Experimental Social Psychology, 46*(3), 494–504.

has prepared for negotiation knows when to walk away and how much is reasonable to concede. The negotiator who has adequately researched the counterparty's BATNA and interests is less likely to be manipulated or confused by the other party. We outlined several issues the negotiator should consider prior to commencing negotiations. A summary preparation form is presented in Exhibit 2-4. We suggest the negotiator use it when preparing for negotiations. The next two chapters focus on pie-slicing and pie-expanding strategies in negotiations.

EXHIBIT 2-4

Preparation Worksheet for Negotiations

Self-Assessment	Assessment of the Other Party	Situation Assessment
• What do I want? (Set a target point)	• Who are the other parties?	• Is the negotiation one shot, long term, or repetitive?
• What is my alternative to reaching agreement in this situation?	• Are the parties monolithic?	• Do the negotiations involve scarce resources, ideologies, or both?
• Determine your reservation point	• Counterparties' interests and position	• Is the negotiation one of necessity or opportunity?
• Be aware of focal points	• Counterparties' BATNA?	• Is the negotiation a transaction or dispute situation?
• Be aware of sunk costs		• Are linkage effects present?
• Do not confuse the target point with your reservation point		• Is agreement required?
		• Is it legal to negotiate?
• Identify the issues in the negotiation		• Is ratification required?
• Identify the alternatives for each issue		• Are time constraints or other time-related costs involved?
• Identify equivalent multi-issue proposals		• Are contracts official or unofficial?
• Assess your risk propensity		• Where do the negotiations take place?
• Endowment effects		• Are negotiations public or private?
• Am I going to regret this?		• Is third-party intervention a possibility?
• Violations of the sure thing principle		• What conventions guide the process of negotiation?
• Do I have appropriate level of confidence?		• Do negotiations involve more than one offer?
		• Do negotiators communicate explicitly or tacitly?
		• Is there a power differential between parties?
		• Is precedent important?

CHAPTER

3

Distributive Negotiation: Slicing the Pie

Some people go to court hoping to win millions of dollars. Tyler and Cameron Winklevoss had already won tens of millions of dollars in court. But more than six years into a bitter legal battle with Facebook founder and CEO Mark Zuckerberg, they wanted more. But that involved a big risk on their part. Not unlike a modern gameshow, they would have to give the money they were previously awarded back for a chance of getting more. The Winklevosses claimed that they along with Divya Narenda (all Harvard students) had the original idea for Facebook and that Zuckerberg stole it. Consequently, they sued Facebook and Zuckerberg in 2004 and settled in 2008 for $20 million in cash and $45 million in Facebook shares. However, days after the dispute was settled, the Winklevosses claimed foul play in that they were misled on the value of the shares they thought they were worth $35.90/each but were actually $8.88/each. Facebook claimed it was under no obligation to disclose the valuation. The Winklevoss twins and Mr. Narendra said that it wasn't about the money, but rather about the principle and the vindication. Facebook saw it differently and said that the Winklevosses suffered from a case of "settler's remorse."[1]

The opening example reveals that when people get emotional in negotiation, it is nearly inevitably about how the pie should be divided. In the case of the Facebook dispute, one party believed they were misled and that they deserved more. In this chapter, we focus on how negotiators can best achieve their outcomes—economic (e.g., money and resources) as well as social (e.g., preserving relationships and building trust). We address the question of how best to claim resources. This chapter discusses who should make the first offer, how to respond to an offer made by the other party, the amount of concessions to make, and how to handle an aggressive negotiator.

---

[1] Helft, M. (2010, December 31). Twins' Facebook fight rages on. *New York Times*, p. B1.

The entire process of making an opening offer and then reaching a mutually agreeable settlement is known as the **negotiation dance**.[2] Unfortunately, most of us have never taken dance lessons or know what to do once we find ourselves on the dance floor. Should we lead? Should we follow? A few hard-and-fast rules of thumb apply, but the negotiator must make many choices that are not so clear-cut. We wrestle with these issues in this chapter.

Although this chapter deals with slicing the pie, most negotiations involve a win-win aspect (*expanding* the pie), which we discuss in detail in the next chapter. However, even in win-win negotiations, the pie of resources created by negotiators eventually has to be sliced.

THE BARGAINING ZONE

Typically, negotiators' target points do not overlap: The seller wants more than the buyer is willing to pay. However, it is often the case that negotiators' reservation points *do* overlap, such that the most the buyer is willing to pay is more than the least the seller is willing to accept. Under such circumstances, mutual settlement is profitable for both parties. *However, the challenge of negotiation is to reach a settlement that is most favorable to oneself and does not give up too much of the bargaining zone.* The **bargaining zone**, or **zone of possible agreements (ZOPA)**, is the range between negotiators' reservation points.[3] The final settlement of a negotiation will fall somewhere above the seller's reservation point and below the buyer's reservation point.[4] The bargaining zone can be either positive or negative (see Exhibits 3-1A and 3-1B).

EXHIBIT 3-1A

Positive Bargaining Zone

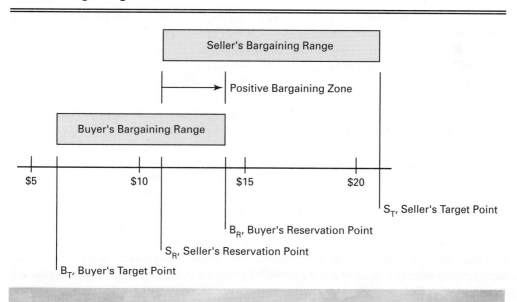

[2] Raiffa, H. (1982). *The art and science of negotiation.* Harvard University Press, Cambridge, MA.
[3] Lax, D. A., & Sebenius, J. K. (1986). *The manager as negotiator.* New York: Free Press.
[4] Raiffa, *The art and science of negotiation.*

EXHIBIT 3-1B

Negative Bargaining Zone

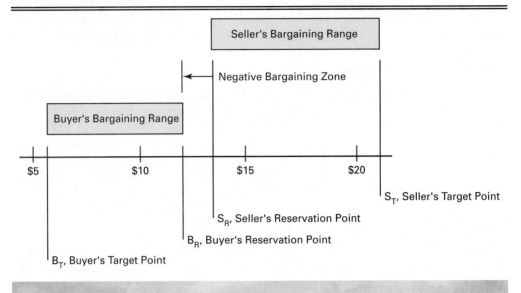

In a positive bargaining zone, negotiators' reservation points overlap: the most the buyer is willing to pay is greater than the least the seller will accept. This overlap means that mutual agreement is better than resorting to BATNAs. Consider the bargaining zone in Exhibit 3-1A. The seller's reservation point is $11; the buyer's reservation point is $14. The most the buyer is willing to pay is $3 greater than the very least the seller is willing to accept. The bargaining zone is between $11 and $14, or $3. If the negotiators reach agreement, the settlement will be somewhere between $11 and $14. If the parties fail to reach agreement in this situation, the outcome is an impasse and is **suboptimal** because negotiators leave money on the table and are worse off by not reaching agreement than reaching agreement.

In some cases, the bargaining zone may be nonexistent or even negative. However, the negotiators may not realize it and may spend fruitless hours trying to reach an agreement. This situation can be costly for negotiators; during the time in which they are negotiating, their opportunities may be worsening (i.e., negotiators have time-related costs; see Chapter 2). For example, consider the bargaining zone in Exhibit 3-1B, in which the seller's reservation point is $14 and the buyer's reservation point is $12. The most the buyer is willing to pay is $2 less than the seller is willing to accept at a minimum. This **negative bargaining zone** indicates that there is no positive overlap between the parties' reservation points. In this situation, negotiators should exercise their best alternatives to agreement. Because negotiations are costly to prolong, it is in both parties' interests to determine whether a positive bargaining zone is possible. If not, the parties should not waste time negotiating; instead, they should pursue other alternatives. For example Facebook CEO Mark Zuckerberg and Apple CEO Steve Jobs spent 18 months discussing a partnership regarding Ping, before walking away from the table. When talks broke down, Jobs was quoted as saying Zuckerberg and Facebook had "onerous terms that we could not agree to."[5]

Bargaining Surplus

Bargaining surplus is the amount of overlap between parties' reservation points. It is a measure of the size of the bargaining zone (what we refer to in this chapter as "the pie"). The bargaining surplus is a measure of the value that a negotiated agreement offers to both parties over the value of not reaching settlement. Skilled negotiators know how to reach agreements even when the bargaining zone is small.

Negotiator's Surplus

Negotiated outcomes will fall somewhere in the bargaining zone. But what determines *where* in this range the settlement will occur? Obviously, each negotiator would like the settlement to be as close to the other party's reservation point as possible, thereby maximizing his or her slice of the pie. In our example in Exhibit 3-1A, the seller would prefer to sell close to $14; the buyer would prefer to buy close to $11. *The best possible economic outcome for the negotiator is one that just meets the counterparty's reservation point, thereby inducing the other party to agree, but allows the focal negotiator to reap as much gain as possible.* This outcome provides the focal negotiator with the greatest possible share of the resources to be divided. In other words, one person gets all or most of the pie.

The positive difference between the settlement outcome and the negotiator's reservation point is the **negotiator's surplus** (see Exhibit 3-2). The total surplus of the two negotiators adds

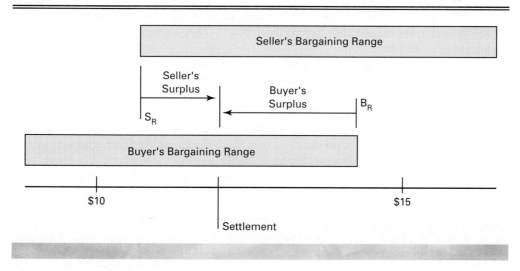

EXHIBIT 3-2

Bargaining Range and Surplus

---

[5] Horn, L. (2010, October 17). Report: Zuckerburg, Jobs dine, talk Ping in Apple CEO's home. *PCMag*.com

up to the size of the ZOPA or bargaining surplus. Obviously, negotiators want to maximize their surplus in negotiations; surplus represents resources in excess of what is possible for negotiators to attain in the absence of negotiated agreement.

The fact that negotiated settlements fall somewhere in the ZOPA and that each negotiator tries to maximize his or her share of the bargaining surplus illustrates the **mixed-motive** nature of negotiation: Negotiators are motivated to *cooperate* with the other party to ensure that settlement is reached in the case of a positive bargaining zone, but they are motivated to *compete* with one another to claim as much of the bargaining surplus as they can.

PIE-SLICING STRATEGIES

The most frequently asked question about negotiation is, "How can I achieve most of the bargaining surplus for myself?" For example, if you are a potential home buyer and you discern that the seller's reservation point is $251,000, that is an ideal offer to make, assuming that your reservation point is much higher. However, the ability to claim bargaining surplus is easier said than done. How do you get information about the other party's reservation point? Most negotiators will not reveal their reservation point, but it may emerge unintentionally. Raiffa cites a humorous story wherein one party opens with a direct request for information about his opponent's reservation price:[6]

> "Tell me the bare minimum you would accept from us, and I'll see if I can throw in something extra." The opponent, not to be taken in, quips, "Why don't you tell us the very maximum that you are willing to pay, and we'll see if we can shave off a bit?"

This quip illustrates the essence of negotiation: How do people make sure they reach agreement if the ZOPA is positive but simultaneously claim as much of the pie as possible?

Another problem emerges as well. Even if someone reveals his or her reservation point, the other party has no way to verify that the first party is telling the truth. Indeed, the most commonly used phrase in any negotiation is "That's my bottom line." When the counterparty tells us his or her reservation point, we are faced with the dilemma of whether the information is valid. The negotiator is always at an information deficit because the other party's reservation point is usually not verifiable (it includes subjective factors) whereas a BATNA is based on objective factors and can therefore be verifiable.

Given that "private" information about reservation points is inherently unverifiable, negotiation seems rather pointless. After all, if you can never tell if the other person is telling the truth, talking is fruitless (economists refer to such discussions as "cheap talk"[7]). However cheap talk does, in fact, matter.[8]

Some conditions allow negotiators to be more *confident* about the counterparty's reservation point. For example, a car buyer openly invites the dealer to call the competitor as a way of verifying that the buyer can indeed get the same car for less money. Similarly, if a person says something that is not in his or her interest, we may have more reason to believe it. For example,

---

[6] Raiffa, *The art and science of negotiation,* p. 40.

[7] Croson, R., Boles, T., & Murnighan, J. K. (2003). Cheap talk in bargaining experiments: Lying and threats in ultimatum games. *Journal of Economic Behavior & Organization, 51*(2), 143–159.

[8] Bazerman, M. H., Gibbons, R., Thompson, L., & Valley, K. L. (1998). Can negotiators outperform game theory? In J. Halpern & R. Stern (Eds.), *Debating rationality: Nonrational aspects of organizational decision making* (pp. 78–98). Ithaca, NY: ILR Press.

if a seller tells us she does not have another buyer and is under pressure to sell, we might believe her because this statement is not in her interest. This factor leads to an important cautionary note: It is not necessarily in your best interest to misrepresent your reservation point because you risk the possibility of disagreement. For example, imagine that you are trying to sell your iPod because you have been given a nicer model as a gift. You would be willing to accept $50 for the used model (your reservation point, based upon a re-seller's offer), but you would ideally like to get $100 (your target point). You place an ad, and a potential buyer calls offering to pay $60. If you tell the caller that you have an offer of $70 (when in fact, you do not), you risk the possibility that the potential buyer will not accept because he or she might have a better BATNA.[9]

With regard to slicing the pie, negotiators should be willing to settle for outcomes that exceed their reservation point and reject offers that are worse than their reservation point. However, people frequently settle for outcomes worse than their BATNA (the agreement bias) and often reject offers that are better than their BATNA (hubris). For example, most strikes are eventually settled on terms that could have been reached earlier, without parties incurring the costs that the strike imposes.[10] The key question is why such irrational behavior occurs. The problem can usually be traced to either cognitive or emotional biases. We will elaborate on some of these biases later in this chapter.

If negotiators follow 10 basic strategies, they can substantially increase the probability they will obtain a favorable slice of the pie.

Strategy 1: Assess Your BATNA and Improve It

Many negotiators do not think about their BATNA before negotiating. Even those who think about their BATNA often do not attempt to improve it. For most negotiators, BATNAs involve some uncertainty (see Chapter 2). However, uncertainty is not a good excuse for failure to assess one's BATNA. *Nothing can help a negotiator get a bigger slice of the pie than having a great BATNA.*

The risk a negotiator takes from not accurately assessing his or her BATNA prior to negotiation is that the negotiator will be unduly influenced by the counterparty. Consequently, negotiators should spend a considerable amount of time attempting to improve their BATNA before entering into a negotiation (remember the "falling in love" principle from Chapter 2).

Strategy 2: Determine Your Reservation Point, but Do Not Reveal It

Do not reveal your BATNA or your reservation price during the course of negotiation, even in the friendliest of situations. If you do, the other has no incentive to offer you more. In only two circumstances do we think it is appropriate to truthfully reveal your reservation price.

SITUATION #1 You have exhausted your time to negotiate and are about to walk out without a deal and you sense that the bargaining zone may be very small or perhaps negative.

SITUATION #2 You have a great BATNA and, consequently, an aggressive reservation price, and you would be happy if the counterparty matched or barely exceeded your reservation point.

---

[9] Farrell, J., & Gibbons, R. (1989). Cheap talk can matter in bargaining. *Journal of Economic Theory, 48,* 221–237.

[10] Keenan, J., & Wilson, R. B. (1993). Bargaining with private information. *Journal of Economic Literature, 31*(1), 45–104; Roth, A. E. (1993). Bargaining experiments. In J. Kagel & A. E. Roth (Eds.), *Handbook of experimental economics.* Princeton, NJ: Princeton University Press.

In this sense, negotiators "signal" their BATNA. Simon Cowell, the notoriously cranky British judge on the long-running blockbuster talent show "American Idol" sought a whopping $108 million dollar pay increase in 2009 which initially seemed unrealistic. However, Cowell had other alternatives beyond "American Idol." Thus, when another show, the "X Factor" made him an offer, he was OK walking away from the $36 million "American Idol" salary.[11]

Consider how another company, AOL, signaled its BATNA. One tactic involved an AOL dealmaker pitching a deal to a prospective dot-com client. The AOL rep's PowerPoint presentation would include the logo of the client's rival—as if AOL had accidentally mixed up some of the slides from another presentation. The AOL rep would then feign embarrassment and apologize. However, the slip was completely intentional and meant to signal to the dot-com that AOL had a BATNA.[12]

Many negotiators reveal their true reservation price if they trust and like the other party or desire a long-term relationship. However, we think this is ill-advised. There are many other ways to demonstrate trust and build a relationship, short of revealing your BATNA. Revealing information about a BATNA or reservation point is not a pie-expanding strategy; it is a pie-slicing strategy, and as a pie-slicing strategy it reduces a negotiator's power in a negotiation.

We do not believe that negotiators should lie about their BATNA or reservation price. Lying is unethical (see Chapter 7). Moreover, if you lie about your reservation price, you effectively reduce the size of the bargaining zone. A positive but small bargaining zone may appear to be negative and result in negotiation impasse. It is difficult to save face in such a situation because you appear foolish if you retract your demand.

Strategy 3: Research the Other Party's BATNA and Estimate Their Reservation Point

Negotiators can use a variety of tactics to garner information that may reveal information about the counterparty's alternatives.

Be careful when the other party discloses, however. When the counterparty discloses his or her BATNA at the outset of the negotiation, negotiators actually make less demanding offers, disclose more truthful information, and settle for less profit than when the counterparty does not disclose a BATNA.[13]

Strategy 4: Set High Aspirations (Be Realistic but Optimistic)

Your aspiration, or target point, defines the upper limit on what you can get in a negotiation. Because you will usually never get more than your first offer, your first offer represents an important **anchor point** in the negotiation. Trian Riceanu, a 30-year-old trained Romanian tailor, knew his skill set was needed in his field where most trained tailors are over the age of 60. This led him to set high aspirations in his salary negotiations with a high-end custom tailor shop in Chicago that only employs classically-trained master tailors. His high salary aspirations were met.[14]

---

[11] Simon Cowell leaving 'American Idol' (2010, January 11). Cnn.com

[12] Klein, A. (2003, June 15). Lord of the flies. *The Washington Post*, p. W06.

[13] Paese, P. W., & Gilin, D. A. (2000). When an adversary is caught telling the truth: Reciprocal cooperation versus self-interest in distributive bargaining. *Personality and Social Psychology Bulletin, 26*(1), 79–90.

[14] Hendershot, S. (2010, July). Hiring an all-star employee can involve tightening your own belt. *Workforce Management.* Workforce.com

According to Raiffa, the final outcome of any negotiation is usually the midpoint between the first two offers that fall within the bargaining zone.[15] For this reason, it does not make sense to make unrealistic offers because they do not influence settlements as much as realistic offers. We use the first offer made by each party as a measure of his or her aspirations.[16] Aspirations or target points determine the "final demands" made by negotiators, more so than do BATNAs.[17] Negotiators who set high aspirations end up with more of the pie than those who set lower aspirations. And negotiators whose aspirations exceed those of the counterparty get more of the bargaining zone.[18] For example, negotiators who have unattractive reservation points and high aspirations actually demand more from their opponents than do negotiators with attractive BATNAs and low aspirations. Thus, it pays to set your aspirations high during a negotiation.

However, this does not mean asking for the outrageous. If you ask for something outrageous, you risk souring the relationship. This is known as the **chilling effect**. Strategically, make your first offer slightly lower than the other party's reservation point, and then you can bargain up to their reservation point. Most people are not going to immediately accept your first offer, but they ultimately might accept an offer that is equivalent to their reservation point.

Setting specific, challenging, and difficult goals results in greater profit than does setting easy or nonspecific goals.[19] Nonspecific or easy goals lead to suboptimal, compromise agreements. High aspirations exert a self-regulating effect on negotiation behavior. Negotiators who are assigned easy goals tend to set harder new goals; however, in spite of adjustments, their new goals are significantly easier than the goals chosen by the difficult-goal negotiators. Thus, it is to a negotiator's advantage to set a high, somewhat difficult aspiration point early in the negotiation. The combination of high goals and cooperation is associated with the highest outcomes.[20]

When a negotiator focuses on his or her target point during negotiation, this increases the value of the outcome he or she ultimately receives.[21] Similarly, negotiators who focus on "ideals" rather than "oughts" do better in terms of slicing the pie.[22] Negotiators who focus on their accomplishments, hopes, and aspirations claim more resources than negotiators who focus on avoiding negative outcomes, holding constant their actual economic positions.[23] However,

---

[15] Raiffa, *The art and science of negotiation.*

[16] Kray, L., Thompson, L., & Galinsky, A. (2001). Battle of the sexes: Gender stereotype confirmation and reactance in negotiations. *Journal of Personality and Social Psychology, 80*(6), 942–958.

[17] Thompson, L. (1995). The impact of minimum goals and aspirations on judgments of success in negotiations. *Group Decision and Negotiation, 4*(6), 513–524.

[18] Chen, Ya-Ru, Mannix, E. A., & Okumura, T. (2003). The importance of who you meet: Effects of self- versus other-concerns among negotiators in the United States, the People's Republic of China, and Japan. *Journal of Experimental Social Psychology, 39*(1), 1–15.

[19] Huber, V. L., & Neale, M. A. (1986). Effects of cognitive heuristics and goals on negotiator performance and subsequent goal setting. *Organizational Behavior and Human Decision Processes, 38*(3), 342–365; Huber, V. L., & Neale, M. A. (1987). Effects of self- and competitor goals on performance in an interdependent bargaining task. *Journal of Applied Psychology, 72*(2), 197–203; Northcraft, G. B., Neale, M. A., & Earley, C. P. (1994). The joint effects of goal-setting and expertise on negotiator performance. *Human Performance, 7*(4), 257–272; Thompson, "The impact of minimum goals."

[20] Halpert, J. A., Stuhlmacher, A. F., Crenshaw, J. L., Litcher, C. D., Bortel, R. (2010). Paths to negotiation success. *Negotiation and Conflict Management Research, 3*(2), 91–116.

[21] Galinsky, A. D., Mussweiler, T., & Medvec, V. H. (2002). Disconnecting outcomes and evaluations: The role of negotiator focus. *Journal of Personality and Social Psychology, 83*(5), 1131–1140; Thompson, "The impact of minimum goals."

[22] Galinsky, A. D., & Mussweiler, T. (2001). First offers as anchors: The role of perspective-taking and negotiator focus. *Journal of Personality and Social Psychology, 81*(4), 657–669.

[23] Galinsky, A. D., Leonardelli, G. J., Okhuysen, G. A., & Mussweiler, T. (2005). Regulatory focus at the bargaining table: Promoting distributive and integrative success. *Personality and Social Psychology Bulletin, 31*(8), 1087–1098.

negotiators who focus on ideals do not *feel* as satisfied as negotiators who focus on their reservation point or BATNA.[24] This is known as the **goal-setting paradox**.[25] Thus, focusing on your targets will lead to an attractive outcome, but it may not feel satisfying. In contrast, focusing on reservation points leads people to *do* worse but *feel* better. If negotiators think about their BATNA after the negotiation, they feel better.[26]

The **winner's curse** occurs when the negotiator's first offer is immediately accepted by the counterparty. Immediate acceptance signals that the negotiator did not set his or her aspirations high enough. Furthermore, we caution negotiators to avoid a strategy known as boulwarism. **Boulwarism** is named after Lemuel Boulware, former CEO of General Electric, who believed in making one's first offer one's final offer. This strategy engenders hostility from the counterparty.

Another piece of advice: Do not become "anchored" by your reservation point. Many negotiators who assess their BATNA and set an appropriate reservation point fail to think about their aspiration or target point. Consequently, the reservation point acts as a psychological anchor and, in most cases, people make insufficient adjustments—they do not set their target high enough.

Strategy 5: Make the First Offer (If You Are Prepared)

Folklore dictates that negotiators should let the counterparty make the first offer. However, there is no scientific support for this advice. In fact, the party who makes the first offer obtains a better final outcome.[27] First offers act as an anchor point and correlate at least .85 with final outcomes.[28]

Negotiators need to consider a number of factors when making an opening offer. First and foremost, an opening offer should not give away too much of the bargaining zone. Second, many people worry they will "insult" the other party if they open too high (if they are selling) or too low (if they are buying). However, the fear of insulting the other party and souring the negotiations is more apparent than real. Indeed, people's perceptions of how assertive they can be with others are notably lower than what others actually believe.[29]

The first offer that falls within the bargaining zone acts as a powerful anchor point in negotiation. Recall the example of people's Social Security numbers affecting estimates of the number of physicians in Manhattan. That was a case of insufficient adjustment from an arbitrary anchor. Making the first offer protects negotiators from falling prey to a similar anchoring effect when they hear the counterparty's offer. Ideally, a negotiator's first offer acts as an anchor for the counterparty's counteroffer.

Your first offer should not be a range. Employers often ask prospective employees to state a range in salary negotiations. Do not fall victim to this bargaining ploy. By stating a range, you give up precious bargaining surplus. The counterparty will consider the lower end of the range as your target and negotiate down from there. A far better strategy is to respond to the counterparty's request for a range by making several offers that are all equally satisfying to you.

---

[24] Thompson, "The impact of minimum goals."

[25] Freshman, C., & Guthrie, C. (2009). Managing the goal-setting paradox: How to get better results from high goals and be happy. *Negotiation Journal, 25*(2), 217–231.

[26] Galinsky, Mussweiler, & Medvec, "Disconnecting outcomes and evaluations."

[27] Galinsky & Mussweiler, "First offers as anchors."

[28] Ibid.

[29] Ames, D. R. (2008). Assertiveness expectancies: How hard people push depends on the consequences they predict. *Journal of Personality and Social Psychology, 95*(6), 1541–1557.

One more thing about making the first offer: If you have made an offer, then you should expect to receive some sort of counteroffer or response. Once you put an offer on the table, be patient. It is time for the counterparty to respond. In certain situations, patience and silence can be important negotiation tools. Many negotiators make what we call **premature concessions**—they make more than one concession in a row before the other party responds or counteroffers. Always wait for a response before making a further concession. For example, Lewis Kravitz, an Atlanta executive coach and former outplacement counselor, advises patience and knowing when not to speak in the heat of negotiations. In one instance, he was coaching a young man who had just been fired by his team. The young man felt desperate and told Kravitz he was willing to take a $2,000 pay cut and accept $28,000 for his next job. Kravitz told the man to be quiet at the bargaining table and let the prospective employer make the first offer. At the man's next job interview, the employer offered him $32,000, stunning the overjoyed job seeker into momentary silence. The employer interpreted the silence as dissatisfaction and increased the offer to $34,000 on the spot.[30]

Strategy 6: Immediately Reanchor if the Other Party Opens First

If the counterparty makes an offer, then the ball is in your court, and it is wise to make a counteroffer in a timely fashion. It is unwise to accept the first offer. Negotiators whose first offers are accepted engage in counterfactual thoughts about how they could have done better (e.g., "What could have been different?") and are less satisfied than negotiators whose first offers are not immediately accepted.[31] CarWoo!, an online car buying website coaches consumers to negotiate when buying a new car by offering anonymous communications with car dealerships, which some deem a "hassle." CarWoo encourages buyers to make counter offers. One first time shopper and negotiator was able to negotiate 5.4% off a new BMW 355is coupe when they counteroffered $53,780 to the original $57,000 sales price.[32]

Counteroffers do two things. First, they diminish the prominence of the counterparty's initial offer as an anchor point in the negotiation. Second, they signal your willingness to negotiate. It is essential that you plan your opening offer before hearing the other party's opening—otherwise you risk being anchored by the other party's offer. In one investigation, some negotiators who received an offer from the other party were coached to focus on information that was inconsistent with that offer; others were not given such coaching.[33] The result? *Thinking* about the opponent's BATNA or reservation price or even one's own target point completely negates the powerful anchoring impact that the other party's first offer might have on you. Above all, do not adjust your BATNA based upon the counterparty's offer, and do not adjust your target. It is extremely important not to be "anchored" by the counterparty's offer. An effective counteroffer moves the focus away from the other party's offer as a reference point.

Strategy 7: Plan Your Concessions

Concessions are the reductions that a negotiator makes during the course of a negotiation. Most negotiators expect to make concessions during negotiation. (One exception is the bargaining style known as **boulwarism**, presented previously.)

---

[30] Lancaster, H. (1998, January 27). You have to negotiate for everything in life, so get good at it. *The Wall Street Journal*, p. B1.
[31] Galinsky, A. D., Seiden, V. L., Kim, P. H., & Medvec, V. H. (2002). The dissatisfaction of having your first offer accepted: The role of counterfactual thinking in negotiations. *Personality and Social Psychology Bulletin, 28*(2), 271–283.
[32] Furchgott, R. (2001, January 18). CarWoo: Demystifying the art of the deal. *New York Times.* Nytimes.com
[33] Galinsky & Mussweiler, "First offers as anchors."

Negotiators need to consider three things when formulating counteroffers and concessions: (1) the **pattern of concessions**, (2) the **magnitude of concessions**, and (3) the **timing of concessions**.

PATTERN OF CONCESSIONS   **Unilateral concessions** are concessions made by one party; in contrast, **bilateral concessions** are concessions made by both sides. Consider unilateral concessions made during negotiations for the University of Michigan's school-naming rights. Alumni donate millions of dollars to their business schools, hoping the school will be named after them. Stephen Ross, a property developer, made the first offer of $50 million to the business school's dean. The dean did not accept. Ross then made an immediate concession by doubling his offer to $100 million and received the naming rights.[34] The haunting question is whether he could have offered less and still received the naming rights. Negotiators who make fewer and smaller concessions maximize their slice of the pie, compared to those who make larger and more frequent concessions.[35] It is an almost universal norm that concessions take place in a quid pro quo fashion, meaning that negotiators expect a back-and-forth exchange of concessions between parties. People expect others to respond to concessions by making concessions in kind. However, negotiators should not offer more than a single concession at a time to the counterparty. Wait for a concession from the counterparty before making further concessions. An exception would be a situation in which you feel that the counterparty's offer is truly at his or her reservation point.

MAGNITUDE OF CONCESSIONS   Even though negotiators may make concessions in a back-and-forth method, this exchange does not say anything about the degree of concessions made by each party. Thus, a second consideration when making concessions is to determine how much to concede. The usual measure of a concession is the amount reduced or added (depending upon whether one is a seller or buyer) from one's previous offer. It is unwise to make consistently greater concessions than the counterparty.

The **graduated reduction in tension (GRIT) model** is a method in which parties avoid escalating conflict to reach mutual settlement within the bargaining zone.[36] The GRIT model, based on the reciprocity principle, calls for one party to make a concession and invites the other party to reciprocate by making a concession. The concession offered by the first party is significant, but not so much that the offering party is tremendously disadvantaged if the counterparty fails to reciprocate.

Hilty and Carnevale examined the degree of concessions made by negotiators over different points in the negotiation process (e.g., early on versus later).[37] They compared black-hat/white-hat (BH/WH) negotiators with white-hat/black-hat (WH/BH) negotiators. BH/WH negotiators began with a tough stance, made few early concessions, and later made larger concessions. WH/BH negotiators did the opposite: They began with generous concessions and then became tough and unyielding. The BH/WH concession strategy proved to be more

---

[34] News from the schools. Name games. (2007, January 23). *Economist.com*

[35] Siegel, S., & Fouraker, L. E. (1960). *Bargaining and group decision making.* New York: McGraw-Hill; Yukl, G. A. (1974). Effects of the opponent's initial offer, concession magnitude and concession frequency on bargaining behavior. *Journal of Personality and Social Psychology, 30*(3), 323–335.

[36] Osgood, C. E. (1962). *An alternative to war or surrender.* Urbana: University of Illinois Press.

[37] Hilty, J. A. & Carnevale, P. J. (1993). Black-hat/white-hat strategy in bilateral negotiation. *Organizational Behavior and Human Decision Processes, 55*(3), 444–469.

effective than the WH/BH strategy in eliciting concessions from the counterparty. Why? The BH-turns-WH sets up a favorable contrast for the receiver. The person who has been dealing with the BH feels relieved to now be dealing with the WH.

TIMING OF CONCESSIONS   The timing of concessions refers to whether they are immediate, gradual, or delayed.[38] In an analysis of buyer-seller negotiations, sellers who made immediate concessions received the most negative reaction from the buyer—who showed least satisfaction and evaluated the object of sale most negatively. In contrast, when the seller made gradual concessions, the buyer's reaction was most positive, with high satisfaction.

Strategy 8: Support Your Offer with Facts

The way in which an offer is presented affects the course of negotiations. Ideally, present a rationale that is objective and invites the counterparty to buy into your rationale. If your proposals are labeled as "fair," "even splits," or "compromises," they carry more impact. Agent Scott Boras represents many of the highest-paid baseball players in the game. When Boras walks into a front office and asks team administration for a price for his player, it is almost always the correct market price. Boras knows the importance of facts and has been known to carry around book-sized binders of every one of his clients' accomplishments including seemingly obscure charts of a player's potential impact on the team's bottom line. By using fact-based arguments, he netted superstar Alex Rodriguez a 10-year, $252 million contract.[39]

Sometimes, the rationale does not even need to make sense to be effective. One investigation examined how often people were successful in terms of negotiating to cut in line at a photocopy machine.[40] Those who did not provide a rationale were the least successful (60%); those who presented a logical rationale were the most successful (94%). People who used a meaningless rationale (e.g., "I have to cut in line because I need to make copies") were remarkably successful (93%).

Strategy 9: Appeal to Norms of Fairness

A variety of norms of fairness exist and that negotiators usually focus on norms of fairness that serve their own interests.[41] Fairness is an arbitrary concept that can be used as a bargaining strategy; the negotiator should simultaneously be prepared to counterargue when the counterparty presents a fairness argument that does not serve his or her own interests. Consider the different fairness standards invoked in United Airlines negotiations with its employees. Back in 2005, US airline employees conceded more than $12 billion a year in wages, benefits, pensions and other concessions. However, when United and Continental merged in 2010 to create the nation's second-largest airline, and airlines showed profitability for the first time in years, employees argued for a bigger piece of the pie in ongoing contract negotiations. Conversely, the airlines argued that domestic airline profit margin was just 1.1 percent for the first half of 2010.[42]

---

[38] Kwon, S., & Weingart, L. R. (2004). Unilateral concessions from the other party: Concession behavior, attributions, and negotiation judgments. *Journal of Applied Psychology, 89*(2), 263–278.

[39] Taibbi, M. (2009, February 23). The devil's doorstep: A visit with Scott Boras. *Men's Journal.* Mensjournal.com

[40] Langer, E. J., Blank, A., & Chanowitz, B. (1978). The mindlessness of ostensibly thoughtful action: The role of placebic information in interpersonal interaction. *Journal of Personality and Social Psychology, 36*(6), 635–642.

[41] Loewenstein, G. F., Thompson, L., & Bazerman, M. H. (1989). Social utility and decision making in interpersonal contexts. *Journal of Personality and Social Psychology, 57*(3), 426–441.

[42] Mouawad, J. (2010, October 27). Airline unions seek a share of the industry gains. *New York Times*, p. B1.

Strategy 10: Do Not Fall for the "Even Split" Ploy

A common technique is the **even split** between whatever two offers are currently on the negotiation table. The concept of the even split has an appealing, almost altruistic flavor to it. So what is the problem with even splits? The problem is that they are based on values arrived at arbitrarily. Consider a car-buying situation. Suppose you initially offered $33,000 for the car, then $34,000, and finally, $34,500. Suppose the salesperson initially requested $35,200, then reduced it to $35,000, and then to $34,600. The salesperson then suggests you split the difference at $34,550, arguing that an even split of the difference would be "fair." However, the pattern of offers up until that point was not "equal" in any sense. You made concessions of $1,500; the salesperson made concessions of $600. Further, even concessions that were of equal magnitude do not guarantee that the middle value is a "fair" value. It behooves a negotiator to begin with a high starting value and make small concessions. Often, the person who suggests the even split is in an advantageous position. Before accepting or proposing an even split, make sure the anchors are favorable to you.

THE MOST COMMONLY ASKED QUESTIONS

Should I Reveal My Reservation Point?

No. If you reveal your reservation price, be prepared for the other party to offer you your reservation price—but not more. Some negotiators reveal their reservation point to demonstrate that they are bargaining in good faith and trust the other party. These negotiators rely on the counterparty's goodwill and trust their opponent not to take advantage of this information. There are more effective ways to build trust. For example, you could show a genuine concern for the needs and interests of the other party. The purpose of negotiation is to maximize your surplus, so why create a conflict of interest by "trusting" the other party with your reservation point?

The most valuable piece of information you can have about the counterparty is his or her reservation point. This knowledge allows you to make the counterparty an offer that barely exceeds his or her reservation point and to claim the entire bargaining surplus for yourself. However, you should assume the counterparty is as smart as you are and therefore not likely to reveal his or her reservation point.

Should I Lie About My Reservation Point?

If negotiators do well for themselves by not revealing their reservation point, perhaps they might do even better by lying, misrepresenting, or exaggerating their reservation point. However, lying is not a good idea for three important reasons.

First, lying is unethical. Lewicki and Stark identified five types of behavior that some consider to be unethical in negotiations, including traditional competitive bargaining (e.g., exaggerating an initial offer or demand); attacking an opponent's network (e.g., attempting to get your opponent fired or threatening to make him or her look foolish); misrepresentation and lying (e.g., denying the validity of information your opponent has that weakens your negotiating position even though the information is valid); misuse of information (e.g., inappropriate information gathering), and false promises (e.g., offering to make future concessions that you know you won't follow through on, and guaranteeing your constituency will uphold the settlement, even though you know they won't).[43]

Our examination of lying revealed that even though 40% of people believed that others in their network lied over a 10-week period, these same people admitted lying only about 22% of the time. Such egocentric perceptions often lead to lawsuits. After Bank of America reached a $150-million settlement with the Securities and Exchange Commission, they were accused of lying to shareholders in 2008 to speed the purchase of Merrill Lynch.[44]

In other cases, negotiators are quick to assume that others have deceived them. For example, when John Mara, owner of the National Football League's New York Giants, said that he was resigned to an NFL season with a salary cap in place—a full month and a half before the deadline the two sides had set for a completion of the deal—the NFL players union accused NFL owners of negotiating in bad faith.[45] And in another case, negotiations to prevent 167 Newark, N.J. police officers from being laid off broke down when conflict arose between the local Fraternal Order of Police and two members of its executive board over whether $9.5 million in temporary cuts to save the positions had actually been agreed upon.[46] In each of these examples, negotiators most likely held self-serving views.

Another example from the world of sports: In 2009, the Pittsburgh Pirates baseball club played hardball with two of their starting players, and the team made take-it-or-leave-it offers to Freddy Sanchez ($10 million deal for the following season) and Jack Wilson (a two-year, $8 million contract). However, both players rejected the "final" offers. The Pirates responded by immediately pulling the offers and trading both players to other teams within the week. Paul Cobbe, Sanchez's agent at the time commented, "The scenario is not set up for a counteroffer. My understanding is, they gave us what they thought is a very strong offer, and there is no room for any significant change."[47]

If you lie about your alternatives and the other party calls your bluff, how do you get back to the table without losing face? Indeed, the most common lie in negotiation is "This is my final offer." It is embarrassing to continue negotiating after making such a statement. Do not back yourself into a corner.

Second, lying hurts your reputation. People in the business community develop reputations that quickly spread via electronic mail, telephone, and word of mouth. People who have a reputation as tough are treated more competitively by others, and have more difficulty claiming resources. "Deceptive cheap talk" that is discovered by the other party negatively impacts a negotiator's outcomes.[48] People who discover that they have been deceived may seek retribution, even though doing so may be costly to themselves, much like the opening example of the Facebook dispute. Experienced negotiators are able to extract more of the pie for themselves, but not when they have a reputation for being "distributive."[49] Misrepresenting your reservation price is a poor substitute for preparation and developing strategy.

---

[43] Lewicki, R. J., & Stark, N. (1996). What's ethically appropriate in negotiations: An empirical examination of bargaining tactics. *Social Justice Research, 9*(1), 69–95.

[44] Popper, N. (2010, February 23). Bank of America's $150-million settlement with SEC gets grudging approval. *Los Angeles Times.* Latimes.com

[45] Battista, J. (2010, January 21). Union responds to Mara's comments. *New York Times,* p. B27.

[46] Giambusso, D. & Queally, J. (2010, November 24). Negotiations break down over 167 police layoffs. *Newark Star-Ledger.* Nj.com

[47] Biertempfel, R. (2009, July 20). Pirates pull offers to SS Wilson, 2B Sanchez, *Pittsburgh Tribune Reivew.* Pittsburghlive.com

[48] Croson, Boles, & Murnighan, "Cheap talk in bargaining experiments."

[49] Tinsley, C. H., O'Connor, K. M., & Sullivan, B. A. (2002). Tough guys finish last: The perils of a distributive reputation. *Organizational Behavior and Human Decision Processes, 88*(2), 621–642.

Should I Try to Manipulate the Counterparty's Reservation Point?

No. Assuming that the counterparty is reasonably intelligent, motivated, and informed (like you), he or she is not likely to fall prey to this transparent negotiation ploy. Such attempts may actually backfire, entrenching the counterparty more steadfastly in his or her position. Furthermore, you want to discourage the other negotiator from using such influence tactics.

Some negotiators are inclined to use scare tactics, such as "If you do not sell your house to us, there will not be another buyer" or "You'll regret not buying this company from me in 10 years when I am a billionaire." In 2009, Microsoft Corp. Chief Executive Officer Steven Ballmer threatened that he would move some employees offshore if President Barack Obama enacted higher taxes on U.S. companies' foreign profits. Obama proposed outlawing or restricting nearly $190 billion in tax breaks over a decade. Following Ballmer's threat, the "Creating American Jobs and Ending Offshoring Act" bill died in the United States Senate in late 2010.[50] However, scare tactics may not always be effective.

Should I Make a "Final Offer" or Commit to a Position?

The phrase "This is my final offer" has much more impact when said later in a negotiation. Making an irrevocable commitment, such as a "final offer," should be done only when you really mean it and are prepared to walk away from the bargaining table. Of course, you should only walk away from the bargaining table if your BATNA is more attractive than the counterparty's offer. Intimidating the other party is risky. It is difficult to make "binding" commitments that are credible. Consider the threat that Newfoundland and Labrador Premier Danny Williams made to Exxon Mobil. Williams was negotiating a multibillion-dollar Hebron offshore oil deal. Williams based his position on the importance of an adequate deal to Newfoundlanders, committed to it and challenged oil companies, "Well, fine. Go somewhere else. We'll still have our oil." Eventually, Exxon Mobil and Chevron gave in and agreed to Williams's terms.[51] In this situation, the threat worked. However, in other situations threats don't work, such as in the case of Yelp. In 2009, Google and Yahoo! each tried to purchase Yelp, the popular review site. Google offered Yelp $500 million, but Yahoo! came in with a financially more attractive offer of nearly $750 million. Yelp negotiators told Google they had received a better offer from Yahoo!, but Google held steady and did not top the Yahoo! bid. However, Yelp had no intention of working with Yahoo! as executives deemed the company a poor fit. Therefore Yelp came away with no deal, and no money. The underlying message is: do not reject an offer if you are not prepared to walk away. In this case, Yelp was not prepared to walk away.[52]

SAVING FACE

"Face," or dignity, in a negotiation has been called "one of an individual's most sacred possessions."[53] **Face** is the value a person places on his or her public image, reputation, and status vis-à-vis other people in the negotiation. Direct threats to face in a negotiation include making ultimatums, criticisms, challenges, and insults. Often, the mere presence of an audience can

---

[50] Donmoyer, R. (2009, June 3). Ballmer says tax would move Microsoft jobs offshore. *Bloomberg.* Bloomberg.com
[51] Campbell, C. (2007, September 10–17). How to win, in a fight with Big Oil. *Maclean's: Toronto, 120*(35/36), p. 62.
[52] Helft, M. (2009, December 21). Who walked? Google or Yelp? *The New York Times.* Nytimes.com
[53] Deutsch, M. (1961). The face of bargaining. *Operations Research, 9*(6), 886–897.

make "saving face" of paramount importance for a negotiator. When a person's face is threatened in a negotiation, it can tip the balance of his or her behavior away from cooperation toward competition, resulting in impasses and lose-lose outcomes.

People differ in terms of how sensitive they are to losing face. A negotiator's face threat sensitivity (FTS) is the likelihood of having a negative reaction to a face threat.[54] People with high FTS have a lower threshold for detecting and responding to face threats. Their emotional responses range from anger or frustration to a feeling of betrayal or sadness. In turn, they may not trust the other party and refuse to share information. We measured negotiators' FTS and the impact it had on their behavior and the quality of their negotiated outcomes.[55] Negotiators were asked how easily their feelings get hurt, the extent to which they are "thin-skinned" and "don't respond well to criticism." In buyer-seller negotiations, fewer win-win agreements were reached when the seller had high FTS. In employment negotiations, job candidates were less likely to make win-win deals if they had high FTS.

The best way to help the other party save face is not indicate that you think he or she has lost face. If the other takes an irrevocable stance, such as labeling an offer as "final," what can you do? First, do not acknowledge their statement as final. Instead of saying "So, if this is your final offer, I guess things are over," you might say "Let me consider your offer and get back to you." By not acknowledging the finality of an offer, you provide the other party with an "out" to resume negotiations later. For example, during the 1985 Geneva Summit meeting, a tense moment occurred when Mikhail Gorbachev of the Soviet Union glumly declared (after hours of negotiating with U.S. President Ronald Reagan), "It looks as if we've reached an impasse."[56] Instead of acknowledging this comment, Reagan quickly suggested that they take a break and proposed taking a walk outside. This suggestion proved to be a critical move in allowing Gorbachev to come back to the table. Said Gorbachev, "Fresh air may bring fresh ideas." Reagan replied, "Maybe we'll find the two go together."[57]

In other situations, you may have to help the other party by finding a face-saving strategy, perhaps achieved by relabeling some of the terms of the negotiation. An excellent example of face saving occurred in the General Motors–Canadian UAW strike talks. The Canadian union had insisted on a wage increase; GM wanted to institute a profit-sharing scheme but keep wages at a minimum, especially because of GM's fear of a slippery slope. A solution was devised such that wages were kept at a minimum but workers were given an incentive-based increase.[58]

THE POWER OF FAIRNESS

Fairness concerns pervade aspects of social life from corporate policy to sibling squabbles.[59]

[54] Tynan, R. O. (2005). The effects of threat sensitivity and face giving on dyadic psychological safety and upward communication. *Journal of Applied Social Psychology*. 35(2), 223–247.
[55] White, J. B., Tynan, R., Galinsky, A. D., & Thompson, L. (2004). Face threat sensitivity in negotiation: Roadblock to agreement and joint gain. *Organizational Behavior and Human Decision Processes, 94*(2), 102–124.
[56] Thomas, E. (1985, December 2). Fencing at the fireside summit: With candor and civility, Reagan and Gorbachev grapple for answers to the arms-race riddle. *Time, 126*(22).
[57] Ibid.
[58] Gunnarsson, S., & Collison, R. (Directors/Producers). (1985). *Final offer.* Montreal: National Film Board of Canada.
[59] Deutsch, M. (1985). *Distributive justice: A social-psychological perspective.* New Haven, CT: Yale University Press.

Multiple Methods of Fair Division

Negotiators often use one of three fairness principles when it comes to slicing the pie: equality, equity, and need:[60]

1. *Equality rule,* or *blind justice,* prescribes equal shares for all. Outcomes are distributed without regard to inputs, and everyone benefits (or suffers) equally. The U.S. education system and legal systems are examples of equality justice: Everyone receives equal entitlement.

2. *Equity rule,* or *proportionality of contributions principle,* prescribes that distribution should be proportional to a person's contribution. The free market system in the United States is an example of the equity principle. In many universities, students bid for classes; those who bid more points are more entitled to a seat in the course.

3. *Needs-based rule,* or *welfare-based allocation,* states that benefits should be proportional to need. The social welfare system in the United States is based on need. In many universities, financial aid is based on need.

Situation-Specific Rules of Fairness

Different fairness rules apply in different situations.[61] For example, most of us believe that our court/penal justice system should be equality-based: Everyone should have the right to an equal and fair trial regardless of income or need (equality principle). In contrast, most believe that academic grades should be assigned on the basis of an equity-based rule: Students who contribute more should be rewarded with higher marks (equity principle). Similarly, most people agree that disabled persons are entitled to parking spaces and easy access to buildings (needs principle). However, sometimes fierce debates arise (e.g., affirmative action, with some arguing it is important for people who have been historically disadvantaged to have equal access and others arguing for pure equity-based, or merit-only, rules).

The goals involved in a negotiation situation often dictate which fairness rule is employed.[62] For example, if the goal is to minimize waste, then a needs-based or social welfare policy is most appropriate.[63] If the goal is to maintain or enhance harmony and group solidarity, equality-based rules are most effective.[64] If the goal is to enhance productivity and performance, equity-based allocation is most effective.[65]

Similarly, a negotiator's relationship to the other party strongly influences the choice of fairness rules. When negotiators share similar attitudes and beliefs, when they are physically close to one another, or when it is likely they will engage in future interaction, they prefer equality rule. When the allocation is public (others know what choices are made), equality is used; when allocation is private, equity is preferred. Friends tend to use equality, whereas

[60] Ibid.

[61] Schwinger, T. (1980). Just allocations of goods: Decisions among three principles. In G. Mikula (Ed.), *Justice and social interaction: Experimental and theoretical contributions from psychological research* (pp. 95–125). New York: Springer-Verlag.

[62] Mikula, G. (1980). On the role of justice in allocation decisions. In G. Mikula (Ed.), *Justice and social interaction: Experimental and theoretical contributions from psychological research* (pp. 127–166). New York: Springer-Verlag.

[63] Berkowitz, L. (1972). Social norms, feelings and other factors affecting helping behavior and altruism. In L. Berkowitz (Ed.), *Advances in experimental social psychology: Vol. 6* (pp. 63–108). New York: Academic Press.

[64] Leventhal, G. S. (1976). The distribution of rewards and resources in groups and organizations. In L. Berkowitz & E. Walster (Eds.), *Advances in experimental social psychology: Vol. 9* (pp. 91–131). New York: Academic Press.

[65] Deutsch, M. (1953). The effects of cooperation and competition upon group processes. In D. Cartwright & A. Zander (Eds.), *Group dynamics* (pp. 319–353). Evanston, IL: Row, Peterson.

non-friends or acquaintances use equity.[66] Further, people in relationships with others do not consistently employ one rule of fairness but, rather, use different fairness rules for specific incidences that occur within relationships. For example, when people in relationships are asked to describe a recent incident from their own relationship that illustrates a particular justice principle (equity, equality, or need), needs-based fairness is related to incidents involving nurturing and personal development, whereas equity and equality-based fairness are related to situations involving the allocation of responsibilities.[67] In general, equality-based pie-slicing strategies are associated with more positive feelings about the decision, the situation, and one's partner.

Fairness rules also depend on whether people are dealing with rewards versus costs (recall our discussion about the framing effect in Chapter 2). Equality is often used to allocate benefits, but equity is more commonly used to allocate burdens.[68] For example, in one investigation people were involved in a two-party negotiation concerning a joint project.[69] In the benefit-sharing condition, negotiators were told that their joint project produced a total earning of 3,000 GL (a hypothetical monetary unit) and their task was to reach an agreement about how to divide this amount with their partner. Participants were told they had personally incurred a cost of 1,350 GL for this project and their final profit would be determined by subtracting 1,350 from the negotiated agreement amount. In the cost-sharing condition, the situation was exactly the same, except participants were told they had personally invested 1,650 GL. Thus, the bargaining situation was identical in both situations, with the exception of the personal investment. Obviously, an equal split of 3,000 GL would mean 1,500 GL apiece, which would result in a gain in the benefit condition and a loss in the cost condition. Negotiators were more demanding and tougher when bargaining how to share costs than benefits. Furthermore, fewer equal-split decisions were reached in the cost condition.

The selection of fairness rules is also influenced by extenuating circumstances. Consider, for example, a physically handicapped person who attains an advanced degree. A person who overcomes external constraints is more highly valued than a person who does not face constraints but contributes the same amount. When a situation is complex, involving multiple inputs in different dimensions, people are more likely to use the equality rule. Thus, groups often split dinner bills equally rather than compute each person's share. This approach can lead to problems. Group members aware of the pervasive use of equality may actually spend more individually. No group member wants to pay for more than he or she gets; if people cannot control the consumption of others, they consume more. Of course, when everyone thinks this way, the costs escalate, leading to irrational group behavior (a topic we discuss in Chapter 11 on social dilemmas).

Different fairness rules are a potential source of conflict and inconsistency.[70] For example, people who are allocating resources choose different rules of fairness than do people who are on the receiving end. Allocators often distribute resources equally, even if they have

---

[66] Austin, W. (1980). Friendship and fairness: Effects of type of relationship and task performance on choice of distribution rules. *Personality and Social Psychology Bulletin, 6*(3), 402–408.

[67] Steil, J. M., & Makowski, D. G. (1989). Equity, equality, and need: A study of the patterns and outcomes associated with their use in intimate relationships. *Social Justice Research, 3*(2), 121–137.

[68] Sondak, H., Neale, M. A., & Pinkley, R. (1995). The negotiated allocation of benefits and burdens: The impact of outcome valence, contribution and relationship. *Organizational Behavior and Human Decision Processes, 64*(3), 249–260.

[69] Ohtsubo, Y., & Kameda, T. (1998). The function of equality heuristic in distributive bargaining: Negotiated allocation of costs and benefits in a demand revelation context. *Journal of Experimental Social Psychology, 34*(1), 90–108.

[70] Deutsch, *Distributive justice.*

different preferences. In contrast, recipients who have been inequitably, but advantageously treated justify their shares—even when they would not have awarded themselves the resources they received.[71]

Social Comparison

Social comparison is an inevitable fact of life in organizations and relationships. How does someone's higher salary, larger office, special opportunities, or grander budget affect us? Are we happy for other people—do we bask in their glory when they achieve successes—or are we threatened and angry?

When we compare ourselves to others, we consider the relevance of the comparison to our self-concept. People have beliefs and values that reflect their central dimensions of the self. Some dimensions are highly self-relevant; others are irrelevant. It all depends on how a person defines himself or herself. The performance of other people can affect our self-evaluation, especially when we are psychologically close to them. When we observe someone who is close to us performing extremely well in an area that we highly identify with, our self-evaluation is threatened. Such "upward" comparisons can lead to envy, frustration, anger, and even sabotage. Upon hearing that a member of one's cohort made some extremely timely investments in companies that have paid off multifold and is now a multimillionaire, people who pride themselves on their financial wizardry probably feel threatened. The fact that our colleague excels in an area that we pride ourselves is unsettling. When another person outperforms us on a behavior that is irrelevant to our self-definition, the better her or his performance and the closer our relationship, the more we take pride in his or her success.

When it comes to pay and compensation, people are more concerned about how much they are paid relative to other people than about the absolute level of their pay (see Exhibit 3-3 for an example of social comparison).[72]

With whom do people compare themselves? Three social comparison targets may be distinguished: upward comparison, downward comparison, and comparison with similar others.

1. *Upward comparison* occurs when people compare themselves to someone who is better off, more accomplished, or higher in status. The young entrepreneur starting his own software company may compare himself to Bill Gates. Oftentimes, people compare themselves upward for inspiration and motivation.

2. *Downward comparison* occurs when people compare themselves to someone who is less fortunate, able, accomplished, or lower in status. For example, when a young manager's marketing campaign proves to be a complete flop, she may compare herself to a colleague whose decisions led to the loss of hundreds of thousands of dollars. Downward comparison often makes people feel better about their own state.

---

[71] Diekmann, K. A., Samuels, S. M., Ross, L., & Bazerman, M. H. (1997). Self-interest and fairness in problems of resource allocation. *Journal of Personality and Social Psychology, 72*(5), 1061–1074.

[72] Adams, S. (1966). Inequity in social exchange. In L. Berkowitz (Ed.), *Advances in experimental social psychology: Vol. 2* (pp. 267–299). New York: Academic Press; Blau, P. M. (1964). *Exchange and power in social life.* New York: Wiley; Deutsch, *Distributive justice*; Homans, G. C. (1961). *Social behavior: Its elementary forms.* New York: Harcourt, Brace, Walster, E., Berscheid, E., & Walster, G. W. (1973). New directions in equity research. *Journal of Personality and Social Psychology, 25*(2), 151–176.

EXHIBIT 3-3

Self-Interest Versus Social Comparison

Imagine that you are being recruited for a position in firm A. Your colleague, Jay, of similar background and skill, is also being recruited by firm A. Firm A has made you and Jay the following salary offers:

Your salary: $75,000

Jay's salary: $95,000

Your other option is to take a position at firm B, which has made you an offer. Firm B has also made your colleague, Ines, an offer:

Your salary: $72,000

Ines's salary: $72,000

Which job offer do you take, firm A's or firm B's? If you follow the principles of rational judgment outlined in Appendix 1, you will take firm A's offer—it pays more money. However, if you are like most people, you prefer firm B's offer because you do not like feeling you are being treated unfairly.

Source: Bazerman, M. H., Loewenstein, G., & White, S. (1992). Reversals of preference in allocating decisions: Judging an alternative versus choosing among alternatives. *Administrative Science Quarterly, 37,* 220–240. Used by permission of Administrative Science Quarterly.

3. *Comparison with similar others* occurs when people choose someone of similar background, skill, and ability with whom to compare themselves. Comparison with similar others is useful when people desire to have accurate appraisals of their abilities.

What drives the choice of the comparison to others? A number of goals and motives may drive social comparison, including the following:

1. *Self-improvement:*   People compare themselves with others who can serve as models of success.[73] For example, a beginning chess player may compare his or her skill level with a grand master. Upward comparison provides inspiration, insight, and challenge, but it can also lead to feelings of discouragement and incompetence.
2. *Self-enhancement:*   The desire to maintain or enhance a positive view of oneself may lead people to bias information in self-serving ways. Rather than seek truth, people seek comparisons that show them in a favorable light. People make downward comparisons with others who are less fortunate, less successful, and so forth.[74]
3. *Accurate self-evaluation:*   The desire for truthful knowledge about oneself (even if the outcome is not favorable).

---

[73] Taylor, S. E., & Lobel, M. (1989). Social comparison activity under threat: Downward evaluation and upward contacts. *Psychological Review, 96*(4), 569–575.
[74] Wills, T. A. (1981). Downward comparison principles in social psychology. *Psychological Bulletin, 90*(2), 245–271.

The Equity Principle

People make judgments about what is fair based on what they are investing in the relationship and what they are getting out of it. Inputs are investments in a relationship that usually entail costs. For example, the person who manages the finances and pays the bills in a relationship incurs time and energy costs. An output is something that a person receives from a relationship. The person who does not pay the bills enjoys the benefits of a financial service. Outputs, or outcomes, may be positive or negative. In many cases, A's input is B's outcome, and B's input is A's outcome. For example, a company pays (input) an employee (outcome) who gives time and expertise (input) to further the company's goals (outcome). Consider the negotiations between the Writers Guild of America (WGA) and its employers. Employers wanted to extend the WGA's existing contract that pays writers residuals based on reuse of their works. However, the writers were frustrated with their compensation and rejected the employers' proposal. The writers created a "Contract Bulletin" that included eight charts emphasizing rising financial profitability at media companies: Growth was evident in almost every single measure of economic performance, including gross revenues in every segment, excellent operating profits, and rising share prices for all six major entertainment companies. In short, the writers argued that their "inputs" were worth more than what the employers gave them.[75]

Equity exists in a relationship if each person's outcomes are proportional to his or her inputs. Equity, therefore, refers to equivalence of the outcome/input ratio of parties; inequity exists when the ratio of outcomes to inputs is unequal. Equity exists when the profits (rewards minus costs) of two actors are equal.[76] However, complications arise if two people have different views of what constitutes a legitimate investment, cost, or reward and how they rank each one. For example, consider salaries paid to players in the National Basketball Association (NBA). With the starting players taking the greatest salaries (capped at a fixed amount per team), little is left over to pay the last three or four players on a 12-person team roster. The minimum salary of $473,604 might seem extraordinarily high to the average person, but in the context of the team such as the Los Angeles Lakers with an average player salary of $6,835,185 for the 2010–2011 season—led by the league's highest paid player Kobe Bryant at $24,806,250—it reflects a sizable disparity.[77] In 2010, the disparity in salaries for the National Football League's Chicago Bears spanned nearly $19.7 million ranging from the highest paid player, Julius Peppers ($20 million), to players such as wide receiver Eric Peterman and defensive end Corey Wooten who made the league minimum salary of $320,000.[78]

Equity exists when a person perceives equality between the ratio of his or her own outcomes (O) to inputs (I) and the ratio of the other person's outcomes to inputs, where a and b represent two people:[79]

$$\frac{O_a}{I_a} = \frac{O_b}{I_b}$$

[75] Hibberd, J., & Krukowski, A. (2007, July 16). WGA salvo kicks off contract talks. *TelevisionWeek, 26*(29), 3–4.
[76] Homans, *Social behavior.*
[77] Badenhausen, K. (2010, November 4). The NBA's highest-paid players. *Forbes.* Forbes.com; *Los Angeles Lakers salaries.* (2010). Hoopshype. Hoopshype.com
[78] Chicago Bears salaries. (2010). *Sports City.* Sportscity.com
[79] Adams, "Inequity in Social Exchange," p. 37.

However, this equity formula is less applicable to situations in which inputs and outcomes might be either positive or negative. The basic equity formula may be reconstructed as follows:

$$\frac{O_a - I_a}{|I_a|^{ka}} = \frac{O_b - I_b}{|I_b|^{kb}}$$

This formula proposes that equity prevails when the disparity between person a's outcomes and inputs and person b's outcomes and inputs are equivalently proportional to the absolute value of each of their inputs. The numerator is "profit," and the denominator adjusts for positive or negative signs of input. Each k takes on the value of either $+1$ or -1, depending on the valence of participants' inputs and gains (outcomes $-$ inputs).

Restoring Equity

Suppose that you were hired by company X last year with an annual salary of $85,000. You felt happy about your salary until you learned that your colleague at the same company, whom you regard to be of equivalent skill and background, is paid $5,000 more per year. How do you deal with this inequity? When people find themselves in an inequitable relationship, they become distressed; the greater the perceived inequity, the more distressed people feel. Distress drives people to attempt to restore equity.

People who believe they are underpaid feel dissatisfied and seek to restore equity.[80] For example, underpaid workers lower their level of effort and productivity to restore equity,[81] and in some cases they leave organizations characterized by inequity to join an organization in which wages are more fairly distributed, even if they are less highly paid in absolute terms.[82] Consider what happened when two vice presidents of a major *Fortune* 100 company were promoted to senior vice president at about the same time.[83] Both of them moved into new offices, but one of them suspected an inequity. He pulled out blueprints and measured the square footage of each office. His suspicions were confirmed when it turned out the other guy's office was bigger than his by a few feet. A former employee said, "He blew a gasket." Walls were moved, and his office was reconfigured to make it as large as his counterpart's.

People use the following six means to eliminate the tension arising from inequity:[84]

1. *Alter the inputs.*   The senior VP could work less hard, take on fewer projects, take more days off, etc.
2. *Alter the outcomes.*   The senior VP could make his office bigger—which he did.
3. *Cognitively distort inputs or outcomes.*   The senior VP could minimize the importance of his contributions and maximize the perceived value of his office—for example, by deciding that his office was quieter than that of his counterpart.
4. *Leave the situation.*   The senior VP could quit his job.

---

[80] Walster, Berscheid, & Walster, "New directions in equity research."
[81] Greenberg, J. (1988). Equity and workplace status: A field experiment. *Journal of Applied Psychology, 73*(4), 606–613.
[82] Schmitt, D. R., & Marwell, G. (1972). Withdrawal and reward reallocation in response to inequity. *Journal of Experimental Social Psychology, 8*(3), 207–221.
[83] Klein, "Lord of the flies."
[84] Adams, "Inequity in social exchange."

5. ***Cognitively distort either the inputs or the outcomes of an exchange partner.*** The senior VP may view the other VP as contributing more, or perhaps regard the big office to be less attractive than it actually is.

6. ***Change the object of comparison.*** The senior VP may stop comparing himself to the other senior VP and start comparing himself to someone else in the company.

The use of the first two strategies depends on whether the person has been over- or under-rewarded. Overrewarded individuals can increase their inputs or decrease their outcomes to restore equal ratios, whereas underrewarded people must decrease their inputs or increase their outcomes. For example, people work harder if they think they are overpaid. Conversely, people may cheat or steal if they are underpaid.[85]

Given the various methods of restoring equity, what determines which method will be used? People engage in a cost-benefit analysis and choose the method that maximizes positive outcomes. Usually, this method minimizes the necessity of increasing any of one's own inputs that are difficult or costly to change and also minimizes the necessity of real changes or cognitive changes in inputs/outcomes that are central to self-concept. Simply put, it is often easier to rationalize a situation than to do something about it. Further, this type of change minimizes the necessity of leaving the situation or changing the object of social comparison once it has stabilized. Thus, we are not likely to ask for a salary cut if we think we are overpaid, but we are more inclined to regard the work we do as more demanding. (See Exhibit 3-4 for an examination of factors that can cause reactions to inequity.)

The equity drive is so strong that people who are denied the opportunity to restore equity will derogate others, thereby restoring **psychological equity**. If distortion must occur, people focus on the other person's inputs or outcomes before distorting their own, especially if such distortion threatens their self-esteem. Leaving the situation and changing the object of comparison involves the highest costs because they disrupt the status quo and violate justice beliefs.

Procedural Justice

In addition to their slice of the pie, people are concerned with the way resources are distributed.[86] People evaluate not only the fairness of outcomes but also the fairness of the procedures by which those outcomes are determined. Listening to the other party, treating them with respect, and explaining oneself is related to outcome satisfaction and the desire for future negotiations.[87] People's evaluations of the fairness of procedures determine their satisfaction and willingness to comply with outcomes. For example, managers who educate employees (i.e., explain to them why change is occurring, such as in the case of a merger) find that it increases employee commitment to the change.[88] Employees who believe they have been

---

[85] Greenberg, J. (1990). Employee theft as a reaction to underpayment inequity: The hidden cost of pay cuts. *Journal of Applied Psychology, 75*(5), 561–568.

[86] Thibaut, J. W., & Walker, L. (1975). *Procedural justice: A psychological analysis.* Hillsdale, NJ: Erlbaum; Thibaut, J., & Walker, L. (1978). A theory of procedure. *California Law Review, 66*(3), 541–566; Leventhal, "The distribution of rewards and resources"; Leventhal, G. S. (1980). What should be done with equity theory? New approaches to the study of fairness in social exchange. In K. Gergen, M. Greenberg, & R. Willis (Eds.), *Social exchange: Advances in theory and research* (pp. 27–55). New York: Plenum Press.

[87] Kass, E. (2008). Interactional justice, negotiator outcome satisfaction, and desire for future negotiations: R-E-S-P-E-C-T at the negotiating table. *International Journal of Conflict Management, 19*(4), 319 – 338.

[88] Kotter, J. P., & Schlesinger, L. A., (1979). Choosing strategies for change. *Harvard Business Review, 57*(2), 106–114.

EXHIBIT 3-4

Distributed Versus Concentrated Unfairness

Within an organizational setting, many acts of unfair or unjust behavior may occur. For example, a person of color may be passed over for a promotion. A woman with managerial skills may be relegated to administrative and secretarial tasks. How do employees react to injustice in the organization? Consider two hypothetical companies: A and B. In each company, the overall incidence of unfair behavior is identical. In company A, the unfair incidences (i.e., percentage of total acts) are targeted toward a single individual—a black female. In company B, the unfair incidences are spread among three individuals—a black female, a Hispanic male, and an older, handicapped white male. The fact that the incidences are concentrated on a single individual or spread out over many organizational members should be irrelevant, if the overall incidence of unfairness in each organization is the same. In practice, however, these situations are viewed quite differently.

In a simulated organization, each of three employees was victimized in one out of three interactions with a manager. In another company, one of the three employees was victimized in all three out of three interactions with a manager; the two other employees were treated fairly. Thus, in both companies, the incidence of unfairness was identical. However, groups' overall judgment of the unfairness of the manager was greater when the injustice was spread across members than when it was concentrated on one individual. Most disconcertingly, targets of discrimination were marginalized by other group members. Blaming-the-victim effects may be more rampant when individuals are the sole targets of discrimination—ironically, when they need the most support.

Source: Lind, E. A., Kray, L., & Thompson, L. (1998). The social construction on injustice: Fairness judgments in response to own and others' unfair treatment by authorities. *Organizational Behavior and Human Decision Processes, 75*(1), 1–22.

mistreated are more likely to exit and exhibit work withdrawal.[89] The process of explaining decisions in a change context helps employees adapt to the change, whereas the lack of an explanation is often regarded by employees as unfair, generating resentment toward management and toward the decision.[90] An investigation of 183 employees of seven private-sector organizations, each of whom had just completed a relocation, revealed that perceived fairness was higher when justification was provided in the case of unfavorable change.[91] Baseball players and fans felt a lack of procedural justice when the World Anti-Doping Agency chief called on Major League Baseball and its players' union to start testing for human growth hormone and accused Major League Baseball of misleading its public by its continued refusal to institute a transparent and rigorous drug testing program. The private ownership

---

[89] Boswell, W., & Olson-Buchanan, J. (2004). Experiencing mistreatment at work: The role of grievance filing, nature of mistreatment and employee withdrawal. *Academy of Management Journal, 47*(1), 129–139.

[90] Daly, J. P., & Geyer, P. D. (1994). The role of fairness in implementing large-scale change: Employee evaluations of process and outcome in seven facility relocations. *Journal of Organizational Behavior, 15,* 623–638.

[91] Daly, J. P. (1995). Explaining changes to employees: The influence of justifications and change outcomes on employees' fairness judgments. *Journal of Applied Behavioral Science, 31*(4), 415–428.

of United States professional sports leagues meant the leagues would have to volunteer for testing, which they regarded to be "unfair."[92]

Fairness in Relationships

Consider the following situation: You and a college friend develop a potentially revolutionary (and profitable) idea for a new kind of water ski.[93] You spend about half a year in your dorm basement developing a prototype of the new invention. Your friend had the original idea; you developed the design and materials and assembled the prototype. The two of you talk to a patent lawyer about getting a patent, and the lawyer tells you a patent is pending on a similar product but the company will offer you $3,000 for one of the innovative features of your design. You and your friend gladly accept. What division of the $3,000 between you and your friend would you find to be most satisfying?

People's preferences for several possible distributions of the money for themselves and the other person were assessed.[94] People's utility functions were *social* rather than *individual,* meaning that individual satisfaction was strongly influenced by the payoffs received by the other, as well as the payoffs received by the self (see Exhibit 3-5). Social utility functions were tent shaped. The most satisfying outcome was equal shares for the self and other ($1,500 apiece). Discrepancies between payoffs to the self versus the other led to lower satisfaction. However, social utility functions were lopsided in that advantageous inequity (self receives more than other) was preferable to disadvantageous inequity (other receives more than self). Further, the relationship people had with the other party mattered: In positive or neutral relationships, people preferred equality; in negative relationships, people preferred advantageous inequity. (See Exhibit 3-6 for an examination of different types of profiles.)

People will reject outcomes that entail one person receiving more than others and settle for a settlement of lower joint value but equal-appearing shares.[95] This arrangement is especially true when resources are "lumpy" (i.e., hard to divide into pieces), such as an Oriental rug.[96]

Egocentrism

Consider a group of three people who go out for dinner. One person orders a bottle of expensive wine, an appetizer, and a pricey main course. Another abstains from drinking and orders an inexpensive side dish. The third orders a moderately priced meal. Then the bill arrives. The wine drinker immediately suggests that the group split the bill into thirds, explaining that this approach is the simplest. The teetotaler winces and suggests that the group ask the waiter to bring three separate bills. The third group member argues that, because he is a student, the two others should cover the bill, and he invites the two over to his house the next week for pizza. This example

---

[92] Associated Press. (2010, August 16). WADA rips MLB's drug policy. *Entertainment Sports Programming Network.* Espn.com

[93] Loewenstein, Thompson, & Bazerman, "Social utility and decision making."

[94] Ibid.

[95] McClelland, G., & Rohrbaugh, J. (1978). Who accepts the Pareto axiom? The role of utility and equity in arbitration decisions. *Behavioral Science, 23*(5), 446–456.

[96] Messick, D. M. (1993). Equality as a decision heuristic. In B. A. Mellers & J. Baron (Eds.), *Psychological perspectives on justice* (pp. 11–31). New York: Cambridge University Press.

EXHIBIT 3-5

Social Utility as a Function of Discrepancy Between Our Own and Others' Outcomes

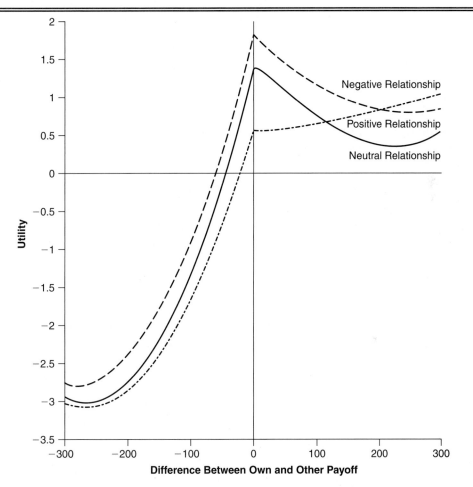

Difference Between Own and Other Payoff

Source: Loewenstein, G. F., Thompson, L., & Bazerman, M. H. (1989). Social utility and decision making in inter-personal contexts. *Journal of Personality and Social Psychology, 57*(3), 426–441.

illustrates that any situation can have as many interpretations of fairness as it has parties involved. Two people may both truly want a fair settlement, but they may have distinctly different and equally justifiable ideas about what is fair. Consider, for example, "fairness opinions" that underpin mergers and acquisitions. Some are written by independent firms unconnected to the deal, but

EXHIBIT 3-6

Profiles of Pie Slicers

Have you ever wondered whether most people are truly interested in other people or are only concerned about their own profit? To examine this question, MBA students were given several hypothetical scenarios, such as the situation involving the ski invention, and asked what division of resources (and, in some cases, costs) they preferred. Further, people made responses for different kinds of relationships: friendly ones, antagonistic ones, and neutral ones. Three types of people were identified:

- *Loyalists* prefer to split resources equally, except in antagonistic relationships (27%).
- *Saints* prefer to split resources equally no matter whether relationships are positive, neutral, or negative (24%).
- *Ruthless competitors* prefer to have more resources than the other party, regardless of relationship (36%).

Source: Loewenstein, G. F., Thompson, L., & Bazerman, M. H. (1989). Social utility and decision making in interpersonal contexts. *Journal of Personality and Social Psychology, 57*(3), 426–441.

the majority aren't.[97] Banks can rack up millions of dollars in fees by acting simultaneously as agents and appraisers, presumably fueled by self-serving interests.

Why are people self-serving? People want or prefer more than what they regard as fair (basic hedonism). In short, our preferences are more primary, or immediate, than our social concerns. People are more in touch with their own preferences than with the concerns of others. We have immediate access to our preferences; fairness is a secondary judgment. For this reason, fairness judgments are likely to be tainted by preferences. Allocating more money to ourselves is only one way that people show egocentric bias. For example, people pay themselves substantially more than they are willing to pay others for doing the same task.[98] People were asked, if they worked for 7 hours and were paid $25, while another person worked for 10 hours, how much did they think the other person should get paid? Most answered that the other person should get paid more for doing more work—about $30.29 on average. Then they switched roles and asked if the other person worked for 7 hours and was paid $25, and they worked for 10 hours, what is a fair wage for them to be paid? The average response was $35.24. The difference between $35.24 and $30.29 is about $5, which illustrates the phenomenon of egocentric bias.

Egocentric judgments of fairness also emerge in other ways. For example, people select fairness rules in a self-serving fashion: When people make minimal contributions, they often prefer equality rather than equity; however, when people's contributions are substantial, they opt for equity rather than equality.[99] Even if people agree to use the same fairness rule, they think it is fair for them to get more than others in a similar situation because they think they would have contributed more.[100]

---

[97] Henry, D. (2003, November 24). A fair deal—but for whom? *BusinessWeek, 3859*, 108–109.
[98] Messick, D. M., & Sentis, K. P. (1979). Fairness and preference. *Journal of Experimental Social Psychology, 15*(4), 418–434.
[99] Van Avermaet, E. (1974). *Equity: A theoretical and experimental analysis.* Unpublished doctoral dissertation, University of California, Santa Barbara.

Another way people can engage in egocentric evaluation is to selectively weigh different aspects of the exchange situation in a way that favors themselves. Consider a situation in which participants are told how many hours they worked on a task of assembling questionnaires, as well as how many questionnaires they completed. The key dimensions are hours worked and productivity. Participants are then asked to indicate what they believe is fair payment for their work. Those who worked long hours but did not complete many questionnaires emphasize the importance of hours; in contrast, those who worked short hours but completed many questionnaires emphasize quantity completed. Thus, people emphasize the dimension that favors themselves.[101]

Appeals to equality can also be self-serving.[102] At a superficial level, equality is simple. Employing equality as a division rule in practice, however, is complex because of the multiple dimensions on which equality may be established.[103] Furthermore, equality is not consistently applied. For example, when the outcome is evenly divisible by the number in the group, people will use equality more than when even division is not possible.[104] The problem with egocentric judgment is that it makes negotiations more difficult to resolve.

The preceding examples suggest that people immediately seize upon any opportunity to favor themselves. However, in many situations, people would ultimately benefit by not having egocentric views. Consider arbitration situations: People's predictions of judges' behavior are biased in a manner that favors their own side. Efforts to eliminate bias among litigants meet with virtually no success. Informing parties of the potential bias or providing them with information about the counterparty's point of view does little to assuage biased perceptions of fairness, suggesting that egocentric biases are deeply ingrained.[105]

People really do care about fairness but usually do not realize that they are behaving in a self-interested fashion. Egocentric judgments of responsibility and fairness are attributable to ways in which people process information. Several cognitive mechanisms allow the development of egocentric judgments:

- *Selective encoding and memory.*   Our own thoughts distract us from thinking about the contributions of others. We rehearse our own actions and fit them into our own cognitive schemas, which facilitates retention and subsequent retrieval. If encoding mechanisms lead to self-serving judgments of fairness, then a person who learns of the facts before knowing which side of a dispute he or she is on should not be egocentric. However, the egocentric effect still emerges even when the direction of self-interest occurs subsequent to the processing of information, suggesting that encoding is not the sole mechanism producing egocentric judgment.
- *Differential retrieval.*   When making judgments of responsibility, people ask themselves "How much did I contribute?" and they attempt to retrieve specific instances.[106] Because

[100] Messick, D. M., & Rutte, C. G. (1992). The provision of public goods by experts: The Groningen study. In W. B. G. Liebrand, D. M. Messick, & H. A. M. Wilke (Eds.), *Social dilemmas: Theoretical issues and research findings* (pp. 101–109). Oxford, England: Pergamon Press.

[101] Van Avermaet, *Equity.*

[102] Messick, "Equality as a decision heuristic."

[103] Harris, R. J., & Joyce, M. A. (1980). What's fair? It depends on how you ask the question. *Journal of Personality and Social Psychology, 38*(1), 165–179.

[104] Allison, S. T., & Messick, D. M. (1990). Social decision heuristics in the use of shared resources. *Journal of Behavioral Decision Making, 3*(3), 195–204.

[105] Babcock, L., Loewenstein, G., Issacharoff, S., & Camerer, C. (1995). Biased judgments of fairness in bargaining. *The American Economic Review, 85*(5), 1337–1343.

[106] Ross, M., & Sicoly, F. (1979). Egocentric biases in availability attribution. *Journal of Personality and Social Psychology, 37*(3), 322–336.

it is easier to retrieve instances involving oneself, a positive correlation exists between recall and responsibility attributions.[107] Not surprisingly, when people are asked to think about how much others contributed to a joint task, egocentrism decreases.[108] However, after considering others' contributions to joint tasks, people report less enjoyment and lower satisfaction.

• *Informational disparity.*   People often are not privy to the contributions made by others, which suggests that information, not goals, mediates the self-serving effect. Even when information is constant but goals are manipulated, self-serving effects emerge,[109] suggesting that information itself is not solely responsible for the egocentric effect.[110]

Most situations are ambiguous enough that people can construe them in a fashion that favors their own interests. One unfortunate consequence is that people develop different perceptions of fairness even when they are presented with the same evidence. Consider a strike situation in which people are provided with background information on a hypothetical teachers union and board of education. The background material is constructed so that some facts favor the teachers and other facts favor the board of education. On balance, the facts are equal. In one condition, both disputants are presented with extensive, identical background information concerning the dispute. In another condition, disputants are presented with abbreviated, much less extensive background information. Those who have extensive information are more likely to go on strikes that last longer and are more costly to both parties, compared to disputants who do not have extensive information, even though the information is identical for both sides.[111] Information, even when shared among parties, creates ambiguity and provides fertile ground for unchecked self-interest to operate.

Reducing egocentrism is not easy. In general, leading people to consider other members' contributions to a joint task reduces self-centered judgments.[112] However, this can backfire by activating egoistic theories of people's behavior and claiming more in subsequent situations.[113]

WISE PIE-SLICING

The distribution of resources (pie-slicing) is an unavoidable and inevitable aspect of negotiation. What principles should we live by when slicing the pie? Messick suggests the following guidelines: consistency, simplicity, effectiveness, and justifiability.[114] We add consensus, generality, and satisfaction.[115]

---

[107] Kahneman, D., & Tversky, A. (1982). On the study of statistical intuitions. *Cognition, 11*(2), 123–141.

[108] Caruso, E. M., Epley, N., & Bazerman, M. H. (2006). The costs and benefits of undoing egocentric responsibility assessments in groups. *Journal of Personality and Social Psychology, 91*(5), 857–871.

[109] Thompson, L., & Loewenstein, G. F. (1992). Egocentric interpretations of fairness and interpersonal conflict. *Organizational Behavior and Human Decision Processes, 51*(2), 176–197.

[110] Camerer, C., & Loewenstein, G. (1993). Information, fairness, and efficiency in bargaining. In B. A. Mellers & J. Baron (Eds.), *Psychological perspectives on justice* (pp. 155–181). Boston: Cambridge University Press.

[111] Thompson & Loewenstein, "Egocentric interpretations."

[112] Caruso, Epley, & Bazerman. "The costs and benefits of undoing egocentric responsibility"; Epley, N., Caruso, E., & Bazerman, M. H. (2006). When perspective taking increases taking: Reactive egoism in social interaction. *Journal of Personality and Social Psychology, 91*(5), 872–889.

[113] Epley, Caruso, & Bazerman, "When perspective taking increases taking."

[114] Messick, "Equality as a decision heuristic."

[115] Levine, J., & Thompson, L. (1996). Conflict in groups. In E. T. Higgins & A. Kruglanski (Eds.), *Social psychology: Handbook of basic principles* (pp. 745–776). New York: Guilford.

Consistency

One of the hallmarks of a good pie-slicing heuristic is consistency or invariance across settings, time, and contacts. For example, most of us would be outraged if those managers up for performance review did better if the meeting was scheduled in the morning rather than the afternoon. This example represents a clear bias of the interviewer. Fairness procedures are often inconsistent because of heuristic decision making. Heuristic judgment processes are necessary when normative decision procedures are absent or when their application would be inefficient. Unfortunately, people are typically unaware of the powerful contextual factors that affect their judgments of fairness.

Simplicity

Pie-slicing procedures should be clearly understood by the individuals who employ them and those who are affected by them. Group members should be able to explain the procedure used to allocate resources. This allows the procedure to be implemented with full understanding and the outcomes of the procedure to be evaluated against a clear criterion.

Effectiveness

Pie-slicing policies should produce a choice, meaning that the allocation procedure should yield a clear decision. If the procedure does not produce such a decision, then conflict may erupt among group members who try to identify and implement a decision post hoc.

Justifiability

Pie-slicing procedures should be justifiable to other parties. A fairness rule may be consistent, simple, and effective, but if it cannot be justified it is not likely to be successful. For example, suppose that a manager of an airline company decides that raises will be based upon hair color: Blondes get big raises, brunettes do not. This policy is consistent, simple, and effective but hardly justifiable.

Consensus

Group members should agree upon the method of allocation. Effective pie-slicing procedures are often internalized by group members, and norms act as strong guidelines for behavior and decision making in groups. Because social justice procedures often outlive current group members, new members are frequently indoctrinated with procedures that the group found useful in the past.[116]

Generalizability

The pie-slicing procedure should be applicable to a wide variety of situations. Procedures and norms develop when intragroup conflict is expected, enduring, or recurrent, and effective policy therefore specifies outcome distribution across situations.

---

[116] Bettenhausen, K., & Murnighan, J. K. (1985). The emergence of norms in competitive decision-making groups. *Administrative Science Quarterly, 30*(3), 350–372; Levine, J. M., & Moreland, R. L. (1994). Group socialization: Theory and research. In I. W. Stroebe & M. Hewstone (Eds.), *The European review of social psychology: Vol. 5* (pp. 305–336). Chichester, England: Wiley.

Satisfaction

To increase the likelihood that negotiators will follow through with their agreements, the pie-slicing procedure should be satisfying to all. For example, when the board of insurance giant AIG forced former executives Maurice Greenberg and Howard Smith to resign in 2005, it set up a nasty long-running legal dispute between the sides that extended all the way to such items as ownership of an expensive Persian rug at AIG's former headquarters. Thus, it was surprising when a settlement was finally reached that very much pleased each of parties involved and was described as a "win-win" by numerous financial observes. The settlement relieved the troubled insurance company and the former executives from crushing legal fees incurred, and also brought Greenberg back into the fold to advise AIG on how to find a way to pay back taxpayers on the hook for bailing out the company during the financial crisis of 2008, as well as aid in the company's continued survival.[117]

CONCLUSION

When it comes to slicing the pie, the most valuable information is a negotiator's best alternative to reaching agreement (BATNA). Nothing can substitute for the power of a strong BATNA. Negotiators can enhance their ability to garner a favorable slice of the pie by engaging in the following strategies: determine their BATNA prior to negotiations and attempt to improve upon it; determine your reservation point; research the other party's BATNA; set high aspirations; make the first offer; immediately re-anchor if the other party opens with an "outrageous" offer, plan your concessions; support your offers with facts; appeal to norms of fairness, and do not fall for the "even split" ploy. Negotiators should not reveal their reservation price (unless it is very attractive) and never lie about their BATNA. A negotiator who is well versed in the psychology of fairness is at a pie-slicing advantage in negotiation.

---

[117] Hoffman, M. A. & McCarthy, C. (2009, December 7). AIG, Greenberg settlement viewed as "win-win" deal. *Business Insurance*. Businessinsurance.com

CHAPTER

4

Win-Win Negotiation: Expanding the Pie

It might not seem possible for environmentalists, energy developers, and state legislators to agree about anything, much less reach an integrative agreement. A long-running battle over aging wind turbines in Northern California pitted the interests of three wildly different parties with opposing motives against one another. But when California Attorney General Jerry Brown brokered a settlement between environmental groups, wind developer NextEra Energy Resources, and the state, it was enthusiastically embraced by all sides. Altamont Pass, east of San Francisco, is a breeding area for raptors and other species and a major migratory route. Tragically, the turbines kill between 1,700 and 4,700 birds each year—the most of any wind farm in the U.S.—and injure or kill federally protected birds such as golden eagles and red-tailed hawks. In the integrative settlement, the environmentalists' interests— the native migratory birds—are protected. Moreover, the state's long-term interests of deriving 33% of its power from clean energy moved a step forward, and the new turbines produced more power more efficiently than the models they replaced. A grand total of 2,400 turbines on the hills of the Altamont Pass operated by NextEra will be replaced or shut down completely by Nov. 1, 2015. The settlement cleared the way for NextEra to begin planning its new wind farm at the site and begin securing deals with utilities, who are required under California's strict renewable energy goals to derive 33 percent of their power from clean sources by 2020.[1]

---

[1] Dearen, J. (2010, December 7). Northern California wind turbines to be upgraded. *Bloomberg Businessweek.* Businessweek.com

T he opening example suggests that even the most contentious negotiations contain potential for win-win agreements. However, win-win negotiation techniques are not intuitive. Many people who regard themselves to be win-win negotiators often leave money on the table without even realizing it. This chapter provides strategies for expanding the pie.

WHAT IS WIN-WIN NEGOTIATION?

Most people erroneously equate win-win negotiations with the fair division of resources. Obviously, allocating resources is always necessary in negotiation, but win-win means something entirely different. Win-win is *not:*

- *Compromise:*   Compromise refers to reaching a middle ground between negotiators' positions. Win-win negotiation does not pertain to how the pie is *divided* (Chapter 3) but, rather, to how the pie is *enlarged* by negotiators.
- *Even split:*   Even splits, like compromises, refer to how the bargaining zone is divided among the negotiators. For example, two sisters who quarrel over an orange and ultimately decide to cut it in half have reached an even split. However, if they fail to realize that one sister wants all the juice and the other wants all of the rind, it is painfully clear that the even split is not win-win.[2]
- *Satisfaction:*   Satisfaction is no guarantee that money and resources have not been wasted; in fact, many "happy" negotiators do not expand the pie.[3]
- *Building a relationship:*   Building a relationship and establishing trust comprise an important aspect of negotiation. However, people with a genuine interest in the other party may not think creatively. In fact, people who would seem to have the most interest in building a relationship with the other party (for example, husbands and wives, dating couples, and long-term partners) often fail to reach integrative agreements.[4]

Win-win negotiation *really* means that all creative opportunities are leveraged and no resources are left on the table. We call these outcomes **integrative negotiations.**

TELLTALE SIGNS OF WIN-WIN POTENTIAL

Integrative potential exists in just about every negotiation situation. However, people often fail to see it because they do not believe that win-win is possible. The following are questions for negotiators to ask when assessing the potential of a negotiation situation.

Does the Negotiation Contain More Than One Issue?

Most negotiations begin as single-issue negotiations. By definition, single-issue negotiations are not win-win because whatever one party gains, the other party loses. However, it is usually

---

[2] Follett, M. (1994). In P. Graham (Ed.), *Mary Parker Follett: Prophet of management—A celebration of writings from the 1920s.* Boston: Harvard Business School Press.
[3] Thompson, L., Valley, K. L., & Kramer, R. M. (1995). The bittersweet feeling of success: An examination of social perception in negotiation. *Journal of Experimental Social Psychology, 31*(6), 467–492.
[4] Fry, W. R., Firestone, I. J., & Williams, D. L. (1983). Negotiation process and outcome of stranger dyads and dating couples: Do lovers lose? *Basic and Applied Social Psychology, 4,* 1–16; Thompson, L., & DeHarpport, T. (1998). Relationships, good incompatibility, and communal orientation in negotiations. *Basic and Applied Social Psychology, 20*(1), 33–44; Kurtzberg, T., & Medvec, V. H. (1999). Can we negotiate and still be friends? *Negotiation Journal, 15*(4), 355–361.

possible to identify more than one issue. The probability that negotiators will have identical preferences across all issues is small, and, *it is differences in preferences, beliefs, and capacities that may be profitably traded off to create joint gain.*[5]

Can Other Issues Be Brought In?

Another strategy is to bring additional issues into the negotiation. As a case in point, Google brought in additional issues when controversy erupted over its search engine in China. At the outset of negotiations, Google refused to censor its search results in China. Google's position on the issue angered the Chinese government who threatened to let Google's operating license expire, potentially forcing the company out of the largest country on Earth and its largest Internet market. Google's key interest was in preventing online censorship. One of China's key interests was to be seen as an international business powerhouse. The negotiation deadlock was resolved by unbundling issues and creating more issues. In the final agreement, China renewed Google's license for a censored website and Internet services in mainland China, and allowed an uncensored website in Hong Kong which Google was permitted to direct Chinese users to.[6] In short, the more moving parts, the better the potential deal.

Can Side Deals Be Made?

In many situations, people are strictly cautioned not to make side deals or side payments. In contrast, the ability to bring other people into negotiations to make side deals may increase the size of the bargaining pie. In the lengthy negotiations towards the national health care law passed in 2010, numerous side deals were made between medical interests and the federal government to reduce costs of the legislation and to put influential industries on board that had historically opposed such a plan. In 2009, the nation's three hospital associations agreed to contribute $155 billion over 10 years to aid the costs of insuring 47 million Americans without health insurance. "Getting health-care reform is absolutely critical," said one hospital negotiator. "This is our attempt to act in good faith." In return, hospital officials understood that in final legislation that included a new government-sponsored insurance program, they will not pay at Medicare or Medicaid reimbursement rates, which they had argued did cover the cost of services.[7]

Do Parties Have Different Preferences Across Negotiation Issues?

If parties have different strengths of preference across the negotiation issues, then a win-win negotiation is possible.[8] Consider the orange-splitting example. Essentially, the situation involves two issues: the juice and the rind. One sister cares more about the juice; the other cares more about the rind. If only a single issue (the orange) was involved or if both sisters wanted the juice much more than the rind, then an integrative agreement would not be possible.

Another example of integrating different preferences occurred in a GM Nexteer-Beijing deal. General Motors steering division, Nexteer, an automotive parts supplier was facing liquidation with many Detroit auto companies. This was hurting the economy and the workers' unions. Chinese companies however saw "tremendous resources" in Detroit, in terms of technology,

[5] Lax, D. A., & Sebenius, J. K. (1986). *The manager as negotiator.* New York: Free Press.

[6] Hudson, J. (2010, June 29). Is Google giving in to China? *The Atlantic Wire.* Theatlanticwire.com

[7] Connolly, C. & Shear, M. (2009, July 7). Hospitals reach deal with administration. *Washington Post.* Washingtonpost.com

[8] Froman, L. A., & Cohen, M. D. (1970). Research reports. Compromise and logroll: Comparing the efficiency of two bargaining processes. *Behavioral Science, 15*(2), 180–183.

talent, and the customer. The Chinese company wanted access to western automotive technology and foreign markets, and the United Auto Workers union wanted jobs.[9]

A PYRAMID MODEL

Truly integrative agreements leave no resources underutilized. We distinguish three "levels" of integrative, or win-win, agreements. The pyramid model presented in Exhibit 4-1 depicts the three levels of integrative agreements. Beginning at the base, each successive level subsumes the properties of the levels below it. Ideally, negotiators should always strive to reach level 3 integrative agreements. Higher levels are progressively more difficult for negotiators to achieve, but they are more beneficial to negotiators.

Level 1 integrative agreements exceed parties' no-agreement possibilities, or reservation points. Reaching an agreement that exceeds parties' no-agreement possibilities creates value relative to their best alternative. Negotiators create value by reaching settlements that are better than their reservation points, or disagreement alternatives.

Level 2 integrative agreements are better for both parties than are other feasible negotiated agreements. In other words, negotiators create value with respect to a given negotiated outcome by finding another outcome that all prefer.

The existence of such agreements, by definition, implies that the bargaining situation is not purely fixed-sum: Some agreements yield higher joint gain than do others. In purely fixed-sum

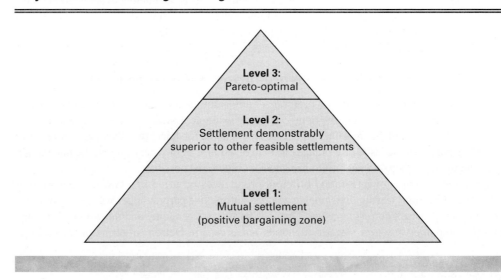

EXHIBIT 4-1

A Pyramid Model of Integrative Agreements

---

9 D' Altorio, T. (2010, December 13). Chinese interest in Detroit creates a win-win situation. *Investment U Research.* Investmentu.com

situations, all outcomes sum to the same joint amount, and, therefore, no alternative agreement exists that improves one party's outcome while simultaneously improving or not reducing the outcome of the other party. If negotiators fail to reach agreement in a fixed-sum negotiation when the bargaining zone is positive, they have failed to reach a level 1 agreement. Unlike the pure fixed-sum case, integrativeness is much more difficult to assess in the more common mixed-motive case.

Level 3 integrative agreements are settlements that lie along the **Pareto-optimal frontier** of agreement, meaning that no other feasible agreement exists that would improve one party's outcome while simultaneously not hurting the other party's outcome. Therefore, *any* agreement reached by negotiators in a purely fixed-sum situation is level 3, leaving no way to improve any negotiator's outcome without making the other party worse off.

Reaching level 3 integrative agreements may sound easy enough, but observation of hundreds of executives' performance in business negotiation simulations reveals that fewer than 25% reach level 3 agreements, and of those, approximately 50% do so by chance.[10]

MOST COMMON PIE-EXPANDING ERRORS

If reaching win-win negotiation agreements is the objective of most negotiators, what prevents them from doing so? Negotiators encounter two key problems, which we describe next.

False Conflict

False conflict, also known as **illusory conflict**, occurs when people believe that their interests are incompatible with the other party's interests when, in fact, they are not. For example, in the Cuban Missile Crisis, unbeknownst to the United States, Russia preferred to constrain the Cubans from provocative behavior and to minimize the contributions of the Chinese—an interest held by the United States.[11] Similarly, in a labor strike at the Dow Chemical Company, both union and management preferred the same wage increase, but neither party realized this fact at the time of the strike.[12]

In 1990, we uncovered a particularly insidious and widespread effect in negotiations: **the lose-lose effect**. A negotiation situation was constructed in which parties had compatible interests on a few of the negotiation issues, meaning both parties wanted the same outcome. At first, it seemed absurd to imagine any outcome occurring other than the parties settling for what was obviously the best solution for themselves and the other party. However, a substantial number of negotiators not only failed to realize that the other party had interests that were completely compatible with their own, but they reached settlements that were less optimal for both parties than some other readily available outcome. The failure to capitalize on compatible interests is known as a lose-lose agreement.[13] In an analysis of 32 different negotiation studies across more than 5,000 people, negotiators failed to realize compatible issues about 50% of the time and fell prey to the lose-lose effect about 20% of the time.[14]

---

[10] These data are based on executives' performance in negotiation simulations that involve integrative (win-win) potential.

[11] Walton, R. E., & McKersie, R. B. (1965). *A behavioral theory of labor relations.* New York: McGraw-Hill.

[12] Balke, W. M., Hammond, K. R., & Meyer, G. D. (1973). An alternate approach to labor-management relations. *Administrative Science Quarterly, 18*(3), 311–327.

[13] Thompson, L., & Hrebec, D. (1996). Lose-lose agreements in interdependent decision making. *Psychological Bulletin, 120*(3), 396–409.

[14] Ibid.

What should negotiators do to avoid lose-lose agreements? First, they should be aware of the fixed-pie perception and not assume that their interests are opposed to the other party. Second, negotiators should avoid making **premature concessions** to the other party (i.e., conceding on issues before even being asked). Third, negotiators should develop an accurate understanding of the other party's interests—a skill we explore shortly.

Fixed-Pie Perception

The **fixed-pie perception** is the belief that the other party's interests are directly and completely opposed to one's own interests.[15] Most untrained negotiators view negotiation as a pie-slicing task: They assume that their interests are incompatible, that impasse is likely, and that issues are settled one by one rather than as packages.[16] For example, in one investigation, negotiators' perceptions of the other party's interests were assessed immediately before, during, and then following a negotiation.[17] Most negotiators (68%) perceived the other's interests to be completely opposed to their own. However, negotiators shared interests that could be profitably traded off and completely compatible.

Unfortunately, banishing the fixed-pie perception is difficult. It is not enough to warn negotiators of its existence.[18] Further, it is not enough for negotiators to have experience.[19] It is not even enough for negotiators to receive feedback about their counterparties' interests to eliminate the fixed-pie perception.[20] We will talk more about how to successfully challenge the fixed-pie perception when we examine biases and creativity (Chapter 8).

Lack of time and effort do not explain lose-lose outcomes and the fixed-pie perception. The biggest detriment to the attainment of integrative agreements is the faulty assumptions we make about the counterparty and the negotiation situation. One of the first realizations negotiators should make is that negotiation is not a purely competitive situation. Rather, most negotiation situations are mixed-motive in nature, meaning that parties' interests are imperfectly correlated with one another. The gains of one party do not represent equal sacrifices by the other. For example, consider a negotiation between two collaborators on a joint project: One is a risk-averse negotiator who values cash up front more than riskier long-term payoffs; the other is more interested in long-term value than in current gains. The two may settle on a contract in which a large lump sum is paid to the risk-averse negotiator, and the other party reaps most of the (riskier) profits in the long term.

Few conflicts are purely win or lose.[21] In most mixed-motive negotiations, parties realize that they have two incentives vis-à-vis the other party: cooperation (so that they can reach an agreement and avoid resorting to their BATNAs) and competition (so that they can claim the largest slice of the pie). However, what this analysis misses is the incentive to create value, which is the key to win-win negotiation.

---

[15] Fisher, R., & Ury. W. (1981). *Getting to yes.* Boston: Houghton Mifflin; Bazerman, M. H., & Neale, M. A. (1983). Heuristics in negotiation: Limitations to effective dispute resolution. In M. Bazerman & R. Lewicki (Eds.), *Negotiating in organizations* (pp. 51–67). Beverly Hills, CA: Sage; Thompson, L., & Hastie, R. (1990). Social perception in negotiation. *Organizational Behavior and Human Decision Processes, 47*(1), 98–123.

[16] O'Connor, K. M., & Adams, A. A. (1999). What novices think about negotiation: A content analysis of scripts. *Negotiation Journal, 15*(2), 135–148.

[17] Thompson & Hastie, "Social perception in negotiation."

[18] Thompson, L. (1991). Information exchange in negotiation. *Journal of Experimental Social Psychology, 27*(2), 161–179.

[19] Thompson, L. (1990). An examination of naïve and experienced negotiators. *Journal of Personality and Social Psychology, 59*(1), 82–90; Thompson, L. (1990). The influence of experience on negotiation performance. *Journal of Experimental Social Psychology, 26*(6), 528–544.

[20] Thompson, L., & DeHarpport, T. (1994). Social judgment, feedback, and interpersonal learning in negotiation. *Organizational Behavior and Human Decision Processes, 58*(3), 327–345.

[21] Deutsch, M. (1973). *The resolution of conflict.* New Haven, CT: Yale University Press.

STRATEGIES THAT DO NOT REALLY WORK

We want to save negotiators time and heartache in their quest to expand the pie by outlining several strategies that might, at first glance, seem to be effective in expanding the pie and reaching win-win agreements but, in fact, do not really work.

Commitment to Reaching a Win-Win Deal

Many negotiators approach the negotiation table committed to reaching a win-win deal. However, commitment to reaching a win-win deal does not guarantee that negotiators will reach a win-win agreement.

Compromise

Negotiators often mistake win-win negotiations for **equal-concession negotiations**. Equal concessions or "splitting the difference" does not really ensure that a win-win negotiation has been reached. Compromise pertains to slicing the pie, not expanding the pie.

Focusing on a Long-Term Relationship

Oftentimes, negotiators believe that focusing on the long-term nature of their relationship with the other party will ensure a win-win deal. Obviously, the long-term relationship is key in negotiation—and we spend an entire chapter (Chapter 6) discussing how to foster the relationship—but establishing a long-term relationship does not guarantee a win-win outcome. Rather, it means that negotiators should have an easier time working to reach win-win.

Adopting a Cooperative Orientation

It is nice when negotiators approach the negotiation table with benevolent attitudes and a cooperative orientation. However, negotiators' intentions to cooperate often keep them from focusing on the right information at the right time. For example, negotiators often attempt to cooperate by revealing their BATNA to the other party. Revealing one's BATNA is a pie-slicing, not a pie-expanding tactic. Negotiators often think cooperation means compromise, and compromises often lead to lose-lose outcomes. For example, in 1996 MasterCard International wanted to determine why it was losing money on some of its promotional deals. Subsequent analysis revealed that MasterCard was attempting to form good relationships with others (i.e., being cooperative), but it was giving away money and promotions and not asking for sufficient compensation in return.[22] Indeed, when both parties to a negotiation hold highly relational goals or views of themselves they are prone to **relational accommodation,** a dynamic resulting in suboptiomal outcomes. This is particularly true when the organizational context focuses on egalitarian values, as opposed to hierarchical relationships.[23]

Taking Extra Time to Negotiate

Extra time does not guarantee that negotiators will reach an integrative agreement (most negotiators wait until the last few moments of a negotiation to reach an agreement). Furthermore, people

---

[22] Kiser, K. (1999, October 1). The new deal. *Training, 36*(10), 116–126.
[23] Curhan, J. R., Elfenbein, H. A., & Kilduff, G. J. (2009). Getting off on the right foot: Subjective value versus economic value in predicting longitudinal job outcomes from job offer negotiations. *Journal of Applied Psychology, 94*(2), 524-534.

tend to work to fill their time.[24] The same is true for negotiation. For example, we recently gave some people 1 hour, others 2 hours, and still others a week (via e-mail) to complete a two-party negotiation exercise. If time really makes a difference in terms of the quality of negotiated agreements, then the one-hour group should have inferior outcomes in terms of expanding the pie. However, this did not happen. In fact, there were no discernible differences among the three groups, which suggest that extra time does not improve the quality of negotiated agreements.

EFFECTIVE PIE-EXPANDING STRATEGIES

The following nine strategies that can help negotiators expand the pie and create win-win negotiations.[25] We present them in terms of the most straightforward and intuitive strategies to strategies that are more sophisticated and even paradoxical. The first few strategies are especially good to use when negotiating with someone who seems cooperative and trustworthy. The strategies that come later on this list are useful when dealing with extremely tough negotiators.

Perspective-Taking

By taking the perspective of the other party, negotiators attempt to see the world through the counterparty's eyes. Indeed, negotiators who take the perspective of the counterparty are more successful in terms of a number of social enterprises, such as coordinating with others.[26] Perspective taking also enhances problem-solving abilities, including the ability to jointly solve problems at the bargaining table.[27] Consider the following example of losing trees in new building construction. Typically, a building site provides the required replacement trees and counties plant the trees in public parks and along streets. Due to heavy construction, Arlington County, Virginia, lost numerous trees but at the same time ran out of suitable free space on public property to plant new trees. By taking the county's perspective and supporting the importance of an urban canopy, developers negotiated a program to use the tree-loss calculation for owed money instead of owed trees. Developers funded the program in which the county gave away trees to residents to plant on their private property.[28] Perspective-taking ability also enhances negotiators' ability to claim resources[29] and react effectively to the anchoring attempts of the counterparty.[30]

Perspective taking is different from empathy. Whereas perspective taking is a *cognitive* ability to consider the world from another's viewpoint, empathy is the ability to *emotionally* connect with another person.[31] It is the cognitive capacity that is most important for negotiation

---

[24] McGrath, J. E., Kelly, J. R., & Machatka, D. E. (1984). The social psychology of time: Entrainment of behavior in social and organizational settings. *Applied Social Psychology Annual, 5,* 21–44.

[25] Bazerman, M. H., & Neale, M. A. (1982). Improving negotiation effectiveness under final offer arbitration: The role of selection and training. *Journal of Applied Psychology, 67*(5), 543–548.

[26] Galinsky, A., Ku, G., & Wang, C. (2005). Perspective-taking: Fostering social bonds and facilitating coordination. *Group Processes and Intergroup Relations, 8,* 109–125; Galinsky, A. D., Wang. C. S., & Ku, G. (2008). Perspective-takers behave more stereotypically. *Journal of Personality and Social Psychology, 95(2),* 404–419.

[27] Richardson, D., Hammock, G., Smith, S., Gardner, W., & Signo, M. (1994). Empathy as a cognitive inhibitor of inter-personal aggression. *Aggressive Behavior, 20,* 275–289.

[28] Schulte, B. (2007, May 31). Sowing a different tomorrow; on a mission to restore urban canopy, Arlington distributes trees to plant on private property. *Washington Post, Virginia Extra,* p. T01.

[29] Bazerman & Neale, "Improving negotiation effectiveness."

[30] Galinsky, A., & Mussweiler, T. (2001). First offers as anchors: The role of perspective-taking and negotiator focus. *Journal of Personality and Social Psychology, 81*(4), 657–669.

[31] Galinsky, A. D., Maddux, W. W., Gilin, D., & White, J. B. (2008). Why it pays to get inside the head of your opponent: The differential effects of perspective-taking and empathy in strategic interactions. *Psychological Science, 19*(4), 378–384.

success. Negotiators who are either high in perspective-taking ability or are prompted to take the perspective of the counterparty are more successful in identifying and reaching integrative outcomes in negotiation. Perspective takers are more likely than empathizers to discover hidden agreements, achieve maximum joint gains, and secure peace. Similarly, people who regret "not following their heart" often give up more resources than do people who regret "not following their head" because they sacrifice for the relationship.[32] For these reasons, it is better to get inside the head (but not heart) of your competitive adversaries.[33]

Ask Questions About Interests and Priorities

A negotiator could ask the other party any number of questions during the negotiation (see Exhibit 4-2). However, of the six types of information listed in Exhibit 4-2 only two are truly helpful types of questions to ask in terms of expanding the pie—questions about underlying interests and questions about priorities.[34] Negotiators who ask the counterparty about their preferences are much more likely to reach integrative agreements than negotiators who do not ask the other party about his or her priorities.[35] However, left to their own devices, negotiators fail to ask diagnostic questions. For example, only about 7% of negotiators seek information about the other party's preferences during negotiation, even though it would be dramatically helpful to know such information.[36]

Why are these questions diagnostic with respect to increasing the likelihood of win-win agreements? Two reasons: First, such questions help negotiators discover where the value is. Second, diagnostic questions do not tempt the other party to lie or to misrepresent himself or herself. Asking the other party about his or her BATNA or reservation price might induce him or her to exaggerate or lie, but it is not immediately clear why or how a negotiator would lie about his or her underlying needs. Thus, diagnostic questions are effective because they do not put negotiators on the defensive.

It is important to ask the right questions; indeed possessing information about a counterparty that is irrelevant to the negotiation task actually impairs negotiators' effectiveness because such knowledge impedes effective information exchange.[37] Negotiators who possess nondiagnostic information about an opponent are more likely to terminate the search for integrative agreements prematurely.

Negotiators who express interest in their opponent's opposing viewpoints are more willing to engage in future interaction with the counterparty and are more receptive. The mere act of preparing questions that ask the counterparty to elaborate leads to more openness and positive attributions.[38] Negotiators who have high *epistemic motivation*—a personal need for structure—are more likely to reach higher joint outcomes because they ask more questions that benefit the dyad as a

---

[32] Crotty, S. & Thompson, L. (2009). When your heart isn't smart: How different types of regret change decisions and profits. *International Journal of Conflict Management, 20*(4), 315–350.
[33] Galinksy, Maddux, Gilin, & White, "Why it pays to get inside the head."
[34] Bazerman, M. H., & Neale, M. A. (1992). *Negotiating rationally.* New York: Free Press.
[35] Thompson, "Information exchange in negotiation."
[36] Ibid.
[37] Wiltermuth, S. & Neale, M. A. (2011). Too much information: The perils of nondiagnostic information in negotiations. *Journal of Applied Psychology, 96*(1), 192–201.
[38] Chen, F. S., Minson, J. A., & Tormala, Z. L. (2010). Tell me more: The effects of expressed interest on receptiveness during dialogue. *Journal of Experimental Social Psychology, 46*(5), 850–853.
[39] Ten Velden, F. S., Beersma, B., De Dreu, C. K. W. (2010). It takes one to tango: The effects of dyads' epistemic motivation composition in negotiation. *Personality and Social Psychology Bulletin, 36*(11), 1454–1466.

EXHIBIT 4-2

Types of Information in Negotiation and How Each Affects Distributive and Integrative Agreements

Type of Information	Definition (example)	Claiming Value	Creating Value
BATNA (and reservation price)	The alternatives a negotiator has outside of the current negotiation (e.g., "If I don't buy your car, I can buy my uncle's car for $2,000.")	Revealing this information severely hurts the ability to maximize negotiator surplus.	Revealing or obtaining this information does not affect ability to reach level 2 or 3 integrative agreements; it might help negotiators reach level 1 integrative agreements.
Position (stated demand)	Usually, a negotiator's opening offer; the behavioral manifestation of his/her target point (e.g., "I will give you $1,500 for your car.")	Opening with an aggressive target point significantly increases the negotiator's surplus (share of the bargaining zone).	This does not affect integrative agreements.
Underlying interests	The underlying needs and reasons a negotiator has for a particular issue (e.g., "I need a car because I need transportation to my job site, which is 15 miles away in a rural zone.")	Revealing this information generally increases the likelihood of obtaining a favorable slice of the pie because negotiators who provide a rationale for their demands are more adept at realizing their targets.	Very important for reaching win-win deals; by (truthfully) revealing underlying interests, negotiators can discover win-win agreements (e.g., one sister tells the other that she wants the orange because she needs to make juice and has no need for rinds).
Priorities	A judgment about the relative importance of the issues to a negotiator (e.g., "I am more concerned about the down payment than I am about the financing for the car.")	Increases a negotiator's surplus indirectly, because if more value is created via sharing priorities, then the probability that a negotiator will get a larger slice of the pie increases.	Vitally important for maximizing the pie (e.g., the sister who said she cared more about the rinds *relative* to the juice created potential for integrative agreement).
Key facts	Pertains to information that bears on the quality and the value of the to-be-negotiated issues (e.g., "The car has a rebuilt engine and has been involved in a major collision." "The oranges are genetically modified.")	This information can affect the slice of the pie the negotiator obtains in that facts either increase or decrease the value of the to-be-negotiated issues.	Affects the quality of win-win agreements in that failure to reveal key information may lead a negotiator to over- or undervalue a particular resource (e.g., someone who sells "fresh organic orange juice" does not want to have genetically modified oranges as an ingredient).
Substantiation	Argument either made to support one's own position or to attack the other party's position (e.g., "You will get lots of dates if you buy my car because women like it.")	Most dominant type of distributive tactic (24% to 27% of all statements[1]); can increase a negotiator's slice of the pie because providing a rationale (even an absurd one) can often be effective in obtaining a demand.	A distributive tactic; does not increase win-win negotiation and may, in fact, reduce the likelihood of win-win.[2]

[1] Carnevale, P. J., & Lawler, E. J. (1986). Time pressure and the development of integrative agreements in bilateral negotiations. *Journal of Conflict Resolution, 30*(4), 636–659.
[2] Pruitt, D. G. (1981). *Negotiation behavior.* New York: Academic Press; Hyder, E. B., Prietula, M. J., & Weingart, L. R. (2000). Getting to best: Efficiency versus optimality in negotiation. *Cognitive Science, 24*(2), 169–204.

whole compared to negotiators who are both low in epistemic motivation.[39] Moreover, negotiators high in epistemic motivation are more likely to benefit from adding and discussing more issues.[40]

Provide Information About Your Interests and Priorities

Negotiation is a paradox because parties are expected to be honest and straightforward, but revealing too much information can put one at a disadvantage. For example, negotiators who are naturally straightforward tend to show greater concern for the other party and make more concessions, especially in purely distributive negotiations, resulting in lower profit.[41] It is a fallacy to believe that negotiators should never provide information to the counterparty.[42] Negotiations would not go anywhere if negotiators did not communicate their interests to the other party. You should negotiate as you would with your fraternal twin: If you do not provide information, neither will the other party. A negotiator should never ask the other party a question that he or she is not willing to answer truthfully. The important question, then, is not *whether* to reveal information but *what* information to reveal.

By signaling your willingness to share information about your interests (not your BATNA), you capitalize on the powerful principle of reciprocity: If you share information, the other party will often share as well. Negotiators who provide information to the other party about their priorities are more likely to reach integrative agreements than negotiators who do not provide this information.[43] The disclosing negotiator is not at a strategic disadvantage, as long as he or she does not reveal information about his or her BATNA or reservation price. The disclosing negotiator does not earn significantly more or less resources than the counterparty.

Negotiators can exchange six key types of information during negotiation. The skilled negotiator knows how to recognize each. Even more important, the skilled negotiator knows what information is safe (and even necessary) to reveal to reach win-win outcomes. The information that negotiators need to share is not information about their BATNAs but, rather, information about their *preferences* and *priorities* across the negotiation issues. (Exhibit 4-2 outlines the six types of information that negotiators can exchange. Exhibit 4-3 supplements Exhibit 4-2 by providing a worksheet to complete prior to negotiation.)

A distinct time course emerges in terms of the unraveling of information during negotiation. Adair and her colleague divided the negotiation into four quarters.[44] During the first quarter, people are more likely to use influence strategies as they battle for power and influence. During the second quarter, priority information peaks as negotiators discuss the issues and share information about their priorities. In the third quarter, negotiators make offers and counteroffers and either support or reject them on the basis of rational argument. In the fourth quarter, negotiators begin to work toward agreement by building on each other's offers.

Even though many negotiators provide information during a negotiation, the counterparty may not necessarily understand the information. This faulty assumption may be traceable to the

---

[40] Ibid.

[41] DeRue, D. S., Conlon, D. E., Moon, H. & Willaby, H. W. (2009). When is straightforwardness a liability in negotiations? The role of integrative potential and structural power. *Journal of Applied Psychology, 94*(4), 1032–1047.

[42] Bazerman & Neale, *Negotiating rationally.*

[43] Thompson, "Information exchange in negotiation."

[44] Adair, W. L., & Brett, J. M. (2005). The negotiation dance: Time, culture and behavioral sequences in negotiation. *Organization Science, 16*(1), 33–51.

EXHIBIT 4-3

Preparation Worksheet

Issue	Self	Other
Salary	position / underlying interest [1]	other party's position on this issue / other party's underlying interest [ ]
Signing Bonus	[3]	[ ]
Job title	[4]	[ ]
Stock options	[2]	[ ]
Company car	[5]	[ ]
Reservation price		
Target		
BATNA		

Instructions:

1. In the far-left column, identify the issues to be negotiated.
2. Then, indicate your "position" in the top part of the triangle and your underlying interest in the lower part of the triangle in the middle column.
3. Next, rank-order the issues from most to least important (using, say, 1 through 5 in the small boxes).
4. Next, make your best assessment of the other party's position, interests, and priorities across the issues.
5. Indicate your reservation price (and attempt to assess the reservation price of the other party).
6. Indicate your target point.
7. Indicate your BATNA (and attempt to assess the other party's BATNA).

Source: Based on Brett, J. (2007). *Negotiating globally: How to negotiate deals, resolve disputes, and make decisions across cultural boundaries* (2nd edition), San Francisco: Jossey-Bass, p. 17.

illusion of transparency.[45] The illusion of transparency occurs when negotiators believe they are revealing more than they actually are (i.e., they believe others have access to information about them when in fact they do not). In one investigation, negotiators judged whether an observer to the negotiation could accurately discern their negotiation goals from their behavior.[46] Negotiators consistently overestimated the transparency of their objectives. Thus, people feel more like an "open book" with respect to their goals and interests in negotiation than they actually are. Negotiators are also not as clear in their messages as they should be. Indeed, when the information exchanged is amenable to multiple interpretations, it can lead to settlement delays and divergent expectations.[47] Conversely, when a single interpretation is obvious, information sharing leads to convergence of expectations and speeds settlement.

Unbundle the Issues

One reason negotiations fail is because negotiators haggle over a single issue, such as price. By definition, if negotiations contain only one issue (e.g., price), they are purely distributive (i.e., fixed-pie). Skilled negotiators are adept at expanding the set of negotiable issues. Adding issues, unbundling issues, and creating new issues can transform a single-issue, fixed-pie negotiation into an integrative, multi-issue negotiation with win-win potential.[48] Integrative agreements require at least two issues. Roger Fisher, co-author of the classic book *Getting to Yes*, recounts a situation when he was helping the president of a company sell a building he owned: "He was retiring and wanted $2 million, which he considered a fair price. He had a buyer, but the buyer wouldn't pay that price. I asked the seller, 'What's the worst thing about selling this building?' And he said, 'All of my papers for 25 years are mixed up in my corner office. When I sell the building, I can't throw everything away. I've got to go through that stuff. That's the nightmare I have.'"[49] Then Fisher asked the buyer why he wanted the building. The buyer explained he hoped to rent it for business. This knowledge gave Fisher the idea of suggesting that the seller offer the buyer a lease with an option to buy with one contingency: that the president's name be on the corner office for three years. The buyer agreed. In this example, an integrative agreement was reached by unbundling the price and the lease option.

Make Package Deals, Not Single-Issue Offers

Most negotiators make the mistake of negotiating each issue one by one. This approach is a mistake for several reasons: First and foremost, negotiating each issue separately does not allow negotiators to make trade-offs between issues. To capitalize on different strengths of preference, negotiators need to compare and contrast issues and trade them off. Second, it may mean that impasse is more likely, especially if the bargaining zone is narrow and trade-offs are necessary to reach a mutually profitable outcome. Single-issue offers lure negotiators into compromise agreements, which, as we have seen, are usually not the best approach for win-win negotiations.

A major and potentially crippling strike was neatly avoided between Pratt Whitney and its Machinists union through the crafting of a package deal. The company's main goal was to

---

[45] Gilovich, T., Savitsky, K., & Medvec, V. H. (1998). The illusion of transparency: Biased assessments of others' ability to read one's emotional states. *Journal of Personality and Social Psychology, 75*(2), 332–346.

[46] Vorauer, J. D., & Claude, S. D. (1998). Perceived versus actual transparency of goals in negotiation. *Personality and Social Psychology Bulletin, 24*(4), 371–385.

[47] Loewenstein, G. F., & Moore, D. A. (2004). When ignorance is bliss: Information exchange and inefficiency in bargaining. *Journal of Legal Studies, 33*(1), 37–58.

[48] Lax & Sebenius, *The manager as negotiator.*

[49] Fisher, R. (2001, September 1). Doctor YES. *CFO: The Magazine for Senior Financial Executives*, p. 66.

eliminate 500 jobs, close two plants and move operations overseas; hardly what union workers wanted. However, Pratt packaged its key interest (closures and job eliminations) in a deal that did not include layoffs, added 75 jobs at the Middletown assembly plants for workers at the targeted facilities, provided a generous early-retirement program, set wage increases of 3% in the first year, along with a $3K signing bonus, and provided job security for workers outside of the targeted facilities.[50]

Make Multiple Offers of Equivalent Value Simultaneously

In some cases, negotiators are disappointed and frustrated to find that their attempts to provide and seek information are not effective. Can negotiators do anything to change the situation? Fortunately, the answer is yes. The strategy of making **multiple offers of equivalent value simultaneously** can be effective even with the most uncooperative of negotiators.[51] The strategy involves presenting the other party with at least two (and preferably more) proposals of *equal value* to oneself. For example, in the Wal-Mart negotiation discussed in Exhibit 4-4, the Sequim county engineer, Don McInnes, responded to the planning director's protests by outlining three different options: (a) widening three roads to a standard 40-foot width, (b) bringing the roadways up to a higher standard (but not to full standard) through a major overhaul, or (c) creating a cul-de-sac at two of the roads.[52]

The multiple-offer strategy is threefold:

1. *Devise multiple-issue offers,* as opposed to single-issue offers (to get away from sequential bargaining, which can lock people into lose-lose outcomes).
2. *Devise offers that are all of equal value to yourself* (leaving yourself many ways to get what you want before making a concession).
3. *Make all the offers at the same time.* This last point is the hardest for most people to do because they negotiate like playing tennis: They make one offer and then wait for the other party to "return" a single offer; then they make a concession, and so on. In the multiple-offer strategy, a negotiator presents a "dessert tray" of offers to the other party and invites a response. *Note:* The other party should be cautioned that cherry-picking (e.g., selecting the terms from each option that most suit a negotiator) is not permissible. Rather, the offers are truly package deals.[53]

Negotiators who make multiple equivalent offers enjoy more profitable negotiated outcomes and are evaluated more favorably by the other party.[54] Specifically, they are seen by the other side as being more flexible, and they are more satisfied at the end of the negotiation. Multiple offers increase the discovery of integrative solutions.[55] When issues are packaged together in

---

[50] Pratt & Whitney Company, Union reach win-win agreement that avoids strike. (2010, December 7). *The Hartford Courant*. Courant.com

[51] Bazerman & Neale, *Negotiating rationally*; Kelley, H. H., & Schenitzki, D. P. (1972). Bargaining. In C. G. McClintock (Ed.), *Experimental social psychology* (pp. 298–337). New York: Holt, Rinehart, and Winston; Kelley, H. H. (1966). A classroom study of dilemmas in interpersonal negotiations. In K. Archibald (Ed.), *Strategic intervention and conflict* (pp. 49–73). Berkeley: University of California, Institute of International Studies.

[52] Ross, D. (2003, July 30). County proposes mall traffic solution. *Sequim Gazette*, p. A7.

[53] Schatzki, M., & Coffey, W. R. (1981). *Negotiation: The art of getting what you want.* New York: New American Library.

[54] Leonardelli, G. J., Medvec, V., Galinsky, A. D., & Claussen-Schulz, A. (2008). Building interpersonal and economic capital by negotiating with multiple equivalent simultaneous offers. Under review at *Organizational Behavior and Human Decision Processes*.

[55] Hyder, E. B., Prietula, M. J., & Weingart, L. R. (2000). Getting to best: Efficiency versus optimality in negotiation. *Cognitive Science, 24*(2), 169–204.

EXHIBIT 4-4

Wal-Mart's Construction Plans

The mayor of Sequim, Washington, and Wal-Mart's attorney fired verbal shots at the county as the appeals hearing for approving Wal-Mart's construction plans concluded. Shortly thereafter, appeals were filed by the Clallam County Department of Community Development, the Jamestown S'Kallam Indian tribe, and the community group, Sequim First, to block the city planning director from allowing a Wal-Mart complex to be built in the small town of Sequim (fewer than 5,000 people). The groups opposed to the new 575,000-square-foot shopping center complex argued that the Wal-Mart would create a traffic nightmare, causing "unsafe driving conditions" on the roads, and the storm-water runoff (from all the concrete and pavement) would put toxins in the city's rivers and streams. They argued that the impact of the huge store could cause anywhere between a 280% and 500% increase in traffic. And they wanted Wal-Mart to pay—in advance—something to the tune of $100 million to fix the roads. However, Wal-Mart and the mayor of Sequim viewed these protests as a thinly veiled ploy to squeeze a "deep pocket to pay for [the city's] neglect [of its roads]." According to Wal-Mart and the mayor, the county's road maintenance around Sequim had been downright negligent and the county had not kept up the roads. A Wal-Mart analysis of the same roads predicted only a 7% traffic increase. For a while it appeared to be a standoff, and the two sides seemed to be working off completely different data. Then a breakthrough solution was proposed by Mayor Walt Schubert: An independent body would conduct an analysis of possible traffic impacts on the country roads, and Wal-Mart would give the city up to $100,000 if substantial traffic impacts were proven through the independent study. Through this plan, the Wal-Mart could be built and the city could have money to fix the roads.

Source: Ross, D. (2003, July 9). Wal-Mart united against county during hearing. *Sequim Gazette*, pp. A1, A5.

a single proposal, rather than considered as separate entities, it is easier to arrange trades and concessions. Moreover, when issues are dealt with individually, negotiators tend to compromise on each issue in a sequential fashion.[56] More important, it is **substantiation** (arguments for one's own position or against the other's position) that interferes the most with win-win agreements. "Substantiation, by its very nature, is a seductive strategy that seems not only to be a default behavior, but a persistent one that feeds upon itself and the cognitive resources of the negotiators."[57] Substantiation begets more substantiation.[58]

Negotiators who make multiple, equivalent offers have an edge in five critical aspects: They can (a) be more aggressive in terms of anchoring the negotiation favorably, (b) gain better

---

[56] Thompson, E. A., Mannix, E. A., & Bazerman, M. H. (1988). Group negotiation: Effects of decision rule, agenda, and aspiration. *Journal of Personality and Social Psychology, 54*(1), 86–95; Weingart, L. R., Bennett, R. J., & Brett, J. M. (1993). The impact of consideration of issues and motivational orientation on group negotiation process and outcome. *Journal of Applied Psychology, 78*(3), 504–517.

[57] Hyder, Prietula, & Weingart, "Getting to best," 194.

[58] Weingart, L. R., Hyder, E. B., & Prietula, M. J. (1996). Knowledge matters: The effect of tactical descriptions on negotiation behavior and outcome. *Journal of Personality and Social Psychology, 70*(6), 1205–1217.

information about the other party, (c) be more persistent, (d) signal their priorities more effectively, and (e) overcome concession aversion on the part of the other side.[59]

BE AGGRESSIVE IN ANCHORING   Consider how Ken Alex, an attorney at a major international law firm, negotiated a business news database.[60] For the law firm, the database was critical and renewal was necessary. Not doing so would mean a lot more research librarian time, and recent staff cutbacks had reduced the number of librarians. The amount the firm paid for the renewal in the previous year was $52,000. Alex had budgeted $58,000 for this year's renewal. Alex's strategy was to use the simultaneous multiple-offer strategy. Because he knew that one of the key issues for the database service was the contracted value of the database, he reasoned that a 2-year contract with a major firm would be quite valuable for the database company. Moreover, signing up for 2 years was a low-risk strategy for him because he was confident that the firm would want the database again next year. Moreover, it also would represent budget certainty for the firm in highly volatile times. Alex made two proposals that he called A and B. Proposal A was a 1-year renewal at $45,000; proposal B was a 2-year renewal for $43,000 for year 1 and $47,000 for year 2. Ultimately, the database company opted for proposal B, the 2-year renewal.

GAIN BETTER INFORMATION ABOUT THE OTHER PARTY   The multiple-offer strategy is based on the strategy of **inductive reasoning**, meaning that a negotiator can deduce what the other party's true interests are and where the joint gains are. (We present more about inductive, as well as deductive, reasoning in Chapter 8 in a discussion of advanced negotiations and creativity.) By listening to the opponent's response, the negotiator learns about the other party's preferences. Thus, the negotiator acts as a "detective" by drawing conclusions based on the counterparties' responses to the multiple offers.

BE PERSISTENT AND PERSUASIVE REGARDING THE VALUE OF AN OFFER   Consider how the multiple-offer strategy helped a team at a major pharmaceutical firm maintain ground in a particularly tense negotiation.[61] "The situation was a divestiture, and we had an issue surface from our side (regarding much more inventory than was originally estimated), a significant surprise that appeared as if we had provided incorrect information at the due diligence stage. The issue was of a very significant magnitude relative to the size of the deal (meaning that they would have to pay a higher amount in some very significant way)." The pharmaceutical firm proposed five options, all of equivalent value, that involved various trade-offs between deferred payment terms, cash on close, and not taking some of the inventory, among other options. The team made the five proposals and then held their collective breath. "We had already had multiday tirades on issues of who owned the pencil sharpeners, so we were braced for the worst attacks." The other team calmly said, "We understand," and the very next day selected one of the options. The pharmaceutical team members reflected, "If we had taken the single-option approach, their obvious position would have been to say 'That is your problem, you misled us...provide us with the excess inventory for free.'" However, this potential deal killer was avoided and the deal closed much more successfully than ever anticipated.

---

[59] Medvec, V. H., & Galinsky, A. D. (2005). Putting more on the table: How making multiple offers can increase the final value of the deal. *HBS negotiation newsletter, 8*(4), 4–6.
[60] Personal communication, December 4, 2002. Names have been altered.
[61] Personal communication, September 14, 2003.

OVERCOME CONCESSION AVERSION   When people perceive themselves as having more choices (as opposed to only one), they may be more likely to comply. For example, when Ross Johnson, a member of the California Senate was faced with a legislative bill that he hated, he did not kill it outright. Rather, he strategically proposed three amendments he knew would not be accepted but which would make legislators aware of some issues Johnson felt were important.[62]

Structure Contingency Contracts by Capitalizing on Differences

Negotiators not only have differences in interests and preferences, but they also view the world differently.[63] A book author may believe that the sales will be high; the publisher may believe they will be more modest. Different interpretations of the facts may threaten already tenuous relations. Attempts to persuade the other person may be met with skepticism, hostility, and an escalating spiral of conflict. Differences in beliefs—or expectations about uncertain events—pave the way toward integrative agreements. For example, in the Wal-Mart negotiation presented in Exhibit 4-4, the parties had widely differing beliefs about the impact the shopping complex would have on local traffic, with the city estimating a 500% increase in traffic and Wal-Mart estimating only 7%. Given these differing predictions, it is somewhat ironic to think they might be leveraged to create a workable solution. In fact, it is differences, rather than commonalities, that can be more advantageous in negotiations.[64] The enlightened negotiator realizes that differences in beliefs, expectations, and tastes can create greater value. Most people are uncomfortable when they encounter differences and, instead of leveraging this opportunity, they either downplay their differences or ignore them.

Negotiators can exploit differences to capitalize on integrative agreements in a variety of ways.[65] Consider the following differences and the opportunities they create:

- Differences in the valuation of the negotiation issues
- Differences in expectations of uncertain events
- Differences in risk attitudes
- Differences in time preferences
- Differences in capabilities

DIFFERENCES IN VALUATION   Negotiators have different strengths of preference for each issue. For example, in a negotiation for scarce office space, one person is more interested in a large office than a nice view; the other negotiator is more interested in a view than having extra space. They reach an agreement in which one person gets a large, windowless office and the other gets a small office with a great view. The strategy of trading off so as to capitalize on different strengths of preference is known as **logrolling**.[66]

DIFFERENCES IN EXPECTATIONS   Because negotiation often involves uncertainty, negotiators differ in their forecasts, or beliefs, about what will happen in the future. Consider the case of a woman and her brother who inherited a tool store from their father[67] The sister expected the profitability of the store to decline steadily; the brother expected the store to succeed. The sister

---

[62] Quach, H. (2002, January 6). "Caveman" and conciliator: Sen. Ross Johnson adroitly plays to both sides of the aisle, and sings, too. *Orange County Register,* p. 1.

[63] Lax & Sebenius, *The manager as negotiator.*

[64] Ibid.

[65] Ibid.

[66] Froman & Cohen, "Compromise and logroll."

[67] Personal communication, April 1993.

wanted to sell the store; the brother wanted to keep it. A contingent contract was constructed: The brother agreed to buy his sister's share of the store over a period of time at a price based on her bleak assessment of its worth. The sister is guaranteed a certain return; the brother's return is based on the success of the store.

DIFFERENCES IN RISK ATTITUDES   In other situations, negotiators agree on the probability of future events but feel differently about taking risks.[68] For example, two colleagues may undertake a collaborative project, such as writing a novel, for which they both agree that the probability of success is only moderate. The colleague with an established career can afford to be risk-seeking; the struggling young novelist may be risk-averse. The two may capitalize on their different risk-taking profiles with a contingent contract: The more risk-averse colleague receives the entire advance on the book; the risk-seeking colleague receives the majority of the risky profits after the publication of the novel. Negotiators who have a **gain-frame** (i.e., see the glass as half full) are more likely to logroll or trade off issues in a win-win fashion; conversely, those with a **loss-frame** (i.e., see the glass as half empty) are more likely to accept a contingent contract.[69]

DIFFERENCES IN TIME PREFERENCES   People may value the same event quite differently depending on when it occurs.[70] If one party is more impatient than the other, mechanisms for optimally sharing the consequences over time may be devised. Two partners in a joint venture might allocate the initial profits to the partner who has high costs for time, whereas the partner who can wait will achieve greater profits over a longer, delayed period.

DIFFERENCES IN CAPABILITIES   People differ not only in their tastes, probability assessments, and risk preferences; they also differ in their capabilities, endowments, and skills. Consider two managers who have different resources, capital, and support staff. One manager has strong quantitative skills and access to state-of-the-art computers; the other has strong marketing and design skills. Together, they may combine their differing skills and expertise in a mutually beneficial way, such as in the design of a new product concept. The development of successful research collaborations is fostered by differences in skills and preferences.[71]

CAUTIONARY NOTE   Capitalizing on differences often entails **contingency contracts**, wherein negotiators make bets based upon different world occurrences. For contingency contracts to be effective, they should satisfy the following four criteria: First, they should not create *a conflict of interest.* For example, if a book author, optimistic about sales, negotiates a contingency contract with her publisher such that royalty rates will be contingent upon sales, the contract should not create an incentive for the publisher to attempt to thwart sales. Second, contingency contracts should be *enforceable* and therefore often may require a written contract. Third, contingency contracts should be *clear, measurable, and readily evaluated,* leaving no room for ambiguity. Conditions and measurement techniques should be spelled out in advance.[72] Further, a date or

---

[68] Lax & Sebenius, *The manager as negotiator.*
[69] Kray, L. J., Paddock, L. E., & Galinsky, A. D., (2008). The effect of past performance on expected control and risk attitudes in integrative negotiations. *Negotiations and Conflict Management Research, 1*(2), 161–178.
[70] Lax & Sebenius, *The manager as negotiator.*
[71] Northcraft, G., & Neale, M. A. (1993). Negotiating successful research collaboration. In J. K. Murnighan (Ed.), *Social psychology in organizations: Advances in theory and research.* Upper Saddle River, NJ: Prentice Hall.
[72] Bazerman, M. H., & Gillespie, J. J. (1999). Betting on the future: The virtues of contingent contracts. *Harvard Business Review, 77*(5), 155–160.

time line should be mutually agreed upon. Finally, contingency contracts require *continued interaction* among parties. We go into more detail about contingency contracts in Chapter 8.

Presettlement Settlements (PreSS)

Presettlement settlements (PreSS) have three characteristics: They are *formal,* in that they encompass specific, binding obligations; *initial,* because they are intended to be replaced by a formal agreement; and *partial,* in that the parties do not address or resolve all outstanding issues.[73] PreSS's involve more than a simple handshake or "gentleman's agreement." Rather, a PreSS occurs in advance of the parties undertaking full-scale negotiations and is designed to be replaced by a long-term agreement. A PreSS resolves only a subset of the issues on which the parties disagree (i.e., partial). In some cases, instead of resolving any of the outstanding issues, a PreSS may simply establish a concrete framework for final negotiations. For example, reaching a workable agreement between United Kingdom broadcasters and independent producers over who owns the rights to exploit TV shows across broadband and mobile platforms could have taken up to a year. Therefore, a quick resolution to generate revenue from new audiences was crucial for both partners. The parties agreed to negotiate an interim code of practice deal before the consensus on a final agreement.[74]

Gillespie and Bazerman note that a famous example of PreSS is the 1993 Oslo Accords between Israel and Palestine.[75] The Oslo Accords sought to establish an incremental process of negotiation and reciprocation that would lead to what both parties termed "final-status" talks. The parties agreed to wait to resolve the most difficult issues (e.g., borders, settlements, Jerusalem) until the final-status talks. As an initial step, the Israelis and Palestinians sought to resolve less difficult issues, thereby establishing a political dialogue and working toward formalized relations. For example, the Israelis agreed to release female prisoners, transfer disputed money, and withdraw from Hebron. The Palestinians agreed to revise their national charter, transfer suspected terrorists, and limit the size of the Palestinian police force. Gillespie and Bazerman also noted that the PreSS framework has subsequently floundered due to heated rhetoric and escalating violence. (For another type of PreSS, see Exhibit 4-5.)

Search for Postsettlement Settlements

A final strategy for expanding the pie is one in which negotiators reach an initial settlement that both agree to but spend additional time attempting to improve upon (each from their own perspective). In the **postsettlement settlement strategy**, negotiators agree to explore other options with the goal of finding another that both prefer more than the current one, or that one party prefers more and to which the other is indifferent.[76] The current settlement becomes both parties' new BATNA. For any future agreement to replace the current one, both parties must be in agreement; otherwise, they revert to the initial agreement. It may seem counterintuitive and perhaps downright counterproductive to resume negotiations once an acceptable agreement has been reached, but the strategy of postsettlement settlements is remarkably effective in improving the quality of negotiated agreements[77] and in moving an agreement from a level 1 agreement to a level 2 or 3 agreement.

---

[73] Gillespie, J. J., & Bazerman, M. H. (1998). Pre-settlement settlement (PreSS): A simple technique for initiating complex negotiations. *Negotiation Journal, 14*(2), 149–159.

[74] Jones, G. (2006, March 2). Pact warns solution to digital media rights could take a year. *NMA Magazine,* p. 4.

[75] Gillespie & Bazerman, "Pre-settlement settlement (PreSS)."

[76] Raiffa, H. (1982). *The art and science of negotiation.* Cambridge, MA: Belknap.

[77] Bazerman, M. H., Russ, L. E., & Yakura, E. (1987). Post-settlement settlements in two-party negotiations. *Negotiation Journal, 3*(3), 283–292.

EXHIBIT 4-5

NO-FIST (Normal Operations with a Financial Strike)

Lax and Sebenius suggested a unique type of presettlement settlement (PreSS) in a letter written to the editor of the *Wall Street Journal*. They cautioned that a planned strike by American Airlines pilots would result in the airline incurring revenue losses of more than $200 million per day. To avoid such a lose-lose outcome, they recommended the following: Once the strike seemed imminent and negotiations reached impasse, the parties should agree to continue normal business operations, but place some or all of their revenues and salaries into an escrow account controlled by a trusted outside entity. By continuing operations but accruing escrow money—no matter how the escrow fund is eventually divided—both parties will inevitably be better off compared to a typical strike situation. In this sense, NO-FIST promotes a Pareto-superior outcome for all concerned parties, including pilots, shareholders, customers, and non-pilot airline employees.

Source: Based on Lax, D. A., & Sebenius, J. K. (1997, February 24). A better way to go on strike. *The Wall Street Journal*, Section A, p. 22.

Because they can safely revert to their previous agreement, the postsettlement settlement strategy allows both parties to reveal their preferences without fear of exploitation. If better terms are found, parties can be more confident they have reached a level 2 or 3 settlement. If no better agreement is found, the parties may be more confident that the current agreement is level 3.

A STRATEGIC FRAMEWORK FOR REACHING INTEGRATIVE AGREEMENTS

The discovery and creation of integrative agreements is much like problem solving, which requires creativity. Integrative agreements are devilishly obvious after the fact but not before. Because negotiation is an ill-structured task, with few constraints and a myriad of possible "moves," a royal road for reaching integrative agreement does not exist. Look at the decision-making model of integrative negotiation in Exhibit 4-6. The model is prescriptive; that is, it focuses on what negotiators *should* do to reach agreement, not what they *actually* do. The model has five major components: resource assessment, assessment of differences, construction of offers and trade-offs, acceptance/rejection of a decision, and renegotiation.

Resource Assessment

Resource assessment involves the identification of the bargaining issues and alternatives. For example, consider an employment negotiation. The bargaining issues may be salary, vacation, and benefits. In this stage, parties identify the issues that are of concern to them in the negotiation. A superset emerges from the combination of both parties' issues.

The union of both parties' issues forms the **issue mix** of the negotiation. In addition to specifying the issue mix, parties also define and clarify the alternatives for each issue. The ultimate set of options for each issue is a superset of both parties' alternatives.

EXHIBIT 4-6

Decision-Making Model of Integrative Negotiation

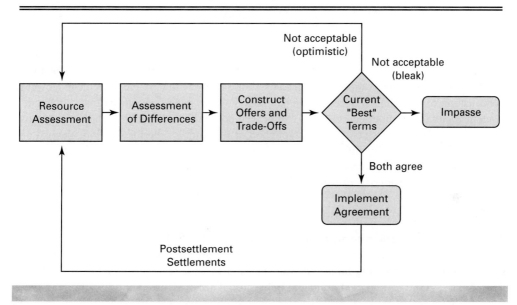

Later stages of resource assessment move beyond the mere identification of issues and alternatives to more sophisticated processes, namely, the **unbundling** of issues and alternatives and the addition of new issues and alternatives. Unbundling[78] issues is important in negotiations that center around a single issue. Because mutually beneficial trade-offs require a minimum of two issues, it is important to fractionate conflict into more than one issue. In other instances, it may be necessary to add new issues and alternatives. The process of adding issues and alternatives is facilitated by discussing parties' interests.

Assessment of Differences

Once the issue mix is identified, we should focus on assessing their differences in valuation, probability assessment, risk preferences, time constraints, and capabilities.[79] Each party should focus on its most important issues. Negotiators most important issues are their interests; the other issues secondary. When negotiators are psychologically distant from one another, they focus on secondary issues more than their primary interests, which facilitates integrative agreement when tradeoff potential resides in these issues.[80]

---

[78] Lax & Sebenius, *The manager as negotiator.*

[79] Ibid.

[80] Giacomantonio, M., De Dreu, C. K. W., Shalvi, S., Sligte, D., & Leder, S. (2010). Psychological distance boosts value-behavior correspondence in ultimatum bargaining and integrative negotiation. *Journal of Experimental Social Psychology, 46*(5), 824–829.

Offers and Trade-Offs

In this phase, parties should consider several potential trade-offs among valuations, forecasts, risks, time preferences, and capabilities, and eliminate those dominated by other alternatives. Parties should focus on issues that are of high value to one party and of low cost for the other party to provide. It makes no sense to pursue a trade-off unless what you are offering is more valuable to the other party than what it costs you to provide.

Acceptance/Rejection Decision

At some point, negotiators may identify a set of terms that both find minimally acceptable: It exceeds both parties' reservation points and constitutes a level 1 integrative agreement. However, identification of a minimally acceptable agreement does not necessarily mean that settlement is efficient. Negotiators should continue to explore the possibilities, depending on their time costs and their subjective assessments of the likelihood of reaching a superior solution. Negotiators' aspirations and goals may influence the search process in negotiation; negotiators who set specific, challenging goals are more likely to continue to search for integrative agreements than do those who do not set goals or who set easy goals.[81]

Prolonging Negotiation and Renegotiation

Two feedback loops emanate from the decision stage: the decision to prolong negotiations and the decision to renegotiate. Negotiators should prolong negotiations when the best agreement on the bargaining table fails to meet both parties' reservation points. Negotiators should reassess the resources by unpacking the initial set of issues and breaking them down into smaller issues that may be traded off. In addition to unpacking issues, negotiators may add issues and alternatives to the bargaining mix. If parties have identified all the issues and alternatives, and they have identified differences to trade off, and yet a mutually agreeable solution has not been found, they should call a halt to the negotiation and pursue their BATNAs. For example, Canadian National Railway representatives met with representatives of the Canadian branch of the United Transportation Union numerous times but could not make any progress toward a national agreement. After 8 months of negotiations, both parties agreed to pursue regional deals as the best alternative to the national agreement.[82]

DO NOT FORGET ABOUT CLAIMING

Sometimes, when negotiators learn about integrative agreements and expanding the pie, they forget about the distributive (pie-slicing) element of negotiation. It is not an effective negotiation strategy to focus exclusively on expanding the pie; the negotiator must simultaneously focus on claiming resources. After all, if a negotiator focused only on expanding the pie, he or she would not benefit because the other party would reap all the added value.

We have witnessed three stages in the evolution of the integrative negotiator. The first stage is what we call the **old-fashioned negotiator**. This type of negotiator comes from the old school of bargaining and believes that one must adopt a tough, hard stance to negotiate successfully.

---

[81] Huber, V. L., & Neale, M. A. (1986). Effects of cognitive heuristics and goals on negotiator performance and subsequent goal setting. *Organizational Behavior and Human Decision Processes, 38*(3), 342–365.
[82] Boyd, J. D. (2007, April 23). CN-UTU rumble on the rails. *Traffic World, 271*(16), 28.

The second stage in the evolution of the negotiator is what we call the **flower child negotiator;** one who gets "turned on" to win-win negotiations and is so busy expanding the pie that he or she forgets to claim resources. Thus, the "flower child" is at a disadvantage in terms of slicing the pie. The third stage is what we call the **enlightened negotiator**, who realizes that negotiation has a pie-expanding aspect but at the same time does not forget to claim resources. Thus, this negotiator protects his or her interests while expanding the pie. If you follow all the strategies outlined in this chapter, you will be an enlightened negotiator.

CONCLUSION

Virtually all negotiators want to reach integrative (or win-win) agreements; however, most negotiators fail to do so, resulting in money and resources being left on the table. In reality, people are usually not aware that their negotiation outcomes are inefficient. The key reasons for lose-lose outcomes are illusory conflict and the fixed-pie perception. The successful creation of win-win negotiation deals involves perspective-taking; asking questions about interests and priorities; providing the counterparty with information about your priorities and preferences (not your BATNA!); unbundling issues; making package deals (not single-issue offers); making multiple offers simultaneously; structuring contingency contracts that capitalize on differences in negotiators' beliefs, expectations, and attitudes, and using pre- and postsettlement settlement strategies. In their attempts to expand the pie, negotiators should not forget about claiming resources.

Part II: Advanced Negotiation Skills

Developing a Negotiating Style

French President Nicolas Sarkozy didn't budge an inch when protests erupted in 2010 after the French government raised the national minimum retirement age from 60 to 62, and full retirement from 65 to 67. Sarkozy's government instigated the change, saying it was needed to save France's hefty pension system, one of the most generous in the world. The French president stuck to his conservative mantra even as tens of thousands of French workers—many of them union employees—caused travel chaos on the ground and in the air, created gas shortages and garbage pileups, set fires, and shut down ports and schools. All 12 fuel-producing refineries in France went on strike. French labor unions' call for action brought more than a million protestors into the street. Despite an approval rating hovering around 30%, the President used emergency legislation to push the bill through. "(I am) fully aware that this is a difficult reform. But I always considered that my duty, and the duty of the government, was to carry it out," he said. Sarkozy and his supporters held the perception that French workers "had it a bit too good," causing Europe to lag while workers in places like China and India continued to push their economies ahead. The unions, however, saw it as an attack on their social protections.[1]

---

[1] Associated Press (2010, November 10). France raises retirement age despite protests. *Msnbc*.msn.com; Daily mail reporter (2010, October 17). Demonstrators take the streets across France to protest retirement age raise...as fuel runs low at Paris airports. Dailymail.co.uk

T he opening example illustrates that negotiators often use power- or rights-based arguments when in the heat of conflict. In this case, the unions responded with protests and demonstrations (power) when they saw the government enacting unfair legislation (rights). In this chapter, we consider the various conflict styles that negotiators bring to the table.

Negotiators often choose between one of two completely different negotiation styles: being tough or being soft.[2] The tough negotiator is unflinching, makes high demands, concedes little, holds out until the very end, and often rejects offers that are within the bargaining zone. In contrast, the soft negotiator typically offers too many concessions, reveals his or her reservation point and is so concerned that the other party feels good about the negotiation that he or she gives away too much of the bargaining zone. About 78% of MBA students describe their style as "cooperative"; 22% describe themselves as "aggressive."[3] Neither approach is particularly effective for expanding the pie. The tough negotiator often walks away from potentially profitable interactions and gains a reputation for being stubborn. The soft negotiator agrees too readily and never reaps much of the bargaining surplus.

This chapter is designed to help you create a comfortable and effective negotiating style that allows you to (a) expand the pie, (b) maximize your slice, and (c) feel good about the negotiation.

This chapter focuses on motivational orientation, the interests, rights, and power model of disputing, and the influence of emotions and emotional knowledge in negotiations. We provide ways of assessing your style and we profile negotiators who characterize each style. Your job is to do an honest self-assessment of your negotiation style. (See Exhibit 5-1 for a description of Carly Fiorina's negotiation style).

EXHIBIT 5-1

Carly Fiorina's Negotiation Style

Carly Fiorina developed a tough image as the CEO of Hewlett-Packard, a best-selling author, a breast cancer survivor, and in 2010, the Republican nominee for one of California's two U.S. Senate seats. Born to working class parents, Fiorina's negotiation prowess began when she was a Kelly girl temp working her way through college. At one job, she absorbed daily yelling and screaming because the company ethos "was to beat you up hard—and often—to see what you were made of." But when her boss went on an abusive, 45-minute rant, Fiorina reciprocated with her own power move, "That's enough, I am sick and f- tired of being yelled at by you." The toxic boss got the message. Years later, in a high-powered executive role with Lucent Technologies, Fiorina developed a reputation as a "her way or no way" negotiator with no false modesties. "One of the most effective moves in anything you can do is to be who you are. It does not pay to act like someone else," Fiorina said. One vendor remembered her as being dead set on chalking up a huge sale, no exceptions because "the press release was very important to her," while Fiorina herself once told a room of attendees at the Woman's Foodservice Forum that she is most often referred to as "one of two B-words—bimbo and that other word."

Source: Marinucci, C. (2010, May 6). Fiorina cultivates image as tough but vulnerable. *The San Francisco Chronicle*, p. A1.; Lockyer, S. (2007). Ex-HP exec Fiorina discusses the art of professional, personal negotiation. *Nation's Restaurant News*. Nrn.com; Woollet, S. (2010, October 15). Carly Fiorina's troubling telecom past. *CNN Money.* Tech.fortune.cnn.com

---

[2] Bazerman, M. H., & Neale, M. A. (1992). *Negotiating rationally.* New York: Free Press.
[3] Lewicki, R. J., & Robinson, R. J. (1998). Ethical and unethical bargaining tactics: An empirical study. *Journal of Business Ethics, 17*(6), 665–682.

Your first response in a negotiation situation is often a good indicator of your instinctive style. Take an honest look at yourself negotiating (audio record or videotape yourself if you have to). Then ask people who are not afraid to give you frank feedback about how they view your style. You will probably be surprised at their responses!

MOTIVATIONAL ORIENTATION

People have different orientations toward the process of negotiation. Some are individualists, seeking only their own gain; others are cooperative, seeking to maximize joint interests, and others are competitive, seeking to maximize differences. Exhibit 5-2 depicts eight distinct

EXHIBIT 5-2

A Circumplex of Social Motivations

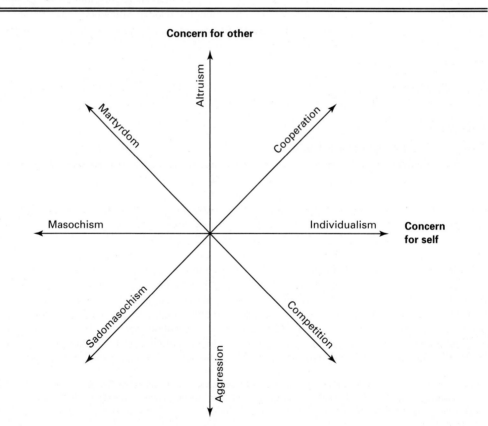

Source: Adapted from McClintock, C. G., & Van Avaermet, E. (1982). Social values and rules of fairness: A theoretical perspective. In V. J. Derlega and J. Grzelak (Eds.), *Cooperation and helping behavior* (pp. 43–71). New York: Academic Press.

motivational orientations, ranging from altruism (high concern for others' interests) to aggression (desire to harm the other party) to masochism (desire to harm oneself) and individualism (desire to further one's own interests). Cooperation represents a midpoint between altruism and individualism; martyrdom represents a midpoint between altruism and masochism; sadomasochism represents a midpoint between masochism and aggression, and competition represents a midpoint between aggression and individualism.

Assessing Your Motivational Style

Although Exhibit 5-2 depicts several motivational orientations, the following three are most common: individualism, competition, and cooperation, so we'll focus most on these. (See Exhibit 5-3, specifically.)

1. The **individualistic** negotiator prefers to maximize his or her own gain and is indifferent to how much the other person is getting.
2. The **competitive** negotiator prefers to maximize the difference between his or her own profits and those of the other party.
3. The **cooperative** negotiator seeks equality and to minimize the difference between negotiators' outcomes.

For a quick assessment of your own motivational orientation, answer the nine questions in Exhibit 5-4.

Richard Shell identified helpful strategies and tips designed for cooperative types and competitive types.[4] According to Shell, if you are a cooperative negotiator, you need to become

EXHIBIT 5-3

Motivational Styles

	Motivational Style		
	Individualistic	**Competitive**	**Cooperative**
Objective	Self-interest	Victory	Joint welfare
View of others	Self-interested	Competitive	Heterogeneous: Some cooperative; some competitive; some individualistic
Situational factors that trigger this motivational orientation	Incentives to maximize own gain	Group competition; when organizations make interpersonal comparisons salient	Social identity; superordinate goals

---

[4] Shell, G. R. (1999). *Bargaining for advantage: Negotiation strategies for reasonable people.* New York: Viking.

EXHIBIT 5-4

Motivational Style Assessment

MOTIVATIONAL STYLE ASSESSMENT

Each question presents three possible distributions of money (A, B, and C) to you and an opponent. Your task is to choose which of these distributions you most prefer. Indicate your true preference, not what you think you should choose. Be honest with yourself and circle only one alternative per question.

	Payoff to You Payoff to Other	A	B	C
1	You	$2,400	$2,700	$2,400
	Other party	$400	$1,400	$2,400
2	You	$2,800	$2,500	$2,500
	Other party	$1,500	$2,500	$500
3	You	$2,600	$2,600	$2,900
	Other party	$2,600	$600	$1,600
4	You	$2,500	$2,800	$2,450
	Other party	$500	$1,500	$2,450
5	You	$2,800	$2,500	$2,450
	Other party	$1,500	$2,500	$450
6	You	$2,500	$2,500	$2,850
	Other party	$2,500	$500	$1,500
7	You	$2,550	$2,800	$2,550
	Other party	$2,550	$1,500	$550
8	You	$2,750	$2,500	$2,500
	Other party	$1,500	$500	$2,500
9	You	$2,400	$2,450	$2,700
	Other party	$2,400	$500	$1,500

Compute your cooperative score by giving yourself one point for:
#1-C, #2-B, #3-A, #4-C, #5-B, #6-A, #7-A, #8-C, #9-A.
Compute your competitive score by giving yourself one point for:
#1-A, #2-C, #3-B, #4-A, #5-C, #6-B, #7-C, #8-B, #9-B.
Compute your individualist score by giving yourself one point for:
#1-B, #2-A, #3-C, #4-B, #5-A, #6-C, #7-B, #8-A, #9-C.

Source: Based on Kuhlman, D. M., & Marshello, A. (1975). Individual differences in the game motives of own, relative, and joint gain. Journal of Research in Personality, 9(3), 240–251.

more assertive, confident, and prudent in negotiations to be more effective at pie-expanding and pie-slicing. Most people assume that they can be assertive up to a point before it will backfire.[5] However people vary quite a bit in terms of how assertive they think they can be before it results in negative returns. Shell outlines seven tools for the overly cooperative negotiator:

1. *Avoid concentrating too much on your bottom line.* Instead, spend extra time preparing your goals and developing high aspirations.
2. *Develop your BATNA.* Know your options to negotiating.
3. *Get an agent and delegate the negotiation task.* It is not an admission of failure to appoint an agent if you think that person can act more assertively for you than you can for yourself.
4. *Bargain on behalf of someone or something else, not yourself.* Sometimes people feel selfish when they negotiate. To get away from this limiting perception, think about other people, such as your family, your staff, even your "retired self," and negotiate on their behalf. Indeed, women who negotiate on behalf of someone else achieve better outcomes than do women who self-advocate, primarily because they fear a backlash if they self-advocate.[6]
5. *Create an audience.* People negotiate more assertively when they have an audience. So, tell someone about your negotiation, make promises, and then report results.
6. *Say "You will have to do better than that because…," not "Yes."* Cooperative people are programmed to say yes to almost anything. Rehearse not saying yes to everything that is proposed. Indeed, a historical analysis of four crises (including the Bay of Pigs and the Cuban Missile Crisis) reveals that leaders with cooperative-affiliative motivation are more likely to offer concessions.[7]
7. *Insist on commitments, not just agreements.* An agreement puts too much trust in the other party; instead, insist upon commitments and specific promises from the other party, with consequences if they are not followed.

Shell also outlines seven tools for competitive people. He cautions that competitive negotiators need to become more aware of others and legitimate their needs.

1. *Think about pie-expansion, not just pie-slicing.* Remember that you can increase your slice of the pie by creating a bigger pie.
2. *Ask more questions than you think you should.* It pays to really understand the other party's objectives and needs.
3. *Rely on standards.* Other people respond well to arguments based upon standards of fairness and objectivity.
4. *Hire a relationship manager.* It is not a sign of failure to consult with someone concerning how to manage the "people side" of negotiations.
5. *Be scrupulously reliable.* Keep your word. Remember the egocentric bias: We see ourselves as more honorable than others do, so we have to go overboard. (Recall the data on the "lying" study presented in Chapter 3.)

---

[5] Ames, D. R. (2008). Assertiveness expectancies: How hard people push depends on the consequences they predict. *Journal of Personality and Social Psychology, 95*(6), 1541–1557.

[6] Amanatullah, E. T., Morris, M. W., & Curhan, J. R. (2008). Negotiators who give too much: Unmitigated communion, relational anxieties, and economic costs in distributive and integrative bargaining. *Journal of Personality and Social Psychology, 95*(3), 723–738.

[7] Langner, C. A., & Winter, D. G. (2001). The motivational basis of concessions and compromise: Archival and laboratory studies. *Journal of Personality and Social Psychology, 81*(4), 711–727.

6. ***Do not haggle when you can negotiate.*** Do not view the negotiation as a contest of wills on every little issue. Spend time thinking about all the issues and the big picture. Remember that trade-offs mean you may lose on some issues in return for big gains on other issues.

7. ***Always acknowledge the other party and protect that person's self-esteem.*** Do not gloat or brag. The word other people most like to hear is their own name. So shower them with honest respect.

Strategic Issues Concerning Motivational Style

Once you know your own (and the other party's) motivational style, how can you best use this information? Several strategic issues are relevant when it comes to motivational style.

THE MYTH OF THE HARD BARGAINER   In Schneider's analysis of more than 700 practicing attorneys, adversarial behavior was regarded by peers to be distinctly ineffective. In fact, more than 50% of the negotiators viewed as adversarial were regarded as ineffective.[8] As negotiators become more irritating, stubborn, and unethical, their effectiveness ratings drop.

When both negotiators have a cooperative orientation, they can be more effective in terms of maximizing the pie.[9] For example, cooperative groups outperform individualists in terms of pie-expansion.[10] Highly cooperative negotiators use more integrative strategies (such as information exchange), make more proposals for mutual coordination, and use fewer distributive tactics.[11] Moreover, the more cooperatively motivated people present in a negotiation, the more integrative (pie-expanding) information is exchanged.[12] When individualistically motivated negotiators are at the table, distributive strategies increase (e.g., positional statements and substantiation). Cooperators and individualists take different roads to reach win-win outcomes.[13] Individualists use the multiple-offer strategy and indirect information exchange; in contrast, cooperators share information about interests and priorities directly.

DO NOT LOSE SIGHT OF YOUR OWN INTERESTS   Negotiators should not turn into "cream puffs."[14] In any negotiation situation, it is important not to lose sight of your own interests. Individualists do not need to worry about this possibility, but cooperators and competitors do. Often, two cooperators end up with a lose-lose agreement because they fail to make their interests known to the other party.[15] Similarly, competitors are often so intent on "beating" the other

---

[8] Schneider, A. K. (2002). Shattering negotiation myths: Empirical evidence on the effectiveness of negotiation style. *Harvard Negotiation Law Review, 7,* 143–233.

[9] Olekalns, M., & Smith, P. L. (1999). Social value orientations and strategy choices in competitive negotiations. *Personality and Social Psychology Bulletin, 25*(6), 657–668; Olekalns, M., & Smith, P. L. (2003). Testing the relationships among negotiators' motivational orientations, strategy choices, and outcomes. *Journal of Experimental Social Psychology, 39*(2), 101–117; Pruitt, D. G., & Lewis, S. A. (1975). Development of integrative solutions in bilateral negotiation. *Journal of Personality and Social Psychology, 31*(4), 621–633; Weingart, L. R., Bennett, R. J., & Brett, J. M. (1993). The impact of consideration of issues and motivational orientation on group negotiation process and outcome. *Journal of Applied Psychology, 78*(3), 504–517; Weingart, L. R., Brett, J. M., Olekalns, M., & Smith, P. L. (2007). Conflicting social motives in negotiating groups. *Journal of Personality and Social Psychology, 93*(6), 994–1010.

[10] Weingart, Bennett, & Brett, "The impact of consideration."

[11] Olekalns & Smith, "Social value orientations."

[12] Weingart, Brett, Olekalns, & Smith, "Conflicting social motives."

[13] Olekalns & Smith, "Testing the relationships."

[14] Glick, S., & Croson, R. (2001). Reputations in negotiation. In S. J. Hoch & H. C. Kunreuther (Eds.), *Wharton on making decisions* (pp. 177–186). New York: Wiley.

[15] Thompson, L., & Deharpport, T. (1998). Relationships, goal incompatibility, and communal orientation in negotiations. *Basic and Applied Social Psychology, 20*(1), 33–44.

side they do not pay attention to their own interests. In a sense, they win the battle but lose the war. Thus, it is important that you maintain a high level of concern for your own interests, as well as those of the other party.[16] Even in populations of successful business executives, negotiators can experience relational anxiety and fear that they need to make concessions to avoid straining relationships.[17] Negotiators who show "unmitigated communion" make large concessions to accommodate the other and reap less profit; when both parties are high in unmitigated communion, joint gains are lower[18] (some gender differences have been documented as well when it comes to motivational orientation; see Exhibit 5-5.)

SOCIAL COMPARISON CAN CAUSE BREAKDOWNS IN NEGOTIATION   In negotiations between United Airlines and its pilots in 1999, the union doubled its pay raise demand from 14.5% to 28% immediately upon learning that pilots at Delta had gotten a 20% jump above industry-leading rates.[19] Houston janitors working in buildings owned by Hines Interests asked for a salary increase and family health care benefits after comparing their pay and benefits to

EXHIBIT 5-5

Why Do Women Settle for Less?

Do men and women communicate differently about the subject of money? The question caught the attention of researcher Lisa Barron when she was a graduate student, after noticing that men in her master of business administration classes spent a lot of time talking about money—and the women didn't. In her research, Barron watched men and women negotiate in mock job interviews. To enhance realism, she had real MBA students negotiate with real hiring managers for marketing positions. She told them to ask for more than the $60,000 starting salary. Men believed that they had to advocate for themselves; in contrast, women believed that if they did a good job the organization would eventually reward them. Whereas 85% of the men felt comfortable measuring their worth in dollars, 83% of the women were uncomfortable doing so and unsure of their monetary value. At least 70% of men believed they were entitled to more than others, but 71% of the women believed that they were entitled to the same as others (cooperative motivation).

Source: Fisher, M. (2003, July 5). Why do women settle for less: A researcher says female job seekers hate to haggle over pay. *Orange County Register*, p. 1; Barron, L. A. (2003). Ask and you shall receive? Gender differences in negotiators' beliefs about requests for a higher salary. *Human Relations, 56*(6), 635.

---

[16] Pruitt, D. G., & Carnevale, P. J. (1993). *Negotiation in social conflict.* Pacific Grove, CA: Brooks-Cole; De Dreu, C. K. W., Weingart, L. R., & Kwon, S. (2000). Influence of social motives on integrative negotiation: A meta-analytic review and test of two theories. *Journal of Personality and Social Psychology, 78*(5), 889–905.

[17] Amanatullah, Morris, & Curhan, "Negotiators who give too much."

[18] Ibid.

[19] Griffin, G., & Leib, J. (2003, June 9). Flying on fumes: A costly pilots contract, the dot-com meltdown and a failed merger put United in a tailspin and sent executives scrambling to recover. *Denver Post,* p. A01.

janitors in other cities. According to the Service Employees International Union, janitors of Hines-owned buildings in Chicago were making $13.80 an hour plus benefits, while those in Houston earned only $5.30 an hour and received no family health care benefits.[20] In one investigation, people were given several choices concerning the division of a pie between themselves and another person (e.g., $300 you/$300 other versus $500 you/$800 other, etc.).[21] They were asked to indicate how satisfactory each division of the pie was. If people were purely individualistic, satisfaction would only be driven by the amount of money for oneself. In fact, people were highly concerned with how much the "other person" received, so much so that people often preferred to earn less money, if it meant that this would equate outcomes between themselves and another person. For example, many people preferred $300 self/$300 other over $500 self/$800 other. When faced with a choice between $300 self/$300 other versus $800 self/$500 other, people still preferred equality but not as strongly as when the self was disadvantaged.

The relationship we have with the other party can affect our own motivational orientation. Consider the following choices:[22]

Choice A: $4,000 for yourself

Choice B: 50% chance at $3,000; 50% chance at $5,000

Which do you choose? We asked 111 MBA students, and most of them (73%) chose the sure thing: choice A. This example confirms the risk-aversion principle we discussed in Chapter 2. We then asked a separate, but comparable, group of MBA students to choose between the following:

Choice C: $4,000 for yourself

　　　　　　　$6,000 for another person

Choice D: Self: 50% chance at $3,000, 50% chance at $5,000

　　　　　　　Other: 50% chance at $7,000, 50% chance at $5,000

A close look at all four choices (A, B, C, and D) reveals that choice C is identical to choice A (except for the payoff to the other person), and choice D is identical to choice B (except for the payoff to the other person). Thus, if people were perfectly rational and consistent, they would choose C over D (given that most choose A over B). However, that's not what happens. People's choices are driven, in large part, by their *relationship* with the other party. Negotiators who have a positive relationship with the other person prefer the sure thing of choice C (56%) over the gamble of choice D; in contrast, those who had a negative relationship with the other person preferred to gamble on D (67%) over C. Perhaps it is this concern for equality that led to the removal of American Airlines CEO Donald Carty in 2003. When Donald Carty became CEO of American Airlines in 1998, he was well-liked. However, in the aftermath of the September 11, 2001 terrorist attacks, Carty was forced from his position because of tainted relations with American's powerful unions and, in the end, his own board of directors. The reason? The union members, who had recently taken serious wage cuts, discovered Carty and other executives had

[20] Sixel, L. M. (2006, September 30). Janitors try to build support: Union asks building owners, managers for help. *Houston Chronicle,* p. 1.

[21] Loewenstein, G. F., Thompson, L., & Bazerman, M. H. (1989). Social utility and decision making in interpersonal contexts. *Journal of Personality and Social Psychology, 57*(3), 426–441.

[22] Ibid.

privately been given bonus plans and lavish pension benefits. It seemed like an inequity of the grandest sort and they would have no part of it.[23]

Distinct differences are evident between the pie-expanding and pie-slicing strategies used by cooperators versus those used by competitors. Cooperators not only increase the size of the pie, they also prefer an equitable division of the pie in comparison to individualists and competitors. Furthermore, cooperation is strongly related to reciprocity: Relative to individualists and competitors, cooperators are more likely to engage in the same level of cooperation as their opponent.[24]

USE REINFORCEMENT TO SHAPE BEHAVIOR   Negotiators can use reinforcement (and punishment) to shape the behavior of their opponents. For example, in one study a lecturer stood in front of a class. Half of the class was instructed to look interested, nod their heads, and smile approvingly (positive reinforcement); the other half of the class was told to look bored and disinterested (punishment). After a short time, the instructor moved to the side of the class that was reinforcing his behavior. It is important to reinforce the behavior immediately after it occurs. Similarly, one of the fastest ways to extinguish a behavior is simply not to respond.

THE POWER OF RECIPROCITY   Integrative (pie-expanding) and distributive (pie-slicing) behaviors tend to be reciprocated.[25] If you want to discourage a competitive motivational orientation in the counterparty, then don't reciprocate.

ANTICIPATE MOTIVATIONAL CLASHES AT THE BARGAINING TABLE   What happens when a person with a cooperative orientation negotiates with a competitive person? The cooperator begins the negotiation in a cooperative fashion, but when she realizes that she is facing a competitor, she changes her own style. People with a cooperative orientation behave competitively when paired with a competitive opponent, whereas competitive players do not change.[26] When different types of players faced a prosocial (cooperative) opponent, prosocial and individualistic players were more likely to cooperate than were competitive players. Prosocials and individualists competed when the other party competed, but competitive players competed regardless of the behavior of the other party.[27]

MOTIVATIONAL CONVERGENCE   During negotiation, people's strategies often change in response to how they view the other party and the situation. In particular, when a cooperator meets a competitor, the cooperator is the one to change. Thus, a strong tendency toward convergence of styles is likely to occur at the bargaining table.[28] Convergence of outcomes, as well as

[23] Kerr, K. (2003, April 25). Carty known as tough CEO who smiled. *Tulsa World,* p. E1.

[24] Van Lange, P. A. M. (1999). The pursuit of joint outcomes and equality in outcomes: An integrative model of social value orientation. *Journal of Personality and Social Psychology, 77*(2), 337–349.

[25] Brett, J. M., Shapiro, D. L., & Lytle, A. L. (1998). Breaking the bonds of reciprocity in negotiations. *Academy of Management Journal, 41*(4), 410–424; Donohue, W. A. (1981). Analyzing negotiation tactics: Development of a negotiation interact system. *Human Communication Research, 7*(3), 273–287; Putnam, L. L. (1983). Small group work climates: A lag-sequential analysis of group interaction. *Small Group Research, 14*(4), 465–494.

[26] Kelley, H. H., & Stahelski, A. J. (1970). Social interaction basis of cooperators' and competitors' beliefs about others. *Journal of Personality and Social Psychology, 16*(1), 66–91.

[27] McClintock, C. G., & Liebrand, W. B. (1988). Role of interdependence structure, individual value orientation, and another's strategy in social decision making: A transformational analysis. *Journal of Personality and Social Psychology, 55*(3), 396–409.

[28] Weingart, Brett, Olekalns, & Smith, "Conflicting social motives."

bargaining styles, occurs in later stages of negotiation.[29] As deadlines approach, people exchange specific proposals and make concessions.[30]

EPISTEMIC MOTIVATION   Epistemic motivation refers to a person's need to understand his or her world.[31] To reach integrative agreements, negotiators should have not only a cooperative (social) orientation but also a deep understanding of the task (epistemic motivation). Negotiators who are high in both epistemic and cooperative motivation develop greater trust and reach more integrative agreements than those low in cooperation or low in epistemic motivation.[32]

INTERESTS, RIGHTS, AND POWER MODEL OF DISPUTING

According to Ury, Brett, and Goldberg, negotiators use one of three types of approaches when in the process of conflict or dispute resolution:[33]

1. *Interests:*   Negotiators who focus on interests attempt to learn about the other party's underlying needs, desires, and concerns.[34] Interests-based negotiators attempt to reconcile differences in a way that addresses parties' most pressing needs and concerns.
2. *Rights:*   Negotiators who focus on rights apply standards of fairness to negotiation, including contracts, legal rights, precedent, or expectations based upon norms.
3. *Power:*   Negotiators who focus on power use status, rank, threats, and intimidation to get their way.

As an example of the difference between interests-, rights-, and power-based approaches, consider this statement made by an employer: "I am afraid I cannot meet your desired salary requirements, but I hope you will realize that working in our company is a wonderful opportunity and join us." Before reading further, take a moment to consider how you would respond if an employer made this statement to you. Three different negotiators might respond to the employer's statement in ways unique to their own approach:

1. *Interests-based response:*   "I am very interested in joining your company if my interests can be met. I would like to share some of my key goals and objectives. I want to learn more about the company's interests from your standpoint. Salary is a key concern for me. I am the single wage earner in my family, and I have a number of educational loans. You did not mention other aspects of the offer, such as stock options, vacations, and flex time. Can we discuss these issues at this point?"
2. *Rights-based response:*   "I am very interested in joining your company if we can come up with a fair employment package. My salary requirements are in line with those of other people joining similar companies. I would think it would be a competitive advantage for your company to offer employment packages that are competitive with those being offered

---

[29] Gulliver, M. P. (1979). The effect of the spatial visualization factor on achievement in operations with fractions. *Dissertation Abstracts International, 39*(9-A), 5381–5382.

[30] Lim, S. G., & Murnighan, J. K. (1994). Phases, deadlines, and the bargaining process. *Organizational Behavior and Human Decision Processes, 58*(2), 153–171; Stuhlmacher, A. F., Gillespie, T. L., & Champagne, M. V. (1998). The impact of time pressure in negotiation: A meta-analysis. *International Journal of Conflict Management, 9*(2), 97–116.

[31] Kruglanski, A. W. (1989). *Lay epistemics and human knowledge: Cognitive and motivational bases.* New York: Plenum Press.

[32] De Dreu, C. K. W., Beersma, B., Stroebe, K., & Euwema, M. C. (2006). Motivated information processing, strategic choice, and the quality of negotiated agreement. *Journal of Personality and Social Psychology, 90*(6), 927–943.

[33] Ury, W. L., Brett, J. M., & Goldberg, S. B. (1988). *Getting disputes resolved: Designing systems to cut the costs of conflict.* San Francisco: Jossey-Bass.

[34] Fisher, R., Ury, W., & Patton, B. (1991). *Getting to yes: Negotiating agreement without giving in* (2nd edition). Boston: Houghton Mifflin.

by other companies. I believe that my record and previous experience mean that a higher salary would be fair in this case."

3. *Power-based response:* "I am very interested in joining your company, but other companies are offering me more attractive deals at this point. I would like to invite you to reconsider the offer so that I do not have to resort to turning your offer down, given that I think that we make a good match for one another. I hope you will be able to make a competitive offer."

(For a more complete description of interests-, rights-, or power-based approaches, see Exhibit 5-6.)

During the process of negotiating or resolving disputes, the focus may shift from interests to rights to power and back again. For example, in one investigation negotiators' statements were recorded during a negotiation. Each statement was coded in terms of whether it reflected an interests-, rights-, or power-based approach.[35] Parties moved frequently among interests, rights,

EXHIBIT 5-6

Approaches to Negotiation

	Approach		
	Interests	**Rights**	**Power**
Goal	Self-interest Dispute resolution Understanding others' concerns	Fairness Justice	Winning Respect
Temporal focus	Present (What needs and interests do we have right now?)	Past (What has been dictated by the past?)	Future (What steps can I take in the future to overpower others?)
Distributive strategies (pie-slicing)	Compromise	Often produces a "winner" and a "loser"; thus, unequal distribution	Often produces a "winner" and a "loser"; thus, unequal distribution
Integrative strategies (pie-expansion)	Most likely to expand the pie via addressing parties' underlying needs	Difficult to expand the pie unless focus is on interests	Difficult to expand the pie unless focus is on interests
Implications for future negotiations and relationship	Greater understanding Satisfaction Stability of agreement	Possible court action	Resentment Possible retaliation Revenge

[35] Lytle, A. L., Brett, J. M., & Shapiro, D. L. (1999). The strategic use of interests, rights and power to resolve disputes. *Negotiation Journal, 15*(1), 31–52.

and power in the same negotiation (23 of 25 dyads), with more emphasis on rights and power in the first and third quarters than in the second and fourth quarters.

Assessing Your Approach

Consider the United Airlines pilots' negotiation of 2000 to analyze the moves in the negotiation in terms of interests, rights, and power:

- *Union power move:*   United's pilots expected a new contract on April 12, 2000, and many were angry when it did not happen. They began refusing to work overtime and started calling in extra sick days. This reaction caused immediate disruptions to United's flight schedule, which required voluntary overtime by pilots to function normally. Management also noticed that pilots were taxiing more slowly, correcting flight plans at the last minute, and insisting on repairs of minor items.
- *Management rights move:*   Management warned that if such tactics were organized by the union, they would be illegal. The company began compiling evidence it could take to court, including union communiqués encouraging pilots to "work to rule" (in other words, to do everything to the letter of the contract).
- *Union power move:*   Pilots stopped conducting training flights for new hires, leaving a pool of 120 pilots who could not fly. In July, 20 California-based first officers called in sick in one day, forcing the company to cancel virtually its entire schedule of Asia-bound fights. In Colorado Springs, pilots abandoned a plane full of passengers on the ramp because their duty time was up, and United couldn't find replacements to get the plane to Denver. A clandestine pilot newsletter, circulated in August, urged pilots to "slow down" and give United "a Labor Day that they'll never forget."
- *Management rights and power move:*   In November, with the busy Thanksgiving weekend approaching, United took its mechanics to court, seeking $66 million in damages (rights). The company also fired and disciplined some of them (power).

Next, we present each approach in greater detail. Which one characterizes you?

INTERESTS   Interests are a person's needs, desires, concerns, fears—in general, the things a person cares about or wants. Interests underlie people's positions in negotiation (the things they *say* they want). Reconciling interests in negotiation is not easy. It involves understanding interests, devising creative solutions, and looking for trade-offs. We discussed some negotiation strategies in Chapters 3 and 4, such as fashioning trade-offs or logrolls among issues, searching for compatible issues, devising bridging solutions, and structuring contingency contracts. It is difficult to immediately address interests in a negotiation because people adopt positional tendencies and because emotions can often conceal interests. Negotiators who use an interests-based approach frequently ask other parties about their needs and concerns and, in turn, disclose their own needs and concerns.[36]

RIGHTS   Consider the following rights-based negotiations:

- Los Angeles Dodgers owner Frank McCourt found himself sharing ownership of the team with his ex-wife, Jamie, when a judge invalidated a disputed marital agreement that would

---

[36] Poitras, J., & Le Tareau, A. (2008). Dispute resolution patterns and organizational dispute states. *International Journal of Conflict Management, 19*(1), 72–87.

have made him sole owner of the franchise. The rights of ownership controversy stemmed from a marital property agreement signed by both parties' years earlier.[37]

- The United Steel Workers (USW) Union is known for invoking successorship clauses to get what it wants. In most cases, these clauses simply require that the potential buyer of a plant adhere to a collective-bargaining agreement. But the USW altered its clauses to state that before a plant can be sold, a successor company must agree on a new labor contract, thereby giving the union the ability to "approve" the sale of a steel plant. When Wheeling-Pittsburgh steel company struck a partnership deal with Brazil's largest steelmaker, CSN, the union did not like the idea. Union leaders believed CSN would benefit significantly while the American workers would receive very little. They used the rights clause to invoke the rights of the workers and effectively rejected the possibility of a merger between the two companies.[38]

These examples illustrate that a common negotiation style is to rely on some independent standard with perceived legitimacy or fairness to determine who is right in a situation. Some rights are formalized by law or contract. Others are socially accepted standards of behavior, such as reciprocity, precedent, equality, and seniority (e.g., "I want a higher salary because it would be consistent with the incentive structure in this organization."). Negotiators who use a rights-based approach frequently say things like "I deserve this" or "this is fair" (see the cartoon in Exhibit 5-7 for a humorous example of a rights-based move).

Rights differ across situations. For example, a productive employee may want a salary increase based upon extreme productivity, yet the organization may focus on seniority. Negotiators may involve a third party to determine who is right. In **adjudication**, disputants present evidence and arguments to a neutral third party with the power to hand down a binding decision.

POWER   Power is the ability to coerce someone to do something he or she would not otherwise do. Exercising power typically means imposing costs on the other side or threatening to do so. Exercising power may manifest itself in acts of aggression, such as sabotage, physical attack, or withholding benefits derived from a relationship. A prime example of a power move occurred when Time Warner yanked ABC stations off its systems in 11 cities at the beginning of the May sweeps period in 2000, a critical time for setting ratings and ad rates. Television viewers saw the words "Disney Has Taken ABC Away from You" scrolling across the screen in block letters.[39] (See Exhibit 5-8 for the complete story.)

Within a relationship of mutual dependence (e.g., labor and management; employee and employer), the question of who is more powerful rests on who is more dependent. In turn, one's degree of dependency on the other party rests on how satisfactory the alternatives are for satisfying one's interests. The better the alternative, the less dependent one is. Power moves include behaviors that range from insults and ridicule to strikes, beatings, and warfare.

Power tactics have the intent to coerce the other side to settle on terms more satisfactory to the wielder of power. For example, Kim Jong II, president of North Korea, is described as "cunning and cruel, with street-fighter instincts."[40] Moreover, he is not above using

---

[37] Bollinger, R. (2010, December 7). Judge invalidates agreement in McCourt case. Major League Baseball. MLB.com
[38] Wysocki Jr., B., Maher, K., & Glader, P. (2007, May 9). New clout—A labor union's power: Blocking takeover bids; steel-company buyers learn they must get USW on their side. *The Wall Street Journal*, p. A1.
[39] Cooper, J. (2000, May 8). Fading to black. *Adweek, 41*(19), C50.
[40] Zielenziger, M. (2003, January 12). Crazy like a fox and steel-tough. *Patriot-News Harrisburg*, p. A20.

EXHIBIT 5-7

Humorous Example of a Rights-Based Move in a Divorce

"Your wife's also asking that you rot in hell for eternity, but I think that's negotiable."

Source: © The New Yorker Collection 1999 Michael Masline from cartoonbank.com. All Rights Reserved.

brinksmanship—threatening to drive himself and others over the edge. However, Wendy Sherman, the former senior U.S. State Department official who negotiated with Kim in the Clinton administration, astutely surmised, "He is not crazy....He is intelligent and he is totally conscious about what he is doing."[41] His strategy is to push just far enough. Just before the U.S. government gets really angry, he stops the provocations and comes to the negotiation table. His son Kim Jong-un, not known to the world until he was 20 years old, seems to have many similar

---

[41] Ibid.

EXHIBIT 5-8

Power Moves

At 12:01 on the morning of May 1, 2000, the TV screen went blue on Time Warner Cable's WABC-TV feed, and a scrolling message in block letters began: "Disney Has Taken ABC Away from You." After four months of fruitless negotiations over the rights to retransmit ABC signals over cable, Time Warner yanked ABC stations off its systems in 11 cities, including Houston, Philadelphia, Raleigh, and New York, during a critical period for setting ratings and ad rates. The "alert" aired on WABC-TV Channel 7 in New York, whose cable subscribers in 3.5 million homes went without their local ABC station. Time Warner said it wanted to extend talks until the end of the year, but ABC only offered an extension through May 24—the end of the sweeps. Time Warner laid blame squarely on Disney, ABC's corporate parent. "Disney is trying to inappropriately use its ownership of ABC television stations to extract excessive and unreasonable terms for its cable TV channels—terms that would add hundreds of millions of dollars in cost for Time Warner and its cable customers," said Fred Dressler, senior vice president of programming for Time Warner Cable. Disney wanted higher fees for the cable rights to ABC and broader distribution by Time Warner for Disney's own cable programming, especially ESPN. The Cable Act of 1992 entitles over-the-air networks to compensation from cable systems that carry network signals. The previous agreement between Disney's ABC and Time Warner Cable expired on December 31, 1999. ABC blamed the impasse on Time Warner: "This is a punitive act, but Time Warner is only punishing their own customers through their cable system," said Tom Kane, president and general manager of WABC.

Source: Fading to Black by M. Larson in *Adweek*, May 8, 2000, *41*(19), p. C50. Reprinted by permission of Nielsen Business Media, Inc.

traits. Reports note his fierce competitive streak when playing basketball with his middle brother, Kim Jong-chul, who was said to be dismissed by his father as too "girlish" to lead.[42]

Two types of power-based approaches are **threats** (in which one or both parties makes a threat) and **contests** (in which parties take action to determine who will prevail).[43] Determining who is more powerful without a decisive and potentially destructive power contest may be difficult because power is ultimately a matter of perception. People may fail to take into account the possibility that the other will invest greater resources in the contest than expected, out of fear that a change in the perceived distribution of power will affect the outcomes of future disputes. Many power contests involve threatening avoidance (e.g., divorce), actually engaging in it temporarily to impose costs on the other side (e.g., striking or breaking off diplomatic relations), or ending the relationship altogether.

---

[42] Demick, B. (2010, September 28). Propagandists tell North Koreans that supreme leader's son is a successor in the making. *The Los Angeles Times.* Articles.latimes.com; Moore, M. (2009, June 2). Kim Jong-un: A profile of North Korea's next leader. *The Telegraph.* Telegraph.co.uk

[43] Ury, Brett, & Goldberg, *Getting disputes resolved.*

Strategic Issues Concerning Approaches

Negotiators should keep in mind the following principles when choosing their approach:

THE PRINCIPLE OF RECIPROCITY   The style you use in negotiation will often be reciprocated by the other party. In one investigation, interests were reciprocated the most (42%), followed by power (27%) and rights (22%).[44]

INTERESTS ARE EFFECTIVE FOR PIE-EXPANSION   Focusing on interests can usually resolve the problem underlying the dispute more effectively than focusing on rights or power. A focus on interests can help uncover "hidden" problems and help identify which issues are of the greatest concern to each party. Put the focus on interests early in the negotiations. This suggestion raises an obvious question: If interests are effective, why doesn't everyone use them? Ury, Brett, and Goldberg identify several reasons, including lack of skill, the tendency to reciprocate rights and power, and strong cultural or organizational norms.[45]

HOW TO REFOCUS YOUR OPPONENT ON INTERESTS (AND MOVE THEM FROM RIGHTS AND POWER)   Suppose you enter a negotiation with an interests-based approach, but your opponent uses rights or power. This makes you angry, and you reciprocate power and rights out of sheer self-defense. Yet, you realize this behavior is creating a lose-lose situation. How do you break out of the spiral? Consider two strategies: personal strategies (that you can use in a face-to-face situation) and structural strategies (steps that an organization can take to create norms that engender an interests-based culture).[46]

Personal Strategies.

Do Not Reciprocate!   Resist the urge to reciprocate.[47] By not reciprocating, you refocus your opponent. In one investigation, when the other negotiator reciprocated, the focal negotiator stayed with rights and power arguments 39% of the time; however, when the other did not reciprocate, the focal negotiator stayed with rights and power arguments only 22% of the time (and, hence, was refocused 78% of the time).[48] For example, Rex Tillerson, CEO of ExxonMobil, led tense negotiations for access to underwater fields off Russia's Sakhalin Island. At one point, a Russian minister let his anger show in a disagreement over a permit and slammed his fist on the bargaining table. Instead of getting angry and reciprocating the minister's behavior, Mr. Tillerson remained calm, realizing the extensive talks required a gentle touch. He feared the Russian officials would be offended by the Exxon leaders, thinking, "Here come the powerful Americans that won the Cold War, and now they're going to come in and tell us all how messed up we are and how we got it all wrong," Mr. Tillerson recalled. "You make yourself very aware of it, and almost go out of your way to make sure there's nothing that conveys such a sentiment."[49]

Provide Opportunities to Meet.   Often, rights- and power-based approaches emerge when parties are out of touch and uncertain about the intentions of the other side. Getting parties

---

[44] Lytle, Brett, & Shapiro, "The strategic use of interests."
[45] Ury, Brett, & Goldberg, *Getting disputes resolved.*
[46] Ibid.
[47] Fisher, Ury, & Patton, *Getting to yes*; Ury, Brett, & Goldberg, *Getting disputes resolved.*
[48] Lytle, Brett, & Shapiro, "The strategic use of interests."
[49] Ball, J. (2006, March 8). The new act at Exxon; CEO Tillerson, prototype of Texas oilman, must focus on delicate global diplomacy. *The Wall Street Journal,* p. B1.

together for informal discussions can move them toward interests. When people are face-to-face, they often can't help but feel some compassion for the other party. Moreover, differences don't have an opportunity to fester. When the Boston Red Sox's top executives thought they were going to lose their chance to sign Daisuke Matsuzaka, the Japanese pitching star, they boarded a private jet to southern California. Unable to come to an agreement and fearful that Scott Boras, Matsuzaka's agent, was not negotiating faithfully, they went on an unsolicited visit to Boras's neighborhood, forcing him to negotiate face-to-face. The tactic worked. Just days later, Matsuzaka boarded the plane back to Boston with the Red Sox executives.[50]

Don't Get Personal: Use Self-Discipline.   Make sure that you stay focused on the conflict and the issues. Many negotiators begin to attack the other party's character. In their classic book, *Getting to Yes,* Fisher and Ury advocate separating the people from the problem. The same principle characterizes successful marriages![51] Gottman and Levenson tracked couples over a 14-year period.[52] Based upon an initial observation of the couples' fighting style early in their marriage, the researchers predicted which couples got divorced and which stayed together with 93% accuracy. The biggest determinant of divorce was not the amount of arguing, nor the amount of anger, but the use of personal attacks.

Use Behavioral Reinforcement.   Make sure that you are not rewarding the other party's rights- or power-based behavior. In other words, if you have been planning to make a concession, do not offer it to the other party immediately after he or she has misused rights or power. If you do, you reward the very behavior you want to extinguish. One of the most effective ways to extinguish a behavior is simply not to react. If you do react, you may unconsciously reward the behavior (e.g., if the other party benefits from the attention associated with a conflict spiral).

Making unilateral concessions is not effective for refocusing negotiations. In one study, concession making was less effective in refocusing negotiations from rights and power (60% refocused), as were other uncontentious communications (77% refocused).[53] Why? A unilateral concession may be seen as a reward for contentious behavior; therefore, it may encourage the repetition of such behavior.

Send a Mixed Message.   Reciprocation is instinctive, especially under stress.[54] Thus, you may find that your opponent is making you angry and you need to "flex your muscles." One effective strategy is to reciprocate rights or power, but *combine* it with interests-based questions or proposals.[55] Sending the counterparty a "mixed message" (rights and interests) gives them a chance to choose what to reciprocate—interests, rights, or power.

Try a Process Intervention.   Process interventions are tactics that are interests-based with the goal of moving the counterparty back to interests-based negotiation. Effective processes can include any of the pie-expanding strategies we discussed in Chapter 4 (e.g., multiple offers, revealing information about priorities, etc.), as well as several other dispute resolution strategies (indicated next). In a direct test of the effectiveness of process interventions, Ury, Brett, and

---

[50] Curry, J. (2006, December 14). After forcing issue, Red Sox on verge of Matsuzaka deal. *New York Times,* p. D1.

[51] Fisher, Ury, & Patton, *Getting to yes.*

[52] Gottman, J. M., & Levenson, R. W. (2000). The timing of divorce: Predicting when a couple will divorce over a 14-year period. *Journal of Marriage & the Family, 62*(3), 737–745.

[53] Lytle, Brett, & Shapiro, "The strategic use of interests."

[54] Lerner, H. G. (1985). *The dance of anger.* New York: Harper and Row.

[55] Ury, Brett, & Goldberg, *Getting disputes resolved.*

Goldberg examined the success rate of various tactics:[56] Least effective was reciprocation (66%); the most effective method was process intervention (82% success rate). Other methods included the mixed-message approach (74% success rate), and simply resisting the urge to reciprocate (self-discipline; 76% success rate).

Let's Talk and Then Fight.   Another strategy is to agree to talk for 20 minutes or so, and then argue. By agreeing up front on a process, both parties commit to listen to one another at least temporarily.

Strategic Cooling-Off Periods.   It is easy to muster a rights-based response or power display in the heat of conflict. An interests-based approach requires deeper levels of cognitive processing. Thus, it often serves parties' interests to build in some cooling-off periods that allow them to better assess their own needs and interests, independent of rights and power issues.

Paraphrasing.   Many times, negotiators struggle in their attempt to transform a rights- or power-based argument into an interests-based discussion. Negotiators should not abandon their interests-based approach but, rather, persist in their attempt to understand the other party's underlying needs. Stephen Covey suggests that parties to conflict should be forced to empathize with each other.[57] He has a strict ground rule: "You can't make your point until you restate the other person's point to his or her satisfaction."[58] People are often so emotionally invested that they cannot listen. According to Covey, they pretend to listen. So he asks the other party, "Do you feel understood?" The other party always says, "No, he mimicked me, but he doesn't understand me." The negotiator gets to state a point only after satisfying the other party. (For an example of this intervention, see Exhibit 5-9).

Label the Process.   If the counterparty uses a rights- or power-based approach after you have tried to focus on interests, it might be useful to label the strategy you see the counterparty using. Recognizing or labeling a tactic as ineffective can neutralize or refocus negotiations.[59]

Structural Strategies.   Ury, Brett, and Goldberg suggest several methods whereby dispute resolution systems can be designed and used within organizations, some of which are described here in detail.[60] Each of these strategies is designed to reduce the costs of handling disputes and to produce satisfying, durable resolutions.

Put the Focus on Interests.   When International Harvester introduced a new procedure for oral (rather than written) handling of grievances at the lowest possible level, the number of written grievances plummeted to almost zero.[61] Some organizations stay focused on interests via use of a **multistep negotiation procedure**, in which a dispute that is not resolved at one level of the organizational hierarchy moves to progressively higher levels. Another strategy is the **wise counselor**, in which senior executives are selected to consider disputes. By creating **multiple points of entry**, negotiators have several points of access for resolving disputes. In some instances, **mandatory negotiations** provide a way for reluctant negotiators to come to the table. By providing **skills**

---

[56] Ibid.

[57] Covey, S. R. (1999). Resolving differences. *Executive Excellence, 16*(4), 5–6.

[58] Ibid.

[59] Fisher, Ury, & Patton, *Getting to yes.*

[60] Ury, Brett, & Goldberg, *Getting disputes resolved,* p. 42.

[61] Ibid.

EXHIBIT 5-9

Resolving Differences

The following is a summary of an intervention led by Steven Covey between two parties who had no trust for one another:

The president of Company A asked Covey to act as a third-party facilitator in a lawsuit with Company B, the key reason being that there was no trust between the parties.

Covey stated that the disputants did not actually need a third party because they possessed the power to handle the conflict themselves. Covey suggested putting all the issues on the table and asking if they would be willing to search for a solution. Covey called the president of Company B and made the invitation. The president of Company B declined the offer and said he wanted the legal process to handle it.

The president of Company A suggested that he send his material and documents to Company B and meet face-to-face. He promised not to bring an attorney and told Company B president that he could bring his attorney if he wished. He further said it was not even necessary that Company B president speak. They could just have lunch. In short, there was nothing to lose and possibly everything to gain.

The presidents met for lunch and Company A president said, "Let me see if I can make your case for you since you are not going to speak." Company A president tried to show genuine empathy and took pains to describe Company B president's position in depth. He then asked if his understanding was correct or not.

At this point, the silence was broken. The president of Company B spoke up and said that the summary was 50% accurate but he wanted to correct some inaccuracies. At that point, the attorney advised Company B president to not say another word. At this juncture Company B president told the attorney to shut up because he could feel the power of the dialogue that was happening.

The lunch meeting progressed with both parties standing shoulder-to-shoulder making notes, using flip charts, and brainstorming alternatives. At the close of the lunch, the disagreement was resolved.

Source: Based on Covey, S. R. (1999). Resolving differences. *Executive Excellence, 16*(4), 5–6.

and training in negotiation, people are better prepared to negotiate in an interests-based fashion. Finally, by providing opportunities for **mediation** in which a third party intervenes, negotiators can often focus on interests.

Build in "Loop-Backs" to Negotiation.   Rights or power contests can be costly and risky, and therefore negotiators need to be able to loop-back to interests:

- *Looping back from rights.*   Some loop-back procedures provide information about a negotiator's rights, as well as the likely outcome of a rights contest. Consider **information procedures** in which databases are created that can be accessed by negotiators who want to research the validity and outcome of their claims. **Advisory arbitration** is a method whereby managers are provided with information that would likely result if arbitration were to be carried out or the dispute were to go to court. **Minitrials** are procedures whereby "lawyers" (high-level executives in the organization who have not been involved previously) represent each side and present evidence and arguments that are heard by a neutral judge or advisor. Minitrials put negotiation in the hands of people who are not emotionally involved in the dispute and who have the perspective to view it in the context of the organization's broad interests.

- *Looping back from a power conflict.*   A variety of strategies can be used to move parties away from power contests back to interests. **Crisis procedures**, or guidelines for emergency communication written in advance, establish communication mechanisms between disputants. For example, in disputes between the United States and the Soviet Union, a hotline served a crisis procedure purpose; in addition, U.S. and Soviet officials established nuclear risk reduction centers, staffed 24 hours in Washington and Moscow, for emergency communications.[62] Finally, **intervention by third parties** can halt power contests. For example, when Detroit public school teachers were unsatisfied with their pay, they went on strike and entered negotiations that went on for more than two weeks. Unable to come to an agreement, Mayor Kwame Kilpatrick stepped in. He called everyone into his office, where negotiations continued for the next 11 hours. They dealt with one issue at a time, finally settling on a definitive agreement.[63]

Provide Low-Cost Rights and Power Backups.   Should interests-based negotiation fail, it is useful to have low-cost rights and power backup systems. **Conventional arbitration** is less costly than court or private adjudication. Ury, Brett, and Goldberg note that 95% of all collective bargaining contracts provide for arbitration of disputes.[64] **Med-arb** is a hybrid model in which, if mediation fails, the mediator serves as an arbitrator. With the threat of arbitration in the air, parties are often encouraged to reach a negotiated solution. In **final-offer arbitration**, the arbitrator does not have authority to compromise between parties' positions but, rather, must accept one of the final offers made. Thus, each party has an incentive to make a final offer appear the most reasonable in the eyes of the neutral third party. **Arb-med** is also a hybrid model traced to South Africa in which an arbitrator makes a decision and places it in a sealed envelope. The threat of the arbitrator's decision sits on a table and is destined to be opened unless the parties reach mutual agreement. Arb-med is more effective than conventional arbitration.[65]

Build in Consultation Beforehand and Feedback Afterward.   **Notification and consultation** between parties prior to taking action can prevent disputes that arise through sheer misunderstanding. They can also reduce the anger and hostility that often result when decisions are made unilaterally and abruptly. **Postdispute analysis and feedback** is a method whereby parties learn from their disputes to prevent similar problems in the future. Similarly, by establishing a **forum**, consultation and postdispute analysis can be institutionalized to create an opportunity for discussion.

Provide Skills and Resources.   People who lack the skills to resolve disputes often resort to rights- and power-based actions (i.e., lawsuits or firings).

---

[62] Ibid.
[63] MacDonald, C., & Jun, C. (2006, September 3). How mayor brokered end of school strike; No wage givebacks, but benefits cut. *Detroit News,* p. A1.
[64] Ury, Brett, & Goldberg, *Getting disputes resolved,* p. 56.
[65] Conlon, D. E., Moon, H., & Ng, K. Y. (2002). Putting the cart before the horse: The benefits of arbitrating before mediating. *Journal of Applied Psychology, 87*(5), 978–984.

HIGH COSTS ASSOCIATED WITH POWER AND RIGHTS   Focusing on who is right or who is more powerful usually leaves at least one person feeling like a loser. Losers often do not give up but instead appeal to higher courts or plot revenge. Rights are less costly than power. Generally, power costs more in resources consumed and opportunities lost. For example, strikes cost more than arbitration, and violence costs more than litigation. Costs are incurred not only in efforts invested but also from the destruction of each side's resources. Power contests often create new injuries and a desire for revenge. Interests are less costly than rights. In summary, focusing on interests, compared to rights and power, produces higher satisfaction with outcomes, better working relationships, and less recurrence; it may also mean lower transaction costs.

KNOW WHEN TO USE RIGHTS AND POWER   Resolving all disputes by reconciling interests is neither possible nor desirable.[66] Rights and power procedures are often used when they are not necessary; a procedure that should be the last resort too often becomes the first move. Rights and power may be appropriate to use in the following situations:[67]

- *The other party refuses to come to the table.*   In this case, no negotiation is taking place, and rights and power are necessary for engagement.
- *Negotiations have broken down and parties are at an impasse.*   A credible threat, especially if combined with an interests-based proposal, may restart negotiations. For example, when union clerical workers at the ports of Los Angeles and Long Beach were unable to come to an agreement in their labor contract negotiations, they threatened a crippling strike. Accounting for 40% of the nation's cargo container traffic and for 12% of southern California's economic activity, a strike at the two ports would be extremely costly, even if it only lasted a few days. A few hours later, all issues were finally resolved, and the strike was averted.[68]
- *The other party needs to know you have power.*   Sometimes, people need to wield power simply to demonstrate they have it.[69] However, threats must be backed up with actions to be credible. Furthermore, the weaker party may fail to fully comply with a resolution based on power, thus requiring the more powerful party to engage in expensive policing.
- *Someone violates a rule or breaks the law.*   In this situation, it is appropriate to use rights or power.
- *Interests are so opposed that agreement is not possible.*   Sometimes, parties' interests are so disparate that agreement is not possible. For example, when fundamental values are at odds (e.g., abortion beliefs), resolution can occur only through a rights contest (a trial) or power contest (a demonstration or legislative battle).
- *Social change is necessary.*   To create social impact, a rights battle may be necessary. For example, consider the case of *Brown v. Board of Education,* which laid important groundwork for the elimination of racial segregation.
- *Negotiators are moving toward agreement and parties are "positioning" themselves.*   In other words, parties are committed to reaching a deal, and now they are dancing in the bargaining zone.

---

[66] Ury, Brett, & Goldberg, *Getting disputes resolved,* p. 15.
[67] Ibid.
[68] White, R. D. (2007, July 27). All hands on board at ports: A tentative contract deal, reached after negotiators declared an impasse, averts a strike by clerical workers. *Los Angeles Times,* p. C1.
[69] Ury, Brett, & Goldberg, *Getting disputes resolved,* p. 16.

KNOW HOW TO USE RIGHTS AND POWER   Consider the following when making a threat:[70]

Threaten the Other Party's Interests.   To effectively make a threat, a negotiator needs to attack the other party's underlying interests. Otherwise, the other party will feel little incentive to comply with your threat. Consider how American Airlines attempted to jump-start negotiations with its union members in 2003 by threatening their most basic interests.[71] Company negotiators gave each union group a written outline, called a "term sheet," that clearly laid out the financial impact of bankruptcy: $500 million in pay and benefit cuts beyond the $1.62 billion the airline requested. The result was that the union leaders became anchored on this number: The pilot's board quickly huddled at union offices and came up with 10 concessions that would raise the needed amount.

Clarity.   Negotiators need to be clear about what actions are needed by the other party. For example, nine days after al-Qaeda's terrorist attacks on the United States in 2001, President George W. Bush issued a clear threat: He demanded that the Taliban turn over Osama bin Laden and the leaders of his terrorist network and shut down terrorist training camps in Afghanistan; otherwise, the United States would "direct every resource at our command—every means of diplomacy, every tool of intelligence, every instrument of law enforcement, every financial influence and every necessary weapon of war—to the destruction and to the defeat of the global terror network."[72]

Credibility.   Power-based approaches typically focus on the future (e.g., "If you do not do such-and-such, I will withdraw your funding"). To be effective, the other party must believe that you have the ability to carry out the threat. If you are not seen as credible, people will call your bluff.

Do Not Burn Bridges.   It is important to leave a pathway back to interests-based discussion. Ury, Brett, and Goldberg call it the "loop-back to interests."[73] Threats are expensive to carry out; thus, it is critical that you are able to turn off a threat, allowing the other party to save face and reopen negotiations. If you do not provide yourself with a loop-back to interests, you force yourself to carry out the threat. Furthermore, after you use your threat, you lose your power and ability to influence. Lytle, Brett, and Shapiro suggest that if you are going to use rights or power, you should use the following sequence: (a) state a specific, detailed demand and deadline; (b) state a specific, detailed, credible threat (which harms the other side's interests); and (c) state a specific, detailed, positive consequence that will follow if the demand is met.[74]

EMOTIONS AND EMOTIONAL KNOWLEDGE

Emotions are inevitable in conflict and negotiations. Moreover, negotiators vary in terms of how accurate they are in assessing the emotional expression of others.

Emotions and Moods

For the purposes of this chapter, **emotions** are relatively fleeting states that are usually fairly intense and often a result of a particular experience. In general, emotions are characterized in

---

[70] Brett, J. M. (2007). *Negotiating globally: How to negotiate deals, resolve disputes, and make decisions across cultural boundaries,* 2nd edition. San Francisco, CA: Jossey-Bass.

[71] Torbenson, E. (2003, April 3). American Airlines pilots agree to plan to avoid bankruptcy. *Dallas Morning News.*

[72] Espo, D. (2001, September 20). Bush says U.S. will use 'every resource' to defeat global terrorism. *Associated Press Newswires.*

[73] Ury, Brett, & Goldberg, *Getting disputes resolved,* p. 52.

[74] Lytle, Brett, & Shapiro, "The strategic use of interests."

terms of pleasantness and activation (see Exhibit 5-10). **Moods** are more chronic and more diffuse, meaning that whereas emotions are a result of, and can be directed at, certain events or people, moods are usually not directed at someone. Unlike emotions, which are very specific, such as anger, regret, relief, gratitude, and so on, moods are often classified as simply "being in a good mood" or a "bad mood." Emotions and moods can be either a consequence or a determinant of negotiation behavior and outcomes.

Expressed Versus Felt Emotion

People vary in terms of their ability and willingness to express (as well as control) their emotions. There are implications for people who express too much emotion and, conversely, for those who attempt to suppress emotions.

Negotiators should resist the urge to gloat or show signs of smugness following negotiation.[75] In one investigation, some negotiators gloated following their negotiation

EXHIBIT 5-10

Distinct Emotions

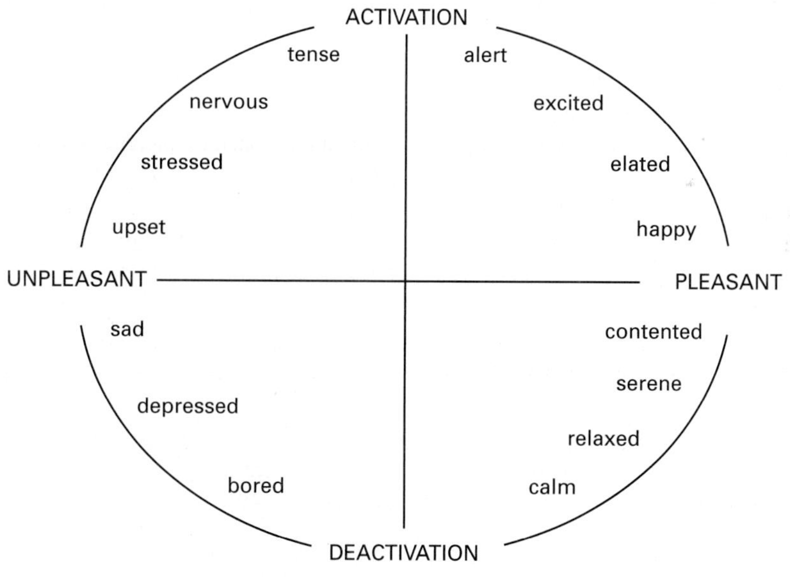

Source: Posner, J. Russell, J. A., & Peterson, B. S. (2005). The circumplex model of affect: Anintegrative approach to affective neuroscience, cognitive development, and psychopathology. *Development and Psychopathology*, 17, 715–734.

---

[75] Raiffa, H. (1982). *The art and science of negotiation.* Cambridge, MA: Belknap.

("I really feel good about the negotiation—I got everything I wanted!"). Other negotiators made self-effacing remarks (such as "I really didn't do that well"). Later, negotiators who overheard the other party gloat or make self-effacing remarks were given an opportunity to provide valuable stock options to these same parties. Those parties who gloated received significantly fewer stock options than those who made the self-effacing remark.[76]

Genuine Versus Strategic Emotion

Perhaps the key question when it comes to emotion at the bargaining table concerns whether emotions are **genuine** (behavioral manifestations of felt emotions) or **strategic** (carefully designed orchestration to take the counterparty off guard). The effectiveness of three different strategic emotions (positive emotion, negative emotion, and poker face [no emotion]) was tested in a distributive bargaining situation.[77] The positive and poker face strategies were distinctly more effective than the negative emotional strategy in obtaining a favorable outcome from a counterparty. (See Exhibits 5-11 and 5-12 to assess your own strategic use of emotion.)

EXHIBIT 5-11

Emotional Styles

	Rational	Positive	Negative
Focus	Conceal or repress emotion	Create positive emotion in other party Create rapport	Use irrational-appearing emotions to intimidate or control other party
Distributive strategies (pie-slicing)	Citing norms of fair distribution	Compromise for the sake of the relationship	Threats; often tough bargaining
Integrative strategies (pie-expansion)	Systematic analysis of interests	Positive emotion stimulates creative thinking	Negative emotion may inhibit integrative bargaining
Implications for future negotiations and relationship	Not likely to say or do anything regrettable, but also may come across as "distant"	Greater feelings of commitment to relationship partner	Pressure to carry out threats or lose credibility

---

[76] Thompson, L., Valley, K. L., & Kramer, R. M. (1995). The bittersweet feeling of success: An examination of social perception in negotiation. *Journal of Experimental Social Psychology, 31*(6), 467–492.
[77] Kopelman, S., Rosette, A. S., & Thompson, L. (2006). The three faces of Eve: Strategic displays of positive, negative, and neutral emotion in negotiations. *Organizational Behavior and Human Decision Processes, 99*(1), 81–101.

EXHIBIT 5-12

Emotional Style Questionnaire

Read each statement, and indicate whether you think it is true or false for you in a negotiation situation. Force yourself to answer each one as generally true or false (i.e., do not respond with "I don't know").

1. In a negotiation situation, it is best to "keep a cool head."
2. I believe that in negotiations you can "catch more flies with honey."
3. It is important to me that I maintain control in a negotiation situation.
4. Establishing a positive sense of rapport with the other party is key to effective negotiation.
5. I am good at displaying emotions in negotiation to get what I want.
6. Emotions are the downfall of effective negotiation.
7. I definitely believe that the "squeaky wheel gets the grease" in many negotiation situations.
8. If you are nice in negotiations, you can get more than if you are cold or neutral.
9. In negotiation, you have to "fight fire with fire."
10. I honestly think better when I am in a good mood.
11. I would never want to let the other party know how I really felt in a negotiation.
12. I believe that in negotiations you can "catch more flies with a flyswatter."
13. I have used emotion to manipulate others in negotiations.
14. I believe that good moods are definitely contagious.
15. It is very important to make a very positive first impression when negotiating.
16. The downfall of many negotiators is that they lose personal control in a negotiation.
17. It is best to keep a "poker face" in negotiation situations.
18. It is very important to get the other person to respect you when negotiating.
19. I definitely want to leave the negotiation with the other party feeling good.
20. If the other party gets emotional, you can use it to your advantage in a negotiation.
21. I believe that it is important to "get on the same wavelength" as the other party.
22. It is important to demonstrate "resolve" in a negotiation.
23. If I sensed that I was not under control, I would call a temporary halt to the negotiation.
24. I would not hesitate to make a threat in a negotiation situation if I felt the other party would believe it.

Scoring Yourself

Computing your "R" score: Look at items #1, #3, #6, #11, #16, #17, #20, #23. Give yourself 1 point for every "true" answer and subtract 1 point for every "false" answer. Then combine your scores for your R score (rational).

Computing your "P" score: Look at items #2, #4, #8, #10, #14, #15, #19, #21. Give yourself 1 point for every "true" answer and subtract 1 point for every "false" answer. Then combine your scores for your P score (positive).

Computing your "N" score: Look at items #5, #7, #9, #12, #13, #18, #22, #24. Give yourself 1 point for every "true" answer and subtract 1 point for every "false" answer. Then combine your scores for your N score (negative).

In another investigation, three strategic uses of emotion were examined: expressing truly felt emotions, hiding felt emotions, and feigning unfelt emotions.[78] Hiding truly felt anger and feigning anger benefits negotiators in terms of monetary outcomes. Feigning rapport with the counterparty is especially useful for garnering concessions, as is feigning resentment. Elation or joy, however, is an emotion that is best kept hidden from the counterparty.

One type of strategic emotion is feigned liking. Presumably negotiators feign liking as a way of gaining favor and achieving their ultimate interaction goals. However, using "fake" emotions can take its toll on the negotiator: People who fake positive emotion are more likely to feel stress and actually get lower service delivery ratings (e.g., ratings by customers).[79]

Negative Emotion

Negotiators who use negative emotion feign temper tantrums as a way of threatening the counterparty to make a concession. It makes a difference whether the anger is "real" or "strategic." Negotiators who are really angry and feel little compassion for the counterparty are less effective in terms of expanding the pie than are happy negotiators.[80] Moreover, they are not as effective in terms of slicing the pie.[81] In contrast, negotiators who are "strategically angry" are more likely to gain concessions from their opponent because the counterparty will assume the angry person is close to their reservation point.[82] Angry negotiators induce fear in their opponent, and their opponents are more likely to succumb when they are motivated.[83] For example, before the annexation of Austria, Hitler met to negotiate with the Austrian chancellor, Kurt von Schuschnigg. At some point, in this dark historical meeting, Hitler's emotional style became very angry:

> [He] became more strident, more shrill. Hitler ranted like a maniac, waved his hands with excitement. At times he must have seemed completely out of control....Hitler may then have made his most extreme coercive threats seem credible....[He threatened to take von Schuschnigg into custody, an act unheard of in the context of diplomacy.] He insisted that von Schuschnigg sign an agreement to accept every one of his demands, or he would immediately order a march into Austria.[84]

The effect of negative emotions on negotiator behavior are also influenced by the alternatives available to negotiators. Recipients who have particularly poor alternatives are most affected by angry displays and therefore make more concessions[85] The motivations and goals of the

---

[78] Levine, R. C., Amanathullah, E. J., & Morris, M. (2009). *Untangling the web of emotional deceit: Measuring strategic use of emotions in negotiations.* Paper presented at the 22nd Annual IACM Conference Kyoto, Japan.

[79] Grandey, A. A. (2003). When "the show must go on": Surface acting and deep acting as determinants of emotional exhaustion and peer-rated service delivery. *Academy of Management Journal, 46*(1), 86–96.

[80] Allred, K. G., Mallozzi, J. S., Matsui, F., & Raia, C. P. (1997). The influence of anger and compassion on negotiation performance. *Organizational Behavior and Human Decision Processes, 70*(3), 175–187.

[81] Allred, K. G. (2000). Anger and retaliation in conflict: The role of attribution. In M. Deutsch & P. T. Coleman (Eds.), *The handbook of conflict resolution: Theory and practice* (pp. 236–255). San Francisco: Jossey-Bass.

[82] Van Kleef, G. A., De Dreu, C. K. W., & Manstead, A. S. R. (2004). The interpersonal effects of anger and happiness in negotiations. *Journal of Personality and Social Psychology, 86*(1), 57–76.

[83] Ibid.

[84] Raven, B. H. (1990). Political applications of the psychology of interpersonal influence and social power. *Political Psychology, 11*(3), 515.

[85] Sinaceur, M., & Tiedens, L. (2006). Get mad and get more than even: When and why anger expression is effective in negotiation. *Journal of Experimental Social Psychology, 42*(3), 314–322.

negotiator also influence the degree to which they react to the counterparty's display of negative emotion. For example, whereas negotiators tend to make more concessions to an angry opponent than to a happy one, this tends to be more true when negotiators are motivated to understand the other party, such as when they are not under time pressure (and, therefore, have resources to engage in thought processing).[86] When expressing anger, negotiators should direct it to a specific behavior rather than another person, thereby separating the people from the problem.[87] Moreover, when negotiators do concede to an angry opponent, they will also tend to concede to that person in the future because they perceive the other as tough.[88]

Communicating anger can sometimes backfire, such as when their opponent has the possibility to deceive them during the negotiation and when the consequences of rejecting the angry negotiator's offer are low.[89] The use of strategic negative emotion is not limited to displays of anger and temper tantrums. Displays of helplessness, pouting, and hurt feelings also can be used to manipulate others. For example, Effa Manley, a female baseball executive and owner of the Newark Eagles baseball franchise in the Negro League in the 1930s and 1940s, was not above shedding tears to get what she wanted at the negotiation table. Pittsburgh sports writer Wendell Smith recalls, "If she did not get what she wanted, Mrs. Manley would wrinkle up her pretty face and turn on the sprinkling system."[90] Acting somewhat insane can achieve similar effects, such as when AOL's Myer Berlow announced to his opponents during the middle of negotiations that his favorite movie was *The Godfather* and quoted his philosopher-hero, Machiavelli, saying "it is safer to be feared than loved."[91]

The type of negative emotion expressed may elicit very different reactions from counterparties. For example, one investigation examined how negotiators responded to an opponent who was disappointed or worried (supplication) with a guilty or regretful opponent (appeasement) versus an unemotional opponent. Negotiators conceded more when the opponent showed supplication (disappointment and worry) and conceded the least when the opponent showed guilt.[92] People who are self-interested (pro-self) are more likely to concede to a disappointed opponent as compared to pro-socials, because they see disappointment as a threat to getting what they want.[93]

Emotional Intelligence

Emotional intelligence is the ability of people (and negotiators) to understand emotions in themselves and others and to use emotional knowledge to effect positive outcomes. Whereas research and theory on emotional intelligence encourage people to be aware of their emotions, a large body of research indicates emotions, especially negative ones, can thwart people's ability to make good decisions. For example, decision makers experiencing high levels of emotional stress

---

[86] Van Kleef, De Dreu, & Manstead, "The interpersonal effects of anger."

[87] Steinel, W., Kleef, G. A., & Harnick, F. (2008). Are you talking to me?! Separating the people from the problem when expressing emotions in negotiation. *Journal of Experimental Social Psychology, 44*(2), 362–369.

[88] Van Kleef, G. A., & De Dreu, C. K. W. (2010). Longer-term consequences of anger expression in negotiation: Retaliation or spillover? *Journal of Experimental Social Psychology, 46*(5), 753–760.

[89] Van Dijk, E., Van Kleef, G.A., Steinel, W., & Van Beest, I. (2008). A social functional approach to emotions in bargaining: When communicating anger pays and when it backfires. *Journal of Personality and Social Psychology, 94*(4), 600–614.

[90] Moritz, O. (2003, June 20). First lady Effa Manley. *New York Daily News*, p. 33.

[91] Klein, A. (2003, June 15). Lord of the flies. *The Washington Post*, p. W06.

[92] Van Kleef, G. A., De Dreu, C. K. W., & Manstead, A. S. R. (2006). Supplication and appeasement in conflict and negotiation: The interpersonal effects of disappointment, worry, guilt and regret. *Journal of Personality and Social Psychology, 91*(1), 124–142.

[93] Van Kleef, G. A., & Van Lange, P. A. M., "What Other's Disappointment May Do the Selfish People: Emotion and Social Value Orientation in a Negotiation Context," *Personality and Social Psychology Bulletin, 34*(8), (2008): 1084–1095.

often undergo incomplete search, appraisal, and contingency-planning thought processes.[94] For this reason, it is important to draw a distinction between *expressing* emotion and *feeling* emotion. Even though a negotiator may feel emotion, he or she may not express that emotion.

Positive Emotion

Expressing positive emotion might have positive consequences in negotiations.[95] People process information differently when in a positive mood, as opposed to a negative or neutral mood.[96] Good moods promote creative thinking,[97] which, in turn, leads to innovative problem solving.[98] For example, in one investigation, negotiators watched a funny movie and were given a gift. These negotiators reached more integrative outcomes and generated more creative ideas than negotiators who did not watch the movie and were not given a gift.[99] Negotiators who are in a positive mood use more cooperative strategies, engage in more information exchange, generate more alternatives, and use fewer contentious tactics than do negative or neutral-mood negotiators.[100]

Emotions in negotiation can create a self-fulfilling prophecy, in which negotiators' emotions stimulate those emotions in the counterparty. In one investigation, people in a job-contract negotiation achieved lower joint gains when they experienced high levels of anger and low levels of compassion toward each other than when they experienced positive emotion.[101] Furthermore, angry negotiators were less willing to work with each other and more likely to retaliate.[102] However, when negotiators express happiness on the counterparty's high-priority issue and anger on the low-priority issue, this reduces the fixed-pie perception and increases integrative behavior.[103]

When people are in a positive mood, they are more creative, generate integrative information, and are more flexible in conveying their thoughts.[104] Why does positive emotion work? It is largely due to a combination of the self-fulfilling prophecy, information processing, and the fact that positive affect is associated with more creative and varied cognitions. For example, people

[94] Janis, I. L., & Mann, L. (1977). *Decision making: A psychological analysis of conflict, choice, and commitment.* New York: Free Press.

[95] Kumar, R. (1997). The role of affect in negotiations: An integrative overview. *Journal of Applied Behavioral Science, 33*(1), 84–100; Kramer, R. M., Pommerenke, P., & Newton, E. (1993). The social context of negotiation: Effects of social identity and interpersonal accountability on negotiator decision making. *Journal of Conflict Resolution, 37*(4), 633–654.

[96] Isen, A. M. (1987). Positive affect, cognitive processes, and social behavior. In L. Berkowitz (Ed.), *Advances in experimental social psychology: Vol. 20* (pp. 203–253). San Diego, CA: Academic Press, Inc.

[97] Isen, A. M. Daubman, K. A., & Nowicki, G. P. (1987). Positive affect facilitates creative problem solving. *Journal of Personality and Social Psychology, 52,* 1122–1129.

[98] Carnevale, P. J. D., & Isen, A. M. (1986). The influence of positive affect and visual access on the discovery of integrative solutions in bilateral negotiation. *Organizational Behavior and Human Decision Processes, 37*(1), 1–13.

[99] Allred, Mallozzi, Matsui, & Raia, "The influence of anger"; Barry, B., & Oliver, R. L. (1996). Affect in dyadic negotiation: A model and propositions. *Organizational Behavior and Human Decision Processes, 67*(2), 127–143. Forgas, J. P. (1996). The role of emotion scripts and transient moods in relationships: Structural and functional perspectives. In G. J. O. Fletcher & J. Fitness (Eds.), *Knowledge structures in close relationships: A social psychological approach* (pp. 275–296). Mahwah, NJ: Erlbaum.

[100] Carnevale & Isen, "The influence of positive affect."

[101] Allred, Mallozzi, Matsui, F., & Raia, "The influence of anger."

[102] Ibid.

[103] Pietroni, D., Van Kleef, G.A., De Dreu, C.K.W., & Pagliaro, S. (2008). Emotions as strategic information: Effects of other's emotional expressions on fixed-pie perception, demands and integrative behavior in negotiation. *Journal of Experimental Social Psychology, 44*(6), 1444–1454.

[104] Baron, R. A. (1990). Environmentally induced positive affect: Its impact on self-efficacy, task performance, negotiation, and conflict. *Journal of Applied Social Psychology, 20*(5), 368–384; Isen, Daubman, & Nowicki, "Positive affect facilitates creative problem solving"; Isen, A. M., Niedenthal, P. M., & Cantor, N. (1992). An influence of positive affect on social categorization. *Motivation and Emotion, 16*(1), 65–78.

who experience positive emotion see relationships among ideas and link together nontypical category exemplars.[105] This response builds rapport, which, in turn, helps to avoid impasse and facilitates the negotiation process.[106]

Emotional Intelligence and Negotiated Outcomes

The relationship between measured emotional intelligence (EQ) and negotiation outcomes is not totally straightforward.[107] On one hand, framing negotiations in affective (as opposed to purely cognitive-intellectual) terms allows negotiators to be more involved and positive, but they simultaneously have lower levels of trust and use of cooperative negotiation tactics.[108] People who are high in measured emotional intelligence experience greater subjective outcomes in negotiation than do people lower in emotional intelligence, however, high EQ negotiators achieve lower objective outcomes.[109] Apparently, people high in emotional intelligence feel better emotionally and create objective value for their counterparty but not for themselves.

ACCURACY   The ability to accurately read emotions in others, particularly the counterparty, is important for successful outcomes. Indeed, a consistent positive correlation exists between emotion recognition accuracy (ERA) and goal-oriented performance.[110] Greater recognition of facial expressions predicted how well negotiators did in a buyer-seller negotiation, in terms of both distributive and integrative outcomes[111]

SELF-EFFICACY   Part of emotional intelligence is a certain degree of self-efficacy and confidence. Whereas no one likes an overly confident, arrogant person, we admire people who have a quiet, steady belief in themselves and a "can do" attitude. Just as there are many types of negotiation skills, it stands to reason that there are many areas of skill about which negotiators may or may not be self-confident. **Distributive self-efficacy** refers to a negotiator's belief in his or her ability to claim resources effectively (e.g., "gain the upper hand"; "persuade others to make the most concessions"); in contrast, **integrative self-efficacy** refers to a negotiator's belief in her or his ability to create resources (e.g., "establish rapport"; "find tradeoffs").[112]

---

[105] Forgas, J. P. (1998). On feeling good and getting your way: Mood effects on negotiator cognition and bargaining strategies. *Journal of Personality and Social Psychology, 74*(3), 565–577; Isen, Niedenthal, & Cantor, "An influence of positive affect on social categorization."

[106] Drolet, A. L., & Morris, M. W. (2000). Rapport in conflict resolution: Accounting for how face-to-face contact fosters cooperation in mixed-motive conflicts. *Journal of Experimental Social Psychology, 36*, 26–50; Moore, D. A., Kurtzberg, T. R., Thompson, L., & Morris, M. W. (1999). Long and short routes to success in electronically mediated negotiations: Group affiliations and good vibrations. *Organizational Behavior and Human Decision Processes, 77*(1), 22–43; Thompson, L., Nadler, J., & Kim, P. H. (1999). Some like it hot: The case for the emotional negotiator. In L. Thompson, J. Levine, & D. M. Messick (Eds.), *Shared cognition in organizations: The management of knowledge* (pp. 139–162). Mahwah, NJ: Erlbaum.

[107] Fulmer, I. S., & Barry, B. (2004). The smart negotiator: Cognitive ability and emotional intelligence in negotiation. *International Journal of Conflict Management, 15*(3), 245–272.

[108] Hunt, C. S., & Kernan, M. C. (2005). Framing negotiations in affective terms: Methodological and preliminary theoretical findings. *International Journal of Conflict Management, 16*(2), 128–156.

[109] Foo, M. D., Elfenbein, H., Tan, H. H., & Aik, V. C. (2004). Emotional intelligence and negotiation: The tension between creating and claiming value. *International Journal of Conflict Management, 15*(4), 411–429.

[110] Elfenbein, H. A., Foo, M. D., White, J., Tan, H. H., & Aik, V. C. (2007). Reading your counterparty: The benefit of emotion recognition accuracy for effectiveness in negotiation. *Journal of Nonverbal Behavior, 31*(4), 205–223.

[111] Elfenbein, Foo, White, Tan, and Aik, "Reading your counterparty."

[112] Sullivan, B. A., O'Connor, K. M., & Burris, E. R. (2006). Negotiator confidence: The impact of self-efficacy on tactics and outcomes. *Journal of Experimental Social Psychology, 42*(5), 567–581.

Strategic Advice for Dealing with Emotions at the Table

Negotiators who understand how emotions work can be more strategic at the bargaining table.

UNDERSTAND INCIDENTAL EMOTIONS   People often do not realize that they are affected by their own transient emotions. As a result, decisions based on a fleeting incidental emotion can become the basis for subsequent decisions and outcomes.[113] Moreover, people are affected by the affective displays of emotion with a given behavior. For example, looking disgusted or frustrated when doing something nice is viewed much less positively; similarly, looking pleased when engaging in a negative behavior does not lead to a positive impression.[114]

BEWARE OF WHAT YOU ARE REINFORCING   People often make concessions to another person just to shut them up. What they may not realize is that this effectively reinforces the very behavior they are trying to extinguish. Negative reinforcement, or escape behavior, explains the increased likelihood of behavior that eliminates or removes an aversive stimulus.[115] For example, if obnoxious music is emanating from a radio, you will turn off the radio, thus eliminating the unpleasant sounds. In a similar vein, because most people find it unpleasant to be around someone who is openly hostile, negative, and unpredictable, they may be willing to capitulate to the other party just to remove themselves from this aversive situation. Unfortunately, this behavior acts as positive reinforcement for the counterparty. If someone acts irrationally and you acquiesce, you increase the likelihood of that person engaging in negative behavior in the future.

REEVALUATION IS MORE EFFECTIVE THAN SUPPRESSION   People often try to suppress emotions. However, suppression may backfire. For example, when people tell themselves not to conjure up certain thoughts, they find it virtually impossible to refrain from thinking those exact thoughts. Indeed, people who spend more time trying to repair their negative moods are the most likely to suffer from persistent emotional problems, such as depression and anxiety.[116] Reevaluation involves acknowledging emotion, but thinking about a different way to view it.

EMOTIONS ARE CONTAGIOUS   If one negotiator conveys positive emotion, the other negotiator is likely to "catch" this positive emotional state and convey positive emotion as well.[117] However, the same is true for negative emotion. Other people's emotions are a significant predictor of our own emotions, even after controlling for our perceptions of other's emotions. Stated another way, we don't need to be consciously aware of somebody else's emotion for it to affect our own emotion and our decision making.[118]

---

[113] Andrade, E. B., & Ariely, D., (2009). The enduring impact of transient emotions on decision making. *Organizational Behavior and Human Decision Processes, 109*(1), 1–8.

[114] Ames, D. R., Johar, G. V. (2009). I'll know what you're like when I see how you feel: How and when affective displays influence behavior-based impressions. *Psychological Science, 20(5), 586–593.*

[115] Skinner, B. F. (1938). *The behavior of organisms: An experimental analysis.* New York, London: D. Appleton Century.

[116] Wegner, D. M., & Wenzlaff, R. M. (1996). Mental control. In E. T. Higgins & A. W. Kruglanski (Eds.), *Social psychology: Handbook of basic principles* (pp. 466–492). New York: Guilford Press.

[117] Hatfield, E., Cacioppo, J. T., & Rapson, R. L. (1992). Primitive emotional contagion. In M. S. Clark (Ed.), *Review of personality and social psychology: Vol. 14, Emotion and social behavior* (pp. 151–177). Newbury Park, CA: Sage.

[118] Parkinson, B. & Simons, G. (2009). Affecting others: Social appraisal and emotion contagion in everyday decision making. *Personality and Social Psychology Bulletin, 35*(8), 1071–1084.

UNDERSTAND EMOTIONAL TRIGGERS   Certain words, when used in negotiation, are loaded and evoke emotion. In one investigation, the emotional impact of six different types of words were measured (see Exhibit 5-13).[119] Of all the different types of words, those that labeled the other person negatively or told the other person what he or she ought to do triggered the greatest anger and frustration.

EXHIBIT 5-13

Emotional Trigger Words and Phrases

Type of Emotional Trigger	Example Phrases	Words
Labeling the other person negatively	"You are lying." "Don't be stupid." "You are being unfair." "It was your fault."	Unfair, silly, liar, stupid
Telling the other person what to do or what they can't do	"No way." "You need to...." "You need to give me a better deal."	Can't, must, never, should
Appealing to a higher source; blaming, abdicating responsibility	"From a legal standpoint...." "This is how we've always done it." "You should have known that." "I don't think you understand."	Fair, ethical, moral, better
Rude: not listening, explicative, insincere praise, sarcasm, educating the other	"Yes, but...." "I like you, but...." "With all due respect...." "It is easy to see that...."	Whatever, you always, you never
Labeling your own behavior as superior	"I'm being reasonable." "This is a good deal." "I know what I'm doing."	Reasonable, deserve
Implied threats	"You either comply or else." "We are going to ruin your reputation."	

Source: Adapted from Schroth, H., Bain-Chekal, J., and Caldwell, D. (2005). Sticks and stones may break bones and words can hurt me: Words and phrases that trigger emotions in negotiations and their effects. *International Journal of Conflict Management, 16*(2), 102–127. Reprinted by permission.

---

[119] Schroth, H. A., Bain-Chekal, J., & Caldwell, D. F. (2005). Sticks and stones may break bones and words can hurt me: Words and phrases that trigger emotions in negotiations and their effects. *International Journal of Conflict Management, 16*(2), 102–127.

CONCLUSION

We considered motivational orientation (individualistic, cooperative, or competitive), the interests-, rights-, and power-based model of disputing, and the role of emotion at the bargaining table. The following are the key messages of this chapter:

Get in touch with your own style in an honest and straightforward way. Ask someone else to appraise you honestly, using the diagnostic tools presented in this chapter.

Know your limits and your strengths. Knowing your own stylistic limits and strengths is important.

Understand the counterparty. Most naive negotiators just assume that the counterparty has the same orientation they do.

Expand your repertoire. People who do not feel comfortable with their bargaining style are not effective. This chapter gives negotiators options for expanding their repertoire, especially at critical points during negotiation.

Establishing Trust and Building a Relationship

Todd Stern, the United States chief climate negotiator, knows when to say "No." When Stern arrived at a climate change summit in Copenhagen in 2009, he immediately called a news conference and blasted the Chinese government for not doing enough to reduce emissions, European governments for making too many demands on the United States, and poor countries for demanding pollution reparations from rich countries. However, Stern knows how to establish relationships at the negotiation table too. Negotiators who have sat at the table with Stern call him "accommodating," "low-key," and "artful." In the pressure cooker that is international climate change diplomacy, Stern needs all of his people and task skills. And it has worked. Jairam Ramesh, India's environment minister and chief climate negotiator remarked about Stern, "Obviously India's stance on climate change is quite different from that of the United States, and there are many things in U.S. policy that I disagree with strongly, but that has not stood in the way of our developing a warm personal rapport." Ramesh took a long walk with Mr. Stern around a lake in Copenhagen during a preliminary meeting to the major climate conference. Although they did not come to agreement during their walk, Ramesh said: "We discussed our differences frankly. He understood me better, I think, and I certainly got a fuller understanding of where he was coming from."[1]

---

[1] Broder, J. M. (2009, December 10). U.S. climate envoy's good cop, bad cop roles. *New York Times*, p. A12.

THE PEOPLE SIDE OF WIN-WIN

Successful negotiation is not just about money. And, making more money may not always make us feel more successful or more satisfied.[2] Despite the fact that rational behavior is often equated with the maximization of monetary wealth, economic models focus on the maximization of utility—which can be defined as money but can include other considerations, such as trust, security, happiness, and peace of mind. Win-win agreements maximize whatever negotiators care about, whether it's money, relationships, trust, or peace of mind. Exhibit 6-1 identifies six different types of resources people can exchange: love, money, services, goods, status, and information.[3] Each of these resources varies in terms of **particularism** (how much utility we derive depends on who is providing it—a kiss from one's own child is valued much more than a kiss from a complete stranger) and **concreteness** (how tangible it is). Love and social status are less concrete than services or goods, for example.

The Subjective Value Inventory **(SVI)** assesses four major concerns held by negotiators: feelings about instrumental outcomes, feelings about themselves, feelings about the process, and

EXHIBIT 6-1

Resources That May Be Exchanged in a Relationship

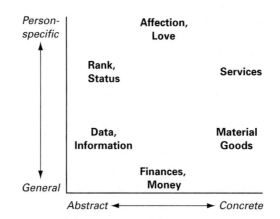

Source: Adapted from Foa, U., & Foa, E. (1975). *Resource theory of social exchange.* Morristown, NJ: General Learning Press.

---

[2] Thompson, L. (1995). The impact of minimum goals and aspirations on judgments of success in negotiations. *Group Decision Making and Negotiation, 4*(6), 513–524; Thompson, L., Valley, K. L., & Kramer, R. M. (1995). The bittersweet feeling of success: An examination of social perception in negotiation. *Journal of Experimental Social Psychology, 31*(6), 467–492; Galinsky, A. D., Mussweiler, T., & Medvec, V. H. (2002). Disconnecting outcomes and evaluations: The role of negotiator focus. *Journal of Personality and Social Psychology, 83*(5), 1131–1140.

[3] Foa, U., & Foa, E. (1975). *Resource theory of social exchange.* Morristown, NJ: General Learning Press.

feelings about their relationships.[4] Subjective value predicts MBA students' satisfaction with their employment compensation, job satisfaction, and reduces intentions to seek a different job a year later.[5] (See Exhibit 6-2 for the Subjective Value Inventory.)

EXHIBIT 6-2

Subjective Value Inventory

Think about your most recent negotiation. Rate your response to each of the following questions on a scale of 1 to 7, with 1 = not at all; 4 = moderately; and 7 = perfectly true or characteristic.

1. How satisfied are you with your own outcome—i.e., the extent to which the terms of your agreement (or lack of agreement) benefit you?
2. How satisfied are you with the balance between your own outcomes and the outcome(s) of your counterpart(s)?
3. Did you feel like you forfeited or "lost" in this negotiation?
4. Do you think the terms of your agreement are consistent with the principles of legitimacy of objective criteria (e.g., common standards of fairness, precedent, industry practice, legality, etc.)?
5. Did you "lose face" (i.e., damage your sense of pride) in the negotiation?
6. Did this negotiation make you feel more or less competent as a negotiator?
7. Did you behave according to your own principles and values?
8. Did this negotiation positively or negatively impact your self-image or your impression of yourself?
9. Did you feel your counterpart(s) listened to your concerns?
10. Would you characterize the negotiation process as fair?
11. How satisfied are you with the ease (or difficulty) of reaching an agreement?
12. Did your counterpart(s) consider your wishes, opinions, or needs?
13. What kind of "overall" impression did your counterpart(s) make on you?
14. How satisfied are you with your relationship with your counterpart(s) as a result of this negotiation?
15. Did the negotiation make you trust your counterpart(s)?
16. Did the negotiation build a good foundation for a future relationship with your counterpart(s)?

Note about scoring:

- Instrumental outcome (reverse score #3; average items 1–4)
- Feelings about oneself (reverse score #5; average items 5–8)
- Feelings about the process (average items 9–12)
- Feelings about the relationship (average items 13–16)

Source: Based on Curhan, J., Elfenbein, H., and Xu, H. (2006). What do people value when they negotiate? Mapping the domain of subjective value in negotiation. *Journal of Personality and Social Psychology, 91*(3), 493–512.

---

[4] Curhan, J. R., Elfenbein, H. A., & Xu, H. (2006). What do people value when they negotiate? Mapping the domain of subjective value in negotiation. *Journal of Personality and Social Psychology, 91*(3), 493–512.
[5] Curhan, J. R., Elfenbein, H. A., & Kilduff, G. J. (2009). Getting off on the right foot: Subjective value versus economic value in predicting longitudinal job outcomes from job offer negotiations. *Journal of Applied Psychology, 94*(2), 524–534.

TRUST AS THE BEDROCK OF RELATIONSHIPS

Trust is essential in any relationship. It is an expression of confidence in another person or group of people that you will not be put at risk, harmed, or injured by their actions.[6] On a practical level, trust means that we could be exploited by someone. Most relationships offer some incentive for people to behave in an untrustworthy fashion.[7]

Three Types of Trust in Relationships

People form three major types of trust relationships with others: deterrence-based trust, knowledge-based trust, and identification-based trust.[8]

DETERRENCE-BASED TRUST   **Deterrence-based trust** is based on consistency of behavior, meaning people will follow through on what they promise to do. Behavioral consistency, or follow-through, is sustained by threats or promises of consequences that will result if consistency and promises are not maintained. The consequences most often used are punishments, sanctions, incentives, rewards, and legal implications. Deterrence-based trust often involves contracts, surveillance, and sometimes punishment. A whopping 77.7% of major U.S. companies keep tabs on employees by checking their email, Internet, phone calls, computer files, or by videotaping them at work.[9] In the Hawthorne plant in the 1940s, the established norm was that workers would not deviate from acceptable levels of production. Whenever a worker was caught over- or underperforming, other plant workers would give him or her a sharp blow to the upper arm (called "binging"). (For another example, see Exhibit 6-3.)

There are two key problems with deterrence-based trust systems. First, they are expensive to develop and maintain (they require development, oversight, maintenance, and monitoring) and second, they can backfire. **Reactance theory** argues that people do not like their freedom taken away and will act to reassert it. For example, signs reading "Do Not Write on These Walls Under Any Circumstances" actually increase the incidence of vandalism (as compared to signs that say "Please Do Not Write on These Walls" or the complete absence of signs).[10] Similarly, people take longer to vacate a parking space when they know someone else is waiting for it.[11] People often have a negative reaction when they perceive that someone is controlling their behavior or limiting their freedom. When people think their behavior is controlled by extrinsic motivators, such as sanctions and rewards, intrinsic motivation is reduced.[12] Thus, surveillance may undermine the behaviors such monitoring is intended to ensure! The fear of monitoring adversely impacted

[6] Axelrod, R. (1984). *The evolution of cooperation.* New York: Basic Books.

[7] Kramer, R. M. (1999). Trust and distrust in organizations: Emerging perspectives, enduring questions. *Annual Review of Psychology, 50,* 569–598; Kramer, R. M., Brewer, M. B., & Hanna, B. A. (1996). Collective trust and collective action: The decision to trust as a social decision. In R. M. Kramer & T. R. Tyler (Eds.), *Trust in organizations* (pp. 357–389). Thousand Oaks, CA: Sage.

[8] Shapiro, D. L., Sheppard, B. H., & Cheraskin, L. (1992). Business on a handshake. *Negotiation Journal, 8*(4), 365–377; Lewicki, R. J., & Bunker, B. B. (1996). Developing and maintaining trust in work relationships. In R. M. Kramer & T. M. Tyler (Eds.), *Trust in organizations: Frontiers of theory and research* (pp. 114–139). Thousand Oaks, CA: Sage.

[9] Office Slacker Stats. (2010). *Staff Monitoring New.* Staffmonitoring.com

[10] Pennebaker, J. W., & Sanders, D. Y. (1976). American graffiti: Effects of authority and reactance arousal. *Personality and Social Psychology Bulletin, 2*(3), 264–267.

[11] Ruback, R. B., & Juieng, D. (1997). Territorial defense in parking lots: Retaliation against waiting drivers. *Journal of Applied Social Psychology, 27*(9), 821–834.

[12] Enzle, M. E., & Anderson, S. C. (1993). Surveillant intentions and intrinsic motivation. *Journal of Personality and Social Psychology, 64*(2), 257–266.

EXHIBIT 6-3

Deterrence-Based Trust

Another striking example of deterrence-based trust is the negotiated agreement between explorer Christopher Columbus and Spain's King Ferdinand and Queen Isabella. Ferdinand and Isabella offered Columbus ships, men, and money to carry the faith and the Spanish flag to the West. However, Columbus refused to agree until his demands were met in writing. He insisted he be knighted and made admiral of the Ocean Sea and Viceroy and Governor General of all the lands he would discover. He further demanded 10% of whatever would be acquired overseas. A handshake would not suffice. He insisted that the deal be set in writing, and so he drafted a lengthy, detailed agreement between himself and the crown. This move was astonishingly bold, considering the king and queen held the power of life and death over him. The haggling went back and forth, and on April 17, 1492, the Pact of Santa Fe was agreed to by the rulers.

Source: Dworetzky, T. (1998, December 11). Explorer Christopher Columbus: How the West's greatest discoverer negotiated his trips' financing. *Investors' Business Daily,* p. 1BD. Copyright © 1998–2008. Investor's Daily, Inc. Republished with permission.

trust among flight attendants at Delta Airlines.[13] Flight attendants came to fear and distrust their passengers because of a policy allowing passengers to write letters of complaint about in-flight service. The climate of distrust was further intensified when flight attendants became suspicious that undercover supervisors were posing as passengers. (We discuss more about deterrence-based trust in Chapter 11.)

KNOWLEDGE-BASED TRUST   **Knowledge-based trust** is grounded in behavioral predictability, and it occurs when a person has enough information about others to understand them and accurately predict their behavior. Whenever informational uncertainty or asymmetry characterizes a relationship, it provides opportunity for deceit, and one or both parties risk exploitation. Paradoxically, if no risk is present in an exchange situation, exploitation cannot occur, but high levels of trust will not develop.[14] Trust is a consequence or response to uncertainty.[15]

An intriguing example of the development of knowledge-based trust among negotiators concerns the sale of rubber and rice in Thailand.[16] For various reasons, the quality of

---

[13] Hochschild, A. R. (1983). *The managed heart: Commercialization of human feeling.* Berkeley: University of California Press.

[14] Thibaut, J. W., & Kelley, H. H. (1959). *The social psychology of groups.* New York: Wiley.

[15] Kollock, P. (1994). The emergence of exchange structures: An experimental study of uncertainty, commitment and trust. *American Journal of Sociology, 100*(2), 313–345; Granovetter, M. (1973). The strength of weak ties. *American Journal of Sociology, 78*(6), 1360–1380.

[16] Siamwalla, A. (1978, June). Farmers and middlemen: Aspects of agricultural marketing in Thailand. *Economic Bulletin for Asia and the Pacific, 29*(1), 38–50; Popkin, S. L. (1981). Public choice and rural development—free riders, lemons, and institutional design. In C. S. Russell & N. K. Nicholson (Eds.), *Public choice and rural development* (pp. 43–80). Washington, DC: Resources for the Future.

rubber cannot be determined at the time of sale but, rather, only months later: When rubber is sold, the seller knows the quality of the rubber, but the buyer does not. This is a classic case of information asymmetry. In contrast, in the rice market, the quality of rice can be readily determined at the time of sale (no informational uncertainty). It would seem that the rubber market, because of its informational asymmetries, would be characterized by exploitation on the part of sellers who would only sell cheap rubber at high prices, creating a market of lemons.[17] However, buyers and sellers in the rubber market abandoned anonymous exchange for long-term exchange relationships between particular buyers and sellers. Within this exchange framework, growers establish reputations for trustworthiness, and rubber of high quality is sold.

Knowledge-based trust increases dependence and commitment among parties.[18] For example, suppliers who regularly negotiate with certain customers develop highly specialized products for those customers. Such product differentiation can create barriers to switching suppliers. In addition to economic dependence, people become emotionally committed to certain relationships. For example, in markets characterized by information asymmetries, once negotiators develop a relationship with someone they find to be trustworthy, they remain committed to the relationship, even when it would be profitable to trade with others.[19] When switching does occur, the party who is "left" feels indignant and violated. People who expect to interact with others in the future are less likely to exploit them, even when given an opportunity.[20] When negotiators anticipate extended relationships, they are more likely to cooperate with customers, colleagues, and suppliers but not with competitors.[21] These relationships and the perception of low mobility among individuals promote development of integrative agreements across interactions, rather than only within given transactions.[22]

IDENTIFICATION-BASED TRUST **Identification-based trust** is grounded in complete empathy with another person's desires and intentions. In identification-based trust systems, trust exists between people because each person understands, agrees with, empathizes with, and takes on the other's values because of the emotional connection between them; thus, they act for each other.[23] Identification-based trust means that other people have adopted your own preferences.

Whereas it may seem that personal relationships would be completely grounded in knowledge-based or identification-based trust, that is not always the case. For example, a deterrence-based trust system is put in place when couples get prenuptial agreements or when husbands or wives hire private investigators to monitor the actions of their spouses.

---

[17] Akerlof, G. A. (1970). The market for "lemons": Quality uncertainty and the market mechanism. *Quarterly Journal of Economics, 84*(3), 488–500.

[18] Dwyer, F. R., Schurr, P. H., & Oh, S. (1987). Developing buyer-seller relationships. *Journal of Marketing, 51*(2), 11–27; Kollock, P. "The emergence of exchange structures."

[19] Kollock, "The emergence of exchange structures."

[20] Marlowe, D., Gergen, K. J., & Doob, A. N. (1966). Opponents' personality, expectation of social interaction and interpersonal bargaining. *Journal of Personality and Social Psychology, 3*(2), 206–213.

[21] Sondak, H., & Moore, M. C. (1994). Relationship frames and cooperation. *Group Decision and Negotiation, 2*(2), 103–118.

[22] Mannix, E. A., Tinsley, C. H., & Bazerman, M. H. (1995). Negotiating over time: Impediments to integrative solutions. *Organizational Behavior and Human Decision Processes, 62*(3), 241–251.

[23] Lewicki & Bunker, "Developing and maintaining trust."

Building Trust: Rational and Deliberate Mechanisms

There are two routes to building trust: the **cognitive route** is based on rational and deliberate thoughts and considerations; the **affective route** is based on intuition and emotion.[24] The cognitive and the affective routes to trust have different triggers and turning points in negotiation.[25]

Let's first consider how to build trust through the cognitive route. (For an examination of how businesspeople attempt to secure trust, see Exhibit 6-4.)

EXHIBIT 6-4

How Managers Secure Commitment in the Absence of Binding Contracts

We surveyed businesspeople on how they attempted to secure trust in relationships. We asked 52 MBA students to "imagine that you are involved in a negotiation situation where you need to get commitment (i.e., follow-through) from one or more of the people involved. The nature of the negotiation does not involve 'binding contracts.' How do you try to instill a sense of commitment in the absence of any binding contracts?" The responses varied dramatically.

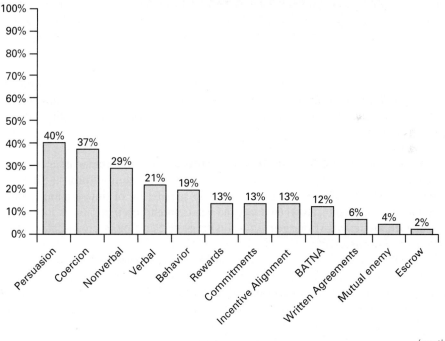

(continued)

---

[24] McAlister, D. (1995). Affect- and cognition-based trust as foundations for interpersonal cooperation in organizations. *Academy of Management Journal, 38*(1), 24–59; Lewis, D. J. & Weigert, A. (1985). Trust as a social reality. *Social Forces, 63*(4), 967–985.

[25] Olekalns, M., & Smith, P. L. (2005). Moments in time: Metacognition, trust, and outcomes in dyadic negotiations. *Personality and Social Psychology Bulletin, 31*(12), 1696–1707.

Review of Categories (Left to Right):

- *Persuasion and consciousness-raising* (e.g., "I would reinforce the idea that this is the beginning of a long-term, multiple-contact relationship, and that it is in my counterparty's best interest to think about the repercussions of reneging on future negotiations")
- *Coercion and threat tactics* (e.g., humiliation, punishment, etc.)
- *Nonverbal strategies* (e.g., handshakes, establishing rapport, "…look people in the eye, have them look at you, and say to you that they will do what you want them to do…", etc.)
- *Verbal agreements*
- *Behavior modification* (e.g., tit for tat; social modeling)
- *Rewards and benefits*
- *Public commitments* (e.g., "…by making the outcome public, the erring party would suffer public embarrassment and suffer loss of reputation…")
- *Alignment of incentives*
- *Collecting information about other's BATNA*
- *Written (nonbinding) agreements*
- *Creation of a mutual enemy*
- *Creating escrow or collateral arrangements*

TRANSFORM PERSONAL CONFLICT INTO TASK CONFLICT   Two basic types of conflict occur in relationships. **Personal conflict**, also known as **emotional conflict**, is rooted in anger, personality clashes, ego, and tension. **Task conflict**, also known as **cognitive conflict**, is largely depersonalized. It consists of argumentation about the merits of ideas, plans, and projects, independent of the identity of the people involved. Task conflict is often effective in stimulating the creativity necessary for integrative agreement because it forces people to rethink problems and arrive at outcomes that everyone can accept. Personal conflict threatens relationships, whereas task conflict enhances relationships, provided that people are comfortable with it.[26]

AGREE ON A COMMON GOAL OR SHARED VISION   The importance of a common goal is summed up in a quote by Steve Jobs, associated with three high-profile Silicon Valley companies—Apple, NeXT, and Pixar: "It's okay to spend a lot of time arguing about which route to take to San Francisco when everyone wants to end up there, but a lot of time gets wasted in such arguments if one person wants to go to San Francisco and another secretly wants to go to San Diego."[27]

The 2005 departure of Carly Fiorina as chief executive of Hewlett-Packard (HP) illustrates how conflicts can also mask the fact that people may never agree on the goals of the company. Escalating disagreements between Fiorina and HP's board of directors led to an open discussion of their differences at a company retreat. Several board members expressed concern about the company's performance under Fiorina's leadership. When a *Wall Street Journal* story leaked details of their discussions, Fiorina was furious and shifted her focus to the leak. Board members

[26] Jehn, K. A. (1997). A qualitative analysis of conflict types and dimensions in organizational groups. *Administrative Science Quarterly, 42,* 530–557.

[27] Eisenhardt, K. M., Kahwajy, J. L., & Bourgeois, L. J., III. (1997). How management teams can have a good fight. *Harvard Business Review, 75*(4), 77–85 (p. 80).

were also outraged by the leak but felt their concerns regarding the performance of the company were more important. They started to believe it had become impossible to work out their differences with Fiorina. Less than 2 weeks later, during a private meeting, the board members voted to dismiss her.[28]

CAPITALIZE ON NETWORK CONNECTIONS Negotiators who do not know each other may attempt to build a more trusting relationship by trying to find a common node in their social networks. Conversely, getting people to talk to someone outside their social network is challenging. An investigation of a weekly business "mixer" revealed that people don't mix as much as would be expected, given the purpose of the mixer.[29] Affect-based trust is high among people who are embedded densely in their networks and among those who provide social support; cognition-based trust is higher in those with whom people engage in instrumental exchanges.[30]

FIND A SHARED PROBLEM OR A SHARED ENEMY It is remarkable how the presence of a common enemy can unite people and build trust.[31] A shared goal was established during the Reagan–Gorbachev summit talks. One evening, President Reagan and Soviet leader Mikhail Gorbachev were drinking coffee after dinner on Lake Geneva. Secretary of State George P. Shultz turned to Georgi Kornienko, the Soviet first deputy foreign minister, and accused him of trying to stall summit negotiations on bilateral issues. "You, Mr. Minister, are responsible for this," Shultz declared. Then, turning to Gorbachev, the secretary of state added forcefully, "This man is not doing what you want him to do. He is not getting done what you want done." Reagan took advantage of the situation to create a common bond and looked at Gorbachev: "To hell with what they're doing. You and I will say, 'We will work together make it come to about.'" Reagan and Gorbachev then shook hands. The moment marked a critical turning point in the summit talk.[32]

FOCUS ON THE FUTURE If negotiators can forget the past and focus on their future, they can go a long way toward building trust. When negotiators expect to have future interaction with the counterparty, they have lower aspirations, expect negotiations to be friendlier, are more satisfied, and predominantly use a problem-solving bargaining style. Moreover, compared to one-time negotiations, those who expect to interact in the future have harmonious expectations and seek mutually beneficial solution.[33] In early 2011, ESPN and the NFL came to agreement on a 10-year, 1.9 billion extension of ESPN's Monday Night Football contact, a huge program for both the network and the NFL. The complex negotiations were completed in a relatively short amount

[28] Murray, A. (2006, September 6). Directors cut: H-P board clash over leaks triggers angry resignation—Perkins slams briefcase, says, "I quit and I'm leaving," as probe fingers a friend—A new era of governance. *Wall Street Journal*, p. A1.

[29] Ingram, P., & Morris, M. W. (2007). Do people mix at mixers? Structure, homophily, and the "life of the party." *Administrative Science Quarterly, 52*(4), 558–585.

[30] Chua, R. Y. J., Ingram, P., & Morris, M. W. (2008). From the head and the heart: Locating cognition- and affect-based trust in managers' professional networks. *Academy of Management Journal, 51*(3), 436–452.

[31] Sherif, M., Harvey, O. J., White, B. J., Hood, W. R., & Sherif, C. W. (1961). *Intergroup conflict and cooperation: The robber's cave experiment.* Norman: University of Oklahoma Press.

[32] Hoffman, D. (1985, November 23). Tense turning point at summit; key Reagan-Gorbachev handshake calmed atmosphere. *Washington Post*, p. A1.

[33] Patton, C., & Balakrishnan, P. V. S. (2010). The impact of expectation of future negotiation interaction on bargaining processes and outcomes. *Journal of Business Research, 63*(8), 809–816.

of time because the parties were able to focus on their future partnership. The negotiations frequently involved friendly meetings between top-level executives from ESPN and the NFL in the league's Manhattan offices. Both sides enjoyed a long working relationship and acknowledged they had much to gain from continued mutual rapport. This allowed for a mutually beneficial tradeoff as the NFL benefitted from ESPN's extensive air time for game highlight packages and from the coverage given to the NFL player draft—an event that ESPN almost singlehandedly shaped into an annual media frenzy.

Building Trust: Psychological Strategies

Psychological mechanisms for building trust are different from the rational, cognitive mechanisms discussed earlier in that people tend not to talk about these factors explicitly; rather, savvy negotiators know how to capitalize on them intuitively.

SIMILARITY People who are similar to each other like one another.[34] Negotiators are more likely to make concessions when negotiating with people they know and like. The **similarity-attraction effect** may occur on the basis of little, and sometimes downright trivial, information. Many sales training programs urge trainees to "mirror and match" the customer's body posture, mood, and verbal style because similarities along each of these dimensions produce positive results.[35] Similarity in dress also has dramatic effects. For example, marchers in a political demonstration not only are more likely to sign the petition of similarly dressed requester, but do so without bothering to read it first.[36] Google's mergers and acquisitions chief David Lawee uses similarity to establish a personal connection, He often arrives at meetings with a backpack in tow. "He's got this laid-back style that says, 'I like you, you like me—one way or another, we're going to work this out,'" said Anthony McCusker, an attorney who represented AdMob during negotiations with Google.[37]

MERE EXPOSURE The more we are exposed to something—a person, object, or idea—the more we like it. The **mere exposure effect** is extremely powerful and occurs below the level of our awareness.[38] For example, fractious political negotiations were smoothed by mere exposure initiated by the "Senate Wives" during the 1950s. The Senate wives met each Tuesday morning and included both Democrats and Republicans. The 50 wives achieved results that went far beyond a morning social club. During the Presidency of Lyndon Baines Johnson, rifts between the adminstration and congressional Republicans, led by Gerald Ford, were often smoothed over by Lady Bird Johnson and Betty Ford, who regularly met socially along with the wives of

---

[34] Griffin, E., & Sparks, G. G. (1990). Friends forever: A longitudinal exploration of intimacy in same-sex friends and platonic pairs. *Journal of Social and Personal Relationships, 7*(1), 29–46.

[35] LaFrance, M. (1985). Postural mirroring and intergroup relations. *Personality and Social Psychology Bulletin, 11*(2), 207–217; Locke, K. D., & Horowitz, L. M. (1990). Satisfaction in interpersonal interactions as a function of similarity in level of dysphoria. *Journal of Personality and Social Psychology, 58*(5), 823–831; Woodside, A. G., & Davenport, J. W., Jr. (1974). The Effects of salesman similarity and expertise on customer purchasing behavior. *Journal of Marketing Research, 11*(2), 198–202.

[36] Suedfeld, P., Bochner, S., & Matas, C. (1971). Petitioners attire and petition signing by peace demonstrators: A field experiment. *Journal of Applied Social Psychology, 1*(3), 278–283.

[37] MacMillan, D. (2010, November 24). So Google's buying your startup. Now what? *Bloomberg*. Bloomberg.com

[38] Zajonc, R. (1968). Attitudinal effects of mere exposure. *Journal of Personality and Social Psychology, 9* (monograph supplement No. 2, Part 2).

EXHIBIT 6-5

Mere Exposure Increases Liking

The effects of mere exposure on liking are demonstrated clearly in the classroom. In one investigation, student A attended 15 sessions of a course. For each session, she arrived before the class began, walked down the aisle, and sat at the front where other students could see her. Student B did the same thing but attended only 10 lectures. Student C came to class only 5 times. Student D never showed up. At the end of the term, the students in the class were shown slides of students A, B, C, and D and were asked to indicate how "familiar" they found each one, how attractive they found each one, and how similar they believed each one was to them. The number of classes attended had a dramatic impact on attraction and similarity but not on familiarity.

Source: Based on Moreland, R. L., & Beach, S. R. (1992). Exposure effects in the classroom: The development of affinity among students. *Journal of Experimental Social Psychology, 28*(3), 255–276.

other leaders. A current club, dubbed the "Senate Spouses," meets less than once a month and fewer than a dozen wives attend. Former Senate majority leader Trent Lott summarized the mere exposure effect this way, "If you live across the street from your political opponent, if you know his kids, if you've been to dinner at his house, it's impossible to go up on the floor of the Senate or House and blast him the next day."[39] (See Exhibit 6-5 for an example of how mere exposure increases liking in classrooms.)

PHYSICAL PRESENCE   When students are seated alphabetically in a classroom, friendships are significantly more likely to form between those whose last names begin with the same or a nearby letter.[40] This is what is called the **propinquity effect**. This may not seem important until you consider the fact that you may meet some of your closest colleagues, and perhaps even a future business partner, merely because of an instructor's seating chart! Similarly, people given a corner seat or an office at the end of a corridor make fewer friends in their organization.[41] If an instructor changes seat assignments once or twice during the semester, each student becomes acquainted with additional colleagues.[42] Consider the entering class of the Maryland State Police Training Academy.[43] Trainees were assigned to their classroom seats and to their dormitory rooms by the alphabetical order of their last names. Sometime later, trainees were asked to name their three best friends in the group; their choices followed the rules of alphabetization almost

---

[39] Miller, L. (2011, January 3). The commuter congress. *Newsweek.* Newsweek.com
[40] Segal, M. W. (1974). Alphabet and attraction: An unobtrusive measure of the effect of propinquity in a field setting. *Journal of Personality and Social Psychology, 30*(5), 654–657.
[41] Maisonneuve, J., Palmade, G., & Fourment, Cl. (1952). Selective choices and propinquity. *Sociometry, 15*(1/2), 135–140.
[42] Byrne, D. (1961). Interpersonal attraction and attitude similarity. *Journal of Abnormal and Social Psychology, 62*(3), 713–715.
[43] Segal, "Alphabet and attraction."

exactly. Larsons were friends with Lees, not with Abromowitzes or Xiernickes, even though they were separated by only a few yards.[44]

For another example, consider friendship formation among couples in apartment buildings. In this particular case, residents had been assigned to their apartments at random as vacancies opened up, and nearly all of them were strangers when they moved in. When asked to name their three closest friends in the entire housing project, 65% named friends in the same building. Among those living in the same building, the propinquity effect was in play: 41% of next-door neighbors indicated they were close friends, compared to only 22% who lived two doors apart and only 10% who lived on the opposite ends of the hall.

Certain aspects of architectural design make it more likely that some people will come into contact with each other more often than with others, even though the physical distance between them might be the same. This is known as **functional distance**. For example, more friendships are made with people on the same floor than on other floors, presumably because climbing stairs requires more effort than walking down the hall.

RECIPROCITY   According to the **reciprocity principle**, we feel obligated to return in kind what others have offered or given to us. This principle is one that all human societies subscribe to—it is a rule permeating exchanges of all kinds.[45] Feelings of indebtedness are so powerful that, if unresolved, they are carried into the future and are passed on to the next generation to repay. People feel upset and distressed if they have received a favor from another person and are prevented from returning it.

Madeleine Albright, former U.S. Secretary of State, knew the power of reciprocity. One of Albright's first public meetings with members of Congress was an appearance to testify before the House Appropriations Subcommittee chaired by Republican Harold Rogers. Albright needed to be on good terms with Rogers because his subcommittee's jurisdiction included the State Department's operating budget. For the occasion, Albright carried with her a big box, gift-wrapped in red, white, and blue ribbon. Inside was a book of photographs. Albright had learned that Rogers had lost all his papers and photographs in a fire at his home, a disaster that had erased many souvenirs of his career and compounded the grief caused by the recent death of his wife. Albright instructed embassies in countries he had visited to provide copies of photos taken and compiled them in an album she bestowed on him right there in the committee hearing room.[46]

Not surprisingly, people are aware of the powerful grip that reciprocity has on them. People often do not accept favors from others because they do not want to feel obligated. For example, suppose the counterparty provides us with a favor, gift, or service that we never invited and perhaps even attempted to avoid. Our attempts to return it have been denied, and we are left with the unwanted gift. Even under these circumstances, the reciprocity rule may operate. Thus, we should beware of the unsolicited gift from our real estate agent, the courtesy token from our business associate, and the free lunch from the consulting firm. When faced with these situations, acknowledge the favor and then, if we still feel indebted, we should return the favor on a similar level.

---

[44] Byrne, "Interpersonal attraction"; Kipnis, D. M. (1957). Interaction between members of bomber crews as a determinant of sociometric choice. *Human Relations, 10*(3), 263–270.

[45] Gouldner, A. W. (1960). The norm of reciprocity: A preliminary statement. *American Sociological Review, 25*(2), 161–178.

[46] Lippman, T. W. (2000, June 3). Madame Secretary. *National Journal, 32*(23), p. 1736.

Reciprocity is made even more difficult when parties place different value on aspects of a relationship. For example, trustors focus primarily on the risk associated with trusting someone, whereas trusted parties (those who are in a position to reciprocate) base their decisions on the level of economic benefits they have received.[47] Unfortunately, neither party is particularly sensitive to the factors that affect their counterpart's decision.

SCHMOOZING   Small talk often seems to serve no obvious function. The exchange of pleasantries about the weather or our favorite basketball team seems to be purposeless. However, **schmoozing** has a dramatic impact on our liking and trust of others. Even a short exchange can lead people to develop trust.[48] Wine and small talk at San Diego convention resulted in a collaboration of millions of research dollars between the Salk Institute for Biological Studies and the French pharmaceutical company Sanofi-Avenits. Sanofi agreed to sponsor huge research discovery grants in areas of interest to both companies, including stem cell research, in exchange for first rights to license intellectual property from discoveries, an educational and business partnership potentially worth hundreds of millions of dollars. And it all began over wine. When two Salk scientists were enjoying a drink at a reception hosted by the French consulate in San Diego, they introduced themselves to a Sanofi scientist and then began to talk research, A meeting was made for a Sanofi executive to tour the Salk facility, and a scientist travelling home to Spain was asked to stop in Paris to talk about the work of Salk. From there interests aligned to the point of the lucrative collaboration.[49]

FLATTERY   People like others who appreciate and admire them. People are more likely to trust others who like them and to respond more favorably when they are flattered. Even if people suspect the flatterer has another reason for flattering them, this behavior can still increase liking and trust.[50] The most strategic type of flattery, in terms of advancing one's own interest, is to flatter another person on a personally important dimension about which he or she feels somewhat insecure.[51] John Wakeham, previous chief whip for British Prime Minister Margaret Thatcher, said about Westminster politics, "I was absolutely fascinated by how Westminster actually works…the smoke-filled rooms, the nods and the winks. As a businessman, I found it more comprehensible than most politicians do. One thing I learnt as chief whip was the infinite capacity of human beings to absorb flattery."[52]

MIMICRY AND MIRRORING   Strategic behavioral mimicry can facilitate the discovery of integrative outcomes. Specifically, negotiators who mimic the mannerisms of their opponents secure better individual outcomes and greater joint gains, compared to negotiators who do not mimic.[53] Negotiators who mimic the mannerisms of the counterparty build trust. More generally,

---

[47] Malhotra, D. (2004). Trust and reciprocity decision: The differing perspectives of trustors and trusted parties. *Organizational Behavior and Human Decision Processes, 94*(2), 61–73.

[48] Morris, M., Nadler, J., Kurtzberg, T., & Thompson, L. (2002). Schmooze or lose: Social friction and lubrication in e-mail negotiations. *Group Dynamics: Theory, Research, and Practice, 6*(1), 89–100.

[49] Somers, T. (2009, March 27). Salk to join forces with drug firm from Paris. *The San Diego Union Tribune,* p. C1.

[50] Jones, E. E., Stires, L. K., Shaver, K. G., & Harris, V. A. (1968). Evaluation of an ingratiator by target persons and bystanders. *Journal of Personality, 36*(3), 349–385.

[51] Ibid.

[52] Perkins, A. (2000, January 15). John Wakeham, Lord fixit. *The Guardian,* p. 6.

[53] Maddux, W. W., Mullen, E., & Galinsky, A.D. (2008). Chameleons bake bigger pies and take bigger pieces: Strategic behavioral mimicry facilitates negotiation outcomes. *Journal of Experimental Social Psychology, 44*(2), 461–468.

parties whose trust in one another is equal or congruent have a special advantage in negotiations. Indeed trust congruence predicts the integrativeness of negotiated outcomes.[54]

SELF-DISCLOSURE   Sharing information about oneself with another person makes oneself vulnerable because the self-disclosing negotiator could potentially be exploited. Self-disclosure also explicitly invites the other person to reciprocate the disclosure, thereby increasing trust.

What Leads to Mistrust?

Distrust involves having negative expectations about another person's motives; suspicion involves ambiguity about another person's motives. Paradoxically, **suspicion** can actually enhance integrative outcomes by generating information search. In one investigation, dyads in which one person was suspicious reached more integrative agreements than when neither party was suspicious or both were suspicious.[55]

One of the biggest threats to trust in a relationship is a **breach** or **defection**. A breach occurs when one or both people violate the trust that has been built between them. For example, on March 19, 2003, U.S. President George W. Bush issued orders to begin "striking selected targets of military importance to undermine Saddam Hussein's ability to wage war." According to the United States, Saddam Hussein had engaged in a breach of trust by placing "Iraqi troops and equipment in civilian areas, attempting to use innocent men and women as shields for his own military," and demonstrating disregard for "conventions of war [and] rules of morality."[56]

MISCOMMUNICATION   In some cases, a real breach of trust does not occur but a miscommunication occurs that causes one or more parties to interpret it as such. Miscommunication is more likely when parties are not in regular contact, especially when they have little face-to-face contact.

DISPOSITIONAL ATTRIBUTIONS   Negotiators often make dispositional, as opposed to situational, attributions for the questionable behavior of the other party, which can threaten trust.[57] A **dispositional attribution** is one that calls into question another person's character and intentions by citing them as the cause of a behavior or incident (e.g., arrogance, greed, etc.). In contrast, a situational attribution cites one or more situational factors as the cause of a behavior or incident (e.g., a traffic jam, the faulty mail-delivery system, etc.). Assigning dispositional attributions to opponents' behaviors can threaten the trust between negotiators. It is much more difficult for people to respond to a dispositional attribution than a situational one. For example, consider how people interpret ambiguous and slightly negative social interactions (i.e., when a person you know does not acknowledge you when you walk past). The

---

[54] Tomlinson, E. C., Dineen, B. R., & Lewicki, R. J. (2009). Trust congruence among integrative negotiators as a predictor of joint-behavioral outcomes. *International Journal of Conflict Management, 20*(2), 173–187.

[55] Sinaceur, M. (2010). Suspending judgment to create value: Suspicion and trust in negotiation. *Journal of Experimental Social Psychology, 46*(3), 543–550.

[56] Bush declares war: U.S. President George W. Bush has announced that war against Iraq has begun (2003, March 19). CNN.com

[57] Morris, M. W., Larrick, R. P., & Su, S. K. (1999). Misperceiving negotiation counterparts: When situationally determined bargaining behaviors are attributed to personality traits. *Journal of Personality and Social Psychology, 77*(1), 52–67.

power or status differential is significant in interpreting these situations. The high-power person who does not acknowledge a colleague usually reported having a busy day or, more often, not even being aware of the other person. In contrast, the low-power person was often extremely paranoid and upset, believing that the high-power person was attempting to ostracize or punish them.[58] Thus, the low-power person pieces together a dispositional attribution for what is really a situational cause.

FOCUSING ON THE "BAD APPLE"   In a team or group, one person may have a reputation for being less trustworthy, tougher, or less easy to work with than other members of the group. We call this person the "bad apple," and bad apples can stand out. Unfortunately, the bad apple can spoil the bunch. For example, in simulated negotiations between labor and management groups, negotiators were significantly less likely to trust the group as a whole than any individual in the group.[59] It seems the "bad apple" in the group called the entire group's trustworthiness into question.

Repairing Broken Trust

When trust has been broken, it is often in both parties' interests to attempt to repair the trust because broken relationships are often costly in terms of the emotions involved and the opportunities lost. Trust that is harmed by untrustworthy behavior can be effectively restored when people observe a consistent series of trustworthy actions. However, trust harmed by the same untrustworthy actions and deception never fully recovers, even when the victim receives a promise and an apology and observes a consistent series of trustworthy actions.[60] Some people are quick to forgive after a trust violation, but others never trust again. A key characteristic that moderates the recovery of trust are beliefs about moral character. People who believe that moral character can change over time are more likely to trust after an apology, but people who don't believe in such change don't trust again.[61]

We outline a process for repairing broken trust. (See Exhibit 6-6 for a summary.)

STEP 1: ARRANGE A PERSONAL MEETING   When trust has been violated, one person (party) either directly or indirectly accuses the other (target) of doing something that was unfair. The target should suggest a face-to-face meeting with the party as quickly as possible. Indeed, verbal explanations are more effective than written explanations.[62]

STEP 2: PUT THE FOCUS ON THE RELATIONSHIP   Instead of launching into discussions of who is right or who is wrong, the focus should be put on what both people care about: the relationship. Often, parties will readily agree the relationship is worth saving. For New

---

[58] Kramer, R. M., & Wei, J. (1999). Social uncertainty and the problem of trust in social groups: The social self in doubt. In T. R. Tyler, R. M. Kramer, & O. P. John (Eds.), *The psychology of the social self: Applied social research* (pp. 145–168). Mahwah, NJ: Erlbaum.

[59] Naquin, C. (1999). Trust and distrust in group negotiations. Unpublished dissertation, Kellogg Graduate School of Management, Northwestern University, Evanston, IL.

[60] Schweitzer, M. E., Hershey, J. C., & Bradlow, E. T. (2006). Promises and lies: Restoring violated trust. *Organizational Behavior and Human Decision Processes, 101*(1), 1–19.

[61] Haselhuhn, M. P., Schweitzer, M. E., & Wood, A. M. (2010). How implicit beliefs influence trust recovery. *Psychological Science, 21*(5), 645–648.

[62] Shapiro, D. L., Buttner, E. H., & Barry, B. (1994). Explanations: What factors enhance their perceived adequacy? *Organizational Behavior and Human Decision Processes, 58*(3), 346–368.

EXHIBIT 6-6

Steps Toward Repairing Broken Trust

Step 1:	Arrange a personal meeting.	**Step 6:**	Ask for clarifying information.
Step 2:	Put the focus on the relationship.	**Step 7:**	Test your understanding.
		Step 8:	Formulate a plan.
Step 3:	Apologize.	**Step 9:**	Think about ways to prevent a future problem.
Step 4:	Let them vent.		
Step 5:	Do not get defensive.	**Step 10:**	Do a relationship checkup.

England Patriots owner Robert Kraft, winning Super Bowls is not just a business; the personal relationships he forges with his players are very important. Kraft has said of his star quarterback, Tom Brady: "We have a very special relationship. He's like a real son." While Brady and Kraft were negotiating for Brady's new deal, Brady slammed his Audi into a minivan. Although Brady was not hurt, Kraft realized that he could have lost Brady and their long-standing personal and professional relationship. Kraft reacted to the near miss by immediately working with Brady and his agent and coming to an agreement on a new deal of $72 million over four years. Kraft explained that in all cases "building bridges and doing the right thing is what I try to do."[63]

STEP 3: APOLOGIZE The expression of remorse following a wrongful act can mitigate punishment. But resist the urge to immediately blurt out an apology: Apologies offered later in a conflict are more impactful and effective than those offered immediately.[64] Later apologies are more effective because the "victim" has had an opportunity for self-expression and feels more understood. If the target does not feel at fault, then he or she should apologize in a way that takes ownership for his or her actions or behavior, yet does not necessarily accept the party's version of the violator's intentions. For example, a target might tell a party "I am very sorry that I did not consult you before preparing the report." By saying this, the target does not agree with the party's accusation that the violator attempted to take more credit for the report; rather, the target only identifies the action as being hurtful for the victim. Indeed, when companies acknowledge they have committed acts that threaten their legitimacy (e.g., newspaper claims of illegal conduct), they are more successful in blunting criticism when they point to external, mitigating circumstances (e.g., company norms, budgetary problems, etc.).[65]

---

[63] Cohan, W. D. (2010, November 3). Football's true patriot. *CNN Money*. Cnnmoney.com

[64] Frantz, C. M., & Bennison, C. (2005). Better late than early: The influence of timing on apology effectiveness. *Journal of Experimental Social Psychology, 41*(2), 201–207.

[65] Elsbach, K. D. (1994). Managing organizational legitimacy in the California cattle industry: The construction and effectiveness of verbal accounts. *Administrative Science Quarterly, 39*(1), 57–88; Bies, R. J., Shapiro, D. L., & Cummings, L. L. (1988). Causal accounts and managing organizational conflict: Is it enough to say it's not my fault? *Communication Research, 15*(4), 381–399.

STEP 4: LET THEM VENT It is important for people to express their anger, rage, disappointment, and feelings of betrayal over an event. Merely talking about negative events can actually be part of the cure.[66] Expressing disappointment often helps people take a significant step in the healing process.[67]

STEP 5: DO NOT GET DEFENSIVE Do not behave defensively, no matter how misinformed or wrong you believe the other party is. It is appropriate to tell the other person you view the situation differently and to point out that the situation can be viewed in many ways. Only after the party has had an opportunity to vent and explain his or her perspective should the violator attempt to tell the party, in clear and simple terms, what his or her intentions were. For example, a target might say, "My intention was to submit the report and not bother too many people with unnecessary requests to edit it."

STEP 6: ASK FOR CLARIFYING INFORMATION Targets should invite the party to provide clarifying information in a nondefensive fashion. For example, a target might say "Am I wrong in thinking you did not ask to be listed on the report?" or "Did you receive the draft copy I sent last week?"

STEP 7: TEST YOUR UNDERSTANDING If a person feels understood, the chances for rebuilding trust are greatly increased. It is helpful if one party can truly empathize with the other's perspective (e.g., "I can understand why you felt out of the loop. I have felt that way before, too."). A negotiator's ability to understand emotion is directly related to how satisfied the other party feels, independent of the monetary value of the outcome.[68]

STEP 8: FORMULATE A PLAN A major stumbling block in the trust rebuilding process is that parties have different ideas about what is fair. The egocentric bias once again rears its ugly head with most harmdoers perceiving themselves as more beneficent than the harmed. However, the mere fact of asking the harmed what he or she needs can go a long way toward rebuilding trust. In an empirical investigation of breaches of trust, harmdoers who asked "What can I do?" were more successful in rebuilding cooperation than those who did not ask or asked "What will it take?"[69] Penance is critical to trust in mixed-motive relationships.[70] Aggravating a counterparty after a breach by making offers of penance that do not seem sincere may further antagonize. In contrast, volunteering to do penance, even in small amounts, is particularly effective.

The speed and amount of "trust recovery" are significantly moderated by the promises that a person makes.[71] No one should underestimate the power of the spoken word, especially when it contains an apology. For example, verbal explanation can dramatically dampen

---

[66] Pennebaker, J. W., Hughes, C. F., & O'Heeron, R. C. (1987). The psychophysiology of confession: Linking inhibitory and psychosomatic processes. *Journal of Personality and Social Psychology, 52*(4), 781–793.

[67] Lind, E. A., & Tyler, T. R. (1988). *The social psychology of procedural justice.* New York: Plenum.

[68] Mueller, J. S., & Curhan, J. R. (2006). Emotional intelligence and counterpart mood induction in a negotiation. *International Journal of Conflict Management, 17*(2), 110–128.

[69] Bottom, W. P., Gibson, K. S., Daniels, S. E., & Murnighan, J. K. (2002). When talk is not cheap: Substantive penance and expressions of intent in rebuilding cooperation, *Organization Science, 13*(5), 497–513.

[70] Ibid.

[71] Schweitzer, Hershey, & Bradlow, "Promises and lies."

people's negative reactions to aversive behavior.[72] However, when it comes to truly rebuilding cooperation, the power of the deed exceeds the power of the spoken word. "Substantive amends have significantly more positive effects than explanations alone [on rebuilding cooperation]."[73]

STEP 9: THINK ABOUT WAYS TO PREVENT A FUTURE PROBLEM   Do not just try to remedy the past; rather, think about a way to make sure this problem, and any others like it, does not occur in the future.

STEP 10: DO A RELATIONSHIP CHECKUP   It is often wise to pull out your planners and decide upon a lunch or coffee meeting in a month or so to discuss how each party is feeling about the situation and occurrences since the breach of trust occurred. It is also helpful to schedule this date during the first meeting because it may seem awkward to bring it up after this time. This step ensures that parties will have a reason to meet and an opportunity to talk things through at a later date.

REPUTATION

One thing a negotiator definitely needs to protect is his or her reputation. According to Glick and Croson, you don't have to be a famous real estate tycoon for others to have an impression of you.[74] Managers' reputations are built fairly quickly in negotiation communities.[75] The reputations people gain affect how others deal with them. As a case in point, they describe the reputation held by Donald Trump:

> Real estate developer Donald Trump has a well-publicized reputation as a hard-line negotiator. In an article describing Trump's negotiations with the Taj Mahal Casino Resort's bondholders, Trump's advisors tell how after a deal is agreed upon, he always comes back requesting something more. Well-informed counterparts, familiar with his reputation, are prepared for this tactic and anticipate it in deciding how many concessions to make during the pre-agreement stage. Similarly, Trump has a reputation for storming out of negotiations in the middle of talks. An anonymous participant in the bondholders negotiation above said, "You know Donald's going to get up and leave, you just don't know when."[76]

Glick and Croson cite Silicon Valley as an example of a negotiation community, where an active technology trade press helps generate a rich flow of information regarding reputations. Because venture capitalists co-invest with various firms, they share information. Moreover, because time is money, you might not even get on a calendar unless your reputation is good. Our impressions of others are formed quickly and immediately, sometimes within the first

[72] Bottom, Gibson, Daniels, & Murnighan, "When talk is not cheap."
[73] Bottom, Gibson, Daniels, & Murnighan, "When talk is not cheap," p. 497.
[74] Glick, S., & Croson, R. (2001). Reputations in negotiation. In S. J. Hoch, H. C. Kunreuther & E. Gunther (Eds.), *Wharton on making decisions* (pp. 177–186). New York: Wiley.
[75] Ibid.
[76] Glick & Croson, "Reputations in negotiation," p. 178.

few minutes of meeting someone, because the judgments we make about people are often automatic.[77]

Reputations are often more extreme and polarized than the person they represent; they can be summed up by four words: **judgmental**, **consistent**, **immediate**, and **inferential**. The reputations assigned to others tend to be highly evaluative, meaning that they are either "good" or "bad."[78] Furthermore, the reputations we assign to others are highly internally consistent. Once we decide that someone is trustworthy, other qualities about this person are perceived as consistent with this favorable impression. This tendency gives rise to the **halo effect**, which is the propensity to believe that people we trust and like are also intelligent and capable.

Of course, the halo effect can work in the opposite direction. The **forked-tail effect** means that once we form a negative impression of someone, we tend to view everything else about them in a negative fashion. For this reason, it is difficult to recover from making a bad impression.

Reputations are based on a combination of firsthand and secondhand information.[79] Firsthand information is based on our direct experience with someone. Secondhand information is based on what we hear about someone else's experience with someone.

Glick and Croson undertook an investigation of the reputations earned by 105 students enrolled in a class.[80] They rated one another, on the basis of firsthand experience, from the least cooperative to the most cooperative:

- *Liar-manipulator* (will do anything for advantage)
- *Tough but honest* (very tough and makes few concessions but will not lie)
- *Nice and reasonable* (makes concessions)
- *Cream puff* (makes concessions and is conciliatory regardless of what the other does)

The major finding from their multiweek investigation was that people act much tougher when dealing with someone who has the reputation of being a liar (61% reported using distributive, pie-slicing tactics with these people). Against tough negotiators, this behavior dropped to 49%, and integrative tactics (pie-expanding tactics) were used 35% of the time. Against nice negotiators, only 30% used distributive tactics and 64% used integrative tactics. Against cream puffs, 40% used distributive tactics, and only 27% used integrative tactics. People use tough or manipulative tactics in a defensive fashion with liars and tough negotiators, and they use them in an opportunistic fashion with cream puffs.

Repairing a tarnished reputation is a lot like attempting to build trust. It is important to act in a trustworthy fashion—not just talk in a trustworthy fashion.

RELATIONSHIPS IN NEGOTIATION

Relationships influence not only the process of how people negotiate but also their choice of an interaction partner.[81] Negotiators who reach impasse find themselves getting caught in "distributive spirals" in which they interpret their performance as unsuccessful, experience

---

[77] Bargh, J. A., Lombardi, W. J., & Higgins, E. T. (1988). Automaticity of chronically accessible constructs in person-situation effects on person perception: It's just a matter of time. *Journal of Personality and Social Psychology, 55*(4), 599–605.

[78] Osgood, C. E., Suci, G. J., & Tannenbaum, P. H. (1957). *The measurement of meaning.* Urbana: University of Illinois Press.

[79] Glick & Croson, "Reputations in negotiation."

[80] Ibid.

[81] McGinn, K. L. (2006). Relationships and negotiations in context. In L. Thompson (Ed.), *Negotiation theory and research: Frontiers of social psychology* (pp. 129–144). New York: Psychology Press.

negative emotions, and develop negative perceptions of their negotiation counterparts and the entire negotiation process.[82] Moreover, negotiators who reach an impasse in a prior negotiation are more likely to do the same in their next negotiation or to reach low-value (lose-lose) deals compared to negotiators who were successful in reaching agreement (i.e., reaching a level 1 agreement).[83] Moreover, this effect holds true even when the negotiator is dealing with a different person. Thus, if a negotiator has "baggage" from the past, it affects his or her ability to go forward. Incidental emotions from the past (e.g., anger stemming from an argument with a spouse) can influence trust even more dramatically in an unrelated setting (e.g., the likelihood of trusting a coworker).[84] In short, anger about anything—even in our past with another person—makes us less likely to trust anyone else in the future.

People often feel better about pie-slicing and are in a better position to expand the pie when they have a good relationship and trust one another. For example, high concern for oneself and the other party is most likely to lead to integrative (win-win) outcomes.[85] Indeed, soldiers experiencing high concern for the needs of their Iraqi counterparts engaged in more problem-solving behavior, had greater trust, and reached more mutually satisfying agreements when their roles were clear, rather than ambiguous.[86] Levels of cooperation decrease as social distance increases between people.[87] When reaching agreement is important, negotiators who have a relationship are more likely to reach a win-win agreement than negotiators who do not have a relationship.[88]

People negotiate with spouses, friends, and neighbors. People also negotiate on a regular basis with others in their personal life who do not necessarily fall into the categories of "friends" or "family" (e.g., homeowners negotiating with contractors, parents negotiating with other parents concerning carpool arrangements, parents negotiating with nannies concerning child care, etc.). In addition to negotiating in our personal lives, we also negotiate in our business lives, with colleagues, supervisors, and staff members. In some cases, our personal life is intermingled with our business life in relationships we cannot easily classify as strictly personal or strictly business. We refer to this type of relationship as an "embedded" relationship.[89] We will expose the relevant implicit norms and rules that lurk under each of these three types of relationships and their implications for trust in negotiations. The behavior of people in relationships is guided by shared sets of rules.[90]

---

[82] O'Connor, K. M., Arnold, J. A. & Burris, E. R. (2005). Negotiators' bargaining histories and their effects on future negotiation performance. *Journal of Applied Psychology, 90*(2), 350–362.

[83] Ibid.

[84] Dunn, J. R., & Schweitzer, M. E. (2005). Feeling and believing: The influence of emotion on trust. *Journal of Personality and Social Psychology, 88*(5), 736–748.

[85] Pruitt, D. G., & Carnevale, P. J. (1993). *Negotiation in social conflict.* Pacific Grove, CA: Brooks-Cole; Rubin, J. Z., Pruitt, D. G., & Kim, S. H. (1994). *Social conflict: Escalation, stalemate and settlement.* New York: McGraw-Hill.

[86] Nobel, O. B., Campbell, D., Hannah, S. T., & Wortinger, B. (2010). Soldiers' negotiations in combat areas: The effects of role clarity and concern for members of the local population. *International Journal of Conflict Management, 21*(2), 202–227.

[87] Buchan, N. R., Croson, R. T. A., & Dawes, R. M. (2002). Swift neighbors and persistent strangers: A cross-cultural investigation of trust and reciprocity in social exchange. *American Journal of Sociology, 108*(1), 168–206.

[88] Kray, L. J., Thompson, L., & Lind, E. A. (2005). It's a bet! A problem solving approach promotes the construction of contingent agreements. *Personality and Social Psychology Bulletin, 31*(8), 1039–1051.

[89] Uzzi, B. (1997). Social structure and competition in interfirm networks: The paradox of embeddedness. *Administrative Science Quarterly, 42,* 35–67.

[90] Argyle, M., & Henderson, M. (1984). The rules of relationships. In S. Duck & D. Perlman (Eds.), *Understanding personal relationships: An interdisciplinary approach.* Beverly Hills, CA: Sage; Clark, M., & Mills, J. (1979). Interpersonal attraction in exchange and communal relationships. *Journal of Personality and Social Psychology, 37,* 12–24.

Negotiating with Friends

We negotiate with our friends all the time. For example, we make childcare arrangements with neighbors, plan parties and vacations together, and even purchase jointly shared equipment together (e.g., snowblowers). Friends don't call these activities "negotiations"; rather, they say they are "working things out," "making plans," "figuring things out," and so on. However, friends and family negotiations may be problematic. Consider how James and Lloyd Maritz decided to negotiate their differences about how to manage their business. In 1950, they decided to cut the company in half and, following Solomon's rule, one brother did the dividing and the other brother got to choose first.[91]

McGinn and Keros examined negotiations among strangers and friends and found that one of three patterns emerges early on:[92]

- *Opening up*   (complete and mutual honesty)
- *Working together*   (cooperative problem solving)
- *Haggling*   (competitive attempt to get the best possible deal for oneself)

These negotiators use one of three dynamic processes: trust-testing, process clarification, and emotional punctuation when they have difficulty moving through the interaction. When strangers interact, they often begin in haggling mode. In contrast, friends begin to open up almost immediately.

WHY PEOPLE ARE UNCOMFORTABLE NEGOTIATING WITH FRIENDS   People often feel uncomfortable negotiating with friends.[93] "Friendship dictates that we should be concerned with fairness and the other person's welfare, while negotiations dictate that we should get a good deal for ourselves."[94] These two dictates are in conflict with one another. Most friendships are built on **communal norms**, which mandate that we should take care of people we love, respond to their needs, and not "keep track" of who has put in what.[95] Thus, the communal norm prescribes that we should be sensitive to the needs of people we love or like and attempt to meet those needs, rather than trying to maximize our own interests. The opposite of communal norms are **exchange norms**, which state that people should keep track of who has invested in a relationship and be compensated based on their inputs. Thus, people need to have a mental accounting system that records who has done what.

FRIENDS ARE LESS COMPETITIVE WITH EACH OTHER   Friends are less competitive with each other than they are with strangers.[96] Friends exchange more information, make more concessions, make fewer demands, and are more generous with one another.[97] Consequently, negotiators in a relationship are often unable to profitably exploit opportunities to create value. The oft-observed pattern in which people in close relationships reach monetarily inefficient outcomes but increase

[91] Bailey, J. (2002, August 12). A CEO's legacy: Sons wage battle over family firm. *Wall Street Journal,* p. A1.

[92] McGinn, K. L., & Keros, A. T. (2002). Improvisation and the logic of exchange in socially embedded transactions. *Administrative Science Quarterly, 47,* 442–473.

[93] Kurtzberg, T., & Medvec, V. H. (1999). Can we negotiate and still be friends? *Negotiation Journal, 15*(4), 355–362.

[94] Kurtzberg, & Medvec, "Can we negotiate and still be friends?" p. 356.

[95] Clark & Mills, "Interpersonal attraction."

[96] Valley, K. L., Neale, M. A., & Mannix, E. A. (1995). Friends, lovers, colleagues, strangers: The effects of relationships on the process and outcome of negotiations. In R. Bies, R. Lewich, & B. Sheppard (Eds.), Research in negotiation in organizations, *5,* 65–94.

[97] Mandel, D. R. (2006). Economic transactions among friends. *Journal of Conflict Resolution, 50*(4), 584–606.

their relational satisfaction is known as the "O. Henry Effect."[98] In O. Henry's story "The Gift of the Magi," the main characters—husband and wife—are madly in love with each other but engage in an inefficient exchange in a desperate attempt to provide each other with a Christmas gift. When relationship partners sacrifice instrumental value, they actually increase their relational satisfaction.

FRIENDS MAY NOT REACH LEVEL 3 INTEGRATIVE AGREEMENTS   Friends and lovers are too willing to compromise.[99] Friends are reluctant to engage in the firm flexibility maxim that is often required to reach level 3 integrative agreements. In short, friends believe that reaching an impasse may permanently damage their relationship, so they settle quickly. Yet, as we have seen in our discussion of integrative agreements in Chapter 4, it is important to focus on differences of interest and maintain high aspirations to reach level 3 integrative outcomes. When people compromise quickly because they want to avoid conflict and minimize the threat of impasse, they are likely to leave value on the table. In short, they satisfice rather than optimize. Too much focus on the relationship can lead to satisficing, rather than optimizing.[100] As can be seen in Exhibit 6-7, when both negotiators have a high relational focus, there is a tendency to satisfice. When one negotiator has a high relationship focus and the other does not, there is distancing; when both are low in relationship focus, there is trading; it is only when both negotiators are moderately focused on the relationship that integrating occurs.

FRIENDSHIP AND THE MISMANAGEMENT OF AGREEMENT   Imagine piling into a steamy car on a 104-degree west Texas afternoon, tempted by the best ice cream in Texas at the other end of a long 50 sun-baked miles across a flat and dust-blown landscape. Your group seems enthusiastic, and says so even though at home it is tolerable with fans, cold drinks, and games. The best ice cream on a hot day: Who wouldn't go for that?! But after the sun-baked trip to the ice cream shoppe in Abilene, the flavors on hand are bland—vanilla, an uninspiring chocolate—and neither as good as remembered. Silence descends as the ice cream is eaten. Hours later, after a return trip across the steamy semi-desert, you arrive back home. No one says anything until you break the silence. "Great trip, right?" you say. "Honestly, no," a friend pipes up, adding that she felt pressured into the trip. "What?!" says another friend. "I went along with it because it seemed like everyone else wanted to go. Who'd want to go 50 miles for ice cream in *that* heat?" In other words, three people had taken a 100-mile round trip for ice cream on a 104-degree day, even though they did not want to do so, because they thought that's what the other people in the group wanted to do. The story of the *Road to Abilene* epitomizes the notion that among family and friends, conflict is to be avoided at all costs, even if it means a lose-lose outcome for all involved.[101] The need for friends to maintain the

---

[98] Curhan, J. R., Neale, M. A., Ross, L., & Rosencranz-Engelmann, J. (2008). Relational accommodation in negotiation: Effects of egalitarianism and gender on economic efficiency and relational capital. *Organizational Behavior and Human Decision Processes, 107*(2), 192–205.

[99] Fry, W. R., Firestone, I. J., & Williams, D. L. (1983). Negotiation process and outcome of stranger dyads and dating couples: Do lovers lose? *Basic and Applied Social Psychology, 4,* 1–16; Thompson, L., & DeHarpport, T. (1998). Relationships, good incompatibility, and communal orientation in negotiations. *Basic and Applied Social Psychology, 20*(1), 33–44.

[100] Gelfand, M. J., Major, V. S., Raver, J. L., Nishii, L. H., & O'Brien, K. (2006). Negotiating relationally: The dynamics of the relational self in negotiations. *Academy of Management Review, 31*(2), 427–451.

[101] Harvey, J. (1974). The Abilene Paradox: The management of agreement. *Organizational Dynamics, 3*(1), 63–80.

EXHIBIT 6-7

Relational Self-Construals (RSC) Dynamics in Negotiation

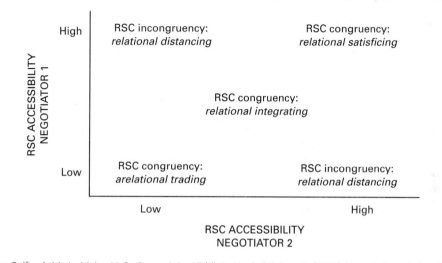

Source: Gelfand, M. J., Major, V. S., Raver, J. L., Nishii, L. H., & O'Brien, K. (2006) Negotiating relationally: The dynamics of the relational self in negotiations. *Academy of Management, 31*(2), 427–451.

illusion of agreement means that important differences in preferences, interests, and beliefs are often downplayed or buried. Paradoxically, it is precisely these kinds of differences that should surface in any negotiation to enable negotiators in personal relationships to fashion value-added trade-offs and develop contingency contracts. Somehow, friends and families need a way to make their differences known so they can capitalize on them in a win-win fashion.

IF WE HAVE TO NEGOTIATE, WE SHOULD DIVIDE IT DOWN THE MIDDLE   When it comes to dividing the pie, friends use an **equality rule** (thereby allocating equal shares to everyone involved), whereas strangers and business associates use an **equity rule**—otherwise known as a **merit-based rule**—in which those who have contributed more are expected to receive more.[102] Unfortunately, equality norms may promote compromise agreements, thereby inhibiting the discovery of integrative trade-offs. However, norms of equality are not blindly applied by people in close relationships. For example, friends who differ in their ability and effort in a joint task will favor the less able but more diligent partner in the allocation of resources.[103]

---

[102] Austin, W. (1980). Friendship and fairness: Effects of type of relationship and task performance on choice of distribution rules. *Personality and Social Psychology Bulletin, 6,* 402–408.

[103] Lamm, H., & Kayser, E. (1978). An analysis of negotiation concerning the allocation of jointly produced profit or loss: The roles of justice norms, politeness, profit maximization, and tactics. *International Journal of Group Tensions, 8,* 64–80.

Similarly, people in communal relationships will meet others' needs, with no expectation of remuneration.[104] Equity, in which outcomes are allocated proportional to inputs, is a hallmark feature of the business world. For example, most of us do not expect to earn the same exact salary as our colleagues; we earn salaries based upon various contributions and inputs to the specific business situation. However, equity does not seem to have a legitimate role in personal relationships.

Negotiating with Businesspeople

In contrast to friendship negotiation, businesspeople are much more likely to use an exchange norm. Exchange norms are rooted in market pricing. **Market pricing** is a method by which everything is reduced to a single value or utility metric that allows for the comparison of many qualitatively and quantitatively diverse factors.[105] Market pricing allows people to negotiate by making references to ratios of this metric, such as percentage share in a business venture. Money is the prototypical medium of market pricing relationships. Capitalism is the ultimate expression of market pricing. In a true market pricing relationship, people will do virtually anything if offered enough money because "Everyone has his price." However, just because this approach is the predominant business mode, it does not mean people will follow it.

WE CHOOSE OUR FRIENDS, BUT NOT OUR COWORKERS   Basically, we (usually) like our friends, but we do not necessarily like the people with whom we do business. Yet this generalization does not excuse us from having to negotiate and deal with them. In fact, we often must deal with people we do not like and may regard to be offensive. For example, a woman might find herself negotiating with a male who is a blatant sexist. It is often difficult for people to separate their feelings about someone as a person from the business at hand. (See Exhibit 6-8 for an example of an uncomfortable business relationship.)

BUSINESS RELATIONSHIPS OFTEN HAVE STATUS AND RANK ISSUES ASSOCIATED WITH THEM   Most friendships are not hierarchical, meaning that people in friendships do not have different status and rank. In contrast, businesses are generally organized around rank and status—either explicitly (e.g., an organizational chart) or implicitly (e.g., salaries, number of supervisees, office space, etc.). In one investigation, an employment negotiation was simulated: When people believed themselves to be in an "egalitarian" (equal status) relationship, they were less likely to expand the pie but liked one another more. In contrast, when people believed themselves to be in a hierarchical relationship (in which one person had more authority), they were more likely to expand the pie but not feel as good about the relationship.[106] As we will see in Chapter 10, in some cultures, it is perfectly acceptable for members of different status and rank to meet each other at the bargaining table. However, in other cultures people find this uncomfortable and insulting.

SWIFT TRUST   Sometimes we need to build trust with people very rapidly, on the basis of little information, and, in many cases, with no expected meaningful future interaction. When design and innovation consultancy Bulldog Drummond worked with the American Eagle

---

[104] Clark & Mills, "Interpersonal attraction."
[105] Fiske, A. P. (1992). The four elementary forms of sociality: Framework for a unified theory of social relations. *Psychological Review, 99*(4), 689–723.
[106] Curhan, Neale, Ross, & Rosencranz-Engelmann, "Relational accommodation in negotiation."

EXHIBIT 6-8

Uncomfortable Business Relationships

Uncomfortable business relationships occur when a negotiation involves engaging in interactions that, in a personal context, would take on a different meaning and, thus, might be regarded as inappropriate. For example, consider two managers, a man and a woman, each married, who have late flights arriving in their destination city and very busy schedules, and nevertheless they need to negotiate. They agree to meet at a bar because it is the only location open late enough. However, when they arrive at the bar, the waitstaff treats them as a couple. The situation is embarrassing for the business associates because their relationship is viewed in a different way by those outside the business context than by those on the "inside." This perception has implications for the negotiation; for example, if the waitstaff presents the check to the man, it can potentially create an uncomfortable power dynamic between them. (We will discuss this further in Chapter 7.) Quite often, business opportunities are conducted in the context of social relationships. For this reason, it is difficult to form close relationships across gender lines if they are built through social activities such as playing golf, going to the theater, or meeting for dinner because these practices often have a different meaning between men and women than they do between persons of the same gender.

Source: Uzzi, B. (1997). Social structure and competition in interfirm networks: The paradox of embeddedness. *Administrative Science Quarterly, 42,* 35–67; Etzkowitz, H., Kemelgor, C., & Uzzi, B. (1999). *Social capital and career dynamics in hard science: Gender, networks, and advancement.* New York: Cambridge University Press.

Outfitters clothing company to quickly create their 77Kids brand, the company dedicated a standalone team to immerse itself in all details of the project. Despite having not worked together before, the team was able to integrate rapidly, learn to trust one another and dive into the project. They built a new successful business in 18 months.[107] The partnership between Bulldog Drummond and American Eagle Outfitters is an example of **swift trust**— the mechanism that allows people to build trust quickly.[108] Many new business relationships require that strangers come together and produce a product, service, or carry out some task and then immediately disband, perhaps never to see one another again. In contrast, our personal relationships are longer term; we have a past history with family and friends, and we expect to have future interactions with them. Business situations increasingly require swift trust, which is necessary among people who have a finite life span in a temporary system. The question is, how do we build trust with no past and no likely future? We deal with this issue in Chapter 11.

THE MYTH OF THE ONE-SHOT BUSINESS SITUATION In the business world, through its web of networked relationships, it is impossible not to experience the consequences of our

---

[107] Parr, S. (2010, December 7). 5 lessons big corporations can learn from startups. *Mashable.* Mashable.com
[108] Meyerson, D., Weick, K. E., & Kramer, R. M. (1996). Swift trust and temporary groups. In R. M. Kramer & T. R. Tyler (Eds.), *Trust in organizations: Frontiers of theory and research* (pp. 166–195). Thousand Oaks, CA: Sage.

interactions with others. Social networks mean that even though the particular people in a business interaction may never interact or see one another again, their companies will interact again, or others in their social network will become apprised of the interaction, which will, in turn, affect the nature of future business interactions. The one-shot business situation may be extinct.

When in Business with Friends and Family

When the Ricketts' family bought the Chicago Cubs baseball team in 2009, the franchise truly became a family operation, but one where the members of the family had distinct differences. Pete Ricketts lived in Omaha and left his post as COO of the family's stock brokerage to run as a Republican for U.S. Senate, running on a conservative family values platform where he was quoted as saying that "Nebraska values' include traditional marriage." That platform put him at odds with his only sister, Laura, who serves on the board of directors of LAMBDA Legal, a national gay and lesbian rights organization, which fought in court to overturn Nebraska's ban on same-sex marriage.[109] When friends and family do business, the relationship is more complex and is known as an **embedded relationship**. This relationship would seem to have several advantages, the most important of which is facilitating the nature of business exchange by initiating self-organizing governance arrangements that operate through expectations of trust and reciprocity, rather than expensive deterrence mechanisms.[110] Firms that embedded their bank exchanges in social attachments were more likely to have access to capital and received more favorable interest rates on loans.[111]

Another example of an embedded relationship was that between Magic Johnson (former Los Angeles Lakers' star basketball player) and Jerry Buss (the Lakers' owner). They socialized away from the basketball court and spent nearly every dinner hour together during home games. Formally, they were employer and employee: The employer would pay, and the employee would play. According to Magic Johnson, the two of them developed a relationship outside of their formal business because "he saw me as one of his kids."[112] Says Johnson, "That's why I've never negotiated with him.... We never had a negotiation. He said, 'I want to give you this.' I said, 'OK.' He said, 'I want you to coach this team.' I said, 'OK.' It's been like that. It's no contract, you just say, 'OK.' That's how we have it.' Buss calls Johnson his hero; Johnson calls Buss his surrogate father.

However, pitfalls to an embedded relationship can also happen. We describe some of them next.

THE EMOTIONAL POTENTIAL IS HIGHER   When business and friendship combine, the emotional potential can often be overwhelming, and interpersonal conflict can result. For example, if someone has a poor exchange with a neighbor that leaves the friendship in question, it is quite disturbing, but the person can at least travel to work knowing the situation is "contained." Similarly, a person may have a terrible day at work and still be able to go

---

[109] Spector, B. (2009, August 31). Cubs family owners' ideologies clash; Mets family owners may have to sell. *Family Business Magazine*. Familybusinessmagazine.com
[110] Uzzi, B. (1999). Embeddedness in the making of financial capital: How social relations and networks benefit firms seeking financing. *American Sociological Review, 64*(4), 481–505.
[111] Ibid.
[112] Howard-Cooper, S. (1996, April 23). The odd couple: From beginning, friendship between Buss, Johnson has transcended usual relationship between owner, player. *Los Angeles Times*, p. 1.

home that evening to take solace in friends and family. Somehow, the separation of work and friendship creates a "buffer zone" for the parties involved. However, when things go awry in an embedded relationship during the course of negotiation, all systems can potentially fail. Consider the Maritz Company, which suffered through three generations of feuding.[113] Before Bill Maritz passed away, he wrote at the end of his memoir, "I still find it virtually impossible to understand and accept the lack of respect and feeling my two sons, Peter and Flip, have shown me." Their mother, Phyllis Maritz said, "It would be my greatest hope to see the company sold and out of the family forever. Then perhaps the family could heal." Similarly, L'Oreal heiress Liliane Bettencourt—Europe's richest woman—and her daughter Francoise Bettencourt-Meyers feuded for several years over Liliane's purported mental frailty after she attempted to adopt the son of a friend to whom she had already given millions of dollars in art and gifts. Bettencourt-Meyers filed a criminal complaint against the son, and the eventual agreement led to an increased role in the company for Bettencourt's son-in-law, Jean Pierre Myers, who was elevated to chief executive.[114]

INTERNAL VALUE CONFLICT   Personal relationships are driven by people's need for acceptance, love, and identity, whereas business relationships are generally guided by a need for achievement and utilitarian goals. In embedded relationships, people often experience more internal value conflict because competence and liking are at battle with one another. For example, we may find someone to be a delightful friend, a wonderful and empathic listener, and a good person with whom to spend time; however, this person may be incompetent at the business task at hand. Conversely, the person who is more competent may be annoying to us. The question is, which of these factors do we respond to in the situation: competence or liking?

MYOPIA   We have seen that embedded relationships can often reduce the costs associated with surveillance. However, embedded relationships may create myopia if people are reluctant to move beyond their own networks. At the extreme, imagine a cliquish network in which people engage only in business matters with their friends. This interaction may eventually result in a myopic view of reality, if people within the network are biased in their perceptions and not connected to others who may have more or better information. These are **sticky ties**—relationships that emanate from ingrained habits of past social interaction.[115] Most people are reluctant to turn to new, untried partners for information, resources, and the variety of interactions that are required in organizations.

CONCLUSION

In negotiation, personal value, which includes goodwill, trust, and respect, is just as important as economic value. Establishing trust and building relationships are essential for effective negotiation. The three types of "trust" relationships discussed in this chapter include

---

[113] Bailey, "A CEO's legacy."

[114] Kroll, L. (2010, December 6). Europe's richest woman ends feud with daughter. *Forbes*. Blogs.forbes.com

[115] Valley, K. L., & Thompson, T. A. (1998). Sticky ties and bad attitudes: Relational and individual bases of resistance to change in organizational structure. In Kramer, R. M., & Neale, M. A. (Eds.), *Power and influence in organizations* (pp. 39–66). Thousand Oaks, CA: Sage.

deterrence-based trust (based on sanctions and monitoring), knowledge-based trust (based on predictability and information), and identification-based trust (based on true empathy). Trust-building and trust-repairing strategies include transforming personal conflict into task conflict, agreeing on a common goal, capitalizing on network connections, recognizing a shared problem, and focusing on the future. Psychological strategies that often engender trust include similarity, mere exposure, physical presence, reciprocity, schmoozing, flattery, and self-disclosure. And the three common types of relationships in negotiation are business only, friendship only, and embedded relationships that involve both.

CHAPTER 7

Power, Persuasion, and Ethics

Lenoir, a quiet town in western North Carolina, seemed an unlikely place for one of the world's leading high-tech companies. Lenoir had stumbled from the loss of more than 2,000 jobs because of the closure of seven furniture factories. Yet, Lenoir had just about everything that Google wanted: lots of inexpensive land, access to cheap electricity, huge and ideal warehouses, and excess water capacity for cooling off computers. By playing an aggressive real estate game, Google elicited a stream of promises from local and state officials, all frantic to lure a mighty tech company. During long months of negotiations, Google never failed to remind those officials that it could go elsewhere. In the course of negotiation, Lenoir agreed to a package of tax breaks, infrastructure upgrades, and other prospects valued at $212 million over 30 years, or more than $1 million for each of the 210 jobs Google hoped to create in Lenoir. Many people felt bullied by the tactics used by the out-of-town technology giant. "It's simply unconscionable from an ethics standpoint for this company to go in from this very unfair bargaining position," said Robert F. Orr, a former North Carolina Supreme Court justice. "These are business decisions by the smartest businesspeople in the world, and it's just exploiting a desperate town." "There were 18 or 20 drafts of contracts, a lot of ticky-tacky stuff," said T. J. Rohr, an attorney and member of Lenoir's city council (who voted against the final deal), "And a lot of the time it seemed like they were saying, 'It's our way or the highway.'" Ultimately, Google opened the facility and hired 200 new workers, many of them former furniture workers whose jobs had been outsourced to China and retrained at the local community college for jobs with Google.[1]

---

[1] Byrnes, N., & Cowan, C. (2007, July 23). The high cost of wooing Google. *Business Week, 4043,* 50–56; Langfitt, F. (2009, December 16). Laid-off furniture workers try to leap to Google. *National Public Radio.* Npr.org

The Google example suggests that negotiators often attempt to get as much of the bargaining zone as possible. Negotiators who have power are in position to claim the lion's share of the resources. The power and persuasion strategies in this chapter can be read from two vantage points. One way is to read it as the *holder* of power. The other way is as the *target* of someone's power. The *counterparty* is reading this or another book; therefore, every strategy and tactic in this chapter could (and probably will) be used against you by the counterparty. Thus, it is important to remember the "fraternal twin" model that we introduced in Chapter 1. At relevant points in this chapter, we present "defense strategies" that negotiators can use to deal with a source of power or a persuasion tactic employed by the other party during the course of negotiation.

YOUR BATNA IS YOUR MOST IMPORTANT SOURCE OF POWER IN NEGOTIATION

When negotiators have a great BATNA, they have a lot of power. For example, consider how Palm improved its bargaining power by creating a bidding war among several suitors, including Apple, Google, RIM (Research in Motion), HP, and Nokia, to buy their company. RIM originally outbid HP, before HP upped its offer. Whereas Google did not know that Apple was bidding, they did not make an official bid. With as many as 11 other buyers on the fringes, Palm could afford to wait for the best deal while the suitors scrambled to outdo one another and drive up the price. HP was the highest bidder and paid $1.2 billion.[2]

Unfortunately, most of the time, people do not have a great BATNA. For this reason, it is imperative that negotiators cultivate and improve their BATNAs prior to negotiating, by doing the following:

- *Keep your options open.*   Keep your options open even after you have come to the negotiation table because negotiations could break down for a variety of reasons at any point prior to mutual settlement. Consider how NBC kept its options open in negotiations with Bay Area TV station KRON in 2002.[3] For several years, KRON was the carrier of NBC programming in the Bay Area. However, in 2002 NBC looked at an alternative station, KNTV. Interestingly, it was KNTV owners who had been following the feud between NBC and KRON and saw an opportunity. Moreover, KNTV suggested that it pay NBC to make the switch to its station—an unusual form of reverse compensation.
- *Signal your BATNA, but do not reveal it.*   If the counterparty does not believe you actually have a BATNA, you should signal that you have options, without revealing their exact value. However, alluding to options you do not actually have is **misrepresentation**, which is unethical. It is not misrepresentation to signal to the other party that you have alternative courses of action (if you actually do). In the NBC–KRON negotiations, KRON mistakenly thought that NBC was bluffing about its alternative (KNTV). Thus, when NBC approached KRON—saying "This is the last chance you have, take it or leave it. Pay us $10 million

---

[2] Frommer, D. (2010, July 15). Apple tried to buy Palm before HP won the bidding war—and RIM completely blew the deal. *Business Insider.* Businessinsider.com
[3] Fost, D. (2002, January 13). How NBC, KRON deal fell apart/ Animosity, mistrust colored negotiations. *San Francisco Chronicle*, p. G1.

or no deal."—KRON responded by distributing a press release saying it was no longer an NBC affiliate. However, NBC was surprised and said, "We're not finished [negotiating]." Five days later, NBC struck a deal with KNTV.

• **Assess the other party's BATNA.**   Do not leave any stone unturned when attempting to assess the counterparty's BATNA. Start your research well before the negotiation begins. Do not wait until you get to the negotiation table. In the NBC example, KRON did not adequately assess NBC's BATNA. They assumed it was worse than it actually was and, thus, no deal was reached. Spend some time before negotiation assessing current data (if you have them), previous years' data, current market trends—anything you can get. Also, use multiple sources. Researching the other party's BATNA is time well spent. Negotiators who *think* about the counterparty's BATNA do better in terms of slicing the pie than those who don't.[4] For example, in the 2009 negotiations that eventually led to Disney buying Marvel for $4 billion and gaining the rights to thousands of new characters, Disney executives had good insight into Marvel's BATNA. In particular, Disney was aware that Marvel's financial clout had taken a hit and not fully recovered after the company fell into bankruptcy in 1997. Knowing that a deal would give Marvel much more financial muscle to make films at a time when credit was still tight, and give CEO Issac Perlmutter—who rescued the company from bankruptcy—a payday in the billions, Disney CFO Thomas Staggs set an aggressive target. Holding firm, Disney and Marvel argued over the stock price of the deal in a final negotiating session that stretched out over 24 hours. Ultimately, Disney got their price because they leveraged the information about Marvel's unattractive BATNA.[5]

SOURCES OF POWER

In addition to a negotiator's BATNA, another source of power is the contribution a negotiator makes to a negotiation.[6] When you bring resources to a negotiation and the other party puts a high value on those resources, your contribution is great. When the bargaining zone is small, BATNAs exert a stronger effect on resource allocation than do contributions; however when the bargaining zone is large, contributions exert a stronger effect than do BATNAs.[7]

ANALYZING YOUR POWER

Power in a negotiation can be analyzed in terms of four vantage points: potential power, perceived power, power tactics, and realized power.[8] A negotiator's **potential power** is the underlying capacity of the negotiator to obtain benefits from an agreement.[9] It is a function of the counterparty's dependence on you. How much someone depends on you in a negotiation is based

[4] Galinsky, A., & Mussweiler, T. (2001). First offers as anchors: The role of perspective-taking and negotiator focus. *Journal of Personality and Social Psychology, 81*(4), 657–669.
[5] Garrett, D. (2010, December 9). Disney-marvel: Anatomy of a deal. *Variety*. Variety.com
[6] Kim, P. H., & Fragale, A. R.(2005). Choosing the path to bargaining power: An empirical comparison of BATNAs and contributions in negotiation. *Journal of Applied Psychology, 90*(2), 373–381.
[7] Ibid.
[8] Kim, P. H., Pinkley, R. L., & Fragale, A. R. (2005). Power dynamics in negotiation. *Academy of Management Review, 30*(4), 799–822.
[9] Ibid.

upon how much he or she values the resources you provide and the value of the alternatives to negotiating with you. **Perceived power** is a negotiator's assessment of each party's potential power, which may or may not square with reality. Whereas a negotiator's alternatives affect the distribution of outcomes, perceived power, as well as actual alternatives, affect the integrativeness of outcomes.[10] **Power tactics** comprise what's commonly studied in negotiation behavior and refer to the behaviors designed to use or change the power relationship. **Realized power** is the extent to which negotiators claim benefits from an interaction.

PERSUASION TACTICS

You do not necessarily have to have power to be persuasive. We identify techniques negotiators can use to induce attitude and behavior change in their opponents. However, we need to caution negotiators that power also can be used against them as well.

Two desires are especially important in negotiation: the need to be liked and approved of, and the need to be rational and accurate. Savvy negotiators prey upon people's need to be approved of and respected by others and their need to believe they are rational and logical. Next, we identify two primary routes to persuasion that tap into these two needs.

Two Routes to Persuasion

The two routes to persuasion roughly correspond to our distinction between the mind and heart of the negotiator.[11] The first route is called the **central route** to persuasion. It is direct, mindful, and information-based. Here, activities such as evaluating the strength or rationality of the counterparty's argument and deciding whether its content agrees or disagrees with a negotiator's beliefs tend to occur. When the counterparty's messages are processed via this central route, persuasion will occur to the extent that the arguments presented are convincing and the facts marshaled on their behalf are strong. The central route is ideal when dealing with analytical people who focus on information, facts, and data.

In contrast to the central route, little cognitive or mindful work is performed when attempting to persuade someone via the **peripheral route**. Rather, persuasion, when it occurs, involves a seemingly automatic response to subtle cues. A person's prestige, credibility, or likeability determine whether they will be successful when navigating the peripheral route. Persuasion is more likely to occur through the peripheral route when the negotiator is distracted or highly emotionally involved in the situation.

In the next sections, we deal with tactics that can be used via the central route and via the peripheral route. Again, we caution negotiators that all of these tactics can and probably will be used against them at some time in their negotiation career. Therefore, when describing each of these tactics, we indicate a defense strategy a negotiator can use if he or she suspects a particular tactic is being used against him or her.

Central Route Persuasion Tactics

Central route persuasion tactics involve rational and deliberate strategies that can be used to organize the content and flow of information during a negotiation.

---

[10] Wolfe, R. J., & McGinn, K. L. (2005). Perceived relative power and its influence on negotiations. *Group Decision and Negotiation, 14*(1), 3–20.

[11] Chaiken, S., Wood, W., & Eagly, A. H. (1996). Principles of persuasion. In E. T. Higgins & A. W. Kruglanski (Eds.), *Social psychology: Handbook of basic principles* (pp. 702–742). New York: Guilford Press.

THE POWER OF AGENDA   In a negotiation, players explicitly or implicitly follow an agenda. Most commonly, negotiators discuss the issues in a one-by-one, "laundry list" fashion. Negotiations often involve a discussion of who will control the agenda. Consider the agenda battle concerning Internet neutrality. Internet neutrality, or the premise that all data on the Web should be treated equally, is a heated issue pitting those who want the Federal Communications Commission to protect neutrality (the idea that any website one visits is allowed to load at the same speed) versus telecommunications giants who would like customers to pay for access to faster speeds or subscription content. Internet service providers have mostly kept to the principles of net neutrality and are prevented from favoring some kinds of content over others. However, as demand for broadband grew and mobile devices like the iPhone and Blackberry became commonplace, telecommunications giants like Verizon, Comcast, and AT&T—who spent hundreds of billions of dollars laying networks through which data travels—were eager to put internet neutrality on the bargaining table as a legitimate issue.[12]

Defense.   It is a good idea to discuss what may seem to be an implicit or unspoken agenda (e.g., "I get the sense that you have an agenda of how you would like to cover the issues. I would like to hear your ideas and then tell you mine. Maybe we can come up with an agenda that makes sense for both of us, after hearing each other out.").

THE POWER OF ALTERNATIVES   Negotiators who generate several alternatives for each issue may have a bargaining advantage because they formulate alternatives that benefit themselves. The savvy negotiator will specify alternatives that are most favorable to himself or herself. Consider a software development deal between two of the fiercest rivals in the industry: Apple and Microsoft. Since 1997, when Microsoft bought a $150 million stake in Apple and began an initial 5-year development deal to release new versions of Microsoft Office for the Mac, the companies subsequently agreed to three extensions of the deal. But it hasn't always been easy to find common ground. In the initial deal in 1997, Apple agreed to replace Netscape with Microsoft's Internet Explorer after Microsoft threatened to back out of the deal. In subsequent years, items such as Apple's Visual Basic and Outlook for Mac were used as bargaining chips before renewing deals.[13]

Defense.   Make sure that you have thought about your own alternatives and get those on the table. Even though it is wise to unbundle single-issue negotiations from multi-issue negotiations, those who negotiate a lot of issues actually feel worse about their outcomes.[14] Why? They are more likely to ponder "what might have been" and experience doubts.

THE POWER OF OPTIONS   In our chapter on integrative bargaining (Chapter 4), we strongly advocated that negotiators generate several options, all of equal value to themselves. The negotiator who generates options has an advantage.

Defense.   If the counterparty suggests several options, it is actually good news because it suggests that your opponent is not a positional negotiator. However, make sure that you do not offer unilateral concessions. The best way to avoid making unilateral concessions is to generate several options to present to the other party.

---

[12] Altman, A. (2010, September 8). Net neutrality and foes of big government. *Time.* Time.com
[13] Miller, D. (2010, February 11). Microsoft announces office for Mac2011. *Macworld.* Macworld.com
[14] Naquin, C. (2003). The agony of opportunity in negotiation: Number of negotiable issues, counterfactual thinking, and feelings of satisfaction. *Organizational Behavior and Human Decision Processes, 91*, 97–107.

ATTITUDINAL STRUCTURING   If a negotiator suspects that the counterparty has an uncertain or unspecified BATNA, he or she can influence the opponent's perception of his or her BATNA. Thus, a negotiator may coax the counterparty to reveal his or her BATNA.

Defense.   The best strategy to use when the counterparty attempts to manipulate your BATNA is to research your BATNA and develop your reservation price *before* negotiating. Oftentimes, negotiators can be manipulated to reveal their BATNA when an opponent makes the assumption that the negotiator's BATNA is weak. Consider the following interchange between negotiators:

NEGOTIATOR A: You know, it is really a buyer's market out there. I would strongly suggest that you think about my offer [on your house] before you turn it down. There may not be any more buyers for a while.

NEGOTIATOR B: Actually, I have received a lot of interest on my house.

NEGOTIATOR A: In this market? That does not sound very likely to me. In fact, my sister is selling her house, and she has not had an offer yet.

NEGOTIATOR B: Actually, just last week, a buyer from out of state saw my house and said he would most likely make an offer of $230,000 this week. You can ask my agent about it, if you do not believe me.

NEGOTIATOR A: That is so interesting. Just last night my spouse and I decided that we would most likely offer $231,000 for your house. Imagine that!

From this interchange, we see negotiator A was successful in taunting negotiator B to reveal her BATNA by challenging it.

THE POWER OF CONTRAST   Negotiators may invent irrelevant alternatives for the counterparty to consider. The negotiator who proposes irrelevant alternatives knows the other party will find them unacceptable, but they nevertheless create a **psychological contrast effect**. To understand how the contrast effect works, consider the behavior of some real estate agents.[15] Agents who want a prospective buyer to make an offer on a house may show the buyer several houses. They arrange a house-showing day during which they first show the prospective buyer some "doghouses" that may have been on the market for several months because they are extremely unattractive or over-priced. The buyer may become somewhat depressed at the sight of these houses or at the high price tags they carry. At this point, the agent will show the buyer the houses he or she wants the buyer to seriously consider. This tactic creates a psychological contrast effect because the potential buyer will view these houses much more favorably than the more dilapidated, overpriced alternatives and will be more motivated to make an offer. In negotiation, contrast is often used when the counterparty makes an extreme initial offer and then follows with an offer that appears more reasonable. Acceptance rates of the second offer are higher when it follows the initial extreme offer.

Defense.   The best defense against the contrast effect is to set a well-defined target point. For example, the prospective home buyer should research the market thoroughly. Negotiators should avoid making premature concessions (i.e., concessions they make before they have tried to get what they want.)

---

[15] Cialdini, R. B. (1993). *Influence: Science and practice.* New York: HarperCollins.

COMMITMENT AND CONSISTENCY The **consistency principle** describes the human need to be consistent in our beliefs, feelings, and behaviors. To contradict ourselves, whether in thought or in deed, is a sign of irrationality. Thus, savvy negotiators will often attempt to get a verbal commitment from the counterparty.

What are the implications of the consistency principle for the negotiator? If a negotiator agrees to something (e.g., a particular set of terms, etc.), he or she is motivated to behave in a fashion consistent with his or her verbal commitment. A common bargaining ploy of salespeople is to ask customers about their intentions to buy (e.g., "Are you ready to buy a car today at the right price?"). Most people would agree to this statement because it does not obligate them to buy a particular car. However, powerful psychological commitment processes begin to operate once we acknowledge ourselves to be a "buyer."

Defense. Be careful what you agree to in a negotiation. If a car seller asks whether you are ready to buy a car, do not immediately say "Yes!" but, rather, "That depends on the terms."

FRAMING EFFECTS: CAPITALIZING ON THE HALF-FULL OR HALF-EMPTY GLASS As we saw in Chapter 2, people are risk-averse for gains and risk-seeking when it comes to losses. The **reference point** defines what is a gain and what is a loss. Savvy negotiators know if they want to induce the counterparty to maintain the status quo—that is, induce risk aversion or conservatism—they should present options as gains relative to a reference point. Similarly, if they want to induce risk-taking (change), they frame choices as losses.

Defense. Determine your reference point prior to entering into a negotiation to avoid being "framed."

FAIRNESS HEURISTICS: CAPITALIZING ON EGOCENTRIC BIAS Fairness is important in negotiation. To the extent that negotiators characterize their offer as "fair," they increase the likelihood that it will be accepted by the other party. However, multiple standards of fairness exist. Moreover, negotiators tend to like proposals that they make or ultimately accept more than other proposals; and they devalue proposals offered by the counterparty, not so much based upon the content of the proposal but upon who is offering it.[16]

Defense. Be aware of the many rules of fairness (e.g., equity, equality, and need). When an opponent puts forth a fairness ploy, be ready to present a counterargument and introduce your preferred fairness criterion.

TIME PRESSURE Intuition suggests that the negotiator who is under the most time pressure is at a disadvantage in a negotiation. Whereas it is true that the negotiator who needs to come to an agreement more quickly (because his or her BATNA may deteriorate with time) is at a disadvantage, time limits may be an advantage for the negotiator.[17]

Defense. Remember that the party who has the deadline sets the deadline for the other party. Set a limit on how long you will negotiate. A final deadline limits the potential time-related costs. If you face a final deadline, whether or not you set it yourself, make sure those with whom

---

[16] Curhan, J., Neale, M., & Ross, L. (2004). Dynamic valuation: Preference changes in the context of face-to-face negotiation. *Journal of Experimental Social Psychology, 40*, 142–151.
[17] Moore, D. A. (2004). The unexpected benefits of final deadlines in negotiation. *Journal of Experimental Social Psychology, 40*, 121–127.

you are negotiating know about the time constraint it puts on them. If they want any deal at all, they will have to reach agreement before the deadline.[18]

With regard to using power, a certain amount of suspicion is advantageous. Negotiators who are suspicious are more effective at the bargaining table because a variety of adaptive defense mechanisms operate. People who are suspicious of the counter-party are better able to guard against influence strategies.[19]

Peripheral Route Persuasion Tactics

The strategies we describe next work through a fundamentally different mechanism: people's inherent need to be liked, approved of, and respected by others. The negotiator who uses the following strategies manipulates the counterparty's sense of his or her own identity and, through these strategies, attempts to change the counterparty's behavior. Marshaling defense strategies is more difficult in the case of peripheral route persuasion tactics because they often catch us off guard. A good defense is an awareness of common strategies.

STATUS   Two types of status are relevant in most negotiation situations: primary status characteristics and secondary status characteristics. **Primary status characteristics** refer to indicators of legitimate authority; for example, a person's rank within an organization, the number of supervisees in that person's unit, and a person's various titles and degrees all denote primary status. The impact of status on the conduct of bargaining can be quite enormous. High-status individuals talk more, even when they do not necessarily know more. A high-status person will also generally control when he or she speaks in a conversation. Furthermore, a low-status person will defer to the high-status person in terms of turn-taking in the conversation. These factors can affect the distribution of resources in negotiation.

When primary status cues (such as rank and status in an organization) are absent, or when people of equal status negotiate, people often pay attention to **secondary status characteristics**, which are cues and characteristics that have no legitimate bearing on the allocation of resources or on the norms of interaction, but nevertheless they exert a powerful influence on behavior. Such **pseudostatus characteristics** include sex, age, ethnicity, status in other groups, and cultural background. The three most common secondary status characteristics are gender, age, and race. Men have more influence than women, older people have more influence than younger people, and Caucasian people have more influence than African American people when it comes to interpersonal interaction.[20] Because men are perceived to be of higher status than women, in a negotiation context, men are given the "right" to offer proposed agreements and to have them viewed as coming from competent source.[21] Although pseudo status characteristics are not legitimate markers of status, people treat them as though they do. Status cues operate quickly, often within minutes after negotiators are seated at the bargaining table. Furthermore, even when a negotiator does not regard these pseudo status cues to be significant (or even rejects them outright), if someone else at the bargaining

---

[18] Ibid.

[19] Oza, S. S., Srivastava, J., & Koukova, N. T. (2010). How suspicion mitigates the effect of influence tactics. *Organizational Behavior and Human Decision Processes, 112*(1), 1–10.

[20] Mazur, A. (1985). A biosocial model of status in face-to-face groups. *Social Forces, 64,* 377–402.

[21] Miles, E. W. & Clenney, E. F. (2010). Gender differences in negotiation: A status characteristics theory view. *Negotiation and Conflict Management Research, 3*(2), 130–144.

table considers them significant, it may create a **self-fulfilling prophesy**. Another pseudostatus cue is posture. Striking a pose that opens up a person's body and takes up space alters hormone levels and makes a person feel more powerful and more willing to take risks.[22] In a complementary fashion, constrictive postures lower a person's sense of power and willingness to take risks.

As a case in point, consider Wendell Primus, who exudes status as one of Capitol Hill's most influential politicians, having served as former Speaker of the House Nancy Pelosi's point man during the 2010 Health Care debates. But he also possesses a number of other secondary-status markers: his gray hair and reading glasses and soft-spoken manner—described as grandfatherly. Even though he is not an elected official, elected officials deferred to him on a regular basis during the debates. "Wendell probably says the fewest words of any person in senior staff and probably says the most," said Rep. Robert E. Andrews.[23]

GENDER   Because gender is a secondary status characteristic, it is worth exploring the question of how men and women fare at the bargaining table. Across the board, men are more successful than women in terms of pie-slicing—they inevitably get a bigger slice.[24] When negotiators believe a negotiation simulation is diagnostic of their true negotiation ability, men do even better. Apparently, highly successful female managers from major companies falter because of the pervasive cultural stereotype that "women are docile." Even though the successful females in our investigation were anything but docile, the mere knowledge that this stereotype about women exists was enough to form a mental roadblock in the negotiations. However, if the cultural stereotype about women was positioned more prominently, perhaps women would be able to attack it mentally. Consequently, when we created a simulation in which the classic female stereotype was explicitly mentioned, the tide turned. Highly competent female MBA students not only actively dismissed the stereotype, but they also claimed more of the pie than did their fellow male MBA students. The message? Stereotypes that lurk below the surface creep into our subconscious and interfere with our performance. By exposing those negative stereotypes—getting them out in the open and then attacking them mentally—women can do much better at the bargaining table. This effect is even stronger when people want to make a good impression on others. In one investigation, men and women in high-status roles responded to impression motivation in a way that contradicted classic gender stereotypes: Men actually became more docile, and women responded by acting more assertively.[25] Women persisted more with male naysayers than with female naysayers, but they did so in a stereotypically low-status (more indirect than direct manner). Moreover, women's persistence with the male naysayers helped close a gender gap in performance.[26]

---

[22] Carney, D. R., Cuddy, A. J. C., & Yap, A. J. (2010). Power posing: Brief nonverbal displays affect neuroendocrine levels and risk tolerance. *Psychological Science, 21*(10), 1363–1368.

[23] Akers, M.A. (2010, June 21). The speaker's liberal brawler. *The Washington Post*, p. A15.

[24] Kray, L., Thompson, L., & Galinsky, A. (2001). Battle of the sexes: Gender stereotype confirmation and reactance in negotiations. *Journal of Personality and Social Psychology, 80*(6), 942–958; Kray, L., Galinsky, A., & Thompson, L. (2002). Reversing the gender gap in negotiations: An exploration of stereotype regeneration. *Organizational Behavior and Human Decision Processes, 87*(2), 386–409.

[25] Curhan, J. R., & Overbeck, J. R. (2008). Making a positive impression in a negotiation: Gender differences in response to impression motivation. *Negotiation and Conflict Management Research, 1*(2), 179–193.

[26] Bowles, H. R. & Flynn, F. (2010). Gender and persistence in negotiation: A dyadic perspective. *Academy of Management Journal, 53*(4), 769–787.

These results gave us the idea of completely turning the stereotype of women on its head. We created a negotiation simulation in which we clearly suggested that success in negotiation requires people skills—listening, verbal prowess, nonverbal acumen, and so on—all the elements of the classic female stereotype. Sure enough, women performed better under these conditions.[27] The key conclusion is that if a task (such as negotiation) can be positively linked to your own gender stereotype, you can perform better. (See also Exhibit 7-1 for an example of how a powerful female leader leveraged her role.)

The greater the amount of situational ambiguity in a given situation, the more a negotiation will be affected by gender.[28] A given situation is less ambiguous to the stereotype-consistent gender and more ambiguous to the other gender.[29]

Unfortunately, women encounter both social and economic backlash when they behave assertively at the bargaining table. The backlash is most evident when gender stereotypes that

EXHIBIT 7-1

The Verbal and Nonverbal Skills of Power

Madeleine Albright served as the first female secretary of state in U.S. history and at that time was also the highest-ranking woman ever to serve in the executive branch of government. The tough-talking, wisecracking, former Georgetown University professor sought the job and accepted it eagerly, making no pretense of reluctance and offering no sham modesty about her stellar credentials. During her reign as secretary of state, "Last Word" Albright compiled an impressive list of powerful accomplishments: She forged an alliance that finally faced down Serb aggression in the Balkans and held it together during the war, and she did it without a total rupture with Moscow. At the same time, she kept the Israeli–Palestinian peace negotiations from falling apart completely while Benjamin Netanyahu was prime minister so that Netanyahu's successor, Ehud Barak, could build on a foundation that was still intact. She nursed a relationship with China and opened the door to better relations with Iran. Her secret to power? "Interrupt!" At least that is the advice she gives to young women: "Don't wait for men to solicit your input" (p. 1736). And she walks the talk: In her course at Georgetown, she instituted a no-hand-raising rule because she believes that if students are told to raise their hands before speaking, women will do so but men will not. Her successes with the variety of people she has dealt with reveal her remarkable persuasive skills and her bargaining power.

Source: Based on Lippman, T. W. (2000, June 3). Madame Secretary. *National Journal, 32*(23),1736–1744.

---

[27] Kray, Galinsky, & Thompson, "Reversing the gender gap."

[28] Bowles, H. R., Babcock, L., & McGinn, K. L.(2005). Constraints and triggers: Situational mechanics of gender in negotiation. *Journal of Personality and Social Psychology, 89*(6), 951–965; Bowles, H. R., & McGinn, K. L. (2005). Claiming authority: Negotiating challenges for women leaders. In D. M. Messick & R. Kramer (Eds.), *The psychology of leadership: Some new approaches,* (191–208). Mahwah, NJ: Erlbaum; Pradel, D. W., Bowles, H. R., & McGinn, K. L. (2005, November). When does gender matter in negotiation? *Negotiation, 8,* 9–10.

[29] Miles, E. W. & Clenney, E. F. (2010). Gender Differences in Negotiation: A Status Characteristics Theory View. *Negotiation and Conflict Management Research, 3*(2), 130–144.

prescribe communal, nurturing behavior are activated.[30] When women behave in a stereotypically feminine way, such as flirting, they are judged as more likeable, but less authentic.[31]

SOCIAL NETWORKS   Whereas information power in a negotiation refers to the power associated with *what* you know, network power refers to the power associated with *who* you know. **Social capital** is the power that results from managers' access to other people within and outside of their organization. Social capital is a value that comes from who, when, and how to coordinate through various contacts within and beyond the organization.[32] When the United States Congress passed the controversial national health care bill into law in 2010, it followed months of behind the scenes wheeling and dealing amongst players in political-social networks. President Barack Obama and White House Chief of Staff Rahm Emanuel stocked the West Wing with an all-star line-up of former congressional insiders. Obama decided he would stay in the background and encourage Congress to come up with a plan, fast track it, relying on good will and personal relationships and network relationships to get it passed. Emanuel and Senate majority leader Harry Reid—at Obama's request—cut deals with Democrats for their vote.[33]

However, you don't have to be a Capitol Hill lobbyist to leverage social networks. Managers with more social capital get higher returns on their human capital because they are positioned to identify and develop more rewarding opportunities.[34] Negotiators with high network power are those who act as **boundary spanners** by bridging functional gaps in organizations and units. They are the critical link between people who otherwise would not be in contact. As boundary spanners, they fill a unique spot within the organizational network by bringing together people, knowledge, and information that would not otherwise be brought together. A negotiator's position as a unique link in a network of relationships means that he or she can broker more opportunities than can other members of the network who do not represent unique links within the organization and beyond. Furthermore, negotiators who are boundary spanners are in a position to make or break opportunities for other people. Negotiators who act as boundary spanners broker the flow of information between people and control information. Negotiators who bridge gaps are the people who know about, have a hand in, and exercise more control over rewarding opportunities. They have broader access to information because of their diverse contacts. This access means they are more often aware of new opportunities and have easier access to these opportunities than do their peers—even their peers of equivalent or greater human capital. For this reason, they are also more likely to be discussed as suitable candidates for inclusion in new opportunities and are more likely to be able to display their capabilities because they have more control over the substance of their work, defined by relationships with subordinates, superiors, and colleagues.

PHYSICAL APPEARANCE   Physically attractive people are more effective in getting what they want than are less physically attractive people, independent of their actual skills. And the work produced by allegedly attractive people is more highly valued than that produced by less-attractive people. In one investigation, men evaluated an essay with a photo of the supposed

---

[30] Tinsley, C. H., Cheldelin, S. I., Schneider, A. K., & Amanatullah, E. T. (2009). Women at the bargaining table: Pitfalls and prospects. *Negotiation Journal, 25*(2), 233–248.

[31] Kray, L. J., & Locke, C. C. (2008). To flirt or not to flirt? Sexual power at the bargaining table. *Negotiation Journal, 24*(4), 483–493.

[32] Burt, R. S. (1997). The contingent value of social capital. *Administrative Science Quarterly, 42*(2), 339–365.

[33] Kirk, M., (writer) & Kirk, M. (director). (2010). Obama's deal [Television series episode]. In M. Kirk, J. Gilmore, M. Wiser (producers), *Frontline*. Boston, MA: PBS.

[34] Burt, R. S. (1992). *The social structure of competition.* Cambridge, MA: Harvard University Press.

author attached—either an attractive or an unattractive woman (as judged by an independent group of people).[35] Even though the essays were identical, men's judgments of the essays were strongly affected by how attractive the woman in each picture was: The more attractive the person in the photo, the better the grade given.[36] People think attractive people are more talented, kind, honest, and intelligent than unattractive people.[37] As a consequence, attractive people are more persuasive in terms of changing attitudes[38] and getting what they want.[39] Physical attractiveness has a favorable impact on sales effectiveness[40] and on income levels across a wide range of occupations.[41] (*Note:* Attractiveness is usually achieved through dress and grooming in most of these investigations.)

The benefits of attractiveness carry through to the negotiation table. Consistent with the idea of a "beauty premium," attractive people are offered more money, but also more is demanded of them.[42]

The evaluation of an employment applicant can be affected by physical attractiveness as well.[43] Attractive people are evaluated more positively and are treated better than unattractive people. Attractive communicators and salespeople are more effective in changing other people's attitudes than unattractive ones.[44] For this reason, sales campaigns often feature an attractive person selling a product or service. Attractive people are often presumed to have other positive qualities as well; for example, they are regarded to be more poised, interesting, sociable, independent, dominant, exciting, sexy, well-adjusted, socially skilled, and successful than unattractive persons.[45] This attribution of positive qualities to attractive people is part of the **halo effect** described in Chapter 6. The underlying message: Be aware of how your judgment (and others') is affected by physical appearance.

DELAYED LIKING   Should you show your liking for the other party immediately or wait awhile? In terms of gaining compliance from the other party, it is far more effective to *grow* to like the other party.[46] The most effective type of liking (in terms of getting what you want from

[35] Feingold, A. (1992). Good-looking people are not what we think. *Psychological Bulletin, 111*(2), 304–341.

[36] Landy, D., & Sigall, H. (1974). Beauty is talent: Task evaluation as a function of the performer's physical attractiveness. *Journal of Personality and Social Psychology, 29*(3), 299–304.

[37] Eagly, A. H., Ashmore, R. D., Makhijani, M. G., & Longo, L. C. (1991). What is beautiful is good, but … : A meta-analytic review of research on the physical attractiveness stereotype. *Psychological Bulletin, 110*(1), 109–128.

[38] Chaiken, S. (1979). Communicator physical attractiveness and persuasion. *Journal of Personality and Social Psychology, 37*(8), 1387–1397.

[39] Benson, P. L., Karabenick, S. A., & Lerner, R. M. (1976). Pretty pleases: The effects of physical attractiveness, race, and sex on receiving help. *Journal of Experimental Social Psychology, 12*(5), 409–415.

[40] Kivisilta, P., Honkaniemi, L., & Sundvi, L. (1994, July 12). *Female employees' physical appearance: A biasing factor in personnel assessment, or a success-producing factor in sales and marketing?* Poster presented at the 23rd International Congress of Applied Psychology, Madrid, Spain; Reingen, P. H., & Kernan, J. B. (1993). Social perception and interpersonal influence: Some consequences of the physical attractiveness stereotype in a personal selling setting. *Journal of Consumer Psychology, 2*(1), 25–38.

[41] Hamermesh, D. S., & Biddle, J. E. (1994). Beauty and the labor market. *The American Economic Review, 84*(5), 1174.

[42] Solnick, S. J., & Schweitzer, M. (1999). The influence of physical attractiveness and gender on ultimatum game decisions. *Organizational Behavior and Human Decision Processes, 79*(3), 199–215.

[43] Dion, K. L. (1972). Physical attractiveness and evaluations of children's transgressions. *Journal of Personality and Social Psychology, 24*(2), 207–213.

[44] Kiesler, C. A., & Kiesler, S. B. (1969). *Conformity.* Reading, MA: Addison-Wesley.

[45] Dion, K. L., & Dion, K. K. (1987). Belief in a just world and physical attractiveness stereotyping. *Journal of Personality and Social Psychology, 52*(4), 775–780; Moore, J. S., Graziano, W. G., & Millar, M. G. (1987). Physical attractiveness, sex role orientation, and the evaluation of adults and children. *Personality and Social Psychology Bulletin, 13*(1), 95–102.

[46] Aronson, E., & Linder, D. (1965). Gain and loss of esteem as determinants of interpersonal attractiveness. *Journal of Experimental Social Psychology, 1*(2), 156–171.

someone) is to not like the other person immediately. Rather, people who *grow* to like someone are more effective in getting what they want than if they show their liking for the other person immediately. Consider an investigation in which people were given one of four types of evaluations by a peer: completely positive, initially negative and then positive, relentlessly negative, and initially positive and then negative. The recipient of the evaluation feedback was then asked to indicate how much he or she liked the other party. Liking was highest for the other party who was initially negative and later became positive.[47]

TO ERR IS HUMAN   Negotiators are naturally suspicious of smooth-talking and attractive negotiators. Therefore, it is important to show the counterparty that you are human and have your own foibles and faults. Showing the other person that you have flaws may endear you to them. For example, in one investigation, people listened to someone who was highly competent (i.e., got 92% of difficult exam questions correct). During a subsequent interview, it was revealed that this person was also very competent in other areas—an honor student, editor of the yearbook, and excellent at sports. In another situation, people heard the same person, but this time he spilled coffee on himself during the interview. Even though the person had identical qualifications in both instances, when he made the human error (spilling coffee), he was liked much more than when he was "perfect." In fact, liking increased by 50%.[48]

PRIMING THE PUMP   People's judgments and behaviors are affected by **unconscious priming**, which refers to the impact subtle cues and information in the environment have on our behavior (at a level below our conscious awareness).

Consider the following hypothetical scenario: You and a business associate are formulating strategy for the next round of negotiations with an important client. The two of you are discussing your strategy at a local bar, where a big-screen TV is broadcasting a particularly vicious boxing match. You and your associate are not really watching the fight but hear the referee's calls and description of the action in the background. You notice your associate talks about "packing a punch" and "hitting below the belt," and you wonder whether the social context is affecting your associate's judgment about negotiation. You suggest that the two of you walk down the street to the Honey Bear Cafe; the local music that night is a folk group called Brotherly Love. As the two of you are sipping coffee, your associate once again starts talking about the upcoming negotiations. You listen as he talks about "harmony" and "building a community" and wonder again whether features of your location are influencing your friend's judgment. This scenario illustrates how people are often manipulated by cues in the environment that act as primes. Sometimes these cues are random or naturally occurring products of the environment (such as in the bar); sometimes they may be "planted" (by a savvy negotiator). Two aspects of the environment—head-to-head rivalry and time pressure—fuel competitive motivations and behavior.[49] Even when winning is costly and does not provide a strategic gain, negotiators will have a desire to win under time pressure and in the presence of rival.[50]

---

[47] Ibid.
[48] Aronson, E., Willerman, B., & Floyd, J. (1966). The effect of a pratfall on increasing interpersonal attractiveness. *Psychonomic Science, 4*, 227–228.
[49] Malhotra, D. (2010). The desire to win: The effects of competitive arousal on motivation and behavior. *Organizational Behavior and Human Decision Processes, 111*(2), 139–146.
[50] Ibid.

RECIPROCITY VERSUS COMPLEMENTARITY   In the previous chapters, we've mentioned the powerful process of reciprocity in negotiation. However, tactics in negotiation are not always met with similar tactics; they can be met with their complement, such as when dominant strategies are met with submissive behavior. Whereas negotiators believe they would behave more competitively with an opponent who acted competitively, they actually behave less competitively, as evidenced by setting lower, less-aggressive reservation prices, making less-demanding counteroffers, and ultimately settling for worse-negotiated outcomes.[51]

SOCIAL PROOF   According to the **social proof principle**, we look to the behavior of others to determine what is desirable, appropriate, and correct. This behavior is sensible in many respects; if we want to get along with others, it only makes sense to know what they expect. However, this fundamental psychological process can work against us in negotiations if we look toward others—especially the counterparty—to determine an appropriate offer or settlement. For example, new-car dealers target the neighbors of recent customers. Bartenders often "seed" their tip jars, and church ushers "prime" collection baskets with coins. Social proof is why advertisers use the slogans "largest-selling" and "fastest-growing." One tactic, called the **list technique**, involves making a request after a target person has been shown a list of similar others who have already complied. For example, college students and homeowners donated money or blood to a charitable cause in much greater numbers when shown a list of others who had already done so.[52] The more ambiguous the situation, the more likely we are to rely on situational cues and the behavior of others to tell us what to do.

REACTANCE TECHNIQUE   **Reactance technique** (also known as **reverse psychology** or the **boomerang effect**) refers to people's desire to assert their individual freedom when others attempt to take it away.[53] Negotiators can use an interesting form of reverse psychology to extract what they want and need from the counterparty. (*Warning:* This technique can be extremely risky to use; we argue that negotiators practice with it before negotiating so as not to make fatal errors.)

One strategy for getting a "reaction" from the counterparty is to paraphrase his or her position in a way that makes it sound more extreme than it actually is. For example, consider the following interchange that occurs after two hours of a negotiation in which each negotiator has stopped making concessions:

NEGOTIATOR A: (*with deep sincerity and respect*): So, what you seem to be saying is that you have put your best offer on the table. That is your final best offer; there are no other possibilities of any kind. Your offer is a line drawn in the sand.

NEGOTIATOR B: (*looking slightly perplexed*): Well, no, it is not entirely like that. I have tried to be clear about my company's position and feel committed to achieving our goals. And the final offer I made reflects my company's goals.

---

[51] Diekmann, K., Tenbrunsel, A., & Galinsky, A. (2003). From self-prediction to self-defeat: Behavioral forecasting, self-fulfilling prophesies, and the effect of competition expectations. *Journal of Personality and Social Psychology, 85*(4), 672–683.
[52] Reingen, P. H. (1982). Test of a list procedure for inducing compliance with a request to donate money. *Journal of Applied Psychology, 67*(1), 110–118.
[53] Brehm, S. S. (1983). Psychological reactance and social differentiation. *Bulletin de Psychologie, 37*(11–14), 471–474.

NEGOTIATOR A: (*with resignation*): I respect a person who makes a commitment, who draws a line in the sand and who will not move an inch from that position. Someone who has the resolve to stick to his guns, and the tenacity and firmness of an army and…

NEGOTIATOR B: (*interrupting negotiator A*): Look, I am not drawing a line in the sand, or anything like that. I am a reasonable person, and I am willing to consider reasonable offers.

NEGOTIATOR A: (*looking incredulous*): You mean you have the power and the freedom to create more options? I was under the impression that you were tied to your position.

NEGOTIATOR B: (*somewhat defensively*): Well, of course, I can do anything I want here—within reason. I can come up with other alternatives.

NEGOTIATOR A: (*with interest*): I am most interested in hearing about your ideas.

FOOT-IN-THE-DOOR TECHNIQUE   In the **foot-in-the-door technique**, a person is asked to agree to a small favor or statement (such as agreeing with a question like "Are you ready to buy a car today at the right price?" or signing a petition). Later, the same person is confronted with a larger request (e.g., buying a car or voting with a particular coalition in a departmental meeting). The probability the person will agree to the larger request increases when the person previously agreed to the smaller request.[54] This strategy plays upon people's need to demonstrate consistent behavior.

DOOR-IN-THE-FACE TECHNIQUE   Another strategy for gaining compliance is called the **door-in-the-face technique** (or the **rejection-then-retreat tactic**), in which a negotiator asks for a very large concession or favor from the other party—one that the counterparty is almost certain to refuse.[55] When the refusal occurs, the negotiator makes a much smaller request, which is, of course, the option he or she wanted all along. We described this principle in Chapter 3, which admonishes negotiators to state high aspirations. The high aspiration creates a contrast effect, in that the counterparty views any request that is less extreme than the original to be more reasonable.

THAT'S-NOT-ALL TECHNIQUE   Many negotiators engage in the **that's-not-all technique** (also known as **sweetening the deal**) by offering to add more to a negotiated package or deal. For example, car dealers often add options to the car in question as a "deal closer." In a study involving a bake sale, when patrons asked about cupcake prices and were told that two cupcakes cost $0.75, 40% bought the cupcakes. However, when they were told that one cupcake cost $0.75 and another cupcake would be "thrown in" for free, 73% bought the cupcakes.[56]

---

[54] Beaman, A. L., Cole, N., Preston, M., Glentz, B., & Steblay, N. M. (1983). Fifteen years of the foot-in-the-door research: A meta-analysis. *Personality and Social Psychology Bulletin, 9,* 181–186.

[55] Cialdini, R. B. (1975). Reciprocal concessions procedure for inducing compliance: The door-in-the-face technique. *Journal of Personality and Social Psychology, 31*(2), 206–215.

[56] Burger, J. M. (1986). Increasing compliance by improving the deal: The that's-not-all technique. *Journal of Personality and Social Psychology, 51,* 277–283.

The Effects of Power on Those Who Hold Power

People with power are often oblivious to people who have less power.[57] People with high power have little or no reason to pay attention to those who are less powerful. After all, the powerful are in control of the situation, and the actions of those who are not as powerful have little effect on the high-power person's well-being. Consequently, those who have more power tend to be less accurate about the situation. People with power have an illusion of control—they feel control over outcomes that they cannot influence.[58] Negotiators who are higher in power (whether it is a legitimate form of power or not) may be less vigilant and thorough in collecting information from those of lesser power. Those with more power also engage in less "self-monitoring," meaning they don't change their behavior to fit the situation.[59] In one investigation, highly powerful people were secretly videotaped as they interacted with less powerful people. The interchange took place at a social gathering where refreshments were being served. High-power people ate more and messier foods, which resulted in a disheveled appearance.[60] Additionally, people with a high-power mindset are more likely to act in a risk-seeking fashion and divulge their interests in a negotiation (a form of risky behavior).[61]

The Effects of Power on Those with Less Power

What are the psychological effects of those who have more power on those who have less power? Those with less power are highly accurate in perceiving the behaviors and attitudes of those with higher power.[62] Less powerful people are dependent upon those of higher power for important organizational rewards. If someone is in a position to control a variety of organizational benefits that could dramatically affect your well-being, you would probably closely scrutinize his or her behavior. However, this greater accuracy may come at a price. Those who are low in power may exhibit signs of paranoia, believing they are being constantly scrutinized and evaluated by those who are higher in power.[63] Moreover, whereas anger helps powerful negotiators, who feel more focused and assertive and claim more value, low-power negotiators are particularly susceptible to the emotions of the other party and consequently lose focus and yield ground when they face a powerful, emotional counterparty.[64]

---

[57] Gruenfeld, D. H., Keltner, D. J., & Anderson, C. (2003). The effects of power on those who possess it: How social structure can affect social cognition. In G. Bodenhausen & A. Lambert (Eds.), *Foundations of social cognition: A festschrift in honor of Robert S. Wyer, Jr.* (pp. 237–261). Mahwah, NJ: Erlbaum.

[58] Fast, N. J., Gruenfeld, D. H., Sivanathan, N., & Galinsky, A. D. (2010). Illusory control: A generative force behind power's far-reaching effects. *Psychological Science, 20*(4), 502–508.

[59] Snyder, M. (1974). Self-monitoring of expressive behavior. *Journal of Personality and Social Psychology, 30,* 526–537; Gruenfeld, Keltner, & Anderson, "The effects of power."

[60] Gruenfeld, Keltner, & Anderson, "The effects of power."

[61] Anderson, C., & Galinsky, A. (2006). Power, optimism, and risk-taking. *European Journal of Social Psychology, 36,* 511–536.

[62] Fiske, S. T., & Dépret, E. (1996). Control, interdependence, and power: Understanding social cognition in its social context. *European Review of Social Psychology, 7,* 31–61.

[63] Kramer, R. M., & Hanna, B. A. (1988). Under the influence? Organizational paranoia and the misperception of others' influence behavior. In R. M. Kramer & M. A. Neale (Eds.), *Power and influence in organizations* (pp. 145–179). Thousand Oaks, CA: Sage.

[64] Overbeck, J. R., Neale, M. A., & Govan, C. L. (2010). I feel, therefore you act: Intrapersonal and interpersonal effects of emotion on negotiation as a function of social power. *Organizational Behavior and Human Decision Processes, 112*(2), 126–139.

NEGOTIATION ETHICS

Negotiation creates incentives for people to violate ethical standards of behavior. Some hard-and-fast rules dictate what is ethical in negotiation, but more often negotiators must deal with ambiguity. Ethics are a manifestation of cultural, contextual, and interpersonal norms that render certain strategies and behaviors unacceptable. Negotiators evaluate tactics on a continuum of "ethically appropriate" to "ethically inappropriate" when deciding whether to use tactics.[65] We address the question of what behaviors are regarded as unethical or questionable in negotiations, what factors give rise to them, and how to develop personal ethical standards.

The question of ethical negotiations was raised when North Carolina-based Duke Energy withdrew a proposed settlement worked out with several Indiana customer groups on approving a controversial $2.88 billion coal gasification plant in downstate Indiana. Duke Energy had been accused of ethics violations with state regulators from the Indiana Utility Regulatory Commission, the agency ultimately responsible for approval of the deal. The company had asked to add $530 million more to what it can recover from customers as part of the deal, and negotiated a settlement with some customer groups on approving the higher costs and working out how Duke could recover the costs in rates. Indiana governor Mitch Daniels then ordered an investigation into the deal.[66]

Lying

More than anything else, lying is regarded to be unethical (as well as illegal in some cases). A given statement may be defined as **fraudulent** when the speaker makes a knowing misrepresentation of a material fact on which the victim reasonably relies and the fact causes damage. Unpacking this definition, we find several key aspects to lying: (a) The speaker is aware he or she is misrepresenting information (b) regarding a material fact. The other party (c) relies on this fact and (d) by doing so is damaged in some way—economically or emotionally. Consider the case in which a New York City landlord told a prospective tenant that if he did not rent the condo, the landlord could rent it immediately to someone else. In this situation, the landlord misrepresented his BATNA. The tenant relied on this fact to make a lease decision and was economically damaged.

Using this standard of lying, let's examine some of the key concepts we have discussed thus far: positions, interests, priorities, BATNAs, reservation prices, and key facts.

1. *Positions.*   Positions are the stated demands made by one party to another. Negotiators are under no obligation to truthfully state their position. However, it is usually wise to clearly signal your position. Keep in mind that most negotiators are not as clear as they think they are in articulating their position.[67] Whereas lying about one's position is not advised, many negotiators exaggerate their position. For example, a prospective employee negotiating a job contract may tell the employer she feels entitled to a salary of $100,000 per year, when in fact she is willing to accept $85,000. Note that this negotiator is not lying about her BATNA, nor is she implying that she has another job offer; she is just stating that she feels entitled to $100,000.

---

[65] Lewicki, R. J., Saunders, D. M., & Barry, B. (2007). *Negotiation: Readings, exercises, and cases* (5th ed.). Boston: McGraw Hill/Irwin.

[66] Downey, J. (2010, December 9). Ethics issue kills Duke Energy deal on Indiana plant cost. *Charlotte Business Journal.* Bizjournal.com

[67] Harinck, F. (2004). Persuasive arguments and beating around the bush in negotiations. *Group Processes and Intergroup Relations, 7*(1), 5–18.

2. *Interests.*   Recall that interests are the underlying "whys" behind negotiators' positions. In negotiation, it is generally assumed that people are self-interested with no "general duty of good faith." Specifically, according to the U.S. Court of Appeals, 7th Circuit:

> In a business transaction, both sides presumably try to get the best deal. That is the essence of bargaining and the free market.... No legal rule bounds the run of business interest. So, one cannot characterize self-interest as bad faith. No particular demand in negotiations could be termed dishonest, even if it seemed outrageous to the other party. The proper recourse is to walk away from the bargaining table, not sue for "bad faith" negotiations.[68]

3. *Priorities and preferences.*   A negotiator is entitled to his or her preferences, however idiosyncratic they might be. A negotiator who misrepresents his or her interests is not lying about a material fact. "Estimates of price or value placed on the subject of a transaction and a party's intentions as to an acceptable settlement of a claim"[69] are not material facts for purposes of the rule prohibiting lawyers from making false statements to a third person.

You can appreciate the complexities of sharing (or failing to share) information with the following example: Consider two people who have been hired to act as a project team in a company. The two associates (A and B) are given a large office to share, and they begin to arrange their workplace. The office contains two desks, and the only window can be enjoyed from one of the desks. A conversation between A and B reveals that A wants the desk with the window view and is ready to make sacrifices on other joint resources to get it—like giving up the close parking space and the storage areas. Unbeknownst to A, B has a terrible fear of heights; the window overlooks a steep precipice outside, and frankly, B prefers the other desk that is near an attractive saltwater aquarium. B considers not mentioning her true preference, hoping that she can *appear* to make a sacrifice, and thus extract more resources. **Passive misrepresentation** occurs when a negotiator does not mention true preferences and allows the other party to arrive at an erroneous conclusion. Now, imagine that A surprises B by asking her point-blank which desk B prefers—the one by the window or the aquarium. Does B lie about her preferences? If so, she commits an act of **active misrepresentation** (if she deliberately misleads her opponent). This strategic manipulation ploy is used about 28% of the time.[70]

4. **BATNAs.**   A negotiator's BATNA *is* material and therefore, subject to litigation. The message: Don't make up offers that don't exist! Negotiators who make up offers that don't exist (or even allude to them) are bluffing. According to Lewicki, a bluff can be a false promise or false threat.[71] A false promise (e.g., "If you do x, I will reward you") and a false threat (e.g., "If you do not do x, I will punish you") are false in the sense that the person stating the threat does not intend to or cannot follow through.

5. *Reservation prices.*   As stated in Chapter 2, a negotiator's reservation price is the quantification of a negotiator's BATNA. A negotiator's stated reservation price (the least or most at which he or she will sell or buy) is not a material fact per se, and thus, whereas it may be reprehensible to lie about one's reservation price, it is not unethical, legally speaking.

[68] *Feldman v. Allegheny International, Inc.,* 850 F.2d 1217 (IL 7th Cir. 1988).
[69] American Bar Association. (2004). Model rules of professional conduct: Transactions with persons other than clients. Abanet.org
[70] O'Connor, K. M., & Carnevale, P. J. (1997). A nasty but effective negotiation strategy: Misrepresentation of a common-value issue. *Personality and Social Psychology Bulletin, 23*(5), 504–515.
[71] Lewicki, R. J. (1983). Lying and deception: A behavioral model. In M. H. Bazerman & R. J. Lewicki (Eds.), *Negotiating in organizations.* Beverly Hills, CA: Sage.

6. *Key facts.* The falsification of erroneous, incorrect information is unethical (and subject to punishment). For example, a home seller who does not disclose known foundation problems is guilty of falsification.

Other Questionable Negotiation Strategies

In addition to lying about positions, interests, preferences, priorities, BATNAs, reservation prices, or material facts, let's consider other strategies negotiators might regard as unethical.

- ***Traditional competitive bargaining.*** In an analysis of MBA students' perceptions of unethical behavior, traditional competitive bargaining behavior, such as hiding one's real bottom line, making very high or low opening offers, and gaining information by asking among one's contacts, was considered to be unethical.[72] And self-rated "aggressive" negotiators are more accepting of such tactics than are self-rated "cooperative" negotiators.[73]

- ***Manipulation of an opponent's network.*** This tactic involves an attempt to weaken an opponent's position by influencing his or her associate or constituency. For example, consider how state labor unions attempted to use access to social networks to defeat an anti-tax initiative in the state of Washington.[74] Labor union groups sent e-mails, pretending to be from campaign supporters who were requesting petitions, signs, and stickers. The idea was to get the protax group to waste a lot of money and time sending people pamphlets, stickers, and other items that would ultimately be thrown away.

- ***Reneging on negotiated agreements.*** In many important negotiations, deals are closed without formal contracts. For example, even in the purchase of houses and cars, an understanding is often reached before official papers have been signed. Even after formal contracts are signed, a period of rescission exists, wherein either party can legally exit from the agreement. However, considerable disagreement and ethical debate concern the issue of whether parties have a right to renege on an agreement once an informal closing (such as a handshake) has occurred.

- ***Retracting an offer.*** According to an unwritten rule, once a negotiator puts an offer on the table, he or she should not retract it. This action would be bargaining in bad faith. Even so, negotiators may need to retract offers because a mistake has been made. For example, a newspaper published winning lottery numbers, but a typo was made, and a large number of people believed themselves, mistakenly, to be winners (see Exhibit 7-2). However, what the offering negotiator may see as an honest mistake is often viewed by the recipient negotiator as bargaining in bad faith.

- ***Nickel-and-diming.*** The strategy of continually asking for "just one more thing" after a deal has been closed is annoying to most people. Most people are reluctant to make concessions when they fear the other party will continue to prolong negotiations. Negotiators are more likely to make concessions if they feel they will be successful in closing the deal. Thus, it is often an effective strategy to inform the other party of the terms you need to make the agreement final. Even better, prepare the official paperwork and indicate that you will "sign today" if your terms are met. The prospect of closing a deal is often enough of an enticement for negotiators to agree to the terms proposed by the other party.

---

[72] Lewicki, Saunders, & Barry, (2007), *Negotiation: Readings, exercises, and cases.*
[73] Ibid.
[74] Postman, D. (2002, April 4). E-mail reveals labor's plot to foil I-776. *Seattle Times,* p. A1.

EXHIBIT 7-2

Retracting an Offer

On November 5, 1999, the *New York Daily News* printed the wrong numbers in a Scratch 'N' Match lottery game. The *News*, citing game rules, said it would not honor "false winners," but it did announce that it would award the day's regular sum of $192,500 in prizes by holding a drawing the next month between all who sent in winning game cards. Not surprisingly, calls of anger and frustration flooded the hotline and telephone system, and people swarmed the lobby of the *News* building in New York. An elderly security guard in the building was punched and suffered a black eye, and irate game players threatened lawsuits.

Source: Based on McFadden, R. D. (1999, November 6). *Daily News* error: $100,000 dreams turn to nightmare. *New York Times*, p. A1.

In sum, there are several predictors of the extent to which a negotiator will engage in each of the strategies listed, including their attitude toward competitive-unethical tactics, the early use of competitive unethical tactics, and the behavior of the counterparty.[75] Personality differences in empathy and perspective-taking differentially affect the use of unethical strategies, such as lies and bribes.[76] Empathy, but not perspective-taking, discourages attacking the opponent's network, misrepresentation, inappropriate information gathering, and feigning emotions to manipulate the other. Thus, unethical bargaining is more likely to be deterred by empathy, as opposed to perspective-taking. Interestingly, negotiators who suppress their emotions are more likely to misrepresent information.[77] To examine your own ethical values, see Exhibit 7-3, which measures a seven-factor model of ethical and unethical bargaining tactics, including: traditional competitive bargaining, attacking an opponent's network, making false promises, misrepresentation, inappropriate information-gathering, strategic misrepresentation of positive emotion, and strategic misrepresentation of negative emotion.[78]

Sins of Omission and Commission

Sins of commission (active lying) are regarded as more unethical than sins of omission. (For an example of the complexity of sins of omission, consider the scenario in Exhibit 7-4.) It is possible to withhold information and not be regarded as unethical, but willful shielding from material information does not exculpate the negotiator. In other words, a businessperson should not refuse to see company reports in order to maintain a stance that the company is in financial health.

---

[75] Volkema, R., Fleck, D. & Hofmeister, A. (2010). Predicting competitive-unethical negotiating behavior and its consequences. *Negotiation Journal 26*(3), 263–286.
[76] Cohen, T. R. (2010). Moral emotions and unethical bargaining: The differential effects of empathy and perspective taking in deterring deceitful negotiation. *Journal of Business Ethics, 94*(4), 569–579.
[77] Yurtserver, G. (2008). Negotiators profit predicted by cognitive reappraisal, suppression of emotions, misrepresentation of information and tolerance of ambiguity. *Perceptual and Motor Skills, 106*(2), 590–608.
[78] Lewicki, Saunders, & Barry, *Negotiation: Readings, exercises, and cases.*

EXHIBIT 7-3

Incidents in Negotiation Questionnaire: SINS II SCALE

For each of the tactics below, indicate how appropriate the tactic would be to use in a negotiation situation in which you will negotiate something very important to you. Assign a rating to each tactic, evaluating how appropriate it would be to use this tactic in the content specified above, based on the following scale.

1	2	3	4	5	6	7
Not at all appropriate			Somewhat appropriate			Very appropriate

1. Promise that good things will happen to your opponent if he/she gives you what you want, even if you know that you can't (or won't) deliver these things when the other's cooperation is obtained.
2. Get the other party to think that you like him/her personally despite the fact that you don't really.
3. Intentionally misrepresent information to your opponent in order to strengthen your negotiating arguments or position.
4. Strategically express anger toward the other party in a situation where you are not really angry.
5. Attempt to get your opponent fired from his/her position so that a new person will take his/her place.
6. Intentionally misrepresent the nature of negotiations to your constituency in order to protect delicate discussions that have occurred.
7. Express sympathy with the other party's plight, although in truth you don't care about their problems.
8. Gain information about an opponent's negotiating position by paying your friends, associates, and contacts to get this information for you.
9. Feign a melancholy mood in order to get the other party to think you are having a bad day.
10. Make an opening demand that is far greater than what you really hope to settle for.
11. Pretend to be disgusted at an opponent's comments.
12. Convey a false impression that you are in absolutely no hurry to come to a negotiated agreement, thereby trying to put time pressure on your opponent to concede quickly.
13. Give the other party the false impression that you are very disappointed with how things are going.
14. In return for concessions from your opponent now, offer to make future concessions which you know you will not follow through on.
15. Threaten to make your opponent look weak or foolish in front of a boss or others to whom he/she is accountable, even if you know that you won't actually carry out the threat.
16. Deny the validity of information which your opponent has that weakens your negotiating position, even though that information is true and valid.
17. Give the other party the (false) impression that you care about his/her personal welfare.
18. Intentionally misrepresent the progress of negotiations to your constituency in order to make your own position appear stronger.
19. Talk directly to the people who your opponent reports to, or is accountable to, and tell them things that will undermine their confidence in your opponent as a negotiator.
20. Stimulate fear on your part so that the other party will think you are tense about negotiating.

(continued)

21. Gain information about an opponent's negotiating position by cultivating his/her friendship through expensive gifts, entertaining, or "personal favors."
22. Pretend to be furious at your opponent.
23. Make an opening demand so high/low that it seriously undermines your opponent's confidence in his/her ability to negotiate a satisfactory settlement.
24. Guarantee that your constituency will uphold the settlement reached, although you know that they will likely violate the agreement later.
25. Gain information about an opponent's negotiating position by trying to recruit or hire one of your opponent's teammates (on the condition that the teammate bring confidential information with him/her).

To complete the scoring, combine and average the following items:

a. Traditional Competitive Bargaining (10, 12, 23)
b. Attacking Opponent's Network (5, 15, 19)
c. False Promises (1, 14, 24)
d. Misrepresentation (3, 6, 16, 18)
e. Inappropriate Information Gathering (8, 21, 25)
f. Strategic Misrepresentation of Positive Emotion (2, 7, 17)
g. Strategic Misrepresentation of Negative Emotion (4, 9, 11, 13, 20, 22)

Source: Lewicki, R. J., Saunders, D. M., & Barry, B. (2007). *Negotiation: Readings, exercises, and cases* (5th ed.). Boston: McGraw Hill/Irwin.

EXHIBIT 7-4

Sins of Omission

A couple interested in purchasing a house had almost all aspects of a deal worked out on House A. The realtor was aware the couple would have strongly preferred to make an offer on House B, which had sold in the previous month to someone else and, therefore, had not been on the market when the couple was house shopping. The realtor showed the couple House A, and the couple made an offer on it that was accepted. Prior to the closing on House A, House B came on the market again due to a set of completely unforeseeable circumstances. The realtor was aware House B was now on the market but did not inform the couple prior to their closing on House A. It was only following the closing (and after a 7.5% commission was paid to the realtor) that the realtor informed the couple that House B was now on the market and asked the couple if they wanted to put their newly purchased House A on the market and purchase House B.

Did the agent engage in unethical behavior? In the eyes of the real estate agent, because House B was not officially listed and because the couple did not inquire about whether House B was on the market, he did not engage in unethical behavior. In the eyes of the couple, it was unethical for the realtor not to inform them that their preferred house had become available when it did.

Costs of Lying

Senator Sam Ervin once remarked that "the problem with lying is you have to remember too damn much."[79] Several costs, or disadvantages, are associated with lying, the first being that the liar can be caught and face criminal charges. Even if the liar is not caught, one's reputation and trustworthiness can be damaged. This event, when it happens repeatedly, can then lead to a culture in which everyone in the organization lies and general suspiciousness increases. Lying also may not be strategic: Because a negotiator who lies about his or her reservation price effectively decreases the size of the bargaining zone, the probability of impasse increases.

Under What Conditions Do People Engage in Deception?

Tenbrunsel and Diekman examined the factors that lead people to engage in deception: the lure of temptation, uncertainty, powerlessness, and anonymity of victims.[80] The more negotiators have to gain economically by lying, the more likely they are to lie.[81] And, the more uncertainty negotiators have about material facts, the more likely they are to lie.

One survey asked MBA students to describe the conditions under which they personally would engage in deception (defined as lying) in negotiations. Most people were able to identify situations in which they would lie. Only two people out of 47 said they would never deceive. More than 25% said that they would use "white lies" or exaggerations in nearly any negotiation. The most common reason for lying is when we think the other party is lying (see Exhibit 7-5). Financial self-interest does not fully explain dishonesty. Rather, dishonesty is influenced by emotional reactions to wealth-based inequity, even when it is personally costly.[82] Negative inequity leads to envy and subsequent hurting behavior; conversely, positive inequity leads to guilt and motivates helping behavior.[83]

Being in a team or group may increase the tendency to lie. Groups are less honest than individuals in the same bargaining situation.[84] In fact, the group "default" response is to lie; whereas the individual "default" response is to be honest. Only by strongly introducing a climate of organizational honesty, do groups move away from their default.

Psychological Bias and Unethical Behavior

Ethics are often a problem in negotiations, not so much because people are inherently evil and make trade-offs between profit and ethics or fail to consider other people's interests and welfare but, rather, because of psychological tendencies that foster poor decision making.[85] People may

---

[79] Senate Watergate Hearings. (1974).

[80] Tenbrunsel, A. E., & Diekmann, K. A. (2007). When you are tempted to deceive. *Negotiation, 10*(7),1–3.

[81] Bazerman, M. H., Tenbrunsel, A. E., & Wade-Benzoni, K. (1998). Negotiating with yourself and losing: Making decisions with competing internal preferences. *Academy of Management Review, 23*(2), 225–241; Grover, S. L. (2005). The truth, the whole truth and nothing but the truth: The causes and management of workplace lying. *Academy of Management Executive, 19*(2), 148–157.

[82] Gino, F., & Pierce, L. (2009). Dishonesty in the name of equity. *Psychological Science, 20*(9), 1153–1160.

[83] Ibid.

[84] Stawiski, S., Tindale, S. R., & Dykema-Engblade, A. (2009) The effects of ethical climate on group and individual level deception in negotiation. *International Journal of Conflict Management, 20*(3) 287–308.

[85] Messick, D. M., & Bazerman, M. H. (1996). Ethical leadership and the psychology of decision making. *Sloan Management Review, 37*(2), 9–22.

EXHIBIT 7-5

Conditions Under Which Negotiators Say They Would Engage in Deception

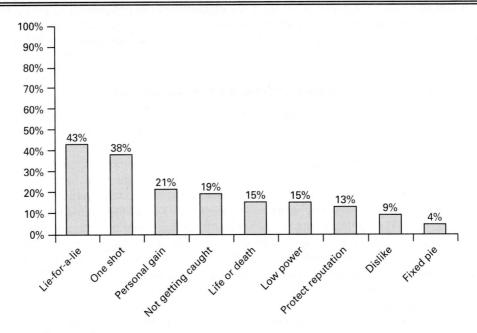

Review of Categories:

- *Lie-for-a-lie:* When I suspect the other party is deceiving me
- *One shot:* In a one-shot situation, with no potential for a long-term relationship
- *Personal gain:* If there was a gain to be had
- *Not getting caught:* If I felt I could get away with it
- *Life or death:* If the situation was "life or death"
- *Low power:* If the other party had more power (i.e., to "level the playing field")
- *Protecting reputation:* When I would not have to worry about my reputation
- *Dislike:* If I did not like the other person
- *Fixed pie:* If the situation was purely distributive

often *believe* they are behaving ethically, but due to self-serving tendencies, problems result and negotiators cry foul.[86]

- **Bounded ethicality.**   Bounded ethicality refers to the limits of people to make ethical decisions because they are either unaware or fail to fully and deliberately process information.[87]

---

[86] Ibid.
[87] Chugh, D., Banaji, M. R., & Bazerman, M. H. (2005). Bounded ethicality as a psychological barrier to recognizing conflicts of interest. In D. A. Moore, D. M. Cain, G. Loewenstein, & M. Bazerman, (Eds.), *Conflicts of interest: Problems and solutions from law, medicine and organizational settings* (pp. 74–95). London: Cambridge University Press.

- *Illusion of superiority.*   People view themselves and their actions much more favorably than others view them.[88] People focus on their positive characteristics and downplay their shortcomings. In relative terms, people believe they are more honest, ethical, capable, intelligent, courteous, insightful, and fair than others.
- *Illusion of control.*   People believe they have more control over events than they really do. For example, in games of chance, people often feel they can control outcomes.[89] Obviously, this thinking can lead to a type of gambler's fallacy in decision making. However, it can also give rise to ethical problems, such as when people make claims of quality control that cannot be met.
- *Overconfidence.*   Most people are overconfident about their knowledge. For example, when people are asked factual questions and then asked to judge the probability that their answers are true, the probability judgments far exceed the accuracy measures of the proportion of correct answers. On average, people claim to be 75% certain, when they are actually correct only 60% of the time.[90] And, people who have unmet goals (presumably because of overconfidence) are more likely to engage in unethical behavior.[91]

Given that our judgments of ethical behavior are often biased, how can negotiators best answer the question of whether a given behavior is ethical? Consider the following:

1. *The front-page test.*   The front-page test, or light-of-day test, poses the following ethical challenge to negotiators: Would you be completely comfortable if your actions and statements were printed in full on the front page of the local newspaper or were reported on the TV news? If not, then your behavior or strategies in question may be regarded as unethical. Another version: "How would I feel if I had to stand before a board of inquiry and describe what I have done?"
2. *Reverse Golden Rule.*   The Golden Rule states, "Do unto others as you would have them do unto you." In this strategy, the negotiator asks himself or herself "If the tables were turned, how would I feel if my opponent did this to me?" If the answer is "I wouldn't like it very much," then it means the behavior in question may be regarded as unethical.
3. *Role modeling.*   "Would I advise others to do this?" or "Would I be proud to see my child act this way?" or "What if everyone bargained this way? Would the resulting society be desirable?"
4. *Third-party advice.*   It is wise to consult a third party (someone who takes an impartial view of the negotiation) to see how that person regards your planned behavior. When consulting the third party, do not reveal your own vote. Describe the event or situation in the third-person voice.
5. *Strengthen your bargaining position.*   Negotiators who have prepared adequately will be less tempted to lie. For example, a negotiator who initiates efforts to improve her BATNA does not need to lie about her BATNA. A negotiator who has thought about the factors that affect his reservation price can simply inform the other party, "It's none of your business." And a negotiator who has considered the facts can express an "opinion" based on the facts.

---

[88] Taylor, S. E., & Brown, J. (1988). Illusion and well-being: A social-psychological perspective. *Psychological Bulletin, 103,* 193–210.
[89] Langer, E. (1975). The illusion of control. *Journal of Personality and Social Psychology, 32,* 311–328.
[90] Fischhoff, B., Slovic, P., & Lichtenstein, S. (1977). Knowing with certainty: The appropriateness of extreme confidence. *Journal of Experimental Psychology: Human Perception and Performance, 3*(4), 552–564.
[91] Schweitzer, M., Ordonez, L., & Douma, B. (2004). Goal setting as a motivator of unethical behavior. *Academy of Management Journal, 47*(3), 422–432.

Some argue that ethics, "far from being a check or drag on negotiator power, can actually help to enhance it." The "samurai negotiator" derives power from ethics and their principles are perceived by the other party as a sign of strength.[92] Consider, for example, how Pizza Hut dropped their key tomato sauce supplier, Hunt-Wesson (HW) in an aggressive cost-cutting move.[93] Pizza Hut threatened HW to drop their price by 2.5 cents or lose the Pizza Hut business. HW refused. Six weeks later, Pizza Hut begged HW to come back to the bargaining table because of quality problems (runny pizza) and asked HW to name its price to reinstate the contract.

CONCLUSION

A negotiator's BATNA is the most important source of power in a negotiation. Having said that, effective use of power is not simply the threat of exercising one's BATNA. The enlightened negotiator knows a larger slice of the pie can be obtained by creating a larger pie. We outlined two types of influence strategies that appeal to the mind and heart, respectively. The central route strategies include: controlling the agenda, generating alternatives within issues, generating options across issues, attitudinal structuring and contrast, consistency, strategic framing, fairness, and time pressure. The peripheral route strategies we discussed included: status, gender, social networks, physical appearance, delaying liking, a certain degree of self-effacing behavior, strategic priming, reciprocity and complementarity, social proof, reactance, and foot-in-the-door, door-in-the-face, and the that's-not-all technique.

All negotiators need to be concerned about ethical behavior in negotiation and know that, as with everything else, we don't always see our actions the way others see them. We discussed the moral and strategic disadvantages of lying with respect to the six things negotiators most often lie about (positions, interests, priorities, BATNAs, reservation prices, and key facts). We discussed how bounded ethicality, the illusion of superiority, the illusion of control, and overconfidence might contribute to a negotiator's decision to engage in deception. We suggest that negotiators engage in five "tests" when struggling to decide whether a given behavior is ethical: the front-page test, reverse Golden Rule, role modeling, third-party advice, and strengthening their bargaining position.

---

[92] Young, M. (2008), Sharks, saints, and samurai: The power of ethics in negotiations. *Negotiation Journal*, *24*(2), 145–155.
[93] Shapiro, R., & Jankowsko, M. (1998). *The power of nice: How to negotiate so everyone wins—especially you*. New York: John Wiley and Sons.

Creativity and Problem Solving in Negotiations

After two years of negotiations among odd bedfellows, a win-win agreement was artfully crafted among PXP (Plains Exploration and Production Company) and two Wyoming advocacy groups, the Wyoming Sportsmen for Fish and Wildlife and the Wyoming Outfitters and Guides Association. On the surface, the positions of the parties were not aligned; in fact, they were downright opposed—PXP wanted drilling and development and the advocacy groups desired to protect big-game habitats and camping. PXP had a lease for development and could have bullied in the negotiation. They decided to listen instead. In the creative agreement, PXP was given the opportunity to drill as many as 136 natural gas wells on 17 well pads across 20,000 acres in return for a substantial mitigation dollar amount. The parties also focused on the future: PXP would not apply for any additional drilling permits, regardless of the volume of natural gas discovered and would pay for more than $6 million to protect the wildlife habitat and monitor air and water quality in the area. There were several keys that allowed for a creative negotiation process. One was a pledge on the part of all parties to agree early in the process that "everything was on the table and open for discussion." The second was the presence of contingency agreements. For example, PXP committed to pay for a million-dollar study to establish baseline water quality data that could be used to determine whether the drilling activity was polluting groundwater. A third was willingness to stay at the table.[1]

---

[1] Streater, S. (2010, December 16). Oil and gas: Industry cedes 28,000 acres of Wyoming range for conservation. *E & E Publishing*, LLC. Eenews.net

CREATIVITY IN NEGOTIATION

The most creative negotiation agreements, like PXP and the Wyoming Fish and Wildlife are often complex agreements that have several moving parts. The creative aspect of negotiation is often ignored by negotiators, who fixate on the competitive aspect of negotiation. This tendency is largely driven by the pervasive **fixed-pie perception**, or the belief that negotiation is a win-or-lose enterprise. Successful negotiation requires creativity and problem solving, and the process of dividing resources is easier when the pie has been enlarged via creative and insightful problem-solving strategies.

This chapter is the "advanced course" in integrative bargaining. It provides negotiators with strategies to transform their negotiations into win-win enterprises. We focus on products of negotiation (such as outcomes), the people involved (i.e., the negotiators), and the processes (or the conditions that connect the people to the product).[2] We invite negotiators to put their problem-solving skills and creativity to the test. We focus on creative agreements in negotiation. Next, we consider the biggest threats to creative problem solving in negotiations.

Test Your Own Creativity

Exhibit 8-1 contains 13 problems. Take 30 minutes right now to try to solve these problems. When in doubt, make your best guess. As you go along, make a mental note of your thoughts about each problem as you try to solve it. Read the rest of this chapter before you look up the answers in Exhibit 8-10 (at the end of this chapter). As you read the chapter, see whether any insights come to you, and make note of them as they arise.

WHAT IS YOUR MENTAL MODEL OF NEGOTIATION?

A mental model is a person's theory about cause and effect. A mental model of negotiation is a personal theory about what behaviors will lead to certain outcomes. Negotiators' mental models shape their behavior and affect the course of negotiation. For example, if you view negotiation as a "dog-eat-dog" enterprise, you are going to be much tougher than if you view negotiation as a "partnership." Consider the following five popular mental models: haggling, cost-benefit analysis, game playing, partnership, and problem solving.[3] As you read about these five mental models, think about which one best characterizes your approach to negotiation.

Haggling

The most common mental model of negotiation is the **haggling model**, in which each negotiator tries to obtain the biggest share of the bargaining zone. The haggling model is based upon a fixed-pie perception of negotiation. For example, before setting out for Dungeness crab season each December, fisherman and processors in Newport, Oregon engage in a time-honored tradition of negotiating an opening price for the crabs, known as "parley" in maritime terminology. Before the 2010 season began, negotiations continued to the last minute over a range of $1.55 to $1.75 per pound, with a final settlement price of $1.65 per pound.[4]

---

[2] Carnevale, P. J. (2006). Creativity in the outcomes of conflict. In M. Deutsch, P. T. Coleman & E. C. Marcus (Eds.), *Handbook of conflict resolution* (2nd ed.). San Francisco: Jossey-Bass.

[3] Thompson, L., & Loewenstein, J. (2003). Mental models of negotiation: Descriptive, prescriptive, and paradigmatic implications. In M. A. Hogg & J. Cooper (Eds.), *Sage handbook of social psychology*. London: Sage.

[4] Dillman, T. (2010 November 29). Haggling over price. *Newport News Times*. Newportnewstimes.com

EXHIBIT 8-1

Creativity Test

Card Decision*

Look at the following numbers/letters. Each number/letter represents a card. On each of the four cards, a letter appears on one side and a number on the other. Your task is to judge the validity of the following rule: *"If a card has a vowel on one side, then it has an even number on the other side."* Your task is to turn over only those cards that have to be turned over for the correctness of the rule to be judged. What cards will you turn over? [*Circle those cards that you will turn over to test the rule.*]

E   K   4   7

Person in a Room Decision†

A person has been chosen at random from a set of 100 people, consisting of 30 engineers and 70 lawyers. What is the probability that the individual chosen at random from the group, Jack, is an engineer?

"Jack is a 45-year-old man. He is married and has four children. He is generally conservative, careful, and ambitious. He shows no interest in political and social issues and spends most of his free time on his many hobbies, which include home carpentry, sailing, and mathematical puzzles."

Jack is [*circle one*]:

an engineer   a lawyer

Betting Decision**

Which gamble would you rather play? [*Circle either A or B.*]

   A: 1/3 chance to win $80,000

   B: 5/6 chance to win $30,000

Now, imagine that you have to choose one of the following gambles. Which one will you play? [*Circle either C or D.*]

   C: 50% chance to win $10,000, and 50% chance to lose $10,000

   D: $0

Water Jugs††

You have been given a set of jugs of various capacities and an unlimited water supply. Your task is to measure out a specified quantity of water. You should assume you have a tap and a sink so

---

* Wason, P. C., & Johnson-Laird, P. N. (1972). *Psychology of reasoning: Structure and content.* Cambridge, MA: Harvard University Press.
† Kahneman, D., & Tversky, A. (1973). On the psychology of prediction. *Psychological Review, 80,* 237–251.
** Tversky, A., & Kahneman, D. (1981). The framing of decisions and the psychology of choice. *Science, 211,* 453–458.
†† Luchins, A. S. (1942). Mechanization in problem solving. *Psychological Monographs, 5*(46), 1–95.

                                                                                    (continued)

that you can fill jugs and empty them. The jugs start out empty. You are allowed only to fill the jugs, empty them, and pour water from one jug to another. As an example, consider the following problems 1 and 2:

Example Problem#	Capacity of Jug A	Capacity of Jug B	Capacity of Jug C	Quantity Desired
1	5 cups	40 cups	18 cups	28 cups
2	21 cups	127 cups	3 cups	100 cups

To solve problem 1, you would fill jug A and pour it into B, fill A again and pour it into B, and fill C and pour it into B. The solution to this problem is denoted by **2A + C**.

To solve problem 2, you would first fill jug B with 127 cups, fill A from B so that 106 cups are left in B, fill C from B so that 103 cups are left in B, and empty C and fill C again from B so that the goal of 100 cups in jug B is achieved. The solution to this problem can be denoted by **B-A-2C**.

Real Problems

Problem #	Capacity of Jug A	Capacity of Jug B	Capacity of Jug C	Desired Quantity	Solution
1	14 cups	163 cups	25 cups	99 cups	
2	18 cups	43 cups	10 cups	5 cups	
3	9 cups	42 cups	6 cups	21 cups	
4	20 cups	59 cups	4 cups	31 cups	
5	23 cups	49 cups	3 cups	20 cups	
6	15 cups	39 cups	3 cups	18 cups	
7	28 cups	76 cups	3 cups	25 cups	
8	18 cups	48 cups	4 cups	22 cups	
9	14 cups	36 cups	8 cups	6 cups	

Stick Problem*

You have six sticks, all of equal length. You need to arrange them to form four triangles that are equilateral and with each side one stick long. (You cannot break any sticks.) Indicate how you would do this.

Letter Sequence[†]

What is the next letter in the following sequence? OTTFFSS____

Chain Problem**

The goal of this task is to make a chain (as depicted in the goal state) from the links you are given (in the given state). Please note that it costs $3 to open a link, $5 to close a link. Your total budget is $25.

---

* Scheer, M. (1963). *Scientific American, 208,* 118–218.
[†] Letter sequence: Source unknown.
** De Bono, E. (1967). *The use of lateral thinking.* New York: Penguin.

(continued)

Given State	Goal State
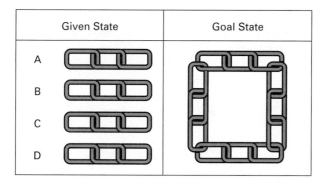	

Susan and Martha

Susan and Martha are discussing their children when Susan asks Martha for the ages of her three sons. Martha says, "The sum of their ages is 13 and the product of their ages is the same as your age." Susan replies, "I still do not know their ages." What must Susan's age be?

    a. 24 b. 27 c. 63 d. 36 e. 48

Necklace*

A woman has four pieces of chain. Each piece is made of three links. She wants to join the pieces into a single closed ring of chain. To open a link costs 2 cents; to close a link costs 3 cents. All links are now closed. She has only 15 cents. How does she do it?

Gold Chain

Isaac is staying at a motel when he runs short of cash. Checking his finances, he discovers that in 23 days he will have plenty of money, but until then he will be broke. The motel owner refuses to let Isaac stay without paying his bill each day, but because Isaac owns a heavy gold chain with 23 links, the owner allows Isaac to pay for each of the 23 days with one gold link. Then, when Isaac receives his money, the motel owner will return the chain. Isaac is very anxious to keep the chain as intact as possible, so he does not want to cut off any more of the links than absolutely necessary. The motel owner, however, insists on payment each day, and he will not accept advance payment. How many links must Isaac cut while still paying the owner one link for each successive day?

_____links

Nine Dot Problem†

Consider the following nine dots. Draw four or fewer straight lines *without lifting your pencil from the paper* so that each of the nine dots has a line through it.

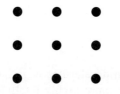

---

* Wickelgren, W. A. (1974). *How to solve problems.* San Francisco: W. H. Freeman.
† Weisberg, R. W., & Alba, J. W. (1981). An examination of the alleged role of "fixation" in the solution of several insight problems. *Journal of Experimental Psychology: General, 110,* 169–192.

(continued)

Pigpen*

Nine pigs are kept in a square pen, as shown in the figure. Build two more square enclosures that would put each pig in a pen by itself.

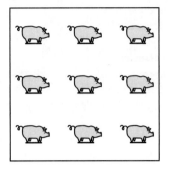

Water Lilies[†]

Water lilies on a certain lake double in area every 24 hours. On the first day of summer, one water lily is on the lake. On the sixtieth day, water lilies completely cover the lake. On what day is the lake half covered?

Bartender Problem**

A man walks into a bar and asks for a glass of water. The bartender points a shotgun at the man. The man says, "Thank you," and walks out. What is going on in this situation?

---

[*] Fixx, J. F. (1972). *More games for the super-intelligent*. New York: Warner Books.
[†] Sternberg, R. J., & Davidson, J. E. (1983). Insight in the gifted. *Educational Psychologist, 18*, 51–57.
[**] Dayton, T., Durso, F. T., & Shepard, J. D. (1990). A measure of the knowledge reorganization underlying insight. In R. W. Schraneveldt (Ed.), *Pathfinder associative networks: Studies in knowledge organization*. Norwood, NJ: Ablex.

Cost-Benefit Analysis

Some negotiators think of negotiation as a rational, decision-making model in which they compute a cost-benefit analysis and attempt to maximize their returns. For example, Robert Rubin, former U.S. Treasury secretary, calculates the odds of almost every decision he faces, using both real and mental yellow pads.[5] He once suggested to the board of the American Ballet Theatre, on which he sat, that it enact a cost reduction by cutting 10% of the swans in *Swan Lake*.

Game Playing

The chess game model of negotiation elevates negotiation from "fighting in the streets" to a battle of wits between two or more highly intelligent people. In game playing, each

---

[5] Loomis, C. (2003, December 22). The larger-than-life life of Robert Rubin. *Fortune*, 114–124.

person has his or her own interests in mind. For example, California Tortilla's customers were invited to challenge cashiers to a game of Rock, Paper, Scissors to get a dollar taken off their bill. The World RPS (Rock, Paper, Scissors) Society posted the following advice on the Internet to size up the counterparty: A seemingly intellectually superior counterparty (thus most likely to play paper) can be beat by playing scissors. Rock being the most aggressive throw, the knuckle-dragging cashier type can be beat by playing paper, which symbolizes "the victory of modern culture over barbarism." A contained, clever, user of tools can be beat by playing rock.

Partnership

A quite different mental model of negotiation is what we call the **partnership model**, embraced by companies and salespeople who treat their clients as partners. Negotiators who ascribe to the partnership model believe it is important to build rapport to nurture a long-term relationship and, in many cases, to make sacrifices in the name of creating long-term goodwill.

Problem Solving

In **problem-solving**, both negotiators sit on the same side of the table and attempt to solve a puzzle together. This model focuses on the collaborative or cooperative aspects of the task and involves a great deal of creativity, reframing, and out-of-the-box thinking.

We investigated negotiators' mental models and how they affect performance.[6] Compared to negotiators who fail to reach win-win outcomes, negotiators who reach win-win outcomes are more accurate in their understanding of the other party's underlying interests. Negotiators who reach win-win outcomes have mental models that are more similar to one another than do negotiators who fail to reach win-win outcomes. Shared metacognition promotes more cooperative negotiation, greater insight into the opponent's values and interest, and greater satisfaction with the negotiation outcome.[7] To achieve such shared cognition, negotiators should explicitly exchange their understanding with one another. Experience-based training allowed negotiators to develop mental models that resemble expert, win-win models; in contrast, didactic lecturing is uniquely ineffective,

CREATIVE NEGOTIATION AGREEMENTS

Creativity in negotiation often follows the pattern of the "Monday morning quarterback," meaning that it is easy in hindsight to see creative opportunity in negotiations; however, it often eludes us in the moment. Next, we outline the hallmark characteristics of truly creative negotiations.[8]

Fractionating Problems into Solvable Parts

Most negotiation situations appear to contain a single issue. Fractionating negotiation issues into solvable parts and creating several issues from what appear to be single-issue negotiations

---

[6] Van Boven, L., & Thompson, L. (2003). A look into the mind of the negotiator: Mental models in negotiation. *Group Processes & Intergroup Relations, 6*(4), 387–404.

[7] Choi, D. W. (2010). Shared metacognition in integrative negotiation. *International Journal of Conflict Management, 21*(3), 309–333.

[8] Pruitt, D. G., & Carnevale, P. J. (1993). *Negotiation in social conflict.* Pacific Grove, CA: Brooks-Cole.

is probably the most important aspect of creative negotiation.[9] For example, consider how the negotiations between members of the United Food and Commercial Workers Local 175 and Wilfred Laurier University went when they avoided a strike, even when they had a $300,000 deficit with which to deal. They fractionated the bargaining issue from a single issue (wage increases) to several issues, including job security, control over uniforms, parking fees, access to athletic facilities, and overtime costs.[10] Also, consider negotiations between Southwest Airlines and AirTran. The most obvious issue—the Southwest and AirTran merger—took precedent. However, the parties also identified seemingly smaller issues as well. For example, because AirTran featured business class seating, and Southwest did not, AirTran raised the seating issue and argued that loyal customers of AirTran might miss their seats.[11]

People are good at solving problems when the problems are presented directly to them; however, they are not very good at *defining* problems. Negotiation requires defining problems before solving them (i.e., searching for differences in such a way that trade-offs can be creative). Psychologists call this task **problem representation**, as opposed to problem solving.

Finding Differences: Issue Alignment and Realignment

Before negotiators can find differences to trade off, they need to align the issues in such a way that permits the issues to be negotiated independently and, ideally, traded off.[12] Skilled negotiators know how to realign issues so as to find pockets of opportunity. Consider, for example, the negotiation between architect Daniel Libeskind and developer Larry Silverstein concerning the rebuilding of the World Trade Center site.[13] By identifying additional issues and realigning issues, a negotiated agreement was reached, ending months of heated battles between Silverstein and Libeskind. The impasse centered on how much influence the architect (Libeskind) would have on the design of the first office building to go up at the site—the 1,776-foot tower that defines the rebuilt Trade Center's presence on the Lower Manhattan skyline. The developer (Silverstein) wanted to involve other architects for the largest tower and make changes to the master plan. An agreement was reached between the two by carving out another issue—namely, the development of commercial design guidelines governing future commercial development on the site. Libeskind won this issue, but Silverstein got to hire another firm to serve as design architect and project manager for the Freedom Tower, the first commercial building constructed on the site. Libeskind drew up diagrams showing how theaters, rehearsal halls and classrooms could be combined with a 35-story apartment building, items that were folded into redevelopment plans.[14]

Expanding the Pie

Expanding the pie is an important method by which to create integrative agreements. However, negotiators who labor under the fixed-pie perception may limit their options unnecessarily.

---

[9] Lax, D. A., & Sebenius, J. K. (1986). *The manager as negotiator.* New York: Free Press.
[10] Simone, R. (2003, July 29). Food workers help WLU trim deficit. *Kitchener-Waterloo Record,* p. D8.
[11] Mutzabaugh, B. (2010, October 5). 'Not for sale' AirTran CEO initially told Southwest. *USA Today.* Travel.usa.com
[12] Lax, & Sebenius, *The manager as negotiator.*
[13] Wyatt, E. (2003, July 16). Officials reach an agreement on rebuilding downtown site. *New York Times,* p. 1.
[14] Dunlap, D. W. (2011, January 12). 10 years after 9/11, Deutsche bank tower vanishes. *New York Times.* Nytimes.com

Consider, for example, how a negotiation between a fire station and an elementary school was transformed from an impasse to a creative arrangement by expanding the pie.[15] Initially, the school wanted to acquire land to expand, but the fire station blocked that move. So the pie was expanded such that each party paid an unrelated third party to acquire a separate parcel of land. In the final deal, the city gave a 3-acre parcel of land to a private owner, who then gave back to the city 7.5 of his own acres (located nearer to the school and fire station). At this point, the fire station and the school successfully expanded the pie of available land to accomplish both of their goals. Thus, by expanding the pie to include another plot of land that could be "swapped," both parties ultimately achieved what they wanted: The school was able to expand, and the firehouse could make its entrances and exits more convenient and safe.

Bridging

Oftentimes, it is not possible for negotiators to find a compromise solution, and expanding the pie does not work. Furthermore, perhaps neither party can get what it wants in a trade-off. A **bridging** solution creates a new alternative that meets parties' underlying interests. Bridging alerts us to yet another reason to understand the other party's interests and avoid positional bargaining. If negotiators understand the basic needs of the counterparty, they are more likely to fashion bridging agreements.

Cost Cutting

Sometimes, people are reluctant to negotiate because reaching a resolution seems costly to them. Most people are risk seeking when it comes to loss, meaning that they are reluctant to make concessions and may behave irrationally when they believe they will have to make concessions. **Cost cutting** is a way of making the other party feel whole by reducing that party's costs. An example of value-added cost cutting occurred in negotiations between The Nature Conservancy and the Great Northern Paper Company.[16] On the surface, we might expect the interests of these two to be a classic fixed-pie—The Nature Conservancy, dedicated to preserving the environment, should hardly want to work with a company that makes its money by cutting down trees for consumer and industrial use. In an unprecedented partnership, The Nature Conservancy assumed $50 million worth of Great Northern's debts. In return, Great Northern Paper agreed to protect a quarter-million acres from development.[17]

Another example of cost-cutting occurred in a heated dispute involving Walgreens and CVS drugstores. In 2010, Walgreens threatened to stop filing or renewing prescriptions from competitor CVS Caremark's huge network because of perceived unpredictable reimbursement rates and prescription plans that favored CVS stores. CVS retaliated by announcing it would pull its network from Walgreens stores within a month. The threats would have blocked millions from filing prescriptions at Walgreens stores. However, a turning point occurred when each company looked at the potential costs. Walgreen's patients accounted for about 10% of CVS' Pharmacy Benefit Manager business, and CVS customers accounted for nearly $4.4 billion of Walgreens' annual sales. The two companies agreed to cut costs via an agreement in which CVS provided

---

[15] Robertson, G. (1998, February 18). Creative negotiations pay off. *Richmond Times-Dispatch,* p. J3.

[16] Analysis: Business deal between great northern paper and the nature conservancy to protect a quarter-million acres of Maine woods from development. (2002, August 28). *NPR org*

[17] Ibid.

financial concessions in return for Walgreens not extracting higher payment for the drugs that CVS Caremark enrollees buy.[18]

Nonspecific Compensation

In a **nonspecific-compensation** agreement, one negotiator receives what he or she wants, and the other is compensated (or paid) by some method that was initially outside the bounds of the negotiation. For example, Phil Jones, managing director of Real Time, a London-based interactive design studio, recalls an instance where he used nonspecific compensation in his negotiations.[19] The problem was that his client, a Formula 1 motor-racing team, wanted to launch Internet web sites but did not have the budget to pay him. However, in Phil Jones's eyes, the client was high profile and had creative, challenging projects with which Real Time wanted to get involved. Formula 1 came up with a non-specific compensation offer to make the deal go through: tickets to some of the major Formula 1 meetings. It worked. Says Phil Jones, "The tickets are like gold dust…and can be used as a pat on the back for staff or as an opportunity to pamper existing clients or woo new ones."

Structuring Contingencies

A major obstacle to reaching negotiated agreements often concerns negotiators' beliefs about some future event or outcome.[20] Impasses often result from conflicting beliefs that are difficult to surmount, especially when each side is confident about the accuracy of his or her prediction and consequently suspicious of the other side's forecasts. Often, compromise is not a viable solution, and each party may be reluctant to change his or her point of view. Contingent contracts can provide a way out of the mire. With a **contingency** (or contingent) **contract**, differences of opinion among negotiators concerning future events do not have to be bridged; instead, they become the core of the agreement.[21] Negotiators can bet on the future rather than argue about it. In some areas of business, contingency contracts are commonplace. For example, some CEOs agree to tie their salary to a company's stock price.

However, in many business negotiations, contingency contracts are either ignored or rejected for several reasons.[22] First, people are unaware of how to construct contingency contracts. Second, contingency contracts are often seen as a form of gambling. Third, no systematic way of thinking about the formulation of such contracts is usually available, meaning that they *appear* to be a good idea, but how to formalize and act upon them remains an enigma. Fourth, many negotiators have a "getting to yes" bias, meaning they focus on reaching common ground with the other party and are reluctant to accept differences of interest, even when this might create viable options for joint gain.[23] The paradoxical view suggested by the contingency contract strategy states that differences are often constructive. With a contingency contract, negotiators can focus on their real

---

[18] Martin, T. W., & Dagher, V. (2010, June 19). Corporate news: CVS, Walgreens settle dispute–fund threatened to block millions from filling prescriptions at Walgreen stores. *The Wall Street Journal*, p. B5; Abelson, R. (2010, June 19). Walgreen and CVS reach deal on filling prescriptions. *New York Times*, p. B3.

[19] Davies, J. (1998, November 1). The art of negotiation. *Management Today*, pp. 126–128.

[20] Lax, & Sebenius, *The manager as negotiator.*

[21] Bazerman, M. H., & Gillespie, J. J. (1999). Betting on the future: The virtues of contingent contracts. *Harvard Business Review, 77*(4), 155–160.

[22] Ibid.

[23] Gibson, K., Thompson, L., & Bazerman, M. H. (1994). Biases and rationality in the mediation process. In L. Heath, F. Bryant, & J. Edwards (Eds.), *Application of heuristics and biases to social issues: Vol. 3.* New York: Plenum.

mutual interests, not on their speculative disagreements.[24] When companies fail to find their way out of differences in beliefs, they often go to court, creating expensive delays, litigation costs, loss of control by both parties, and deteriorating BATNAs. Consider how a contingent contract might have changed the course of one of the century's most famous and most fruitless antitrust cases. In 1969, the U.S. Department of Justice [DOJ] filed a suit against IBM, alleging monopolistic behavior. More than a decade later, the case was still bogged down in litigation. Some 65 million pages of documents had been produced, and each side had spent millions of dollars in legal expenses. The DOJ finally dropped the case in 1982, when it had become clear that IBM's once-dominant share of the computer market was eroding rapidly.

During the case's 13 futile years, IBM and the government essentially argued over differences in their expectations about future events. IBM assumed that its market share would decrease in coming years as competition for the lucrative computer market increased. The government assumed that IBM, as a monopolist, would hold its large market share for the foreseeable future. Neither felt the other's view was valid, and so neither had a basis for compromise.

An efficient and rational way to settle this dispute would have been for IBM and the government to have negotiated a contingent contract whose purpose would have been to place a wager on the future. They might have agreed, for example, that if by 1975 IBM still held at least 70% of the market—its share in 1969—it would pay a set fine and divest itself of certain businesses. If, however, its market share had dropped to 50% or lower, the government would not pursue antitrust actions. If its share fell somewhere between 50% and 70%, another type of contingency would take effect.

Constructing such a contingent contract would not have been easy. There were, after all, an infinite number of feasible permutations, and many details would need to be hammered out. But it would have been far more rational—and far cheaper—to have the two sides' lawyers devote a few weeks to arguing over how to structure a contingent contract than it was for them to spend years filing motions, taking depositions, and reviewing documents.[25]

Another advantage of contingency contracts is they provide a nearly perfect lie-detection device. Contingency contracts allow negotiators to test the counterparty's veracity in a nonconfrontational manner, thereby allowing parties to save face. Contingency contracts also allow parties who are concerned about being cheated to safeguard themselves. This fear of being cheated is precisely what Christopher Columbus was worried about when he negotiated an agreement about the New World with Queen Isabella and King Ferdinand of Spain. Worried he would risk life and opportunity and gain nothing, Christopher Columbus insisted he be offered an opportunity to contribute one-eighth of the costs of future expeditions and be guaranteed one-eighth of all profits. Unfortunately, the crowns reneged on the deal upon his return, and Columbus had to go to court.[26]

By the same token, contingency contracts build trust and good faith between negotiators because incentives can be provided for each company to deliver exceptional performance. Therefore, contingency contracts provide a safety net, limiting each company's losses should an agreement go awry unexpectedly. (For a summary of the benefits of contingency contracts, see Exhibit 8-2.)

---

[24] Bazerman, & Gillespie, "Betting on the future."

[25] Ibid.

[26] Dworetzky, T. (1998, December 11). Explorer Christopher Columbus: How the West's greatest discoverer negotiated his trips' financing. *Investors' Business Daily,* p. 1BD.

EXHIBIT 8-2

The Six Benefits of Contingency Contracts

1. Contingency contracts allow negotiators to *build on their differences*, rather than arguing about them. Do not argue over the future. Bet on it.
2. Contingency contracts allow negotiators to *manage decision-making biases*. Although over-confidence and egocentrism can be barriers to effective agreements, contingency contracts use these biases to create a bet.
3. Contingency contracts allow negotiators to *solve problems of trust*, when one side has infor-mation that the other side lacks. The less-informed party can create a contingency to protect itself against the unknown information possessed by the other side.
4. Contingency contracts allow negotiators to *diagnose the honesty of the other side*. When one party makes a claim that the other party does not believe, a bet can be created to protect a negotiator against the lie.
5. Contingency contracts allow negotiators to *reduce risk through risk sharing*. The sharing of upside gains and losses not only can reduce risk, but can also create goodwill by increasing the partnership between the parties.
6. Contingency contracts allow negotiators to *increase the incentive of the parties to perform* at or above contractually specified levels. Contingency contracts should be specifically considered when the motivation of one of the parties is in question.

Source: Based on Bazerman, M. H. & Gillespie, J. J. (1999). *Betting on the future: The virtues of contingent contracts.* Cambridge, MA: Harvard Business School Publishing Corporation.

Although we believe contingency contracts can be valuable in many kinds of business negotiations, they are not always the right strategy to use. Bazerman and Gillespie suggest three key criteria for assessing the viability and usefulness of contingency contracts in negotiation:[27]

1. Contingency contracts require *some degree of continued interaction between the parties.* Because the final terms of the contract will not be determined until sometime after the initial agreement is signed, some amount of future interaction between parties is neces-sary, thereby allowing them to assess the terms of their agreement. Therefore, if the future seems highly uncertain, or if one of the parties is suspected of preparing to leave the situa-tion permanently, contingency contracts may not be wise.
2. Parties need to think about the *enforceability* of the contingency contract. Under a contingency contract, one or more of the parties will probably not be correct about the out-come because the contract often functions as a bet. This outcome creates a problem for the "loser" of the bet, who may be reluctant to reimburse the other party when things do not go his or her way. For this reason, the money in question might well be placed in escrow, thereby removing each party's temptation to defect.

---

[27] Bazerman & Gillespie, "Betting on the future."

3. Contingency contracts require a high degree of *clarity* and *measurability*. If an event is ambiguous, nonmeasurable, or of a subjective nature, overconfidence, egocentric bias, and a variety of other self-serving biases can make the objective appraisal of a contingency contract a matter of some opinion. Parties should agree up front on clear, specific measures concerning how the contract will be evaluated. For this reason, it is often wise to consult a third party.

THREATS TO EFFECTIVE PROBLEM SOLVING AND CREATIVITY

A variety of human biases and shortcomings threaten people's ability to think creatively. A key first step to preventing these biases is *awareness* of their existence.

The Inert Knowledge Problem

People's ability to solve problems in new contexts depends on the accessibility of their relevant knowledge. If a manager is confronted with new business challenges, he or she often consults his or her knowledge base for previous problems in an attempt to see which previous problem solving strategies might be useful in solving the new problem. The **inert knowledge problem** is the inability to access relevant knowledge when we most need it.[28] The information necessary to solve a new problem is part of a manager's cognitive repertoire but is not accessible at the right time. This unavailability is not due to senility or amnesia but, rather, to the peculiar way that our long-term memories are constructed.

A striking dissociation occurs between what is most *accessible* in our memories and what is most *useful* in human problem solving and reasoning. People often fail to recall what is ultimately most valuable for solving new problems.[29] In one investigation, people studied examples containing principles of probability theory and then attempted to solve problems requiring the use of those principles.[30] If the study and test stories were from the *same* context, people were more likely to be reminded of them than if the stories were from *different* contexts. In another investigation, participants were given a story to read about a hawk giving feathers to a hunter.[31] Participants were then given one of four stories resulting from combining surface and structural similarities (i.e., a story with similar characters and plot, different characters but same plot, similar characters but different plot, or different characters and different plot). People were more than four times more likely to recall the original story when later shown a story with similar characters than when shown a story with different characters, suggesting that people often fail to recall what is ultimately most valuable for solving new problems.[32] Upon being informed of the correct approach to a negotiation, management students often express regret: "*I knew that. I just did not think to use it.*"

Unfortunately, negotiators in the real world typically do not experience regret because they are not told when they have made learning and application errors. The ability of managers to transfer knowledge from one context to another is highly limited. **Transfer** is the

---

[28] Whitehead, A. N. (1929). *The aims of education.* New York: Macmillan.
[29] Forbus, K. D., Gentner, D., & Law, K. (1995). MAC/FAC: A model of similarity-based retrieval. *Cognitive Science, 19*(2), 141–205; Gentner, D., Rattermann, M. J., & Forbus, K. D. (1993). The roles of similarity in transfer: Separating retrievability from inferential soundness. *Cognitive Psychology, 25*(4), 524–575.
[30] Ross, B. H. (1987). This is like that: The use of earlier problems and the separation of similarity effects. *Journal of Experimental Psychology: Learning, Memory and Cognition, 13*(4), 629–639.
[31] Gentner, Rattermann, & Forbus, "The roles of similarity in transfer."
[32] Forbus, Gentner, & Law, "MAC/FAC"; Gentner, Rattermann, & Forbus, "The roles of similarity in transfer."

ability to apply a strategy or idea learned in one situation to solve a problem in a different, but relevant, situation. **Surface-level transfer** occurs when a person attempts to transfer a solution from one context to a superficially similar context. However, in most situations it is desirable for people to engage in **deep-level transfer** by applying solutions and strategies that have meaningful similarities, rather than superficial ones. Unfortunately, this task proves to be quite difficult for most managers to do. In general, if two problems have similar surface (or superficial) features, managers are more likely to transfer knowledge from one problem situation to the other. Ideally, managers must transfer solutions to problems that have similar deep (or structural) features but have significantly different superficial features.

As a case in point, consider the "tumor problem" presented in Exhibit 8-3. When presented with this problem, few people successfully solve it; if it is preceded by the fortress problem in Exhibit 8-4, the solution rate rises dramatically.[33] Even though a similar solution can be applied in both problems, because the surface information in each problem is quite different (one deals with a medical situation; the other, a political situation), people are often unable to access their knowledge about one of these problems to help them solve the other.

The same problem occurs in negotiation. Studies of MBA students, executives, and consultants acquiring negotiation skills reveal a dramatic inert knowledge problem.[34] Transfer rates are quite low when a key principle needs to be applied to different negotiation situations that

---

EXHIBIT 8-3

The Tumor Problem

Suppose you are a doctor faced with a patient who has a malignant tumor in his stomach. It is impossible to operate on the patient, but unless the tumor is destroyed, the patient will die. A kind of ray can be used to destroy the tumor. If the rays reach the tumor all at once at a sufficiently high intensity, the tumor will be destroyed. Unfortunately, at this intensity, the healthy tissue the rays pass through on the way to the tumor will also be destroyed. At lower intensities, the rays are harmless to healthy tissue, but they will not affect the tumor either. What type of procedure might be used to destroy the tumor with the rays and, at the same time, avoid destroying the healthy tissue?

Source: Based on Gick, M. L., & Holyoak, K. J. (1980). Analogical problem solving. *Cognitive Psychology, 12,* 306–355.

---

[33] Gick, M. L., & Holyoak, K. J. (1980). Analogical problem solving. *Cognitive Psychology, 12,* 306–355.

[34] Loewenstein, J., Thompson, L., & Gentner, D. (1999). Analogical encoding facilitates transfer in negotiation. *Psychonomic Bulletin and Review, 6*(4), 586–597; Loewenstein, J., Thompson, L., & Gentner, D. (2003). Analogical learning in negotiation teams: Comparing cases promotes learning and transfer. *Academy of Management Learning and Education, 2*(2), 119–127; Thompson, L., Loewenstein, J., & Gentner, D. (2000). Avoiding missed opportunities in managerial life: Analogical training more powerful than case-based training. *Organizational Behavior and Human Decision Processes, 82*(1), 60–75; Gentner, D., Loewenstein, J., & Thompson, L. (2003). Learning and transfer: A general role for analogical encoding. *Journal of Educational Psychology, 95*(2), 393–408; for a review, see Loewenstein, J., & Thompson, L. (2000). The challenge of learning. *Negotiation Journal, 16*(4), 399–408; Gentner, D., Loewenstein, J., Thompson, L., & Forbus, K. D. (2009). Reviving inert knowledge: Analogical abstraction supports relational retrieval of past events. *Cognitive Science, 33*(8), 1343–1382.

involve different surface features. For example, when people are challenged with a negotiation situation involving a theater company that contains the potential for a contingency contract, they are often unable to employ the principle of contingency contracts even when they have received extensive training on this principle in a negotiation case involving a different context, such as a family-owned farm. This occurs because we tend to use our previous knowledge only when it seems similar to a new problem. People are not able to recognize problems that may benefit from similar problem solving principles and strategies.

The obvious question is: What decreases the inert knowledge problem and increases people's ability to transfer knowledge they possess when faced with a situation that could potentially benefit from that knowledge? One answer appears to be quite simple and powerful. It involves making an explicit *comparison* between two or more relevant cases.[35] To the extent that people mentally compare cases or situations, they are able to create a problem-solving schema that is uncluttered by irrelevant surface information. Thus, problem-solving schemas created through this process of mental comparison are more portable and more likely to be called upon when negotiators are challenged with a novel problem. In the absence of comparison, it is not clear to negotiators which information about a situation is relevant or irrelevant. Furthermore, as helpful as making comparisons can be, recognizing *when* to make them is not always obvious. For example, in our training of MBA students and executives, we frequently present negotiators with several training cases, usually on the same printed page. Very rarely do negotiators actively compare the cases printed on the same page, even though they contain a similar underlying principle. Thus, the key appears to be making comparisons among experiences, a strategy we elaborate upon later.

The preceding strategy focused on enhancing knowledge transfer by providing negotiators with very similar, specific examples. However, diverse analogical training, wherein negotiators compare several different value-creating strategies, may be more effective.[36] Negotiators who are prompted to compare (rather than simply read) examples are not only able to profitably transfer their learning to a new negotiation situation, they are able to remember negotiation situations from their own life that illustrate the key learning principle.[37] In a related investigation, negotiators were able to engage in successful knowledge transfer by focusing on differences in seemingly unrelated tasks.[38] Specifically, negotiators who were able to think about how others made decisions in versions of the "Monty Hall" game[39] and the multiparty "Ultimatum" game,[40] were more accurate in analyzing a new problem.[41]

Availability Heuristic

Which is more common: words that start with the letter *K*—for example, *king*—or words with *K* as the third letter—for example, *awkward*?[42] In the English language, more than twice as many

[35] Thompson, Loewenstein, & Gentner, "Avoiding missed opportunities."

[36] Moran, S., Bereby-Meyer, Y., & Bazerman, M. H. (2008). Stretching the effectiveness of analogical training in negotiations: Teaching diverse principles for creating value. *Negotiation and Conflict Management Research, 1*(2), 99–134.

[37] Gentner, Loewenstein, Thompson, & Forbus, "Reviving inert knowledge."

[38] Idson, L., Chugh, D., Bereby-Meyer, Y., Moran, S., Grosskopf, B., & Bazerman, M. (2004). Overcoming focusing failures in competitive environments. *Journal of Behavioral Decision Making, 17,* 159–172.

[39] Nalebuff, B. (1987, Autumn). Puzzles: Choose a curtain, duelity, two point conversions, and more. *Journal of Economic Perspectives, 1,* 157–163.

[40] Messick, D. M., Moore, D. A., & Bazerman, M. H. (1997). Ultimatum bargaining with a group: Underestimating the importance of the decision rule. *Organizational Behavior and Human Decision Processes, 69*(2), 87–101.

[41] Samuelson, W. F., & Bazerman, M. H. (1985). Negotiating under the winner's curse. In V. Smith (Ed.), *Research in experimental economics: Vol. 3* (pp. 105–137). Greenwich, CT: JAI Press.

[42] Kahneman, D., & Tversky, A. (1982). On the study of statistical intuitions. *Cognition, 11*(2), 123–141.

words have K as the third letter than have K as the first letter. Despite this fact, the majority of people guess incorrectly (they assume that more words have K as the first letter), due to the **availability heuristic**. According to the availability heuristic, the more prevalent a group or category is judged to be, the easier it is for people to bring instances of this group or category to mind. This heuristic affects the quality of negotiators' judgments in that they may be biased by the ease with which information can be brought to mind. In another investigation, people were presented with a list of 39 names of well-known people.[43] Nineteen of the people on the list were female; 20 were male. The women happened to be more famous than the men. Afterward, people were asked to judge how many women's names appeared on the list. People dramatically over-estimated the number of female names, presumably because they were easier to recall—another illustration of the availability heuristic.

The availability heuristic is associated with the **false consensus effect**.[44] The false consensus effect refers to the fact that most people think others agree with them more than is actually warranted. For example, people who smoke estimate that 51% of others are smokers, but nonsmokers' estimate that only 38% of people are smokers.[45] Furthermore, people overestimate the proportion of people who agree with them about their attitudes concerning drugs, abortion, seatbelt use, politics, and even certain brand-name crackers.[46] When a negotiator falls victim to the availability heuristic, the likelihood of employing creative strategies (which are often less available) is severely undermined.

Representativeness

Imagine that you have just met your new boss. She is thin, wears glasses, is soft-spoken, and dresses conservatively. Does your supervisor enjoy poetry or sports? In answering such questions, people make judgments on the basis of a relatively simple rule: The more similar a person is to a group stereotype, the more likely he or she is to also belong to that group. Most people assume the supervisor enjoys poetry. Basically, the more a person looks like the stereotype of a group member, the more we are inclined to stereotype them as belonging to that group. The **representativeness heuristic** is based on stereotypes of people, which often have a basis in reality but are frequently outdated and wrong. Furthermore, reliance on stereotypical information leads people to overlook other types of information that could potentially be useful in negotiations. The most important type of information is related to base rates. **Base rates** are the frequency with which some event or pattern occurs in a general population. For example, consider a negotiator interested in purchasing a new car. One source of information concerning the new car is a popular consumer report. This report is based upon thousands of consumer data points and research and therefore is highly reliable. However, in addition to consulting this source, people interested in purchasing a new car often consult their neighbors and friends. Sometimes, a neighbor or friend may have had a personal experience with a car that is quite different from what is reported in the consumer report magazine. Oftentimes, however, people who consult their neighbors and friends often discount perfectly valid information (i.e., the base

---

[43] Tversky, A., & Kahneman, D. (1973). Availability: A heuristic for judging frequency and probability. *Cognitive Psychology, 5,* 207–232.

[44] Sherman, S. J., Presson, C. C., & Chassin, L. (1984). Mechanisms underlying the false consensus effect: The special role of threats to the self. *Personality and Social Psychology Bulletin, 10,* 127–138.

[45] Ibid.

[46] Nisbett, R. E., Krantz, D. H., Jepson, C., & Kunda, Z. (1995). The use of statistical heuristics in everyday inductive reasoning. In R. E. Nisbett (Ed.), *Rules for reasoning* (pp. 15–54). Hillsdale, NJ: Erlbaum.

rate information) and choose to rely upon a single, vivid data point. This error is known as the **base rate fallacy**.

Faulty judgments of probability are associated with what is known as the **gambler's fallacy**, the tendency to treat chance events as though they have a built-in, evening-out mechanism. As an example, consider the following problem: Suppose you flip a coin and it comes up heads five times in a row. What do you think the next outcome will be? Most people feel that the probability is high that the coin will come up tails. Of course, the probability of a heads or tails outcome is always the same (50%) for each flip, regardless of the previous result. However, most people think that some sequences (such as heads, tails, heads, tails) are far more likely to occur than others (such as a string of heads or a string of tails).[47]

Anchoring and Adjustment

Job candidates are often asked by recruiters to state their salary range. The job candidate, wanting to maximize his or her salary but at the same time not remove himself or herself from consideration because of unrealistic demands, faces a quandary. Similarly, the prospective home buyer struggles with what to make as an opening offer. What factors determine how we make such assessments of value?

People use a reference point as an anchor and then adjust that value up or down as deemed appropriate.[48] For example, a prospective job recruit may have a roommate who just landed a job with a salary of $80,000. The candidate decides to use $80,000 as a starting point. Two fundamental concerns arise with the anchoring-and-adjustment process. First, the anchors we use to make such judgments are often arbitrary.[49] Oftentimes, anchors are selected on the basis of their temporal proximity, not their relevance to the judgment in question. Second, we tend to make insufficient adjustments away from the anchor; we are weighed down by the anchor. (Remember how people's estimates of the number of doctors in Manhattan were affected by their Social Security number!) The message for the negotiator is clear: Carefully select anchors, and be wary if the counterparty attempts to anchor you.

Unwarranted Causation

Consider the following facts:

- Women living in the San Francisco area have a higher rate of breast cancer.
- Women of lower socioeconomic status are less likely to breast-feed their babies.
- People who marry at a later point in life are less likely to divorce.

Before reading further, attempt to explain each fact. When people are asked to do so, they frequently conclude the following:

- Living in San Francisco causes breast cancer.
- People of lower socioeconomic status are not given postnatal care.
- People become wiser as they grow older.

All of these explanations are reasonable, but they are all unwarranted based upon the information given. The tendency to infer a **causal relationship** between two events is unwarranted

---

[47] Tversky, A., & Kahneman, D. (1974). Judgment under uncertainty: Heuristics and biases. *Science, 185,* 1124–1131.
[48] Ibid.
[49] Ibid.

because we do not know the direction of causality (for example, it is possible that more older women live in the Bay Area). Further, a third variable could be the cause of the event (for example, people who marry later may be richer or more educated). Maybe women of lower socioeconomic status are younger and less comfortable breast-feeding, more likely to be targeted by formula companies, or less likely to get maternity leave. There is a myriad of possible explanations.

Belief Perseverance

The **perseverance effect** is the tendency of people to continue to believe that something is true even when it is revealed to be false or has been disproved.[50] For example, imagine that you have taken an aptitude test and have been told you scored poorly. Later, you learn the exam was misscored. Are you able to erase this experience? Not if you are like most college students, who continue to persevere in their beliefs.[51] Why is this tendency so prevalent? Once a causal explanation is constructed, it is difficult to change it. If you or your counterparty has an erroneous belief about the other, even when it is proven wrong, the belief may still prevail. The important implication is to carefully examine the beliefs you hold about the counterparty and be cognizant of faulty beliefs they may have about you.

Illusory Correlation

Illusory correlation is the tendency to see invalid correlations between events. For example, people often perceive relationships between distinct pieces of information as a mere consequence of their being presented at the same time.[52] For example, in one investigation, people read diagnoses of mental patients.[53] Specifically, people were shown pictures allegedly drawn by these patients and then were given the patients' diagnoses to read. In actuality, there was no correlation between the types of pictures the patients allegedly drew and the nature of their diagnoses (paranoia, schizophrenia). Nevertheless, the people reviewing the evidence believed they saw correlations—for example, between a diagnosis of paranoia and a drawing of a very large eye. Even when people are presented with contradictory or ambiguous evidence, they are extremely reluctant to revise their judgments. As another example, suppose you learn during the course of a negotiation with a business representative from country X that 60% of country X's male population is uneducated. Suppose the same day you learn 60% of crimes committed in that country are violent. Although no logical relation connects the two statistics, most people assume a correlation; that is, they assume that uneducated men from country X are responsible for violent crimes. In fact, no relationship exists between the two—it is illusory. Such correlations between separate facts are illusory because they lack an objective basis for the relationships. Rather, our implicit theories are constructed so that we interpret relations between temporally proximate events.

---

[50] Ross, L., & Lepper, M. R. (1980). The perseverance of beliefs: Empirical and normative considerations. In R. A. Shweder (Ed.), *New directions for methodology of behavioral science: Fallible judgment in behavioral research.* San Francisco: Jossey-Bass.
[51] Ibid.
[52] Hamilton, D. L., & Gifford, R. K. (1976). Illusory correlation in interpersonal perception: A cognitive basis of stereotypic judgments. *Journal of Experimental Social Psychology, 12,* 392–407.
[53] Chapman, L. J., & Chapman, J. P. (1967). Genesis of popular but erroneous diagnostic observations. *Journal of Abnormal Psychology, 72,* 193–204; Chapman, L. J., & Chapman, J. P. (1969). Illusory correlation as an obstacle to the use of valid psychodiagnostic signs. *Journal of Abnormal Psychology, 74*(3), 271–280.

Just World

Most people believe the world is a fair place: People get out of life what they deserve and deserve what happens to them.[54] This mind-set leads to positive evaluations of others who have good things happen to them; for example, most people believe "good" people are likely to win lotteries. Unwarranted negative impressions are produced when others suffer misfortune; for instance, we assume that bad people or ignorant people are victims of crimes.[55] **Blaming-the-victim attributions** are **defensive attributions** because they enable observers to deal with perceived inequities in others' lives and maintain the belief that the world is just.[56] In short, if we believe bad things could easily happen to us (e.g., dying in an airplane crash or losing a limb), the world seems scary and less predictable.

Hindsight Bias

The **hindsight bias** refers to a pervasive human tendency for people to be remarkably adept at inferring a process once the outcome is known but to be unable to predict outcomes when only the processes and precipitating events are known.[57] The hindsight bias, or the "I knew it all along" effect, makes integrative solutions to negotiation situations appear obvious when we see them in retrospect, although before they were discovered, the situation appeared to be fixed-sum.

We are frequently called upon to explain the causes of events, such as the demise of an organization or the success of a particular company. We often perceive events that have already occurred as inevitable. Stated another way, once we know the outcome of an event, we perceive the outcome to be an inevitable consequence of the factors leading to the outcome. This **creeping determinism**[58] accounts for the "Monday morning quarterback" or the "I knew it all along" phenomenon. Therefore, once someone knows the outcome, the events leading up to it seem obvious. The hindsight bias also accounts for why negotiators often think integrative agreements are obvious after the fact but fail to see them when encountering a novel negotiation.

Functional Fixedness

Functional fixedness occurs when a problem solver bases a strategy on familiar methods.[59] The problem with functional fixedness is that previously learned problem-solving strategies hinder the development of effective strategies in new situations. The person fixates on one strategy and cannot readily switch to another method of solving a problem. In other words, experience in one domain produces in-the-box thinking in another domain. Reliance on compromise as a negotiation strategy may produce functional fixedness.

Our past experience can limit problem solving. Consider the tumor problem presented in Exhibit 8-3. The solution rate, when people are given the problem by itself, is 37%; however, when people are shown a diagram of an arrow going through a black dot and then given the

---

[54] Lerner, M. (1980). *The belief in a just world: The fundamental delusion.* New York: Plenum.

[55] Saunders, D. G., & Size, P. B. (1986). Attitudes about woman abuse among police officers, victims, and victim advocates. *Journal of Interpersonal Violence, 1,* 25–42.

[56] Thornton, B. (1992). Repression and its mediating influence on the defensive attribution of responsibility. *Journal of Research in Personality, 26,* 44–57.

[57] Fischhoff, B. (1975). Hindsight does not equal foresight: The effect of outcome knowledge on judgment under uncertainty. *Journal of Experimental Psychology: Human Perception and Performance, 1,* 288–299.

[58] Ibid.

[59] Adamson, R. E., & Taylor, D. W. (1954). Functional fixedness as related to elapsed time and situation. *Journal of Experimental Psychology, 47,* 122–216.

problem, the solution rate drops to 9%.[60] The diagram of the arrow going through the black dot depicted the function of the X-ray as a single line going through the human body; thus, it blocked people's ability to think of several rays focused on the tumor. Functional fixedness occurs when people have a mental block against using an object in a new way to solve a problem. In another example, people are challenged with the problem of how to mount a candle vertically on a nearby screen to function as a lamp. The only materials they are given are a box of matches, a box of candles, and a box of tacks. The creative solution is to mount the candle on top of the matchbox by melting the wax onto the box and sticking the candle to it, then tacking the box to the screen. This elegant solution is much harder to discover when the people are presented with the boxes filled with tacks (i.e., the way the boxes are normally used), rather than emptied of their contents.[61]

Set Effect

Closely related to the problem of functional fixedness is the **set effect**, in which prior experience can also have negative effects in new problem-solving situations. Also known as **negative transfer**, prior experience can limit a manager's ability to develop strategies of sufficient breadth and

EXHIBIT 8-4

The Fortress Story

A small country fell under the iron rule of a dictator. The dictator ruled the country from a strong fortress. The fortress was situated in the middle of the country, surrounded by farms and villages. Many roads radiated outward from the fortress like spokes on a wheel. A great general arose, who raised a large army at the border and vowed to capture the fortress and free the country of the dictator. The general knew that if his entire army could attack the fortress at once, it could be captured. His troops were poised at the head of one of the roads leading to the fortress, ready to attack. However, a spy brought the general a disturbing report. The ruthless dictator had planted mines on each of the roads. The mines were set so that small bodies of men could pass over them safely because the dictator needed to be able to move troops and workers to and from the fortress. However, any large force would detonate the mines. Not only would this blow up the road and render it impassable, but the dictator would destroy many villages in retaliation. A full-scale direct attack on the fortress therefore appeared impossible.

The general, however, was undaunted. He divided his army into small groups and dispatched each group to the head of a different road. When all was ready, he gave the signal, and each group charged down a different road. All of the small groups passed safely over the mines, and the army then attacked the fortress in full strength. In this way, the general was able to capture the fortress and overthrow the dictator.

Source: Based on Gick, M. L., & Holyoak, K. J. (1980). Analogical problem solving. *Cognitive Psychology, 12,* 306–355.

---

[60] Duncker, K. (1945). On problem solving. *Psychological Monographs, 58,* 270.
[61] Anderson, J. R. (1995). *Cognitive psychology and its implications* (4th ed.). New York: Freeman.

generality. Consider the water jug problem presented in Exhibit 8-1. People who had the experience of working on all the water problems typically used a longer, costlier method to solve the problems. People without the experience of solving the problems almost always discovered the short, direct solution. Set effects also plague coalitions. Because war policies can become institutionalized over time, there is a very strong link between coalition shifts and war termination.[62] Changes in coalitions are often necessary to kick-start an updating process.

Selective Attention

In negotiations, we are bombarded with information—the counterparty's physical appearance, his or her opening remarks, hearsay knowledge, nonverbal behavior, and so on. However, we perceive about 1% of all information in our visual field.[63] Thus, we perceive only a tiny fraction of what happens in the negotiation room. How do we know if we are paying attention to the right cues?

The basic function of our sensory information buffers is to parse and code stimulus information into recognizable symbols. Because external stimuli cannot get directly inside our heads, we cognitively represent stimuli as internal symbols and their interrelations as symbol structures. The sensory buffers—visual, auditory, and tactile—maintain the stimulus as an image or icon while its features are extracted. This activity occurs rapidly and below our threshold of awareness. The features extracted from a given stimulus object comprises a coded description of the object. For example, our interaction with a colleague concerning a joint venture is an event that is real, but our minds are not video cameras that record everything; rather, we use a process known as **selective attention**.

Overconfidence

Consider a situation in which you are assessing the probability that a particular company will be successful. Some people might think the probability is quite good; others might think the probability is low; others might make middle-of-the-road assessments. For the decision maker, what matters most is making an assessment that is accurate. How accurate are people in judging probability? How do they make assessments of likelihood, especially when full, objective information is unavailable?

Judgments of likelihood for certain types of events are often more optimistic than is warranted. The **overconfidence effect** refers to unwarranted levels of confidence in people's judgment of their abilities and the occurrence of positive events and underestimates of the likelihood of negative events. For example, in negotiations involving third-party dispute resolution, negotiators on each side believe the neutral third party will adjudicate in their favor.[64] Obviously, this outcome cannot happen; the third party cannot adjudicate in favor of both parties. Similarly, in final-offer arbitration, wherein parties each submit their final bid to a third party

---

[62] Stanley, E. A., & Sawyer J. P. (2009). The equifinality of war termination: Multiple paths to ending war. *The Journal of Conflict Resolution, 53*(5), 651–676.

[63] Kaplan, S., & Kaplan, R. (1982). *Cognition and environment: Functioning in an uncertain world.* New York: Praeger.

[64] Farber, H. S. (1981). Splitting the difference in interest arbitration. *Industrial and Labor Relations Review, 35,* 70–77; Farber, H. S., & Bazerman, M. H. (1986). The general basis of arbitrator behavior: An empirical analysis of conventional and final offer arbitration. *Econometrica, 54,* 1503–1528; Farber, H. S., & Bazerman, M. H. (1989). Divergent expectations as a cause of disagreement in bargaining: Evidence from a comparison of arbitration schemes. *Quarterly Journal of Economics, 104,* 99–120.

who then makes a binding decision between the two proposals, negotiators consistently over-estimate the probability that the neutral arbitrator will choose their own offer.[65] Obviously, the probability is only 50% that a final offer will be accepted; nevertheless, typically, both parties' estimates sum to a number greater than 100%. The message is to be aware of the overconfidence effect. When we find ourselves to be highly confident of a particular outcome occurring (whether it be the counterparty caving in to us, a senior manager supporting our decision, and so on), it is important to examine why.

Perspective taking has been a common treatment to remedy a number of faulty beliefs in negotiation, such as overconfidence and egocentric behavior. Indeed, leading people to consider other peoples' thoughts reduces self-centered judgments such that people claim it is fair for them to take less from a common pool of resources, yet their behavior actually becomes more selfish![66] Moreover, people seem completely unaware of the fact that their personal beliefs about what is fair do not align with their behavior.

The Limits of Short-Term Memory

Short-term memory is the part of our mind that holds the information currently in the focus of our attention and conscious processing. Unfortunately, short-term memory has severely limited capacity; only about five to nine symbols or coded items may be currently active. The "seven plus-or-minus two" rule extends to just about everything we try to remember.[67] Consider, for example, an interaction you might have with the president of a company concerning the details of a consulting engagement. The president tells you many facts about her company; you will recall, on average, five to nine pieces of information. Without deliberate rehearsal, the information in your short-term memory will disappear and be replaced with new information perceived by your sensory registers. Obviously, we perceive much more information than we ultimately store and remember.

CREATIVE NEGOTIATION STRATEGIES

The following strategies are designed to sharpen your creative mind. Thus, they are not specific to negotiation; rather, they are an exercise program for enhancing creativity.

Analogical Training

We have carefully examined the ability of managers to apply what they learn in the classroom to their real-life negotiations. The rates of "positive transfer" (applying knowledge learned in one situation to another) are markedly limited.[68] Moreover, even the ability to benefit from our own experience is limited. For example, 100% of the respondents who read a negotiation case that

---

[65] Neale, M. A., & Bazerman, M. H. (1983). The role of perspective taking ability in negotiating under different forms of arbitration. *Industrial and Labor Relations Review, 36,* 378–388; Bazerman, M. H., & Neale, M. A. (1982). Improving negotiation effectiveness under final offer arbitration: The role of selection and training. *Journal of Applied Psychology, 67*(5), 543–548.

[66] Epley, N., Caruso, E., & Bazerman, M. H. (2006). When perspective taking increases taking: Reactive egoism in social interaction. *Journal of Personality and Social Psychology, 91*(5), 872–889.

[67] Miller, G. A. (1956). The magical number seven plus or minus two: Some limits on our capacity for processing information. *Psychological Review, 63,* 81–97.

[68] Thompson, Loewenstein, & Gentner, "Avoiding missed opportunities"; Loewenstein, Thompson, & Gentner, "Analogical learning in negotiation teams."

contained win-win potential suggested (suboptimal) compromises.[69] When attempting to learn something new (e.g., a key strategy, principle, etc.), it is important to have two (or more) cases or examples, rather than just one. The reason is clear: What is essential about any example or case taught in a business school is not the *superficial* details of the case but rather the *underlying* idea. The ability of a manager to separate the wheat from the chaff, or the core idea from the idiosyncrasies of the example, is limited if embedded in only one case. In fact, one case is no more effective than no cases at all.[70] However, it is not enough simply to be presented with two cases; the manager needs to actively mentally compare the two cases. Moreover, even if the instructor does not provide more than one case, if the manager (or trainee) can think of examples from his or her own experience, it can help significantly. Diverse analogical training, wherein negotiators compared several different value-creating strategies, such as logrolling and contingent contracts is more effective for learning broad, underlying value-creating principles than more narrow training, in which negotiators are only exposed to one type of pie-expanding strategy.[71]

Feedback

Feedback is essential for learning. Even professional golfers regularly seek feedback on their swings. When it comes to learning, the more intense and pointed the feedback is, the better. For example, power golf guru Jim McLean charges $500 per hour to give business leaders such as Henry Kravis, Charles Schwab, Ken Chenault, and David Rockefeller direct feedback on just how bad their swing looks.[72] His teaching style is simple and powerful: analyze, be direct, and focus on what needs work. Says McLean, "These [business] people are used to getting results on the job. They want the same from their golf games."[73] If we consider the fact that a near-perfect correlation exists between our ability to negotiate and our ability to successfully run a company, doesn't it make sense to seek feedback on our negotiation ability?

Feedback improves a negotiator's ability to negotiate.[74] Experience accompanied by a debriefing is more effective in improving performance than experience without debriefing.[75] The type and method of feedback matter. For example, in one investigation of business managers' negotiations, negotiators were given one of four types of feedback (allegedly from their counterparty) following a negotiation, ranging from positive to negative, which focused on their abilities or their ethics:[76]

- *Positive-ability feedback* ("What a skilled negotiator you seem to be.")
- *Negative-ability feedback* ("What an unskilled negotiator you seem to be.")
- *Positive-ethicality feedback* ("What an ethical negotiator you seem to be.")
- *Negative-ethicality feedback* ("What an unethical negotiator you seem to be.")

[69] Gentner, Loewenstein, & Thompson, "Learning and transfer."

[70] Loewenstein, Thompson, & Gentner, "Analogical learning in negotiation teams."

[71] Moran, Bereby-Meyer, & Bazerman, "Stretching the effectiveness."

[72] Rynecki, D. (2003, August 11). Field guide to power: Power golf guru. *Fortune, 148*(3), 126.

[73] Ibid.

[74] Thompson, L., & DeHarpport, T. (1994). Social judgment, feedback, and interpersonal learning in negotiation. *Organizational Behavior and Human Decision Processes, 58*(3), 327–345; Nadler, J., Thompson, L., & Van Boven, L. (2003). Learning negotiation skills: Four models of knowledge creation and transfer. *Management Science, 49*(4), 529–540.

[75] Bereby-Meyer, Y., Moran, S., & Sattler, L. (2010). The effects of achievement motivational goals and of debriefing on the transfer of skills in integrative negotiations. *Negotiation and Conflict Management Research, 3*(1), 64–86.

[76] Kim, P. H., Diekmann, K. A., & Tenbrunsel, A. E. (2003). Flattery may get you somewhere: The strategic implications of providing positive vs. negative feedback about ability vs. ethicality in negotiation. *Organizational Behavior and Human Decision Processes, 90,* 225–243.

The key question was how the feedback would affect the performance of the negotiators in a subsequent negotiation situation. Negotiators who received the negative-ability feedback were the least competitive and achieved the worst individual performance. Negotiators who received the negative-ethicality feedback were the most honest. Negotiators who received the positive-ethicality feedback were the most cooperative.[77]

In addition to the type of feedback negotiators give to one another, we examined the type of feedback a coach might give to a negotiator.[78] We first measured managers' baseline performance in an initial negotiation. Then we separated them into one of five different "feedback groups": no feedback (our scientific "control" condition), traditional lecture-style feedback (also known as "didactic feedback"), information-based feedback (wherein negotiators learned about the other party's underlying interests), observational feedback (wherein negotiators watched experts-in-action via video for about 15 minutes), and analogical learning (wherein negotiators were given relevant cases that all depicted a key negotiation skill). The results? Nearly everything is better than no feedback at all, and nearly anything is better than traditional, classroom-style, didactic learning (see Exhibit 8-5).[79]

In an in-depth analysis of feedback in negotiation, two types of information were focused on: how well negotiators understand the counterparty's general priorities among the issues under negotiation, and how much the counterparty gained for a particular offer. Both types of understanding are important for negotiators to improve: Understanding the counterparty's interests is not sufficient to reach integrative outcomes; the additional step of assessment of their gains for each offer is key.[80]

Counter-Factual Reflection

Counter-factual reflection is the process of thinking about the past. Negotiators who reflect on "additive" counter-factual (e.g., "if only I had…") learn more than negotiators who reflect on subtractive counter-factuals (e.g., "If only I had not…").[81] Generating additive counter-factuals about a previous negotiation led to a distinct advantage for negotiators as compared to subtractive counter-factuals in terms of distributive and creative agreements.

Incubation

Excellent problem solvers frequently report that after trying to solve a problem and getting nowhere, they put the problem aside for hours, days, even weeks, and upon returning to it, they can see the solution quickly. (For a real-life example of the incubation effect, see Exhibit 8-6.) The incubation phase is usually one step in a process of problem solving detailed in the following list:

1. ***Preparation.***   During the preparation phase, the problem solver gathers information and makes preliminary attempts to arrive at a solution. The key is to understand and define the problem. As we have noted, finding a good problem is the essence of effective negotiation.

[77] Ibid.

[78] Nadler, Thompson, & Van Boven, "Learning negotiation skills."

[79] For another illustration of how experience-based training is better than instruction-based training, see also Van Boven & Thompson, "A look into the mind of the negotiator."

[80] Moran, S., & Ritov, I. (2007). Experience in integrative negotiations: What needs to be learned? *Journal of Experimental Social Psychology, 43*(1), 77–90.

[81] Kray, L. J., Galinsky, A. D., & Markman, K. D. (2009). Counterfactual structure and learning from experience in negotiations. *Journal of Experimental Social Psychology, 45*(4), 979–982.

EXHIBIT 8-5

Effect of Learning Method on Negotiation Performance

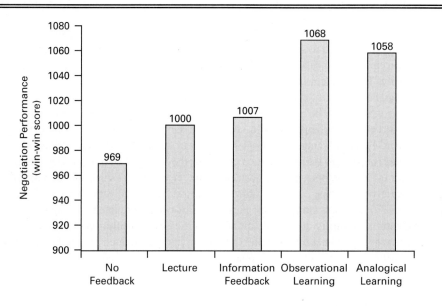

Source: Reprinted by permission, Nadler, J., Thompson, L., & Van Boven, L., "Learning Negotiation Skills: Four Models of Knowledge Creation and Transfer," *Management Science, 49*(4), pp. 529–540. Copyright © 2003, The Institute for Operations Research and the Management Sciences, 901 Elkridge Landing Road, Suite 400, Linthicum, MD 21090 USA.

EXHIBIT 8-6

Incubation Effects

Numerous examples of incubation were reported by the famous French mathematician Poincaré including the following: "Then I turned my attention to the study of some arithmetical questions apparently without much success and without a suspicion of any connection with my preceding researches. Disgusted with my failure, I went to spend a few days at the seaside, and thought of something else. One morning, walking on the bluff, the idea came to me, with just the same characteristics of brevity, suddenness, and immediate certainty, that the arithmetic transformations of indeterminate ternary quadratic forms were identical with those of non-Euclidean geometry." (p. 388)

Source: Poincaré, H. (1929). *The foundations of sciences.* New York: Science House.

2. *Incubation.* When initial attempts to solve the problem have failed, problem solvers may put the problem aside to work on other activities or even to sleep. Indeed, negotiators were more likely to reach high-quality, integrative agreements after they took a break in which they were cognitively busy with a distraction task than after a break in which they could reflect upon the negotiation.[82] Another example: think about the necklace problem you were challenged with in Exhibit 8-1, in which you are given four chains to make one necklace on a limited budget. Three groups of people worked on this problem.[83] One group spent 30 minutes trying to solve it, with a solution rate of 55%. A different group spent 30 minutes trying to solve it but was interrupted during the solving period with a 30-minute break. In this group, 64% of participants solved the problem. A third group spent 30 minutes trying to solve the problem but were interrupted in the solving process by a 4-hour break. Of this group, 85% solved the problem. Whereas we do not guarantee that difficult negotiation situations will always be met with illumination after putting the problem aside, it certainly cannot hurt to try. Difficult issues in negotiation can stymie negotiations and even threaten agreement. Perhaps facing such obstacles can lead negotiators to step back and look at the big picture, or perhaps if they face such obstacles, they become so myopic they don't see other possibilities. Negotiators who face obstacles head on tend to get stuck and are less able to create integrative solutions.[84] Negotiators with a "distal" (e.g., "10 years from now") rather than "proximal" (e.g., "next month") time perspective reached more integrative agreements.

3. *Illumination.* During the illumination phase, the key to a solution often appears. It often happens when people are doing something completely unrelated to solving the problem.

4. *Verification.* In the verification phase, problem solvers need to check the solution to make sure it works.

Rational Problem-Solving Model

The rational problem-solving model, patterned after Pólya, also describes four steps for solving a problem.[85] However, unlike the incubation method, the rational problem-solving model is deliberate and systematic:

1. *Understand the problem.* In this step, the negotiator needs to ask himself or herself: *What is known? What is unknown? What are the data I am using? What are my assumptions?*

2. *Devising a plan.* During this step, the negotiator may ask himself or herself whether past experience is a profitable means of finding a solution method, engaging in a search for similar problems, or perhaps restating the goal of the problem.

3. *Carrying out the plan.* In this step, the negotiator carries out the plan and tests it.

4. *Looking back.* In this step, the negotiator asks himself or herself whether he or she can obtain the result by using another method and looks at how it all fits together. In this step, it is important the negotiator ask what the key takeaway is.

---

[82] Harinck, F., & De Dreu, C. K. W. (2008). Take a break! or not? The impact of mindsets during breaks on negotiation processes and outcomes. *Journal of Experimental Social Psychology, 44*(2), 397–404.

[83] Silveira, J. M. (1972). Incubation: The effect of interruption timing and length on problem solution and quality of problem processing. *Dissertation Abstracts International, 32*(9-B), 5500.

[84] De Dreu, C. K. W., Giacomantonio, M., Shalvi, S., & Sligte, D. (2009). Getting stuck or stepping back: Effects of obstacles and construal level in the negotiation of creative solutions. *Journal of Experimental Social Psychology, 45*(3), 542–548.

[85] Pólya, G. (1957). *How to solve it: A new aspect of mathematical method* (2nd ed.). New York: Doubleday; Pólya, G. (1968). *Mathematical discovery: Vol. II: On understanding, learning, and teaching problem solving.* New York: Wiley.

Fluency, Flexibility, and Originality

What is creativity? What constitutes a creative idea? To be considered creative, an idea must be highly original and useful. That usefulness is the challenge—many people can come up with totally bizarre but useless ideas. One common way of evaluating creativity is via three indexes: fluency, flexibility, and originality.[86]

- *Fluency.* The ability to generate *many solutions* that all fit some requirement; a negotiator who is able to think of several solutions to a conflict (which matches the notion of strength in numbers).
- *Flexibility.* The ability to change approaches to a problem, such as being able to solve a series of tasks requiring a different strategy for each; a negotiator who is able to generate many *different kinds of solutions.*
- *Originality.* The ability to generate *unusual solutions,* such as coming up with unique answers; a negotiator who is able to think of solutions that elude other people.

As a way of thinking about these three indexes of creativity, do the following exercise: See how many possible uses you can think of for a cardboard box. (Give yourself about 10 minutes for this exercise.) Suppose one person who completed this exercise, Geoff, generated two ideas: using the box as a cage for a hamster and as a kennel for a dog. Geoff would receive two points for fluency of ideas because he offered two different ideas, but only one point for flexibility because the ideas are of the same category (i.e., a home for animals). Creative people generate more novel and unusual ways to use a cardboard box. Another person, Avi, generated these unusual ideas for a cardboard box: using it as a god, using it as a telephone (e.g., two boxes and some string), and trading it as currency. Avi would get a score of three points for fluency and three points for flexibility because three separate categories of ideas for use, involving religion, communication, and economics, were used. In addition, Avi's ideas are extremely original.

It is easy to see how flexibility in thought (that is, thinking about different categories of use) can influence originality. Thus, one key for enhancing creativity is to **diversify the use of categories**. By listing possible categories of use for a cardboard box (containers, shelter, building material, therapy, religion, politics, weaponry, communication, etc.), a person's score on these three dimensions increases dramatically. Thus, a key strategy is to think in terms of *categories* of ideas—not just *number* of ideas. This approach can often help negotiators out of a narrow perspective on a conflict and open up new opportunities for creative solutions.

Brainstorming

Alex Osborn, an advertising executive in the 1950s, wanted to increase the creativity of organizations. He believed one of the main blocks to creativity was the premature evaluation of ideas. He was convinced two heads were better than one when it came to generating ideas— but only if people could be trained to defer judgment of their own and others' ideas during the idea-generation process. Therefore, Osborn developed the most widespread strategy used by organizations to encourage creative thought: brainstorming.

Brainstorming is a technique used by a large number of companies and organizations to unleash the creative group mind and avoid the negative impact of group dynamics on creativity.

---

[86] Guilford, J. P. (1959). *Personality.* New York: McGraw-Hill; Guilford, J. P. (1967). The nature of human intelligence. *Intelligence, 1,* 274–280.

The goal of brainstorming is to maximize the quantity and quality of ideas. Osborn aptly noted that quantity is a good predictor of quality: A group is more likely to discover a really good idea if it has a lot of ideas from which to choose, but brainstorming involves more than mere quantity. Osborn believed that the ideas generated by one person in a team could stimulate ideas in other people in a synergistic fashion.

Osborn believed the collective product could be greater than the sum of the individual parts if certain conditions were met. Hence, he developed rules for brainstorming. Contrary to popular corporate lore that brainstorming sessions are wild and crazy free-for-alls where anything goes, brainstorming has defined rules,[87] which are still widely used today. In fact, several companies post the brainstorming guidelines and roles prominently in their meeting rooms (see Exhibit 8-7). However, people do not often use these rules for negotiations.

Convergent Versus Divergent Thinking

Two key skills are involved in creative thinking: divergent thinking and convergent thinking.[88] **Convergent thinking** proceeds toward a single answer, such as the expected value of a 70% chance of earning $1,000 is obtained by multiplying $1,000 by 0.7 to reach $700. **Divergent thinking** moves outward from the problem in many possible directions and involves thinking without boundaries. It is related to the notion of flexibility of categories and originality of thought. Divergent thinking *is* out-of-the-box thinking.

Many of the factors that make up creative problem solving seem most closely related to divergent thinking. However, ideas eventually need to be evaluated and acted upon, which is

EXHIBIT 8-7

Rules for Brainstorming

Expressiveness: Group members should express any idea that comes to mind, no matter how strange, weird, or fanciful. Group members are encouraged not to be constrained nor timid. They should freewheel whenever possible.

Nonevaluation: Do not criticize ideas. Group members should not evaluate any of the ideas in any way during the generation phase; all ideas should be considered valuable.

Quantity: Group members should generate as many ideas as possible. Groups should strive for quantity; the more ideas, the better. Quantity of ideas increases the probability of finding excellent solutions.

Building: Because all of the ideas belong to the group, members should try to modify and extend the ideas suggested by other members whenever possible.

Source: Based on Osborn, A. F. (1957). *Applied imagination:* (Rev. Ed.). New York: Scribner.

---

[87] Osborn, A. F. (1957). *Applied imagination.* New York: Scribner; Osborn, A. F. (1963). *Applied imagination* (3rd ed.). New York: Scribner.
[88] Guilford, *Personality*; Guilford, "Nature of human intelligence."

where convergent thinking comes in. In convergent thinking, a negotiator judges and evaluates the various ideas presented in relation to their feasibility, practicality, and overall merit.

People working independently excel at divergent thinking because no cognitive or social pressures constrain their thought. In short, they are not subject to conformity pressures. In contrast, people are much less proficient at divergent thinking. To avoid social censure, people assess the norms of the situation and conform to them. In contrast, groups excel compared to individuals when it comes to convergent thinking. Groups are better at judging the quality of ideas. This ability suggests that an effective design for promoting creativity in negotiation involves separating the generation of ideas—leaving this task to individual team members—and then evaluating and discussing the ideas as a team. However, divergent thinking (or creative thinking) is often not rewarded in schools or organizations. Teachers prefer students who have high IQs but are not high in creativity. High-IQ students and managers tend to gauge success by conventional standards (i.e., to behave as teachers expect them to and seek careers that conform to what others expect of them). In contrast, highly creative people use unconventional standards for determining success, and their career choices do not usually conform to expectations. Most educational training, including that of MBAs, favors logical or convergent thinking and does not nurture creative or divergent thinking.[89]

Deductive Reasoning

To be effective at negotiation, negotiators must be good at deductive, as well as inductive, reasoning. First we take up the topic of **deductive reasoning**, or the process of drawing logical conclusions. For example, most people have some kind of training in solving logical syllogisms, such as the ones in Exhibit 8-8. The difficulty in solving these syllogisms does not imply that managers are unintelligent; rather, it indicates that formal logic and individual (or psychological) processes are not necessarily the same. However, many people violate rules of logic on a regular basis. Some of the most common violations of the rules of logic are the following:

- *Agreement with a conclusion.*   The desirability of the conclusion often drives people's appraisal of reality. This behavior, of course, is a form of wishful thinking, as well as an egocentric bias. The tendency is strong for people to judge the conclusions they agree with as valid, and the conclusions they disagree with as invalid.
- *Cognitive consistency.*   People have a tendency to interpret information in a fashion that is consistent with information they already know. The tendency for people to judge conclusions to be true, based upon whether the information agrees with what they already know to be true, illustrates the need for consistency in one's belief structure.
- *Confirmation bias.*   People have a strong tendency to seek information that confirms what they already know. A good example of this bias is the card task presented in Exhibit 8-1.

Inductive Reasoning

Inductive reasoning is a form of hypothesis testing, or trial and error. In general, people are not especially good at testing hypotheses, and they tend to use confirmatory methods. Another example is the availability heuristic we discussed previously, which states that judgments of frequency tend to be biased by the ease with which information can be called to mind.

---

[89] Getzels, J. W., & Jackson, P. W. (1962). *Creativity and intelligence: Explorations with gifted students.* New York: Wiley.

EXHIBIT 8-8

Sample Syllogisms

Pick the conclusions about which you can be sure:

1. All S are M. All M are P. Therefore,
   a. All S are P.
   b. All S are not P.
   c. Some S are P.
   d. Some S are not P.
   e. None of these conclusions is valid.

2. As technology advances and natural petroleum resources are depleted, the securing of petroleum from unconventional sources becomes more imperative. One such source is the Athabasca tar sands of northern Alberta, Canada. Because some tar sands are sources of refinable hydrocarbons, these deposits are worthy of commercial investigation. Some kerogen deposits are also sources of refinable hydrocarbons. Therefore:
   a. All kerogen deposits are tar sands.
   b. No kerogen deposits are tar sands.
   c. Some kerogen deposits are tar sands.
   d. Some kerogen deposits are not tar sands.
   e. None of the above.

3. The delicate Glorias of Argentina, which open only in cool weather, are all Sassoids. Some of the equally delicate Fragilas, found only in damp areas, are not Glorias. What can you infer from these statements?
   a. All Fragilas are Sassoids.
   b. No Fragilas are Sassoids.
   c. Some Fragilas are Sassoids.
   d. Some Fragilas are not Sassoids.
   e. None of the above.

   If you think like most people, you think that problem 1 is probably the easiest to solve (the answer is a). However, problems 2 and 3 generate much higher error rates (75% error rate for problem 2, with most errors due to picking answer c instead of e; 90% error rate for problem 3, mainly due to picking d instead of e).

Source: Based on Stratton, R. P. (1983). Atmosphere and conversion errors in syllogistic reasoning with contextual material and the effect of differential training. Unpublished master's thesis, Michigan State University, East Lansing. In R. E. Mayer (Ed.), *Thinking, problem-solving, and cognition.* New York: W. H. Freeman and Company.

For example, people make inaccurate judgments when estimating probabilities. Consider the problem in Exhibit 8-9.[90] When people are asked to answer this question, 22% select the first answer (i.e., the larger hospital), 22% select the second answer (i.e., the smaller hospital), and 56% select the third answer (i.e., both hospitals). They seem to make no compensation for large

---

[90] Tversky & Kahneman, "Judgment under uncertainty."

EXHIBIT 8-9

The Hospital Problem

A certain town is served by two hospitals. In the larger hospital, about 45 babies are born each day, and in the smaller hospital, about 15 babies are born each day. As you know, about 50% of all babies are boys. However, the exact percentage varies from day to day. Sometimes it may be higher than 50%, sometimes lower. For a period of one year, each hospital recorded the days in which more than 60% of the babies born were boys. Which hospital do you think recorded more such days?

1. The larger hospital
2. The smaller hospital
3. About the same (within 5% of each other)

Source: Tversky, A., & Kahneman, D. (1974). Judgment under uncertainty: Heuristics and biases. *Science, 185*, 1124–1131. Used with permission from AAAS.

versus small sample sizes. They believe that an extreme event (for example, 60% of births being male) is just as likely in a large hospital as in a small one. In fact, it is actually far more likely for an extreme event to occur within a small sample because fewer cases are included in the average. People often fail to take sample size into account when they make an inference.

In summary, managers do not form generalizations (reason inductively) in ways that statistics and logic suggest. When people make inferences about events based on their experience in the real world, they do not behave like statisticians. Rather, they seem to be heavily influenced by salient features that stand out in their memory, and they are swayed by extreme events even when the sample size is small.

Flow

According to Csikszentmihalyi, **autotelic experience**, or **flow**, is a particular kind of experience so engrossing and enjoyable that it becomes worth doing, even though it may have no consequences beyond its own context.[91] Creative activities in life, such as music, sports, games, and so on, are typical sources for this kind of experience. Of course, people never do anything purely for its own sake—their motives are always a combination of intrinsic and extrinsic considerations. For example, filmmakers may make films for the joy of creating something artistic but also because the film may make money or win an Academy Award. Similarly, managers and executives create new products and ideas not only because they enjoy doing so but also because the products will make the company more profitable. However, if people are only motivated by extrinsic rewards, they are missing a key ingredient in terms of experience. In addition to external rewards, they can also enjoy an activity, such as negotiation, for its own sake.

---

[91] Csikszentmihalyi, M. (1997). *Finding flow: The psychology of engagement with everyday life.* New York: Basic Books.

This kind of intense flow experience is not limited to creative endeavors. It is also found in the most mundane activities in the personal and business world, such as going to work every day, interacting with people, and so on. An important condition for the flow experience is that a person feels his or her abilities match the opportunities for action. If the challenges are too great for a person's skill, intense anxiety, or **choking**, can occur. However, if the person's skills outweigh the challenges of the experience, he or she may feel bored. In a negotiation, this effect of flow means the process of working through differences, satisfying underlying needs, and creating value is more important than the content of the particular negotiation. To the extent that negotiation is viewed as unpleasant, uncomfortable, or a struggle, flow (and the creative process that can ensue from flow) is less likely to occur.

CONCLUSION

Effective negotiation requires creative thinking. The ability to think creatively is affected by a negotiator's mental model of negotiation. We identified five common mental models: haggling, cost-benefit analysis, game playing, partnership, and problem solving. Creative negotiations involve fractionating problems into several, simpler parts, finding differences to exploit, expanding the pie, bridging, cost cutting, nonspecific compensation, and structuring contingency contracts. We reviewed several of the biggest threats to creativity in negotiation, including the inert knowledge problem, availability bias, representativeness, anchoring and adjustment, unwarranted causation, illusory correlation, hindsight bias, functional fixedness, selective attention, and overconfidence. We described several strategies for rethinking almost any negotiation problem, including feedback, incubation, brainstorming, divergent (as opposed to convergent) thinking, deductive as well as inductive reasoning, and psychological flow.

EXHIBIT 8-10

Answers to Creativity Test

Card Decision*

Correct answer: E and 7.
Averaging over a large number of experiments,[†] it has been found that 89% of people select E, which is a logically correct choice because an odd number on the other side would disconfirm the rule. However, 62% also choose to turn over the 4, which is not logically informative because neither a vowel nor a consonant on the other side would have falsified the rule. Only 25% elect to turn over the 7, which is a logically informative choice because a vowel behind the 7 would have falsified the rule. Only 16% elect to turn over K, which would not be an informative choice.

---

[*] Wason, P. C., & Johnson-Laird, P. N. (1972). *Psychology of reasoning: Structure and content.* Cambridge, MA: Harvard University Press.
[†] Oaksford, M., & Chater, N. (1994). A rational analysis of the selection task as optimal data selection. *Psychological Review, 101*(4), 608–631.

(continued)

Person in a Room Decision*

Correct answer: Jack is a lawyer.

This problem illustrates a classic base-rate problem. We are given information that the probability of any one person selected is equivalent to the stated base rates; the normatively appropriate solution is 30%, thus making it more likely that Jack is a lawyer. Yet, most people choose to ignore base rate information and assume that Jack is an engineer. An answer that goes against explicitly stated probability theory runs the risk of being one based on stereotypes. Groups may be more likely to defend the stereotype decision.

Betting Decision†

Correct answer: A (for the first bet).

The normatively appropriate logic here is to use expected value theory, in which the expected value of a risky choice is determined by the value of the payoff multiplied by its probability. Using this technique, the expected value of bet A is $8 \times 0.3333 = \$2.66$. The expected value of bet B is ($\$3 \times 0.8333 = \$2.5$). Thus, bet A maximizes expected value. However, many people overweight high probabilities and end up choosing bet B. Groups tend to be riskier than individuals, so groups often choose riskier decisions, whether they are normatively appropriate or not. For the second bet, either answer is normatively correct because their expected values are the same.

Water Jugs**

Problem solvers can become biased by their experiences to prefer certain problem solving operators in solving a problem. Such biasing of the problem solution is known as a **set effect**. Also known as the **Einstellung effect**, or **mechanization of thought**, this can paradoxically lead to worsened performance. The Einstellung effect involves remembering a particular sequence of operations, and it is memory for this sequence that is blinding managers to other possibilities. In this series of problems, all problems except 8 can be solved by using the B-2C-A method. For problems 1 through 5, this solution is the simplest, but for problems 7 and 9, the simpler solution of A + C also applies. Problem 8 cannot be solved by the B-2C-A method but can be solved by the simpler solution of A-C. Problems 6 and 10 are also solved more simply as A-C than B-2C-A.

Of the participants who received the whole setup of 10 problems, 83% used the B-2C-A method on problems 6 and 7, 64% failed to solve problem 8, and 79% used the B-2C-A method for problems 9 and 10. The performance of people who worked on all 10 problems was compared with the performance of people who saw only the last 5 problems. These people did not see the biasing B-2C-A problems. Fewer than 1% of these people used B-2C-A solutions, and only 5% failed to solve problem 8. Thus, the first 5 problems can create a powerful bias for a particular solution. This bias hurt solution of problems 6 through 10.

Stick Problem††

Correct answer: Form a tetrahedron (something like a pyramid).

Most people take the six sticks and form a square with an X in it. However, this solution is not acceptable because the triangles are not equilateral—each has a 90-degree angle. Another incorrect

---

* Kahneman, D., & Tversky, A. (1973). On the psychology of prediction. *Psychological Review, 80,* 237–251.
† Tversky, A., & Kahneman, D. (1981). The framing of decisions and the psychology of choice. *Science, 211,* 453–458.
** Luchins, A. S. (1942). Mechanization in problem solving. *Psychological Monographs, 5*(46), 1–95.
†† Scheer, M. (1963). *Scientific American, 208,* 118–218.

(continued)

answer that is common is to form three of the sticks in a triangle and overlay them on another triangle upside down; this produces four triangles, but the sides of the triangle are not one stick in length. To solve the problem, the solver must think in three dimensions, making a pyramid with a triangle base. This is a general class of problem situations that often involve "insight"—a rearrangement of the parts in a certain way to solve a problem.

Letter Sequence*

Correct answer: E.
The answer to this Eureka problem is E. The letters are the first seven letters of the first eight digits: one, two, three, four, five, six, seven, and eight.

Chain Problem[†]

Open one chain and put links between the other three.

Susan and Martha

Correct answer: 36.
This is a disjunctive decision task. It is a Eureka problem, and the answer must be calculated. Only 14 combinations yield a total of 13 (e.g., 1, 1, 11; 1, 2, 10; 1, 3, 9, etc.), and only two of these have the identical product (1, 6, 6 and 2, 2, 9). If we assume Susan knows her own age, she would still be confused only if she were 36.

Necklace**

Initially, people tend to break a link on each chain, attach it to another chain, and then close it. The more elegant (and cheaper) solution is to break a single three-link piece and use its links to attach others. It costs 6 cents to open three links. The total connection cost is 9 cents, yielding a 15-cent necklace.

Gold Chain

Correct answer: 2.

The chain puzzle is a Eureka problem. Many groups answer 11 because that would involve cutting only every other link. The correct answer, however, is 2. If the fourth and eleventh links are cut, all the values from 1 to 23 can be obtained by getting "change" back from the motel owner. Separate links (the fourth and the eleventh) are given on days 1 and 2, but on day 3 the three-link unit is given to the owner, who returns the separate links. These links are then used to pay on days 4 and 5, but on day 6 the six-link unit is used, and the owner returns the others as change. The process can be continued for 23 days.

Nine Dot Problem[††]

Correct answer: See Panels 3 and 4.
Most people implicitly assume that the lines must be drawn within an imaginary boundary, as shown in the second panel of the diagram. One possible solution that is preferred by "experts" is given in

---

* Source unknown.
[†] De Bono, E. (1967). *The use of lateral thinking.* New York: Penguin
** Wickelgren, W. A. (1974). *How to solve problems.* San Francisco, CA: W. H. Freeman.
[††] Weisberg, R. W., & Alba, J. W. (1981). An examination of the alleged role of "fixation" in the solution of several insight problems. *Journal of Experimental Psychology: General, 110,* 169–192.

(continued)

the third panel of the diagram. The problem solver must go outside the self-imposed square boundary. Another creative solution uses lines that do not go through the center of the dots, as shown in the fourth panel of the diagram. This solution involves overcoming another self-imposed limit on the problem—namely, realizing it is not necessary to draw the lines through the center of each dot.

Thus, one major kind of conceptual block is the tendency to impose too many constraints on the problem (that is, to represent the problem in a way that limits the potential kinds of solutions). Overcoming the conceptual blocks is similar to overcoming functional fixedness or Einstellung; instead, look for alternative ways of representing the problem.

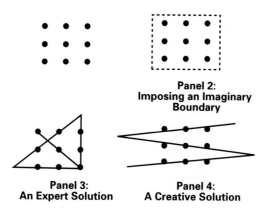

Panel 2:
Imposing an Imaginary
Boundary

Panel 3:
An Expert Solution

Panel 4:
A Creative Solution

Pigpen*

Correct answer: See diagram.

This is an "insight" problem. Most people assume that each pigpen must be square. The solution involves diamond-shaped pens.

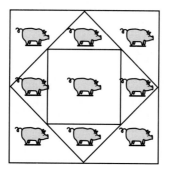

Waterlilies[†]

Correct answer: Day 59.

This is a pure "insight" problem. People initially approach the problem as one involving a linearly increasing quantity and simply divide the total time in half. However, because the lilies increase

---

* Fixx, J. F. (1972). *More games for the super-intelligent.* New York: Warner Books.
[†] Sternberg, R. J., & Davidson, J. E. (1983). Insight in the gifted. *Educational Psychologist, 18,* 51–57.

(continued)

exponentially in area, this approach is incorrect, and another representation is needed. Such a change in representation can occur when the participant tries to imagine what happens as the pond fills up and he or she works backward from the last day, rather than carrying out a formal analysis of the problem.

Bartender Problem*

The man who walked into the bar had the hiccups. The bartender realized this and attempted to scare the daylights out of the man by pointing a gun at him. Some people are able to solve this problem immediately; others are not. This is a Eureka problem.

---

* Dayton, T., Durso, F. T., & Shepard, J. D. (1990). A measure of the knowledge reorganization underlying insight. In R. W. Schraneveldt (Ed.), *Pathfinder associative networks: Studies in knowledge organization*. Norwood, NJ: Ablex.

Part III: Applications and Special Scenarios

Multiple Parties, Coalitions, and Teams

In May 2003, CEOs at every company on the *Fortune* 1000 and *Fortune* Global 500 opened a letter to discover they would be sued if anyone anywhere in their company had used Linux—the free, open-source operating system. A little known company named SCO Group, headquartered in Lindon, Utah, had sent the letter. Two months earlier, SCO had filed a $1 billion lawsuit against IBM, claiming that Big Blue had taken chunks of SCO-owned Unix code and sprinkled it into Linux. According to Darl McBride, the CEO of SCO, some companies were misusing Unix code by inserting it into other programs they were using, a privilege they needed to pay SCO for in the form of an additional license. The leverage that SCO had in fighting IBM was by involving IBM's customers. The more SCO could scare Big Blue's customers, the more power SCO had. To make things more complicated, Ralph Yarro, the head of Canopy Group, owned 43% of SCO. Canopy, owned by Noorda, is made up of 35 start-up companies. When McBride got rebuffed by IBM, he flew to the Florida office of Boies, Schiller, and Flexner for a meeting with the anti-Microsoft litigator David Boies, who agreed to take up the case on a combination contingency and hourly-fee basis. In the meantime, Microsoft called BayStar Capital managing partner Lawrence Goldfarb to ask if he would consider investing in SCO. In 2007 a federal court in Utah ruled that Novell, not SCO, owned the copyright to Unix. The ruling stated that SCO had only licensed Unix from Novell and declared that Novell had the authority to force SCO to drop its claim against IBM. In mid-2010, a judge in U.S. District Court ruled against SCO's claims of slander and breach of implied

(Continued)

covenant and good faith and stated that SCO was obligated to recognize Novell's waiver of SCO's claims against IBM and other companies that use Linux. The case was ordered closed.[1]

T he opening example indicates that negotiation situations often involve more than two parties. The other people may include negotiators, agents, constituents, and third parties. To negotiate effectively in complex situations, negotiators need all of the skills we have described thus far, and then some. We discuss skills specific to multiparty negotiation in this chapter.

ANALYZING MULTIPARTY NEGOTIATIONS

How might we analyze the negotiation between SCO and IBM? The negotiation involves a myriad of players, relationships, and issues. In Exhibit 9-1, two principals are involved in the multiparty negotiation: SCO and IBM. That is the primary table. Noorda, the Canopy Group, BayStar Capital,

EXHIBIT 9-1

SCO-IBM Negotiations Structure

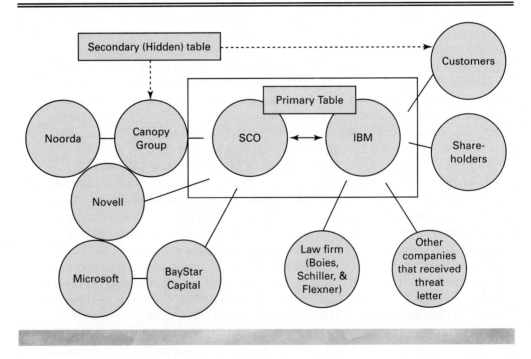

[1] Lashinsky, A. (2003, July 21). Penguin slayer. *Fortune, 148*(2), 85–90; Kerstetter, J., Green, J., & Sager, I. (2004, March 22). Microsoft versus Linux. *Business Week, 3875,* 14; Winstein, K. J., & Bulkeley, W. M. (2007, August 11). Court ruling gives Novell copyright in Unix system. *Wall Street Journal,* p. A3; Gohring, N. (2010, June 11). Novell wins final judgment in SCO battle. *Reuters.* Reuters.com

and Novell are potential principals. When IBM became a reluctant negotiator, SCO put leverage on IBM's hidden or secondary table—its customers. SCO's second table included the Canopy Group, which is the extension of Noorda, and BayStar Capital, which was connected to SCO. Ultimately, Novell entered the negotiation. A coalition could include SCO and Microsoft, SCO and IBM customers, or IBM and Novell. Further, other companies in positions similar to IBM (in terms of receiving the letter) could act as coalition partners. The opening example indicates that negotiations within and between organizations are embedded in an intricate web of interdependent relationships and interests. Just as a complete understanding of human anatomy requires analyses at the levels of cell chemistry, tissues, organs, and organ systems, a complete understanding of negotiation within and between organizations requires analysis at several levels.[2]

In this chapter, we review six levels of analysis beyond one-on-one negotiation: (1) multiparty negotiations, (2) coalitions, (3) principal-agent relationships, (4) constituencies, (5) team negotiation, and (6) team-on-team negotiations, or intergroup negotiations (see Exhibit 9-2). For each level, we identify key challenges and suggest practical advice and strategies for maximizing negotiation effectiveness.

Multiparty Negotiations

A **multiparty negotiation** is formed when a group of three or more individuals, each representing his or her own interests, attempts to resolve perceived differences of interest.[3] The involvement of more than two principals at the negotiation table complicates the situation enormously. Social interactions become more complex, information-processing demands increase exponentially, and coalitions form. Despite all these obstacles, groups make more accurate judgments and more readily aggregate information than do individuals.[4]

Key Challenges of Multiparty Negotiations

We present four key challenges of multiparty negotiations and follow with some practical advice.

DEALING WITH COALITIONS   A key difference between two-party and group negotiations is the potential for two or more parties within a group to form a coalition to pool their resources and exert greater influence on outcomes.[5] A **coalition** is a (sub) group of two or more individuals who join together in using their resources to affect the outcome of a decision in a mixed-motive situation[6] involving at least three parties.[7] Coalition formation is one way that otherwise weak group members may marshal a greater share of resources. Coalitions involve both cooperation in terms of attracting members and competition in terms of dividing resources.

---

[2] Thompson, L., & Fox, C. R. (2001). Negotiation within and between groups in organizations: Levels of analysis. In M. E. Turner (Ed.), *Groups at work: Theory and research*. Hillsdale, NJ: Erlbaum.

[3] Bazerman, M. H., Mannix, E., & Thompson, L. (1988). Groups as mixed-motive negotiations. In E. J. Lawler & B. Markovsky (Eds.), *Advances in group processes: Theory and research: Vol. 5*. Greenwich, CT: JAI Press; Kramer, R. M. (1991). The more the merrier? Social psychological aspects of multiparty negotiations in organizations. In M. H. Bazerman, R. J. Lewicki, & B. H. Sheppard (Eds.), *Research on negotiations in organizations: Handbook of negotiation research, Vol. 3* (pp. 307–332). Greenwich, CT: JAI Press.

[4] Bottom, W. P., Ladha, K., & Miller, G. J. (2002). Propagation of individual bias through group judgment: Error in the treatment of asymmetrically informative signals. *Journal of Risk and Uncertainty, 25*(2), 147–163.

[5] Komorita, S. S., & Parks, C. D. (1995). Interpersonal relations: Mixed-motive interaction. *Annual Review of Psychology, 46*, 183–207.

[6] Komorita & Parks, "Interpersonal relations"; Murnighan, J. K. (1978). Models of coalition behavior: Game theoretic, social psychological, and political perspectives. *Psychological Bulletin, 85*, 1130–1153.

[7] Gamson, W. (1964). Experimental studies in coalition formation. In L. Berkowitz (Ed.), *Advances in experimental social psychology: Vol. 1*. New York: Academic Press.

EXHIBIT 9-2

Levels of Analysis in Multiparty Negotiation

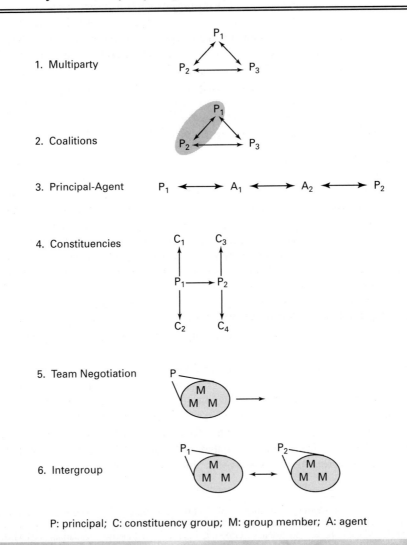

1. Multiparty

2. Coalitions

3. Principal-Agent

4. Constituencies

5. Team Negotiation

6. Intergroup

P: principal; C: constituency group; M: group member; A: agent

FORMULATING TRADE-OFFS In a multiparty negotiation, integrative trade-offs may be achieved either through circular or reciprocal logrolling.[8] **Circular logrolling** involves trade-offs that require each group member to offer another member a concession on one issue while receiving a concession from yet another group member on a different issue. A circular trade-off

---

[8] Palmer, L. G., & Thompson, L. (1995). Negotiation in triads: Communication constraints and tradeoff structure. *Journal of Experimental Psychology: Applied, 2,* 83–94.

is typified by the tradition of drawing names from a hat to give holiday gifts to people. People receive a gift from one person and give a gift to yet another person. Ideally, we give gifts that are more appreciated by the recipient than by the giver. In contrast, **reciprocal trade-offs** are fashioned between two members of a larger group. Reciprocal trade-offs are typified in the more traditional form of exchanging presents. Circular trade-offs are more risky than reciprocal trade-offs because they involve the cooperation of more than two group members.

VOTING AND MAJORITY RULE Groups often simplify the negotiation of multiple issues among multiple parties through voting and decision rules. However, if not used wisely, decision rules can thwart effective negotiation, both in terms of pie-expansion and pie-slicing. A number of problems are associated with voting and majority rule.[9]

Problems with Voting and Majority Rule. The most common procedure used to aggregate preferences of team members is **majority rule**. Despite its democratic appeal, majority rule fails to recognize the strength of individual preferences. One person in a group may feel very strongly about an issue, but his or her vote counts the same as the vote of someone who does not have a strong opinion about the issue. Consequently, majority rule does not promote integrative trade-offs among issues. Groups negotiating under unanimous rule reach more efficient outcomes than groups operating under majority rule.[10] Groups whose members multi-task reach lower joint profits under majority rule, but not unanimity rule.[11]

Although **unanimity rule** is time-consuming, it encourages group members to consider creative alternatives to expand the size of the pie and satisfy the interests of all group members. Because strength of preference is a key component in fashioning integrative agreements, majority rule hinders the development of mutually beneficial trade-offs. Voting in combination with other decision aids, such as agendas, may be especially detrimental to the attainment of efficient outcomes because it prevents logrolling.[12]

Other problems arise with voting. Within groups that demonstrate pro-self motives (as opposed to pro-social motives), majority rule leads to more distributive and less integrative behavior.[13] Group members may not agree upon a method for voting; for example, some members may insist upon unanimity, others may argue for a simple majority rule, and still others may advocate a weighted majority rule. Even if a voting method is agreed upon, it may not yield a choice if the group is evenly split. Voting does not eliminate conflicts of interest but, instead, provides a way for group members to live with conflicts of interest; for this reason, majority rule decisions may not be stable. In this sense, voting hides disagreement within groups, which threatens long-term group and organizational effectiveness.

---

[9] Bottom, W. P., Eavey, C. L., Miller, G. J., & Victor, J. N. (2000). The institutional effect on majority rule instability: Bicameralism in spatial policy decisions. *American Journal of Political Science, 44*(3), 523–540; Bottom, W. P., Handlin, L., King, R. R., & Miller, G. J. (2002). Institutional modifications of majority rule. In C. Plott & V. Smith (Eds.), *Handbook of experimental economics results.* Amsterdam: North Holland.

[10] Beersma, B., & De Dreu, C. K. W. (2002). Integrative and distributive negotiation in small groups: Effects of task structure, decision rule, and social motive. *Organizational Behavior and Human Decision Processes, 87*(2), 227–252; Mannix, E. A., Thompson, L., & Bazerman, M. H. (1989). Negotiation in small groups. *Journal of Applied Psychology, 74*(3), 508–517; Thompson, L., Mannix, E., & Bazerman, M. H. (1988). Group negotiation: Effects of decision rule, agenda, and aspiration. *Journal of Personality and Social Psychology, 54,* 86–95.

[11] Mohammed, S., Rizzuto, T., Hiller, N. T., Newman, D. A., & Chen, T. (2008). Individual differences and group negotiation: The role of polychronicity, dominance, and decision rule. *Negotiation and Conflict Management Research, 1*(3), 282–307.

[12] Mannix, Thompson, & Bazerman, "Negotiation in small groups"; Thompson, Mannix, & Bazerman, "Group negotiation."

[13] Beersma & De Dreu, "Integrative and distributive negotiation."

EXHIBIT 9-3

Managers' Preferences for Product Designs

Manager	Design A	Design B	Design C
Raines	1	2	3
Warner	2	3	1
Lassiter	3	1	2

Voting Paradoxes.   Consider a three-person (Raines, Warner, and Lassiter) product-development team. The three are in conflict over which design to use—A, B, or C. The preference ordering is depicted in Exhibit 9-3. As a way of resolving the conflict, Warner suggests voting between designs A and B. In that vote, A wins and B is discarded. Warner then proposes that the group vote between A and C. In that vote, C wins. Warner then declares that design C be implemented. Lassiter concludes that the group vote was fair and agrees to develop design C. However, Raines is perplexed and suggests taking another vote. Warner laughs and says, "We just took a vote and you lost—so just accept the outcome!" Raines glares at Warner and says, "Let's do the vote again, and I will agree to accept the outcome. However, this time I want us to vote between B and C first." Warner has no choice but to go along. In this vote, B is the clear winner and C is eliminated. Next, the vote is between A and B, and A beats B. Raines happily declares A the winner. Lassiter then declares the voting process fraudulent but cannot explain why.

Raines, Warner, and Lassiter are victims of the **Condorcet paradox**, which demonstrates that the winners of majority rule elections will change as a function of the order in which alternatives are proposed. Alternatives that are proposed later, as opposed to earlier, are more likely to survive sequential voting.[14] Thus, clever negotiators arrange to have their preferred alternatives entered at later stages of a sequential voting process.

The unstable voting outcomes of the product development team point to a larger concern known as the **impossibility theorem**.[15] This theorem states that the derivation of group preference from individual preference is indeterminate. Simply put, no method can combine group members' preferences in a way that guarantees group preference is maximized when groups contain three or more members and are facing three or more options. In other words, even though each manager's preferences are transitive, the group-level preference is intransitive.

---

[14] May, K. (1982). A set of independent, necessary and sufficient conditions for simple majority decisions. In B. Barry & R. Hardin (Eds.), *Rational man and irrational society.* Beverly Hills, CA: Sage.

[15] Arrow, K. J. (1963). *Social choice and individual values.* New Haven, CT: Yale University Press.

Strategic Voting. The problem of indeterminate group choice is further compounded by the temptation for members to **strategically misrepresent** their true preferences so that a preferred option is more likely to be favored by the group.[16] For example, a group member may vote for his least-preferred option to ensure that the second choice option is eliminated. Raines could have voted strategically in the first election to ensure that his preferred strategy was not eliminated in the first round.

Consensus Agreements. *Consensus agreements* require the consent of all parties to the negotiation before an agreement is binding. However, consensus agreements do not imply unanimity. Consensus agreements imply that parties agree *publicly* to a particular settlement, even though their *private* views about the situation may be in conflict.

Although consensus agreements are desirable, they precipitate several problems. They are time-consuming because they require the consent of all members, who are often not in agreement. Second, they often lead to compromise, in which parties identify a lowest-common denominator acceptable to all. Compromise agreements are an extremely easy method of reaching agreement and are compelling because they appear to be fair, but they are usually inefficient because they fail to exploit potential Pareto-improving trade-offs.[17]

COMMUNICATION BREAKDOWNS When a sender transmits a message, errors are possible at three different points: The sender may fail to send a message, the message may be sent but is inaccurate or distorted, or an accurate message is sent but is distorted or not received by the recipient. In a multiparty environment, the complexity grows when several people simultaneously send and receive messages. The extent to which communication is restricted influences how the pie is divided. For example, parties with weaker BATNAs benefit from a more constrained communication structure, especially if they are the conduit of communication; in contrast, negotiators with stronger BATNAs benefit from a more public communication structure that promotes competitive bidding.[18]

Private Caucusing. When groups grow large, communication among all parties is difficult. One way of simplifying negotiations is for negotiators to communicate in smaller groups, thereby avoiding full-group communication. Group members often form private caucuses for strategic purposes. However, private caucusing may cause problems. Full-group communication is more time-consuming but enhances equality of group members' outcomes, increases joint profitability, and minimizes perceptions of competition.[19] However, when the task structure requires group members to logroll in a reciprocal fashion (as opposed to a circular fashion), restricted communication leads to higher joint outcomes than full communication. Private caucusing can take many different forms. For example, Oregon congressman Peter DeFazio created a House Small

---

[16] Chechile, R. (1984). Logical foundations for a fair and rational method of voting. In W. Swapp (Ed.), *Group decision making.* Beverly Hills, CA: Sage; Ordeshook, P. (1986). *Game theory and political theory: An introduction.* Cambridge, England: Cambridge University Press; Plott, C. (1976). Axiomatic social choice theory: An overview and interpretation. *American Journal of Political Science, 20,* 511–596; Plott, C., & Levine, M. (1978). A model of agenda influence on committee decisions. *American Economic Review, 68,* 146–160.

[17] Mnookin, R. H. (2003). Strategic barriers to dispute resolution: A comparison of bilateral and multilateral negotiation. *Journal of Institutional and Theoretical Economics, 159*(1), 199–220.

[18] Bolton, G. E., Chatterjee, K., & McGinn, K. L. (2003). How communication links influence coalition bargaining: A laboratory investigation. *Management Science, 49*(5), 583–598.

[19] Palmer & Thompson, "Negotiation in triads."

Brewers Caucus to represent and advocate the interests of small brewers, including commodities prices and labeling laws.[20]

Biased Interpretation.   People often hear what they want to hear when receiving messages, especially ambiguous ones. For example, when people are given neutral information about a product, they interpret it in a way that is favorable toward their own position. Furthermore, they pay attention to information that favors their initial point of view and ignore or misinterpret information that contradicts their position.

Perspective-Taking Failures.   People are remarkably poor at taking the perspective of others. For example, people who are privy to information and knowledge that they know others are not aware of nevertheless act as if others are aware of it, even though it would be impossible for the receiver to have this knowledge.[21] This problem is known as the **curse of knowledge**.[22] For example, in a simulation, traders who possessed privileged information that could have been used to their advantage behaved as if their trading partners also had access to the privileged information. Perspective-taking deficiencies also explain why some instructors who understand an idea perfectly are unable to teach students the same idea.

Indirect Speech Acts.   **Indirect speech acts** are the ways in which people ask others to do things—but in indirect ways. For example, consider the various ways of requesting that a person shut a door (see Exhibit 9-4). Each statement can serve as a request to perform that act even though the sentence forms (except for "Close the door") are not requests but assertions and questions. Thus, statements 2 through 9 are indirect speech acts; a listener's understanding of the intention behind a communicator's intention requires an extra cognitive step or two, which can often fail, especially under stress.

Indirect speech acts are a function of the magnitude of the request being made (i.e., trivial requests, such as asking someone for the time of day, are easy to accommodate; asking someone if you can have a job is much more difficult to accommodate), the power the recipient has over the sender, and the social distance in the culture.[23] Thus, as the magnitude of requests increases, the power distance increases, and as the social distance increases, requests made by negotiators will become more indirect.

Multiple Audience Problem.   In some negotiation situations, negotiators need to communicate with another person in the presence of someone who should not understand the message. For example, consider a couple selling a house having a face-to-face discussion with a potential buyer. Ideally, the couple wants to communicate information to one another in a way that the spouse understands but the buyer does not—better yet, in such a way that the buyer is not even aware that a surreptitious communication is taking place. This is the **multiple audience problem**.[24]

---

[20] McSherry, A. (2010, May 17). Beer caucus brews up consensus. *Rollcall.* Rollcall.com

[21] Keysar, B. (1998). Language users as problem solvers: Just what ambiguity problem do they solve? In S. R. Fussell & R. J. Kreuz (Eds.), *Social and cognitive approaches to interpersonal communication* (pp. 175–200). Mahwah, NJ: Erlbaum.

[22] Camerer, C. F., Loewenstein, G., & Weber, M. (1989). The curse of knowledge in economic settings: An experimental analysis. *Journal of Political Economy, 97,* 1232–1254.

[23] Brown, P., & Levinson, S. (1987). *Politeness: Some universals in language use.* Cambridge, England: Cambridge University Press.

[24] Fleming, J. H., & Darley, J. M. (1991). Mixed messages: The multiple audience problem and strategic communication. *Social Cognition, 9*(1), 25–46.

EXHIBIT 9-4

Different Ways to Make Requests That Require Progressively More Inferences and Assumed Common Knowledge on the Part of the Receiver

1. Close the door.
2. Can you close the door?
3. Would you close the door?
4. It might help to close the door.
5. Would you mind awfully if I asked you to close the door?
6. Did you forget the door?
7. How about a little less breeze?
8. It's getting cold in here.
9. I really don't want the cats to get out of the house.

Source: Adapted from Krauss, R. M., & Fussell, S. R. (1996). Social psychological models of interpersonal communication. In E. T. Higgins & A. W. Kruglanski (Eds.), *Social psychology: Handbook of basic principles* (pp. 766–701). New York: Guilford; Levinson, S. C. (1983). *Pragmatics* (p. 264). Cambridge, England: Cambridge University Press.

People are quite skilled at communicating information to the intended recipient without the other party being aware.[25] For example, former U.S. president Ronald Reagan was gifted in his ability to send different messages to different audiences within the same speech. Reagan's "evil empire" speech of March 8, 1983, to the National Association of Evangelicals (and, indirectly, the whole world) is a case in point. In the early sections of this speech, Reagan established identification with the evangelical audience through an ethos that exemplified their ideals, even using their technical vocabulary (e.g., "I believe in intercessionary prayer"). The section of his speech dealing with foreign policy was addressed to a complex array of audiences, foreign as well as domestic. The "evil empire" phrase had strong resonance not only with evangelicals but also with opponents of the Soviet Union everywhere, including those in Poland and Czechoslovakia. For the benefit of his diplomatic audiences, however, Reagan carefully avoided specific references to evil actions of the Soviet Union, personally deleting from early drafts all references to chemical warfare in Afghanistan. And the speech's attack on the nuclear freeze movement of that time was balanced with a call for "an honest freeze," a term that created "presence" for his proposal for "extensive prior negotiations on the systems and numbers to be limited and on the measures to ensure effective verification and compliance."[26] To his audience in the international, diplomatic, and arms control communities, including those within the Soviet Union, such praise alluded to extratextual facts that gave this part of the message a pragmatic connotation.[27]

---

[25] Ibid.

[26] Myers, F. (1999, February). Political argumentation and the composite audience: A case study (p. 65). *Quarterly Journal of Speech, 85*(1), 55–65.

[27] Ibid.

Key Strategies for Multiparty Negotiations

Given that multiparty negotiations are complex and present special challenges, what strategies and practices should negotiators put into place to enhance their ability to expand and slice the pie in a multiparty context? Consider the following strategies.

KNOW WHO WILL BE AT THE TABLE   Know who will be at the table and understand the interests of the constituencies they represent (the hidden table). Consider the following example. Yucaipa, led by Los Angeles billionaire Ron Burkle, stirred up controversy after purchasing a controlling stake in Allied, North America's largest hauler in bankruptcy proceedings. Yucaipa was allowed to assist Allied and its investors in Burkle's Hawk Opportunity Fund during concession talks with the Teamsters. However, Teamsters representatives claimed, "We were getting conflicting proposals from Yucaipa and the company; "We didn't know who we were negotiating with." Several outside investors and Allied directors claimed that during the talks Yucaipa was trying to push through its own reorganization plan. Eventually, Yucaipa was asked to leave the negotiations, and in 2007 Hawk Opportunity Fund sued Yucaipa, charging it with racketeering in Yucaipa's takeover of Allied and stating that Yucaipa and the Teamsters "colluded" to "manipulate and abuse" the bankruptcy/reorganization process "for their own benefit."[28]

MANAGE THE INFORMATION AND SYSTEMATIZE PROPOSAL MAKING   People experience "information overload" when dealing with multiple parties and multiple issues. It is nearly impossible to keep track of the issues, alternatives, and preferences of each party without some kind of information management device. Negotiators are well advised to develop a matrix that lists each party (along the rows) and each issue (along the columns), and then record each person's preferences for each issue. To the extent that this information can be publicly displayed, it can greatly enhance the ability of the group to find win-win agreements.

Negotiating groups often severely mismanage their time. For example, negotiating groups begin by engaging in distributive bargaining and then transition into integrative bargaining.[29] Groups tend not to make proposals and explore options and alternatives in a systematic fashion. This can lead to **tunnel vision**, or the tendency for people in group negotiations to underestimate the number of feasible options available. For example, in one of our investigations, we asked people who had just completed a multiparty negotiation how many feasible agreements they thought were possible (the negotiation contained five issues and four to five alternatives within each issue). The modal response was one. On average, people estimated approximately four feasible outcomes for the group (the highest estimate was 12). In fact, there were over 50 feasible outcomes! This example illustrates the tunnel vision (and ensuing desperation) that can overtake a group if members fail to systematize their proposal making. We strongly encourage members to make several multi-issue proposals and to keep a record of which proposals have been considered.

---

[28] Emshwiller, J. R. (2007, May 2). Politics & economics: Controversy, by the truckload-battle for car hauler puts spotlight on Burkle's dealings. *Wall Street Journal*, p. A4.
[29] Olekalns, M., Brett, J. M., & Weingart, L. R. (2004). Phases, transitions and interruptions and interruptions: The processes that shape agreement in multi-party negotiations. *International Journal of Conflict Management: Special Issue on Processes in Negotiation, 14,* 191–211.

USE BRAINSTORMING WISELY   We also encourage groups to use brainstorming wisely. Most groups suggest fewer and lower-quality ideas than do individuals thinking independently.[30] **Brainwriting**, or **solitary brainstorming**, is a strategy whereby group members independently write down ideas for resolving negotiations and then, later, when the group meets, they share those ideas. Brainwriting capitalizes on the fact that individuals are better at generating ideas but groups are superior in terms of evaluating ideas.

DEVELOP AND ASSIGN PROCESS ROLES   Multiparty negotiations need a timekeeper, a process manager, and a recorder of information. These roles can be rotated, so as not to give any particular member an advantage or disadvantage.

STAY AT THE TABLE   It is unwise for group members to leave the table when all parties need to reach agreement.[31] When groups leave the table, coalitions are more likely to form, which can be detrimental for the group.[32]

STRIVE FOR EQUAL PARTICIPATION   The problem of **uneven participation**, wherein one or two people do all the talking, thwarts information exchange in groups.

ALLOW FOR SOME POINTS OF AGREEMENT, EVEN IF ONLY ON PROCESS   Group negotiations are more complex than dyadic negotiations. Group negotiation can be studied in terms of the acts of individuals, sequences between individuals, phrases of multiple actors, and breakpoints that signal transitions.[33] Sometimes group negotiations can get bogged down because it takes longer for parties to reach agreements—even on a single issue. Failure to reach agreement on negotiation issues can make group members feel they are not making progress and that negotiations are stalemated. The more persistent cooperative negotiators are in their use of integrative strategies, the better they do for themselves.[34] Avoid reaching agreement just for the sake of reaching settlement but, instead, agree on the process of reaching settlement. For example, a group member may suggest something like the following:

> I know we have been working for over 2 hours and have not been able to agree on a single issue. We could take this as a sign of failure or ill will, but I do not think that would be wise. I suggest that we take 10 minutes as a group to revisit all of the proposals that we have considered and then independently rank them in terms of their favorability. This ranking may give us some sense of where to look for possible agreements.

AVOID THE "EQUAL SHARES" BIAS   A tendency often emerges in group negotiations to divide things equally among the parties involved (see also Chapter 3, on pie-slicing). This bias is problematic for several reasons. First and foremost, as we saw in Chapter 3, no fair method of

[30] Diehl, M., & Stroebe, W. (1987). Productivity loss in brainstorming groups: Toward the solution of a riddle. *Journal of Personality and Social Psychology, 61,* 392–403.

[31] Palmer & Thompson, "Negotiation in triads."

[32] Mannix, E. (1993). Organizations as resource dilemmas: The effects of power balance on coalition formation in small groups. *Organizational Behavior and Human Decision Processes, 55,* 1–22.

[33] Brett, J., Weingart, L., & Olekans, M. (2004). Baubles, bangles and beads: Modeling the evolution of negotiating groups over time. In E. Mannix, M. A. Neale, & S. Blount-Lyon (Eds.), *Research on managing groups and teams: Vol. 6* (pp. 39–64), New York: Elsevier.

[34] Kern, M. C., Brett, J. M., & Weingart, L. R. (2005). Getting the floor: Motive-consistent strategy and individual outcomes in multi-party negotiations. *Group Decision and Negotiation, 14*(1), 21–41.

allocation is universally acceptable. Second, pressure is strong in many groups to behave in an egalitarian fashion, but privately, people are not inclined to be egalitarian.

AVOID THE AGREEMENT BIAS   The **agreement bias** occurs when negotiators focus on reaching common ground with the other party and are reluctant to accept differences of interest, even when such acceptance might create viable options for joint gain.

Another word of warning: Don't assume everyone wants to "get to yes." In some negotiation situations, people are paid to break deals and stall agreement.

AVOID SEQUENTIAL BARGAINING   Groups often use **sequential bargaining** (i.e., discuss one issue at a time) rather than simultaneous bargaining (where several issues are under consideration at any given time). By independently discussing and voting on each issue, negotiators cannot fashion win-win trade-offs among issues.[35]

COALITIONS

Coalitions face three sets of challenges: (1) the formation of the coalition, (2) coalition maintenance, and (3) the distribution of resources among coalition members. We take up these challenges and provide strategies for maximizing coalition effectiveness.

Key Challenges of Coalitions

OPTIMAL COALITION SIZE   Ideally, coalitions should contain the minimum number of people necessary to achieve a desired goal. Coalitions are difficult to maintain because members are tempted by other members to join other coalitions, and because agreements are not enforceable.[36]

TRUST AND TEMPTATION IN COALITIONS   Coalitional integrity is a function of the costs and rewards of coalitional membership; when coalitions are no longer rewarding, people will leave them. Nevertheless, members of coalitions experience a strong pull to remain intact even when it is not rational to do so.[37] According to the **status quo bias**, even when a new coalition structure that offers greater gain is possible, members are influenced by a norm of **coalitional integrity**, such that they stick with their current coalition.[38] Negotiators should form coalitions early so as not to be left without coalitional partners. Negotiators should also monitor their negative emotions when forming coalitions. Negotiators form negative impressions of people who use anger and exclude them from coalitions and coalition resources.[39] On the rare occasions when people do form coalitions with "angry" partners, they tend to make deep concessions.

DIVIDING THE PIE   The distribution of resources among members of coalitions is complex because a normative method of fair allocation does not exist.[40] Novice negotiators often settle for

---

[35] Mannix, Thompson, & Bazerman, "Negotiation in small groups"; Thompson, Mannix, & Bazerman, "Group negotiation."

[36] Mannix, E., & Loewenstein, G. (1993). Managerial time horizons and inter-firm mobility: An experimental investigation. *Organizational Behavior and Human Decision Processes, 56,* 266–284.

[37] Bottom, W. P., Eavey, C. L., & Miller, G. J. (1996). Getting to the core: Coalitional integrity as a constraint on the power of agenda setters. *Journal of Conflict Resolution, 40*(2), 298–319.

[38] Ibid.

[39] Beest, I., Van Kleef, G. A., & Van Dijk, E. (2008). Get angry, get out: The interpersonal effects of anger communication in multiparty negotiation. *Journal of Experimental Social Psychology, 44*(4), 993–1002.

[40] Raiffa, H. (1982). *The art and science of negotiation.* Cambridge, MA: Belknap.

"equal division," but experienced negotiators never do so.[41] Experienced negotiators are much more willing and able to exploit differences in their relative bargaining power. Veteran U.S. politicians such as Sam Rayburn, Lyndon Johnson, and Dan Rostenkowski were known for their ability to exploit their sources of power and build winning coalitions around policy initiatives.[42] To illustrate this observation, consider the following example. Lindholm, Tepe, and Clauson are three small firms producing specialized products, equipment, and research for the rehabilitation medicine community.[43] This area has become a critical, high-growth industry, and each firm is exploring ways to expand and improve its technologies through innovations in the research and development (R&D) divisions. Each firm recently applied for R&D funding from the National Rehabilitation Medicine Research Council (NRMR).

The NRMR is a government agency dedicated to funding research in rehabilitation medicine and treatment. The NRMR is willing to provide funds for the proposed research, but because the firms' requests are so similar, they will fund only a consortium of two or three firms. The NRMR will not grant funding to Lindholm, Tepe, or Clauson alone.

The largest of the three firms is Lindholm, followed by Tepe, and then Clauson. The NRMR took a variety of factors into consideration when it put caps on funding, as shown in Exhibit 9-5.

The NRMR strictly stipulated that for a consortium of firms to receive funding, the parties in the consortium (either two or three firms) must be in complete agreement concerning the allocation of resources among firms.

EXHIBIT 9-5

Maximum Funding Caps as a Function of Parties in a Consortium

Organizations in Consortium	Cap for R&D Funding
Lindholm alone	0
Tepe alone	0
Clauson alone	0
Lindholm and Tepe	$220,000
Lindholm and Clauson	$190,000
Tepe and Clauson	$150,000
Lindholm, Tepe, and Clauson	$240,000

---

[41] Bottom, W. P., Holloway, J., McClurg, S., & Miller, G. J. (2000). Negotiating a coalition: Risk, quota shaving, and learning to bargain. *Journal of Conflict Resolution, 44*(2), 147–169.

[42] Ibid.

[43] This example is based on the case Federated Science Fund, written by Elizabeth Mannix, available through the Dispute Resolution Research Center, Kellogg School of Management, Northwestern University (e-mail: drrc@kellogg.northwestern.edu); and the Social Services case, by Raiffa, *The art and science of negotiation.*

If you are Lindholm, what consortium would you consider to be the best for you? Obviously, you want to be in on some consortium, with either Tepe or Clauson or both, to avoid being excluded. But what is the best division of resources within each of those consortiums? Suppose you approach Tepe about a two-way venture, and Tepe proposes receiving half of the $220,000 or $110,000. You argue that you should earn more because you are bigger and bring more synergy to the agreement. You demand $200,000 for yourself, leaving $20,000 for Tepe. At this point, Tepe threatens to leave you and approach Clauson. Tepe argues that Tepe and Clauson can command $150,000 as a consortium without you, and each can receive $75,000. At this point, you argue that you can outbid Tepe's offer to Clauson with $80,000 and keep $110,000 for yourself. Just as Tepe is threatening to overbid you for Clauson, Clauson steps in and tells Tepe that Clauson would want at least $100,000 of the $150,000 pie that Clauson and Tepe together could command. Tepe is frustrated but relents.

You get nervous in your role as Lindholm. You certainly do not want to be excluded. You could attempt to get Clauson or Tepe in a consortium. Then a new thought occurs to you: Maybe all three of you can be in a consortium. After all, all three firms command the greatest amount of funding ($240,000). But how should the $240,000 be divided between the three of you? You are the biggest firm, so you propose that you keep half of the $240,000 (or $120,000), that Tepe get $80,000, and that Clauson get $40,000. This allocation strikes you as fair. At this point, Clauson gets upset and tells you that Clauson and Tepe can team up and get $150,000. Clauson thinks your share is unfair and should be reduced to something less than $90,000. You then remind Clauson that you and Tepe can get $190,000 together, of which you certainly deserve at least half, which is better than the $90,000 offer. Then the three of you are at it again in a vicious circle of coalition formation and demolition.

The negotiation between Lindholm, Tepe, and Clauson illustrates the unstable nature of coalitions. In this example, the excluded party is always able to approach one of the two parties in the coalition and offer a better deal, which can then be beaten by the remaining party, ad infinitum. Furthermore, splitting the pie three ways seems to offer no obvious solution. So, what should the three parties do? Is there a solution? Or are the parties destined to go around in circles forever?

Getting Out of the Vicious Circle.   As a way out of the vicious circle, let's conceptualize the problem as a system of simultaneous equations to solve. Namely,

$$L + T = \$220,000$$
$$L + C = \$190,000$$
$$T + C = \$150,000$$
$$L + T + C = \$240,000$$
$$L + T + C = (\$220,000 + \$190,000 + \$150,000)/2$$
$$= \$560,000/2$$
$$= \$280,000 \text{ total funds needed}$$

However, it is impossible to solve all simultaneous equations. We are $40,000 short of satisfying each party's minimum needs. What should we do? Consider the following three solutions: the core solution, the Shapley solution, and a hybrid model.[44]

---

[44] Raiffa, *The art and science of negotiation.*

The Core Solution. The core solution is a set of alternatives that are undominated.[45] An alternative is in the core if no coalition has both the power and desire to overthrow it.

The first step in computing the core solution is to determine what would be each party's share if shortage of funds were not an issue. Thus, we solve for L, T, and C shares as follows:

$$(L + T) - (L + C) = \$220,000 - \$190,000$$
$$= (T - C) = \$30,000$$
$$(L + T) - (T + C) = \$220,000 - \$150,000$$
$$= (L - C) = \$70,000$$
$$(T + C) + (T - C) = \$150,000 + \$30,000$$
$$2T = \$180,000$$
$$T = \$90,000$$
$$L + T = \$220,000$$
$$L + \$90,000 = \$220,000$$
$$L = \$220,000 - \$90,000$$
$$L = \$130,000$$
$$L + C = \$190,000$$
$$\$130,000 + C = \$190,000$$
$$C = \$190,000 - \$130,000$$
$$C = \$60,000$$
$$\underline{check}:$$
$$L = \$130,000$$
$$T = \$90,000$$
$$C = \$60,000$$
$$Total = \$280,000$$

Thus, if we had a total of $280,000, we could solve each equation. But, the harsh reality is that we do not. So, the second step is to get the total down to $240,000 by deducting $40,000 from somewhere. In the absence of any particular argument as to why one party's share should be cut, we deduct an equal amount, $13,333, from each party's share. In the final step, we compute the "core" shares as follows:

Lindholm:	$116,670
Tepe:	$76,670
Clauson:	$46,670

As Lindholm, you are delighted. Tepe agrees, but Clauson is not happy. Clauson thinks that $46,670 is too little and hires a consultant to evaluate the situation. The consultant proposes a different method, called the Shapley model.

[45] McKelvey, R. D., & Ordeshook, P. C. (1980). Vote trading: An experimental study. *Public Choice, 35,* 151–184.

EXHIBIT 9-6

Analysis of Pivotal Power in the Shapley Model

Order of Joining	Lindholm Added Value	Tepe Added Value	Clauson Added Value
LTC	0	$220,000	$ 20,000
LCT	0	50,000	190,000
TLC	$220,000	0	20,000
TCL	90,000	0	150,000
CLT	190,000	50,000	0
CTL	90,000	150,000	0
Shapley (average)*	98,333	78,333	63,333

*These figures are rounded slightly.

The Shapley Model.   Consider a coalition formation in which one player starts out alone and then is joined by a second and third player. The Shapley model determines the overall payoff a player can expect on the basis of his or her **pivotal power**, or the ability to change a losing coalition into a winning coalition. The consultant considers all possible permutations of players joining coalitions one at a time. The marginal value added to each coalition's outcome is attributed to the pivotal player. The Shapley value is the mean of a player's added value (see Exhibit 9-6). When all players bring equal resources, the Shapley value is the total amount of resources divided by the total number of people. This outcome, of course, is the **equal division principle**, as well as the **equity principle**.

When Clauson's consultant presents this report, Clauson is delighted with a share that increased by almost $20,000. Lindholm is nonplussed with a share that decreased. Tepe is tired of all the bickering and proposes a settlement in between the two proposed solutions.

Raiffa's Hybrid Model.   We have presented two models to solve for shares in coalition situations. The medium-power player's share in both models is identical, but the high- and low-power player's shares fluctuate quite dramatically. It is possible that an egocentric argument could ensue between Lindholm and Clauson as to which model to employ. One solution is a hybrid model in which the mean of the Shapley and core values is computed.[46] This model yields the following shares:

Lindholm:	$107,500
Tepe:	$77,500
Clauson:	$55,000

---

[46] Raiffa, *The art and science of negotiation.*

Tips for Low-Power Players.   Each of the three preceding models of fair solutions is compelling and defensible because each makes explicit the logic underlying the division of resources. It is easy to be a high-power player in coalition situations. However, the real trick is to know how to be an effective low-power player. Weakness can be power if you can recognize and disrupt unstable coalitions. Power is intimately involved in the formation of coalitions and the allocation of resources among coalition members. Power imbalance among coalition members can be detrimental for the group. Compared to egalitarian power relationships, unbalanced power relationships produce more coalitions defecting from the larger group,[47] fewer integrative agreements,[48] greater likelihood of bargaining impasse,[49] and more competitive behavior.[50] Power imbalance makes power issues salient to group members, whose primary concern is to protect their own interests. What is best for the coalition is often not what is best for the organization.

Can an optimal way be found for multiple parties to allocate resources so that group members are not tempted to form coalitions that may hinder group welfare? Usually not. Although several defensible methods can be used to allocate resources among coalition members, no single best way exists.[51]

Strategies for Maximizing Coalitional Effectiveness

What follows are some interpersonal strategies for effectively navigating coalitions.[52]

MAKE YOUR CONTACTS EARLY   Because of the commitment process, people tend to feel obligated to others with whom they have made explicit or implicit agreements. For this reason, it is important to make contact with key parties early in the process of multiparty negotiation before they become committed to others.

SEEK VERBAL COMMITMENTS   Most people feel obligated to follow through with promises they make to others, even when verbal commitments are not legally binding.[53]

USE UNBIASED-APPEARING RATIONALE TO DIVIDE THE PIE   If one or more members of the coalition regard the proposed allocation of resources to be unfair, the coalition will be less stable, and they will be likely to renege. To the extent to which coalitional members feel that the distribution of the pie is fair, they are more likely to resist persuasion from others to leave the coalition.

PRINCIPAL-AGENT NEGOTIATIONS

The reason why principal-agent negotiations are problematic is that "a risk-neutral principal must negotiate an incentive contract to motivate a risk-averse agent to undertake costly actions that cannot be observed."[54] An agent has a stake in the outcome (e.g., a real estate agent earns a commission on

---

[47] Mannix, "Organizations as resource dilemmas."
[48] Mannix, "Organizations as resource dilemmas"; McAlister, L., Bazerman, M. H., & Fader, P. (1986). Power and goal setting in channel negotiations. *Journal of Marketing Research, 23,* 238–263.
[49] Mannix, "Organizations as resource dilemmas."
[50] McClintock, C. G., & Liebrand, W. B. (1988). Role of interdependence structure, individual value orientation, and another's strategy in social decision making: A transformational analysis. *Journal of Personality and Social Psychology, 55*(3), 396–409.
[51] Raiffa, *The art and science of negotiation.*
[52] Bottom, Eavey, Miller, & Victor, "The institutional effect on majority rule."
[53] Cialdini, R. B. (1993). *Influence: Science and practice.* New York: HarperCollins.
[54] Bottom, W. P., Holloway, J., Miller, G. J., Mislin, A., & Whitford, A. B. (2006). Building pathways to cooperation: Negotiation and social exchange between principal and agent. *Administrative Science Quarterly, 51*(1), 29–58.

the sale of a house). In the SCO negotiation, CEO Darl McBride was an intermediary between SCO and IBM and also between SCO and the Canopy Group, and potentially Noorda.

Many advantages can be realized by using agents to represent one's interests:[55]

- *Expertise.*   Agents usually have more expertise in the negotiation process (e.g., a real estate agent).
- *Substantive knowledge.*   Agents may have more information than the principal about certain areas. For example, a tax attorney has a wealth of information about tax law and exemptions.
- *Networks and special influence.*   Often, people work through agents because they do not know what potential principals might be interested in their product or service.
- *Emotional detachment.*   Agents can provide emotional detachment and tactical flexibility. For example "divorce planner" is not an attorney, but rather a person who can act as an agent and bring rationality and perspective to an otherwise too-hot emotional process.[56]
- *Ratification.*   Precisely because an agent does not have authority to make or accept offers (unless directed to do so by the principal), the agent has power in the same way that a car salesperson has limited authority to offer price reductions (without the approval of the owner-manager).
- *Face-saving.*   Agents can provide a face-saving buffer for principals.

However, agency also comes with costs. Because they are usually compensated for their services, agents diminish the resources to be divided among the principals. In addition, ineffective agents complicate the negotiation dynamic and thereby inhibit settlement. Most problematic, the agent's interests may be at odds with those of the principals.[57]

Consider a typical home sale involving two principals and two agents. Is it wise for a home buyer to tell her agent her BATNA (how much she is willing to spend for a particular house)? Similarly, should a seller tell his agent the least amount of money he would accept for his home? No! Selling prices are lowest when the agent knows only the seller's reservation price and highest when the agent knows only the buyer's reservation price.[58] Not surprisingly, when buyers don't reveal their reservation price, their agent spends more time asking them about it.[59]

Agents increase the likelihood of impasse.[60] Agents may be maximally effective only when their interests are aligned with those of the principal. The social relationship the agent has with the principal affects how much effort the principal exerts.[61] The extent to which the agent believes the principal is a "benevolent individual" is directly related to the wage a principal offers an agent. However, money matters as well: The size of the bonus principals offer agents predicts how much effort agents exert.

---

[55] Rubin, J. Z., & Sander, F. E. A. (1988). When should we use agents? Direct vs. representative negotiation. *Negotiation Journal, 4*(4), 395–401.

[56] Grondhal, P. (2003, March 9). Offering a lifeline at marriage's end. *Times Union-Albany,* p. C17.

[57] Jensen, M. C., & Meckling, W. H. (1976). Theory of the firm: Managerial behavior, agency costs, and ownership structure. *Journal of Financial Economics, 3,* 305–360.

[58] Valley, K. L., White, S. B., Neale, M. A., & Bazerman, M. H. (1992). Agents as information brokers: The effects of information disclosure on negotiated outcomes. [Special issue: Decision processes in negotiation.] *Organizational Behavior and Human Decision Processes, 51*(2), 220–236.

[59] Valley, K. L., White, S. B., & Iacobucci, D. (1992). The process of assisted negotiations: A network analysis. *Group Decision and Negotiation, 2,* 117–135.

[60] Bazerman, M. H., Neale, M. A., Valley, K., Zajac, E., & Kim, P. (1992). The effect of agents and mediators on negotiation outcomes. *Organizational Behavior and Human Decision Processes, 53,* 55–73.

[61] Bottom, Holloway, Miller, Mislin, & Whitford, "Pathways to cooperation."

Disadvantages of Agents

SHRINKING ZOPA   Using an agent means more parties are claiming a fixed bargaining surplus. A small bargaining zone increases the likelihood of an impasse. (For an example, see Exhibit 9-7.)

EXHIBIT 9-7

The Bargaining Zone, Maximum Surplus, and Agent Commission Rates for a House Sale

Commission	Seller RP* [adjusted from $410,000/ (1 − c)]	Bargaining Zone [Buyer RP ($440,000) − Seller RP*]	Buyer Maximum Surplus	Seller Maximum Surplus	Agents' Surplus Range
0% (for sale by owner)	$410,000	$30,000	$30,000	$30,000	$0
2%	$418,367	$21,633	$21,633	$21,200	$8,367–$8,800
4%	$427,083	$12,917	$12,917	$12,400	$17,083–$17,600
5%	$431,578	$8,422	$8,422	$8,000	$21,579–$22,000
6%	$436,170	$3,830	$3,830	$3,600	$26,170–$26,400

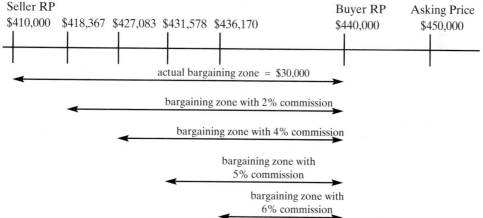

*Note: RP=reservation price. In this example, assume that the house is originally listed for sale at $450,000; assume that the buyer's reservation price is $440,000 and the seller's reservation price is $410,000. If no agency fees were involved, the bargaining range is $30,000 (i.e., any price between $410,000 and $440,000). The agent commission fees mean that the seller must adjust his or her reservation price upward. For example, if the agent commission rate is 6%, the seller cannot sell below $436,170.

INCOMPATIBLE INCENTIVE STRUCTURE   It is unwise to trust someone to effectively represent your interests when their incentives are not aligned with yours. Ultimately, an agent's job is to broker a deal, and thus, agents are motivated to apply pressure to whomever is motivated to reach a deal. Agents have an incentive to make transactions happen. For example, in home buying, a buyer's agent is really an employee of the selling company. The agent's preference is the higher price because he or she gets a commission. Furthermore, an agent may give biased information to get an agreement from his or her constituency.

A key question for agents is whether to align with their principal or to align with the other agent.[62] Obviously, certain laws and regulations govern disclosure, but the question is which social bond is most important for the final agreement. Agents initially show greater loyalty to their principals, but over time their loyalty to the other agent is greater. Moreover, to the extent that the across-the-table relationship among agents is strong, the likelihood of agreement is greater and settlements occur in the middle of the bargaining zone. Most notably, to the extent that the agents are socially similar (i.e., graduated from the same school, etc.) and familiar with each other, they are more likely to forge a bond. Agents who are "securely" attached to their principals negotiate more effectively and are less pro-self than are agents who are not securely attached.[63]

COMMUNICATION DISTORTION   Because agents often do the negotiating (rather than the principal), more communication distortion may occur. **Message tuning** refers to how senders tailor messages for specific recipients. People who send messages (e.g., "I have no fuel"; "I did not receive the attached file") edit their messages in a way they think best suits the recipient. For example, people give longer and more elaborate street directions and instructions to people whom they presume to be nonnatives or unfamiliar with a city.[64] Also, senders capitalize on the knowledge that they believe the recipient to already hold. For this reason, negotiators may send shorter, less complete messages to one another because they believe that they can capitalize on an existing shared knowledge base. However, negotiators often overestimate the commonality of information they share with others. Consequently, the messages they send become less clear.

Message senders present information that they believe will be favorably received by the recipient, and therefore they distort messages.[65] For example, when people present a message to an audience they believe is either for or against a particular topic, they err in the direction of adopting the audience's point of view.

LOSS OF CONTROL   Because an agent is negotiating in your stead, you are giving up control over the process of negotiation and, ultimately, the outcome. Indeed, agents are more active in a negotiation than principals.[66]

---

[62] Kurtzberg, T., Dunn-Jensen, L., & Matsibekker, C. L. Z. (2005). Multiparty e-negotiations: Agents, alliances, and negotiation success. *International Journal of Conflict Management, 16*(3), 245–264.

[63] Lee, S. & Thompson, L. (2011). Do agents negotiate for the best (or worst) interest of principals? Secure, anxious and avoidant principal-agent attachment. *Journal of Experimental Social Psychology, 47*(3), 681–684.

[64] Krauss, R. M., & Fussell, S. R. (1991). Perspective-taking in communication: Representations of others' knowledge in reference. *Social Cognition, 9*, 2–24.

[65] Higgins, E. T. (1999). "Saying is believing" effects: When sharing reality about something biases knowledge and evaluations. In L. Thompson, J. M. Levine, & D. M. Messick (Eds.), *Shared cognition in organizations: The management of knowledge.* Mahwah, NJ: Erlbaum.

[66] Valley, White, & Iacobucci, "Process of assisted negotiations."

AGREEMENT AT ANY COST   Because agents have an incentive to reach agreement, they may fall prey to the **getting to yes bias** in which agreement becomes more important than the contents of the deal.[67]

Strategies for Working Effectively with Agents

SHOP AROUND   Do not assume the first agent you meet is uniquely qualified to represent you. Ask the agent how he or she will successfully represent your interests. Ask the agent about what is expected of you. Ask the agent about the nature of your relationship and what obligations, if any, you have to one another. Many real estate agents have easy-exit clauses that allow principals to remove agents without difficulty; in the absence of this clause, a principal might be committed to an agent for a lengthy period of time. Free agent pitcher Cliff Lee was the hottest commodity on Major League Baseball's free agent market in the winter of 2010. Courted by numerous clubs, he eventually signed a 5-year, $120 million deal with the Philadelphia Phillies that included a sixth year option that would pay Lee $27.5 million. The money was a record for a major league pitcher. The agent behind Lee's deal was Darek Braunecker, described as both "cocky" and "amenable". The pitcher and the agent share a long friendship that dates back more than a decade; Lee and Braunecker regularly hunt together; their wives play tennis together; their daughters are in the same elementary school class.[68] Ask agents about their negotiation training and strategies. (See Exhibit 9-8 for some suggested questions to ask an agent.)

KNOW YOUR BATNA BEFORE MEETING WITH YOUR AGENT   Do your homework before meeting with your agent. Know your own BATNA. Prepare questions to ask your agent that allow you to test the accuracy of your BATNA, but do not reveal your BATNA. For example,

EXHIBIT 9-8

Questions That Potential Home Buyers Should Ask Real-Estate Agents

1. Can you represent me as a buyer's agent?
2. How will you find me homes?
3. How can you leverage my down payment, interest rate, and monthly payment?
4. What different points will you be able to negotiate on my behalf?
5. How long have you been selling real estate full time?
6. What can I expect in terms of communication?
7. Does your contract have an "easy exit" clause in it?
8. Under what conditions will you cut your commission?

Source: Based on Ron Holdridge, Re/Max Metro Realty, Seattle, Washington.

[67] Gibson, K., Thompson, L., & Bazerman, M. H. (1994). Biases and rationality in the mediation process. In L. Heath, F. Bryant, & J. Edwards (Eds.), *Application of heuristics and biases to social issues: Vol. 3.* New York: Plenum.
[68] Waldstein, D. (2010, December 13). Darek Braunecker, agent for Cliff Lee, is getting noticed. *New York Times.* Nytimes.com; Crasnick, J. (2010, December 15). Cliff Lee, Phillies get their wish. *ESPN.* ESPN.com

a home seller might say, "I would like to find out what average sale prices are for this type of home."

COMMUNICATE YOUR INTERESTS TO YOUR AGENT WITHOUT GIVING AWAY YOUR BATNA   One of the most challenging tasks for a negotiator is to communicate his or her interests, priorities, and preferences but not reveal his or her BATNA. Help your agent by prioritizing your key interests and what you perceive to be the alternatives for meeting those interests. Anticipate that your agent will ask you about your BATNA. When this question comes up (and it will!), focus on your priorities (e.g., "I am not sure how helpful it is to tell you the most money I am willing to pay for the house you showed me today. However, I am really interested in a home within this school district, and a double garage. In fact, I would be willing to pay more for those features than I would a master suite and an updated kitchen.").

CAPITALIZE ON THE AGENT'S EXPERTISE   Good agents have a wealth of expertise. Ask them about their key strategies for targeting opportunities for you and closing deals.

TAP INTO YOUR AGENT'S SOURCES OF INFORMATION   Agents, by virtue of their professional affiliations and networks, have access to a lot of information. If your agent is unwilling or unable to obtain information, interview another agent and see whether he or she can provide the information.

DISCUSS RATIFICATION   By nature of the principal-agent relationship, an agent's authority is limited with respect to making certain concessions or types of agreements (i.e., your agent cannot reduce or increase your offer without explicit direction from you).

USE YOUR AGENT TO HELP SAVE FACE   Sometimes, negotiators make what they regard to be perfectly reasonable proposals that are insulting to the other party. When this situation happens (and if the counterparty is insulted), negotiations may start on a losing course. In an agent-mediated negotiation, you can attempt to salvage damaged egos and relationships by blaming your agent.

USE YOUR AGENT TO BUFFER EMOTIONS   Agents can provide an emotional buffer between parties who may either dislike one another or are irrational (see Chapter 5 on bargaining styles). Effective agents will put a positive "spin" on the communications by each party and effectively "tune into" their principal's needs.

CONSTITUENT RELATIONSHIPS

When a negotiating party is embedded within an organization, several peripheral players may have an indirect stake in the outcome and may influence the negotiation process. A **constituent** is on the "same side" as a principal but exerts an independent influence on the outcome through the principal. Constituents can be used to exert pressure on the other side of the table.

Consider the pressure that Zappos CEO Tony Hsieh felt from his board of directors constituency. Before Zappos was bought by Amazon in 2009, Hsieh's board was largely focused on profitability and getting the best price for the sale, while Hsieh was concerned about the unique Zappos culture. There was a possibility that if profitability dropped Hsieh would be fired and replaced by a more profit-minded CEO. In the midst of the internal negotiations, Amazon CEO Jeff Bezos approached Hsieh about selling the company to Amazon. After the $1.2 billion sale,

Zappos board was replaced by a management committee that included the two CEO's plus two Zappos and Amazon executives.[69]

We distinguish three types of constituencies: superiors, who have authority over principals, subordinates, who are under the authority of principals, and constituencies, the party whom the principal represents—that is, for whom the principal is responsible and to whom the principal is accountable (constituencies are represented by *C* in Exhibit 9-2). In the chapter opening example, IBM is accountable to its major shareholders and customers, who are ostensibly on their side but may have interests of their own. Further, the SCO group has dual accountability to the Canopy Group (as 43% owners), as well as its investor BayStar Capital, and ultimately to Noorda as the parent company of Canopy.

Challenges for Constituent Relationships

IDENTIFICATION   Constituent representatives must think about how they want to identify themselves/their side in a negotiation. One choice involves using personal language (e.g., "I believe") or collective language (e.g., "we believe"). Ironically, collective language is not always preferred by constituency members. When constituency members are not highly identified with their group, they rate advocates as more likeable and more effective when they use personal rather than collective language.[70]

ACCOUNTABILITY   Negotiators at the bargaining table comprise the primary relationship in negotiation. The relationship parties share with their constituents is the **second table**.[71] Constituents do not have to be physically present at the negotiation table for their presence to be strongly felt.[72] Negotiators who are accountable to their constituents make higher demands and are less willing to compromise than those not accountable to constituents.[73] Gender affects accountability. Women, as compared to men, believe they are more generous when representing a group; conversely, men don't believe this. When it comes to actual behavior, men are significantly more self-interested when they are responsible for a group as compared to when they are acting only on behalf of themselves; female representatives don't behave differently whether they are representing a group or just themselves.[74] Male constituency representatives tend to explain and justify their successes and not their failures; whereas women tend to justify their failures but not their successes.[75]

[69] Hsieh, T. (2010, June 1). Why I sold Zappos. *Inc.* Inc.com
[70] Hornsey, M. J., Blackwood, L., & O'Brien, A. T. (2005). Speaking for others: The pros and cons of group advocates using collective language. *Group Processes and Intergroup Relations, 8*(3), 245–257.
[71] Ancona, D. G., Friedman, R. A., & Kolb, D. M. (1991). The group and what happens on the way to "yes." *Negotiation Journal, 7*(2), 155–173.
[72] Kramer, R., Pommerenke, P., & Newton, E. (1993). The social context of negotiation: Effects of social identity and accountability on negotiator judgment and decision making. *Journal of Conflict Resolution, 37,* 633–654; Pruitt, D. G., & Carnevale, P. J. (1993). *Negotiation in social conflict.* Pacific Grove, CA: Brooks-Cole; Tetlock, P. E. (1985). Accountability: A social check on the fundamental attribution error. *Social Psychology Quarterly, 48,* 227–236.
[73] Ben-Yoav, O., & Pruitt, D. G. (1984). Accountability to constituents: A two-edged sword. *Organizational Behavior and Human Processes, 34,* 282–295; Carnevale, P. J., Pruitt, D. G., & Britton, S. (1979). Looking tough: The negotiator under constituent surveillance. *Personality and Social Psychology Bulletin, 5,* 118–121; O'Connor, K. M. (1997). Groups and solos in context: The effects of accountability on team negotiation. *Organizational Behavior and Human Decision Processes, 72,* 384–407.
[74] Song, F., Cadsby, C., & Morris, T. (2004). Other-regarding behavior and behavioral forecasts: Females versus males as individuals and as group representatives. *International Journal of Conflict Management, 15*(4), 340–363.
[75] Medina, F. J., Povedano, A., Martinez, I., & Munduate, L. (2009) How do we approach accountability with our constituency?: Gender differences in the use of influence tactics, *International Journal of Conflict Management, 20*(1), 46–59.

The second table has a paradoxical effect on the primary table. Representatives of constituents often are not given power to enact agreements; that is, they are not monolithic.[76] Whereas this would seem to reduce one's power at the bargaining table, the negotiator whose "hands are tied" is often more effective than the negotiator who has the power to ratify agreements. Anyone who has ever negotiated a deal on a new car has probably experienced the "My hands are tied" or "Let me take it to the boss" ploy, in which the salesperson induces the customer to commit to a price that requires approval before a deal is finalized.

Accountability to collateral actors is an inevitable aspect of organizational life.[77] At least two motivational processes are triggered by accountability: decision-making vigilance and evaluation apprehension.

Decision-Making Vigilance.   Decision makers who are accountable for their actions consider relevant information and alternatives more carefully.[78] Accountability increases thoughtful, deliberate processing of information and decreases automatic, heuristic processing.[79]

However, decision accountability may not always promote more thorough and unbiased processing of information if organizational actors are partisan to a particular view.[80] Imagine a situation in which an observer watches a video of people negotiating. Some observers are told to take an objective and impartial view of the situation; other observers are instructed to take the perspective of one of the parties. Further, some observers are told they are accountable for their actions and behaviors (e.g., they must justify their decisions to others who will question them), whereas others are not accountable. After watching the tape, observers indicate what they think each negotiator wanted. Accountable partisans fall prey to the fixed-pie assumption because they are motivated to reach a particular conclusion. However, nonpartisan observers are willing to reach whatever conclusion the data will allow, and their judgments are therefore driven by the evidence, not their desires.

Evaluation Apprehension and Face-Saving.   When people are concerned what others will think, they use face-saving strategies and make their actions appear more favorable to relevant others. Negotiators who want to save face will be more aggressive and uncompromising so they will not be viewed as weak. For this reason, negotiators who are accountable to constituents are more likely to maintain a tough bargaining stance, make fewer concessions, and hold out for more favorable agreements compared to those who are not accountable.[81] A **diffusion of responsibility** occurs within members of the team.[82]

CONFLICTS OF INTEREST   It is important to understand the relationships negotiators share across the bargaining table and the hidden table of constituent relationships.[83] Consider a negotiation involving teams of two people who are either personally acquainted or strangers to

---

[76] Raiffa, *The art and science of negotiation.*

[77] Tetlock, "Accountability"; Tetlock, P. E. (1992). The impact of accountability on judgment and choice: Toward a social contingency model. *Advances in Experimental Social Psychology, 25,* 331–376.

[78] Ibid.

[79] Chaiken, S. (1980). Heuristic versus systematic information processing and the use of source versus message cues in persuasion. *Journal of Personality and Social Psychology, 39*(5), 752–766; Fiske, S. T., & Neuberg, S. L. (1990). A continuum of impression formation, from category-based to individuating processes: Influences of information and motivation on attention and interpretation. In M. P. Zanna (Ed.), *Advances in experimental social psychology: Vol. 23* (pp. 1–74). New York: Academic Press.

[80] Thompson, L. (1995). "They saw a negotiation": Partisanship and involvement. *Journal of Personality and Social Psychology, 68*(5), 839–853.

[81] Carnevale, P. J., & Pruitt, D. G. (1992). Negotiation and mediation. *Annual Review of Psychology, 43,* 531–582.

[82] O'Connor, "Groups and solos in context."

[83] Kolb, D. (1983). *The mediators.* Cambridge, MA: MIT Press.

one another. Each team reports to a manager. Some teams report to a "profit-oriented" manager who instructs the team to "serve the interests of the group at all costs." Some teams report to a "people-oriented" manager who instructs the team to maximize interests while maintaining harmonious intergroup relations. Teams who report to the "profit" supervisor claim a greater share of the resources than do teams who report to the "people" supervisor and teams not accountable to a manager.[84] When team members are acquainted, no differences occur in relative profitability. Why? Negotiators are more likely to maximize profit when the goal is clear and they do not share a previous relationship.

Strategies for Improving Constituent Relationships

COMMUNICATE WITH YOUR CONSTITUENTS   Representatives need to understand their constituents' interests, not just their positions. Moreover, when constituents feel heard, they are less likely to take extreme action. In many cases, representatives act too early (before they understand their constituency's real needs) so as to demonstrate their competence. For example, a minority of "hawks" (people who support competitive behavior) is sufficient to induce constituency representatives to act in a competitive way, even when the majority are "doves" (people who support cooperative behavior).[85] Constituency representatives unconsciously accord more weight to hawkish than to dovish messages.

DO NOT EXPECT HOMOGENEITY OF CONSTITUENT VIEWS   Constituencies are often composed of individuals and subgroups with different needs and interests.

EDUCATE YOUR CONSTITUENTS ON YOUR ROLE AND YOUR LIMITATIONS   Constituents, like other people, suffer from egocentric bias, and want you to educate the other side with your position. It is important to clearly define your role to your constituents early on in the process. Set realistic expectations. Do not characterize yourself as an "evangelist" for their "crusade." Share with your constituents all possible outcomes, not just the favorable ones.

HELP YOUR CONSTITUENTS DO HORIZON THINKING   Horizon thinking involves making projections about future outcomes. People have a difficult time thinking about future events,[86] tend to under- or overestimate the duration of future emotional states,[87] and fail to account for positive or negative circumstances that could arise.[88] Help your constituents develop a sound BATNA and realistic aspirations by engaging in horizon thinking.

---

[84] Peterson, E., & Thompson, L. (1997). Negotiation teamwork: The impact of information distribution and accountability on performance depends on the relationship among team members. *Organizational Behavior and Human Decision Processes, 72*(3), 364–383.

[85] Steinel, W., De Dreu, C. K. W., Ouwehand, E., & Ramirez-Marin, J. Y. (2009). When constituencies speak in multiple tounges: The relative persuasiveness of hawkish minorities in representative negotiation. *Organizational Behavior and Human Decision Processes, 109*(1), 67–78.

[86] Gilbert, D. T., & Wilson, T. D. (2000). Miswanting: Some problems in the forecasting of future affective states. In J. P. Forgas (Ed.), *Feeling and thinking: The role of affect in social cognition. Studies in emotion and social interaction, Second series* (pp. 178–197). New York: Cambridge University Press.

[87] Gilbert, D. T., Pinel, E. C., Wilson, T. D., Blumberg, S. J., & Wheatley, T. P. (1998). Immune neglect: A source of durability bias in affective forecasting. *Journal of Personality and Social Psychology, 75*(3), 617–638.

[88] Loewenstein, G. F., & Schkade, D. (1999). Wouldn't it be nice? Predicting future feelings. In D. Kahneman & E. Diener (Eds.), *Well-being: The foundations of hedonic psychology* (pp. 85–105). New York: Russell Sage Foundation; Schkade, D. A., & Kahneman, D. (1998). Does living in California make people happy? A focusing illusion in judgments of life satisfaction. *Psychological Science, 9*(5), 340–346; Wilson, T. D., Wheatley, T. P., Meyers, J., Gilbert, D. T., & Axsom, D. (2000). Focalism: A source of durability bias in affective forecasting. *Journal of Personality and Social Psychology, 78*, 821–836.

TEAM NEGOTIATION

Consider the following situations:

- A husband and wife negotiate with a salesperson on the price of a new car
- A group of disgruntled employees approach management about wages and working conditions
- A large software company approaches a small software company about an acquisition

In all of these examples, people join together on one side of the bargaining table as a team. Unlike solo negotiators, members of negotiating teams may play different roles for strategic reasons, such as "good cop–bad cop."[89]

Are teams effective at exploiting integrative potential at the bargaining table? A comparison of three types of negotiation configurations (team vs. team, team vs. solo, and solo vs. solo negotiations) revealed that the presence of at least one team at the bargaining table increased the size of the pie.[90] Why are teams so effective? Negotiators exchange much more information about their interests and priorities when at least one team is at the bargaining table than when two individuals negotiate.[91] Information exchange leads to greater judgment accuracy about parties' interests,[92] which promotes integrative agreement.[93] The **team effect** is quite robust: It is not even necessary that team members privately caucus with one another to be effective.[94] In negotiations with integrative potential, teams outperform solos; however, in extremely competitive tasks, teams are more likely to behave in a competitive fashion.[95]

The presence of a team at the bargaining table increases the integrativeness of joint agreements,[96] but what about the distributive component? Do teams outperform their solo counterparts? Not necessarily. Nevertheless, both teams and solo players believe teams have an advantage—a **team efficacy effect**.[97] Even in situations in which teams reap greater shares of profit than their solo counterparts, solos are still better off negotiating with a team than with another solo player. The solo negotiator earns less than the team, but the amount of jointly available resources is greater in the team-solo negotiation than in the solo-solo negotiation. The **team halo effect** refers to the fact that teams tend not to be blamed for their failures, as much as do individuals, holding constant the nature of the failure.[98] Rather, teams are given a lot of credit for their successes but are not blamed for their failures. The reason is that people have an easier

---

[89] Brodt, S., & Tuchinsky, M. (2000). Working together but in opposition: An examination of the "good cop/bad cop" negotiating team tactic. *Organizational Behavior and Human Decision Processes, 81*(2), 155–177.

[90] Thompson, L., Peterson, E., & Brodt, S. (1996). Team negotiation: An examination of integrative and distributive bargaining. *Journal of Personality and Social Psychology, 70*(1), 66–78; Morgan, P., & Tindale, R. S. (2002). Group vs. individual performance in mixed-motive situations: Exploring the inconsistency. *Organizational Behavior and Human Decision Processes, 87*(1), 44–65.

[91] O'Connor, "Groups and solos in context"; Carnevale, P. J. (2008). Positive affect and decision frame in negotiation. *Group Decision and Negotiation, 17(1)*, 51–63; Thompson, Peterson, & Brodt, "Team negotiation."

[92] Ibid.

[93] Thompson, L. (1991). Information exchange in negotiation. *Journal of Experimental Social Psychology, 27*(2), 161–179.

[94] Thompson, Peterson, & Brodt, "Team negotiation."

[95] Morgan & Tindale, "Group vs. individual performance."

[96] Morgan & Tindale, "Group vs. individual performance"; O'Connor, "Groups and solos in context"; Carnevale, *Team effects in bilateral negotiation.*

[97] O'Connor, "Groups and solos in context"; Carnevale, "Positive affect and decision frame in negotiation"; Thompson, Peterson, & Brodt, "Team negotiation."

[98] Naquin, C., & Tynan, R. (2003). The team halo effect: Why teams are not blamed for their failures. *Journal of Applied Psychology, 88*(2), 332–340.

time imagining how an *individual* might have done something better than imagining how a *team* might have done something better.

Challenges That Face Negotiating Teams

For a comprehensive review, see Brodt and Thompson.[99]

SELECTING YOUR TEAMMATES   Consider the following criteria for choosing and evaluating teammates:

1. *Negotiation expertise.*   People with good negotiation skills may be able to devise an integrative solution to a complex conflict situation. A negotiation expert can streamline preparation, ensure the team avoids the four major traps of negotiation (see Chapter 1), avoids destructive conflict strategies, and instigates a creative problem-solving process.
2. *Technical expertise.*   It helps to have someone with technical expertise in the domain of interest. For example, when house buying, it is valuable to have someone skilled in architecture, plumbing, electricity, and so on.
3. *Interpersonal skills.*   Negotiation involves many interpersonal skills, such as the ability to establish rapport, communicate effectively, and redirect a power- or rights-based argument to one focusing on interests.[100]

HOW MANY ON THE TEAM?   Two or three heads can be better than one, but at some point conformity pressures increase with group size, peaking at about five and then leveling off.[101] As teams grow in size, coordination problems increase.

COMMUNICATION ON THE TEAM   Communication, or **information pooling**, is facilitated if members are acquaintances or share a relationship. For example, when the clues for solving a murder mystery game are distributed among group members, groups of friends are more likely to pool their diverse information than are groups of strangers.[102]

TEAM COHESION   **Cohesion** is the strength of positive relations within a team,[103] the sum of pressures acting to keep individuals in a group,[104] and the result of all forces acting on members to remain in a group.[105] Cohesive groups perform better than less cohesive groups.[106] The three sources of cohesion are (a) attraction to the group or resistance to leaving the group, (b) morale and motivation, and (c) coordination of efforts.

---

[99] Brodt, S., & Thompson, L. (2001). Negotiating teams: A levels of analysis approach. *Group Dynamics: Theory, Research, and Practice, 5*(3), 208–219.

[100] Ury, W. L., Brett, J. M., & Goldberg, S. B. (1988). *Getting disputes resolved: Designing systems to cut the costs of conflict.* San Francisco: Jossey-Bass.

[101] Latané, B. (1981). The psychology of social impact. *American Psychologist, 36,* 343–356.

[102] Gruenfeld, D. H., Mannix, E. A., Williams, K., & Neale, M. A. (1996). Group composition and decision making: How member familiarity and information distribution affect process and performance. *Organizational Behavior and Human Decision Processes, 67*(1), 1–15.

[103] Evans, C. R., & Dion, K. L. (1991). Group cohesion and performance: A meta-analysis. *Small Group Research, 22,* 175–186.

[104] Back, K. W. (1951). Influence through social communication. *Journal of Abnormal Social Psychology, 46,* 9–23.

[105] Festinger, L. (1950). Informal social communication. *Psychological Review, 57,* 271–282.

[106] Evans & Dion, "Group cohesion and performance."

Different kinds of bonds keep teams together. **Common-identity groups** are composed of members who are attracted to the group; the individual members may come and go. **Common-bond groups** are composed of members who are attracted to particular members in the group.[107]

INFORMATION PROCESSING   Organizational members often negotiate as a team or a group because no single person has the requisite knowledge and expertise required to negotiate effectively. Thus, knowledge is distributed among team members. How effective are teams at utilizing knowledge that is distributed among members?

It is more efficient for each team member to be responsible for a particular piece of information so that each member is not overwhelmed by too much data. However, as storage space is minimized, so are the chances of successfully retrieving the desired information. Furthermore, groups are less likely to consider and discuss information that is shared only by a subset of its members. They suffer from the **common information bias**.[108]

Members of groups are not privy to the same facts and information. People rely on others for information. Teams can be more efficient by dividing the labor among members. However, distributed cognition is risky because information may be lost to the entire group if a team loses one of its members. Thus, groups face a dilemma: divide responsibility, which increases members' dependence upon each individual member, or share information, which is clumsy and redundant.

Strategies for Improving Team Negotiations

GOAL AND STRATEGY ALIGNMENT   A large experiment with 80 4-person teams revealed that conflict between subgroups exerted a detrimental effect on negotiation performance.[109] The higher the level of team identification, the lower the level of task and relationship conflict in teams.[110] For example, top management teams that have high trust have greater agreement-seeking behavior and collaboration than low-trust-teams.[111]

PREPARE TOGETHER   Team preparation is so important that we developed a worksheet for effective team preparation (see Exhibit 9-9). Preparing together creates a transactive memory system in which group members understand the information others have and how and when to access it. For example, groups in one investigation were given instructions on how to assemble a transistor radio. Some groups trained together; in other groups, individuals trained individually (or with a different group). When it came to actual performance, groups who had trained together outperformed those who had trained individually or with different groups.[112]

---

[107] Prentice, D. A., Miller, D. T., & Lightdale, J. R. (1994). Asymmetries in attachments to groups and to their members: Distinguishing between common-identity and common-bond groups. *Personality and Social Psychology Bulletin, 20,* 484–493.

[108] Gigone, D., & Hastie, R. (1993). The common knowledge effect: Information sharing and group judgment. *Journal of Personality and Social Psychology, 65,* 959–974; Stasser, G. (1992). Pooling of unshared information during group discussion. In S. Worchel, W. Wood & J. A. Simpson (Eds.), *Group processes and productivity* (pp. 48–67). Newbury Park, CA: Sage.

[109] Halevy, N. (2008). Team negotiation: Social, epistemic, economic, and psychological consequences of subgroup conflict. *Personality and Social Psychology Bulletin, 34*(12), 1687–1702.

[110] Guohong, H. and Harms, P. D. (2010) Team identification, trust and conflict: A mediation model. *International Journal of Conflict Management, 21*(1), 20–43.

[111] Parayitam, S., Olson, B. J., & Bao, Y. (2010). Task conflict, relationship conflict and agreement-seeking behavior in Chinese top management teams. *International Journal of Conflict Management. (21)*1, 94–116.

[112] Moreland, R. L., Argote, L., & Krishnan, R. (1996). Socially shared cognition at work. In J. L. Nye & A. M. Brower (Eds.), *What's social about social cognition?* Thousand Oaks, CA: Sage.

EXHIBIT 9-9

Preparing for Your Team-on-Team Negotiation

Team-on-team negotiation can be an advantage over solo negotiation if the team prepares properly. Here are some guidelines:

Step 1:   Individual Preparation

- Identify the issues.
- Identify your BATNA.
- Determine what you believe to be your team's "worst-case" scenario.
- Determine what you believe to be your team's "best-case" scenario.
- Write down these scenarios and be prepared to share them with the members of your team.

Step 2:   As a Team, Decide on Your Procedures for Running the Preparation Meeting

- Who is going to run the meeting (i.e., who is going to summarize, synthesize, etc.)?
- What materials do you need to be effective (calculator, flipcharts, computer, etc.), and who is bringing them?
- What is your timeline, and who will enforce it so that the team arrives at the negotiation table prepared and refreshed?

Step 3:   As a Team, Clarify Facts and Information (*Note:* You are not discussing strategy yet!)

- Develop a "Positions and Interests" chart.
- Prioritize your issues. Understand the reasons for your priorities.
- Identify what you think the other party's priorities are.
- Identify what information you need from the other party.
- Determine your BATNA.
- What do you know about the other party's BATNA?
- Identify your worst-case scenario (reservation price).
- Identify your best-case scenario (target).
- As you complete the preceding tasks, make a list of questions to research.
- Identify information that is too sensitive to reveal at any point under any condition (get clarification and closure within the team on this point).
- Identify information that you are willing to share with the other team if they inquire (get clarification and closure within the team on this point).

Step 4:   Strategy

- As a team, plan your OPENING OFFER. (*Note:* It is not advisable to simply want the "other party" to open; you need to be able to put something on the table at some point.)
- Choose a *lead negotiator* (speaker).
- Choose a *lead strategist* (listener and strategic watchdog).
- Choose an *accountant* to run the numbers.
- Choose a *scribe* to keep track of offers. Decide on a signal to adjourn for a private caucus.

PLAN SCHEDULED BREAKS   Make sure that you schedule breaks into your negotiation to allow team members to meet privately. Admiral Mike Mullen, Chairman of the U.S. Joint Chiefs of Staff, and General Ashfaq Parvez Kayani, who heads Pakistan's Army, differed over strategies for fighting insurgents. However, they came together after U.S. airstrikes on targets in Pakistan and eventually forged a working relationship built on a tense international platform. Mullen casually brought sides together by strategically engineering breaks into the negotiations. During secret meetings in the Indian Ocean aboard an American aircraft carrier, Mullen's team, worried that Kavani, a chain smoker would balk at the ship's no-smoking rule, scheduled regular negotiation breaks and permitted Kayani to smoke on the ship deck. At dusk, the men would gather to watch warplanes take off for missions over Afghanistan and during these "breaks" several issues were discussed.[113]

A word of caution: Many teams spend too much time in private caucus and not enough time at the table. This behavior is ultimately not effective for negotiation.

ASSESS ACCOUNTABILITY   It is important to assess the extent to which team members are accountable to others outside of the team. For example, when teams are accountable to a supervisor, they are more effective than when they negotiate strictly on their own behalf.[114]

INTERGROUP NEGOTIATION

Intergroup negotiation involves everyday life as well as complex political and international relations.[115] For example, members of a student council and university administrators, union and management negotiators, and groups of students from rival universities are all examples of intergroup negotiators. On a larger scale, nations negotiate with other nations. The toll in death, suffering, and displacement caused by intergroup conflict has reached staggering proportions. Through January, 2011, the number of American casualties in the United States-Iraq war reached 4,408.[116]

Challenges of Intergroup Negotiations

STEREOTYPING   In intergroup negotiations, parties identify with their organization and often hold negative impressions about members of the other organizations.[117]

CHANGING IDENTITIES   People identify with many different social groups.[118] For example, a student might consider a relevant group to be the other students in his or her study group, the class as a whole, marketing majors in general, or the entire student body. At any given time, one group

---

[113] Ephron, D. (2009, February 28). Try a little tea and sympathy. *Newsweek.* Newsweek.com
[114] Peterson & Thompson, "Negotiation teamwork."
[115] Deutsch, M. (1973). *The resolution of conflict.* New Haven, CT: Yale University Press; Klar, Y., Bar-Tal, D., & Kruglanski, A. W. (1988). Conflict as a cognitive schema: Toward a social cognitive analysis of conflict and conflict termination. In W. Stroebe, A. Kruglanski, D. Bar-Tal, & M. Hewstone (Eds.), *The social psychology of intergroup conflict.* Berlin: Springer-Verlag; Sherif, M. (1936). *The psychology of social norms.* New York: Harper and Row; Narlikar, A. (2010). *Deadlocks in multilateral negotiations: Causes and solutions.* Cambridge, UK: Cambridge University Press.
[116] ("Casualty Reports, 2011"). Defense.gov/news/casualty.pdf
[117] Kramer, R. M. (1991). The more the merrier? Social psychological aspects of multiparty negotiations in organizations. In M. H. Bazerman, R. J. Lewicki, & B. H. Sheppard (Eds.), *Research on negotiations in organizations: Handbook of negotiation research: Vol. 3* (pp. 307–332). Greenwich, CT: JAI Press; Stroebe, W., Kruglanski, A. W., Bar-Tal, D., & Hewstone, M. (Eds.). (1988). *The social psychology of intergroup conflict.* Berlin: Springer-Verlag; Worchel, S., & Austin, W. G. (Eds). (1986). *Psychology of intergroup relations.* Chicago: Nelson-Hall.
[118] Kramer, "The more the merrier?"

might be more or less salient to the student: At a football game, students might identify most strongly with the entire student body; in a dining hall, students might identify most strongly with a particular dorm or floor.

Imagine you are in an organization in which marketing and finance are distinct subgroups located on different floors of a building. Contrast that arrangement to a situation in which marketing and finance are not separate functional units but, instead, are part of the same product team. What happens in the case in which a marketing manager negotiates with a financial manager? Negotiations among individuals representing different social groups are less mutually beneficial than negotiations among individuals who perceive themselves as belonging to a larger social organization—one that encompasses all those present at the bargaining table.[119] When people define their social identity at the level of the organization, they are more likely to make more organizationally beneficial choices than when social identity is defined at an individual or subgroup level. For example, when group members are instructed to consider features they have in common with another group, behavior toward out-groups is much more generous than when they consider features that are distinct.[120]

IN-GROUP BIAS   Five beliefs propel groups toward conflict: superiority, injustice, vulnerability, distrust, and helplessness.[121] These deeply entrenched beliefs can trigger destructive action. Moreover, to the extent that groups receive social support from their fellow in-group members, such beliefs can lead to even greater intergroup conflict.[122] Group distinctions and social boundaries may be created on the basis of completely arbitrary distinctions.[123] In one investigation, participants were divided into two groups on the basis of an arbitrary procedure (random draws from a box).[124] Then, individuals negotiated with either a member of their "own group" or the "other group." Even though the information concerning the negotiation situation was identical in both respects, negotiations with members of out-groups were anticipated to be more contentious than negotiations with members of in-groups; further, the mere anticipation of negotiation with an out-group member led to increased **in-group bias**, positive evaluations of one's own group relative to the out-group. In another investigation, people allocating money between their group and a competing group took a significantly greater share of the monetary funds than people allocating between themselves and a competing individual.

When we anticipate negotiations with out-group members, we often engage in **downward social comparison**.[125] We evaluate the competitor to be less attractive on a number of organizationally relevant dimensions (such as intelligence, competence, and trustworthiness) than members of our group. However, after successful negotiation with out-groups, intergroup relations improve, and downward social comparison virtually disappears.[126] Negotiation with out-group

---

[119] Ibid.

[120] Kramer, R. M., & Brewer, M. (1984). Effects of group identity on resource use in a simulated commons dilemma. *Journal of Personality and Social Psychology, 46,* 1044–1057.

[121] Eidelson, R. J., & Eidelson, J. I. (2003). Dangerous ideas: Five beliefs that propel groups toward conflict. *American Psychologist, 58*(3), 182–192.

[122] Wildschut, T., Insko, C. A., & Gaertner, L. (2002). Intragroup social influence and intergroup competition. *Journal of Personality and Social Psychology, 82*(6), 975–992.

[123] Tajfel, H. (1970). Experiments in intergroup discrimination. *Scientific American, 223,* 96–102.

[124] Thompson, L. (1993). The impact of negotiation on intergroup relations. *Journal of Experimental Social Psychology, 29*(4), 304–325.

[125] Wills, T. A. (1981). Downward comparison principles in social psychology. *Psychological Bulletin, 90,* 245–271.

[126] Thompson, L. (1993). The impact of negotiation on intergroup relations. *Journal of Experimental Social Psychology, 29*(4), 304–325.

members is threatening to organizational actors, but to the extent that integrative agreements are feasible, negotiation has remarkable potential for improving intergroup relations. Although our initial expectations may be quite pessimistic, interactions with members of opposing groups often have a beneficial impact on intergroup relations if several key conditions are met, such as mutual dependence for goal attainment.

People of high status, those of low status who have few alternatives, and members of groups who have an opportunity to improve their group are most likely to identify with their own group. Members of groups with lower perceived status display more in-group bias than members of groups with higher perceived status.[127] However, high-status group members show more in-group bias on group status-related dimensions, whereas low-status group members consider the in-group superior on alternative dimensions.

EXTREMISM   Groups in conflict do not have an accurate understanding of the views of the other party and exaggerate the position of the other side in a way that promotes the perception of conflict.[128] Each side views the other as holding more extreme and opposing views than is actually the case. And people perceive more disagreement with rivals about values that are central to their own party's ideological position than those that are central to their rival's position.[129] Moreover, people believe their adversaries are actually motivated by their opposition to their own core values rather than by the promotion of the adversaries' core values.

Consider the 1986 Howard Beach incident involving the death of a young African-American man who was struck by a passing car as he attempted to escape from a group of white pursuers in the Howard Beach neighborhood of Queens. A trial ultimately led to the conviction of some (but not all) of the young man's pursuers. Many details of the case were ambiguous and controversial, leading each party to have exaggerated perceptions of the other parties' views, thereby exacerbating the perception of differences in opinion. Partisans on either side of the affirmative action debate greatly overestimate the liberalism of proponents and the conservatism of opponents.[130] The same polarization effect is found for other policy issues, such as abortion and immigration.

Why does this extremism occur? According to the **naïve realism** principle, people expect others to hold views of the world similar to their own.[131] When conflict erupts, people are initially inclined to sway the other party with evidence. When this tactic fails to bridge interests, people regard dissenters as extremists who are out of touch with reality.

Strategies for Optimizing Intergroup Negotiations

Consider the following strategies in intergroup negotiations.

---

[127] Ellemers, N., Van Rijswijk, W., Roefs, M., & Simons, C. (1997). Bias in intergroup perceptions: Balancing group identity with social reality. *Personality and Social Psychology Bulletin, 23*(2), 186–198.

[128] Robinson, R. J., Keltner, D., Ward, A., & Ross, L. (1994). Actual versus assumed differences in construal: "Naïve realism" in intergroup perception and conflict. *Journal of Personality and Social Psychology, 68,* 404–417; Ross, L., & Ward, A. (1996). Naïve realism in everyday life: Implications for social conflict and misunderstanding. In T. Brown, E. S. Reed, & E. Turiel (Eds), *Values and knowledge. The Jean Piaget symposium series* (pp. 103–135). Mahwah, NJ: Erlbaum.

[129] Chambers, J. R., & Melnyk, D. (2007). Why do I hate thee? Conflict misperceptions and intergroup mistrust. *Personality and Social Psychology Bulletin, 32*(10), 1295–1311.

[130] Sherman, D. K., Nelson, L. D., & Ross, L. D. (2003). Naïve realism and affirmative action: Adversaries are more similar than they think. *Basic and Applied Social Psychology, 25*(4), 275–289.

[131] Ross & Ward, "Naïve realism in everyday life."

SEPARATE CONFLICT OF INTEREST FROM SYMBOLIC CONFLICT   Many conflicts between groups do not have their roots in resource scarcity but, rather, in fundamental differences in values.[132] For example, conflicts are judged as more difficult to resolve when they occur between members of different groups than members of the same group, holding constant the nature of the conflict.[133] Consider for example, the strong protests made against busing by people whose lives are not affected by it.[134] Presumably, people who do not have children or grandchildren are not affected by busing. However, they tend to have strong feelings about it. Busing does not represent an economic issue to them but, rather, a symbolic issue. It is important to understand which issues are symbolic and which are economic. Moreover, adversaries are more optimistic about intergroup negotiation when they are exposed to the actual, rather than assumed, views of their counterparts.

SEARCH FOR COMMON IDENTITY   To the extent groups in conflict share a common identity, conflict and competition decreases dramatically.[135] People in organizations can identify at different levels within their organization (e.g., person, group, department, unit, organization as a whole, etc.). In one investigation, groups were told to focus on their group identities. Other groups who were involved in an objectively identical conflict were told to focus on the collective organization. Cooperation increased when groups focused on the collective, rather than their group, identities. Moreover, the stronger the group identification, the more likely it is that groups develop a shared understanding that leads to more integrative outcomes.[136] Finding common identity may be more efficacious when dealing with outgroup members than actually understanding their underlying interests. Negotiations with in-group members are more cooperative when they share information about their underlying self-interests. Conversely, negotiations with out-group members are more cooperative when they don't share information about their underlying interests.[137]

AVOID THE OUT-GROUP HOMOGENEITY BIAS   Suppose three white managers watch a video of a discussion among members of a mixed-race group, composed of three African-American men and three Caucasian men. After watching the video, the managers are presented with the actual text of the conversation and asked to indicate who said what. They are very good at remembering whether an African-American or Caucasian person made a particular comment, but their ability to remember which African-American male said what is abysmal.[138] Within-race (or within-group) errors are more prevalent than between-race errors because people categorize members of out-groups not as individuals but, simply, as "African-American." It is important for people to treat members of out-groups as individuals.

[132] Bobo, L. (1983). Whites' opposition to busing: Symbolic racism or realistic group conflict? *Journal of Personality and Social Psychology, 45*(6), 1196–1210.

[133] Ybarra, O., & Ramon, A. (2004). Diagnosing the difficulty of conflict resolution between individuals from the same and different social groups. *Journal of Experimental Social Psychology, 40,* 815–822.

[134] Sears, D. O., & Allen, H. M., Jr. (1984). The trajectory of local desegregation controversies and Whites' opposition to busing. In N. Miller & M. Brewer (Eds.), *Groups in contact: The psychology of desegregation* (pp. 123–151). New York: Academic Press.

[135] Kramer, R. M., & Brewer, M. (1986). Social group identity and the emergence of cooperation in resource conservation dilemmas. In H. Wilke, C. Rutte, & D. Messick (Eds.), *Experimental studies of social dilemmas.* Frankfurt, Germany: Peter Lang.

[136] Swaab, R., Postmes, T., van Beest, I., & Spears, R. (2007). Shared cognition as a product of, and precursor to, shared identity in negotiations. *Personality and Social Psychology Bulletin, 33*(2), 187–199.

[137] Harinck, F., & Ellemers, N. (2006). Hide and seek: The effects of revealing one's personal interests in intra- and intergroup negotiations. *European Journal of Social Psychology, 36*(6), 791–813.

[138] Linville, P. W., Fischer, G. W., & Salovey, P. (1989). Perceived distributions of the characteristics of in-group and out-group members: Empirical evidence and a computer simulation. *Journal of Personality and Social Psychology, 57,* 165–188.

CONTACT   The **mere contact** strategy is based on the principle that greater contact among members of diverse groups increases cooperation among group members. Unfortunately, contact does not always lead to better intergroup relations, and in some cases it may even exacerbate negative relations among groups. For example, contact between African-Americans and Caucasians in desegregated schools does not reduce racial prejudice,[139] little relationship is noted between interdepartmental contact and conflict in organizations,[140] and college students studying in foreign countries become increasingly negative toward their host countries the longer they remain in them.[141]

Several conditions need to be in place before contact can have its desired effect of reducing prejudice.

- *Social and institutional support.*   For contact to work, a framework of social and institutional support is needed. That is, people in positions of authority should be unambiguous in their endorsement of the goals of the integration policies. This support fosters the development of a social climate in which more tolerant norms can emerge.
- *Acquaintance potential.*   Successful contact must be of sufficient frequency, duration, and closeness to permit the development of meaningful relationships between members of the groups concerned. Infrequent, short, and casual interaction will do little to foster more favorable attitudes and may even make them worse.[142] This type of close interaction will lead to the discovery of similarities and disconfirm negative stereotypes.
- *Equal status.*   The third condition necessary for contact to be successful is that participants have equal status. Many stereotypes of out-groups comprise beliefs about the inferior ability of out-group members to perform various tasks. If the contact situation involves an unequal-status relationship between men and women—for example, with women in the subordinate role (e.g., taking notes, acting as secretaries)—stereotypes are likely to be reinforced rather than weakened.[143] If, however, the group members work on equal footing, prejudiced beliefs become hard to sustain in the face of repeated experience of task competence by the out-group member.
- *Shared goal.*   When members of different groups depend on each other for the achievement of a jointly desired objective, they have instrumental reasons to develop better relationships. The importance of a shared group goal is a key determinant of intergroup relations. Sometimes a common enemy is a catalyst for bonding among diverse people and groups. For example, by "waging a war against cancer," members of different medical groups and laboratories work together.
- *Cross-group friendships.*   Sometimes it is not necessary for groups to have real contact with one another to improve intergroup relations. If group members know that another member of their own group has a friendship or relationship with a member of the out-group, or a cross-group friendship, in-group members have less negative attitudes

[139] Gerard, H. (1983). School desegregation: The social science role. *American Psychologist, 38,* 869–878; Schofield, J. W. (1986). Black and white contact in desegregated schools. In M. Hewstone & R. J. Brown (Eds.), *Contact and conflict in intergroup encounters* (pp. 79–92). Oxford, England: Blackwell.

[140] Brown, R. J., Condor, F., Mathew, A., Wade, G., & Williams, J. A. (1986). Explaining intergroup differentiation in an industrial organization. *Journal of Occupational Psychology, 59,* 273–286.

[141] Stroebe, W., Lenkert, A., & Jonas, K. (1988). Familiarity may breed contempt: The impact of student exchange on national stereotypes and attitudes. In W. Stroebe, A. W. Kruglanski, D. Bar-Tal, & M. Hewstone (Eds.), *The Social psychology of intergroup conflict* (pp. 167–187). New York: Springer-Verlag.

[142] Brewer, M. B., & Brown, R. J. (1998). Intergroup relations. In D. T. Gilbert, S. T. Fiske, & G. Lindzey (Eds.), *The handbook of social psychology: Vol. 2* (4th ed.) (pp. 554–594). New York: McGraw-Hill.

[143] Bradford, D. L., & Cohen, A. R. (1984). *Managing for excellence.* New York: Wiley.

toward the out-group.[144] It is not necessary that all members of a group have cross-group friendships; merely knowing that one member of the group does can go a long way toward reducing negative out-group attitudes.

Many of these strategies are preventative and can help ward off unhealthy, destructive competition between groups. What steps can a manager leader take to deal with conflict after it has erupted?

THE GRIT STRATEGY   The Graduated and Reciprocal Initiative in Tension Reduction, or **GRIT model**, is a model of conflict reduction for warring groups. Originally developed as a program for international disarmament negotiations, it also can be used to deescalate intergroup problems on a smaller, domestic scale.[145] The goals of this strategy are to increase communication and reciprocity between groups while reducing mistrust, thereby allowing for deescalation of hostility and creation of a greater array of possible outcomes. The model prescribes a series of steps that call for specific communication between groups in the hope of establishing the "rules of the game." Other stages are designed to increase trust between the two groups as the consistency in each group's responses demonstrates credibility and honesty. Some steps are necessary only in extremely intense conflict situations in which the breakdown of intergroup relations implies a danger for the group members.

Mikhail Gorbachev's decisions in the period from 1986 to 1989 closely resemble the GRIT model.[146] Gorbachev made a number of unilateral concessions that resulted in serious deescalation of world tensions in this period. On two occasions, the Soviets stalled resumption of atmospheric nuclear testing despite their inability to extend the prior treaty with the Reagan administration. They then agreed twice to summit meetings, despite the Reagan administration's refusal to discuss the Star Wars defense system. They then agreed to the Intermediate-Range Nuclear Forces (INF) Treaty (exceeding the United States' requests for verification) with continued refusal by the United States to bargain about Star Wars. Next came agreements on the Berlin Wall and the unification of Germany. Eventually, even the staunchly anti-Communist/anti-Soviet Reagan-Bush regime had to take notice. These events led to a period of mellowing tensions between these two superpowers (see Exhibit 9-10).

Although the GRIT model may seem overly elaborate and therefore inapplicable to most organizational conflicts, the model clarifies the difficulties inherent in establishing mutual trust between parties that have been involved in prolonged conflict. Although some of the stages are not applicable to all conflicts, the importance of clearly announcing intentions, making promised concessions, and matching reciprocation are relevant to all but the most transitory conflicts.

CONCLUSION

Multiparty negotiations require all of the pie-slicing and pie-expanding skills of two-party negotiations, and then some. The key challenges of multiparty negotiations are the development and management of coalitions, the complexity of information management, voting rules, and communication breakdowns. We discussed several different levels of analysis involved in multiparty

---

[144] Wright, S. C., Aron, A., McLaughlin-Volpe, T., & Ropp, S. A. (1997). The extended contact effect: Knowledge of cross-group friendships and prejudice. *Journal of Personality and Social Psychology, 73*(1), 73–90.

[145] Osgood, C. E. (1979). GRIT 1 (Vol. 8, No. 1, 0553–4283). Dundas, Ontario: Peace Research Reviews.

[146] Barron, R. S., Kerr, N. L., & Miller, N. (1992). *Group process, group decision, group action.* Pacific Grove, CA: Brooks/Cole.

EXHIBIT 9-10

GRIT Strategy: Gradual Reduction in Tension

1. Announce your general intentions to de-escalate conflict and your specific intention to make an initial concession.
2. Execute your initial concession unilaterally, completely, and publicly. Provide as much verification and documentation as possible.
3. Invite reciprocity from the other party. Expect the other party to react to these steps with mistrust and skepticism. To overcome this, consider making another concession.
4. Match any reciprocal concessions made by the other party. Invite more.
5. Diversify the nature of your concessions.
6. Maintain your ability to retaliate if the other party escalates conflict. Any such retaliation should be carefully calibrated to match the intensity of the other party's actions.

Source: Based on Barron, R. S., Kerr, N. L., & Miller, N. (1992). *Group process, group decision, group action* (p. 151). Pacific Grove, CA: Brooks/Cole.

negotiations and key strategies to finesse each situation, including coalition management, principal-agent relationships, team negotiation, intergroup negotiation, and dealing with constituencies. Exhibit 9-11 summarizes the six levels of analysis, the key challenges facing the negotiator at each level, and the best strategies to surmount these challenges.

EXHIBIT 9-11

Summary of Challenges and Strategies for Each Level of Multiparty Analysis

Level of Analysis	Challenges	Strategies
Multiparty negotiation	Coalition formation	Know who will be at the table
	Difficulty formulating trade-offs	Systematize proposal making
	Voting paradoxes	Use brainstorming wisely
	• Strategic voting	Develop and assign process roles
	• Majority rule suppresses strength of preference	Stay at the table
		Strive for equal participation
	Communication breakdowns	Allow for some points of agreement
	• Private caucusing	Avoid the "equal shares" bias
	• Biased interpretation	Avoid the "agreement bias"
	• Perspective-taking failures	Avoid sequential bargaining

(continued)

- Indirect speech acts
- Multiple audience problem

Coalitions	Optimal coalition size	Core solution
	Trust and temptation	Shapley model
	Dividing the pie	Raiffa's hybrid model
		Make contacts early
		Seek verbal commitments
		Use unbiased-appearing rationale to divide the pie
Principal-agent negotiations	Conflicting incentives	Shop around
	Shrinking bargaining zone	Know your BATNA before meeting your agent
	Communication distortion	Communicate interests, but do not reveal your BATNA
	Loss of control	Capitalize on agent's expertise
	Agreement at any cost	Tap into agent's sources of information
		Discuss ratification
		Use agent for saving face
		Use agent to buffer emotions
Principal-constituency relationships	Identification	Communicate with your constituencies
	Accountability	Do not expect homogeneity within constituencies
	• Vigilance	Educate constituents on your role and limitations
	• Face-saving	Help constituents do horizon thinking
	Conflicts of interest	
Team negotiation	Choosing teammates	Prepare together
	How many on the team?	Goal and strategy alignment
	Communication within the team	Plan scheduled breaks (to regroup)
	Team cohesion	Determine accountability
	Information processing	
Intergroup negotiation	Stereotyping	Separate conflict of interest from symbolic conflict
	Changing identities	Search for common identity
	In-group bias	Avoid outgroup homogeneity bias
	Extremism	Contact
		GRIT strategy

10

Cross-Cultural Negotiation

When President Barack Obama greeted King Abdullah of Saudi Arabia with what appeared to be a bow, conservative politicians were outraged. Whereas the White House denied that the president bowed to the 84-year-old king, controversy and debate erupted. Nonverbal experts analyzed video and dissected the moves. Newspapers such as the conservative *Washington Times* described the act as a "traditional obeisance befitting a king's subjects," others noted that no rule existed related to bowing presidents. Lloyd Hand, the former chief of protocol for President Lyndon B. Johnson, put the greetings of foreign dignitaries in perspective: "Protocol is 95% common sense judgment and 5% specific rules and that has nothing to do with bowing."[1]

Negotiations between people of different cultures often stir up deeply held values and beliefs; behaviors that seem normative in one culture often create controversy and even legal action in other cultures. Cultural intelligence is essential for effective negotiation because most managers cannot expect to negotiate only with people of their own country or culture throughout their career. North Americans are a minority—about 5% of the world's population. If the Earth's population were a village of 100 people, with all existing human ratios remaining the same, there would be 61 Asians, 13 Africans, 12 Europeans, 9 people from South America and the Caribbean, and 5 from North America.[2]

---

[1] Obama's apparent bow to Saudi King outrages conservatives. (2009, April 10). *Fox News.* Foxnews.com
[2] Kastle, K. (2011, January 17). World population. *Nations Online.* Nationsonline.org

When people from different cultures get together to negotiate, they may fail to reach integrative agreements.[3] Often, value is left on the table because people are not prepared for the challenges of cross-cultural negotiation. This chapter provides a business plan for effective cross-cultural negotiation. We begin by defining culture; then we identify the key dimensions by which culture affects judgment, motivation, and behavior at the bargaining table. Next, we identify the biggest barriers to effective intercultural negotiation and provide strategies for effective cross-cultural negotiation.

LEARNING ABOUT CULTURES

We do not offer advice on a country-by-country basis for two reasons.

First, doing so would be contrary to the book's focus, which is to provide negotiation skills that work across people and situations. We do not want to promote cultural stereotypes. By making a generic list of characteristics for cultures, we magnify stereotypes, which is neither practical nor informative. People prefer to be considered unique individuals.

We distinguish **stereotypes** from **prototypes**. A stereotype is a faulty belief that everyone from a given culture is exactly alike. In contrast, prototypes recognize that substantial variation is likely even within a culture.[4] Within cultures, key personality traits vary, and different traits are associated with better performance within certain cultures but not others.[5] A cultural framework is sensitive to heterogeneity within cultural groups.

Second, most cultures are different today than they were 10 years ago. A dynamic framework allows us to learn how cultures change and grow. This chapter provides a means by which to expose our own cultural beliefs and those of others, how to avoid mistakes, and how to profit from intercultural negotiations.[6]

Defining Culture

Culture is the unique character of a social group; the values and norms shared by its members set it apart from other social groups.[7] Culture encompasses economic, social, political, and religious institutions. It also reflects the unique products produced by these groups—art, architecture, music, theatre, and literature.[8] Cultural institutions preserve and promote a culture's ideologies. Culture influences our mental models of how things work, behavior, and cause-and-effect relationships. Consider the possible cultural differences contained in all of the following:

- Families
- Social groups and departments in an organization
- Organizations
- Industries

---

[3] Brett, J. M. (2007). *Negotiating globally: How to negotiate deals, resolve disputes, and make decisions across cultural boundaries* (2nd ed). San Francisco: Jossey-Bass.
[4] Ibid.
[5] Liu, L. A., Friedman, R. A., & Chi, S.-C. (2005). "Ren Qing" versus the "Big Five": The role of culturally sensitive measures of individual difference in distributive negotiations. *Management and Organization Review, 1*(2), 225–247.
[6] Brett, *Negotiating globally.*
[7] Lytle, A. L., Brett, J. M., & Shapiro, D. L. (1999). The strategic use of interests, rights and power to resolve disputes. *Negotiation Journal, 15*(1), 31–52.
[8] Brett, *Negotiating globally.*

- States
- Regions
- Countries
- Societies (e.g., foraging, horticultural, pastoral, agrarian, industrial, service, information)
- Continents
- Hemispheres

Nations, occupational groups, social classes, genders, races, tribes, corporations, clubs, and social movements may become the bases of specific subcultures. When thinking about culture and diversity, avoid the temptation to think of it as a single dimension (e.g., country of origin); culture is a complex whole, and it is best to use many criteria to discern one culture from another.

Culture as an Iceberg

We use French and Bell's model of culture as an iceberg.[9] Typically, about one-ninth of an iceberg is visible; the rest is submerged. As Exhibit 10-1 indicates, the top (visible) part of the cultural iceberg is the behaviors, artifacts, and institutions that characterize a culture. This portion includes traditions, customs, habits, and other immediately visible stimuli. These behaviors and artifacts are an expression of deeper-held values, beliefs, and norms. Driving these values and norms are fundamental assumptions about the world and humanity. The artifacts and customs

EXHIBIT 10-1

Culture as an Iceberg

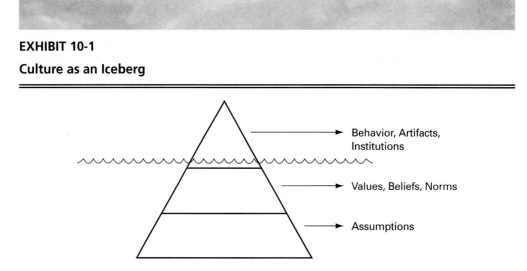

Source: Adapted from French, W. L., & Bell, C. H. (1923). *Organization Development behavioral science in interventions for organization improvement* (p. 18). New Jersey: Prentice-Hall.

---

[9] French, W. L., & Bell, C. H. (1923). *Organization Development behavioral science in interventions for organization improvement* (p. 18). New Jersey: Prentice-Hall.

that characterize a culture are not arbitrary; rather, they are manifestations about fundamental values and beliefs about the world.

CULTURAL VALUES AND NEGOTIATION NORMS

Consider three dimensions of culture (see Exhibit 10-2):[10]

- Individualism versus collectivism
- Egalitarianism versus hierarchy
- Direct versus indirect communication

These three dimensions refer to motivation, influence, and information, respectively.[11] **Individualism-collectivism** refers to the basic human motive concerning preservation of the self

EXHIBIT 10-2

Dimensions of Culture

Cultural Dimension		
Goal:	*Individualists/Competitors:*	*Collectivists/Cooperators:*
Individual versus collective orientation	Key goal is to maximize own gain (and perhaps the difference between oneself and others); source of identity is the self; people regard themselves as free agents and independent actors.	Key goal is to maximize the welfare of the group or collective; source of identity is the group; individuals regard themselves as group members; focus is on social relations.
Influence:	*Egalitarians:*	*Hierarchists:*
Egalitarianism versus hierarchy	Do not perceive many social obligations; often regard BATNA to be major source of bargaining power.	Regard social order to be important in determining conflict management strategies; subordinates are expected to defer to superiors; superiors are expected to look out for subordinates.
Communication:	*Direct Communicators:*	*Indirect Communicators:*
Direct versus indirect	Engage in explicit, direct information exchange; ask direct questions; not affected by situational constraints; face-saving issues likely to arise.	Engage in tacit information exchange such as storytelling, inference-making; situational norms.

Source: Based on Brett, J. M. (2007). *Negotiating globally: How to negotiate deals, resolve disputes, and make decisions across cultural boundaries.* (2nd ed.) San Francisco: Jossey-Bass.

---

[10] Brett, *Negotiating globally;* Gelfand, M. J., & Brett, J. M. (Eds.) (2004). *The handbook of negotiation and culture: Theoretical advances and cultural perspectives.* Palo Alto, CA: Stanford University Press.
[11] Brett, *Negotiating globally.*

versus the collective.[12] **Egalitarianism-hierarchy** refers to the means by which people influence others, either laterally or hierarchically. Finally, **direct-indirect communication** refers to the manner in which people exchange information and messages.

Individualism Versus Collectivism

INDIVIDUALISM In the discussion in Chapter 5 on bargaining style, we outlined three motivational orientations: individualistic, competitive, and cooperative. Individualism, as a cultural style, epitomizes the individualistic motivational orientation.[13] In individualistic cultures, the pursuit of happiness and regard for personal welfare are paramount. People in individualistic cultures give priority to their personal goals, even when these goals conflict with those of their family, work group, or country. Individual happiness and expression are valued more than collective and group needs. People from individualistic cultures enjoy having influence and control over their world and others. Consequently, individual accomplishments are rewarded by economic and social institutions. Furthermore, legal institutions in individualist cultures are designed to protect individual rights. One implication of individualism concerns the use of distributive tactics. People who are more self-interested are motivated to use more tactics that increase their bargaining power. Indeed, U.S. MBA students are more tolerant of certain kinds of ethically questionable tactics than are non-U.S. MBA students studying in the United States.[14] Specifically, U.S. MBA students are more accepting of competitive bargaining tactics and bluffing, which raises the possibility that U.S. negotiators may be perceived as less ethical by their international counterparts.[15] On the other hand, U.S. negotiators are significantly less accepting of misrepresentation to the counterparty's network.

COLLECTIVISM Collectivist cultures are rooted in social groups, and individuals are viewed as members of groups. People in collectivist cultures give priority to in-group goals. People of collectivist cultures view their work groups and organizations as fundamental parts of themselves. Collectivists are concerned about how the results of their actions affect members of their in-group; they share resources with in-group members, feel interdependent with in-group members, and feel involved in the lives of in-group members.[16] In contrast to individualistic cultures that focus on influence and control, people from collectivist cultures emphasize the importance of adjustment. Collectivist cultures are more concerned with maintaining harmony in interpersonal

---

[12] Triandis, *Culture and social behavior;* Hofstede, G. (1980). *Culture's consequences: International differences in work-related values.* Beverly Hills, CA: Sage; Schwartz, S. (1994). Beyond individualism/collectivism: New cultural dimensions of values. In H. C. Triandis, U. Kim, & G. Yoon (Eds.), *Individualism and collectivism* (pp. 85–117). London: Sage; Gelfand, M. J., Bhawuk, D. P. S., Nishii, L. H., & Bechtold, D. (2004). Individualism and collectivism: Multilevel perspectives and implications for leadership. In R. J. House, P. J. Hanges, M. Javidan, P. W. Dorfman, & Vipin Gupta (Eds.), *Culture, leadership, and organizations: The GLOBE study of 62 cultures.* Thousand Oaks, CA: Sage.

[13] For simplicity, we include competitive style with individual style.

[14] Lewicki, R. J., & Robinson, R. J. (1998). Ethical and unethical bargaining tactics: An empirical study. *Journal of Business Ethics, 17*(6), 665–682.

[15] Ibid.

[16] Billings, D. K. (1989). Individualism and group orientation. In D. M. Keats, D. Munroe, & L. Mann (Eds.), *Heterogeneity in cross-cultural psychology* (pp. 22–103); Hofstede, G. (1991). Empirical models of cultural differences. In N. Bleichrodt & P. J. D. Drenth (Eds.), *Contemporary issues in cross-cultural psychology* (pp. 4–20). Netherlands: Swets and Zeitlinger; Hui, C. H., & Triandis, H. C. (1986). Individualism-collectivism: A study of cross-cultural researchers. *Journal of Cultural Psychology, 17,* 225–248.

relationships with the in-group than are individualistic cultures. Social norms and institutions promote the interdependence of individuals through emphasis on social obligations and the sacrifice of personal needs for the greater good. Legal institutions place the greater good of the collective above the rights of the individual, and political and economic institutions reward groups as opposed to individuals.[17]

Whereas individualists want to save face and are concerned with their personal outcomes, collectivists are concerned with others' outcomes. An analysis of U.S. and Hong Kong negotiations reveal that U.S. negotiators are more likely to subscribe to self-interest and joint problem-solving norms, whereas Hong Kong Chinese negotiators are more likely to subscribe to an equality norm.[18] U.S. negotiators are more satisfied when they maximize joint gain; Hong Kong Chinese negotiators are happier when they achieve outcome parity. In one investigation of Canadians (individualists) and Japanese (collectivists), behaviors were covertly measured.[19] Canadians were reluctant to conclude they had performed worse than their average classmate (self-enhancement); in contrast, Japanese negotiators were hesitant to conclude that they had performed better. Individualism and collectivism represent a continuum with substantial within-culture variation. One factor that can push people toward behaving more in line with their native cultural values is **accountability pressure**—simply the extent to which they are answerable for conducting themselves in a certain manner.[20]

IMPLICATIONS FOR NEGOTIATION   Individualism-collectivism involves a variety of implications for the conduct of negotiation, including:

- Social networks
- Cooperation
- In-group favoritism
- Social loafing versus social striving
- Emotion and inner experience
- Dispositionalism versus situationalism
- Preferences for dispute resolution

Social Networks.   Members of different cultures differ in terms of the density of their work friendships (i.e., how many friendships they share at work), the overlap of instrumental and socioemotional ties (i.e., whether the people they seek for information are also the ones whom they seek for comfort and emotional support), the closeness of the tie, the longevity of the tie, and whether the network relationships are directed upward, laterally, or downward. For example, interpersonal trust is an important element of Chinese **guanxi** networks, which are networks of deep trust built over the years, if not decades. China, as is the case with many developing economies, exists in a low-trust environment and as a result, Chinese build trust networks based typically on familial lines. And as a result, others find it virtually impossible to enter into these networks unless they have spent years in China.[21] Affect-and cognition-based trust are more interconnected

---

[17] Brett, *Negotiating globally.*
[18] Tinsley, C. H., & Pillutla, M. M. (1998). Negotiating in the United States and Hong Kong. *Journal of International Business Studies, 29*(4), 711–728.
[19] Heine, S. J., Takata, T., & Lehman, D. R. (2000). Beyond self-presentation: Evidence for self-criticism among Japanese. *Personality and Social Psychology Bulletin, 26*(1), 71–78.
[20] Gelfand, M. J., & Realo, A. (1999). Individualism-collectivism and accountability in intergroup negotiations. *Journal of Applied Psychology, 84*(5), 721–736.
[21] Rein, S. (2010, June 25). How not to run a business in China. *Business Week.* Businessweek.com

among Chinese managers than U.S. managers.[22] In one study, U.S. and Hong Kong students negotiated with someone whom they believed to be a friend or a stranger from their own culture. The Hong Kong students changed their behavior more when interacting with a friend than did the U.S. students.[23] Whereas U.S. managers are equally likely to trust and reciprocate with a partner, as well as with someone in the network (whom they don't know directly), collectivist managers only trust and reciprocate when interacting within the relationship.[24] Perhaps this is why many realty agents report that Hispanics are often perplexed by the U.S. culture's habit of not meeting the seller of a home they are buying.[25] Similarly, agents with whom the Hispanic principal works are often treated as part of the extended family, with invitations to life cycle events.

Cultures develop social networks within the organization according to different sets of norms (see Exhibit 10-3).[26] North American business relationships are characterized by a market orientation in which people form relationships according to the market standard of whether it is profitable. North Americans form ties without the prior basis of friendship, paying attention only to instrumentality. Chinese business relationships are characterized by a familial orientation, in which employees make sacrifices for the welfare of the organization. Sharing resources within the in-group, loyalty, and deference to superiors characterize network relationships. German business relationships are characterized by legal-bureaucratic orientation, formal categories, and rules. In addition, Spanish business relationships are characterized by affiliative orientations, such as sociability and friendliness. A controlled cross-national comparison of network relationships within Citibank supported these network norms.[27]

Cooperation.   People from collectivist cultural traditions engage in more cooperative behavior in mixed-motive interactions than do people from individualistic cultures.[28] For example, Japanese negotiators are more cooperative (and, in turn, expect others to be more cooperative) than are U.S. negotiators.[29] People from collectivist cultures place greater emphasis on the needs and goals of their group and are more likely to sacrifice personal interests for the attainment of group goals. Americans are more likely to remember situations in which they *influenced* others; in contrast, Japanese people are more likely to remember situations in which they *adjusted* to others (a form of cooperation).[30] An examination of Japanese and U.S. newspaper stories on conflict revealed that Japanese newspapers more frequently make reference to mutual blame than do U.S. newspapers, presumably because ascribing blame to both parties affords the maintenance of the

---

[22] Chua, R. Y. J., Morris, M. W., & Ingram, P. (2009). Guanxi versus networking: Distinctive configurations of affect- and cognition-based trust in the networks of Chinese and American managers. *Journal of International Business Studies, 40*(3), 490–508.

[23] Chan, D. K. S., Triandis, H. C., Carnevale, P. J., Tam, A., & Bond, M. H. (1994). Comparing negotiation across cultures: Effects of collectivism, relationship between negotiators, and concession pattern on negotiation behavior. Unpublished manuscript, Department of Psychology, University of Illinois at Urbana–Champaign.

[24] Buchan, N., Croson, R., & Dawes, R. M. (2002). Swift neighbors and persistent strangers: A cross-cultural investigation of trust and reciprocity in social exchange. *American Journal of Sociology, 108*(1), 168–206.

[25] Gendler, N. (2003, June 14). Hispanic home buyers. *Star-Tribune*, p. 4H.

[26] Morris, M. W., Podolny, J. M., & Ariel S. (2000). Missing relations: Incorporating relational constructs into models of culture. In P. C. Earley & H. Singh (Eds.), *Innovations in international and cross-cultural management* (pp. 52–90). Thousand Oaks, CA: Sage Publications.

[27] Ibid.

[28] Cox, T. H., Lobel, S. A., & McLeod, P. L. (1991). Effects of ethnic group cultural differences in cooperative and competitive behavior on a group task. *Academy of Management Journal, 34*(4), 827–847.

[29] Wade-Benzoni, K. A., Okumura, T., Brett, J. M., Moore, D., Tenbrunsel, A. E., & Bazerman, M. H. (2002). Cognitions and behavior in asymmetric social dilemmas: A comparison of two cultures. *Journal of Applied Psychology, 87*, 87–95.

[30] Morling, B., Kitayama, S., & Miyamoto, Y. (2002). Cultural practices emphasize influence in the United States and adjustment in Japan. *Personality and Social Psychology Bulletin, 28*(3), 311–323.

EXHIBIT 10-3

Dominant Norms of Business Relations

Culture	Dominant Attitude	Business Relationships
North American: *Market norms*	Economic individualism	Short-lived Low-multiplexity
Chinese: *Familial norms*	Filial loyalty Economic collectivism	Directed upward to powerful
German: *Legal-bureaucratic norms*	Economic collectivism	Bounded by formal rules Low affectivity
Spanish: *Affiliative norms*	Self-expressive collectivism	Long-lived High affectivity

Source: Based on Morris, M. W., Podolny, J. M., & Ariel S. (2000). Missing relations: Incorporating relational constructs into models of culture. In P. C. Earley, & H. Singh (Eds.), *Innovations in International and cross-cultural management* (pp. 52–90). Thousand Oaks, CA: Sage; Morris, M. W., Podolny, J., & Sullivan, B. N. (2008). Culture and coworker relations: Interpersonal patters in American, Chinese, German, and Spanish division of global retail bank. *Organization Science, 19*(4), 517–532.

social unit and is less threatening to the collective.[31] Moreover, Americans who successfully influenced others reported feeling very *efficacious* (a typical individualistic emotion), whereas Japanese people who adjusted reported feeling *related* (a collectivist emotion).

Awareness of different cultural norms can be a powerful bargaining strategy. For example, consider the negotiations that took place in Kyoto in 1997 to reach a pact on global warming initiatives. For more than a week, the negotiators at the Kyoto climate-change conference haggled over the terms of a treaty that would focus on reducing global warming. In the last hours of the negotiation, all of the world's industrialized nations had agreed to firm targets for reducing six different greenhouse gases—all but Japan, that is. The Japanese had been assigned the most modest goal: cut emissions 6% below 1990 levels by the year 2012, compared with 7% for the United States and 8% for the 15 nations of the European Union. But the Japanese would not budge. Their limit was 5%. So the U.S. delegation called Washington to report the impasse, and at 2:00 a.m. an exhausted Vice President Al Gore got on the phone with Japanese Prime Minister Ryutaro Hashimoto. Gore's cross-cultural skills were sharp: He first praised Hashimoto for Japan's leadership in playing host to the conference (focusing on hierarchical cultural norms), and then he pointed out how bad it would look for the host country to derail the agreement over a measly percentage point (focusing on collective well-being). It worked.[32]

---

[31] Gelfand, M. J., Nishii, L. H., Holcombe, K. M., Dyer, N., Ohbuchi, K–I., & Fukuno, M. (2001). Cultural influences on cognitive representations of conflict: Interpretations of conflict episodes in the United States and Japan. *Journal of Applied Psychology, 86*(6), 1059–1074.

[32] Lemonick, M. (1997, December 22). Turning down the heat. *Time*, p. 23.

In-Group Favoritism.   In-group favoritism is the strong tendency to favor the members of one's own group more than those in other groups, even when one has no logical basis for doing so. Members of collectivist cultures display more in-group favoritism than members of individualistic cultures. For example, making group boundaries salient creates more competitive behavior among members of collectivist cultures than among members of individualistic cultures.[33] Moreover, members of collectivistic cultures become more competitive when they perceive their group to be in the minority.[34] In-group favoritism often has positive effects for members of in-groups, but it can be deleterious for members of out-groups and for intergroup relations (see Chapter 9 for more on intergroup negotiation). However, according to Gabriel and Gardner, you don't have to be from a collectivist culture to show collectivist behavior, such as in-group favoritism; rather, everyone has an "interdependent" and an "independent" self, which can be "triggered."[35] Bicultural individuals are often able to spontaneously trigger either self, depending upon which cultural cue is present.[36] (See Exhibit 10-4 for an example of how priming works.)

Social Loafing Versus Social Striving.   **Social loafing** is the tendency for people to work less hard and contribute less effort and resources in a group context than when working alone. For example, people clap less loudly, work less hard, and contribute less when working in a group, as opposed to working alone.[37] Social loafing should occur less in collectivist cultures than in individualist cultures, presumably because individualistic cultures do not reward group effort but collectivist cultures do. In a study of social loafing among management trainees in the United States and the People's Republic of China, American students loafed (individual performance declined in a group setting), but Chinese students did not.[38] In fact, among Japanese participants, the opposite pattern occurred in the group: **Social striving**—collectivist concerns for the welfare of the group—increased people's motivation and performance.[39] Self-serving biases, such as egocentrism (as discussed in Chapter 3) are more prevalent in individualistic cultures, such as the United States, in which the self is served by focusing on positive attributes and desire to stand out and be better than others. In contrast, members of collectivist cultures are less likely to hold a biased, self-serving view of themselves; rather, the self is served by focusing on negative characteristics in order to "blend in."[40]

Emotion and Inner Experience.   Collectivists and individualists differ in the ways they describe emotional experience, with Chinese using more somatic and social words than Americans.

---

[33] Espinoza, J. A., & Garza, R. T. (1985). Social group salience and interethnic cooperation. *Journal of Experimental Social Psychology, 21,* 380–392.

[34] Ibid.

[35] Gabriel, S., & Gardner, W. L. (1999). Are there "his" and "her" types of interdependence? The implications of gender differences in collective and relational interdependence for affect, behavior, and cognition. *Journal of Personality and Social Psychology, 75,* 642–655.

[36] Fu, H-y., Chiu, C-y., Morris, M. W., & Young, M. J. (2007). Spontaneous inferences from cultural cues: Varying responses of cultural insiders and outsiders. *Journal of Cross-Cultural Psychology, 38*(1), 58–75.

[37] Kerr, N. L. (1983). Motivation losses in small groups: A social dilemma analysis. *Journal of Personality and Social Psychology, 45,* 819–828.

[38] Earley, P. C. (1989). Social loafing and collectivism: A comparison of the United States and the People's Republic of China. *Administrative Science Quarterly, 34,* 565–581.

[39] Shirakashi, S. (1985). Social loafing of Japanese students. *Hiroshima Forum for Psychology, 10,* 35–40; Yamaguchi, S., Okamoto, K., & Oka, T. (1985). Effects of coactors' presence: Social loafing and social facilitation. *Japanese Psychological Research, 27,* 215–222.

[40] Gelfand, M. J., Higgins, M., Nishii, L. H., Raver, J. L., Dominguez, A., Murakami, F., Yamaguchi, S., & Toyama, M. (2002). Culture and egocentric perceptions of fairness in conflict and negotiation. *Journal of Applied Psychology, 87*(5), 833–845.

EXHIBIT 10-4

Priming Individualism and Collectivism

Everyone needs to be individualistic at times and more collectivistic, or group-focused, at other times. In a series of investigations, we "primed" U.S. managers to be either individualistic (focused on the self) or relational (focused on others). To create this focus, we had the U.S. managers read a story about a leader who had an important decision to make—choosing a successor. In one version of the story, the leader chooses someone on the basis of personal talent and merit (individualistic value); in the other version of the story, the leader chooses someone on the basis of his relationship to him (collectivistic value). Then, we watched how the U.S. managers resolved a dispute. The U.S. managers who were in a position of power in a dispute were significantly more generous and cooperative if they had previously read the collectivistic story. In contrast, the U.S. managers who had read the individualistic story were significantly more self-interested.

In another twist, we then had teams of managers negotiate against other teams. We hypothesized that if we used the same collectivistic prime, it would increase the negotiator's loyalty to his or her team but would lead to significantly more in-group favoritism and less generosity across the table. That's exactly what happened. Negotiators were more generous when they were "primed" with interdependence (rather than independence) in a one-on-one (dyadic) negotiation (see panel A). However, the tables turned when the priming occurred in a group setting: Negotiators primed with interdependence were less generous. In panel B, we see the likelihood of impasse follows the same pattern: With interdependent negotiators, they are *least* likely to impasse when they are one-on-one and *most* likely to impasse when they are team-on-team.

The message? Self-interested or other-focused behavior can be triggered in negotiations with subtle primes. Triggering collectivism in a two-party situation will lead the powerful person to be more generous across the table. However, in a team situation, collectivism leads to greater in-group

Panel A

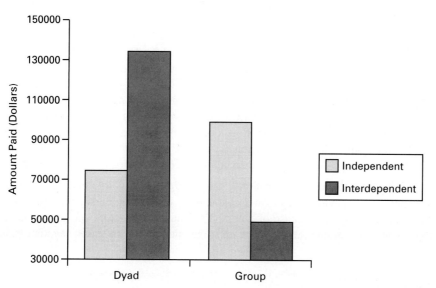

(Continued)

Panel B

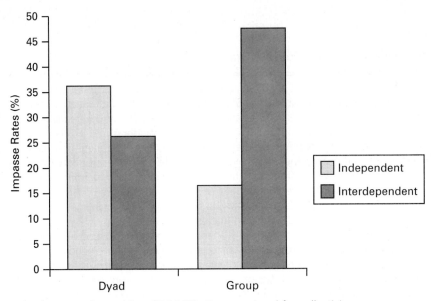

favoritism (to the tune of more than $80,000). Groups primed for collectivism were more successful in avoiding costly court action than were those who were primed to be independent—even though the facts in the situation, their bargaining reservation prices, and other details were objectively identical. In fact, no one who was primed with interdependence escalated to court action, but 20% of those with an independent focus did.

Source: Adapted from Howard, E., Thompson, L., & Gardner, W. (2007). The role of the self-concept and the social context in determining the behavior of power holders: Self-construal in intergroup versus dyadic dispute resolution negotiations. *Journal of Personality and Social Psychology, 93*(4), 614–631.

For example, when Chinese and Americans are both speaking English during emotional events, Chinese Americans used more somatic (e.g., dizzy) and more social (e.g., friend) words than European Americans.[41]

Expressing anger elicits larger concessions from European American negotiators, but smaller concessions from Asian and Asian-American negotiators.[42] This is due to cultural norms about the appropriateness of anger expression in negotiation. When anger is regarded as appropriate, Asian negotiators made as large a concession as did the Euro-Americans. When anger is regarded as inappropriate, the Euro-Americans made much smaller concessions, matching those of Asians.

Dispositionalism Versus Situationalism.   **Dispositionalism** is the tendency to ascribe the cause of a person's behavior to his or her character or underlying personality. **Situationalism** is the tendency to ascribe the cause of a person's behavior to factors and forces outside of a person's control. For example, suppose you are in the midst of a high-stakes negotiation, and you

---

[41] Tsai, J. L., Simeonova, D. I., & Watanabe, J. T. (2004). Somatic and social: Chinese Americans talk about emotion. *Personality and Social Psychology Bulletin, 30*(9), 1226–1238.
[42] Adam, H., Shirako, A., & Maddux, W. W. (2010). Cultural variance in the interpersonal effects of anger in negotiations. *Psychological Science, 21*(6), 882–889.

place an urgent call to your negotiation partner. Your partner does not return your call; yet you know your partner is in town. What is causing your partner's behavior? It is possible our partner is irresponsible (dispositionalism); similarly, it is possible your partner never got your message (situationalism). Depending upon what you think is the true cause, your behavior toward your partner will be different—anger versus forgiveness, perhaps.[43]

People from individualistic cultures view causality differently than do members of collectivist cultures. Dispositionalism is more widespread in individualistic than in collectivist cultures. To see how deep-seated these cultural differences are, look at Exhibit 10-5, panels A and B.

EXHIBIT 10-5

Dispositionalism Versus Situationalism

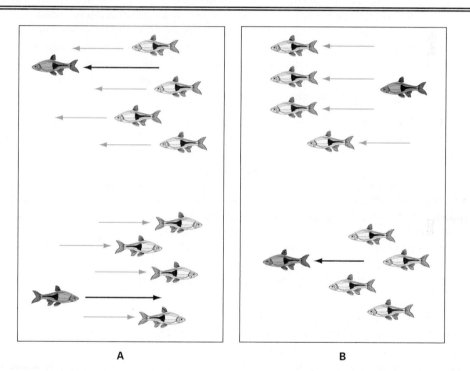

A   B

Diagrams showing trajectories of fish. The dark fishes have the darkest arrows in these diagrams. In A, the group joins the individual (top), and the individual joins the group (bottom); In B, the group leaves the individual (top), and the individual leaves the group (bottom).

Source: Adapted from Morris, M. W., & Peng, K. (1994). Culture and cause: American and Chinese attributions for social and physical events. *Journal of Personality and Social Psychology, 67*(6), 949–971.

---

[43] Rosette, A. S., Brett, J. M., Barsness, Z. I., & Lytle, A. L. (2008). When cultures clash electronically: The impact of email and culture on negotiation behavior. Under review at *Journal of International Business Studies.*

In Exhibit 10-5, panels A and B, the dark fish swims on a trajectory that deviates from that of others (indicated by the darkest arrows). When asked to describe what was going on in videotapes of swimming fish whose movements were similar to those illustrated in Exhibit 10-5, members of individualistic cultures (Americans) perceived more influence of internal factors (dispositionalism), whereas members of collectivist cultures (Chinese) perceived more external influence (situationalism) on the dark fish's motions.[44] Specifically, Chinese people were more likely to view the fish as wanting to achieve harmony, whereas Americans were more likely to view the dark fish as striking out on its own. Similarly, an investigation of stories in American and Chinese newspapers reveals that English-language newspapers are more dispositional and Chinese-language newspapers are more situational when explaining the same crime stories.[45] Specifically, when newspaper articles about "rogue trader" scandals were analyzed, U.S. papers made more mention of the individual trader involved, whereas Japanese papers referred more to the organization.[46] Similarly, when a team member behaves in a maladjusted way, U.S. participants are more likely to focus on the member's traits, whereas the Hong Kong participants focus on situational factors. East Asians, for example, are more sensitive to both external constraints and group influences (as compared to Westerners), but only when there is information about the situation to discount personality traits.[47] Moreover, East Asian people first assign responsibility for events to the collectivity or organizational unit and then extend responsibility to the manager representing that group, thus leaders are held responsible through proxy logic.[48] Dispositionalism also affects biases. People from individualistic cultures, such as the United States, are more likely to fall prey to the fixed-pie bias than are people from collectivistic cultures, such as Greece.[49]

Preferences for Dispute Resolution.   Four types of dispute resolution procedures characterize how different cultures resolve disputes: bargaining, mediation, adversarial adjudication, and inquisitorial adjudication. In **bargaining**, or negotiation, two disputants retain full control over the discussion process and settlement outcome. In **mediation**, disputants retain control over the final decision, but a third party guides the process. In **adversarial adjudication**, a judge makes a binding settlement decision, but disputants retain control of the process. In **inquisitorial adjudication**, disputants yield to a third party control over both the process and the final decision. Collectivist cultures such as China differ from individualistic cultures such as the United States in terms of preferences for dispute resolution.[50] For example, when it comes to resolving conflict, Japanese managers prefer to defer to a higher-status person, Germans prefer to regulate behavior via rules, and Americans prefer an interests model that relies on resolving

---

[44] Morris, M. W., & Peng, K. (1994). Culture and cause: American and Chinese attributions for social and physical events. *Journal of Personality and Social Psychology, 67*(6), 949–971.

[45] Ibid.

[46] Menon, T., Morris, M. W., Chiu, C., & Hong, Y. (1999). Culture and construal of agency: Attribution to individual versus group dispositions. *Journal of Personality and Social Psychology, 76*(5), 701–717.

[47] Valenzuela, A., Srivastava, J., & Lee, S. (2005). The role of cultural orientation in bargaining under incomplete information: Differences in causal attributions. *Organizational Behavior and Human Decision Processes, 96*(1), 72–88.

[48] Zemba, Y., Young, M. J., & Morris, M. W. (2006). Blaming leaders for organizational accidents: Proxy logic in collective- versus individual-agency cultures. *Organizational Behavior and Human Decision Processes, 101*(1), 36–51.

[49] Gelfand, M. J., & Christakopolou, S. (1999). Culture and negotiator cognition: Judgment accuracy and negotiation processes in individualistic and collectivistic cultures. *Organizational Behavior and Human Decision Processes, 79*(3), 248–269.

[50] Leung, K. (1987). Some determinants of reactions to procedural models for conflict resolution: A cross-national study. *Journal of Personality and Social Psychology, 53*(5), 898–908; Morris, M. W., Leung, K., & Iyengar, S. S. (2004). Person perception in the heat of conflict: Negative trait attributions affect procedural preferences and account for situational and cultural differences. *Asian Journal of Social Psychology, 7*(2), 127–147.

underlying interests.[51] One investigation examined differences between Chinese and American commercial arbitrators. Chinese arbitrators make higher awards for interfirm contract violations than do Americans, presumably because the Chinese arbitrators actually make greater internal attributions, even when observing the actions of a group.[52] Furthermore, cultural differences in attributional tendencies (i.e., collectivists view behavior as a function of the situation; individualists view behavior as a function of disposition) create even more of a gap between preferences. Specifically, when negotiators encounter a disagreeable person across the bargaining table, individualists attribute that person's behavior to an underlying disposition and desire more formal dispute resolution procedures; in contrast, collectivists are more likely to ascribe behavior to situational factors and prefer informal procedures.[53]

Egalitarianism Versus Hierarchy

A key factor that influences behavior across cultures is the means by which people influence others and use of power in relationships. Some cultures have relatively permeable status boundaries and are egalitarian. Other cultures have relatively fixed status boundaries in which influence is determined by existing hierarchical relationships.

EGALITARIAN POWER RELATIONSHIPS   In egalitarian power relationships, everyone expects to be treated equally. Egalitarian power relationships do not mean that everyone is of equal status, but rather, that status differences are easily permeated. Egalitarian cultures empower members to resolve conflict themselves. Furthermore, the base of power in negotiations may differ; in egalitarian cultures, one's BATNA and information are key sources of power (status and rank are irrelevant). This same power base is not necessarily valid in hierarchical cultures.

HIERARCHICAL POWER RELATIONSHIPS   In some cultures, great deference is paid to status; status implies social power and is not easily permeated or changed. Social inferiors are expected to defer to social superiors who, in return for privilege, are obligated to look out for the needs of social inferiors.[54] Conflict threatens the stability of a hierarchical society because it implies either that social inferiors have not met expectations or that social superiors have not met the needs of social inferiors.[55] The norm in hierarchical cultures is not to challenge high-status members; thus, conflict is less frequent between members of different social ranks than in egalitarian cultures.[56] Furthermore, conflict between members of the same social rank in hierarchical cultures is more likely to be handled by deference to a superior than by direct confrontation between social equals.[57] Hierarchy reduces conflict by providing norms for interaction. For this reason, superiors intervene in conflicts (in China and Japan), behave more autocratically and decide on more conservative outcomes; conversely, superiors in Western cultures generally involve the disputants themselves and obtain integrative outcomes that go beyond contract-related mandates.[58]

---

[51] Tinsley, C. H. (1998). Models of conflict resolution in Japanese, German, and American cultures. *Journal of Applied Psychology, 83*(2), 316–323; Tinsley, C. H. (2001). How we get to yes: Predicting the constellation of strategies used across cultures to negotiate conflict. *Journal of Applied Psychology, 86*(4), 583–593.
[52] Friedman, R., Liu, W., Chen, C. C., & Chi, S-C., S. (2007). Casual attribution for interfirm contract violation: A comparative study of Chinese and American commercial arbitrators. *Journal of Applied Psychology, 92*(3), 856–864.
[53] Morris, Leung, & Iyengar, "Person perception."
[54] Leung, "Some determinants of reactions."
[55] Brett, *Negotiating globally.*
[56] Ibid.
[57] Leung, "Some determinants of reactions."
[58] Brett, J. M., Tinsley, C. H., Shapiro, D. L., & Okumura, T. (2007). Intervening in employee disputes: How and when will managers from China, Japan, and the US act differently? *Management and Organization Review, 3*(2), 183–204.

Hoftstede examined 73 countries in terms of power distance and individualism-collectivism.[59] Exhibit 10-6 reveals where different countries fall in terms of individualism and power distance. Power distance reflects the tendency to see a large distance between those in the upper part of a social structure and those in the lower part of that structure.

Exhibit 10-6 reveals that individualism and power distance are related: Countries high in collectivism are also high in power distance. The most collectivist high-power countries included Guatemala, Panama, and Ecuador. The most individualistic, low-power-distance countries included Great Britain, the United States, and Australia.

IMPLICATIONS FOR NEGOTIATION

Choose Your Representative.   One of the first issues that negotiators must consider prior to intercultural negotiations is determining who will do the negotiating. In egalitarian cultures, power is usually determined by one's BATNA, and it is not unusual for persons of different status to find themselves at the bargaining table. In contrast, in hierarchical cultures power is associated with one's position and rank, and it is insulting to send a lower-rank employee to meet with a CEO.

Understand the Network of Relationships.   In cultures that have hierarchical power relationships, negotiations often require several levels of approval, all the way to the top. For example, in one failed negotiation, the central government of China voided the long-standing agreement of McDonald's with the Beijing city government because leases of longer than 10 years required central government approval.[60] In the centralized Chinese authority structure, negotiators seldom have the authority to approve the final deal. One by-product of this authority structure is that Chinese negotiators will attempt to secure a deal that is clearly weighted in their favor, so it will be easier to persuade the higher authorities that the Chinese "won" the negotiation.

Face Concerns.   Saving and giving face are important in hierarchical cultures.[61] A study of four cultures (China, Japan, Germany, and the United States) revealed that saving another person's face is associated with remaining calm, apologizing, and giving in; whereas saving one's own face is related with defending positively.[62] In Western culture, people whose face is threatened act more assertively; in contrast, members of Eastern cultures act more passively.[63] Flattery is a common form of Chinese face-saving.[64] Pachtman cautions:

> Be aware of the effect flattery has on you; the proper response is not "thank you," but a denial and an even bigger compliment in return. Apologies are another powerful way to give face, but can obligate the apologizer; be prepared with a token concession in case the Chinese decide to "cash in" on your apology. (p. 25)[65]

---

[59] Hofstede, G., Hofstede, G. J., & Minkov, M. (2010). *Cultures and Organizations, Software of the Mind (3rd Ed)*. Chicago: McGraw-Hill.

[60] Pachtman, A. (1998, July 1). Getting to "hao!" *International Business*, pp. 24–26.

[61] Ting-Toomey, S. (1988). Intercultural conflict styles: A face negotiation theory. In Y. Kim & W. Gudykunst (Eds.), *Theories in intercultural communication* (pp. 213–235). Newbury Park, CA: Sage.

[62] Oetzel, J., Garcia, A. J., & Ting-Toomey, S. (2008). An analysis of the relationships among face concerns and facework behaviors in perceived conflict situations: A four-culture investigation. *International Journal of Conflict Management, 19*(4), 382–403.

[63] Brew, F. P., & Cairns, D. R. (2004). Styles of managing interpersonal workplace conflict in relation to status and face concerns: A study with Anglos and Chinese. *International Journal of Conflict Management, 15*(1), 27–56.

[64] Pachtman, "Getting to 'hao!'"

[65] Ibid.

EXHIBIT 10-6

Position of Countries on Power Distance and Individualism

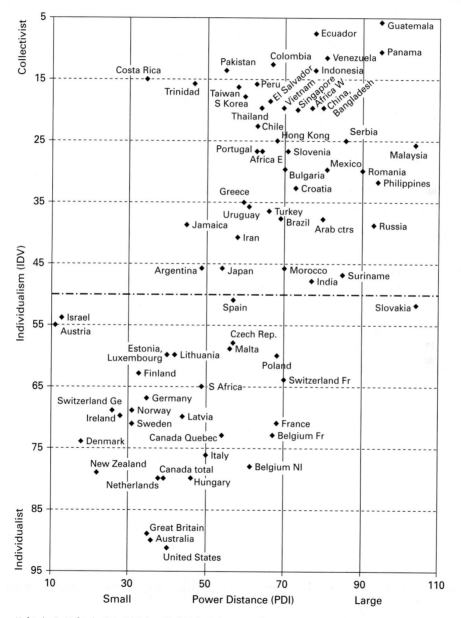

Source: Hofstede, G., Hofstede, G. J., & Minkov, M. (2010). *Cultures and Organizations, Software of the Mind* (3rd Ed). Chicago: McGraw-Hill.

The Conduct of Negotiation.   A Western view of negotiation holds that each party is expected to voice its own interests, and a back-and-forth exchange will occur. An Eastern view of negotiation is quite different. For example, negotiation among Japanese persons is similar to that of father and son, according to Adler.[66] The status relationship is explicit and important. The son (seller) carefully explains his situation and asks for as much as possible because he will have no chance to bicker once the father (buyer) decides. The son (seller) accepts the decision because it would hurt the relationship to argue and because he trusts the father (buyer) to care for his needs.

Direct Versus Indirect Communications

Direct versus indirect information sharing is a cultural dimension that refers to the amount of information contained in an explicit message versus implicit contextual cues.[67] Some cultures' norms favor direct communication, whereas in other cultures, people communicate in an indirect, discreet fashion. The indirect-direct communication dimension has implications for how much people should rely on contextual cues.[68]

DIRECT COMMUNICATION   In a direct communication culture, such as the United States, messages are transmitted explicitly and directly, and communications are action-oriented and solution-minded.[69] The meaning is contained in the message; information is provided explicitly, without nuance.[70] Furthermore, information is **context-free**, meaning the message has the same meaning regardless of the context. Negotiators often ask direct questions about interests and alternatives.

INDIRECT COMMUNICATION   In some cultures, people avoid direct confrontation when conflict occurs. The meaning of communication is inferred rather than directly interpreted; the context of the message stimulates pre-existing knowledge that is then used to gain understanding.[71] (For a classification of direct and indirect communication cultures, see Exhibit 10-7.)

Making a lot of proposals is a form of indirect communication.[72] The pattern of proposals allows inferences to be made about what is important to each party and where points of concession might be. Indirect cultures (such as Japan) transmit messages indirectly and implicitly, and communication is elusive.[73] For example, Japanese negotiators are less likely to say "No" and more likely to remain silent than U.S. negotiators when confronted with an option that is not favorable.[74]

Negotiators from direct cultures prefer sharing information directly, asking questions, and getting (in return for giving) answers. In contrast, negotiators from indirect cultures prefer

---

[66] Adler, N. J. (1991). *International dimensions of organizational behavior*. Boston: PWS-Kent.

[67] Hall, E. T. (1976). *Beyond culture*. Garden City, NJ: Anchor Press.

[68] Hall, E. T., & Hall, M. R. (1990). *Understanding cultural differences*. Yarmouth, ME: Intercultural Press; Cohen, R. (1991). *Negotiating across cultures: Communication obstacles in international diplomacy*. Washington, DC: United States Institute of Peace Press.

[69] Ting-Toomey, "Intercultural conflict styles."

[70] Brett, *Negotiating globally*.

[71] Ibid.

[72] Brett, J. M., Shapiro, D. L., & Lytle, A. (1998). Breaking the bonds of reciprocity in negotiations. *Academy of Management Journal, 41*(4), 410–424.

[73] Ting-Toomey, "Intercultural conflict styles."

[74] Graham, J. L., & Sano, Y. (1984). *Smart bargaining: Doing business with the Japanese*. Cambridge, MA: Ballinger; March, R. M. (1990). *The Japanese negotiator: Subtlety and strategy beyond Western logic* (1st paperback ed.). New York: Kodansha International.

EXHIBIT 10-7

Direct and Indirect Communication Cultures

Direct Communication Cultures	Indirect Communication Cultures
Germany	Japan
United States	Russia
Switzerland	France
Scandinavian cultures	Arabs
	Mediterranean peoples
	In general, cultures in which people have extensive information networks among family, friends, colleagues, and clients and in which people are involved in close, personal relationships

Source: Based on Brett, J. M. (2007). *Negotiating globally: How to negotiate deals, resolve disputes, and make decisions across cultural boundaries* (2nd ed.). San Francisco: Jossey-Bass.

sharing information indirectly, telling stories in an attempt to influence their opponents, and gleaning information from proposals.[75] Cultural norms and values have implications for the reciprocity principle in negotiation. In an investigation of intracultural and intercultural negotiation between the United States and Japan, negotiators reciprocated culturally normative behaviors.[76] U.S. negotiators were more likely to reciprocate direct information exchange; in contrast, Japanese negotiators were more likely to reciprocate indirect information exchange.

IMPLICATIONS FOR NEGOTIATION

Information Necessary to Reach Integrative Agreements.   Getting information out on the table is critical for expanding the pie; relying on context alone to convey information necessary to craft integrative agreements is not enough.[77] Adair examined integrative sequences in same and mixed-culture negotiations. Managers from Hong Kong, Japan, Russia, and Thailand used more indirect integrative strategies (e.g., making multiple offers at the same time); in contrast, managers from Israel, Germany, Sweden, and the United States used direct integrative strategies (e.g., asking for priority information).[78] People from indirect cultures seamlessly enter into a

[75] Brett, J. M., Adair, W. A., Lempereur, A., Okumura, T., Shikhirev, P., Tinsley, C., & Lytle, A. (1998). Culture and joint gains in negotiation. *Negotiation Journal, 14*(1), 61–86.

[76] Adair, W. L., & Brett, J. M. (2005). The Negotiation dance: Time, culture, and behavioral sequences in negotiations. *Organization Science, 16*(1), 33–51.

[77] Brett, Adair, Lempereur, Okumura, Shikhirev, Tinsley, & Lytle, "Culture and joint gains in negotiation."

[78] Adair, W. (2003). Integrative sequences and negotiation outcome in same- and mixed-culture negotiation. *International Journal Conflict Management, 14,* 273–296.

"dance" of complementary, indirect information exchange.[79] For example, by complementing priority information and offers, negotiators from indirect cultures supplement the information that may not have been sufficiently conveyed through reciprocal offers.

Because indirect communication requires more complex and subtle communication skills, direct communicators often find it difficult or impossible; in contrast, indirect communicators can be direct when necessary.[80]

Brett and colleagues investigated negotiation strategies in six countries: France, Russia, Japan, Hong Kong, Brazil, and the United States. Cultures that used direct (as opposed to indirect) information-sharing strategies or a combination of direct and indirect strategies reached the most integrative, pie-expanding agreements.[81] Exchanging information about preferences and priorities was insufficient. For example, in the same study of intracultural negotiations involving the United States, Japan, Brazil, France, Russia, and Hong Kong, negotiators from Russia and Hong Kong generated the lowest joint gains, or integrative agreements.[82] Russia and Hong Kong are indirect communication countries. However, Japanese negotiators had high joint gains, even though they also are an indirect communication culture. Japanese negotiators engaged in more direct information exchange (i.e., asking questions) than the negotiators from Russia or Hong Kong. Thus, making comparisons and contrasts to identify trade-offs and direct reactions appears to be essential.[83] Moreover, offers have different effects across cultures. Early offers generate higher joint gains for Japanese negotiators but lower joint gains for U.S. negotiators.[84] Conversely, direct exchange of information about interests and issues generates higher joint gains for U.S. negotiators but lower joint gains for Japanese negotiators.[85]

In direct cultures, the process of deal-making comes first; in other cultures, the relationship comes first and provides a context for making deals. Frank Lee, a native of Taiwan, who launched Global Intelligence Consultation in San Diego, says, "In negotiations with Chinese, the first 30 minutes are just warming up." If Americans force Chinese negotiators to get down to business too quickly, conflicts can arise.[86]

Dispute Resolution Preferences.   U.S. managers often feel satisfied with their outcomes following interests-based negotiations.[87] However, other cultures use different dispute resolution strategies, often with equally satisfying results.[88] For example, U.S. managers prefer to use interests-based methods, such as discussing parties' interests and synthesizing multiple issues.[89] In one investigation, U.S. managers were more likely than Hong Kong Chinese managers to resolve a greater number of issues and reach more integrative outcomes; in contrast, Hong Kong Chinese managers were more likely to involve higher management in conflict resolution[90] and

---

[79] Adair, & Brett, "The negotiation dance."
[80] Hall, *Beyond culture.*
[81] Brett, Adair, Lempereur, Okumura, Shikhirev, Tinsley, & Lytle, "Culture and joint gains in negotiation."
[82] Ibid.
[83] Ibid.
[84] Adair, W. L., Weingart, L., & Brett, J. (2007). The timing and function of offers in U.S. and Japanese negotiations. *Journal of Applied Psychology, 92*(4), 1056–1068.
[85] Ibid.
[86] Simons, C. (2005, September 6). Companies try to learn China's ways. *Atlanta Journal-Constitution,* p. C1.
[87] Tinsley, "How we get to yes."
[88] Ibid.
[89] Tinsley, C. H., & Brett, J. M. (2001). Managing workplace conflict in the United States and Hong Kong. *Organizational Behavior and Human Decision Processes, 85*(2), 360–381.
[90] Ibid.

choose a relationally connected third party.[91] One way people from indirect cultures communicate their disapproval is by shaming others. For example, Chinese managers show a stronger desire to shame and teach moral lessons compared to U.S. managers.[92] In collectivist cultures, shaming is a common form of social control.[93] In contrast, U.S. managers are more likely to choose a direct approach in response to conflict.

KEY CHALLENGES OF INTERCULTURAL NEGOTIATION

Next, we consider the intercultural challenges of expanding the pie, dividing the pie, sacred values, biased punctuation of conflict, ethnocentrism, affiliation bias, faulty perceptions of conciliation and coercion, and naïve realism.

Expanding the Pie

Negotiators have more difficulty expanding the pie when negotiating across cultures than within a culture. A landmark study of five countries (Japan, Hong Kong, Germany, Israel, and the United States), examined intracultural (within the same culture) negotiations versus intercultural (across cultures) negotiations. Negotiations between Japan and the United States resulted in a smaller expansion of the pie than did intracultural negotiations (Japan–Japan and U.S.–U.S. negotiations).[94] Another study examined joint gains in intra- and intercultural negotiations between Japanese and U.S. negotiators and found that joint gains were significantly lower in intercultural negotiations, as opposed to intracultural negotiations.[95] The key reason appeared to be the degree to which parties understood the priorities of the counterparties and the opportunity for exploiting compatible issues. In cross-cultural negotiations, negotiators' bargaining styles did not match, meaning they had less understanding of the counterparty's priorities and consequently did not create as much value. Each culture expected the other culture to adopt its own style of negotiating. For example, North Americans expected others to talk directly, whereas people from indirect cultures expected to use implicit forms of communication, such as heuristic trial and error. U.S. negotiators exchange information directly and avoid using influence strategies when negotiating intra- and interculturally. In contrast, Japanese negotiators exchange information indirectly and use influence when negotiating intraculturally but adapt their behaviors when negotiating interculturally.[96]

Dividing the Pie

As compared to other cultures, people from the United States are more unabashedly self-interested and, consequently, often have higher aspirations. Aspirations influence opening offers,

[91] Fu, J. Ho-y., Morris, M. W., Lee, S-I., Chao, M., Chiu, C-y., & Hong, Y-y. (2007). Epistemic motives and cultural conformity: Need for closure, culture, and context and determinants of conflict judgments. *Journal of Personality and Social Psychology, 92*(2), 191–207.

[92] Tinsley, C. H., & Weldon, E. (2003). Responses to a normative conflict among American and Chinese managers. *International Journal of Cross-Cultural Management, 3*(2), 183–234.

[93] Creighton, M. R. (1990). Revisiting shame and guilt cultures: A forty-year pilgrimage. *Ethos, 18,* 279–307; Demos, J. (1996). Shame and guilt in early New England. In R. Harre & W. G. Parrott (Eds.), *The emotions* (pp. 74–88). London: Sage.

[94] Brett, *Negotiating globally.*

[95] Brett, J. M., & Okumura, T. (1998). Inter- and intracultural negotiation: U.S. and Japanese negotiators. *Academy of Management Journal, 41*(5), 495–510.

[96] Adair, W., Okumura, T., & Brett, J. M. (2001). Negotiation behavior when cultures collide: The U.S. and Japan. *Journal of Applied Psychology, 86*(3), 371–385.

and are strongly predictive of the ultimate slice of the pie negotiators receive. Indeed, U.S. negotiators who have higher aspirations than their opponents achieve greater profit than managers from China and Japan, primarily because these collectivist cultures are not as self-interested.[97]

Sacred Values and Taboo Trade-Offs

Sacred values, or protected values, are the beliefs, customs, and assumptions that form the basis of a group or culture's belief system.[98] Sacred values are, by definition, those values and beliefs people regard to be so fundamental that they are not discussible nor debatable. Sacred values resist trade-offs with other values, particularly economic values. When people contemplate buying or selling "sacred objects," they are more likely to distort the price, refuse to answer questions, and express moral outrage and cognitive confusion.[99] However, when it is in their economic interest, people may turn a blind eye to taboo trade-offs.[100] Consider the reaction for a mosque proposed for the site near ground zero in lower Manhattan. Before being approved by the city's Landmarks Preservation Commission with Mayor Michael R. Bloomberg hailing the decision with a speech on religious liberty, an array of opponents, including the Anti-Defamation League, and prominent Republican politicians including Sarah Palin and Newt Gingrich, led a highly-publicized fight over the placement of the mosque just blocks away from the former site of the World Trade Center. Opponents wrapped emotional arguments in religious and patriotic symbolism and insisted that mosques nurture terrorist bombers.[101]

To study sacred values, Baron and Spranca developed a list of actions that people might oppose on moral or ethical grounds.[102] Participants were asked to respond, "yes" if they were in favor of an action and were willing to accept a great deal of money to see the action carried out, and "no" or "not sure" if they were not in favor. Some of the actions included:

- Destruction of natural forests by human activity, resulting in the extinction of plant and animal species forever
- Raising the IQ of normal children by giving them (completely safe) drugs
- Using genetic engineering to make people more intelligent
- Performing abortions of normal fetuses in the early stages of pregnancy
- Performing abortions of normal fetuses in the second trimester of pregnancy
- Fishing in a way that leads to the painful death of dolphins
- Forcing women to have abortions for the purposes of population control
- Putting people in jail for expressing nonviolent political views
- Letting people sell their organs (for example, a kidney or an eye) for whatever price they could command

---

[97] Chen, Y., Mannix, E., & Okumura, T. (2003). The importance of who you meet: Effects of self- versus other-concerns among negotiators in the United States, the People's Republic of China, and Japan. *Journal of Experimental Social Psychology, 39,* 1–15.

[98] Baron, J., & Spranca, M. (1997). Protected values. *Organizational Behavior and Human Decision Processes, 70*(1), 1–16; Tetlock, P. E., Peterson, R., & Lerner, J. (1996). Revising the value pluralism model: Incorporating social content and context postulates. In C. Seligman, J. Olson, & M. Zanna (Eds.), *The psychology of values: The Ontario Symposium* (Vol. 8). Mahwah, NJ: Erlbaum.

[99] McGraw, A. P. & Tetlock, P. E. (2005). Taboo trade-offs, relational framing, and the acceptability of exchanges. *Journal of Consumer Psychology, 15*(1), 2–15.

[100] Ibid.

[101] Goodstein, L. (2010, August 8). Across nation, Mosque projects meet opposition. *New York Times*, p.A1.

[102] Baron, J., & Spranca, M. (1997). Protected values. *Organizational Behavior and Human Decision Processes, 70*(1), 1–16.

- Refusing to treat someone who needs a kidney transplant because he or she cannot afford it
- Letting a doctor assist in the suicide of a consenting terminally ill patient
- Letting parents sell their daughter in a bride auction (i.e., the daughter becomes the bride of the highest bidder)
- Punishing people for expressing nonviolent political opinions

Sacred values are the opposite of **secular values**, which are issues and resources that can be traded and exchanged. Within a culture, a near-universal ascription to sacred values generally exists, with some notable exceptions. However, between cultures, extreme conflict may occur when one culture regards an issue to be sacred and another treats it as secular. Taboo trade-offs take place when sacred values are proposed for exchange or trade.[103]

The trade-off principle is ideal for handling scarce resource conflicts containing issues that are fungible. Principles of rationality (see Appendix 1) assume people can compare and trade resources in a way that maximizes their outcomes. Rational bargaining theory assumes everything is comparable and has a price (see Appendix 1). However, the notion of trading becomes unconscionable in some conflict situations.[104] People sometimes refuse to place a monetary value on a good or even think of trading it. Attaching a monetary value to a bottle of wine, a house, or the services of a gardener can be a cognitively demanding task, but it raises no questions about the morality of the individual who proposes the sale or trade. In contrast, attaching monetary value to human life, familial obligations, national honor, and the ecosystem seriously undermines one's social identity or standing in the eyes of others.[105] In a dispute concerning the construction of a dam that would remove native Americans from their ancestral land, a Yavapai teenager said, "The land is our mother. You don't sell your mother."[106]

Proposals to exchange sacred values (e.g., body organs) for secular ones (e.g., money, time, or convenience) constitute taboo trade-offs. Given the inherently sacred values that operate in many countries, the familiar notions of trading and logrolling, so important to interests-based negotiation, are likely to be considered unacceptable and reprehensible to members of different cultures. The extent to which sacred issues negatively impact negotiations depends on the BATNAs of parties.[107] When parties have a strong BATNA, sacred issues produce impasses, lower joint outcomes and more negative perceptions; however when negotiators do not have attractive BATNAs, they can't afford to stand on principle. A study of the Isreali-Palestianian conflict revealed that when negotiators focus on the *losses* inherent in standing on principle and continuing the conflict, they are more willing to acquire new information about possible solutions to the conflict, reevaluate their current positions, and support compromise than when they focus on the *gains* of their position.[108]

Sacred and secular issues are culturally defined, with no absolutes.[109] Sociocultural norms affect the sacredness of certain positions, such as smoking, which is now generally considered

---

[103] Tetlock, Peterson, & Lerner, "Revising the value pluralism model."

[104] Ibid.

[105] Schlenker, B. R. (1980). *Impression management: The self-concept, social identity, and interpersonal relations.* Belmont, CA: Brooks-Cole.

[106] Espeland, W. (1994). Legally mediated identity: The national environmental policy act and the bureaucratic construction of interests. *Law and Society Review, 28*(5), 1149–1179.

[107] Tenbrunsel, A. E., Wade-Benzoni, K. A., Tost, L. P, Medvec, V. H., Thompson, L., & Bazerman, M. H. (2009). The reality and myth of sacred issues in negotiations. *Negotiation and Conflict Management Research, 2*(3), 263–284.

[108] Gayer, C. C., Landman, S., Halperin, E., & Bar-Tal, D. (2009). Overcoming psychological barriers to peaceful conflict resolution: The role of arguments about losses. *Journal of Conflict Resolution, 53*(6), 951–975.

[109] Tetlock, Peterson, & Lerner, "Revising the value pluralism model."

baneful but in the recent past was completely acceptable. The sanctity of issues is also influenced by the labels and names used to define conflicts. The government of Iran took offense when the U.S. Navy's official online style guide referred to the "Persian Gulf" as the "Arabian Gulf." Outrage flowed from Iranian advocacy groups, the Iranian government, and Facebook protesters, heightening an already tense relationship between the two countries. "This is an ethnically divisive term.... It's very troubling," said Jamal Abdi, policy director with the National Iranian American Council. The Persian Gulf name had become a point of cultural pride over the decades, after some Arab nations began calling it the Arabian Gulf in the 1960s—though it was known for centuries as the Persian Gulf and continues to be labeled as that. Iran's government, representing the land formerly known as Persia, has scolded any country that uses the "Arabian" moniker.[110]

The term **sacred** describes people's preferences on issues on which they view themselves as uncompromising. It immediately becomes obvious, however, that labeling an issue as sacred may be a negotiation ploy, rather than a reflection of heartfelt value. The strategy is similar to the irrevocable commitment strategy.[111] We refer to issues that are not really sacred, but are positioned as such, as **pseudosacred**.[112]

Biased Punctuation of Conflict

The **biased punctuation of conflict** occurs when people interpret interactions with their adversaries in self-serving and other derogating terms.[113] An actor, A, perceives the history of conflict with another actor, B, as a sequence of B-A, B-A, B-A, in which the initial hostile or aggressive move was made by B, causing A to engage in defensive and legitimate retaliatory actions. Actor B punctuates the same history of interaction as A-B, A-B, A-B, however, reversing the roles of aggressor and defender. The biased punctuation of conflict is a frequent cause of warfare. Consider the long, sad history of international conflict between the Arabs and Israelis. Each country chooses different historical moments of origin to justify its own claims to land and thus casts the other country in the role of the invader.

Negotiation behaviors are a continuous stream of cause-and-effect relationships in which each person's actions influence the actions of others.[114] To an outside observer, their interaction is an uninterrupted sequence of interchanges. However, people who are actively engaged in conflict do not always see things this way. Instead, they organize their interactions into a series of discrete, causal chunks,[115] a process known as **causal chunking** or **punctuation**.[116] Causal chunks influence the extent to which people are aware of their influence on others, as well as their impressions

---

[110] Berger, J. (2010, December 10). U.S. Navy rankles Iranians for calling Persian Gulf Arabian Gulf. *Fox News*. Foxnews.com

[111] Schelling, T. (1960). *The strategy of conflict*. Cambridge, MA: Harvard University Press.

[112] We are indebted to Max Bazerman for this term; Thompson, L., & Gonzalez, R. (1997). Environmental disputes: Competition for scarce resources and clashing of values. In M. Bazerman, D. Messick, A. Tenbrunsel, & K. Wade-Benzoni (Eds.), *Environment, ethics, and behavior* (pp. 75–104). San Francisco: New Lexington Press; Wade-Benzoni, Okumura, Brett, Moore, Tenbrunsel, & Bazerman, "Cognitions and behavior."

[113] Kahn, R. L., & Kramer, R. M. (1990). *Untying the knot: De-escalatory processes in international conflict*. San Francisco: Jossey-Bass.

[114] Jones, E. E., & Gerard, H. B. (1967). *Foundations of social psychology*. New York: Wiley.

[115] Swann, W. B., Pelham, B. W., & Roberts, D. C. (1987). Causal chunking: Memory and inference in ongoing interaction. *Journal of Personality and Social Psychology, 53*(5), 858–865.

[116] Whorf, B. L. (1956). Science and linguistics. In J. B. Carroll (Ed.), *Language, thought, and reality: Selected writings of Benjamin Whorf*. New York: Wiley.

of others. Two kinds of chunking patterns are self-causal and other-causal. People form self-causal chunks (e.g., "My action causes my partner's action") when they possess an offensive set, other-causal chunks when they possess a defensive set. Disagreement about how to punctuate a sequence of events and a conflict relationship is at the root of many cross-cultural disputes.

Ethnocentrism

If egocentrism refers to unwarranted positive beliefs about oneself relative to others, then **ethnocentrism** refers to unwarranted positive beliefs about one's own group relative to other groups.[117] Ethnocentrism, or the universal strong liking of one's own group and the simultaneous negative evaluation of out-groups, generates a set of universal reciprocal stereotypes in which each culture sees itself as good and the other culture as bad, even when both groups engage in the same behaviors. The behavior may be similar, but the interpretation is not: "We are loyal, they are clannish; we are brave and willing to defend our rights, they are hostile and arrogant."

Even when members of groups do not know one another and never interact, people show in-group favoritism.[118] However, conflict between groups and intergroup bias do not always arise from competition over scarce resources. Much intergroup bias stems from fundamental differences in cultural values. Symbolic conflict can occur between cultural groups due to clashes of values and fundamental beliefs.

One unfortunate by-product of in-group favoritism is the tendency to view people from different cultures as more alike than they really are. Thus, the pejorative phrase, "They all look alike" suggests that within-race and within-culture errors are more prevalent than between-race or between-cultural errors because people categorize members of other cultures not as individuals but as part of a group. As an example, consider the long-standing conflict between pro-choice and pro-life activists on the abortion issue (see Exhibit 10-8).

Stereotypes are another manifestation of ethnocentrism. Stereotypes of cultural groups are common. However, they often do not have a basis in reality. The problem is that if people act as if stereotypes are true, they are likely to create a self-fulfilling prophecy. For example, Americans described their Japanese counterparts as being "poker-faced" or displaying no facial expressions in a negotiation simulation. However, in the laboratory, a camera focused on each person's face during an intercultural negotiation recorded all facial expressions and revealed no differences in the number of facial expressions (smiles and frowns) between the Americans and Japanese. Americans are not able to "read" Japanese expressions, and they wrongly describe them as "expressionless."[119]

Affiliation Bias

Affiliation bias occurs when people evaluate a person's actions on the basis of his or her affiliations rather than on the merits of the behavior itself. For example, when football fans watch a game, they believe the other side commits more infractions than does their own team.[120] Consider

---

[117] LeVine, R. A., & Campbell, D. T. (1972). *Ethnocentrism: Theories of conflict, ethnic attitudes, and group behavior.* New York: Wiley.

[118] Brewer, M. (1979). In-group bias in the minimal intergroup situation: A cognitive-motivational analysis. *Psychological Bulletin, 86,* 307–324; Tajfel, "Social psychology"; Tajfel, H., & Turner, J. (1986). The social identity theory of intergroup behavior. In S. Worchel & W. Austin (Eds.), *Psychology of intergroup relations* (pp. 7–24). Chicago: Nelson-Hall.

[119] Graham, J. L. (1993). The Japanese negotiation style: Characteristics of a distinct approach. *Negotiation Journal, 9*(2), 123–140.

[120] Hastorf, A., & Cantril, H. (1954). They saw a game: A case study. *Journal of Abnormal and Social Psychology, 49,* 129–134.

EXHIBIT 10-8

Stereotyping the Other Party

As an example of how members of groups tend to stereotype the other party, consider the conversation that occurred between Naomi Wolf, author of the best-seller *The Beauty Myth,* and Frederica Mathewes-Green, a syndicated religion columnist and author of a book titled *Right Choices.* Try to figure out which woman made which of the following comments during a discussion in 1996:

> Where the pro-life movement has made its mistake is to focus only on the baby, and not the woman.... You can boil 25 years of the pro-life rhetoric down to three words: "It's a baby."

> There's a whole industry to promote bonding with the wanted fetus, yet unwanted fetuses are treated as though they are unwanted lumps of batter.

The criticism of the pro-life movement's "It's a baby" focus came from Mathewes-Green, one of the movement's own. The criticism of the pro-choice movement's "unwanted lumps of batter" rhetoric came from Wolf, a staunch abortion-rights supporter.

When Wolf and Mathewes-Green met to talk, Wolf said it was the first time she had ever "knowingly been in the presence of a pro-lifer." To her surprise, the other side was willing to have a conversation. Mathewes-Green acknowledged that the pro-life movement had invited stereotypes by "focusing only on the baby and not the woman."

Source: Shirk, M. (1996, June 10.) Women go beyond rhetoric. *St. Louis Post-Dispatch*, p. 11B. Reprinted by permission of St. Louis Post-Dispatch.

the following actions a country could take: establishing a rocket base close to the borders of a country with whom it has strained relations, testing a new assault weapon, or establishing trade relations with a powerful country. People's perceptions of the acceptability of these actions differ dramatically as a function of the perceived agent. For example, during the time of the Cold War, U.S. citizens regarded the preceding actions to be much more beneficial when the United States was the one responsible than when the former U.S.S.R. engaged in the same actions.[121] People perceive the same objective behavior as either sinister or benign, merely as a consequence of the agent's affiliation.

Faulty Perceptions of Conciliation and Coercion

During World War II, the American journalist Edward R. Murrow broadcasted nightly from London, reporting on the psychological and physical consequences of the Nazi bombing of British cities.[122] Contrary to Nazi intent, the bombing did not move the British toward surrender.

---

[121] Oskamp, S. (1965). Attitudes toward U.S. and Russian actions: A double standard. *Psychological Reports, 16,* 43–46.
[122] Rothbart, M., & Hallmark, W. (1988). In-group and out-group differences in the perceived efficacy of coercion and conciliation in resolving social conflict. *Journal of Personality and Social Psychology, 55,* 248–257.

It had quite the opposite effect, strengthening rather than diminishing British resolve to resist German domination. Shortly after the United States entered World War II, the Americans joined the British in launching costly bombing raids over Germany. In part, the intent was to decrease the German people's will to resist. Later research reported by the Office of Strategic Services that compared lightly and heavily bombed areas found only minimal differences in civilians' will to resist.

Several other conflicts follow the same psychological pattern, such as Pearl Harbor, South Africa, and North Vietnam. All of these instances point to important differences in countries' perceptions of what will be effective in motivating an enemy, and what will be effective in motivating themselves or their allies. Coercion is viewed as more effective with our enemies than with ourselves, whereas conciliation is viewed as more effective with ourselves than with our enemies. The unfortunate consequence is that this perception encourages aggressive rather than constructive action.

Three key reasons explain why this behavior occurs.[123] A preference for punitive strategies with one's enemies may reflect a desire to inflict injury or pain, as well as a desire to influence behavior in a desired direction. The relative preference for punishment is based on an incompatible desire to both injure and modify the behavior of the enemy. Alternatively, people may be inclined to use more coercive strategies with a counterparty because the appearance of toughness conveys information about their motives and intentions, which, in the long run, may bring about the desired result. Finally, the mere creation of mutually exclusive, exhaustive social categories (e.g., "them" and "us") leads to different assumptions about members of such groups: More favorable attributes are assigned to ingroup than to outgroup members.[124] Social categorization processes may be particularly powerful in cross-cultural disputes because of stereotypes.

Naïve Realism

A heated debate among English teachers concerns which books should be on the required reading list for U.S. high school students. The Western Canon Debate features traditionalists, who prefer to have classics on the reading list, and revisionists, who believe the reading list should be more racially, ethnically, and gender diversified. In one study, traditionalists and revisionists were interviewed about their own and the other party's preferred books.[125] Most strikingly, each party exaggerates the views of the other side in a way that made their differences bigger rather than smaller. Traditionalists viewed revisionists to be much more extreme than they really were; revisionists viewed traditionalists to be much more conservative. In fact, the groups agreed on 7 out of the 15 books on the reading list! Nevertheless, each group greatly exaggerated the difference between their own and the other's belief systems in a way that exacerbated the conflict. Further, people perceived the other side to be more uniform in their views, whereas they perceived their own views to be more varied and heterogeneous.[126] This faulty perception,

---

[123] Ibid.

[124] Brewer, "In-group bias"; Tajfel, H. (1970). Experiments in intergroup discrimination. *Scientific American, 223,* 96–102.

[125] Robinson, R. J., & Keltner, D. (1996). Much ado about nothing? Revisionists and traditionalists choose an introductory English syllabus. *Psychological Science, 7*(1), 18–24.

[126] Linville, P. W., Fischer, G. W., & Salovey, P. (1989). Perceived distributions of the characteristics of in-group and out-group members: Empirical evidence and a computer simulation. *Journal of Personality and Social Psychology, 57,* 165–188.

of course, leads to beliefs such as "They're all alike." Ideological conflict is often exacerbated unnecessarily as partisans construe the other person's values to be more extremist and unbending than they really are.

The **fundamental attribution error** occurs when people explain the causes of the behavior of others in terms of their underlying dispositions and discount the role of situational factors.[127] Many environmental disputes involve a group that is believed to be interested in the economic development of the environment and an opposing group that represents the interests of the ecosystem. According to the fundamental attribution error, when each group is asked to name the cause of the dispute, each attributes the negative aspects of conflict to the dispositions of the other party. Specifically, developers regard environmentalists to be fanatic lunatics; environmentalists regard developers to be sinister and greedy.

PREDICTORS OF SUCCESS IN INTERCULTURAL INTERACTIONS

Your pharmaceutical company wants to expand its international base. You are charged with the task of selecting a few managers to participate in a special global initiatives assignment in various countries. You know that failure rates as high as 70% can be avoided.[128] These costs include not only the lost salary of an executive, the cost of transporting the family, and the cost of setting up an office abroad, but also damage to your organization, lost sales, on-the-job mistakes, and loss of goodwill. Unfortunately, ready-made personality measures are not good predictors of success abroad. The following characteristics predict success:[129]

- Conceptual complexity (people who are conceptually complex, think in terms of shades of gray, rather than black and white show less social distance to different others)[130]
- Broad categorization (people who use broad categories adjust to new environments better than do narrow categorizers)[131]
- Empathy
- Sociability
- Critical acceptance of stereotypes
- Openness to different points of view
- Interest in the host culture
- Task orientation
- Cultural flexibility (the ability to substitute activities in the host culture for own culture-valued activities)
- Social orientation (the ability to establish new intercultural relationships)
- Willingness to communicate (e.g., use the host language without fear of making mistakes)
- Patience (suspend judgment)
- Intercultural sensitivity

---

[127] Ross, L. (1977). The intuitive psychologist and his shortcomings: Distortions in the attribution process. In L. Berkowitz (Ed.), *Advances in experimental social psychology* (Vol. 10) (pp. 173–220). Orlando, FL: Academic Press.
[128] Copeland, L., & Griggs, L. (1985). *Going international.* New York: Random House.
[129] Martin, J. N. (1989). Intercultural communication competence. *International Journal of Intercultural Relations, 13,* 227–428; Triandis, *Culture and social behavior.*
[130] Gardiner, G. S. (1972). *Aggression.* Morristown, NJ: General Learning Corp.
[131] Detweiler, R. (1980). The categorization of the actions of people from another culture: A conceptual analysis and behavioral outcome. *International Journal of Intercultural Relations, 4,* 275–293.

- Tolerance for differences among people
- Sense of humor
- Skills in collaborative conflict resolution

ADVICE FOR CROSS-CULTURAL NEGOTIATIONS

Global negotiations are characterized by differences that emerge at interpersonal behavioral levels and are manifestations of more deep-seated societal and institutional differences.[132] Negotiators should avoid arguing about the inherent legitimacy of a social system and instead focus on understanding at the interpersonal level. Indeed, the cultural intelligence (CQ) of negotiators measured a week prior to negotiation predicts the extent to which negotiators engage in integrative behaviors and maximize joint profit in intercultural negotiations, controlling for other types of intelligence.[133] Moreover, the quality of integrative negotiation was more a function of the lower-scoring, rather than the high-scoring negotiator, suggesting that both parties in conflict should have cultural intelligence. The QCE, or **Quality of Communication Experience**, measures the nature and quality of intra- and intercultural communications.[134] Indeed, QCE is lower in intercultural negotiation than intra-cultural negotiation. Importantly, the higher the QCE, the better the negotiation outcomes.

Brett researched and proposed several strategies to improve cross-cultural effectiveness.[135] (See Exhibit 10-9 for similar suggestions.)

EXHIBIT 10-9

Advice for International Negotiators

1. Acknowledge differences at the individual and societal levels.
2. Trade off differences in preferences and abilities.
3. Ask questions to ensure understanding of the other party's perspective.
4. Understand the norms and the meaning underlying them.
5. Avoid arguing the inherent legitimacy of a social system.
6. Be prepared to manage bureaucratic interactions with governments.

Source: Tinsley, C. H., Curhan, J. R., & Kwak, R. S. (1999). Adopting a dual lens approach for examining the dilemma of differences in international business negotiations. *International Negotiation.*

---

[132] Tinsley, C. H., Curhan, J. R., & Kwak, R. S. (1999). Adopting a dual lens approach for examining the dilemma of differences in international business negotiations. *International Negotiation, 4,* 5–22.

[133] Imai, L., & Gelfand, M. J. (2010). The culturally intelligent negotiator: The impact of cultural intelligence (CQ) on negotiation sequences and outcomes. *Organizational Behavior and Human Decision Processes, 112*(2), 83–98.

[134] Liu, L. A., Chua, C. H., & Stahl, G. K. K. (2010). Quality of communication experience: Definition, measurement, and implications for intercultural negotiations. *Journal of Applied Psychology, 95*(3), 469–487.

[135] Brett, *Negotiating globally,* 5–22.

Anticipate Differences in Strategy and Tactics That May Cause Misunderstandings

The negotiator who is able to anticipate differences in terms of these three dimensions will have a pie-expanding and pie-slicing advantage in intercultural negotiations. Further, when encountering differences, the negotiator who is aware of cultural differences does not make negative attributions about the counterparty but instead views discomfort as a natural consequence of different cultural styles.

Analyze Cultural Differences to Identify Differences in Values That Expand the Pie

Differences between negotiators can open windows for expanding the pie and creating joint gain. Presumably, more degrees of difference are present between members of different cultures than members of the same culture. The level of differences means the amount of integrative, or win-win potential is higher in intercultural negotiations, as opposed to intracultural negotiations. The culturally enlightened negotiator will search for differences in beliefs, values, risk profiles, expectations, and abilities that can be used to leverage opportunities for joint gain, such as through the creation of value-added trade-offs (logrolling) and the construction of contingency contracts.

Recognize That the Other Party May Not Share Your View of What Constitutes Power

When negotiating with members of hierarchical cultures, be prepared to present information about your company and products, even if you think such information should have no bearing on the outcome. In failing to make a presentation comparable to the one made by the negotiator from the hierarchical culture, negotiators from egalitarian cultures risk appearing weak. By the same token, negotiators from hierarchical cultures should be aware that power-based persuasion, although normative in deal-making negotiations in their own cultures, is not normative in egalitarian cultures. Furthermore, power-based persuasion is likely to be reciprocated in negotiation and may lead to impasse.[136] One American businessperson suffered due to a lack of understanding about cultural behavioral styles. After long, hard bargaining, a U.S. firm landed a large contract with a Japanese firm. At the signing ceremony, however, the Japanese executive began reading the contract intently. His scrutiny seemed endless. The American panicked and offered to take $100 off each item. What the U.S. executive did not know was that the Japanese president was merely demonstrating authority, not backing out.[137]

Avoid Attribution Errors

An **attribution error** is the tendency to ascribe someone's behavior or the occurrence of an event to the wrong cause. For example, people often attribute behaviors of others to their underlying personality (e.g., a smile from another person is often attributed to a "good" disposition; similarly, a frown is presumed to be a manifestation of a grouchy personality).[138] However, the behavior of others is more often a reflection of particular features of the situation, rather than enduring personality traits.

---

[136] Brett & Okumura, "Inter- and intracultural negotiation."

[137] Cultural differences can make or break a deal. (1986, February 10). *Chicago Sun-Times,* p. 60.

[138] Ross, B. H. (1987). This is like that: The use of earlier problems and the separation of similarity effects. *Journal of Experimental Psychology: Learning, Memory and Cognition, 13*(4), 629–639.

Find Out How to Show Respect in the Other Culture

One of the most important preparatory steps a negotiator can take when commencing intercultural negotiation is to find out how to show respect in the other culture. It is a fallacy to assume that the other culture will have the same customs as one's own culture and that ignorance of customs will be forgiven. For example, when the Walt Disney Company undertook a $5 billion EuroDisney theme park project in Paris in 1992, it began with great visions of a united workforce wearing Disney dress and adopting American grooming. Behavioral codes banned alcohol in the park, and meetings were conducted in English. The French perceived these requirements and restrictions as an unnecessary cultural imposition. They retaliated with insults, stormed out of training meetings, and initiated lawsuits. The French press joined in by launching an anti-Disney campaign, and for months French railroad workers regularly initiated strikes from the Paris-EuroDisney train. Annual employee turnover hit a crippling 25%, pushing up labor costs by 40%. Disney paid a heavy price before making amends.[139]

In a complementary fashion, intercultural negotiations may fail, not because negotiators stay anchored to their own cultural assumptions and styles, but rather because they try to adjust to their counterpart's cultural assumptions about negotiating. This phenomenon is called **schematic overcompensation**.[140] In a study of 100 experienced Japanese and U.S. negotiators, there was a clash on six of nine elements, such that the parties had significantly different expectations about what it was like to negotiate with the other. (Also see Exhibit 10-10).

EXHIBIT 10-10

An Experiment in Cultural Perspective-Taking

Two professors—Shyam Kamath and Martin Desmaras—arranged for a realistic mock negotiation between U.S. managers and Brazilians. Most of the time, executives from different cultures are not prepared for one another, but the managers in this situation went overboard: Each party carefully researched the other party's cultural style and decided to adapt its own bargaining style to it. The strange result was a situation in which the Brazilians wanted to get down to business immediately and the Americans avoided negotiations while attempting to establish relationships before talking about any contract details. Said one American, "What really surprised us was that they wanted to get down to business right away. We knew better than to push them into a decision at the start, but they came in with their price offer right away." Said the Brazilians, "They [the Americans] seemed to want to take more time at the start. Our side acted more like Americans." Kim Smith, business development manager for Hertz Corp., said, "I began to worry that if their side acted like Americans and we acted like Brazilians, we wouldn't get anything done."

Source: Based on Transnational executive education exercise shows Brazilians, Americans must negotiate past cultural difference. (2003, June 5). *AScribe News.* Ascribe.org

---

[139] Mishra, B. & Sinha, N. (1999, November 8). Cross-cultural booby traps. *Economic Times.*
[140] Adair, W. L., Taylor, M. S., & Tinsley, C. H. (2009). Starting out on the right foot: Negotiation schemas when cultures collide. *Negotiation and Conflict Management Research, 2*(2), 138–163.

Find Out How Time Is Perceived in the Other Culture

Perceptions of time differ dramatically across cultures.[141] Consider, for example, the lengthy negotiations between the Chinese government and Philip Morris International. After more than three years of negotiations, the Chinese government selected three domestic cigarette brands of the hundreds sold to market abroad in partnership with PMI. According to PMI Chief Executive Andre Calantzopoulos, the negotiations were delayed partly because of cultural differences. "By Chinese standards, urgency is in terms of decades, versus U.S. companies, where urgency is next quarter."[142]

Cooperative and competitive behaviors in global negotiations wax and wane across four stages: relational positioning, identifying the problem, generating solutions, and reaching agreement.[143] Cultural differences occur at these stages, perhaps the most notable being that direct cultures use more rational arguments in stages 3 and 4. Differences in how time unfolds may lead Westerners to want to talk (i.e., discuss their feelings with the goal of repairing frayed relationships); however, the meaning of such talk may not be shared by people from culturally different backgrounds.[144]

Know Your Options for Change

Succeeding in international business requires that people gain international, as well as business, competence.[145] However, cultural differences may conflict with your own values and norms. For example, a 2010 report from the Corporate Women Directors International indicated that in the Saudi Arabia, where Muslim law demands strict gender separation, just 0.1% of company directors are women. Female executives from the United States who do business in the Kingdom are expected to dress conservatively in long skirts with sleeves at elbow length and to do business in the presence of their American male counterparts at all times, but they are not typically allowed to appear in public places with their colleagues. In 2008, an American woman who worked for a finance company in the Saudi capital of Riydah was arrested for sitting with a male colleague in a Starbucks.[146]

Berry described four ways for two cultures to relate to each other (see Exhibit 10-11).[147] The first issue is whether the individual (or group) finds it valuable to maintain distinct cultural identity and characteristics. The second issue is whether the individual (or group) desires to maintain relationships with other (cultural) groups.

- *Integration*   is a type of acculturation whereby each group maintains its own culture and also maintains contact with the other culture.
- *Assimilation*   occurs when a group or person does not maintain its culture but does maintain contact with the other culture.

---

[141] Alon, I., & Brett, J. M. (2007, January). Perceptions of time and their impact on negotiations in the Arabic-speaking Islamic world. *Negotiation Journal, 23*(1), 55–73.

[142] Zamiska, N., Ye, J., & O'Connell V. (2008, January 30). Chinese cigarettes to go global. *Wall Street Journal,* p. B4.

[143] Adair & Brett, "The negotiation dance," 33–51.

[144] Glinow, M. A., Shapiro, D. L., & Brett, J. M. (2004). Can we talk, and should we? Managing emotional conflict in multicultural teams. *Academy of Management Review, 29*(4), 578–592.

[145] Matsumoto, D. (1996). *Culture and psychology.* Pacific Grove, CA: Brooks-Cole.

[146] Tatlow, D. K. (2010, May 27). Unlocking access to the boardrooms. *New York Times.* Nytimes.com; Business and social customs in Saudi Arabia (2011). The Saudi Network: *United States of Commerce.* Buyusa.gov; Associated Press. (2008, Feburary 7). Saudi cops grab U.S. woman in Starbucks. *CBS News.* Cbsnews.com

[147] Berry, J. W. (1980). Acculturation as varieties of adaptation. In A. Padilla (Ed.), *Acculturation: Theory, models, and some new findings.* Boulder, CO: Westview.

EXHIBIT 10-11

Acculturation Framework

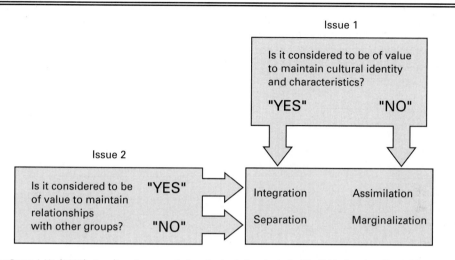

Issue 1

Is it considered to be of value to maintain cultural identity and characteristics?

"YES"   "NO"

Issue 2

Is it considered to be of value to maintain relationships with other groups?   "YES"   "NO"

Integration   Assimilation

Separation   Marginalization

Source: Berry, J. W. (1980). Acculturation as varieties of adaptation. In A. Padilla (Ed.), *Acculturation: Theory, models, and some new findings.* Boulder, CO: Westview. Reprinted with permission.

- *Separation* occurs when a group or individual maintains its culture but does not maintain contact with the other culture.
- *Marginalization* occurs when neither maintenance of the group's own culture nor contact with the other culture is attempted. Marginalization is the most unfavorable condition.[148]

Sometimes, options for change are driven by skill sets—or lack thereof. Most Americans are monolingual, compared to other cultures. Furthermore, members of other cultures know that Americans are monolingual, and so they adapt accordingly. For example, in interactions between North Americans and Mexicans, Mexican bilingual managers immediately switched to English when interacting with North Americans; however, North American linguistic accommodation was a rare occurrence.[149]

CONCLUSION

Negotiating across cultures is a necessity for success in the business world because globalization is a major objective of most companies. Unfortunately, cross-cultural negotiations frequently result in less effective pie expansion than do intracultural negotiations. Part of the

---

[148] Berry, J. W., Poortinga, Y. H., Segall, M. H., & Dasen, P. R. (1992). *Cross-cultural psychology: Research and applications.* New York: Cambridge University Press.
[149] Lindsley, S. L. (1999, June). A layered model of problematic intercultural communication in U.S. owned maquiladoras in Mexico. *Communication Monographs, 66*(2), 145–167.

problem is a lack of understanding cultural differences. We used Brett's tripartite model of culture and identified individualism-collectivism, egalitarianism-hierarchy, and direct-indirect communication as key dimensions of cultural differences.[150] Key challenges of intercultural negotiation are expanding the pie, dividing the pie, dealing with sacred values and taboo trade-offs, biased punctuation of conflict, ethnocentrism, the affiliation bias, faulty perceptions of conciliation and coercion, and naïve realism. Negotiators should analyze cultural differences to identify differences in values that could expand the pie, recognize different conceptions of power, avoid attribution errors, find out how to show respect in other cultures, find out how time is perceived, and assess options for change, including integration, assimilation, separation, and marginalization.

---

[150] Brett, *Negotiating globally.*

Tacit Negotiations and Social Dilemmas

The United Nations Kyoto Protocol, first negotiated in 1997, asked developed countries to cut emissions by an average of five percent (compared with 1990 levels) by 2012. There was initial cooperation. However, as the clock ticked towards the treaty's second commitment period, Japan threatened to pull out of the treaty saying it would not declare emission targets for the next seven years. Developing countries, not beholden to binding emission targets, said the Kyoto Protocol was non-negotiable for the citizens of the world. The conflict exposed disparate ideas on the value of the original treaty. For example, Brazil pledged to reduce its carbon dioxide output by 36 percent over the following decade by protecting its forests, but Brazilian lawmakers had not yet passed laws to that aim. Canada, eager to flee the Kyoto Protocol, cited Japanese resistance as a reason to not declare its own emission targets. The United States opposed the proposed $30 billion fund from 2013 to 2020 from developed countries to developing countries. The first phase of the 1997 treaty only required developed countries to cut emissions. However, because the first phase of the treaty came to an end in 2012, developing countries demanded that wealthy countries submit new targets for a second phase. Wealthy countries resisted because the U.S. was not a party to Kyoto, and powerful, developing countries like China, were not bound to legal commitments. The U.S. flatly refused to enter a treaty that did not treat China, India and other emerging economies as legal equals. These countries responded by refusing to enter any legally binding treaties when the U.S had no plan to cut carbon.[1]

---

[1] Friedman, L. (2010, December 9). Negotiators start round-the-clock sessions to save Kyoto protocol. *New York Times.* Nytimes.com; Friedman, L. (2011, April 22). US negotiator warns Kyoto fight could derail climate talks. *New York Times,* p. ADD.

The previous chapters focused on negotiation situations in which people seek to reach mutual agreement via binding contract, called **explicit negotiations**. In contrast, many negotiations are conducted by actions and pledges, in the absence of a binding contract, such as the Kyoto Protocol. We call these situations **tacit negotiations**.[2] In tacit negotiations, negotiators are interdependent with respect to outcomes, but they make independent decisions. Negotiators' outcomes are determined by the actions they take and the actions taken by others. People can either behave in a cooperative fashion (e.g., agreeing to reduce emissions) or in a competitive fashion (e.g., refusing to reduce emissions).

The distinction between these two different types of negotiation situations was first articulated by the famous mathematician John Nash, who referred to one branch of negotiations as "cooperative games" and the other as "noncooperative games."[3] In using the terms "cooperative" and "noncooperative," Nash was not referring to the motivations or behaviors of the parties involved but, rather, to how the underlying situation was structured. (See Exhibit 11-1.)

In negotiations, our outcomes depend on the actions of others. The situation that results when people engage in behaviors that maximize self-interest but lead to collective disaster, such as a bidding war, greenhouse gases, or negative campaigning, is a **social dilemma**. In this chapter, we discuss two kinds of social dilemmas: two-person dilemmas and multiperson dilemmas. The two-person dilemma is the **prisoner's dilemma**; the multiperson dilemma is a social dilemma. They are dilemmas because the choices available to negotiators are risky. Some choices risk exploitation; others risk antagonizing others. We discuss how dilemmas may be effectively handled by individuals, teams, and even countries.

EXHIBIT 11-1

Two Major Types of Negotiation Situations

Cooperative Negotiations	Noncooperative Negotiations
• Contract is explicit.	• Contract is tacit.
• Mutual understanding (people know what they are getting before they agree).	• People often do not know what others will do.
• People negotiate via proposals and counterproposals and can use words to explain and justify their offers.	• People negotiate through their behaviors and actions (rather than their promises of what they will do).
• People usually come to the table voluntarily.	• People are often pulled into negotiations without wanting to be involved.

---

[2] Schelling, T. (1960). *The strategy of conflict.* Cambridge, MA: Harvard University Press.
[3] Nash, J. (1951). Non-cooperative games. *Annals of Mathematics, 54*(2), 286–295; Nash, J. (1953). Two-person cooperative games. *Econometrica, 21,* 129–140.

BUSINESS AS A SOCIAL DILEMMA

Business competitors routinely face social dilemmas. Some industries are particularly vicious, such as telecommunications companies. An example of the cutthroat nature of industry rivals took place in China when software giant Tencent shut down its messaging service QQ on computers installed with the antivirus software 360 Safe, created by rival Qihoo 360. A battle between the companies began months earlier when Qihoo 360 accused Tencent's QQ software of leaking users' private information and offered its own service to prevent such leaks. Tencent publically accused Qihoo of slander and bad business practices. As a result, more than 78% of Chinese Internet users felt the companies had stopped looking out for the needs of its clients. Eventually, the rivals realized that they needed one another and forged an alliance by restarting the messaging service.[4]

In contrast, other industries have attempted to find points of cooperation that can align their competitive goals. For example, in 2010 Apple and Verizon Wireless teamed up to make the iPhone available on Verizon networks. For three years iPhone had only been available on AT&T networks. The partnership was a direct attempt to capture the market of the more popular Google Android software, which accounted for 32% of the smartphone market in the United States in late 2010 compared to 25% for the iPhone software package.[5] Similarly, two national dairy companies using separate advertising campaigns agreed to create a single marketing plan to increase milk sales in the United States. Dairy Management, Inc., which used the "Got Milk?" campaign, and the National Fluid Milk Processor Promotion Board, which used a popular collection of advertisements in which celebrities wear milk mustaches, coordinated campaigns to increase total fluid milk sales by 4% by the year 2000.[6] Willingness to engage in generic advertising (e.g., advertising the local mall instead of one's own store) is a common form of interfirm cooperation. Simulations reveal that companies confronting a declining trend contribute significantly more dollars to generic advertising; moreover, it positively influences their expectations that others will contribute as well.[7]

THE PRISONER'S DILEMMA

Thelma and Louise are common criminals who have just been arrested on suspicion of burglary. Law enforcement has enough evidence to convict each suspect of a minor breaking and entering crime but insufficient evidence to convict the suspects on a more serious felony charge of burglary and assault. The district attorney immediately separates Thelma and Louise after their arrest. Each suspect is approached separately and presented with two options: confess to the serious burglary charge or remain silent (do not confess). The consequences of each course of action depend on what the other decides to do. Thelma and Louise must make their choices independently. They cannot communicate prior to making an independent, irrevocable decision. The decision each suspect faces is illustrated in Exhibit 11-2, which indicates Thelma and Louise will go to prison for as many as 15 years, depending upon what the other partner chooses. Imagine you are advising Thelma. Your concern is not morality or ethics, you are simply trying to get her a shorter sentence. What do you advise her to do?

---

[4] Xinhua News Agency. (2010, November 4). QQ shut down as fight with Qihoo 360 escalates. *China Daily.* Chinadaily.com
[5] Helft, M. (2010, October 9). Apple plans to offer iPhone on Verizon. *New York Times*, B1.
[6] Elliott, S. (1998, February 6). Milk promoters agree to cooperate. *New York Times,* D17.
[7] Krishnamurthy, S., Bottom, W. P., & Rao, A. G. (2003). Adaptive aspirations and contributions to a public good: Generic advertising as a response to decline. *Organizational Behavior and Human Decision Processes, 92,* 22–33.

EXHIBIT 11-2

Consequences of Thelma and Louise's Behaviors

Thelma

		Do not confess (remain silent)	Confess
Louise	Do not confess (remain silent)	**A** Thelma: 1 yr Louise: 1 yr	**B** Thelma: 0 yrs Louise: 15 yrs
	Confess	**C** Thelma: 15 yrs Louise: 0 yrs	**D** Thelma: 10 yrs Louise: 10 yrs

Note: Entries represent prison term length.

Ideally, it is desirable for both suspects to not confess, thereby minimizing the prison sentence to 1 year for each (cell A). This option is risky, however. If one confesses, then the suspect who does not confess goes to prison for the maximum sentence of 15 years—an extremely undesirable outcome (cell B or C). In fact, the most desirable situation from the standpoint of each suspect is to confess, but have the other person not confess. Then, the confessing suspect would be released, and his or her partner goes to prison for the maximum sentence of 15 years. Given these contingencies, what should Thelma do? Before reading further, stop and think about what is her best course of action.

When each person pursues the course of action that is most rational from her point of view, the result is mutual disaster. That is, both Thelma and Louise go to prison for 10 years (cell D). The paradox of the prisoner's dilemma is that the pursuit of individual self-interest leads to collective disaster. It is easy for Thelma and Louise to see that each could do better by cooperating, but it is not easy to know how to implement this behavior.

Cooperation and Defection as Unilateral Choices

We will use the prisoner's dilemma situation depicted in Exhibit 11-2 to analyze decision making. We will refer to the choices that players make in this game as **cooperation** and **defection**, depending upon whether they remain silent or confess. The language of cooperation and defection allows the prisoner's dilemma game structure to be meaningfully extended to other situations that do not involve criminals but nevertheless have the same underlying structure, such as whether an airline company should bid for a smaller company, whether a cola company or politician should engage in negative advertising or whether countries should agree to reduce emissions. However, prisoner's dilemmas don't just describe criminals and business strategy. In fact, the prisoner's dilemma was initially developed to analyze the 'arms race' between the United States and the Soviet Union. Each country sought to develop and deploy arsenals of nuclear arms they thought necessary for military defense. Studies of nuclear proliferation are crucial for policy making and debate.[8]

Rational Analysis

We use the logic of game theory to provide a rational analysis of this situation. We consider three different cases: (a) one-shot, non-repeated play situations (as in the case of Thelma and Louise), (b) the case in which the decision is repeated for a finite number of times, and (c) the case in which the decision is repeated for a potentially infinite number of trials or the end is unknown.

CASE 1: ONE-SHOT DECISION   Game theoretic analysis relies on the principle of **dominance detection**: A dominant strategy results in a better outcome for player 1 no matter what player 2 does.

To illustrate the dominance principle, suppose you are Thelma and your partner in crime is Louise. First, consider what happens if Louise remains silent (does not confess). Thus, we are focusing on the first row in Exhibit 11-2. Remaining silent puts you in cell A: You both get 1 year. This outcome is not too bad, but maybe you could do better. Suppose you decide to confess. In cell B, you get 0 years and Louise gets 15 years. Certainly no prison sentence is much better than a 1-year sentence, so confession seems like the optimal choice for you to make, given that Louise does not confess.

Now, what happens if Louise confesses? In this situation, we focus on row 2. Remaining silent puts you in cell C: You get 15 years, and Louise gets 0 years, which is not very good for you. Now, suppose you confess. In cell D, you both get 10 years. Neither outcome is attractive, but 10 years is certainly better than 15 years. Given that Louise confesses, what do you want to do? The choice amounts to whether you want to go to prison for 15 years or 10 years. Again, confession is the optimal choice for you.

No matter what Louise does (remains silent or confesses), it is better for Thelma to confess. Confession is a dominant strategy because under all possible states of the world, players should choose to confess. We know that Louise is smart and has looked at the situation the same way as Thelma and has reached the same conclusion. In this sense, mutual defection is an **equilibrium outcome**, meaning no player can unilaterally (single-handedly) improve her outcome by making a different choice.

Thus, both Thelma and Louise are led through rational analysis to confess, and they collectively end up in cell D, where they both go to prison for a long time. This outcome is both unfortunate and avoidable. Certainly, both suspects would prefer to be in cell A than in cell D. Is escape possible from the tragic outcomes produced by the prisoner's dilemma? It would seem that players might extricate themselves from the dilemma if they could communicate, but we already noted that communication is outside the bounds of the noncooperative game. Further, because the game structure is noncooperative, any deals that players might make with

---

[8] Montgomery, A. H., & Sagan, S. D. (2009). The perils of predicting proliferation. *Journal of Conflict Resolution, 53*(2), 302–328.

one another are nonbinding. For example, antitrust legislation prohibits companies from price fixing, which means any communication that occurs between companies regarding price fixing is unenforceable, not to mention punishable by law.

What other mechanism might allow parties in such situations to avoid the disastrous outcome produced by mutual defection? One possibility is to have both parties make those decisions over time, thereby allowing them to influence one another. Suppose the parties did not make a single choice but instead made a series of choices and received feedback about the other player's choice after each of their decisions. Perhaps repeated interaction with the other person would provide a mechanism for parties to coordinate their actions. If the game is to be played more than once, players might learn that cooperation may be elicited in subsequent periods by cooperating on the first round. We consider that situation next.

CASE 2: REPEATED INTERACTION OVER A FIXED NUMBER OF TRIALS   Instead of making a single choice and living with the consequence, suppose Thelma and Louise were to play the game in Exhibit 11-2 a total of 5 times. It might seem strange to think about criminals repeating a particular interaction, so it may be useful to think about two political candidates deciding whether to engage in negative campaigning (hereafter referred to as "campaigning"). Term limits in their state dictate that they can run and hold office for a maximum of 5 years. An election is held every year. During any election period, each candidate makes an independent choice (to campaign or not), then learns of the other's choice (to campaign or not). After the election, the candidates consider the same alternatives once again and make an independent choice; this interaction continues for five separate elections.

We use the concept of dominance as applied previously to analyze this situation, but we need another tool that tells us how to analyze the repeated nature of the game. **Backward induction** is the mechanism by which a person decides what to do in a repeated game situation by looking backward from the last stage of the game.

We begin by examining what players should do in election 5 (the last election). If the candidates are making their choices in the last election, the game is identical to that analyzed in case 1, the one-shot case. Thus, the logic of dominant strategies applies, and we are left with the conclusion that each candidate will choose to campaign. Now, given that we know each candidate will campaign in the last election, what will they do in the fourth election?

From a candidate's standpoint, the only reason to cooperate (or to not campaign) is to influence the behavior of the other party in the subsequent election. In other words, a player might signal a willingness to cooperate by making a cooperative choice in the preceding period. We have already determined that it is a foregone conclusion that both candidates will defect (choose to campaign) in the last election, so it is futile to choose the cooperative (no campaigning) strategy in the fourth election. So, what about the third election? Given that candidates will not cooperate in the last election, nor in the second-to-last election, they would find little point to cooperating in the third-to-last election for the same reason that cooperation was deemed to be ineffective in the second-to-last election. As it turns out, this logic can be applied to every election in such a backward fashion. Moreover, this reasoning is true in any situation with a finite number of elections. This realization leaves us with the conclusion that defection remains the dominant strategy even in the repeated trial case.[9]

---

[9] Formally, if the prisoner's dilemma is repeated finitely, all Nash equilibria of the resulting sequential games have the property that the noncooperative outcome, which is Pareto-inferior, occurs in each period, no matter how large the number of periods.

This conclusion is disappointing. It suggests that cooperation is not possible even in long-term relationships. However, it runs counter to intuition, observation, and logic. We must consider another case, arguably more realistic of the situations we want to study in most circumstances, in which repeated interaction continues for an infinite or indefinite amount of time.

CASE 3: REPEATED INTERACTION FOR AN INFINITE OR INDEFINITE AMOUNT OF TIME   In the case in which parties interact with one another for an infinite or indefinite amount of time, the logic of backward induction breaks down. Because no identifiable endpoint from which to reason backward exists, we are left with forward-thinking logic.

If we anticipate playing a prisoner's dilemma game with another person for an infinitely long or uncertain length of time, we reason that we might influence their behavior with our own behavior. We may signal a desire to cooperate on a mutual basis by making a cooperative choice in an early trial. Similarly, we can reward and punish their behavior through our actions.

Under such conditions, the game theoretic analysis indicates that cooperation in the first period is the optimal choice.[10] Should our strategy be to cooperate no matter what? No! If a person adopted cooperation as a general strategy, it would surely lead to exploitation. So, what strategy would be optimal to adopt? Before reading further, stop and indicate what strategy you think is best.

THE TOURNAMENT OF CHAMPIONS   In 1981, Robert Axelrod, a leading game theorist invited members of the scientific community to submit a strategy to play in a prisoner's dilemma tournament. To play in the tournament, a person had to submit a strategy (a plan that instructed a decision maker of what to do in every trial under all possible conditions) in the form of a computer program written in FORTRAN code. Axelrod explained that each strategy would play all other strategies across 200 trials of a prisoner's dilemma game. He further explained that the strategies would be evaluated in terms of the maximization of gains across all opponents. Hundreds of strategies were submitted by eminent scholars from around the world.

THE WINNER IS A LOSER   The winning strategy of the tournament was the simplest strategy submitted. The FORTRAN code was only four lines long. The strategy was called **tit-for-tat** and was submitted by Anatol Rapoport. Tit-for-tat accumulated the greatest number of points across all trials with all of its opponents. The basic principle for tit-for-tat is simple: Tit-for-tat always cooperates on the first trial, and on subsequent trials it does whatever its opponent did on the previous trial. For example, suppose tit-for-tat played against someone who cooperated on the first trial, defected on the second trial, and then cooperated on the third trial. Tit-for-tat would cooperate on the first trial and the second trial, defect on the third trial, and cooperate on the fourth trial.

Tit-for-tat never beat any of the strategies it played against. Because it cooperates on the first trial, it can never do better than its opponent. The most tit-for-tat can do is earn as much as its opponent. If it never wins, how can tit-for-tat be so successful in maximizing its overall gains? The answer is that it induces cooperation from its opponents.

Psychological Analysis of Why Tit-for-Tat Is Effective

NOT ENVIOUS   One reason why tit-for-tat is effective is that it is not an envious strategy. Tit-for-tat never aims to beat its opponent. Tit-for-tat can never earn more than any strategy

---

[10] Kreps, D. M., Milgrom, P., Roberts, J., & Wilson, R. (1982). Rational cooperation in the finitely repeated prisoner's dilemma. *Journal of Economic Theory, 27,* 245–252.

it plays against. Rather, the tit-for-tat strategy seeks to maximize its own gain in the long run. Unfortunately, people are often preoccupied with how much the other party is earning. And fairness becomes a more important concern than self-interest when negotiation involves negative payoff than when it involves positive payoffs.[11]

NICE   Tit-for-tat always begins the interaction by cooperating. Furthermore, because it is never the first to defect, tit-for-tat is a nice strategy. This feature is important because it is difficult for people to recover from initial defections. Competitive, aggressive behavior often sours a relationship. Moreover, aggression often begets aggression. The tit-for-tat strategy neatly avoids the costly mutual escalation trap.

TOUGH   A strategy of solid cooperation would be easily exploitable by an opponent. Tit-for-tat can be provoked: It will defect if the opponent invites competition. By reciprocating defection, tit-for-tat conveys the message that it cannot be taken advantage of. Indeed, tit-for-tat players effectively move competitive players away from them, thus minimizing noncooperative inter-action.[12] Analyses of strategic rivalries from 1816–1999 revealed that a state has an incentive to initiate and escalate conflicts to maintain a reputation of 'resolute behavior' important for general and immediate deterrence.[13]

FORGIVING   Tit-for-tat is a forgiving strategy in the sense that it reciprocates cooperation, an-other important feature. It is often difficult for people in conflict to recover from defection and end an escalating spiral of aggression. Tit-for-tat's eye-for-an-eye strategy ensures its response to aggression will never be greater than what it received.

SIMPLE   Another reason why tit-for-tat is so effective is that it is simple. People can quickly figure out what to expect from a player who follows it. When people are uncertain or unclear about what to expect, they are more likely to engage in defensive behavior. When uncertainty is high, people often assume the worst about another person.

In summary, tit-for-tat is an extremely stable strategy. Negotiators who follow it often induce their opponents to cooperate. However, few who play prisoner's dilemma games actually follow tit-for-tat. For example, in our analysis of more than 600 executives playing the prison-er's dilemma game, the defection rate is nearly 40%, and average profits are only one-tenth of the possible maximum! But tit-for-tat is not uniquely stable; other strategies are stable as well. For example, solid defection is a stable strategy. Two players who defect on every trial have little reason to do anything else. Once someone has defected, it is difficult to renew cooperation.

RECOVERING FROM DEFECTION   The beer industry is highly competitive, with different companies trying to capture market share by using negative campaigning. The computer industry is also highly competitive, with companies trying to capture market share using the same tactic of negative campaigning. In 2010, Apple released a series of commercials for its Macintosh computer where the Mac was portrayed as a hip, young man while PC's were represented by a socially inept, blandly-dressed middle aged man.[14] Similarly, rivals Coke and Pepsi have spent

---

[11] Leliveld, M. C., Van Dijk, E., & Van Beest, I. (2008). Initial ownership in bargaining: Introducing the giving, splitting, and taking ultimatum bargaining game. *Personality and Social Psychology Bulletin, 34*(9), 1214–1225.

[12] Van Lange, P. A. M., & Visser, K. (1999). Locomotion in social dilemmas: How people adapt to cooperative, tit-for-tat and non-cooperative partners. *Journal of Personality and Social Psychology, 77*(4), 762–773.

[13] Clare, J. & Danilovic, V. (2010). Multiple audiences and reputation building in international conflicts. *The Journal of Conflict Resolution, 54*(6), 860–882.

[14] YouTube. (2011, January 19). Mac vs PC. Youtube.com

decades as the world's Number 1 and 2 soft drink makers, and an equal amount of time tweaking one another in advertising. One Pepsi Max ad portrayed delivery drivers from the rival soft drink makers forming a short-lived friendship in a diner over the song *"Why Can't We Be Friends"* by the band War. The Pepsi Max driver and the Coke Zero driver sample each other's drinks and the Coca-Cola driver prefers the Pepsi drink. When the Pepsi driver snaps a picture of the Coke driver enjoying the drink, a cartoonish fight erupts.[15] Hundreds of thousands of dollars are spent on negative advertising—a form of defection. How can an escalating spiral of defection be brought to an end? Consider the following strategies:

Make Situational Attributions.   We often blame conflict escalation on others' ill will and evil intentions. We fail to realize that we might have done the same thing as our competitor had we been in his or her shoes. Why? We punctuate events differently than do our opponents. We see our behavior as a defensive response to the other. In contrast, we view the other as engaging in unprovoked acts of aggression. The solution is to see the other side's behavior as a response to our own actions. In the preceding situation, your competitor's negative ad campaign may be a payback for your campaign a year ago.

One Step at a Time.   Once destroyed, trust takes time to rebuild. Rebuild trust incrementally by taking a series of small steps that effectively "reward" the other party if they behave cooperatively. For example, the GRIT (graduated reduction in tension relations) strategy (reviewed in Chapter 9) calls for parties in conflict to offer small concessions.[16] This approach reduces the risk for the party making the concession.

Getting Even and Catching Up.   As we saw in Chapter 3, people are especially concerned with fairness. One way of rebuilding trust is to let the other party "get even" and catch up. Repairing a damaged relationship may depend on repentance on the part of the injurer and forgiveness on the part of the injured.[17] Even more surprising is that small amends are as effective as large amends in generating future cooperation.

Make Your Decisions at the Same Time.   Imagine you are playing a prisoner's dilemma game like that described in the Thelma and Louise case. You are told about the contingencies and payoffs in the game and then asked to make a choice. The twist in the situation is that you are either told that your opponent (a) has already made her choice earlier that day, (b) will make her choice later that day, or (c) will make her choice at the same time as you. In all cases, you will not know the other person's choice before making your own. When faced with this situation, people are more likely to cooperate when their opponent's decision is temporally contiguous with their own decision (i.e., when the opponent makes her decision at the same time).[18] Temporal contiguity fosters a causal illusion: the idea that our behavior at a given time can influence the behavior of others. This logical impossibility is not permissible in the time-delayed decisions.

In the prisoner's dilemma game, people make choices simultaneously; therefore, one's choice cannot influence the choice the other person makes on a given trial, only in subsequent trials. That is, when Thelma makes her decision to confess or not, it does not influence Louise, unless she is telepathic. Nevertheless, people act as if their behavior influences the behavior of others, even though it logically cannot.

---

[15] Fredrix, E. (2010, July 20). Cola wars return: Pepsi MAX vs Coke Zero. *The Christian Science Monitor.* CSmonitor.com
[16] Osgood, C. E. (1979). GRIT 1 (vol. 8, no. 1, 0553–4283). Dundas, Ontario: Peace Research Reviews.
[17] Bottom, W., Daniels, S., Gibson, K. S., & Murnighan, J. K. (2002). When talk is not cheap: Substantive penance and expressions of intent in rebuilding cooperation. *Organization Science, 13*(5), 497–513.
[18] Morris, M. W., Sim, D. L. H., & Girrotto, V. (1995). Time of decision, ethical obligation, and causal illusion: Temporal cues and social heuristics in the prisoner's dilemma. In R. M. Kramer & D. M. Messick (Eds.), *Negotiation as a social process* (pp. 209–239). Thousand Oaks, CA: Sage.

In an intriguing analysis of this perception, Douglas Hofstadter wrote a letter, published in *Scientific American,* to 20 friends (see Exhibit 11-3). Hofstadter raised the question of whether one person's action in this situation can be taken as an indication of what all people will do. He concluded that if players are indeed rational, they will either all choose to defect or all choose to cooperate. Given that all players are going to submit the same answer, which choice

EXHIBIT 11-3

Letter from Douglas Hofstadter to 20 Friends in *Scientific American*

Dear_____ :

I am sending this letter by special delivery to 20 of you (namely, various friends of mine around the country). I am proposing to all of you a one-round Prisoner's Dilemma game, the payoffs to be monetary (provided by *Scientific American*). It is very simple. Here is how it goes.

Each of you is to give me a single letter: *C* or *D*, standing for "cooperate" or "defect." This will be used as your move in a Prisoner's Dilemma with *each* of the 19 other players.

Thus, if everyone sends in *C*, everyone will get $57, whereas if everyone sends in *D*, everyone will get $19. You can't lose! And, of course, anyone who sends in *D* will get at least as much as everyone else. If, for example, 11 people send in *C* and nine send in *D*, then the 11 *C*-ers will get $3 apiece from each of the other *C*-ers (making $30) and will get nothing from the *D*-ers. Therefore, *C*-ers will get $30 each. The *D*-ers in contrast, will pick up $5 apiece from each of the *C*-ers (making $55) and will get $1 from each of the other *D*-ers (making $8), for a grand total of $63. No matter what the distribution is, *D*-ers always do better than *C*-ers. Of course, the more *C*-ers there are, the better *everyone* will do!

By the way, I should make it clear that in making your choice you should not aim to be the *winner* but simply to get as much *money* for yourself as possible. Thus, you should be happier to get $30 (say, as a result of saying *C* along with 10 others, even though the nine *D*-sayers get more than you) than to get $19 (by saying *D* along with everyone else, so that nobody "beats" you). Furthermore, you are not supposed to think that at some later time you will meet with and be able to share the goods with your co-participants. You are not aiming at maximizing the total number of dollars *Scientific American* shells out, only at maximizing the number of dollars that come to *you*!

Of course, your hope is to be the *unique* defector, thereby really cleaning up: with 19 *C*-ers, you will get $95 and they will each get 18 times $3, namely $54. But why am I doing the multiplication or any of this figuring for you? You are very bright. So are the others. All about equally bright, I would say. Therefore, all you need to do is tell me your choice. I want all answers by telephone (call collect, please) *the day you receive this letter.*

It is to be understood (it *almost* goes without saying, but not quite) that you are not to try to consult with others who you guess have been asked to participate. In fact, please consult with no one at all. The purpose is to see what people will do on their own, in isolation. Finally, I would appreciate a short statement to go along with your choice, telling me *why* you made this particular one.

Yours,
Doug H.

Source: Hofstadter, D. R. (1983). Metamagical themes, *Scientific American, 248*(6), 14–28.

would be more logical? It would seem that cooperation is best (each player gets $57 when they all cooperate and only $19 when they all defect). At this point, the logic seems like magical thinking: A person's choice at a given time influences the behavior of others at the same time. Another example: People explain that they have decided to vote in an election so that others will, too. Of course, it is impossible that one person's voting behavior could affect others in a given election, but people act as if it does. Hofstadter argues that decision makers wrestling with such choices must give others credit for seeing the logic they themselves have seen. Thus, we need to believe that others are rational (like ourselves) and that they believe that everyone is rational. Hofstadter calls this rationality **superrationality**. For this reason, choosing to defect undermines the very reasons for choosing it. In Hofstadter's game, 14 people defected, and 6 cooperated. The defectors received $43; the cooperators received $15. Robert Axelrod was one of the participants who defected, and he remarked that a one-shot game offers no reason to cooperate.

SOCIAL DILEMMAS

Sometimes, managers find themselves involved in a prisoner's dilemma that contains several people. In these types of situations, negotiators find themselves choosing between cooperative strategies and self-interested strategies. The multiperson prisoner's dilemma is known as a social dilemma. (See Exhibits 11-4 and 11-5 for volunteer dilemmas and ultimatum dilemmas.) In general, people behave more competitively (in a self-interested fashion) in social dilemmas as compared to prisoner's dilemmas. Why do they act this way?

EXHIBIT 11-4

Volunteer Dilemma

The volunteer dilemma is a situation in which at least one person in a group must sacrifice his or her own interests to better the group. An example is a group of friends who want to go out for an evening of drinking and celebration. The problem is that not all can drink if one person must safely drive everyone home. A "designated" driver is a volunteer for the group. Most organized entities would not function if no one volunteered. The act of volunteering strengthens group ties.

Source: Based on Murnighan, J. K., Kim, J. W., & Metzger, A. R. (1993). The volunteer dilemma. *Administrative Science Quarterly, 38*(4), 515–538.

EXHIBIT 11-5

Ultimatum Dilemma

In an ultimatum bargaining situation, one person makes a final offer—an ultimatum—to another person. If the other person accepts the offer, then the first player receives the demand that he or she made, and the other player agrees to accept what was offered to him or her. If the offer is refused, then no settlement is reached (i.e., an impasse occurs) and negotiators receive their respective reservation points.

(continued)

How should we negotiate in ultimatum situations? What kind of a final offer should we make to another person? When the tables are turned, on what basis should we accept or refuse a final offer someone makes to us?

Suppose someone with a $100 bill in hand approaches you and the person sitting on the bus beside you. This person explains that the $100 is yours to share with the other person if you can propose a split to which the other person will agree. The only hitch is that the division you propose is a once-and-for-all decision: You cannot discuss it with the other person, and you have to propose a take-it-or-leave-it split. If the other person accepts your proposal, the $100 will be allocated accordingly. If the other person rejects your proposal, no one gets any money, and you do not have the opportunity to propose another offer. Faced with this situation, what should you do? (Before reading further, indicate what you would do and why.)

It is useful for us to solve this problem using the principles of decision theory and then see whether the solution squares with our intuition. Once again, we use the concept of backward induction, working backward from the last period of the game. The last decision in this game is an ultimatum. In this game, player 2 (the person beside you on the bus) must decide whether to accept the proposal offered by you or reject the offer and receive nothing. From a rational standpoint, player 2 should accept any positive offer you make to him or her because, after all, something (even 1 cent) is better than nothing.

Now we can examine the next-to-last decision in the game and ask what proposal player 1 (you) should make. Because you know that player 2 should accept any positive offer greater than $0, the game theoretic solution is for you to offer $0.01 to player 2 and demand $99.99 for yourself. This proposal is a **subgame perfect equilibrium** because it is rational within each period of the game.[A] In other words, even if the game had additional periods to be played in the future, your offer of $99.99 (to you) and $0.01 to the other person would still be rational at this point.

Contrary to game theoretic predictions, most people do not behave in this way. That is, most player 1's propose amounts substantially greater than $0.01 for player 2, often around the midpoint, or $50. Further, player 2's often reject offers that are not 50–50 splits.[B] Thus, some player 2's choose to have $0 rather than $1 or $2—or even $49. Player 1s act nonrationally, and so do player 2's. This response seems completely counter to one's interests, but as we saw in Chapter 2, people are often more concerned with how their outcomes compare to others than with the absolute value of their outcomes.[C]

Croson also found that acceptance rates are driven by how much information the responder has about the size of the total pie.[D] When the responder does not know the size of the pie and receives a dollar offer, she is much more likely to reject it. Framing can matter, too. Ultimatum games can be framed as "taking" or "giving." Allocations to recipients are highest when the game is framed as "taking"; and allocations are lowest when the game is framed as "giving."[E] Deadlines can matter. Responders usually set deadlines that are too short; a better strategy in the case of uncertainty about the other party's deadline is to set a longer deadline.[F] Feelings can mater. Compared with proposers who are not dependent on their feelings, those who are dependent on their feelings make less generous offers.[G]

[A] Selten, R. (1975). Re-examination of the perfectness concept for equilibrium points in extensive games. *International Journal of Game Theory, 4,* 25–55.

[B] Pillutla, M. M., & Murnighan, J. K. (1995). Being fair or appearing fair: Strategic behavior in ultimatum bargaining. *Academy of Management Journal, 38*(5), 1408–1426.

[C] See Loewenstein, G. F., Thompson, L., & Bazerman, M. H. (1989). Social utility and decision making in interpersonal contexts. *Journal of Personality and Social Psychology, 57*(3), 426–441; Messick, D. M., & Sentis, K. P. (1979). Fairness and preference. *Journal of Experimental Social Psychology, 15*(4), 418–434.

[D] Croson, R. (1996). Information in ultimatum games: An experimental study. *Journal of Economic Behavior & Organization, 30,* 197–212.

[E] Leliveld, Van Dijk, & Beest, "Initial ownership in bargaining."

[F] Tang, W., Bearden, J. N., Tsetlin, I. (2009). Ultimatum deadlines. *Management Science, 55*(8) 1423–1437.

[G] Stephen, A. T., & Pham, M. T. (2008). On feelings as a heuristic for making offers in ultimatum negotiations. *Psychological Science, 19*(10), 1051–1058.

First, the prisoner's dilemma involves two parties; the social dilemma involves *several people*. People behave more competitively in groups than in two-person situations.[19]

Second, the *costs of defection are spread out*, rather than concentrated upon one person. Simply stated, when one person makes a self-interested choice and others choose to cooperate, everyone but the defector absorbs some (but not all) of the cost. Thus, the defecting person can rationalize that everyone is suffering a little bit, rather than a lot. This mindset may lead people to be more inclined to serve their own interests.

Third, social dilemmas are *riskier* than prisoner's dilemmas. In the two-person dilemma, a certain minimal payoff to parties can be anticipated in advance. However, this outcome is not true in a social dilemma. The worst-case scenario is when the negotiator chooses to cooperate and everyone else defects. The costs of this situation are great. Greater risk and more uncertainty lead people to behave in a more self-interested, competitive fashion.

Fourth, social dilemmas *provide anonymity* that prisoner's dilemmas do not. Whereas anonymity is impossible in two-party situations, in social dilemmas people can "hide among the group." When people feel less accountable, they are more inclined to behave in a self-interested, competitive fashion.

Finally, people in social dilemmas *have less control* over the situation. In a classic, two-party prisoner's dilemma, people can directly shape and modify the behavior of the other person. Specifically, by choosing defection, one person may punish the other; by choosing cooperation, he or she can reward the other. This is the beauty of the tit-for-tat strategy. However, in a social dilemma, if someone defects, one person cannot necessarily punish the other on the next round because others will also be affected, and as we have seen, the costs of defection are spread out. For example, consider a classic social dilemma as illustrated by the Organization of the Petroleum Exporting Countries (OPEC). OPEC is a group of mostly Middle Eastern nations that have all agreed to reduce their production of oil. Lowering the volume of available oil creates greater demand, and oil prices go up. Obviously, each member of OPEC has an incentive to increase its production of oil, thus creating greater profit for itself. However, if all members violate the OPEC agreement and increase the production of oil, demand decreases, and so does the price of oil, thus driving down profits for the entire group.

The Tragedy of the Commons

Imagine you are a farmer. You own several cows and share a grazing pasture known as a "commons" with other farmers. One hundred farmers share the pasture. Each farmer is allowed to have one cow graze. Because the commons is not policed, it is tempting for you to add one more cow. By adding another cow, you can double your utility, and no one will really suffer. If everyone does the same thing, however, the commons will be overrun and the grazing area depleted. The cumulative result will be disastrous. What should you do in this situation if you want to keep your family secure?

The analysis of the **tragedy of the commons**[20] may be applied to many real-world problems, such as pollution, use of natural resources, and overpopulation. In these situations, people are tempted to maximize their own gain, reasoning that their pollution, failure to

[19] Insko, C. A., Schopler, J., Graetz, K. A., Drigotas, S. M., Currey, D. P., Smith, S. L., Brazil, D., & Bornstein, G. (1994). Interindividual-intergroup discontinuity in the prisoner's dilemma game. *Journal of Conflict Resolution, 38*(1), 87–116.
[20] Hardin, G. (1968). The tragedy of the commons. *Science, 162,* 1243–1248.

vote, and using polystyrene cups will not have a measurable impact on others. However, if everyone engages in this behavior, the collective outcome is disastrous: Air will be unbreathable, not enough votes will support a particular candidate in an election, and landfills will be overrun. Thus, in the social dilemma the rational pursuit of self-interest produces collective disaster.

In the social dilemma situation, each person makes behavioral choices similar to those in the prisoner's dilemma: to benefit oneself or the group. As in the prisoner's dilemma, the choices are referred to as "cooperation" and "defection." The defecting choice always results in better personal outcomes, at least in the immediate future, but universal defection results in poorer outcomes for everyone than with universal cooperation.

A hallmark characteristic of social dilemmas is that the rational pursuit of self-interest is detrimental to collective welfare. This factor has serious and potentially disastrous implications. (In this sense, social dilemmas contradict the principle of hedonism and laissez-faire economics.) Unless some limits are placed on the pursuit of personal goals, the entire society may suffer.

Types of Social Dilemmas

The two major forms of the social dilemma are **resource conservation dilemmas** (also known as **collective traps**) and **public goods dilemmas** (also known as **collective fences**).[21] In the resource conservation dilemma, people take or harvest resources from a common pool (like the farmers in the commons). Examples of the detrimental effects of individual interest include: pollution, harvesting (of fossil fuels), burning of fossil fuels, water shortages, and negative advertising (see Exhibits 11-6a and 11-6b for actual ads). The defecting choice occurs when people consume too much. For groups to sustain themselves, the rate of consumption cannot exceed the rate of replenishment of resources.

In public goods dilemmas, people contribute or give resources to a common pool or community. Examples include donating to public radio and television, paying taxes, voting,

EXHIBIT 11-6a

Example of Negative (Competitive) Advertising

Since the 1970s, in the trend toward "comparative advertising," companies have compared their product with competitors' products and pointed out the advantages of their own product and the disadvantages of the competitors' products. Hardly any industry has managed to avoid comparative advertising. Advertisers have battled over milk quality, fish oil, beer taste, electric shavers, cola, coffee, magazines, cars, telephone service, banking, credit cards, and peanut butter. The ads attack the

---

[21] Messick, D. M., & Brewer, M. (1983). Solving social dilemmas: A review. In L. Wheeler & P. Shaver (Eds.), *Review of personality and social psychology: Vol. 4* (pp. 11–44). Beverly Hills, CA: Sage.

products and services of other companies. What is the effect of the attack ad? For the consumer, the attack ad keeps prices down and quality high. However, it can also lead to consumer resentment toward the industry. The effect is much more serious for the advertisers, who can effectively run each other out of business.

YOU WON'T FIND THE FASTEST GROWING DOCUMENT OUTPUT COMPANY UNDER X.

(You won't find it under C or M for that matter, either.)

Here's an interesting fact. The name of the fastest growing major document output company isn't Xerox, Canon, or Mita. It's Savin. That's right, Savin.

After all, Savin not only has the award-winning, multi-functional digital imaging systems today's networked offices require, we're also committed to becoming the fastest, most responsive name in the business. With smart, energetic, highly-trained Savin professionals willing to do whatever it takes to give you the satisfaction and service you deserve.

To find out more about Savin's full line of black & white and full-color digital imaging solutions, as well as our unshakable commitment to service, contact us at **1-800-234-1900** or www.savin.com. Or look in your card file under S.

WE'VE GOT WHAT IT TAKES TO WIN YOU OVER™
SAVIN CORPORATION, 333 LUDLOW ST., STAMFORD, CT 06904

©1999 Savin Corporation

Source: Courtesy of The Savin Corporation, Stamford, Connecticut.

EXHIBIT 11-6b

Example of Explicit Comparative Advertising

Business Class Legroom	
Delta BusinessElite	36.5"
Continental	31"
British Airways	24"
Lufthansa	23"
American Airlines	22"

Business Class Recline	
Delta BusinessElite	160°
Continental	152°
British Airways	140°
Lufthansa	135°
American Airlines	132°

Nonstop European Destinations	
Delta BusinessElite	23
Continental	17
American Airlines	12
British Airways	3
Lufthansa	3

Nonstop destinations from the U.S.

Concierge Service At Every Gateway	
Delta BusinessElite	Yes
Continental	No
British Airways	No
Lufthansa	No
American Airlines	No

Looks great on paper.
Feels even better in person.

Presenting Delta BusinessElite.™

There are a lot of reasons to fly Delta's new BusinessElite,

but don't take our word for it. Experience it for yourself.

With more personal space than other leading airlines' business

classes, and our convenient BusinessElite Concierge service at all

32 intercontinental destinations, we think you'll agree. BusinessElite

to Europe, Japan, India and Brazil simply outclasses business class.

BUSINESS*elite*
▲ **Delta Air Lines**

For reservations, visit us at www.bizelite.com or call Delta Air Lines at 1-800-241-4141. Or see your Travel Agent today.

Personal space is defined as the sum of legroom and recline. Legroom based on measurements taken from the foremost point of the bottom seat cushion to the back of the seat in front of it using non-bulkhead seats on a widebody aircraft of Continental (DC10-30), British Airways (747-200), Lufthansa (A340-300) and American Airlines (767-300). ©1999 Delta Air Lines, Inc.

Source: Courtesy of Delta Air Lines, Atlanta, Georgia.

doing committee work, and joining unions. The defecting choice is to not contribute. Those who fail to contribute are known as **defectors** or **free riders**. Those who pay while others free ride are affectionately known as **suckers**.

Think of resource conservation dilemmas as situations in which people *take* things; and think of public goods dilemmas as situations in which people must *contribute*. Moreover, both kinds of dilemmas—taking too much and failing to contribute—can occur within an organization or between different organizations (see Exhibit 11-7 for examples).

How to Build Cooperation in Social Dilemmas

Most groups in organizations could be characterized as social dilemma situations.[22] Members are left to their own devices to decide how much to take or contribute for common benefit. Consider an organization in which access to supplies and equipment—such as computers, photocopy paper, stamps, and envelopes—is not regulated. Each member may be tempted to overuse or hoard resources, thereby contributing to a rapid depletion of supply.

Many individual characteristics of people have been studied, such as gender, race, Machiavellianism, status, age, and so forth.[23] Few, if any, individual differences reliably predict behavior in a prisoner's dilemma game. In fact, people cooperate more than rational analysis would predict. Many investigations use a single trial or fixed number of trials in which the rational strategy is solid defection. When the game is infinite or the number of trials is indefinite, however, people cooperate less than they should. What steps can the negotiator take to build greater cooperation and trust among organization members? Two major types of approaches for maximizing cooperation are **structural strategies** (which are often institutional changes) and **psychological strategies** (which are usually engaged in by the organizational actor; see Exhibit 11-8).

EXHIBIT 11-7

Different Kinds of Social Dilemmas

	Taking	Contributing
Internal (intraorganizational)	Resources (e.g., money, real estate, staffing) Budget fudging	Committee work Recognition
External (interorganizational)	Price competition Brand competition Overharvesting Pollution	Paying taxes Public television

[22] Kopelman, S., Weber, J. M., & Messick, D. M. (2002). Factors influencing cooperation in commons dilemmas: A review of experimental psychological research. In E. Ostrom et al. (Eds.), *The drama of the commons* (pp. 113–156). Washington, DC: National Academy Press; Mannix, E. (1993). Organizations as resource dilemmas: The effects of power balance on coalition formation in small groups. *Organizational Behavior and Human Decision Processes, 55,* 1–22.
[23] Kopelman, Weber, & Messick, "Factors influencing cooperation."

EXHIBIT 11-8

Summary of Strategies for Maximizing Cooperation in Social Dilemmas

Structural Strategies	Psychological Strategies
Align incentives	Psychological contracts
Monitor behavior	Superordinate goals
Regulation	Communication
Privatization	Personalize others
Tradable permits	Social sanctions
	Focus on benefits of cooperation

Source: Brett, J., & Thompson, L. (2011). *Negotiation strategies for managers.* Executive course, Kellogg School of Management, Northwestern University, Evanston, IL. Reprinted by permission of Jeanne Brett.

STRUCTURAL STRATEGIES   Structural strategies involve fundamental changes in the way that social dilemmas are constructed. They are usually the result of thoughtful problem solving and often produce a change in incentives.

Align Incentives.   Monetary incentives for cooperation, privatization of resources, and a monitoring system increase the incidence of cooperation. For example, by putting in "high-occupancy vehicle" lanes on major highways, single drivers are motivated to carpool. However, realignment of incentives can be time-consuming and expensive.

Often, defectors are reluctant to cooperate because the costs of cooperation seem exorbitantly high. For example, people often defect by not paying their parking tickets because the price is high and they have several tickets. In some cases, city officials introduce amnesty delays for delinquent parking tickets, whereby people can cooperate at a cost less than they expected. Some U.S. cities have adopted similar policies to induce people to return borrowed library books.

Cooperation can also be induced through reward and recognition in organizations. Recognition awards, such as gold stars, employee-of-the-month awards and the like, are designed to induce cooperation rather than defection in a variety of organizational social dilemmas.

In some instances, cooperation can be induced by increasing the risk associated with defection. For example, some people do not pay their state or federal income tax in the United States. This behavior is illegal, and if a defector is caught he or she can be convicted of a crime. The threat of spending years in jail often lessens the temptation of defection. However, most tacit negotiations in organizations are not policed in this fashion, and, therefore, defection is more tempting for would-be defectors.

Monitor Behavior.   When we monitor people's behavior, they often conform to group norms. The same beneficial effects also occur when people monitor their own behavior. For example, when people meter their water consumption during a water shortage, they use less water.[24] Moreover, people who meter their water usage express greater concern with the collective costs of overconsumption during a drought.

One method of monitoring behavior is to elect a leader. For example, people often favor electing a leader when they receive feedback that their group has failed at restricting harvests from a collective resource.[25] When a leader is introduced into a social dilemma situation, especially an autocratic leader, individual group members might fear restriction of their freedom.[26] People are more reluctant to install leaders in public goods situations (contributing) than in common resource situations (taking) because it is more threatening to give up decision freedom over private property than over collective property.[27]

Regulation. Regulation involves government intervention to correct market imperfections, with the idea of improving social welfare. Examples include rationing, in which limits are placed on access to a common-pool resource (i.e., water use). Regulation also occurs in other markets, such as agriculture. The telephone industry in the United States is a heavily regulated industry. In 1934 Congress created the Federal Communications Commission (FCC) to oversee all wire and radio communication (e.g., radio, broadcast, telephone). Even though regulation does not always result in a system that encourages responsible behavior (for example, the moral hazard problem created by the Federal Deposit Insurance Corporation system), the intent of regulation is to protect public (social) interests.

Privatization. The basic idea of privatization is to put public resources under the control of specific individuals or groups: public lands in private hands. The rationale is that public resources will be better protected if they are under the control of private groups or individuals. For example, the city of Chicago privatized its parking meters in 2008, signing a 75-year, $1.15 billion lease with an outside company. However, the administration of Mayor Richard Daley spent most of the one-time payment in just two years. Undaunted, and facing a $655 million budget shortfall, the city sought potential deals to privatize everything from recycling services to city festivals. City officials pointed out that privatizing services shifts future financial and operating risk to a private operator.[28] Another example: The Tulsa (Oklahoma) Zoo transferred $1.1 million from city to the private entity, Tulsa Zoo Management, Inc., a non-profit group with a 13-member board composed of the mayor as well as local business and community leaders. Struggling with funding for the zoo for several years, the city transferred operations and financial management to the private group. Tulsa Mayor Dewey Bartlett noted, "City government does a lot of good things, but in some areas it doesn't quite perform as well as the private sector."[29]

Tradable Permits. Tradable environmental allowance (TEA) governance structures are another way of navigating social dilemmas. In TEA arrangements, instead of competing for scarce resources (like the right to pollute), companies purchase the rights to pollute or to use scarce

---

[24] Van Vugt, M., & Samuelson, C. D. (1999). The impact of personal metering in the management of a natural resource crisis: A social dilemma analysis. *Personality and Social Psychology Bulletin, 25*(6), 731–745.

[25] Messick, D. M., Wilke, H., Brewer, M. B., Kramer, R. M., Zemke, P. E., & Lui, L. (1983). Individual adaptations and structural change as solutions to social dilemmas. *Journal of Personality and Social Psychology, 44*(2), 294–309; Rutte, C. G., & Wilke, H. A. M. (1984). Social dilemmas and leadership. *European Journal of Social Psychology, 14,* 105–121.

[26] Van Vugt, M., & De Cremer, D. (1999). Leadership in social dilemmas: The effects of group identification on collective actions to provide public goods. *Journal of Personality and Social Psychology, 76*(4), 587–599.

[27] Van Dijk, E., Wilke, H., & Wit, A. (2003). Preferences for leadership in social dilemmas: Public good dilemmas versus common resource dilemmas. *Journal of Experimental Social Psychology, 39,* 170–176.

[28] Dardick, H. (2010, August 31). Boxed in by parking deal? *Chicago Tribune.* Chicagotribune.com

[29] Lassek, P. J. (2010, December 16). Tulsa moves towards change in zoo ownership. *Tulsa World.* Tulsaworld.com

resources.[30] Users treat these rights as they would conventional property and, thus, conserve resources carefully.[31] Tradable permits have been successfully used for managing fisheries, water supply, and air and water pollution in many different countries.[32] For example, in the fishing industry, the total allowable catch (or TAC) is set by government agencies and subsequently allocated to associations or individual users. As in the case of pollution, these allocations can be traded by individuals or companies.

PSYCHOLOGICAL STRATEGIES   In contrast to structural strategies, which often require an act of government or layers of bureaucracy to enact, psychological strategies are inexpensive and only require the wits of the influence agent.

Psychological Contracts.   Legal contracts involve paperwork and are similar to the deterrence-based trust mechanisms we discussed in Chapter 6. In contrast, **psychological contracts** are commonly known as "handshake deals." They are not binding in a court of law, but they create a psychological pressure to commit. People are more likely to cooperate when they promise to cooperate. Although such promises are nonbinding and are therefore "cheap talk," people nevertheless act as if they are binding. The reason for this behavior, according to the **norm of commitment**, is that people feel psychologically committed to follow through with their word.[33] The norm of commitment is so powerful that people often do things that are completely at odds with their preferences or that are highly inconvenient. For example, once people agree to let a salesperson demonstrate a product in their home, they are more likely to buy it. Homeowners are more likely to consent to have a large (over 10 foot tall), obtrusive sign in their front yard that says "Drive Carefully" when they agree to a small request made the week before.[34]

Superordinate Goals.   Our behavior in social dilemmas is influenced by our perceptions about what kinds of behavior are appropriate and expected in a given context. In an intriguing examination of this idea, people engaged in a prisoner's dilemma task. In one condition, the game was called the "Wall Street game," and in another condition, the game was called the "Community game."[35] Otherwise, the game, the choices, and the outcomes were identical. Although rational analysis predicts that defection is the optimal strategy no matter what the name, in fact, the incidence of cooperation was three times as high in the community game as in the Wall Street game, indicating that people are sensitive to situational cues as trivial as the name of the game. Indeed, people behave more competitively in social dilemmas involving economic decisions compared to those involving noneconomic decisions.[36]

---

[30] Brett, J. M., & Kopelman, S. (2004). Cross-cultural perspectives on cooperation in social dilemmas. In M. Gelfand & J. Brett (Eds.), *The handbook of negotiation and culture: Theoretical advances and cultural perspectives* (pp. 395–411). Palo Alto, CA: Stanford University Press.

[31] Ackerman, B. A., & Stewart, R. B. (1988). Reforming environmental law: The democratic case for market incentives. *Columbia Journal of Environmental Law, 13,* 171–199; Kriz, M. (1998). After Argentina. *National Journal, 30*(49), 2848–2853; Tipton, C. A. (1995). Protecting tomorrow's harvest: Developing a national system of individual transferable quotas to conserve ocean resources. *Virginia Environmental Law Journal, 14,* 381–421.

[32] Tietenberg, T. (2002). The tradable permits approach to protecting the commons: What have we learned. In E. Ostrom, T. Dietz, N. Dolsak, P. C. Stern, S. Sonich, & E. U. Weber (Eds.), *The drama of the commons* (pp. 197–232). Washington, DC: National Academy Press.

[33] Cialdini, R. B. (1993). *Influence: Science and practice.* New York: HarperCollins.

[34] Freedman, J. L., & Fraser, S. C. (1966). Compliance without pressure: The foot-in-the-door technique. *Journal of Personality and Social Psychology, 4,* 195–203.

[35] Liberman, V., Samuels, S. M., & Ross, L. (2004). The name of the game: Predictive power of reputations versus situational labels in determining prisoner's dilemma game moves. *Personality and Social Psychology Bulletin, 30,* 1175–1185.

[36] Pillutla, M. M., & Chen, X. (1999). Social norms and cooperation in social dilemmas: The effects of context and feedback. *Organizational Behavior and Human Decision Processes, 78*(2), 81–103.

Communication.   A key determinant of cooperation is communication.[37] When people are allowed to communicate with the members of the group prior to making their choices, cooperation increases dramatically.[38] The type of communication matters as well. Task-related communication (as opposed to non-task-related communication) promotes greater cooperation by activating interpersonal norms related to fairness and trust.[39]

Two reasons explain this increase in cooperation.[40] First, communication enhances group identity or solidarity. Second, communication allows group members to make public commitments to cooperate. Verbal commitments in such situations indicate the willingness of others to cooperate. They reduce the uncertainty people have about others in such situations and provide a measure of reassurance to decision makers. Of the two explanations, it is the commitment factor that is most important.[41]

In our investigations on the relative effectiveness of verbal face-to-face communication as compared to written-only or no communication, people who communicate face-to-face are much more likely to reach a mutually profitable deal because they are able to coordinate on a price above each party's BATNA.[42] Commitments also shape subsequent behavior. People are extremely reluctant to break their word, even when their words are nonbinding. If people are prevented from making verbal commitments, they attempt to make nonverbal ones.

The other reason why communication is effective in engendering cooperation is that it allows group members to develop a shared group identity. Communication allows people to get to know one another and feel more attached to their group. People derive a sense of identity from their relationships to social groups.[43] When our identity is traced to the relationships we have with others in groups, we seek to further the interests of these groups. This identification leads to more cooperative, or group-welfare, choices in social dilemmas.

Social identity is often built through relationships. For example, as a consequence of population growth, the politics of water distribution, and five years of drought, California had widespread water shortages in 1991. Residents of many areas were encouraged to voluntarily conserve water and were subjected to regulations imposed by the State's Public Utilities Commission. A telephone survey of hundreds of residents of the San Francisco area revealed that people were more willing to support authorities when they had strong relational bonds to the authorities.[44] The effectiveness of authorities in eliciting cooperation in water-shortage dilemmas is linked to the social bonds they share with community members.

---

[37] Komorita, S. S., & Parks, C. D. (1994). *Social dilemmas.* Madison, WI: Brown and Benchmark; Liebrand, W. B. G., Messick, D. M., & Wilke, H., Eds. (1992). *Social dilemmas: Theoretical issues and research findings.* Oxford, England: Pergamon Press; Messick & Brewer, "Solving social dilemmas"; Sally, D. F. (1995). Conversation and cooperation in social dilemmas: Experimental evidence from 1958 to 1992. *Rationality and Society, 7*(1), 58–92.

[38] Sally, "Conversation and cooperation in social dilemmas."

[39] Cohen, T. R, Wildschut, T., & Insko, C. A. (2010). How communication increases interpersonal cooperation in mixed-motive situations. *Journal of Experimental Social Psychology, 46*(1), 39–50.

[40] Dawes, R. M., van de Kragt, A. J. C., & Orbell, J. M. (1990). Cooperation for the benefit of us—Not me, or my conscience. In J. Mansbridge (Ed.), *Beyond self-interest* (pp. 97–110). Chicago: University of Chicago Press.

[41] Kerr, N. L., & Kaufman-Gilliland, C. M. (1994). Communication, commitment, and cooperation in social dilemma. *Journal of Personality and Social Psychology, 66*(3), 513–529.

[42] Valley, K., Thompson, L., Gibbons, R., & Bazerman, M. H. (2002). How communication improves efficiency in bargaining games. *Games and Economic Behavior, 38,* 127–155.

[43] Tajfel, H. (1979). The exit of social mobility and the voice of social change: Notes on the social psychology of intergroup relations. *Przeglad Psychologiczny, 22*(1), 17–38.

[44] Tyler, T. R., & Degoey, P. (1995). Collective restraint in social dilemmas: Procedural justice and social identification effects on support for authorities. *Journal of Personality and Social Psychology, 69*(3), 482–497.

Personalize Others.   People often behave as if they were interacting with an entity or organization rather than a person. For example, an embittered customer claims that the *airline* refused to refund her when in fact it was a representative of the airline who did not issue a refund. To the extent that others can be personalized, people are more motivated to cooperate than if they believe they are dealing with a dehumanized bureaucracy. Even more important is that people see you as a cooperator. People cooperate more when others have cooperated in a previous situation.[45]

For example, Knez and Camerer created a simulation that resembled the transfer of cooperative norms in small firms which are largely cooperative. As firms grow larger they become more like prisoner's dilemmas which pit self-interest against cooperation.[46] Some managers shared a history of coordinating their behavior; others did not. Those who had a history of coordinating their actions were more likely to cooperate in a subsequent prisoner's dilemma situation. Further, the difference was dramatic: Those who had a previous history cooperated in the prisoner's dilemma game about 71% of the time, whereas those without a history only cooperated 15% to 30% of the time.

Still another reason why people cooperate is that they want to believe they are nice. For example, one person attributed his decision to make a cooperative choice in the 20-person prisoner's dilemma game to the fact that he did not want the readers of *Scientific American* to think he was a defector.[47] This behavior is a type of **impression management**.[48] Impression management raises the question of whether people's behavior is different when it is anonymous than when it is public. The answer appears to be yes. However, it is not always the case that public behavior is more cooperative than private behavior. For example, negotiators who are accountable to a constituency often bargain harder and are more competitive than when they are accountable for only their behavior.[49]

Social Sanctions.   Social sanctions are punishments that are administered in a community or a group when defection occurs. Unlike legal sanctions, social sanctions are not economic penalties and fines but, rather, might be a form of reprimand. Long-time U.S. Representative Charles Rangel was the first member of the House to be censured in three decades when the chamber overwhelmingly voted to reprimand him for failure to pay income taxes and misusing his office to solicit fund-raising donations. Censure, the highest form of punishment short of outright expulsion from the House, was an embarrassment to one of the longest-serving and most highly regarded elected officials in the United States, and served as a clear warning against the abuse of power by House members. "I know in my heart I am not going to be judged by this Congress. I'll be judged by my life in its entirety," Rangel said after the punishment was handed down.[50]

Focus on Benefits of Cooperation.   The probability that a person will make a particular choice in a social dilemma is a function of the attraction of that choice in terms of its ability to

---

[45] Pillutla & Chen, "Social norms and cooperation."

[46] Knez, M., & Camerer, C. (2000). Increasing cooperation in prisoner's dilemmas by establishing a precedent of efficiency in coordination games. *Organizational Behavior and Human Decision Processes, 82*(2), 194–216.

[47] Hofstadter, D. (1983). Metamagical thinking. *Scientific American, 248,* 14–28.

[48] Goffman, E. (1959). *The presentation of self in everyday life.* Garden City, NY: Doubleday.

[49] Carnevale, P. J., Pruitt, D. G., & Seilheimmer, S. (1981). Looking and competing: Accountability and visual access in integrative bargaining. *Journal of Personality and Social Psychology, 40,* 111–120.

[50] Kocieniewski, D. (2010, December 3). Rangel censured over violations of ethics rules. *New York Times,* A1.

return a desirable outcome immediately.[51] Our attraction to a choice is usually a reflection of our ability to imagine or mentally simulate good outcomes.[52] In a direct examination of people's ability to think positively in a prisoner's dilemma game, participants were instructed to think about some alternatives that were "worse" or "better" than what actually happened, then they played some more. The results were startling: Negotiators' subsequent cooperation with their partner was directly related to the number of best-case scenarios they generated, and negotiators who generated worst-case scenarios defected a lot.[53] The message? Thinking about how good we can be greatly increases cooperation.

How to Encourage Cooperation in Social Dilemmas When Parties Should Not Collude

In the examples thus far, we've suggested ways negotiators can entice others to cooperate. However, in many situations, it is illegal for parties to cooperate. Consider the problem of price-fixing among companies within an industry. One example concerns how a pharmaceutical company might respond to the entry of a new competitor in a particular class of a drug. Brett suggests the following principles to encourage cooperation in social dilemmas when companies should not privately collude:[54]

- *Keep your strategy simple.*   The simpler your strategy, the easier it is for your competitors to predict your behavior. The correspondence is nearly one-to-one between uncertainty and competitive behavior: Greater uncertainty leads to more competitive behavior;[55] thus it helps to minimize uncertainty for your competitors.
- *Signal via actions.*   The adage that behaviors speak louder than words is important.
- *Do not be the first to defect.*   It is difficult to recover from escalating spirals of defection. Thus, do not be the first to defect.
- *Focus on your own payoffs, not your payoffs relative to others.*   Social dilemmas trigger competitive motives (as discussed in Chapter 5). The competitive motive is a desire to "beat" the other party. Instead, focus on your profits.
- *Be sensitive to egocentric bias.*   Most people view their own behavior as more cooperative than that of others. We see ourselves as more virtuous, more ethical, and less competitive than others see us. When planning your strategy, consider the fact that your competitors will see you less favorably than you perceive yourself.

[51] Anderson, C. M., & Camerer, C. (2000). Experience-weighted attraction learning in sender-receiver signaling games. *Economic Theory, 16,* 689–718; Camerer, C., & Ho, T. H. (1998). Experience-weighted attraction learning in coordination games: Probability rules, heterogeneity, and time-variation. *Journal of Mathematical Psychology, 42,* 305–326; Camerer, C., & Ho, T. H. (1999). Experience-weighted attraction learning in games: Estimates from weak-link games. In D. V. Budescu, I. Erev, & R. Zwick (Eds.), *Games and human behavior* (pp. 31–51). Mahwah, NJ: Erlbaum; Camerer, C., & Ho, T. H. (1999). Experience-weighted attraction learning in normal form games. *Econometrica, 67,* 827–874.

[52] Parks, C. D., Sanna, L. J., & Posey, D. C. (2003). Retrospection in social dilemmas: How thinking about the past affects future cooperation. *Journal of Personality and Social Psychology, 84*(5), 988–996.

[53] Ibid.

[54] Brett, J. M. (2007). *Negotiating globally: How to negotiate deals, resolve disputes, and make decisions across cultural boundaries* (2nd ed.). San Francisco: Jossey-Bass.

[55] Kopelman, Weber, & Messick, "Factors influencing cooperation."

ESCALATION OF COMMITMENT

Suppose you make a small investment in a start-up Internet company that seems to have great potential. After the first quarter, you learn that the company suffered an operating loss. You cannot recover your investment; your goal is to maximize your long-term wealth. Should you continue to invest in the company? Consider two possible choices in this situation:

1. Losing the small amount of money you have already invested.
2. Taking additional risk by investing more money in the company, which could turn around and make a large profit or plummet even further.

The reference point effect described in Chapter 2 would predict that most negotiators would continue to invest in the company because they have already adopted a "loss frame" based upon their initial investment. Suppose you recognize that the Internet company did not perform well in the first period and you consider your initial investment to be a sunk cost—that is, water under the bridge. In short, you adapt your reference point. Now, ask yourself which of the following would be the wiser choice:

1. Not invest in the company at this point (a sure outcome of $0).
2. Take a gamble and invest more money in a company that has not shown good performance in the recent past.

Under these circumstances, most people choose not to invest in the company because they would rather have a sure thing than a loss. A negotiator's psychological reference point also influences the tendency to fall into the escalation trap. Recall that negotiators are risk-seeking when it comes to losses and risk-averse for gains. When negotiators see themselves as trying to recover from a losing position, chances are they engage in greater risk than if they see themselves as starting with a clean slate. Like the gambler in Las Vegas, negotiators who are hoping to hold out longer than their opponent (as in a strike) have fallen into the escalation trap. Most decision makers and negotiators do not readjust their reference point. Rather, they fail to adapt their reference point and continue to make risky decisions, which often prove unprofitable.

The **escalation of commitment** refers to the unfortunate tendency of negotiators to persist with a losing course of action, even in the face of clear evidence that their behaviors are not working and the negotiation situation is quickly deteriorating. The two types of escalation dilemmas are personal and interpersonal. In both cases, the dilemma is revealed when a person would do something different if he or she had not already been involved in the situation.

Personal escalation dilemmas involve only one person, and the dilemma concerns whether to continue with what appears to be a losing course of action or to cut one's losses. Continuing to gamble after losing a lot of money, investing money in a car or house that continues to malfunction or deteriorate, and waiting in long lines that are not moving are examples of personal escalation dilemmas. To stop, in some sense, is to admit failure and accept a sure loss. Continuing to invest holds the possibility of recouping losses.

Interpersonal escalation dilemmas involve two or more people, often in a competitive relationship, such as negotiation. Union strikes are often escalation dilemmas, and so is war. Consider the situation faced by Lyndon Johnson during the early years of the Vietnam War. Johnson received the following memo from George Ball, then Undersecretary of State:

> The decision you face now is crucial. Once large numbers of U.S. troops are committed to direct combat, they will begin to take heavy casualties in a war they

are ill-equipped to fight in a non-cooperative if not downright hostile countryside. Once we suffer large casualties, we will have started a well-nigh irreversible process. Our involvement will be so great that we cannot—without national humiliation— stop short of achieving our complete objectives. Of the two possibilities I think humiliation will be more likely than the achievement of our objectives—even after we have paid terrible costs.[56]

In escalation dilemmas, negotiators commit further resources to what appears to unbiased observers to be a failing course of action. In most cases, people fall into escalation traps because initially the situation does not appear to be a losing enterprise. The situation becomes an escalation dilemma when the persons involved in the decision would make a different decision if they had not been involved up until that point or when objective decision makers would not choose that course of action. Often, in escalation situations, a decision is made to commit further resources to "turn the situation around," such as in the case of gambling (personal dilemma) or making a final offer (interpersonal dilemma). The bigger the investment and the more severe the possible loss, the more prone people are to try to turn things around.

The escalation of commitment process is illustrated in Exhibit 11-9.[57] In the first stage of the escalation of commitment, a person is confronted with questionable or negative outcomes (e.g., a rejection of one's offer by the counterparty, decrease in market share, poor performance evaluation, a malfunction, or hostile behavior from a competitor). This external event prompts a reexamination of the negotiator's current course of action, in which the utility of continuing is weighed against the utility of withdrawing or changing course. This decision determines the negotiator's commitment to his or her current course of action. If this commitment is low, the negotiator may make a concession, engage in integrative negotiations (rather than distributive negotiations), or possibly revert to his or her BATNA. If this commitment is high, however, the negotiator will continue commitment and continue to cycle through the decision stages.

When negotiators receive indication that the outcomes of a negotiation may be negative, they should ask themselves, "What are the personal rewards for me in this situation?" In many cases, the *process* of the negotiation itself, rather than the *outcome* of the negotiation, becomes the reason for commencing or continuing negotiations. This reasoning leads to a self-perpetuating reinforcement trap, wherein the rewards for continuing are not aligned with the actual objectives of the negotiator. Ironically, people who have high, rather than low, self-esteem are more likely to become victimized by psychological forces; people with high self-esteem have much more invested in their ego and its maintenance than do those with low self-esteem.[58] Sometimes face-saving concerns lead negotiators to escalate commitment; some negotiators worry they will look silly or stupid if they back down from an initial position. Ego protection often becomes a higher priority than the success of the negotiation.

---

[56] *The Pentagon papers.* (1971). As published by *The New York Times,* based on the investigative reporting by Neil Sheehan, written by Neil Sheehan [and others]. Articles and documents edited by G. Gold, A. M. Siegal, and S. Abt. New York, Toronto: Bantam.

[57] Ross, J., & Staw, B. M. (1993, August). Organizational escalation and exit: Lessons from the Shoreham Nuclear Power Plant. *Academy of Management Journal, 36*(4), 701–732.

[58] Taylor, S. E., & Brown, J. (1988). Illusion and well-being: A social-psychological perspective. *Psychological Bulletin, 103,* 193–210.

EXHIBIT 11-9

Escalation of Commitment

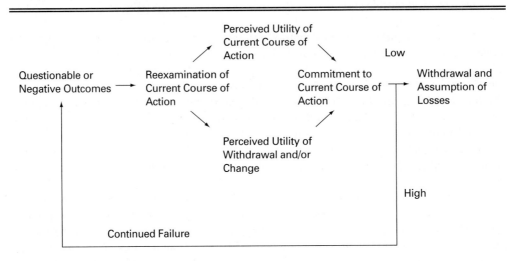

Source: Adapted from Staw, B. M., & Ross, J. (1987). Behavior in escalation situations: Antecedents, prototypes, and solutions. In L. L. Cummings & B. M. Staw (Eds.), *Research in organizational behavior* (Vol. 9, p.45). Greenwich, CT: Jai Press Inc.

Avoiding the Escalation of Commitment in Negotiations

Most negotiators do not realize they are in an escalation dilemma until it is too late. Complicating matters is the fact that, in most escalation dilemmas, a negotiator (like a gambler) might have some early "wins" or good signs that reinforce their initial position. How can a negotiator best get out of an escalation dilemma?

The best advice is to adopt a policy of risk management: Be aware of the risks involved in the situation, learn how to best manage these risks, and set limits, effectively capping losses at a tolerable level. It is also important to find ways to get information and feedback about the negotiation from a different perspective.

SET LIMITS   Ideally, a negotiator should have a clearly defined BATNA. At no point should a negotiator make or accept an offer that is worse than his or her BATNA.

AVOID DECISION MYOPIA   A negotiator should get several perspectives on the situation. Ask people who are not personally involved in the negotiation for their appraisal. Be careful not to bias their evaluation with your own views, hopes, expectations, or other details, such as the cost of extricating yourself from the situation, because that will only predispose them toward your point of view, which is not what you want—you want an honest, critical assessment.

RECOGNIZE SUNK COSTS   Probably the most powerful way to escape escalation of commitment is to simply recognize and accept **sunk costs**, which are basically water under the bridge: money (or other commitments) previously spent that cannot be recovered. It is often helpful for negotiators to consider removal of the project, product, or program. In this way, the situation is redefined as one in which a decision will be made immediately about whether to invest; that is, if you were making the initial decision today, would you make the investment currently under consideration (as a continuing investment), or would you choose another course of action? If the decision is not one you would choose anew, think about how to terminate the project and move on to the next one.

DIVERSIFY RESPONSIBILITY AND AUTHORITY   In some cases, it is necessary to remove or replace the original negotiators from deliberations precisely because they are biased. One way to carry out such a removal is with an external review: appointing someone who does not have a personal stake in the situation.

REDEFINE THE SITUATION   Often, it helps to view the situation not as the "same old problem" but as a new one. Washington D.C. teachers dramatically redefined the situation when they ratified a new contract in 2010, which expanded the ability of administrators to remove poor teachers from classrooms based on student results, an idea once unthinkable to the educators. Initially, many of the proposals—performance pay linked to test score growth, weakening of seniority and tenure—were vehemently opposed. But through persistent efforts, the ideas got incorporated into mainstream thinking that effectively changed the status quo expectations.[59]

CONCLUSION

Prisoner's dilemmas and social dilemmas are characterized by the absence of contracts and enforcement mechanisms. In these dilemmas, people choose between acting in a self-interested fashion or in a cooperative fashion, which makes the negotiator vulnerable to exploitation. Strategic pie-expanding and pie-slicing strategies in the two-person prisoner's dilemma can be achieved via the tit-for-tat strategy, but tit-for-tat works only with two players in a repeated game. However, many tacit negotiations within and between organizations involve more than two players and are called social dilemmas. The best way to ensure cooperation in social dilemmas is to align incentives, monitor behavior, practice regulation and privatization, use tradable permits, communicate with involved parties, personalize others, and focus on the benefits of cooperation. Escalation dilemmas occur when people invest in what is (by any objective standards) a losing course of action. People can deescalate via setting limits, getting several perspectives, recognizing sunk costs, diversifying responsibility, and redefining the situation.

---

[59] Turque. B. (2010, June 3). District teachers approve contract. *Washington Post,* A01.

CHAPTER

12

Negotiating Via Information Technology

When WikiLeaks founder Julian Assange released tens of thousands of classified United States military and other diplomatic documents in 2010, it set in motion a frenzy of secret negotiations to stop the site. According to WikiLeaks, the U.S. military contacted WikiLeaks to remove sensitive information from more than 15,000 threatened-to-be-released documents—some including the name of informants in the war in Afghanistan. However, the Pentagon denied contacting WikiLeaks. Assange used a power strategy and threatened to release thousands more sensitive diplomatic cables if legal action were taken against him or his organization. The United States moved cautiously; less than 1% of the diplomatic cables known to be held by WikiLeaks had been released. The American authorities were negotiating on new technological ground. First, there was no way to retrieve all copies of the cable. Second, there were no obvious legal grounds on which to prosecute Assange. The U.S. Department of Justice considered indicting Assange under the Espionage Act, but the fact that this had never been successfully used to prosecute a third-party recipient of a leak was a negotiation weakness. As a result of the prosecution attention in the media, WikiLeaks released a cable listing sites around the world—from hydroelectric dams in Canada to vaccine factories in Denmark—considered crucial to American national security. Rumors of secret negotiations between the parties percolated.[1]

[1] Shane, S. (2010, December 7). WikiLeaks founder warns about more dispatches. *New York Times*, A13; Agency France Presse. (2010, August 18). Pentagon rules out WikiLeaks negotiations. *MSN.* Msn.com

The WikiLeaks incident raised several issues about the Internet and how the new world of information technology affects negotiation. This chapter examines the impact of information technology on negotiation, with a particular focus on electronic negotiations (e-negotiations). The place-time model focuses on negotiators who negotiate either in the same or different physical location and at the same or different time. For each of these cases, we describe what to expect and ways to deal with the limitations of that communication mode. We follow this discussion with a section on how information technology affects negotiation behavior. We then describe strategies to help negotiators expand and divide the pie effectively.

PLACE-TIME MODEL OF SOCIAL INTERACTION

The **place-time model** describes four modes of interaction that vary in richness: same place + same time; different place + different time; same place + different time; different place + same time (Exhibit 12-1).[2] **Richness** is the potential information-carrying capacity of the communication medium.[3] Face-to-face communication is relatively "rich," whereas formal, written messages, such as memos and business correspondence, are relatively "lean" (see Exhibit 12-2).[4] Face-to-face communication conveys the richest information because it allows for the simultaneous observation of multiple cues, including body language, facial expression, and tone of voice, thereby providing people with a greater awareness of context. In contrast, formal numerical documentation conveys the least-rich information, providing few cues about the context. In addition, geographical propinquity and time constraints affect negotiations.

EXHIBIT 12-1

Place-Time Model of Interaction

	Same Place	Different Place
Same Time	Face-to-face	Telephone Videoconference
Different Time	Single text editing Shift work	E-mail Voice mail

---

[2] Englebart, D. (1989, November). Bootstrapping organizations into the 21st century. Paper presented at a seminar at the Software Engineering Institute, Pittsburgh, PA; Johansen, R. (1988). *Groupware: Computer support for business teams.* New York: Free Press.

[3] Drolet, A. L., & Morris, M. W. (2000). Rapport in conflict resolution: Accounting for how nonverbal exchange fosters cooperation on mutually beneficial settlements to mixed-motive conflicts. *Journal of Experimental Social Psychology, 36,* 26–50.

[4] Daft, R. L., & Lengel, R. H. (1984). Information richness: A new approach to managerial behavior and organization design. *Research in Organization Behavior, 6,* 191–223; Daft, R. L., Lengel, R. H., & Trevino, L. K. (1987). Message equivocality, media selection, and manager performance: Implications for information systems. *MIS Quarterly, 11*(3), 355–366.

EXHIBIT 12-2

Psychological Distancing Model

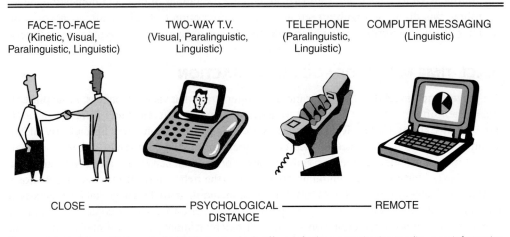

FACE-TO-FACE
(Kinetic, Visual,
Paralinguistic, Linguistic)

TWO-WAY T.V.
(Visual, Paralinguistic,
Linguistic)

TELEPHONE
(Paralinguistic,
Linguistic)

COMPUTER MESSAGING
(Linguistic)

CLOSE ———————— PSYCHOLOGICAL ———————— REMOTE
DISTANCE

Source: Adapted from Wellens, A. R. (1989, September). Effects of telecommunication media upon information sharing and team performance: Some theoretical and empirical findings. *IEEE AES Magazine,* p. 14.

Let's consider each of the four types of communications in the place-time model in greater detail.

Face-to-Face Communication

Face-to-face negotiation is the clear preference of most negotiators and rightly so. Face-to-face contact is crucial in the initiation of relationships and collaborations. Face-to-face negotiations are particularly important when negotiators meet for the first time, when norms of interaction are established. Negotiators are more cooperative when interacting face-to-face than over the telephone.[5] Face-to-face communication (as opposed to using the telephone) fosters the development of interpersonal synchrony and rapport and thus leads to more trusting, cooperative behavior.[6] Face-to-face meetings are ideal for wrestling with complex negotiations. Face-to-face negotiators reach more integrative (win-win) outcomes and more balanced distributions of surplus (even pie-slicing) than writing-only (e-mail) or telephone negotiations.[7] Further, writing-only (e-mail) negotiations have a higher incidence of impasse, and telephone negotiations increase the likelihood of losing buyers and highly profitable sellers.

---

[5] Drolet & Morris, "Rapport in conflict resolution."
[6] Ibid.
[7] Valley, K. L., Moag, J., & Bazerman, M. H. (1998). A matter of trust: Effects of communication on the efficiency and distribution of outcomes (p. 212). *Journal of Economic Behavior and Organizations, 34,* 211–238.

The incidence and frequency of face-to-face communication is determined by how closely people are located to one another: Employees who work in the same office or on the same floor communicate much more frequently than those located on different floors or in different buildings. A few paces can have a huge impact. For example, communication frequency between R&D researchers drops off logarithmically after only 5 to 10 meters of distance between offices.[8] Workers in adjacent offices communicate twice as often as those in offices on the same floor, including via e-mail and telephone transmissions.[9]

Face-to-face communication is easier and therefore more likely to occur than are other forms of communication. Many negotiations occur from chance encounters, which virtually never happen in any mode but face-to-face because of perceived effort. Negotiations of opportunity are very important for long-term business success.

People rely primarily on nonverbal signals to help them conduct social interactions. One estimate is that 93% of the meaning of messages is contained in the nonverbal part of communication, such as voice intonation.[10] (See also Appendix 2 on nonverbal communication.) When President Obama addressed the nation at his inauguration in 2008, he used nonverbal communication to project confidence and leadership. The President used hand gestures to emphasize key concepts of his speech and changed the tone of his voice to suit the message or issue. His voice became louder and delivery more straightforward when he declared that the problems facing the nation would be met.[11]

Nonverbal communication can even extend to choices of clothing and artifacts. For example, President Obama caused a national media stir when he failed to wear an American flag pin lapel on his suit jacket at a Presidential campaign stop. Former Secretary of State Madeline Albright strategically chose pins for various diplomatic occasions. When an Iraqi-state controlled newspaper referred to her as an "unparallelled serpent" after her criticism of former Iraqi leader Saddam Hussein's failure to comply with weapons inspections, she wore a pin featuring a snake wrapped around a branch to her next meeting with Iraqi officials. Her point was made. "Before long and without intending it, I found that jewelry had become part of my personal diplomatic arsenal," Albright said.

Important behavioral, cognitive, and emotional processes are set into motion when people meet face-to-face. Face-to-face negotiation allows people to develop rapport—the feeling of being "in sync" or "on the same wavelength" with another person. Nonverbal (body orientation, gesture, eye contact, head nodding) and paraverbal (speech fluency, use of "uh-huhs," etc.) behaviors are key to building rapport. When the person we are negotiating with sits at a greater distance, has an indirect body orientation, backward lean, and crossed arms, and avoids eye contact, we feel less rapport than when the same person sits with a forward lean, an open body posture and maintains steady eye contact. However, there also appear to be gender differences. When females negotiate, their agreements are of higher quality when they have visual contact, however, the opposite is true for males, who reach better agreements in absence of visual contact.[12]

---

[8] Allen, T. J. (1977). *Managing the flow of technology: Technology transfer and the dissemination of technological information within the R&D organization.* Cambridge, MA: MIT Press.

[9] Galegher, J., Kraut, R. E., & Egido, C. (Eds.) (1990). *Intellectual teamwork: Social and technological foundations of cooperative work.* Hillsdale, NJ: Erlbaum.

[10] Meherabian, A. (1971). *Silent messages.* Belmont, CA: Wadsworth.

[11] Gentry, W. A. (2009, January 20). Nonverbal Obama: Aside from his words. *Bloomberg Businessweek.* Businessweek. com; O'Sullivan, M. (2010, July 9). Never one to be pinned down. *Washington Post.* Washingtonpost.com

[12] Swaab, R. I., & Swaab, D. F. (2009). Sex differences in the effects of visual contact and eye contact in negotiations. *Journal of Experimental Social Psychology, 45*(1), 129–136.

However, we do not always have the luxury of meeting face-to-face. People often turn to the telephone, but even then, people do not always reach their party. Some estimates suggest up to 70% of initial telephone attempts fail to reach the intended party.[13]

Same Time, Different Place

The same time, different place mode, in which people negotiate in real time but are not physically in the same place, is often the alternative to face-to-face negotiations. The most common means is via telephone (telephone tag is different time, different place); videoconferencing is another example. Interestingly, when negotiators are not face-to-face, they reach more integrative agreements when they believe that the other party is physically far away (i.e., several thousand feet away) rather than nearby.[14] Apparently, feeling far away creates a more big-picture construal in the mind of the negotiator.

The United States' Department of Veterans Affairs uses a nationwide videoconferencing network for its 400 information security officers that saves nearly $3 million per year in travel expenses. Because the main office and four regional offices are geographically spaced throughout the country, the department relies on same time, different place technology.[15] In telephone conversations, people lack facial cues; in videoconferencing, they lack real-time social cues, such as pauses, mutual gaze, and another person's nonverbal response to what is being said (looking away, rolling their eyes, or shaking or nodding their head).

Next, we identify four key challenges to same time, different place negotiations.

LOSS OF INFORMAL COMMUNICATION   Probably the most limiting aspect of same time, different place negotiations is the inability to chat informally in the hall or inside offices. The impromptu and casual conversations that negotiators have in a restroom, by a water cooler, or walking back from lunch are often where the most difficult problems are solved and the most important interpersonal issues are addressed. Many companies clearly realize that the informal communication that occurs in their organizations is what is most important and most critical, and they are doing something about it. For example, instant messaging is used on an increasing basis among employees in companies. Written as short, rapid responses, instant messages are used to schedule one-on-one meetings and for "back channel" communications during sales calls.[16] However, they can be more prone to spontaneous emotion than e-mail.

LOST OPPORTUNITY   Negotiations do not occur just when people are in disagreement and haggling over scarce resources. In fact, many negotiations are negotiations of opportunity—something like entrepreneurial joint ventures. Negotiations of opportunity, because they are not planned, usually occur during informal, chance encounters.

---

[13] Philip, G., & Young, E. S. (1987). Man-machine interaction by voice: Developments in speech technology. Part I: The state-of-the-art. *Journal of Information Science, 13,* 3–14.

[14] Henderson, M. D. (2011). Mere physical distance and integrative agreements: When more space improves negotiation outcomes. *Journal of Experimental Social Psychology, 47*(1), 7–15.

[15] Neal, R. (2010, April 6). Videoconferencing centers simplify IT training, cut VA expenses. *Federal Times.* Federaltimes.com

[16] Shaw, R. (2003, November 12). Workplace messaging offers rewards, risks. *Investors' Business Daily.*

SEPARATION OF FEEDBACK   Another negative impact of physical separation is the absence of feedback. Greater distance tends to block the corrective feedback loops provided in face-to-face negotiations. One manager contrasted how employees who worked in his home office negotiated with him, compared to employees 15 kilometers away.[17] Engineers in the home office would drop by and catch him in the hall or at lunch: "I heard you were planning to change project X," they would say. "Let me tell you why that would be stupid." The manager would listen to their points, clarify some details, and all would part ways better informed. In contrast, employees at the remote site would greet his weekly visit with formally prepared objections, which took much longer to discuss and were rarely resolved as completely as the more informal hallway discussions. In short, negotiators interacting remotely do not get the coincidental chances to detect and correct problems on a casual basis.

Friedman and Currall's model of the four key problems with e-mail cite diminished feedback as a key, causal determinant of conflict escalation, along with minimized social cues, excessively long e-mails, and anger.[18]

NEGOTIATION TIMING   Conflicts are expressed, recognized, and addressed more quickly if negotiators work in close proximity. A manager can spot a problem and "nip it in the bud" if he or she works near his or her employees. When people are physically separated, the issues are more likely to go unresolved; this tendency contributes to an escalating cycle of destructive negotiation behavior.

Distance is not always a liability for negotiators. The formality of a scheduled phone meeting may compel parties to better prepare for the negotiation. Distance also creates a "buffer zone" between parties, meaning it might be a good thing if one party does not see the other rolling his or her eyes. Moreover, people are more likely to assume that the behavior of task group members is driven by common goals for physically distant groups, rather than near groups.[19]

Different Time, Same Place

In the different time, same place mode, negotiators interact asynchronously but have access to the same physical document or space. An example might be shift workers who pick up the task left for them by the previous shift; another example would be two collaborators working on the same electronic document. One colleague finishes and then gives the text to a partner, who further edits and develops it.

Different Place, Different Time

In the different place, different time model, negotiators communicate asynchronously in different places. Just as the telephone became an important medium for working out deals, the Internet

---

[17] Armstrong, D. J., & Cole, P. (1995). Managing distances and differences in geographically distributed work groups. In S. E. Jackson & M. N. Ruderman (Eds.), *Diversity in work teams: Research paradigms for a changing workplace* (pp. 187–215). Washington, DC: American Psychological Association.
[18] Friedman, R., & Currall, S. (2003). Conflict escalation: Dispute exacerbating elements of e-mail communication. *Human Relations, 56*(11), 1325–1347.
[19] Henderson, M. D. (2009). Psychological distance and group judgments: The effect of physical distance on beliefs about common goals. *Personality and Social Psychology Bulletin, 35*(10), 1330–1341.

is the medium of choice for many "technobargainers."[20] For example, 61% of Americans comparison-shopped for mortgages online in 2011.[21] When borrowers are ready to buy a home, they may submit financial information on Web sites such as *LowerMyBills.com* and *LendingTree.com* and then receive loan offers, via e-mail, from lenders and brokers.[22]

Technology made it possible for poor migrants in China without high school educations to stage a tech-savvy strike. Hours into the strike, workers posted detailed accounts of the walkout online across China. Armed with desktop computers, they uploaded videos of Honda Lock's security guards roughing up employees, outwitting official censors. When the company deleted the blog posts, workers began using their own cell phones and initiated code words to discuss protest gatherings. In so doing, they tapped into a broader communications web, enabling the working class throughout China to share grievances and negotiation strategies.[23]

Similarly, the Internet allowed demonstrators to quickly organize in Egypt during the 2011 uprising that toppled the three-decade reign of the government of Hosni Mubarak. Egyptian activists used Facebook to organize demonstrations in the capital of Cairo. The Egyptian government was so concerned with the spread of protests that it cut off Internet use and text service to the entire country, a first for any world government. It didn't work. On February 1, a service called SpeakToTweet, was launched by Google and Twitter bringing voices of Egyptians to Twitter by way of a phone number. The messages in Arabic were translated by Small World News. On February 2, with protestors undaunted by the blackout and increasing in number even without the organizing power of instant communications, the government once again turned on the country's communications network. Nine days later, with protests still raging, Mubarak resigned.[24]

We identify four key biases that affect the ability of people to negotiate via e-mail.

TEMPORAL SYNCHRONY BIAS   The **temporal synchrony bias** is the tendency for negotiators to behave as if they are communicating synchronously when in fact they are not. One of the aspects of negotiation that people like is the ability to make proposals and counteroffers, almost in a tennis-game-like fashion. Raiffa refers to this interaction as the "negotiation dance."[25] However, e-negotiations disrupt the natural rhythm of face-to-face negotiation. There is less turn-taking in negotiations conducted via e-mail than in face-to-face negotiations.[26] Moreover, the volume of turn-taking or "dancing" within negotiations predicts schmoozing behavior (e.g., small talk) and facilitates trust and rapport.[27]

---

[20] Kiser, K. (1999, October 1). The new deal. *Training, 36*(10), 116–126; For an overview of the dynamics of e-mail negotiation, Nadler, J., & Shestowsky, D. (2006). Negotiation, information technology, and the problem of the faceless other. In L. Thompson (Ed.), *Negotiation theory and research* (pp. 145–172), New York: Psychology Press, Taylor & Francis Group; Thompson, L., & Nadler, J. (2002). Negotiating via information technology: Theory and application. *Journal of Social Issues, 58*(1), 109–124; McGinn, K. L., & Wilson, E. J. (2004, March). How to negotiate successfully online. *Negotiation, 2*(3), 3–5; McGinn, K. L., & Croson, R. (2004). What do communication media mean for negotiations? A question of social awareness. In M. Gelfand & J. Brett (Eds.), *The handbook of negotiation and culture: Theoretical advances and cultural perspectives and negotiation* (pp. 334–349). Palo Alto, CA: Stanford University Press.

[21] Browning, L. (2011, February 6). Online mortgages shopping made easier. *The New York Times*, p. RE6.

[22] Tedeschi, B. (2008, January 13). Mortages; Getting started, via the Web. *The New York Times* (Real Estate Desk), p. 6.

[23] Barboza, D. & Bradsher, K. (2010, June 17). A labor movement enabled by technology. *New York Times*, B1.

[24] Rothman, W. (2011, February 11). How the Internet brought down a dictator. MSNBC. Technology. Msnbc.msn.com

[25] Raiffa, H. (1982). *The art and science of negotiation.* Cambridge, MA: Belknap.

[26] Morris, M. W., Nadler, J., Kurtzberg, T., & Thompson, L. (2002). Schmooze or lose: Social friction and lubrication in e-mail negotiations. *Group Dynamics: Theory, Research, and Practice, 6*(1), 89–100.

[27] Ibid.

Conversational turn-taking makes the process of negotiation seem smoother and more natural, but it also serves an important informational function: It allows people to correct misunderstandings immediately. In face-to-face interactions, receivers and senders typically engage in a process of rapid correction of information.[28] However, in e-negotiations, negotiators are faced with the mysterious task of interpreting impoverished communication without the opportunity for clarification. Thus, e-negotiators are forced to make more assumptions than face-to-face negotiators. Indeed, e-negotiators ask fewer clarifying questions than do face-to-face negotiators.[29]

EXIT BIAS   The exit bias refers to the perception that negotiation is unstable and should be terminated. In contrast, the **continuation norm** refers to the belief that negotiations are worth continuing.[30] Lack of visual information and increasing spatial distance reduces anticipation of retaliation and may prompt negotiators to exit from the current negotiation. Both visual anonymity and remote distance inhibit the activation of the continuation norm and lead negotiators to terminate the current negotiation.

FLAMING BIAS   The flaming bias is the tendency for negotiators to adopt an adversarial negotiation style (similar to the demanding, negative emotional style described in Chapter 5) when communicating via e-mail—whereas the same negotiator might use a positive emotional style in a face-to-face interaction. Indeed, people are more likely to engage in counter-normative social behavior when interacting via e-mail.[31] Rude, impulsive behavior, such as "flaming" increases when people interact through e-mail, in part because people pay more attention to the content of the message and less attention to the style of the message. For example, bad news is conveyed to superiors with less delay through e-mail than in face-to-face encounters.[32] In a direct comparison of face-to-face negotiations versus e-negotiations, people negotiating via e-mail were more likely to negatively confront one other.[33] One investigation of flaming suggests that people are eight times more likely to flame in e-communication than in face-to-face communication.[34] Similarly, evaluators giving performance appraisals offer more negative feedback to peers when using e-mail than when using traditional paper-form methods.[35] Conversely, people in face-to-face negotiations often follow a politeness ritual, which sets the stage for trust and rapport.

In a study of disputes on SquareTrade, an online mediation service that deals with disputes that arise on eBay, the expression of anger by disputants decreases the likelihood that they

---

[28] Higgins, E. T. (1999). "Saying is believing" effects: When sharing reality about something biases knowledge and evaluations. In L. Thompson, J. M. Levine, & D. M. Messick (Eds.), *Shared cognition in organizations: The management of knowledge.* Mahwah, NJ: Erlbaum; Krauss, R. M., & Chiu, C. (1998). Language and social behavior. In D. T. Gilbert, S. T. Fiske, & G. Lindzey (Eds.), *The handbook of social psychology* (4th ed.) (pp. 41–88). New York: McGraw-Hill.

[29] Morris, Nadler, Kurtzberg, & Thompson, "Schmooze or lose."

[30] Hatta, T., & Ken-ichi, O. (2008). Effects of visual cue and spatial distance on exitability in electronic negotiation. *Computers in Human Behavior, 24*(4), 1542–1551.

[31] Kiesler, S., & Sproull, L. (1992). Group decision making and communication technology. *Organizational Behavior and Human Decision Processes, 52,* 96–123.

[32] Sproull, L. & Kiesler, S. (1991). *Connections: New ways of working in the networked organization.* Cambridge: The MIT Press.

[33] Morris, Nadler, Kurtzberg, & Thompson, "Schmooze or lose."

[34] Dubrovsky, V. J., Kiesler, S., & Sethna, B. N. (1991). The equalization phenomenon: Status effects in computer-mediated and face-to-face decision-making groups. *Human-Computer Interaction, 6*(2), 119–146.

[35] Kurtzberg, T. R., Naquin, C. E., & Belkin, L. Y. (2005). Electronic performance appraisals: The effects of e-mail communication on peer ratings in actual and simulated environments. *Organizational Behavior and Human Decision Processes, 98*(2), 216–226.

will resolve their dispute. Anger expressed by one party generates an angry response from the other party.[36] Examinations of the text data from these eBay disputes among buyers and sellers revealed a higher likelihood of settlement when people provided a causal account of the dispute, but a lower likelihood of settlement when they expressed negative emotions or made commands.[37]

When social context cues are missing or weak, people feel distant from others and somewhat anonymous. They are less concerned about making a good impression, and humor tends to fall apart or to be misinterpreted. The expression of negative emotion is no longer minimized because factors that keep people from expressing negative emotion are not in place when they communicate via information technology. Simply, in the absence of social norms that prescribe the expression of positive emotion, people are more likely to express negative emotion. One MBA student lost a job when he sent his supervisor an e-mail message that was perceived as insensitive. The student used e-mail to renegotiate his job responsibilities and proceeded to outline what he saw as problems within the organization and the people who were running it. Shortly thereafter, he was called into a meeting with the senior staff, and everyone was holding a copy of his e-mail.[38]

SINISTER ATTRIBUTION BIAS   People often misattribute the behavior of others to their underlying character traits while ignoring the influence of temporary, situational factors.[39] The **sinister attribution bias** refers to the tendency for e-communicators to ascribe diabolical intentions to the other party.[40] The "sinister attribution error" is the tendency for people to attribute malevolent motives to people they don't know or who represent the out-group.[41] Attributing sinister motives to out-group members is especially prevalent in e-communication in which the absence of social cues leads to feelings of social isolation and distance. Indeed, e-negotiators are more likely to suspect the other party of lying or deceiving them, relative to negotiators interacting face-to-face.[42] Yet e-negotiators are in fact, no more likely than face-to-face negotiators to deceive the other party. In short, the situation provided no factual basis to fuel the increased suspicion of the other party.

A key question concerns how information technology affects negotiation performance. Exhibit 12-3 summarizes the main findings concerning how information technology—and in particular, e-negotiations—affects economic measures of performance (level 1 integrative agreements, distributive outcomes) and social measures of performance (e.g., trust, respect, etc.).[43] Negotiators who communicate face-to-face are more likely to reach deals and avoid impasses than are e-negotiators. Further, the likelihood of reaching a mutually profitable negotiation (and

---

[36] Friedman, R., Anderson, C., Brett, J., Olekalns, M., Goates, N., & Lisco, C. (2004). The positive and negative effects of anger on dispute resolution: Evidence from electronically mediated disputes. *Journal of Applied Psychology, 89*(2), 369–376.

[37] Brett, J. M., Olekalns, M., Friedman, R., Goates, N., Anderson, C., & Lisco, C. C. (2007). Sticks and stones: Language, face, and online dispute resolution. *The Academy of Management Journal, 50*(1), 85–99.

[38] Kaiser, "The new deal."

[39] Ross, L. (1977). The intuitive psychologist and his shortcomings: Distortions in the attribution process. In L. Berkowitz (Ed.), *Advances in experimental social psychology: Vol. 10* (pp. 173–220). Orlando, FL: Academic Press.

[40] Thompson & Nadler, "Negotiating via information technology."

[41] Kramer, R. M. (1995). Dubious battle: Heightened accountability, dysphoric cognition, and self-defeating bargaining behavior. In R. Kramer & D. Messick (Eds.), *Negotiation as a social process* (pp. 95–120). Thousand Oaks, CA: Sage.

[42] Fortune, A., & Brodt, S. (2000). Face to face or virtually, for the second time around: The influence of task, past experience, and media on trust and deception in negotiation. Working paper, Duke University, Fuqua School of Business, Durham, NC.

[43] McGinn, & Croson, "What do communication media mean for negotiations?"

EXHIBIT 12-3

Information Technology's Effect on Negotiator Performance

	E-negotiations vs. Face-to-Face	Enhanced e-negotiations (via schmoozing, in-group status, etc.) vs. Non-enhanced e-negotiations
Impasse rates (finding the ZOPA)		Brief personal disclosure over e-mail reduces likelihood of impasse. Out-group negotiations result in more impasses than in-group negotiations.
Integrative behavior (e.g., multi-issue offers)	E-negotiators make more multi-issue offers.	Brief telephone call prior to e-negotiations improves joint outcomes.
Pie size (expanding the pie)	Mixed results, with some investigations finding that face-to-face results in better joint profits; other studies indicating no difference.	
Distributive behaviors (e.g., threats, etc.)		Negotiators concerned about group's reputation use more aggressive strategies, leading to lower outcomes than negotiators focused on own reputation.
Pie-slicing (distributive outcomes)	Computer-mediated negotiations result in more equal pie-slices than do face-to-face.	
Trust and rapport	Less rapport in e-negotiations.	Brief telephone call prior to e-negotiation increases cooperation and relationship quality. Negotiators who attempt to build rapport build more trust than those who try to dominate.

Source: Table partially based on Thompson, L., & Nadler, J. (2002). Negotiating via information technology: Theory and application. *Journal of Social Issues, 58*(1), 109–124.

avoiding impasse) is a function of the richness of the communication. For example, when negotiators are allowed to communicate in writing or face-to-face, they are more likely to settle in the ZOPA as compared to negotiators who do not interact and just make offers.[44] Considerable debate continues to surround the question of whether information technology hurts or hinders the ability of negotiators to expand the pie. When face-to-face negotiations were compared with computer-mediated negotiations, computer-mediated outcomes were equally or more integrative than were face-to-face outcomes.[45] Computer-mediated negotiations resulted in outcomes that were more fair, as judged in terms of being more equal in value.[46]

INFORMATION TECHNOLOGY AND ITS EFFECTS ON SOCIAL BEHAVIOR

In addition to affecting negotiated outcomes, information technology has an extremely powerful effect on social behavior in general.[47] To be successful, negotiators must understand how their own behavior is affected by technology.

Trust

Relative to face-to-face negotiations, people who negotiate online trust each other less even before beginning the negotiation, and trust each other less after the online interaction.[48] The low levels of trust negotiators have for one another before the negotiation suggest that negotiators bring different expectations to electronic bargaining than to face-to-face negotiations. Not surprisingly, online negotiators report less desire for future relationships with the other party, less confidence in their performance, and less overall satisfaction.

Status and Power: The "Weak Get Strong" Effect

Walk into any classroom, lunch discussion, or business meeting, and it will be immediately obvious that one person in a two-party group does most of the talking, and a handful of people do more than 75% of the talking in a larger group. For example, in a typical four-person group, two people do more than 62% of the talking, in a six-person group, three people do over 70% of the talking, and in a group of eight, three people do 70% of the talking.[49] Even when performance depends on contributions, participation is not equal.

Who dominates most face-to-face discussions and negotiations? Almost without exception, status predicts domination. Higher-status people talk more, even if they are not experts on the subject. Not surprisingly, managers speak more than subordinates, and men speak more than women. In the absence of legitimate status, gender, age, and race affect speaking. Situational factors also affect perceived status. The person who sits at the head of the table talks more than those on the sides, even if the seating arrangement is arbitrary.[50] Those in business suits talk

---

[44] McGinn, K. L., Thompson, L., & Bazerman, M. H. (2003). Dyadic processes of disclosure and reciprocity in bargaining with communication. *Journal of Behavioral Decision Making, 16,* 17–34.

[45] Croson, R. (1999). Look at me when you say that: An electronic negotiation simulation. *Simulation and Gaming, 30*(1), 23–37.

[46] Ibid.

[47] Kiesler & Sproull, "Group decision making."

[48] Naquin, C., & Paulson, G. (2003). Online bargaining and interpersonal trust. *Journal of Applied Psychology, 88*(1), 113–120.

[49] Shaw, M. E. (1981). *Group dynamics: The psychology of small group behavior* (3rd ed.). New York: McGraw-Hill.

[50] Strodtbeck, F. L., & Hook, L. H. (1961). The social dimensions of a 12-man jury table. *Sociometry, 24*(4), 397–415.

more than others. Dynamic cues can define status, such as nodding in approval, touching (high-status people touch those of lower status but not vice versa), hesitating, and frowning. Leaders such as Steve Jobs are masters at nonverbal communication cues, such as stepping out from behind the lectern, fully facing the audience, making eye contact, and keeping body movements relaxed and natural—all signs of high competence. Conversely, when Sony USA CEO Howard Stringer—normally a strong speaker—met with journalists in Tokyo he played with a ballpoint pen as he spoke and appeared nervous and disjointed to his audience.[51]

What happens when negotiators interact via technology, such as electronic mail? The traditional status cues are missing, and the dynamic has less impact. Consequently, power and status differences are minimized. People in traditionally weak positions in face-to-face negotiations become more powerful when communicating via information technology because status cues are harder to read.[52] In a direct test of this idea, some managers negotiated via e-mail and some negotiated via instant messaging.[53] Instant messaging is more like face-to-face interaction because negotiators need to respond quickly and in real time. Therefore, we hypothesized that instant messaging would be an advantage when negotiators had a strong bargaining position but would backfire when negotiators had a weak bargaining position because they would be "exposed" and could not easily adapt. Indeed, sellers who had strong arguments for their product fared particularly well in instant messaging because they could verbally dominate the buyers. However, sellers who had weaker arguments were not able to counter-argue when using instant messaging and did much better negotiating via traditional e-mail. The message: If you have a strong bargaining position, face-to-face interaction is ideal; if you have a weak bargaining position, impoverished media provide an important buffer.

People who would normally not approach others in person are much more likely to initiate e-mail exchange. Traditional status cues such as position and title are not as obvious in e-mail. It is often impossible to tell whether you are communicating with a president or a clerk on e-mail because addresses are often shortened and may be difficult to comprehend. Even when they can be deciphered, e-mail addresses identify the organization, but not necessarily job titles, social importance, or level in the organization of the sender. Dynamic status cues, such as dress, mannerisms, age, and gender, are also missing in e-mail. In this sense, e-mail acts as an equalizer because it is difficult for high-status people to dominate the discussion. The absence of these cues leads people to respond more openly and less hesitatingly than in face-to-face interaction. People are less likely to conform to social norms and other people when interacting via electronic communication.

Overall, the amount of participation will be less in electronic versus face-to-face communication, but the contributions of members will be more equal.[54] For example, when groups of executives meet face-to-face, men are five times more likely than women to make the first decision proposal. When those same groups meet via computer, women make the first proposal as often as men do.[55] Furthermore, the time to complete a task is longer on e-mail than in face-to-face interaction, probably because people talk much faster than they write.

---

[51] Goman, C. K. (2009, July 17). Body language: Mastering the silent language of leadership. *The Washington Post.* Washingtonpost.com

[52] Sproull & Kiesler, *Connections.*

[53] Loewenstein, J., Morris, M. W., Chakravarti, A., Thompson, L., & Kopelman, S. (2005). At a loss for words: Dominating the conversation and the outcome in negotiation as a function of intricate arguments and communication media. *Organizational Behavior and Human Decision Processes, 98*(1), 28–38.

[54] McGrath, J. E., & Hollingshead, A. B. (1994). *Groups interacting with technology.* Thousand Oaks, CA: Sage.

[55] McGuire, T., Kiesler, S., & Siegel, J. (1987). Group and computer-mediated discussion effects in risk decision-making. *Journal of Personality and Social Psychology, 52*(5), 917–930.

Social Networks

In traditional organizations, social networks are determined by who talks to whom; in the new organization, social networks are determined by who communicates with whom via technology. People on the periphery who communicate electronically become better integrated into their organization.[56] Computerized interaction increases the resources of low-network people.

The nature of social networks that shape negotiation behavior change dramatically when information technology enters the picture as a form of communication. E-mail networks, or connections between people who communicate via e-mail, increase the information resources of low-network people. When people need assistance (e.g., information or resources), they often turn to their immediate social network. When such help is not available, they use weak ties—such as relationships with acquaintances or strangers—to seek help that is unavailable from friends or colleagues. However, in the absence of personal relationships or the expectation of direct reciprocity, help from weak ties might not be forthcoming or could be of low quality.

Some companies, particularly global companies and those in the fields of information technology and communications, rely on e-mail and employees within the company forming connections with each other on the basis of no physical contact. The incentives for taking the time to assist someone who is dealing with a problem and is located in a different part of the world are quite minuscule.

Another possibility is to catalog or store information in some easily accessible database. In a technical company, this database would include published reports and scientific manuals. However, engineers and managers do not like to consult technical reports to obtain needed information; most of the information they use to solve their problems is obtained through face-to-face discussions. People in organizations usually prefer to exchange help through strong collegial ties, which develop through physical proximity, similarity, and familiarity. For example, 80% of companies indicated they intend to increase their use of personal network hiring methods in the future, including the use of employee referrals and contacts made through such sites as Facebook or LinkedIn. These same companies decreased their use of broad-range job boards such as Monster and CareerBuilder, where a posted position can garner thousands of resumes from unknown, and often unqualified, applicants.[57] Is it sending or receiving messages that expand one's social network and ultimate organizational commitment? The amount of e-mail a person sends (but not receives) predicts commitment.[58] Thus, e-mail can provide an alternate route to letting people have a voice if they are low contributors in face-to-face meetings.

Risk Taking

Consider the following choices:

> Option 1: $20,000 return over 2 years
> Option 2: 50% chance of $40,000 return; 50% chance of nothing

Obviously, option 1 is the "safe" (riskless) choice; option 2 is the risky choice. However, these two options are mathematically identical, meaning people should not favor one option over the other

---

[56] Eveland, J. D., & Bikson, T. K. (1988). Work group structures and computer support: A field experiment. *Transactions on Office Information Systems, 6*(4), 354–379.
[57] Light, J. (2011, January 18). Recruiters rethink online playbook. *The Wall Street Journal.* Wsj.com
[58] Sproull & Kiesler, *Connections.*

(see also Appendix 1). When posed with these choices, most people are risk-averse, meaning they select the option that has the sure payoff as opposed to holding out for the chance to win big (or, equally as likely, not win at all). Consider what happens when the following choice is proposed:

Option 1: Sure loss of $20,000 over 2 years
Option 2: 50% chance of losing $40,000; 50% of losing nothing

Most managers are risk-seeking and choose option 2. Why? According to the **framing effect** (see Chapter 2), people are risk-averse for gains and risk-seeking for losses.[59] This tendency can lead to preference reversals. By manipulating a reference point, a person will exhibit inconsistent choice.

Groups tend to make riskier decisions than do individuals given the same choice. Thus, risk-seeking is greatly exaggerated in groups who meet face-to-face. Paradoxically, groups who make decisions via electronic communication are risk-seeking for both gains and losses.[60] Furthermore, executives are just as confident of their decisions whether they are made through electronic communication or face-to-face communication. For example, in comparisons of people negotiating face-to-face, by e-mail, or through a combination of both, people who use only e-mail reach more impasses.[61]

Rapport and Social Norms

Building trust and rapport is critical for negotiation success. The greater the face-to-face contact between negotiators and the greater the rapport, the more integrative the outcomes are likely to be. Rapport is more difficult to establish with impoverished mediums of communication. In one investigation, some negotiators were instructed to stand face-to-face or side-by-side (unable to see each other) in a simulated strike negotiation. Face-to-face negotiators were more likely to coordinate on a settlement early in the strike, resulting in higher joint gains.[62] Further, rapport was higher between face-to-face negotiators than between side-by-side negotiators. In a different investigation, comparisons were made between face-to-face, videoconference, and audio-only negotiation interactions.[63] Face-to-face negotiators felt a greater amount of rapport than did negotiators in the videoconference and audio-only conditions. Further, independent observers judged face-to-face negotiators to be more "in sync" with each other. Face-to-face negotiators trusted each other more and were more successful at coordinating their decisions.

Paranoia

On the TV show *Saturday Night Live,* Pat (Julia Sweeney) was a character whose sex was unknown. Pat had an androgynous name, wore baggy clothes, and did not display any stereotypical male or female characteristics or preferences. Most people found it maddening to interact with Pat without knowing his or her gender. Gender ambiguity also happens when interacting via technology. It is generally impolite to ask someone whether he or she is a man or woman. Therefore, we are left feeling uncertain. Uncertainty, consequently, increases paranoia. Paranoid people are more likely to assume the worst about another person or situation.[64]

---

[59] Kahneman, D., & Tversky, A. (1979). Prospect theory: An analysis of decision under risk. *Econometrica, 47,* 263–291.
[60] McGuire, Kiesler, & Siegel, "Group and computer-mediated discussion."
[61] Shell, G. R. (1999). *Bargaining for advantage: Negotiation strategies for reasonable people.* New York: Viking.
[62] Drolet & Morris, "Rapport in conflict resolution."
[63] Ibid.
[64] Kramer, "Dubious battle."

When technological change creates new social situations, people invent new ways of behaving. Today's electronic technology is impoverished in social cues and shared experience. People "talk" to other people, but they do so alone.[65] As a result, their messages are likely to display less social awareness. The advantage is that social posturing and sycophancy decline. The disadvantage is that politeness and concern for others also decline. Two characteristics of computer-based communication—the plain text and perceived ephemerality of messages—make it relatively easy for a person to forget or ignore his or her audience and consequently send messages that ignore social boundaries, disclose the self, and are too blunt.[66]

Did the following exchange occur in a meeting room or via the Internet?

NEGOTIATOR A: If I do not get your answer by tomorrow, then I assume that you agree with my proposal.

NEGOTIATOR B: From my perspective, I do not see any rationale or any incentive to transfer this revolutionary technology to your division.

NEGOTIATOR A: I do not have to remind you that pushing the issue up the corporate ladder can prejudice both our careers.

NEGOTIATOR B: Your offer is ridiculous.

NEGOTIATOR A: It is my final offer.

Most people correctly note that this exchange occurred on the Internet. The phenomenon of flaming suggests that through electronic mail, actions and decisions (not just messages) might become more extreme and impulsive.[67]

STRATEGIES FOR ENHANCING TECHNOLOGY-MEDIATED NEGOTIATIONS

Often, negotiators do not have the luxury of face-to-face meetings for the duration of their negotiations. Under such circumstances, what strategies can be employed to enhance successful pie-expansion and pie-slicing? Consider the following tactics.

Initial Face-to-Face Experience

The effectiveness of virtual and face-to-face teams was compared as they worked on a brainstorming exercise and a negotiation exercise.[68] Virtual teams worked better on the brainstorming exercise, but face-to-face teams did better on the negotiation exercise. Moreover, even though the face-to-face teams communicated better initially (during the early stages of a project), as virtual teams gained experience, they communicated as openly and shared information as effectively as face-to-face teams.[69] According to Alge, "A manager who wants to put a working group together for a long, complex project should choose a team whose members are in the same location, or initially invest the resources to give the team members an opportunity to get to know each other. Then, as teams become more experienced and familiar with each other and the technology, they can exchange ideas more effectively using 'lean' Internet media

---

[65] Sproull & Kiesler, *Connections.*
[66] Ibid.
[67] Ibid.
[68] Alge, B. J., Wiethoff, C., & Klein, H. J. (2003). When does the medium matter? Knowledge-building experiences and opportunities in decision-making teams. *Organizational Behavior and Human Decision Processes, 91,* 26–37.
[69] Ibid.

that lack the nonverbal communication, social cues, and nuances that exist in face-to-face interactions."[70]

Oftentimes, people develop rapport on the basis of a short face-to-face meeting, which can reduce uncertainty and build trust. Face-to-face contact humanizes people and creates expectations for negotiators to use in their subsequent long-distance work together. A full 59% of executives surveyed said while their use of technology-driven meetings had increased during the recession, nearly 80% indicated they approved of in-person contact. "The art of negotiation takes the kind of nuance that is only present in an in-person meeting," said Dan L'Ecuyer, Vice President of Sales and Marketing at CSP Technologies. "I don't think you can really get at strategies without face-to-face time."[71]

One-Day Videoconference/Teleconference

If an initial, face-to-face meeting is out of the question, an alternative may be to get everyone online so that at least people can attach a name to a face. Depending upon the size of the team and locations of different members, this alternative may be more feasible than a face-to-face meeting. For example, in one investigation, negotiators who had never met one another were instructed to have a short phone call prior to commencing e-mail only negotiations.[72] The sole purpose of the phone call was to get to know the other person. Negotiators were expressly forbidden to discuss any aspect of the negotiation. The simple act of chatting and exchanging personal information built rapport and overcame some of the communication difficulties associated with the impoverished medium of e-mail. Another group did not have an initial phone call with the counterparty. Negotiators who engaged in the initial phone conversation found that their attitudes toward their opponents changed; negotiators who had chatted with their opponent felt less competitive and more cooperative before the negotiation began, compared with negotiators who had not chatted with their opponent. In the end, negotiators who had made personal contact with their opponent felt more confident that future interaction with the same person would go smoothly. Trust was thus developed through the rapport-building phone call prior to the negotiation. Not surprisingly, negotiators who had an initial phone call were less likely to impasse and achieved higher joint gains compared to those who did not have the initial phone call. The simple act of making an effort to establish a personal relationship through telephone contact before engaging in e-mail negotiations can have dramatic positive consequences.

Schmoozing

Schmoozing (as described in Chapter 6) is our name for non–task-related contact between people, which has the psychological effect of having established a relationship with someone.[73] The effectiveness of electronic schmoozing has been put to the test, and the results are dramatic: Schmoozing increases liking and rapport and results in more profitable business deals than when people simply "get down to business."[74] Negotiators who schmoozed (on the phone) developed more realistic goals, resulting in a larger range of possible outcomes, and were less likely to reach an impasse compared to non-schmoozers. The key mediating factor was rapport. Moreover, the

[70] Lillich, M. (2003, April 23). Researcher details management challenge: Getting real results from virtual teams. *Ascribe Higher Education News Service.*
[71] The case for face-to-face. (2009). *Forbes Insight.* Images.forbes.com
[72] Morris, Nadler, Kurtzberg, & Thompson, "Schmooze or lose."
[73] Moore, D. A., Kurtzberg, T., Thompson, L., & Morris, M. W. (1999). Long and short routes to success in electronically mediated negotiations: Group affiliations and good vibrations. *Organizational Behavior and Human Decision Processes, 77*(1), 22–43; Morris, Nadler, Kurtzberg, & Thompson, "Schmooze or lose."
[74] Moore, Kurtzberg, Thompson, & Morris, "Long and short routes."

negotiators who schmoozed on the phone prior to getting down to the business of e-negotiation expressed greater optimism about a future working relationship with the other party, compared to negotiators who did not schmooze.[75]

Another route to building trust and rapport is to build a shared social identity. For example, e-negotiations between managers at the same university (company) versus negotiations between competitor universities (other companies) reveals that membership in the same university (company) reduces the likelihood of impasse in e-negotiations.[76] In contrast, negotiators who do not share social ties with their counterpart consistently underperform on the key measures of negotiator performance.

Perhaps the most attractive aspects of schmoozing are that it is relatively low cost and it is efficient. Merely exchanging a few short e-mails describing yourself can lead to better business relations. However, people do not naturally schmooze on e-mail. Instead, team members working remotely have a tendency to get down to business. As a start toward schmoozing, tell the other person something about yourself that does not necessarily relate to the business at hand (e.g., "I really enjoy sea kayaking"); also, provide a context for your own work space (e.g., "It is very late in the day, and there are 20 people at my door, so I do not have time to write a long message"). Furthermore, ask questions that show you are interested in the other party as a person; this approach is an excellent way to search for points of similarity. Finally, provide the link for the next e-mail or exchange (e.g., "I will look forward to hearing your reactions on the preliminary report, and I will also send you the files you requested").

Humor

The use of humor is particularly important in e-negotiations. The earlier negotiators use humor, the better. Beginning an e-mail negotiation with humor results in increased trust and satisfaction, as well as higher joint and individual gains for the party who initiates the humorous exchange.[77] Moreover, when the negotiations are purely distributive, negotiators who use humor in their first offers are more likely to have first offers in the bargaining zone and final settlements more equally distributed.

CONCLUSION

We used the place-time model of social interaction to examine how the medium of communication affects negotiation. We examined how the use of information technology affects social behavior. In particular, we focused on how non–face-to-face interaction results in more actual airtime than does the same group meeting face-to-face. Part of the reason is that cues about someone's status and authority are not as evident when not face-to-face. We discussed social networks and how information technology effectively expands the potential reach and influence of managers. We noted that people are more likely to display risk-seeking behavior (i.e., choosing gambles over sure things) when interacting via information technology, as opposed to face-to-face. Probably the biggest threat to effective negotiation in non–face-to-face settings is the loss of rapport and the tendency for people to be less conscious of social norms, such as politeness rituals. We discussed several methods for enhancing technology-mediated negotiations, including an initial face-to-face experience (so that negotiators can establish social norms), a one-day videoconference, and schmoozing.

---

[75] Morris, Nadler, Kurtzberg, & Thompson, "Schmooze or lose."

[76] Moore, Kurtzberg, Thompson, & Morris, "Long and short routes."

[77] Kurtzberg, T. R., Naquin, C. E., & Belkin, L. Y. (2009) Humor as a relationship-building tool in online negotiations. *International Journal of Conflict Management, 20*(4), 377–397.

APPENDIX 1

Are You a Rational Person? Check Yourself

The purpose of this appendix is to help you assess your own rationality. First, we present the key principles of **individual rationality**, which focuses on how people make independent decisions. Then we present and discuss **game theoretic rationality**, which focuses on how people make interdependent decisions.

WHY IS IT IMPORTANT TO BE RATIONAL?

Let's first consider why it is important for a negotiator to be rational. Rational models of behavior offer a number of important advantages for the negotiator:

- *Pie-expansion and pie-slicing.* Models of rational behavior are based upon the principle of maximization such that the course of action followed guarantees the negotiator will maximize his or her interests (whether that interest is monetary gain, career advancement, prestige, etc.). In short, the best way to maximize one's interests is to follow the prescriptions of a rational model.
- *Learning and personal growth.* The rational models we present in this appendix make clear and definitive statements regarding the superiority of some decisions over others. Thus, they do not allow you to justify or rationalize your behavior. The truth may hurt sometimes, but it is a great learning experience.
- *Measure of perfection.* Rational models provide a measure of perfection or optimality. If rational models did not exist, we would have no way of evaluating how well people perform in negotiations nor what they should strive to do. We would not be able to offer advice to negotiators because we would not have consensus about what is a "good" outcome. Rational models provide an ideal.
- *Diagnosis.* Rational models serve a useful diagnostic purpose because they often reveal where negotiators make mistakes. Because rational models are built on a well-constructed theory of decision making, they offer insight into the mind of the negotiator.
- *Dealing with irrational people.* Negotiators often follow the norm of reciprocity. A negotiator who is well-versed in rational behavior can often deal more effectively with irrational people.
- *Consistency.* Rational models can help us be consistent. Inconsistency in our behavior can inhibit learning. Furthermore, it can send the counterparty ambiguous messages. When people are confused or uncertain they are more defensive and trust diminishes.
- *Decision making.* Rational models provide a straightforward method for thinking about decisions and provide a way of choosing among options, which will produce the "best" outcome for the chooser, maximizing his or her own preferences (as we will see in this appendix).

INDIVIDUAL DECISION MAKING

Negotiation is ultimately about making decisions. If we cannot make good decisions on our own, joint decision making will be even more difficult. Sometimes our decisions are trivial, such as whether to have chocolate cake or cherry pie for dessert. Other times, our decisions are of great consequence, such as choosing a career or a spouse. Our decisions about how to spend the weekend may seem fundamentally different from deciding what to do with our entire life, but some generalities cut across domains. Rational decision making models provide the tools necessary for analyzing any decision. The three main types of decisions are riskless choice, decision making under uncertainty, and risky choice.

Riskless Choice

Riskless choice, or decision making under certainty, involves choosing between two or more readily available options. For example, a choice between two apartments is a riskless choice, as is choosing among 31 flavors of ice cream or selecting a book to read. Often, we do not consider these events to be decisions because they are so simple and easy. However, at other times, we struggle when choosing among jobs or careers, and we find ourselves in a state of indecision.

Imagine you have been accepted into the MBA program at your top two choices: university X and university Y. This enviable situation is an **approach-approach conflict**, meaning that in some sense you cannot lose—both options are attractive; you need only to decide which alternative is best for you. You have to make your final choice by next week. To analyze this decision situation, we will employ a method known as **multiattribute utility technique** (or **MAUT**).[1] According to MAUT, a decision maker should follow five steps: (a) identify the alternatives, (b) identify dimensions or attributes of the alternatives, (c) evaluate the utility associated with each dimension, (d) weight or prioritize each dimension in terms of importance, and (e) make a final choice.

IDENTIFICATION OF ALTERNATIVES The first step is usually quite straightforward. The decision maker simply identifies the relevant alternatives. For example, you would identify the schools to which you had been accepted. In other situations, the alternatives may not be as obvious. In the case that you did not get any acceptance letters, you must brainstorm new options.

IDENTIFICATION OF ATTRIBUTES The second step is more complex and involves identifying the key attributes associated with the alternatives. The attributes are the features of an alternative that make it appealing or not. For example, when choosing among schools, relevant attributes might include the cost of tuition, reputation of the program, course requirements, placement options, weather, cultural aspects, family, and faculty.

UTILITY The next step is to evaluate the relative utility or value of each alternative for each attribute. For example, you might use a 1-to-5 scale to evaluate how each school ranks on each of your identified attributes. You might evaluate the reputation of university X very highly (5) but the weather as very unattractive (1); you might evaluate university Y's reputation to be moderately high (3) but the weather to be fabulous (5). MAUT assumes preferential independence of attributes (i.e., the value of one attribute is independent of the value of others).

---

[1] Baron, J. (1988). *Thinking and deciding* (pp. 330–351). Boston: Cambridge University Press.

WEIGHT   In addition to determining the evaluation of each attribute, the decision maker also evaluates how important that attribute is to him or her. The importance of each attribute is referred to as **weight** in the decision process. Again, we can use a simple numbering system, with 1 representing relatively unimportant attributes and 5 representing very important attributes. For example, you might consider the reputation of the school to be very important (5) but the cultural attributes of the city to be insignificant (1).

MAKING A DECISION   The final step in the MAUT procedure is to compute a single, overall evaluation of each alternative. For this task, first multiply the utility evaluation of each attribute by its corresponding weight, and then sum the weighted scores across each attribute. Finally, select the option that has the highest overall score.

We can see from the hypothetical example in Exhibit A1-1 that university X is a better choice for the student compared to university Y. However, it is a close decision. If the importance of any of the attributes were to change (e.g., tuition cost, reputation, climate, or culture), then the overall decision could change. Similarly, if the evaluation of any attributes changes, then the final choice may change. Decision theory can tell us how to choose, but it cannot tell us how to weigh the attributes that go into making choices.

According to the **dominance principle**, one alternative dominates another if it is strictly better on at least one dimension and at least as good on all others. For example, imagine university Y had been evaluated as a 5 in terms of tuition cost, a 5 in reputation, a 4 in climate, and a 4 in culture, and university X had been evaluated as a 1, 5, 4, and 3, respectively. In this case, we can quickly see that university Y is just as good as university X on two dimensions (reputation and climate) and better on the two remaining dimensions (tuition cost and culture). Thus, university Y dominates university X. Identifying a dominant alternative greatly simplifies decision making: If one alternative dominates the other, we should select the dominant option.

The example seems simple enough. In many situations, however, we are faced with considering many more alternatives, each having different dimensions. It may not be easy to spot a

EXHIBIT A1-1

Multiattribute Decision Making

Attribute (weight)	University Y (evaluation)	University X (evaluation)
Tuition cost (4)	Inexpensive (5)	Expensive (1)
Reputation (5)	Medium (3)	High (5)
Climate (3)	Lousy (1)	Great (5)
Culture (1)	Good (4)	Poor (1)

Utility of University (Y) = (4*5) + (5*3) + (3*1) + (1*4) = 42
Utility of University (X) = (4*1) + (5*5) + (3*5) + (1*1) = 45

dominant alternative. What should we do in this case? The first step is to eliminate from consideration all options dominated by others and to choose among the nondominated alternatives that remain.

The dominance principle as a method of choice seems quite compelling, but it applies only to situations in which one alternative is clearly superior to others. It does not help us with the agonizing task of choosing among options that involve trade-offs among highly valued aspects. Some people may use "random" choice. The wisdom of choosing randomly depends on whether the choice set is among "noncomparable" or "indifferent" options: systematic randomization among "noncomparable" options may lead to a chain of decisions resulting in monetary loss, but not when choosing among indifferent options.[2] We now turn to situations that defy MAUT and dominance detection.

Decision Making Under Uncertainty

Sometimes we must make decisions when the alternatives are uncertain or unknown. These situations are known as **decision making under uncertainty** or **decision making in ignorance**.[3] In such situations, the decision maker has no idea about the likelihood of events. Consider, for example, a decision to plan a social event outdoors or indoors. If the weather is sunny and warm, it would be better to hold the event outdoors; if it is rainy and cold, it is better to plan the event indoors. The plans must be made a month in advance, but the weather cannot be predicted a month in advance. The distinction between risk and uncertainty hinges upon whether probabilities are known exactly (e.g., as in games of chance) or whether they must be judged by the decision maker with some degree of imprecision (e.g., almost everything else). Hence, "ignorance" might be viewed merely as an extreme degree of uncertainty when the decision maker has no clue (e.g., probability that the closing price of Dai Ichi stock tomorrow on the Tokyo stock exchange is above 1,600 yen).

Risky Choice

In decision making under uncertainty, the likelihood of events is unknown; in **risky choice** situations, the probabilities are known. Most theories of decision making are based on an assessment of the probability that some event will take place. Because the outcomes of risky choice situations are not fully known, outcomes are often referred to as "prospects." Many people cannot compute risk accurately, even when the odds are perfectly known, as in the case of gambling. (See Exhibit A1-2 for some odds associated with winning the lottery.)

Negotiation is a risky choice situation because parties cannot be completely certain about the occurrence of a particular event. For instance, a negotiator cannot be certain that mutual settlement will be reached because negotiations could break off as each party opts for his or her BATNA. To understand risky choice decision making in negotiations, we need to understand **expected utility theory.**

EXPECTED UTILITY THEORY   Utility theory has a long history, dating back to the sixteenth century when French noblemen commissioned their court mathematicians to help them

---

[2] Danan, E. (2010). Randomization vs. selection: How to choose in the absence of preference? *Management Science, 56*(3), 503–518.
[3] Yates, J. F. (1990). *Judgment and decision making.* Upper Saddle River, NJ: Prentice Hall.

EXHIBIT A1-2

Understanding Risk and Probability

Every day, millions of people purchase lottery tickets and gamble. But do they really understand the stakes? Consider these statistics:

- If you toss a coin 26 times, your odds of getting 26 heads in a row are greater than the chance that your Powerball ticket will win you the jackpot.
- To have a reasonable chance of winning the Massachusetts lottery by purchasing a lottery ticket each week, you would need to persist for 1.6 million years.
- If you drive 10 miles to buy a Powerball ticket, you are 16 times more likely to die en route in a car crash than to win.
- If you are an average British citizen who buys a ticket in Britain's National Lottery on Monday, you are 2,500 times more likely to die before the Saturday draw than to win the jackpot.
- Viewers of the lottery draw are 3 times more likely to die during the 20-minute program than to win.

Source: Adapted from Myers, D. G. (2002). *Intuition: Its powers and perils,* (p. 224). Yale University Press: New Haven, CT.

gamble. Modern utility theory is expressed in the form of gambles, probabilities, and payoffs. Why do we need to know about gambling to be effective negotiators? Virtually all negotiations involve choices, and many choices involve uncertainty, which makes them gambles. Before we can negotiate effectively, we need to be clear about our own preferences. Utility theory helps us do that.

EU is a theory of choices made by an individual actor.[4] It prescribes a theory of "rational behavior." Behavior is rational if a person acts in a way that maximizes his or her decision utility or the anticipated satisfaction from a particular outcome. The maximization of utility is often equated with the maximization of monetary gain, but satisfaction can come in many nonmonetary forms as well. Obviously, people care about things other than money. For example, weather, culture, quality of life, and personal esteem are all factors that bear on a job decision, in addition to salary.

EU is based on revealed preferences. People's preferences or utilities are not directly observable but must be inferred from their choices and willful behavior. To understand what a person really wants and values, we have to see what choices he or she makes. Actions speak louder than words. In this sense, utility maximization is a tautological statement: A person's choices reflect personal utilities; therefore, all behaviors may be represented by the maximization of this hypothetical utility scale.

---

[4] von Neumann, J., & Morgenstern, O. (1947). *Theory of games and economic behavior.* Princeton, NJ: Princeton University Press.

EU is based on a set of axioms about preferences among gambles. The basic result of the theory is summarized by a theorem stating that if a person's preferences satisfy the specified axioms, then the person's behavior maximizes the expected utility. Next, we explore utility functions.

UTILITY FUNCTION   A **utility function** is the quantification of a person's preferences with respect to certain objects such as jobs, potential mates, and ice cream flavors. Utility functions assign numbers to objects and gambles that have objects as their prizes (e.g., flip a coin and win a trip to Hawaii or free groceries). For example, a manager's choice to stay at her current company could be assigned an overall value, such as a 7 on a 10-point scale. Her option to take a new job might be assigned a value of either 10 or 2, depending on how things work out for her at the new job. One's current job is the sure thing; the alternative job, because of its uncertainty, is a gamble. How should we rationally make a decision between the two?

We first need to examine our utility function. The following seven axioms guarantee the existence of a utility function. The axioms are formulated in terms of preference-or-indifference relations defined over a set of outcomes.[5] As will become clear, the following axioms provide the foundation for individual decision making, as well as negotiation or joint decision making.

Comparability.   A key assumption of EU is that everything is comparable. That is, given any two objects, a person must prefer one to the other or be indifferent to both; no two objects are incomparable. For example, a person may compare a dime and a nickel or a cheeseburger and a dime. We might compare a job offer in the Midwest to a job offer on the West Coast. Utility theory implies a single, underlying dimension of "satisfaction" associated with everything. We can recall instances in which we refused to make comparisons, which often happens in the case of social or emotional issues such as having to do with marriage and children. However, according to utility theory, we need to be able to compare everything to be truly rational. Many people are uncomfortable with this idea, just as people can be in conflict about what is negotiable.

Closure.   The **closure property** states that if x and y are available alternatives, then so are all of the gambles of the form (x, p, y) that can be formed with x and y as outcomes. In this formulation, x and y refer to available alternatives; p refers to the probability that x will occur. Therefore, (x, p, y) states that x will occur with probability p, otherwise y will occur. The converse must also be true: $(x, p, y) = (y, 1 - p, x)$, or y will occur with probability $(1 - p)$, otherwise x will occur.

For example, imagine you assess the probability of receiving a raise from your current employer to be about 30%. The closure property states that the situation expressed as a 30% chance of receiving a raise (otherwise, no raise) is identical to the statement that you have a 70% chance of not receiving a raise (otherwise, receiving a raise).

So far, utility theory may seem to be so obvious and simple that it is absurd to spell it out in any detail. However, we will soon see how people violate basic "common sense" all the time and, hence, behave irrationally.

---

[5] Coombs, C. H., Dawes, R. M., & Tversky, A. (1970). *Mathematical psychology: An elementary introduction.* Upper Saddle River, NJ: Prentice Hall.

Transitivity.   Transitivity means that if we prefer *x* to *y* and *y* to *z,* then we should prefer *x* to *z.* Similarly, if we are indifferent between *x* and *y* and *y* and *z,* then we will be indifferent between *x* and *z.*

Suppose your employer offers you one of three options: a transfer to Seattle, a transfer to Pittsburgh, or a raise of $5,000. You prefer a raise of $5,000 over a move to Pittsburgh, and you prefer a move to Seattle more than a $5,000 raise. The **transitivity property** states that you should therefore prefer a move to Seattle over a move to Pittsburgh. If your preferences were not transitive, you would always want to move somewhere else. Further, a third party could become rich by continuously "selling" your preferred options to you.

Reducibility.   The **reducibility axiom** refers to a person's attitude toward a compound lottery, in which the prizes may be tickets to other lotteries. According to the reducibility axiom, a person's attitude toward a compound lottery depends only on the ultimate prizes and the chance of getting them as determined by the laws of probability; the actual gambling mechanism is irrelevant:

$$(x, pq, y) = [(x, p, y), q, y]$$

Suppose that the dean of admissions at your top university choice tells you that you have a 25% chance of getting accepted to the MBA program. How do you feel about the situation? Now, suppose the dean tells you that you have a 50% chance of not being accepted and a 50% chance you will have to face a lottery-type admission procedure, wherein half the applicants will get accepted and half will not. In which situation do you prefer to be? According to the reducibility axiom, both situations are identical. Your chances of getting admitted into graduate school are the same in each case: exactly 25%. The difference between the two situations is that one involves a **compound gamble** and the other does not.

Compound gambles differ from simple gambles ones in that their outcomes are themselves gambles rather than pure outcomes. Furthermore, probabilities are the same in both gambles. If people have an aversion or attraction to gambling, however, these outcomes may not seem the same. This axiom has important implications for negotiation; the format by which alternatives are presented to negotiators—in other words, in terms of gambles or compound gambles—strongly affects our behavior.

Substitutability.   The **substitutability axiom** states that gambles that have prizes about which people are indifferent are interchangeable. For example, suppose one prize is substituted for another in a lottery but the lottery is left otherwise unchanged. If you are indifferent to both the old and the new prizes, you should be indifferent about the lotteries. If you prefer one prize to the other, you will prefer the lottery that offers the preferred prize.

For example, imagine you work in the finance division of a company and your supervisor asks you how you feel about transferring to either the marketing or sales division in your company. You respond that you are indifferent. Then your supervisor presents you with a choice: You can be transferred to the sales division, or you can move to a finance position in an out-of-state parent branch of the company. After wrestling with the decision, you decide you prefer to move out of state rather than transfer to the sales division. A few days later, your supervisor surprises you by asking whether you prefer to be transferred to marketing or to be transferred out of state. According to the substitutability axiom, you should prefer to transfer because, as you previously indicated, you are indifferent to marketing and sales; they are substitutable choices.

Betweenness.   The **betweenness axiom** asserts that if x is preferred to y, then x must be preferred to any probability mixture of x and y, which in turn must be preferred to y. This principle is certainly not objectionable for monetary outcomes. For example, most of us would rather have a dime than a nickel and would rather have a probability of either a dime or a nickel than the nickel itself. But consider nonmonetary outcomes, such as skydiving, Russian roulette, and bungee jumping. To an outside observer, people who skydive apparently prefer a probability mixture of living and dying over either one of them alone; otherwise, one can easily either stay alive or kill oneself without ever skydiving. People who like to risk their lives appear to contradict the betweenness axiom. A more careful analysis reveals, however, that this situation, strange as it may be, is not incompatible with the betweenness axiom. The actual outcomes involved in skydiving are (a) staying alive after skydiving, (b) staying alive without skydiving, or (c) dying while skydiving. In choosing to skydive, therefore, a person prefers a probability mix of (a) and (c) over (b). This analysis reveals that "experience" has a utility.

Continuity or Solvability.   Suppose that of three objects—A, B, and C—you prefer A to B and B to C. Now, consider a lottery in which there is a probability, p, of getting A and a probability of $1 - p$ of getting C. If $p = 0$, the lottery is equivalent to C; if $p = 1$, the lottery is equivalent to A. In the first case, you prefer B to the lottery; in the second case, you prefer the lottery to B. According to the **continuity axiom**, a value, p, which falls between 0 and 1 indicates your indifference between B and the lottery. This sounds reasonable enough.

Now consider the following example involving three outcomes: receiving a dime, receiving a nickel, and being shot at dawn.[6] Certainly, most of us prefer a dime to a nickel and a nickel to being shot. The continuity axiom, however, states that at some point of inversion, some probability mixture involving receiving a dime and being shot at dawn is equivalent to receiving a nickel. This derivation seems particularly disdainful for most people because no price is equal to risking one's life. However, the counterintuitive nature of this example stems from an inability to understand very small probabilities. In the abstract, people believe they would never choose to risk their life but, in reality, people do so all the time. For example, we cross the street to buy some product for a nickel less, although by doing so we risk getting hit by a car and being killed.

In summary, whenever these axioms hold, a utility function exists that (a) preserves a person's preferences among options and gambles and (b) satisfies the **expectation principle**: The utility of a gamble equals the expected utility of its outcomes. This utility scale is uniquely determined except for an origin and a unit of measurement.

EXPECTED VALUE PRINCIPLE   Imagine you have a rare opportunity to invest in a highly innovative start-up company. The company has developed a new technology that allows cars to run without gasoline. The cars are fuel efficient, environmentally clean, and less expensive to maintain than regular gasoline-fueled cars. On the other hand, the technology is new and unproven. Further, the company does not have the resources to compete with the established automakers. Nevertheless, if this technology is successful, an investment in the company at this point will have a 30-fold return. Suppose you just inherited $5,000 from your aunt. You could invest the money in the company and possibly earn $150,000—a risky choice. Or you could keep the money and pass up the investment opportunity. You assess the probability of success to be about 20%. (A minimum investment of $5,000 is required.) What do you do?

---

[6] von Neumann & Morgenstern, *Theory of games and economic behavior.*

The dominance principle does not offer a solution to this decision situation because it provides no clearly dominant alternatives. But the situation contains the necessary elements to use the **expected value principle**, which applies when a decision maker must choose among two or more prospects, as in the previous example. The "expectation" or "expected value" of a prospect is the sum of the objective values of the outcomes multiplied by the probability of their occurrence.

For a variety of reasons, you believe there is a 20% chance the investment could result in a return of $150,000, which mathematically is $0.2 \times \$150,000 = \$30,000$. There is an 80% chance the investment will not yield a return, or $0.8 \times \$0 = \$0$. Thus, the expected value of this gamble is $30,000 minus the cost, or $- \$5,000, = \$25,000$.

The expected value principle dictates that the decision maker should select the prospect with the greatest expected value. In this case, the risky option (with an expected value of $30,000) has a greater expected value than the sure option (expected value of $0).

A related principle applies to evaluation decisions, or situations in which decision makers must state, and be willing to act upon, the subjective worth of a given alternative. Suppose you could choose to "sell" to another person your opportunity to invest. What would you consider to be a fair price to do so? According to the expected-value evaluation principle, the evaluation of a prospect should be equal to its expected value. That is, the "fair price" for such a gamble would be $25,000. Similarly, the opposite holds: Suppose your next door neighbor held the opportunity but was willing to sell the option to you. According to the expected value principle, people would pay up to $25,000 for the opportunity to gamble.

The expected value principle is intuitively appealing, but should we use it to make decisions? To answer this question, it is helpful to examine the rationale for using expected value as a prescription. Let's consider the short-term and long-term consequences.[7] Imagine that you will inherit $5,000 every year for the next 50 years. Each year, you must decide whether to invest the inheritance in a start-up company (risky choice) or keep the money (the sure choice). The expected value of a prospect is its long-run average value. This principle is derived from a fundamental principle: the **law of large numbers**.[8] The law of large numbers states that the mean return will get closer and closer to its expected value the more times a gamble is repeated. Thus, we can be fairly sure that after 50 years of investing your money, the average return would be about $25,000. Some years you would lose, others you would make money, but on average your return would be $25,000. When you look at the gamble this way, it seems reasonable to invest.

Now imagine the investment decision is a once-in-a-lifetime opportunity. In this case, the law of large numbers does not apply to the expected-value decision principle. You will either make $150,000, make nothing, or keep $5,000. No in-between options are possible. Under such circumstances, you can often find good reasons to reject the guidance of the expected value principle.[9] For example, suppose you need a new car. If the gamble is successful, buying a car is no problem. But if the gamble is unsuccessful, you will have no money at all. Therefore, you may decide that buying a used car at or under $5,000 is a more sensible choice.

The expected value concept is the basis for a standard way of labeling risk-taking behavior. For example, in the previous situation you could either take the investment gamble or receive $25,000 from selling the opportunity to someone else. In this case, the "value" of the sure thing

---

[7] Yates, *Judgment and decision making.*
[8] Feller, W. (1968). *An introduction to probability theory and its applications: Vol. 1* (3rd ed.). New York: Wiley; Woodroofe, M. (1975). *Probability with applications.* New York, McGraw-Hill.
[9] Yates, *Judgment and decision making.*

(i.e., receiving $25,000) is identical to the expected value of the gamble. Therefore, the "objective worth" of both alternatives is identical. What would you rather do? Your choice reveals your **risk attitude**. If you are indifferent to the two choices and are content to decide on the basis of a coin flip, you are **risk-neutral** or **risk-indifferent**. If you prefer the sure thing, then your behavior may be described as **risk-averse**. If you choose to gamble, your behavior is classified as **risk-seeking**.

Although some individual differences occur in people's risk attitudes, people do not exhibit consistent risk-seeking or risk-averse behavior.[10] Rather, risk attitudes are highly context dependent. The four-fold pattern of risk attitudes predicts people will be risk-averse for moderate- to high-probability gains and low-probability losses, and risk-seeking for low-probability gains and moderate- to high-probability losses.[11]

EXPECTED UTILITY PRINCIPLE   How much money would you be willing to pay to play a game with the following two rules: (a) An unbiased coin is tossed until it lands on heads; (b) the player of the game is paid $2 if heads appears on the opening toss, $4 if heads first appears on the second toss, $8 on the third toss, $16 on the fourth toss, and so on. Before reading further, indicate how much you would be willing to pay to play the game.

To make a decision based upon rational analysis, let's calculate the expected value of the game by multiplying the payoff for each possible outcome by the probability that it will occur. Although the probability of the first head appearing on toss n becomes progressively smaller as n increases, the probability never becomes zero. In this case, note that the probability of heads for the first time on any given toss is $(1/2)^n$, and the payoff in each case is (2^n); hence, each term of the infinite series has an expected value of $1. The implication is that the value of the game is infinite.[12] Even though the value of this game is infinite, most people are seldom willing to pay more than a few dollars to play it. Most people believe the expected value principle produces an absurd conclusion in this case. The observed reluctance to pay to play the game, despite its objective attractiveness, is known as the **St. Petersburg paradox**.[13]

How can we explain such an enigma? Expected value is an undefined quantity when the variance of outcomes is infinite. The person or organization offering the game could not guarantee a payoff greater than its total assets, the game was unimaginable, except in truncated and therefore finite form.[14] So what do we do when offered such a choice? To value it as "priceless" or even to pay hundreds of thousands of dollars would be absurd. So, how should managers reason about such situations?

Diminishing Marginal Utility.   The reactions people have to the St. Petersburg game are consistent with the proposition that people decide among prospects not according to their expected objective values but, rather, according to their expected subjective values. In other

[10] Slovic, P. (1962). Convergent validation of risk taking measures. *Journal of Abnormal and Social Psychology, 65*(1), 68–71; Slovic, P. (1964). Assessment of risk taking behavior. *Psychological Bulletin, 61*(3), 220–233.

[11] Tversky, A., & Kahneman, D. (1992). Advances in prospect theory: Cumulative representation of uncertainty. *Journal of Risk and Uncertainty, 5,* 297–323; Tversky, A., & Fox, C. (1995). Weighing risk and uncertainty. *Psychological Review, 102*(2), 269–283.

[12] Lee, W. (1971). *Decision theory and human behavior.* New York: Wiley.

[13] Bernoulli, D. (L. Sommer, Trans.). (1954). Exposition of a new theory on the measurement of risk. (Original work published in 1738.) *Econometrica, 22,* 23–36.

[14] Shapley, L. S. (1977). The St. Petersburg paradox: A con game? *Journal of Economic Theory, 14,* 353–409.

words, the psychological value of money does not increase proportionally as the objective amount increases. To be sure, virtually all of us like more money rather than less money, but we do not necessarily like $20 twice as much as $10. And the difference in our happiness when our $20,000 salary is raised to $50,000 is not the same as when our $600,000 salary is raised to $630,000. Bernoulli proposed a logarithmic function relating the utility of money, *u,* to the amount of money, *x.* This function is **concave**, meaning that the utility of money decreases marginally. Constant additions to monetary amounts result in less and less increased utility. The principle of **diminishing marginal utility** is related to a fundamental principle of psychophysics, wherein good things satiate and bad things escalate. The first bite of a pizza is the best; as we get full, each bite brings less and less utility.

The principle of diminishing marginal utility is simple, yet profound. It is known as the **everyman's utility function (EU)**.[15] According to Bernoulli, a fair price for a gamble should not be determined by its expected (monetary) value but, rather, by its expected utility. Thus, the logarithmic utility function in Exhibit A1-3 yields a finite price for the gamble.

According to EU, each of the possible outcomes of a prospect has a utility (subjective value) that is represented numerically. The more appealing an outcome is, the higher its utility. The expected utility of a prospect is the sum of the utilities of the potential outcomes, each weighted by its probability. According to EU, when choosing among two or more prospects, people should select the option with the highest expected utility. Further, in evaluation situations, risky prospects should have an expected utility equal to the corresponding "sure choice" alternative.

EXHIBIT A1-3

Utility as a Function of Value

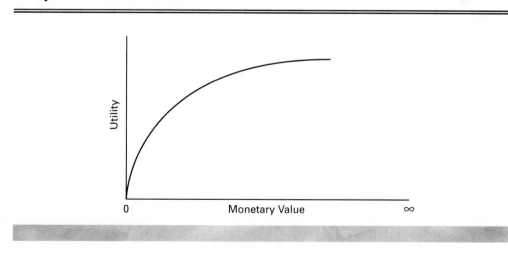

[15] Bernoulli, "Exposition of a new theory."

EU principles have essentially the same form as expected value (EV) principles. The difference is that expectations are computed using objective (dollar) values in EV models as opposed to subjective values (utility) in EU models.

Risk-Taking.   A person's utility function for various prospects reveals something about his or her risk-taking tendencies. If a utility function is concave, a decision maker will always choose a sure thing over a prospect whose expected value is identical to that sure thing. The decision maker's behavior is risk-averse (Exhibit A1-4, Panel A). The risk-averse decision maker would prefer a sure $5 over a 50–50 chance of winning $10 or nothing—even though the expected value of the gamble [0.5($10) + 0.5($0) = $5] is equal to that of the sure thing. If a person's utility function is convex, he or she will choose the risky option (Exhibit A1-4, Panel B). If the utility function is linear, his or her decisions will be risk-neutral and, of course, identical to those predicted by expected value maximization (Exhibit A1-4, Panel C).

If most peoples' utility for gains are concave (i.e., risk-averse), then why would people ever choose to gamble? Bets that offer small probabilities of winning large sums of money (e.g., lotteries, roulette wheels) ought to be especially unattractive, given that the concave utility function that drives the worth of the large prize is considerably lower than the value warranting a very small probability of obtaining the prize.

Consider the following two options. Which would you choose?
Option A: 80% probability of earning $4,000, otherwise $0
Option B: Earn $3,000 for sure

If you are like most people, you chose B. Only a small number of people (20%) choose A.

EXHIBIT A1-4

Risk Attitudes

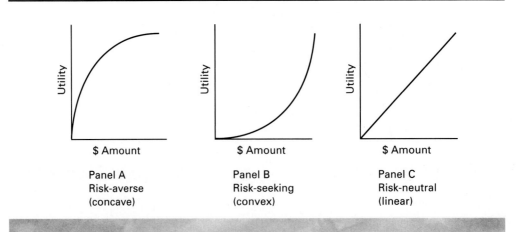

Panel A	Panel B	Panel C
Risk-averse	Risk-seeking	Risk-neutral
(concave)	(convex)	(linear)

Now, consider two different options:

Option C: 20% probability of earning $4,000, otherwise $0

Option D: 25% probability of earning $3,000, otherwise $0

Faced with this choice, a clear majority (65%) choose option C over option D (the smaller, more likely payoff).[16]

However, in this example, the decision maker violates EU, which requires consistency between the A versus B choice and the C versus D choice. In Exhibit A1-5, Branch 1 depicts the C versus D choice [i.e., 25% chance of making $3,000 (otherwise $0) or 20% chance of making $4,000 (otherwise $0)]. In Branch 2 of Exhibit A1-5, another stage has been added to the gamble between A and B, which effectively makes the two-stage gamble in Branch 2 identical to the one-stage gamble in Branch 1. Because Branch 1 is objectively identical to Branch 2, the decision maker should not make different choices. Stated another way, in the A versus B and C versus D choices, the ratio is the same: $(0.8/1) = (0.20/0.25)$. However, people's preferences usually reverse. According to the **certainty effect**, people have a

EXHIBIT A1-5

Allais' Paradox Decision Tree

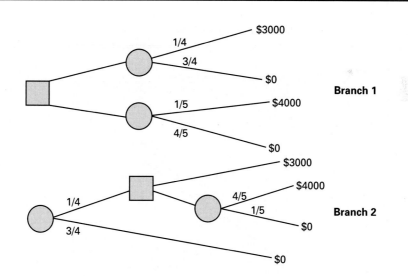

Source: Adapted from Kahneman, D., & Tversky, A. (1979). Prospect theory: An analysis of decision under risk. *Econometrica, 47,* 263–291.

---

[16] Adapted from Kahneman, D., & Tversky, A. (1979). Prospect theory: An analysis of decision under risk. *Econometrica, 47,* 263–291.

tendency to overweight certain outcomes relative to outcomes that are merely probable. The reduction in probability from certainty (1) to a degree of uncertainty (0.8) produces a more pronounced loss in attractiveness than a corresponding reduction from one level of uncertainty (0.25) to another (0.2). People do not think rationally about probabilities. Those close to 1 are often (mistakenly) considered sure things. On the flip side is the **possibility effect**: the tendency to overweight outcomes that are possible relative to outcomes that are impossible.

DECISION WEIGHTS   Decision makers transform probabilities into psychological decision weights. The decision weights are then applied to the subjective values. Prospect theory proposes a relationship between the probabilities' potential outcomes and the weights those probabilities have in the decision process.

Exhibit A1-6 illustrates the **probability weighting function** proposed by cumulative prospect theory. It is an inverted-S function that is concave near 0 and convex near 1. The probability-weighting function offers several noteworthy features.

Extremity Effect.   People tend to overweight low probabilities and underweight high probabilities.

EXHIBIT A1-6

A Weighting Function for Decision Under Risk

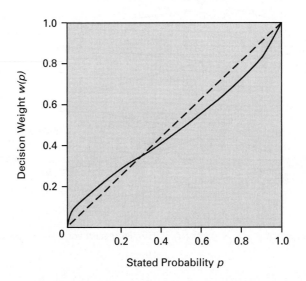

Source: Based on Fox, C. R., & Tversky, A. (1998). A belief-based model of decision under uncertainty. *Management Science, 44,* 879–896. Copyright © by The Econometric Society.

Crossover Point. The **crossover probability** is the point at which objective probabilities and subjective weights coincide. Prospect theory does not pinpoint where the crossover occurs, but it is definitely lower than 50%.[17]

Subadditivity. Adding two probabilities, p_1 and p_2, should yield a probability $p_3 = p_1 + p_2$. For example, suppose you are an investor considering three stocks: A, B, and C. You assess the probability that stock A will close 2 points higher today than yesterday to be 20%, and you assess the probability that stock B will close 2 points higher today than yesterday to be 15%. The stocks are two different companies in two different industries and are completely independent. Now consider the price of stock C, which you believe has a 35% probability of closing 2 points higher today. The likelihood of a 2-point increase in either stock A or B should be identical to the likelihood of a 2-point increase in stock C. The probability-weighting relationship, however, does not exhibit additivity. That is, for small probabilities, weights are subadditive, as we see from the extreme flatness at the lower end of the curve. It means that most decision makers consider the likely increase of either stocks A or B to be less likely than an increase in stock C.

Subcertainty. Except for guaranteed or impossible events, weights for complementary events do not sum to 1. One implication of the **subcertainty** feature of the probability-weight relationship is that for all probabilities, p, with $0 < p < 1$, $\mathrm{p}(p) + \mathrm{p}(1 - p) < 1$.

Regressiveness. According to the **regressiveness principle**, extreme values of some quantity do not deviate very much from the average value of that quantity. The relative flatness of the probability-weighting curve is a special type of regressiveness, suggesting that people's decisions are not as responsive to changes in uncertainty as are the associated probabilities. Another aspect is that nonextreme high probabilities are underweighted and low ones are overweighted.

The subjective value associated with a prospect depends on the decision weights and the subjective values of potential outcomes. Prospect theory makes specific claims about the form of the relationship between various amounts of an outcome and their subjective values.[18] Exhibit A1-7 illustrates the generic prospect theory value function.

Three characteristics of the value function are noteworthy. The first pertains to the decision maker's reference point. At some focal amount of the pertinent outcome, smaller amounts are considered losses and larger amounts gains. That focal amount is the negotiator's reference point. People are sensitive to changes in wealth.

A second feature is that the shape of the function changes markedly at the reference point. For gains, the value function is concave, exhibiting diminishing marginal value. As the starting point for increases in gains becomes larger, the significance of a constant increase lessens. A complementary phenomenon occurs in the domain of losses: Constant changes in the negative direction away from the reference point also assume diminishing significance the farther from the reference point the starting point happens to be.

Finally, the value function is noticeably steeper for losses than for gains. Stated another way, gains and losses of identical magnitude have different significance for people; losses are considered more important. We are much more disappointed about losing $75 than we are happy about making $75.

---

[17] Kahneman & Tversky, "Prospect theory."
[18] Ibid.

EXHIBIT A1-7

A Hypothetical Value Function

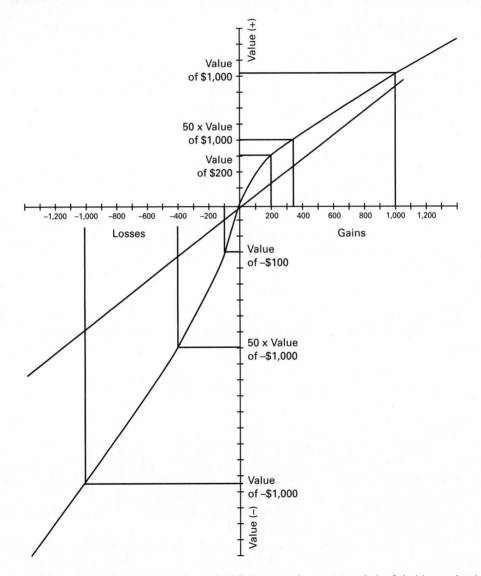

Source: Based on Kahneman, D., & Tversky, A. (1979). Prospect theory: An analysis of decision under risk. *Econometrica, 47,* 263–291.

COMBINATION RULES How do decision weights and outcome values combine to determine the subjective value of a prospect? The amounts that are effective for the decision maker are not the *actual* sums that would be awarded or taken away but are instead the *differences* between those sums and the decision maker's reference point.

Summing Up: Individual Decision Making

Decisions may sometimes be faulty or irrational if probabilities are not carefully considered. A negotiator's assessment of probabilities affects how he or she negotiates. Clever negotiators are aware of how their *own* decisions may be biased, as well as how the decisions of others may be manipulated to their own advantage. Now that we know about how individuals make decisions, we are ready to explore multiparty, or interdependent, decision making.

GAME THEORETIC RATIONALITY

Each outcome in a negotiation situation may be identified in terms of its utility for each party. In Exhibit A1-8, for example, party 1's utility function is represented as u_1; party 2's utility function is represented as u_2. Remember that utility payoffs represent the satisfaction parties derive from particular commodities or outcomes, not the actual monetary outcomes or payoffs themselves. A bargaining situation like the one in Exhibit A1-8 has a feasible set of utility outcomes, or F, defined as the set of all its possible utility outcomes for party 1 and party 2 and by its conflict point, c, where $c = (c_1, c_2)$; c represents the point at which both parties would prefer not to reach agreement (the reservation points of both parties).

EXHIBIT A1-8

Set of Feasible Bargaining Outcomes for Two Negotiators

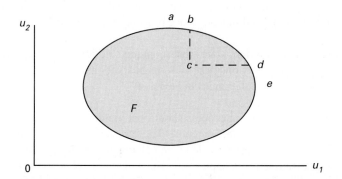

Source: Harsanyi, J. C. (1987). Bargaining. In J. Eatwell, M. Milgate, & P. Newman (Eds.), *The new palgrave: A dictionary of economics* (pp. 191–192). London: MacMillan Press.

Two key issues concern rationality at the negotiation table: one pertains to pie-slicing and one pertains to pie expansion. First, people should not agree to a utility payoff smaller than their reservation point; second, negotiators should not agree on an outcome if another outcome exists that is Pareto-superior, that is, an outcome that is more preferable to one party and does not decrease utility for the other party (e.g., level 3 integrative agreements discussed in Chapter 4).

For example, in Exhibit A1-8, the area *F* is the feasible set of alternative outcomes expressed in terms of each negotiator's utility function. The triangular area *bcd* is the set of all points satisfying the individual rationality requirement. The upper-right boundary *abde* of *F* is the set of all points that satisfy the joint rationality requirement. The intersection of the area *bcd* and of the boundary line *abde* is the arc *bd:* It is the set of all points satisfying both rationality requirements. As we can see, *b* is the least favorable outcome party 1 will accept; *d* is the least favorable outcome party 2 will accept.

The individual rationality and joint rationality assumptions do not tell us how negotiators should divide the pie. Rather, they tell us only that negotiators should make the pie as big as possible before dividing it. How much of the pie should you have?

Nash Bargaining Theory

Nash's bargaining theory specifies how negotiators should divide the pie, which involves "a determination of the amount of satisfaction each individual should expect to get from the situation or, rather, a determination of how much it should be worth to each of these individuals to have this opportunity to bargain."[19] Nash's theory makes a *specific* point prediction of the outcome of negotiation, the **Nash solution**, which specifies the outcome of a negotiation if negotiators behave rationally.

Nash's theory makes several important assumptions: Negotiators are rational; that is, they act to maximize their utility. The only significant differences between negotiators are those included in the mathematical description of the game. Further, negotiators have full knowledge of the tastes and preferences of each other.

Nash's theory builds on the axioms named in EU by specifying additional axioms. By specifying enough properties, we exclude all possible settlements in a negotiation, except one. Nash postulates that the agreement point, *u,* of a negotiation, known as the Nash solution, will satisfy the following five axioms: uniqueness, Pareto-optimality, symmetry, independence of equivalent utility representations, and independence of irrelevant alternatives.

UNIQUENESS   The **uniqueness axiom** states that a unique solution exists for each bargaining situation. Simply stated, one and only one best solution exists for a given bargaining situation or game. In Exhibit A1-9, the unique solution is denoted as *u.*

PARETO-OPTIMALITY   The bargaining process should not yield any outcome that both people find less desirable than some other feasible outcome. The Pareto-optimality (or efficiency) axiom is simply the joint rationality assumption made by von Neumann and Morgenstern and the level 3 integrative agreement discussed in Chapter 4.[20] The **Pareto-efficient frontier** is the set of

---

[19] Nash, J. (1950). The bargaining problem. *Econometrica, 18,* 155–162.
[20] von Neumann & Morgenstern, *Theory of games and economic behavior.*

EXHIBIT A1-9

A Weighting Function for Decision Under Risk

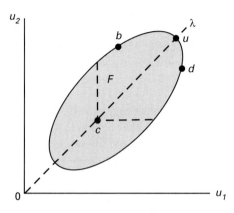

Source: Harsanyi, J. C. (1987). Bargaining. In J. Eatwell, M. Milgate, & P. Newman (Eds.), *The new palgrave: A dictionary of economics* (pp. 191–192). London: MacMillan Press.

outcomes corresponding to the entire set of agreements that leaves no portion of the total amount of resources unallocated. A given option, x, is a member of the Pareto frontier if, and only if, no option y exists such that y is preferred to x by at least one party and is at least as good as x for the other party.

Consider Exhibit A1-9: Both people prefer settlement point u (u_1, u_2), which eliminates c (c_1, c_2) from the frontier. Therefore, settlement points that lie on the interior of the arc bd are Pareto-inefficient. Options that are not on the Pareto frontier are dominated; settlements that are dominated clearly violate the utility principle of maximization. The resolution of any negotiation should be an option from the Pareto-efficient set because any other option unnecessarily requires more concessions on the part of one or both negotiators.

Another way of thinking about the importance of Pareto-optimality is to imagine that in *every* negotiation, whether it be for a car, a job, a house, a merger, or some other situation, a table sits with hundreds, thousands, and in some cases, millions of dollars on it. The money is yours to keep, provided you and the other party (e.g., a car dealer, employer, seller, business associate, etc.) agree how to divide it. Obviously, you want to get as much money as you can, which is the distributive aspect of negotiation. Imagine for a moment you and the other negotiator settle upon a division of the money that both of you find acceptable. However, imagine you leave half or one-third or some other amount of money on the table. A fire starts in the building, and the money burns. This scenario is equivalent to failing to reach a Pareto-optimal agreement. Most of us would never imagine allowing such an unfortunate event to happen. However, in many negotiation situations, people do just that—they leave money to burn.

SYMMETRY   In a **symmetric bargaining** situation, the two players have exactly the same strategic possibilities and bargaining power. Therefore, neither player has any reason to accept an agreement that yields a lower payoff than that of the opponent.

Another way of thinking about symmetry is to imagine interchanging the two players. This alteration should not change the outcome. In Exhibit A1-9, symmetry means that u_1 will be equal to u_2. The feasible set of outcomes must be symmetrical with respect to a hypothetical 45-degree line, λ, which begins at the origin 0 and passes through the point c, thereby implying that $c_1 = c_2$. Extending this line out to the farthest feasible point, u, gives us the Nash point, wherein parties' utilities are symmetric.

The symmetry principle is often considered to be the fundamental postulate of bargaining theory.[21] When parties' utilities are known, the solution to the game is straightforward.[22] As we already noted, however, players' utilities are usually not known. This uncertainty reduces the usefulness of the symmetry principle. That is, symmetry cannot be achieved if a negotiator has only half of the information.[23]

The Pareto-optimality and symmetry axioms uniquely define the agreement points of a symmetrical game. The remaining two axioms extend the theory to asymmetrical games in which the bargaining power is asymmetric.

INDEPENDENCE OF EQUIVALENT UTILITY REPRESENTATIONS   Many utility functions can represent the same preference. Utility functions are behaviorally equivalent if one can be obtained from the other by an order-preserving linear transformation (for example, by shifting the zero point of the utility scale or by changing the utility unit). A distinguishing feature of the Nash solution outcome is that it is independent of the exchange rate between two players' utility scales; it is invariant with respect to any fixed weights we might attach to their respective utilities.

The solution to the bargaining game is not sensitive to positive linear transformations of parties' payoffs because utility is defined on an interval scale. Interval scales, such as temperature, preserve units of measurement but have an arbitrary origin (i.e., zero point) and unit of measurement. The utility scales for player 1 and player 2 in Exhibit A1-9 have an arbitrary origin and unit of measurement.

For example, suppose you and a friend are negotiating to divide 100 poker chips. The poker chips are worth $1 each if redeemed by you and worth $1 each if redeemed by your friend. The question is this: How should the two of you divide the poker chips? The Nash solution predicts that the two of you should divide all the chips and not leave any on the table (Pareto-optimality principle). Further, the Nash solution predicts that you should receive 50 chips and your friend should receive 50 chips (symmetry principle). So far, the Nash solution sounds fine. Now, suppose the situation is slightly changed. Imagine the chips are worth $1 each if redeemed

---

[21] Harsanyi, J. (1962). Bargaining in ignorance of the opponent's utility function. *Journal of Conflict Resolution, 6,* 29–38.
[22] Nash, "The bargaining problem."
[23] Schelling, T. (1960). *The strategy of conflict.* Cambridge, MA: Harvard University Press.

by you, but they are worth $5 each if redeemed by your friend. (The rules of the game do not permit any kind of side payments or renegotiation of redemption values.) Now, how should the chips be divided? All we have done is transform your friend's utilities using an order-preserving linear transformation (multiply all her values by 5) while keeping your utilities the same. The Nash solution states that you should still divide the chips 50–50 because your friend's utilities have not changed; rather, they are represented by a different, but nevertheless equivalent, linear transformation.

Some people have a hard time with this axiom. After all, if you and your friend are really "symmetric," one of you should not come out richer in the deal. But consider the arguments that could be made for one of you receiving a greater share of the chips. One of you could have a seriously ill parent and need the money for an operation, one of you might be independently wealthy and not need the money, or one of you could be a foolish spendthrift and not deserve the money. Moreover, there could be a disagreement: One of you regards yourself to be thoughtful and prudent but is regarded as silly and imprudent by the other person. All of these arguments are outside the realm of Nash's theory because they are **indeterminate**. Dividing resources to achieve monetary equality is as arbitrary as flipping a coin.

But in negotiation, doesn't everything really boil down to dollars? No. In Nash's theory, each person's utility function may be normalized on a scale of 0 to 1 so that his or her "best outcome" = 1 and "worst outcome" = 0. Therefore, because the choices of origin and scale for each person's utility function are unrelated to one another, actual numerical levels have no standing in theory, and no comparisons of numerical levels can affect the outcome.

This axiom has serious implications. Permitting the transformation of one player's utilities without any transformation of the other player's utilities destroys the possibility that the outcome should depend on interpersonal utility comparisons. Stated simply, it is meaningless for people to compare their utility with another. The same logic applies for comparing salaries, the size of offices, or anything else.

However, people do engage in interpersonal comparisons of utility (Chapter 3). The important point is that interpersonal comparisons and arguments based on "fairness" are inherently subjective, which leaves no rational method for fair division.

INDEPENDENCE OF IRRELEVANT ALTERNATIVES   The **independence of irrelevant alternatives** axiom states that the best outcome in a feasible set of outcomes will also be the best outcome in any smaller subset of feasible outcomes that still contains that outcome. For example, a subset of a bargaining game may be obtained by excluding some of the irrelevant alternatives from the original game, without excluding the original agreement point itself. The exclusion of irrelevant alternatives does not change the settlement.

Consider Exhibit A1-9: The Nash solution is point *u*. Imagine the settlement options in the half-ellipse below the 45-degree line are eliminated. According to the independence of irrelevant alternatives axiom, this change should not affect the settlement outcome, which should still be *u*.

This axiom allows a point prediction to be made in asymmetric games by allowing them to be enlarged to be symmetric. For example, imagine that the game parties play is an asymmetric one like that just described (that is, the half-ellipse below the 45-degree line is eliminated). Such a bargaining problem would be asymmetric, perhaps with player 2 having an advantage. According to Nash, it is useful to expand the asymmetric game to be one that is symmetric—for example, by including the points in the lower half of the ellipse that mirrors the half-ellipse above the 45-degree line. Once these points are included, the game is symmetric, and the Nash solution may be identified. Of course, the settlement outcome yielded by the new, expanded game must also be present in the original game.

The independence of irrelevant alternatives axiom is motivated by the way negotiation unfolds.[24] Through a process of voluntary mutual concessions, the set of possible outcomes under consideration gradually decreases to just those around the eventual agreement point. This axiom asserts that the winnowing process does not change the agreement point.

In summary, Nash's theorem states that the unique solution possesses these properties. Nash's solution selects the unique point that maximizes the geometric average (i.e., the product) of the gains available to people as measured against their reservation points. For this reason, the Nash solution is also known as the **Nash product**. If all possible outcomes are plotted on a graph whose rectangular coordinates measure the utilities that the two players derive from them, as in Exhibit A1-8 and Exhibit A1-9, the solution is a unique point on the upper-right boundary of the region. The point is unique because two solution points could be joined by a straight line representing available alternative outcomes achievable by mixing, with various odds, the probabilities of the original two outcomes, and the points on the line connecting them would yield higher products of the two players' utilities. In other words, the region is presumed convex by reason of the possibility of probability mixtures, and the convex region has a single maximum-utility-product point, or Nash point.

---

[24] Harsanyi, J. C. (1990). Bargaining. In J. Eatwell, M. Milgate, & P. Newman (Eds.), *The new Palgrave: A dictionary of economics* (pp. 54–67). New York: Norton.

APPENDIX 2

Nonverbal Communication and Lie Detection

The purpose of this appendix is to help you (a) be a better reader of nonverbal communication and (b) be a better sender of nonverbal communication.

WHAT ARE WE LOOKING FOR IN NONVERBAL COMMUNICATION?

Nonverbal communication is anything that is "not words." Specifically, it includes the following:

- *Vocal cues or paralinguistic cues.* Paralinguistic cues include pauses, intonation, and fluency. Vocal cues, such as tone and inflection, are nonverbal; they include speech volume, pace, and pitch.
- *Facial expressions.* Smiling, frowning, or expressing surprise
- *Eye contact.* A high level of held gazing can be interpreted as a sign of liking or friendliness. However, in other cultures, prolonged eye contact is a sign of dominance or aggression.[1]
- *Interpersonal spacing.* The distance between people when they talk or communicate.
- *Posture.* How people hold and orient their body, including opening their arms and chest, etc.
- *Body movements.* When people are experiencing greater arousal, or nervousness, they tend to make more movements.
- *Gesture.* The three basic kinds of gestures are (a) **emblems,** which symbolize certain messages, such as the North American thumbs-up for "okay," and the finger on the lips for "quiet," (b) **illustrators,** which embellish a verbal message, such as the widening of hands and arms when talking about something that is large, and (c) **adaptors,** which include things like touching one's nose or twitching in such a way that does not embellish or illustrate a particular point.
- *Touching.* Touching another person (in an appropriate way) often leads to positive reactions.

Nonverbal communication is informative because it is relatively irrepressible in that people cannot control it. What nonverbal signals do negotiators look for, and what do they reveal? To address this question, we conducted a survey of 50 MBA students who had recently completed a multiparty negotiation. The majority of students relied on three nonverbal cues as a window into other party's true feelings and intentions: (a) eye contact ("people who are lying avoid looking the other party straight in the eyes"), (b) closed body posture ("When he leans toward me while he talks, I tend to trust him more"), and (c) nervousness, twitching, and fidgeting ("if people play with their shoestrings, tap their pen, bite their lip, or indicate any other nervous tension, it usually signals anxiety and nervousness"). Other indicators mentioned, although much less frequently included, are lack of gestures (too much stillness), emotional outbursts, and autonomic responses, such as sweating and blushing.

What particular nonverbal behaviors do negotiators notice that lead them to distrust someone? (See Exhibit A2-1 for a list of such behaviors.)

---

[1] Ellsworth, P. C., & Carlsmith, J. M. (1973). Eye contact and gaze aversion in aggressive encounters. *Journal of Personality and Social Psychology, 33,* 117–122.

EXHIBIT A2-1

Nonverbal Behaviors

What nonverbal behaviors mean you should not trust someone?

- Fidgeting
- Excessive smiling; sheepish smiles
- Overly serious tone; lack of emotion
- Averting eyes; lack of eye contact
- Being too quiet

What nonverbal behaviors mean you should trust someone?

- Direct speech
- Open gestures and behavior
- Smiling
- Pointing

Note: These behaviors are perceived to be linked to trust; they are not actually indicative of trust.

Next, we consider three aspects of nonverbal communication that can affect the nature and outcome of negotiation: (a) gender differences, in terms of ability and accuracy, (b) nonverbal abilities of powerful and dominant people, and (c) nonverbal abilities of charismatic people.[2] Obviously, power and charisma have implications for success at the bargaining table.

Are Women More "Nonverbally Gifted" Than Men?

Popular culture suggests women are more nonverbally sensitive than men. And scientific evidence backs up this claim: Women *are* more skilled in terms of **nonverbal expression.**[3] In general, women are more open, expressive, approachable, and actively involved in social interaction than men. Their faces are more readable than men's, and they smile and gaze at other people and approach them more closely than do men. Women are also gazed at more, and approached more closely than men.[4] During interactions, women seem more focused on the other person, and they also elicit more warmth and less anxiety from others.[5] However, the sexes are held to different standards of appropriate expressivity; women are typically considered more expressive, and men are viewed as more composed.[6] Women anticipate greater costs and

---

[2] DePaulo, B. M., & Friedman, H. S. (1997). Nonverbal communication. In D. T. Gilbert, S. T. Fiske, & G. Lindzey (Eds.), *The handbook of social psychology* (4th Ed.). New York: McGraw–Hill.

[3] DePaulo & Friedman, "Nonverbal communication"; Hall, J. A. (1984). *Nonverbal sex differences: Communication accuracy and expressive style.* Baltimore: Johns Hopkins University Press.

[4] Hall, *Nonverbal sex differences.*

[5] Abramowitz, C. V., Abramowitz, S. I., & Weitz, L. J. (1976). Are men therapists soft on empathy? Two studies in feminine understanding. *Journal of Clinical Psychology, 32*(2), 434–437.

[6] Hall, *Nonverbal sex differences.*

fewer rewards than men if they fail to express positive emotion in response to someone else's good news.[7]

Nonverbal expressiveness is linked with social power. Greater expressivity is required by those of lower social status and power.[8] In many organizations, women traditionally have lower social status than men. Indeed, in studies of visual dominance (measured as the ratio of time a person spends looking at his or her partner while speaking relative to the time spent looking while listening), women are often less dominant. High-power people are more visually dominant than low-power people.[9] When women have uncertain support in a leadership position, men express more visual dominance than women.[10] When people show more visual dominance, they are perceived as more powerful. Furthermore, when women and men are assigned to different power roles, low-power people (regardless of gender) are better able to read their partner's cues.[11]

In terms of **nonverbal reception,** women are no better than men at recognizing covert messages, such as discrepant communication (which we discuss later). However, when people are being truthful, women are more accurate than men; however, when people are being deceptive (i.e., when the negotiator is pretending to like someone), women are less accurate than men.[12]

In short, women are better at detecting feelings but are not necessarily better at detecting deception, because anyone who is inferior in status is more sensitive to states of mind of superiors. For example, when women and men are assigned to be supervisors or subordinates in organizational simulations, no differences are evident in emotional sensitivity between genders: Subordinates, regardless of gender, are more sensitive than their superiors.

Dominance

People often assert dominance and power through nonverbal cues. Dominant people sit higher, stand taller, talk louder, and have more space and more resources than non-dominant people. Dominant people are more likely to invade others' space (e.g., putting their feet up on their own or someone else's desk), make more expansive gestures, walk in front of others, sit in front of others or sit at the head of a table, interrupt more often, control time, and stare at the other party more, but they tend to look away more often when the other party is speaking.[13]

---

[7] Stoppard, J. M., & Gun-Gruchy, C. (1993). Gender, context, and expression of positive emotion. *Personality and Social Psychology Bulletin, 19*(2), 143–150.

[8] Henley, N. M. (1977). *Body politics: Power, sex, and non-verbal communication.* Upper Saddle River, NJ: Prentice Hall.

[9] Dovidio, J. F., & Ellyson, S. L. (1982). Decoding visual dominance: Attributions of power based on relative percentages of looking while speaking and looking while listening. *Social Psychology Quarterly, 45*(2), 106–113.

[10] Brown, C. E., Dovidio, J. F., & Ellyson, S. L. (1990). Reducing sex differences in visual displays of dominance: Knowledge is power. *Personality and Social Psychology Bulletin, 16*(2), 358–368.

[11] Snodgrass, S. E. (1985). Women's intuition: The effect of subordinate role on interpersonal sensitivity. *Journal of Personality and Social Psychology, 49*(1), 146–155; Snodgrass, S. E. (1992). Further effects of role versus gender on interpersonal sensitivity. *Journal of Personality and Social Psychology, 62*(1), 154–158.

[12] DePaulo, B. M., Epstein, J. A., & Wyer, M. M. (1993). Sex differences in lying: How women and men deal with the dilemma of deceit. In M. Lewis & C. Saarni (Eds.), *Lying and deception in everyday life* (pp. 126–147). New York: Guilford Press; Rosenthal, R., & DePaulo, B. M. (1979). Sex differences in accommodation in nonverbal communication. In R. Rosenthal (Ed.), *Skill in nonverbal communication: Individual differences* (pp. 68–103). Cambridge, MA: Oelgeschlager, Gunn, and Hain; Rosenthal, R., & DePaulo, B. M. (1979). Sex differences in eavesdropping on nonverbal cues. *Journal of Personality and Social Psychology, 37*(2), 273–285.

[13] DePaulo & Friedman, "Nonverbal communication."

High social power is reliably indicated by patterns of looking while speaking and listening. People with less power look more when listening than when speaking. In contrast, more powerful people look about the same amount when listening as when speaking.[14] When people interact with a dominant person, they often respond by decreasing their postural stance (i.e., they often behave more submissively); in contrast, people who interact with a submissive person often increase their stance (i.e., they behave more assertively).[15] Interestingly, people like each other more when the interaction is complementary as opposed to reciprocal. Thus, dominance in response to submission and submission in response to dominance results in greater liking between people than dominance in response to dominance and submission in response to submissiveness.

When men and women have equal knowledge, power, and expertise (or when men have more), men behave *visually* as though they really are more powerful. However, when women have the advantage, they "look" like powerful people more often than men.[16]

Personal Charisma

Charisma is a social skill having to do with verbal and nonverbal expressiveness. People vary strikingly in the intensity, expansiveness, animation, and dynamism of their nonverbal (and verbal) behaviors.[17] Differences in expressiveness are linked directly to affection, empathy, influence, and professional success, as well as to interpersonal experiences, such as the regulation of one's own emotional experiences and physical and mental health.

Expressiveness, or **spontaneous sending,** is the ease with which people's feelings can be read from their nonverbal expressive behaviors when they are not trying to deliberately communicate their feelings to others.[18] Expressiveness instantly makes a difference in setting the tone of social interactions. Even commonplace interpersonal behaviors, such as walking into a room and initiating a conversation[19] or greeting someone who is approaching,[20] suggest this social skill is immediately influential. Why? Expressive people make better first impressions and, over time, they are better liked than unexpressive people.[21] Expressive people are considered to

---

[14] Exline, R. V., Ellyson, S. L., & Long, B. (1975). Visual behavior as an aspect of power role relationships. In P. Pliner, L. Krames, & T. Alloway (Eds.), *Advances in the study of communication and affect: Vol. 2. Nonverbal communication of aggression* (pp. 21–52). New York: Plenum.

[15] Tiedens, L. Z., & Fragale, A. R. (2003). Power moves: Complementary in dominant and submissive nonverbal behavior. *Journal of Personality and Social Psychology, 84*(3), 558–568.

[16] Dovidio, J. F., Brown, C. E., Heltman, K., Ellyson, S. L., & Keating, C. F. (1988). Power displays between women and men in discussions of gender-linked tasks: A multichannel study. *Journal of Personality and Social Psychology, 55*(4), 580–587; Dovidio, J. F., Ellyson, S. L., Keating, C. F., Heltman, K., & Brown, Clifford E. (1988). The relationship of social power to visual displays of dominance between men and women. *Journal of Personality and Social Psychology, 54*(2), 233–242.

[17] Friedman, H. S., Prince, L. M., Riggio, R. E., & DiMatteo, M. R. (1980). Understanding and assessing nonverbal expressiveness: The Affective Communication Test. *Journal of Personality and Social Psychology, 39*(2), 333–351; Halberstadt, A. G. (1991). Toward an ecology of expressiveness: Family socialization in particular and a model in general. In R. S. Feldman & B. Rime (Eds.), *Fundamentals of nonverbal behavior: Studies in emotion and social interaction* (pp. 106–160). New York: Cambridge University Press; Manstead, A. S. R. (1991). Expressiveness as an individual difference. In R. S. Feldman & B. Rime (Eds.), *Fundamentals of nonverbal behavior: Studies in emotion and social interaction* (pp. 285–328). New York: Cambridge University Press.

[18] Buck, R. (1984). On the definition of emotion: Functional and structural considerations. *Cahiers de Psychologie Cognitive, 4*(1), 44–47; Notarius, C. I., & Levenson, R. W. (1979). Expressive tendencies and physiological response to stress. *Journal of Personality and Social Psychology, 37*(7), 1204–1210.

[19] Friedman, H. S., Riggio, R. E., & Casella, D. F. (1988). Nonverbal skill, personal charisma, and initial attraction. *Personality and Social Psychology Bulletin, 14*(1), 203–211.

[20] DiMatteo, M. R., Friedman, H. S., & Taranta, A. (1979). Sensitivity to bodily nonverbal communication as a factor in practitioner-patient rapport. *Journal of Nonverbal Behavior, 4*(1), 18–26.

[21] Cunningham, M. R. (1986). Measuring the physical in physical attractiveness: Quasi-experiments on the sociobiology of female facial beauty. *Journal of Personality and Social Psychology, 50,* 925–935.

be more attractive than unexpressive people.[22] Furthermore, expressive people capture people's attention[23] and then "turn on" the expressive behavior of other people.[24] Expressive people are good actors, feigning convincing expressions of feelings they are not actually experiencing.[25] It follows that they are also good liars.[26]

The most interpersonally successful communicators are nonverbally sensitive, nonverbally expressive, nonverbally self-controlled, and motivated to perform for their "audiences."[27] In social interactions, expressive people can "set the tone and frame the field."[28]

DETECTING DECEPTION

Nonverbal sensitivity (in terms of accuracy) is an advantage in negotiation, as it is in most social interaction. For instance, doctors who are good at reading body language have more satisfied patients.[29] Students who are nonverbally sensitive learn more than less sensitive students.[30] However, nonverbal sensitivity is difficult to achieve. As a skill, it is not correlated with intelligence, and it is very "channel-specific." Skill at understanding facial expression and body movements is measurably different from skill at understanding tone of voice.[31] Nonverbal sensitivity improves with age.[32] (See Exhibit A2-2 for nonverbal visual cues correlated with deception.)

Reading and sending nonverbal messages in negotiation is one thing; detecting deception (and pulling off deception) is another.[33] Obviously, it is to a negotiator's advantage to accurately detect deception at the negotiation table. In fact, relying on nonverbal cues may be our only hope of detecting deception. People believe that liars either cannot control their nonverbal behaviors and therefore these behaviors will "leak out" and betray the liar's true feelings, or liars simply will not control all of their nonverbal cues.[34]

Unfortunately, foolproof nonverbal indicators of deception have not been discovered. In fact, most people cannot tell from demeanor when others are lying.[35] Accuracy rates are close

---

[22] DePaulo, B. M., Blank, A. L., Swaim, G. W., & Hairfield, J. G. (1992). Expressiveness and expressive control. *Personality and Social Psychology Bulletin, 18*(3), 276–285.

[23] Sullins, E. S. (1989). Perceptual salience as a function of nonverbal expressiveness. *Personality and Social Psychology Bulletin, 15*(4), 584–595.

[24] Buck, "On the definition of emotion."

[25] Buck, R. (1975). Nonverbal communication of affect in children. *Journal of Personality and Social Psychology, 31*(4), 644–653.

[26] DePaulo, Blank, Swaim, & Hairfield, "Expressiveness and expressive control."

[27] DePaulo & Friedman, "Nonverbal communication."

[28] DePaulo & Friedman, "Nonverbal communication," 14.

[29] DiMatteo, M. R., Hays, R. D., & Prince, L. M. (1986). Relationship of physicians' nonverbal communication skill to patient satisfaction, appointment noncompliance, and physician workload. *Health Psychology, 5*(6), 581–594.

[30] Bernieri, F. J. (1991). Interpersonal sensitivity in teaching interactions. *Personality and Social Psychology Bulletin, 17*(1), 98–103.

[31] DePaulo, B. M., & Rosenthal, R. (1979). Telling lies. *Journal of Personality and Social Psychology, 37*(10), 1713–1722.

[32] Buck, "On the definition of emotion"; Zuckerman, M., Blanck, P. D., DePaulo, B. M., & Rosenthal, R. (1980). Developmental changes in decoding discrepant and nondiscrepant nonverbal cues. *Developmental Psychology, 16*(3), 220–228.

[33] Croson, R. (2005). Deception of economics experiments. In C. Gerschlager (Ed.), *Deception in markets: An economic analysis* (pp. 113–130). Basingstoke, England: Palgrave-Macmillan; Schweitzer, M. (2001). Deception in negotiations. In S. Hoch & H. Kunreuther (Eds.), *Wharton on making decisions* (pp. 187–200). New York: Wiley.

[34] Ekman, P., & Friesen, W. V. (1969). Nonverbal leakage and clues to deception. *Psychiatry, 32*(1), 88–106.

[35] Ekman, P., O'Sullivan, M. O., & Frank, M. G. (1999). A few can catch a liar. *Psychological Science, 10*(3), 263–266.

EXHIBIT A2-2

Correlations of Nonverbal Visual Cues and Deception

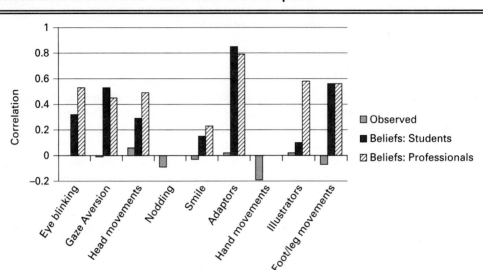

Source: Adapted from Sporer, S. & Schwandt, B. (2007). Moderators of nonverbal indicators of deception: A meta-analytic synthesis. *Psychology, Public Policy, and Law, 13*(1), 1–34.

to chance levels.[36] People who have been professionally trained (e.g., law enforcement groups) are more accurate.[37] For example, law enforcement officers and clinical psychologists are very accurate in judging videos of people who are lying or telling the truth.[38]

There are many things to lie about in negotiation. Some lies may be complete falsifications (such as falsifying an inspection report or pretending another buyer will be calling at any moment with an offer); other lies may be exaggerations (exaggerating the appraised value of a property, exaggerating the attractiveness of one's BATNA). It is more difficult for liars to successfully carry off hard lies (i.e., complete falsifications of information) than to carry off easy lies (exaggerations). Consequently, it is easier for negotiators to detect complete falsifications.

What should you do to maximize the chances of catching a lie in negotiation? Several direct methods, as well as some indirect methods, may be helpful.[39]

---

[36] DePaulo, B. M. (1994). Spotting lies: Can humans learn to do better? *Current Directions in Psychological Science, 3*(3), 83–86; DePaulo, B. M., Lassiter, G. D., & Stone, J. I. (1982). Attentional determinants of success at detecting deception and truth. *Personality and Social Psychology Bulletin, 8*(2), 273–279; Zuckerman, M., Koestner, R., & Driver, R. (1981). Beliefs about cues associated with deception. *Journal of Nonverbal Behavior, 6*(2), 105–114.

[37] Ekman, O'Sullivan, & Frank, "A few can catch a liar."

[38] Ibid.

[39] Schweitzer, "Deception in negotiations."

Direct Methods

TRIANGULATION   One of the best methods of lie detection is questioning. The process of asking several questions, all designed as cross-checks on one another, is known as **triangulation.** For example, if a person wants to accurately assess the time of day, relying on only one clock can be risky. A better method is to use two or three clocks or different timepieces. Similarly, if a person wants to "catch" a liar, a good strategy is to examine nonverbal cues, verbal cues, and perhaps outside evidence as well.

Direct questions are particularly effective in curtailing lies of omission, however, they may actually increase lies of commission.[40] Detectives and lawyers ask several questions of people they think might be lying. Their questions are designed so that inconsistencies emerge if a person is lying. It is very difficult for even the best of liars to be perfectly consistent in all aspects of a lie.

OBJECTIVE EVIDENCE   Another strategy is to focus on inconsistencies and vagueness. In the case of inconsistency, ask for evidence; if appropriate, suggest contingencies. When people buy a used car, they often don't simply rely on the owner's claims of its reliability; rather, they seek an objective, expert opinion. For example, they often have an experienced mechanic inspect the car.

LINGUISTIC STYLE   Telling lies often requires creating a story about an experience or attitude that does not exist. Consequently, false stories are qualitatively different from true stories. Compared to truth-tellers, liars have less cognitive complexity (shades of gray) in their stories, use fewer self-references and fewer other-references, and use more negative-emotion words.[41] Liars hesitate more and have more speech errors. Further, their response length to questions is shorter.

Indirect Methods

ENRICH THE MODE OF COMMUNICATION   It is usually easier to catch a liar when communicating face-to-face than when communicating via telephone or e-mail. If negotiations have been proceeding by phone, written correspondence, or e-mail, the negotiator who wants to catch a lie should insist on a face-to-face interaction. First, people are less likely to lie face-to-face than when communicating by telephone or e-mail. Second, it is easier to detect a lie in a face-to-face interaction partly because it is much more difficult for liars to monitor themselves when the communication modality is multichanneled (as it is in face-to-face negotiations). Telltale signs of lying are often found in nonverbal "leakage," such as in the hands or body, rather than the face or words, which liars usually carefully monitor.[42] For example, liars tend to touch themselves more and blink more than truth-tellers.

DO NOT RELY ON A PERSON'S FACE   Most people look at a person's face when they want to detect deception, but this focus is not always effective. Perceivers are able to detect deception at greater-than-chance levels from every individual channel or combination of channels with the

---

[40] Schweitzer, M., & Croson, R. (1999). Curtailing deception: The impact of direct questions on lies and omissions. *International Journal of Conflict Management, 10,* 225–248.
[41] Newman, M. L., Pennebaker, J. W., Berry, D. S., & Richards, J. M. (2003). Lying words: Predicting deception from linguistic styles. *Personality and Social Psychology Bulletin, 29*(5), 665–675.
[42] Ekman, P. (1984). The nature and function of the expression of emotion. In K. Scherer & P. Ekman (Eds.), *Approaches to emotion.* Hillsdale, NJ: Erlbaum.

exception of one: the face.[43] In fact, people are better off when they cannot see another's face. Facial expressions are misleading at worst and, at best, are of qualified use as clues to deceit. Gaze is not diagnostic in detecting a liar.

TONE OF VOICE   Paying attention to tone of voice is a better indicator of deception than is facial expression.[44] Useful information can come through the voice, which people do not often consider or detect. People's pitch is higher when they are lying than when they are telling the truth; they speak more slowly and with less fluency and engage in more sentence repairs.[45] (See Exhibit A2-3 for meta-analysis of paraverbal indicators of deception.)

MICROEXPRESSIONS   Deception can be detected in the face if you are specially trained to look for microexpressions (or if you have a video you can play back to look for microexpressions). **Microexpressions** are expressions people show on their face for about one-tenth of a second. These expressions reveal how a person is truly feeling, but because of social pressure and self-presentation concerns they are quickly wiped away. As an example, consider an investigation in which the facial expressions of men and women participants were secretly observed while they were interacting with male and female assistants specially trained to act as leaders during

EXHIBIT A2-3

Meta-analysis of Paraverbal Indicators of Deception

Cue	Reliably associated with Deception?	Notes
Message Duration	YES (weak), $r = -.057$	Liars have shorter messages
Speech rate	NO	
Filled pauses	NO	
Unfilled pauses	NO	
Pitch	YES, $r = .101$	Liars have higher pitch
Response latency	YES, $r = .106$	Liars take longer to respond
Speech errors	YES (weak), $r = .059$	Liars make more speech errors
Repetitions	NO	
Number of words	NO	

Source: Based on Sporer, S. & Schwandt, B. (2006). Paraverbal indicators of deception: A meta-analytic synthesis. *Applied Cognitive Psychology, 20,* 421–446.

---

[43] Zuckerman, M., DePaulo, B. M., & Rosenthal, R. (1981). Verbal and nonverbal communication of deception. In L. Berkowitz (Ed.), *Advances in experimental social psychology: Vol. 14* (pp. 1–59). New York: Academic Press.

[44] DePaulo, Lassiter, & Stone, "Attentional determinants of success."

[45] Ekman, P. (2001). *Telling lies: Clues to deceit in the marketplace, politics, and marriage* (3rd ed.). New York: Norton.

a group discussion.[46] The results were clear: Female leaders received more negative nonverbal cues (microexpressions) from other members of the group than did male leaders. Moreover, male leaders also received more positive nonverbal cues per minute than did female leaders. These findings emerged even though participants strongly denied any bias against females.

INTERCHANNEL DISCREPANCIES   To detect deception, look for inconsistencies among these channels, such as tone of voice, body movements, gestures, and so on. As a general rule, watch the body, not the face, and look for clusters of clues. **Illustrators** are another type of body movement that can provide clues about deception.[47] Illustrators depict speech as it is spoken. It is the hands that usually illustrate speech—giving emphasis to a word or phrase, tracing the flow of thought in the air, drawing a picture in space, or showing an action can repeat or amplify what is being said. Eyebrow and upper eyelid movements can also provide emphasis illustrators, as can the entire body or upper torso. Illustrators are used to help explain ideas that are difficult to put into words. For example, people are more likely to illustrate when asked to define the word "zigzag" than the word "chair." Illustrators increase when people are more involved with what is being said; people illustrate less than usual when they are uninvolved, bored, disinterested, or deeply saddened. Illustrators are often confused with emblems, but it is important to distinguish them because these two kinds of body movements may change in opposite ways when people lie: emblematic slips may increase, whereas illustrators will usually decrease. People who feign concern or enthusiasm can be betrayed by the failure to accompany their speech with increased illustrators, and illustrators decrease when a person does not know exactly what to say. For example, if a liar has not adequately worked out a lie in advance, the liar will have to be cautious and carefully consider each word before it is spoken.

EYE CONTACT   People who are lying blink more often and have more dilated pupils than truth-tellers. However, blinking rates and dilation of pupils are almost impossible to detect with the naked eye (which is why "gaze aversion" is listed as *not* diagnostic in Exhibit A2-2). Although eye contact is the primary cue used by MBA students to detect deceit, it is not reliable; often, it is irrelevant, primarily because it is something that people can control too readily.

BE AWARE OF EGOCENTRIC BIASES   Most negotiators regard themselves as truthful and honest and their opponents as dishonest, indicating an egocentric bias. For example, in our investigation, MBA students thought they deceived others in a 10-week negotiation course 22% of the time, whereas they thought they had been deceived by others 40% of the time.

How Motivation and Temptation Affect Lying and Deception

People are more likely to be deceptive when they are likely to get away with it and especially when their potential gain from deception is highest. In one investigation, people were given enticing prospects for large monetary gain in an ultimatum game if they deceived.[48] Although "proposers" and "responders" chose deceptive strategies almost equally, proposers told more

---

[46] Butler, D., & Geis, F. L. (1990). Nonverbal affect responses to male and female leaders: Implications for leadership evaluations. *Journal of Personality and Social Psychology, 58*(1), 48–59.

[47] Ekman, *Telling lies.*

[48] Boles, T., Croson, R., & Murnighan, J. K. (2000). Deception and retribution in repeated ultimatum bargaining. *Organizational Behavior and Human Decision Processes, 83*(2), 235–259.

outright lies.[49] Moreover, proposers were more deceptive when their potential profits were highest. Proposers deceived about 13.6% of the time, and responders deceived about 13.9% of the time.[50] **Motivated communication** is not purely opportunistic: If liars feel that they can "justify" a lie (such as when some uncertainty is involved), they are more likely to lie, even when the costs and benefits for misrepresentation are held constant.[51]

Consider two types of lies: monitoring-dependent and monitoring-independent.[52] **Monitoring-dependent lies** require that the liar monitor the reaction of the target for the lie to be effective; conversely, **monitoring-independent lies** do not require the liar to monitor. If someone wants to lie about a closing date, it would be important to determine what kind of closing date is preferred by the target (one cannot assume early or late). Conversely, if one is attempting to lie about interest rates, it is safe to assume that mortgage holders would uniformly want lower rates; and thus, it is not as important to monitor their reaction to this type of statement. Liars are more likely to tell monitoring-dependent lies when they have visual access (than when they don't). The use of monitoring-independent lies is the same, with or without visual access. In this sense, visual access can actually harm potential targets of deception by increasing their risk of being deceived.

When potential deceivers have high incentives to deceive, they are more emotional.[53] It is hard to conceal these feelings. An exception might be people who have great practice at lying and few qualms about the appropriateness of stretching the truth in a selling context, such as experienced salespersons.[54]

Deception and Secrecy Can Create a Life of Their Own

People who are told to keep a secret can become preoccupied with the secret.[55] The secret becomes more accessible in their memory and absorbs their consciousness (as judged by word association and reaction times). Why? Keeping a secret takes mental control. Often, secrecy is linked to obsession and attraction.[56] For example, in a card-playing game, some pairs were told to engage in "nonverbal communication" with their feet to try to influence the game. They were told to either keep it a secret from the other couple or let it be known. After the game, those players who engaged in more nonverbal, secret communication reported more attraction to the other party than those who did not engage in the secretive behavior.[57]

---

[49] Ibid.

[50] Croson, "Deception of economics experiments."

[51] Schweitzer, M., & Hsee, C. (2002). Stretching the truth: Elastic justification and motivated communication of uncertain information. *Journal of Risk and Uncertainty, 25*(2), 185–201.

[52] Schweitzer, M., Brodt, S., & Croson, R. (2002). Seeing and believing: Visual access and the strategic use of deception. *International Journal of Conflict Management, 13*(3), 258–275.

[53] DePaulo, B. M., & Kirkendol, S. E. (1989). The motivational impairment effect in the communication of deception. In J. C. Yuille (Ed.), *Credibility assessment* (pp. 51–70). Dordrecht, The Netherlands: Kluwer.

[54] DePaulo, P. J., & DePaulo, B. M. (1989). Can deception by salespersons and customers be detected through nonverbal behavioral cues? *Journal of Applied Social Psychology, 19*(18, pt. 2), 1552–1577.

[55] Wegner, D. M. (1994). Ironic processes of mental control. *Psychological Review, 101,* 34–52.

[56] Wegner, D. M., Lane, J. D., & Dimitri, S. (1994). The allure of secret relationships. *Journal of Personality and Social Psychology, 66*(2), 287–300.

[57] Wegner, D. M., Shortt, J. W., Blake, A. W., & Page, M. S. (1990). The suppression of exciting thoughts. *Journal of Personality and Social Psychology, 58,* 409–418.

APPENDIX 3

Third-Party Intervention

Sometimes, despite the best of intentions, the bargaining process breaks down, and negotiators are unable to reach an agreement on their own. When the bargaining process breaks down at the international level, war can result. Indeed, 434 international crises occurred between December 1918 and December 2005.[1] When impasse occurs at the individual level, negotiators may pursue legal action. Sometimes parties try third-party intervention in an effort to avoid court action. Third-party intervention can be an excellent means of reaching settlement when the costs of disagreement are high.

Some negotiators make mediation-arbitration contingencies in the event of disagreement, thereby promising in advance to avoid legal action. For example, since 2000, most credit card companies included mandatory arbitration in card contracts, forcing consumers to arbitrate rather than use the court. However, in 2009, a lawsuit was brought by the state of Minnesota against the National Arbitration Forum, the largest arbitration firm involved in adjudicating delinquent credit-card debts. Accused of consumer fraud, deceptive trade practices, and false advertising, the company pulled out of the business. Numerous banks who used the service also dropped their requirements after the suit.[2]

On an international front, mediation has grown rapidly and positioned governments to adopt new mediation regulations. For example, in China, the law encourages parties to settle their disputes by talking and suspends pending lawsuits to give disputants a chance to first resolve them. Mediated settled agreements are enforceable as contracts in courts of law.[3]

We review the roles of third parties, key challenges facing third parties, and strategies for enhancing the effectiveness of third-party intervention.

COMMON THIRD-PARTY ROLES

A third party may intervene in a dispute in a number of ways.[4]

Mediation

Mediation is a procedure whereby a third party assists disputants in achieving a voluntary settlement (i.e., the mediator cannot impose a settlement on the disputants). Mediation offers the possibility of discovering underlying issues and promoting integrative agreements.[5] Mediation

---

[1] Brecher, Michael, & Jonathan Wilkenfeld. International Crisis Behavior Project, 1918–2004 [Computer file]. ICPSR09286-v7. College Park, MD: Michael Brecher and Jonathan Wilkenfeld, University of Maryland [producers], 2007. Ann Arbor, MI: Inter-university Consortium for Political and Social Research [distributor], 2007–12–14.
[2] Berner, R. (2009, July 19). Big arbitration firm pulls out of credit card business. *Business Week.* Businessweek.com; Class discipline; Litigation in America. (2011, January 29). *The Economist.* Economist.com
[3] Mealey-Lohmann, L. (2010, May 28). Using mediation to resolve disputes—Differences between China and the United States. *China Insight.* Chinainsight.com
[4] Rubin, J. Z., Pruitt, D. G., & Kim, S. H. (1994). *Social conflict: Escalation, stalemate and settlement.* New York: McGraw-Hill; McGrath, J. E. (1966). A social psychological approach to the study of negotiations. In R. V. Bowers (Ed.), *Studies on behavior in organizations* (pp. 101–134). Athens: University of Georgia Press.
[5] McEwen, C. A., & Maiman, R. J. (1984). Mediation in small claims court: Achieving compliance through consent. *Law and Society Review, 18,* 11–49.

produces a high settlement rate (typically 60–80%), though settlement is not guaranteed.[6] Mediation serves an important face-saving function: Each party can make concessions without appearing weak.[7] Disputants often see mediation procedures as fair.[8]

Arbitration

Arbitration is a procedure whereby a third party holds a hearing, at which time disputants state their position on the issues, call witnesses, and offer supporting evidence for their respective positions.[9] After the hearing, the arbitrator issues a binding settlement. The greatest advantage of arbitration is that it always produces a settlement. Moreover, the mere threat of arbitration often motivates parties to settle voluntarily.[10] Like mediation, arbitration allows disputants to "save face" with their constituents because they can always blame the arbitrator if the imposed settlement is unsatisfactory.[11] The two major types of arbitration are traditional arbitration and final-offer arbitration.

TRADITIONAL ARBITRATION   In **traditional arbitration**, each side submits a proposed settlement to the arbitrator, who is at liberty to come up with settlement terms to which both sides must agree. Oftentimes, the final settlement may be a midpoint between the settlement terms submitted by either party. For example, on *Cybersettle.com*, an online out-of-court settlement service, the algorithm immediately imposes a final settlement outcome that is midway between the last two offers submitted by either party. Thus, each side has an incentive to shape the arbitrator's final judgment by submitting an offer that is self-serving.

An obvious disadvantage of traditional arbitration is that parties may reason that the third party will impose a settlement midway between the two final proposals submitted. This expectation leads the parties to submit extreme final proposals. The tendency for disputants to exaggerate their demands and reduce their level of concession making is known as the **chilling effect**.[12]

FINAL-OFFER ARBITRATION   Final-offer arbitration was developed in response to the chilling-effect problem of traditional arbitration.[13] In **final-offer arbitration**, the disputants submit final proposals to the arbitrator, who then chooses one of the two final settlements to impose. Thus,

---

[6] Hoh, R. (1984). The effectiveness of mediation in public-sector arbitration systems: The Iowa experience. *Arbitration Journal, 39*(2), 30–40; Kochan, T. A. (1979). Dynamics of dispute resolution in the public sector. In B. Aaron, J. R. Grodin, & J. L. Stern (Eds.), *Public-sector bargaining* (pp. 150–190). Washington, DC: BNA Books; Kressel, K., & Pruitt, D. G. (1989). Conclusion: A research perspective on the mediation of social conflict. In K. Kressel & D. G. Pruitt (Eds.), *Mediation research* (pp. 394–435). San Francisco: Jossey-Bass.
[7] Ross, W. H., & Conlon, D. E. (2000). Hybrid forms of third-party dispute resolution: Theoretical implications of combining mediation and arbitration. *Academy of Management Review, 25*(2), 416–427.
[8] Karambayya, R., & Brett, J. M. (1989). Managers handling disputes: Third-party roles and perceptions of fairness. *Academy of Management Journal, 32,* 687–704; Pierce, R. S., Pruitt, D. G., & Czaja, S. J. (1993). Complainant-respondent differences in procedural choice. *International Journal of Conflict Management, 4,* 199–122; Ross, W. H., Conlon, D. E., & Lind, E. A. (1990). The mediator as leader: Effects of behavioral style and deadline certainty on negotiator behavior. *Group and Organization Studies, 15,* 105–124.
[9] Ross & Conlon, "Hybrid forms."
[10] Farber, H. S., & Katz, H. (1979). Why is there disagreement in bargaining? *American Economic Review, 77,* 347–352.
[11] Marmo, M. (1995). The role of fact finding and interest arbitration in "selling" a settlement. *Journal of Collective Negotiations in the Public Sector, 14,* 77–97; Rose, J. B., & Manuel, C. (1996). Attitudes toward collective bargaining and compulsory arbitration. *Journal of Collective Negotiations in the Public Sector, 25,* 287–310.
[12] Notz, W. W., & Starke, F. A. (1987). Arbitration and distributive justice: Equity or equality? *Journal of Applied Psychology, 72,* 359–365.
[13] Farber, H. S. (1981). Splitting the difference in interest arbitration. *Industrial and Labor Relations Review, 35,* 70–77.

the incentive of the parties involved is to submit a settlement that will be viewed as most fair in the eyes of the arbitrator.

Mediation-Arbitration

Recognizing the strengths (and weaknesses) of mediation and arbitration, some scholars and practitioners have advocated the adoption of hybrid procedures: mediation-arbitration and arbitration-mediation.[14] **Mediation-arbitration** (hereafter **med-arb**) consists of two phases: (a) mediation followed by (b) arbitration, if mediation fails to secure an agreement by a predetermined deadline. The same third party serves as both mediator and arbitrator.[15] Thus, arbitration is only engaged if mediation fails.

Arbitration-Mediation

Arbitration-mediation (hereafter **arb-med**) consists of three phases.[16] In phase one, the third party holds an **arbitration hearing**. At the end of this phase, the third party makes a decision, which is placed in a sealed envelope and is not revealed to the parties. The second phase consists of **mediation**. The sealed envelope containing the third party's decision is displayed prominently during the mediation phase. Only if mediation fails to produce a voluntary agreement by a specified deadline do the parties enter the third phase, called the **ruling phase**. Here, the third party removes the ruling from the envelope and reveals the binding ruling to the disputants.[17] To ensure that the envelope contains the original ruling and not a later decision (e.g., a ruling created after the mediation phase), the third party can ask a disputant from each side to sign the envelope across the seal at the beginning of mediation. The greatest benefit of arb-med is that it encourages disputants to settle their differences themselves.[18]

In a direct test of the effectiveness of med-arb and arb-med, disputants in the arb-med procedures settled in the mediation phase of their procedure more frequently and achieved settlements of higher joint benefit than did disputants in the med-arb procedure.[19]

KEY CHOICE POINTS IN THIRD-PARTY INTERVENTION

Each of the four key types of third-party intervention are formal but more informal types of intervention are also possible. We now consider some key choice points of third-party intervention.

Outcome Versus Process Control

A key aspect in any type of third-party intervention involves the control held by the third party. The ability to control the outcome is the key distinction between mediation and arbitration. **Outcome control** refers to the ability of the third party to impose a final, binding settlement

---

[14] Ross & Conlon, "Hybrid forms."

[15] Kagel, J. (1976). Comment. In H. Anderson (Ed.), *New techniques in labor dispute resolution* (pp. 185–190). Washington, DC: BNA Books.

[16] Ross & Conlon, "Hybrid forms."

[17] Cobbledick, G. (1992). Arb-med: An alternative approach to expediting settlement. Unpublished manuscript, Harvard Program on Negotiation, Harvard University, Boston; Sander, F. E. A. (1993). The courthouse and alternative dispute resolution. In L. Hall (Ed.), *Negotiation: Strategies for mutual gain* (pp. 43–60). Newbury Park, CA: Sage.

[18] Ross & Conlon, "Hybrid forms."

[19] Conlon, D. E., Moon, H., & Ng, K. Y. (2002). Putting the cart before the horse: The benefits of arbitrating before mediating. *Journal of Applied Psychology, 87*(5), 978–984.

on the parties. In contrast, **process control** refers to the ability of the third party to control the discussions, questions, and process of communication.

The mediator has process control but not outcome control (i.e., the power to impose a settlement). In arbitration, third parties have process and outcome control. Arbitration may be passive or inquisitive, and the arbitrator can have full discretion to impose any kind of settlement or can have constraints, such as the requirement to choose one side's final offer.

Formal Versus Informal

The roles of many, perhaps most, third parties are defined on the basis of some formal understanding among the disputants or on the basis of legal precedents or licensing and certification procedures. Third-party roles are effective to the extent that they are acknowledged by the disputants as implying a legitimate right to be in the business of resolving conflicts. Formal roles include professional mediator, arbitrator, or ombudsperson. However, a variety of informal third-party roles exist, such as a friend who intervenes in a marriage dispute.

Invited Versus Uninvited

Most commonly, a third party intervenes at the request of one or both of the principals. For example, divorcing couples may seek the services of a divorce mediator. Such invited roles are effective for two reasons: First, the invitation to intervene suggests that at least one of the parties is motivated to address the dispute in question. Second, the invitation makes the third party appropriate, acceptable, and desirable, thereby increasing clout and legitimacy. An example of an uninvited role is a customer in an airport witnessing a conflict between a flight agent and a passenger.

Interpersonal Versus Intergroup

Third parties typically intervene in disputes between individuals. In more complex situations, third-party intervention can occur in disputes between groups or nations.

Content Versus Process Orientation

Some third-party roles focus primarily on the content of a dispute, such as the issues or resources under consideration. Others focus more on the process of decision making and on the way in which decisions are taking place. Arbitrators (and to a lesser extent, mediators) are typically content oriented. In contrast, marriage counselors are more process focused (i.e., they try to get each party to listen to one another, etc.).

Facilitation, Formulation, or Manipulation

Mediators use any of three styles: facilitation, formulation and manipulation.[20] **Facilitation**, also known as communication, is characterized by mediators who serve as a channel of communication among disputing parties. Mediators who are facilitators occasionally reveal information they have gathered independently and thereby clarify misconceptions. For example, in a 1990 crisis between India and Pakistan, the U.S. delegation to Pakistan communicated that Pakistan's military was inferior and that the United States did not intend to help Pakistan in a war.[21]

---

[20] Beardsley, K. C., Quinn, D. M., Biswas, B., & Wilkenfeld, J. (2006). Mediation style and crisis outcomes. *The Journal of Conflict Resolution, 50*(1), 58-86.
[21] Ibid.

In contrast, **formulation** involves a substantive contribution to negotiations by conceiving and proposing new solutions. For example, during the 1992 crisis between Liberia and Sierra Leone, the Economic Community of West African States (ECOWAS) successfully structured the bargaining process and proposed the outcome to which the parties ultimately agreed. Finally, **manipulation** occurs when the mediator uses his or her position and leverage to influence the bargaining process, such as by offering incentives or even threats. For example, during the 1972 crisis between North Yemen and South Yemen, the mediator, Colonel Moammar Qaddhafi of Libya, threatened to hold captive the delegation leaders of both sides if they did not reach agreement. Moreover, he offered both sides nearly $50 million in annual aid if they did reach agreement. In a test of the effectiveness of each style in international crisis mediations, manipulation had the strongest effect on the likelihood of reaching a formal agreement and contributing to crisis abatement. Facilitation had the greatest influence on increasing the prospects for lasting tension reduction.[22]

Disputant Preferences

What types of mediation are most preferred by disputants? Participants in mediation generally prefer (a) control over outcome, such that a neutral third party would help disputants reach a mutually satisfactory resolution, (b) control over process such that disputants would relay information on their own behalf without the help of a representative, and (c) either substantive rules that disputants would have agreed to before the resolution process or the rules typically used in court.[23]

Mediators and Gender

A comparison of male versus female mediators revealed that females were more transformative, but no less instrumental than male mediators, in their view of the goals of mediation.[24] Female mediators were more facilitative, whereas male mediators were more directive. Perceptions of mediator effectiveness, however, reveal a gender bias. Male mediators are perceived more favorably than their female counterparts.[25]

CHALLENGES FACING THIRD PARTIES

A number of challenges face the third party.[26]

Meeting Disputants' Expectations

The expectations of mediators go beyond helping parties reach settlement. The success of a mediation program should include the following five dimensions as assessed by disputants: mediator's usefulness, procedural justice, satisfaction with the agreement, confidence in the agreement, and reconciliation between parties.[27] The trust between mediators and parties is a key

---

[22] Ibid.

[23] Shestowsky, D. (2004). Procedural differences in alternative dispute resolution. *Psychology, Public Policy and the Law, 10*(3), 211–249.

[24] Nelson, N. (2010). Transformative women, problem-solving men? Not quite: Gender and mediators' perceptions of mediation. *Negotiation Journal, 26*(3), 287–308.

[25] Stuhlmacher, A. F., & Morrissett, M. G. (2008). Men and women as mediators: disputant perceptions. *International Journal of Conflict Management, 19*(3), 249–261.

[26] Bazerman, M. H., & Neale, M. A. (1992). *Negotiating rationally*. New York: Free Press.

[27] Poitras, J., & Le Tareau, A. (2008). Dispute resolution patterns and organizational dispute states. *International Journal of Conflict Management, 19*(1). 72–87.

element in the mediation process. The five key factors that determine whether disputants trust mediators include: degree of mastery over the process, explanation of the process, warmth and consideration, chemistry with the parties, and lack of bias toward either party.[28]

Increasing the Likelihood That Parties Reach an Agreement if a Positive Bargaining Zone Exists

Effective third-party intervention not only assesses whether a positive bargaining zone exists, but it also helps parties reach agreement if it does. If settlement is not likely, it is to both parties' advantage to realize this quickly and exercise their BATNAs. For example, an increasing number of divorcing couples settle their financial disputes through face-to-face cooperation rather than courtroom confrontations.[29] The benefit of mediation, as opposed to the courtroom, is that the parties can talk and, as a result, often reach settlement quicker. One man estimated that he saved more than $10,000 in attorney fees by settling financial issues with his wife during a pair of 2-hour mediation sessions. Moreover, rather than focusing on their "legal rights," they focused on their "future needs" (i.e., an interests rather than a rights focus; see Chapter 5). However, if the divorcing couple is emotional, it may not work.

Promoting a Pareto-Efficient Outcome

It is not enough for third parties to help negotiators reach agreement. Ideally, they should strive for Pareto-optimal win-win agreements. Obviously, this type of agreement will not happen if the third party is not properly trained in integrative bargaining strategies or places a higher premium on reaching agreement over reaching a win-win agreement. Third parties should not let the desperation of the negotiators narrow their own view of the possibilities for integrative agreement.

Promoting Outcomes That Are Perceived as Fair in the Eyes of Disputants

When people feel that a deal is fair, they are more likely to agree to it, less likely to renege on it, and more likely to come to the table in the future. Mediators' interventions are most likely to be win-win when the relationship among the negotiators is positive and genuine; conversely, mediators are more likely to propose fixed-pie solutions when the negotiators' relationship is negative and not genuine.[30] When disputants in conflict have asymmetrical conflict perceptions, they are more likely to view the mediator as biased, and they are less satisfied.[31] Moreover, the disputant who felt greater conflict is more likely to recommend mediation to their coworkers.

Improving the Relationship Between Parties

Ideally, effective third-party intervention should increase the level of trust between parties.

Empowering Parties in the Negotiation Process

A skilled mediator not only helps parties reach integrative settlements but also improves the ability of parties to reach settlements on their own. Ideally, the ability of negotiators to

---

[28] Poitras, J. (2009). What makes parties trust mediators? *Negotiation Journal, 25*(3), 307–325.

[29] Silverman, S. (2003, June 22). Divorce mediation gains popularity. *The Pantagraph,* p. A1.

[30] Thompson, L., & Kim, P. H. (2000). How the quality of third parties' settlement solutions are affected by the relationship between negotiators. *Journal of Experimental Psychology: Applied, 6*(1), 1–16.

[31] Jehn, K. A., Rupert, J., Nauta, A., & Van Den Bossche, S. (2010). Crooked conflicts: The effects of conflict asymmetry in mediation. *Negotiation and Conflict Management Research, 3*(4), 338–357.

effectively resolve conflict and reach effective outcomes should be enhanced via the influence of a third party.

Debiasing Negotiators

Biased perceptions run rampant among negotiators. When conflict escalates and parties are emotional, biased perceptions escalate further. Third parties should attempt, whenever possible, to debias negotiations. The most common biases include:

EXAGGERATION OF CONFLICT BIAS This bias occurs when parties exaggerate differences between themselves and the opposing party (in negotiation) and even in third parties (in mediation).[32] For example, when students from rival universities watch the same videotape of a football game, they perceive their own team as committing fewer infractions than those attributed to their team by the opposing side.[33] When recipients view a proposer's behavior to be "negative," they regard the proposer to have more negative intentions than an observer watching the same proposer.[34]

Examination of partisans of both sides of contemporary social conflict (e.g., liberal versus conservative groups, pro-life versus pro-choice groups) reveal that partisans overestimate the extremity and consistency of the view of the other side.[35] Consider a deep-rooted conflict between the Nez Perce Tribe and local nontribal governments that operate within the boundaries of the Nez Perce Reservation.[36] Overall, disputants in the conflict were more defensive than offensive. **Offensive behavior** is any attempted actions that benefit one's own side relative to the other side, and **defensive behavior** is antipathy toward actions that harm one's own side to the other side's benefit.[37] Disputants consistently exaggerated the offensiveness of the other side and underestimated the defensiveness of the other side.

HOSTILE MEDIA BIAS Sometimes, parties on both sides of a conflict will view an even-handed media report to be partial to the other side. For example, news accounts of the 1982 Beirut Massacre were judged by partisans on both sides of the Arab-Israeli conflict to be partial to the other side.[38] Similarly, in another investigation, negotiators role-played an organizational mediation. Both sides to the conflict perceived the mediator to be partial to the opponent. Even when a mediator is partial to a particular side, that party often fails to realize this partiality and assumes the mediator is biased against it.

OVERCONFIDENCE BIAS In general, disputants overestimate the extent to which their beliefs are shared by a third party. For example, when negotiators are asked to estimate the likelihood

---

[32] Morris, M. W. (1995). Through a glass darkly: Cognitive and motivational processes that obscure social perception in conflicts. Paper presented at the Academy of Management Meetings, Vancouver, BC.

[33] Hastorf, A., & Cantril, H. (1954). They saw a game: A case study. *Journal of Abnormal and Social Psychology, 49,* 129–134.

[34] Dickson, E. S. (2009). Do participants and observers assess intentions differently during bargaining and conflict? *American Journal of Political Science, 53*(4), 910–930

[35] Robinson, R. J., Keltner, D., Ward, A., & Ross, L. (1994). Actual versus assumed differences in construal: "Naïve realism" in intergroup perception and conflict. *Journal of Personality and Social Psychology, 68,* 404–417.

[36] Allred, K. G., Hong, K., & Kalt, J. P. (2002). Partisan misperceptions and conflict escalation: Survey evidence from a tribal/local government conflict. Paper presented at the International Association of Conflict Management, Park City, UT.

[37] Ibid.

[38] Vallone, R. P., Ross, L., & Lepper, M. (1985). The hostile media phenomenon: Biased perception and perceptions of media bias in coverage of the "Beirut Massacre." *Journal of Personality and Social Psychology, 49,* 577–585.

of prevailing in final-offer arbitration, they are overconfident that the third party will favor their proposal.[39] Parties on both sides of the dispute estimate a greater than 50% chance of prevailing. Obviously, they cannot both be right.

The hostile media bias and the overconfidence bias may appear contradictory. How can people feel the mediator is simultaneously taking the view of the other side and also agreeing with their own position? The apparent inconsistency stems from the nature of the judgment made by negotiators. In a direct test of this question, negotiators' perceptions of mediator behavior were examined in a realistic organizational simulation.[40] Each negotiator simultaneously displayed an egocentric (overconfidence) bias, evaluating his or her behavior as more successful than that of the counterparty. However, when asked about the amount and content of the mediator's attention to disputants, they saw themselves as coming up short. Each party believed that the mediator spent more time talking and listening to the counterparty, allowed more faulty arguments from the counterparty, and showed less resistance to the counterparty's persuasion attempts. Also, both sides perceived the mediator as less receptive to their concerns and less active in exploring their interests than those of the counterparty.

Maintaining Neutrality

Nothing guarantees that third parties are neutral.[41] In fact, third parties evince many of the biases that plague principals, such as framing effects.[42] Even a neutral mediator may be mistakenly viewed as partial to one's adversary.[43] Also, third parties may have a bias to broker an agreement at any cost, which may be disadvantageous to the principals if no positive bargaining zone exists. Finally, the threat of third-party intervention may inhibit settlement if principals believe an arbitrator is inclined to impose a compromise settlement. For this reason, final-offer arbitration may be more effective than traditional arbitration.[44]

In an empirical analysis of 124 peace agreements between 1989 and 2004, neutral mediators, who were engaged primarily because of their interest to end war, had incentives to reach agreement at the expense of quality. In contrast, "biased mediators" seeking to protect their groups, worked to ensure that their party's interests were met.[45] Thus, a biased mediation process is actually more likely than a neutral mediation process to lead to elaborated institutional agreements that benefit democracy and durable peace.

Managers are often called on to resolve disputes in organizations.[46] In contrast to traditional arbitrators and mediators, managers may have a direct stake in the outcome and an ongoing

---

[39] Bazerman & Neale, *Negotiating rationally*; Neale, M. A., & Bazerman, M. H. (1983). The role of perspective taking ability in negotiating under different forms of arbitration. *Industrial and Labor Relations Review, 36,* 378–388.

[40] Morris, M. W., & Su, S. K. (1999). The hostile mediator phenomenon: Egocentric standards of fairness lead disputants to see mediators as favoring the opponent. Unpublished manuscript, Stanford University.

[41] Gibson, K., Thompson, L., & Bazerman, M. H. (1994). Biases and rationality in the mediation process. In L. Heath, F. Bryant, & J. Edwards (Eds.), *Application of heuristics and biases to social issues: Vol. 3.* New York: Plenum.

[42] Carnevale, P. J. (1995). Property, culture, and negotiation. In R. M. Kramer & D. M. Messick (Eds.), *Negotiation as a social process: New trends in theory and research* (pp. 309–323). Thousand Oaks, CA: Sage.

[43] Morris, & Su, "The hostile mediator phenomenon."

[44] Farber, "Splitting the difference"; Chelius, J. R., & Dworkin, J. B. (1980). The economic analysis of final-offer arbitration as a conflict resolution device. *Journal of Conflict Resolution, 24,* 293–310; Raiffa, H. (1982). *The art and science of negotiation.* Cambridge, MA: Belknap.

[45] Svensson, I. (2009). Who brings which peace?: Neutral versus biased mediation and institutional peace arrangements in civil wars. *Journal of Conflict Resolution, 53*(3), 446–469.

[46] Tornow, W. W., & Pinto, P. R. (1976). The development of a managerial job taxonomy: A system for describing, classifying, and evaluating executive positions. *Journal of Applied Psychology, 61,* 410–418.

relationship with the disputants. In addition, managers are more likely to have technical expertise and background knowledge about the dispute. Although several intervention techniques are available to managers, they often choose techniques that maximize their own control over the outcome.[47]

STRATEGIES FOR ENHANCING EFFECTIVENESS OF THIRD-PARTY INTERVENTION

What steps can negotiators take to maximize the effectiveness of third-party intervention?

Accept Your Share of Responsibility

Mediators often struggle to get parties to accept their share of responsibility for conflict. When parties acknowledge their share of responsibility, settlement rates and reconciliation increase.[48]

Test Your Own Position

A good scientist will set up an experiment that includes "blinds." For example, in testing the effectiveness of a particular drug, one group of patients might be given the drug and the other group a placebo or sugar pill. The experimenters further blind themselves to which group was given what and assesses the outcome. The same should be true for your own negotiation position. For example, if you find yourself in a dispute with a merchant or neighbor, describe the situation to the third party in such a way so as not to indicate what role you are playing in the dispute. Then ask the third party for an honest opinion.

Role-Play a Third Party in Your Own Dispute

Describe your negotiation situation to some colleagues who might be willing to play the roles involved. Then take on the role of a third party in the situation. Try to come up with a solution that both parties find agreeable.

Training in Win-Win Negotiation

Perhaps no other skill is as important as the ability to focus on expanding the size of the bargaining zone by discovering interests and then fashioning value-added trade-offs.

---

[47] Karambayya & Brett, "Managers handling disputes"; Sheppard, B. H. (1984). Third-party intervention: A procedural framework. In B. M. Staw & L. L. Cummings (Eds.), *Research in organizational behavior: Vol. 6.* Greenwich, CT: JAI Press.
[48] Poitras, J. (2010). Mediation: Depolarizing responsibilities to facilitate reconciliation. *International Journal of Conflict Management, 21*(1), 4–19.

APPENDIX 4

Negotiating a Job Offer

When negotiating a job, you need all the essential skills covered in Part I (Chapters 1, 2, 3, and 4). In addition, you should be comfortable with your own bargaining style (and know its limits; see Chapter 5). You should be well-versed in building trust and rapport (Chapter 6) and know the dynamics of power (Chapter 7) and how to increase creativity (Chapter 8). This appendix is designed to provide specific strategies for this all-important negotiation that will recur throughout your life. We organized this appendix into three phases: preparation, in vivo process, and postoffer.

PREPARATION

Salary negotiations are extremely important because they affect your livelihood and welfare for years to come. Think of it this way: assuming an average annual pay increase of 5%, an employee whose starting annual salary is $55,000 rather than $50,000 would earn an additional $600,000+ over the course of a 40-year career.[1] The people who choose to negotiate their starting salaries increase it by an average of $5,000.

Step 1: Figure Out What You Really Want

This step sounds easy enough, but for a 28-year-old, it means an ability to project forward in time and to be concerned with things such as retirement and benefits. Karen Cates of Northwestern University's Kellogg School of Management recommends working through a checklist of needs and wants (see Exhibit A4-1).[2] Cates further suggests a practical, step-by-step approach to compensation and benefits (see Exhibit A4-2).

Step 2: Do Your Homework

Research the company and the industry. The Internet allows people to get information quickly and easily, especially when it comes to salaries. Several websites offer salary surveys, job listings with specified pay levels, and even customized compensation analyses. However, for many jobs, web-based pay information represents only a starting point. In other words, websites can tell you if you are in the ballpark and can stop you from underbidding yourself.

It is important to do your homework so you don't ask for something that has already been institutionalized. For example, many companies have on-site chefs because they realized it just does not make sense to break at noon, have everyone get in cars, and go elsewhere for lunch.

Step 3: Determine Your BATNA and Your Aspiration Point

A negotiator always has a BATNA. Some students will claim agitatedly that they do not have a BATNA because they do not have any job offers in hand. They may not have an *attractive* BATNA, but they inevitably have courses of action if they do not get a job offer. Perhaps they will simply "extend" their job search indefinitely; perhaps they will travel abroad; perhaps they

---

[1] Marks, M., & Harold C. (2009). Who asks and who receives in salary negotiation. *Journal of Organizational Behavior.*
[2] Cates, K. (1997). Tips for negotiating a job offer. Unpublished manuscript, Kellogg School of Management, Northwestern University, Evanston, IL.

EXHIBIT A4-1

Checklist of Needs and Wants

Necessary Living Expenses	Additional Living Expenses
Housing (including utilities)	Recreation and entertainment (vacations, events, activities, books, etc.)
Auto	
Computer	Services (professional and household)
Child care	Continuing education
Insurance (auto, home, life, professional)	Children's expenses (lessons, schooling)
Personal (food, medical, clothing, household)	Gifts, charity
Student loan debt service	
Taxes (income, property, etc.)	

Source: Cates, K. (1997). Tips for negotiating a job offer. Unpublished manuscript, Kellogg School of Management, Northwestern University, Evanston, IL. Used by permission of Karen Cates.

EXHIBIT A4-2

Compensation and Benefits

Compensation	Retirement	Paid Leave	Protection
Salary	Pension/401K	Vacation, sick, and personal days	Insurance (life, disability, health, other)
Bonus	Guaranteed pay plans (supplemental unemployment)	Training time	
Other variable pay			
Stock/equity interest		Holidays and special travel considerations	Care plans (child, elder)
	Savings plans		Wellness programs

Source: Cates, K. (1997). Tips for negotiating a job offer. Unpublished manuscript, Kellogg School of Management, Northwestern University, Evanston, IL. Used by permission of Karen Cates.

will do freelance or volunteer work, take a research assistantship at a university, or search for a non-professional job while they continue their career search. All of these options are possible BATNAs; they should be assessed and the best one focused upon and evaluated carefully.

Our BATNAs are never as attractive as we would like them to be. The rare times when we have two or more fabulous job offers in hand, two bids on our house, and lucrative investment opportunities, we can afford to push for a lot more in negotiations. Obviously, you are in a much better position to successfully negotiate an attractive compensation package if your BATNA is attractive. As we stated in Chapter 2, your BATNA is dynamic, and it is important not to be passive about it.

It is important to think about how we might improve our BATNA. Most negotiators do not spend adequate time attempting to improve their current situation. As a result, they approach negotiations feeling more desperate than they should.

Step 4: Research the Employer's BATNA

Developing your BATNA is only half the work that needs to be done before the negotiation. The next step is to determine the other party's BATNA, which requires tapping into multiple sources of information.

Step 5: Determine the Issue Mix

You have made your best assessment of the employer's BATNA. The negotiation is fast approaching. Now what? The next step is to determine the issues that are important to you in this negotiation. Do not make the mistake of letting the employer define the issues for you. Be ready to talk about your interests and needs.

After you determine which issues are important from your perspective, go back through your list and attempt to create an even more detailed list, breaking down each of the issues into smaller and smaller subsets. Breaking up the issues into smaller subsets does two things. First, it allows the negotiator (you) to be much more specific about what is important (e.g., the paid aspect of a vacation or the number of days allowed off). Second, it provides greater opportunity for creative agreements.

In addition to focusing on the issues and concerns of importance to you, anticipate the other party's perspective. Again, information and research are essential.

Step 6: Prepare Several Scenarios

Most likely, the negotiations will not go as planned. Rather than being caught off guard, prepare your response to several different scenarios, including the following:

- The employer agrees immediately to your counteroffer.
- The employer makes a low-ball offer (in your eyes) and flatly states, "This is our final offer."
- The employer makes one small concession.
- The employer asks you to make a reasonable offer.

Step 7: Consider Getting a "Coach"

Job coaches can help people advance their careers and achieve their compensation goals. They are people who help managers plan their future. The way that Peter Goodman, CEO of MyJobCoach, puts it, "If you have a legal issue, you go to a lawyer for advice. When doing financial planning, you go to an accountant. So why would you not go to a career coach when planning your career, the area where you spend over 70% of your waking life?"[3]

---

[3] Business Week. (2011). *Job Coaches* [video]. Businessweek.com

Lexus Nexus Legal Markets provides job coaches for new employees with the idea that the new hire will successfully integrate his or her own ideas into the company culture and make the company stronger, with their stake within it more rewarding.[4] CEOs have always taken coaching seriously, at least when it comes to negotiating their compensation packages. For example, lawyer Joseph Bachelder has negotiated top contracts for top corporate executives for more than 25 years, pioneering the idea of CEO contract negotiation. When Wachovia Corp. former chief executive Ken Thompson retired from the nation's fourth-largest bank while being under fire for plunging stock prices and huge losses, Thompson negotiated a $28 million compensation package despite stock prices that had fallen to a 13-year low. Bachelder negotiated deals for departing CEO's of companies including Bank One, IBM, Lucent, and Eastman Kodak.[5]

IN VIVO: DURING THE NEGOTIATION ITSELF

You have done your preparation. Now it is time for the actual negotiation.

Think About the Best Way to Position and Present Your Opening Offer

Remember to back up your offer with a compelling rationale. Use objective standards. Focus and select those standards that are favorable to you and be prepared to indicate why standards unfavorable to you are inappropriate.

Assume the Offer Is Negotiable

Do not ask "Can I negotiate the offer you have made?" Always assume the offer is negotiable and articulate your needs and interests. Cates advises saying the following: "I have some questions about the insurance coverage that I would like to talk about if we can" or "I have some concerns about the moving allowance, and I need to talk to you about it."[6] A survey conducted by careerbuilder.com indicated that 31% of employers were willing to negotiate salary increases with current employees and more than half (51%) planned to leave some negotiating "wiggle room" when extending first offers to new employees. Also, 21% were willing to extend two or more offers to the same candidate. Additionally, many employers who reported they were unable to provide raises indicated that they were willing to negotiate non-monetary perks such as flexible work hours, bonuses, and training.[7] Most job applicants do not push employers at the negotiating table. The failure to negotiate a first offer from an employer can cost workers a lot of money. "A 22-year-old who secures a $2,000 increase in annual salary at his or her first job will, because of the compounding effects of years of raises to follow, most likely generates roughly $150,000 in extra income over the course of a 40-year career."[8] The effect is even more dramatic for an MBA student negotiating a $90,000 job offer. What's more, if you do not negotiate what you want in that brief window between your receipt of a job offer and your acceptance of it, you may never get it. Your power is greatest when you are

[4] Ibid.

[5] Anders, G. (2003, June 25). Upping the ante: As some decry lavish CEO pay, Joe Bachelder makes it happen. *Wall Street Journal*, p. A1; Rothacker, R. (2008, June 4). CEO's pay hurt by stock fall but Wachoivia's Ken Thompson still walks away with $28 million in pension, stock and severance. *Charlotte Observer*, D1.

[6] Cates, "Tips for negotiating a job offer."

[7] Grasz, J. (2010, November 10). Nearly one-third of employers willing to negotiate salary increases for current employees for 2011. *Career Builder*. Careerbuilder.com

[8] Clark, K. (1999, November 1). Gimme, gimme, gimme: Job seekers don't realize they can ask for more—lots more. *U. S. News & World Report*, 88–92.

EXHIBIT A4-3

Things to Ask for When Negotiating an Offer

Some things to ask for when negotiating an offer (other than a higher salary, which is always worth asking for):

- Extra vacation days
- Flexible scheduling
- Telecommuting
- Delaying your start date to have time off between jobs
- Personal days and parental leaves
- Gas reimbursement
- Public transportation reimbursement
- Increased family benefits
- Supplemental insurance coverage
- Increased job training
- Gym memberships
- Food delivery
- Concierge services
- Dry cleaning services
- Education grants
- Tuition reimbursement
- Adoption assistance

Source: Brandon, E. (2006, June 14). Negotiating for job perks; ask and you might receive. *US News and World Report.* Usnews.com; Liveten, S. (2006, October 6). The power of the perk. *Forbes.com*

responding to "their offer" because it is the one time the employer may want you more than you want them.[9] (For a list of things to ask for in your negotiation, see Exhibit A4-3.)

Immediately Reanchor the Interviewer by Reviewing Your Needs and Your Rationale

Indicate your interest in working for the company, and tell the interviewer how your needs (and wants) can be met in a variety of ways. Many negotiations result in impasse because employers falsely assumed that the candidates did not want the job when they actually did. Thus, keep

---

[9] Ibid.

reiterating your heartfelt interest in the company. Cates advises to "get your requests on the table and keep them there."[10] According to Cates, salary negotiations are really about candidates helping recruiters to solve their problems. In other words, let the employer know what would make their offer more appealing. This offer of information may even come to sharing your own prioritization and MAUT analysis of the issues.

Reveal Neither Your BATNA nor Your Reservation Point

Negotiators have a million ways of asking people about their BATNAs. Asking a potential job recruit about his or her current salary and wage package is one of them. Remember that this information is your business, not the recruiter's. If you are currently employed, redirect the discussion by indicating what it is going to take to move you (e.g., a more exciting job and a wage package commensurate with the job). If you are not employed, explain what it will take to hire you. Ward off direct attacks about your previous salary by explaining that your acceptance of a position depends on the nature of the job offer and wage package.

You should be prepared to take the initiative in the conversation. Practice by role-playing. If the employer attempts to get you to talk about why you are leaving a former job, avoid falling into the trap of trashing a former employer, even if you did have a miserable experience. It is a small world, and a relationship you do not immediately see may be involved. Even more important, the employer will probably get the wrong impression about you (e.g., regard you as a troublemaker or overly critical).

If you have not yet been offered the job but sense that the employer wants to find out what you desire in a job offer, avoid talking about salary or specific terms until you have an offer. You are in a much weaker position to negotiate before you have a job offer than after you are offered a position. If you have been told "Things will work out" or "A job offer is coming," express appreciation and inquire when you will receive formal notice. After that, schedule a meeting to talk about the terms. While you are negotiating, you should assume that everything is negotiable. If you are told that some aspect of the job is "not negotiable," ask questions, such as whether everyone (new hires and veterans) receives the same treatment.

Rehearse and Practice

It is important to plan for negotiation. According to global online compensation company PayScale, negotiating for a raise requires a three-part action plan of proving worth, building PR, and then practice in asking for the raise by pretending that a friend or a loved one is the boss. It might even be helpful to state your case to a mirror![11]

Imagine You Are Negotiating on Behalf of Someone Else (Not Just Yourself)

Many people are reluctant to negotiate their job offer because they feel greedy or have a hard time being assertive. However, these same people are quite effective when negotiating for a company or for someone else. One solution is to approach a job negotiation as if you were negotiating on behalf of an important company: your own family. If we think about the direct effect our salary will have on our ability to provide for our children, our spouse, and our parents, we can be much more effective. Even the unmarried student without children is well

[10] Cates, "Tips for negotiating a job offer."
[11] Rosner, B. & Campbell, S. (2011). Recession proof your career. *Pay Scale.* Payscale.com

advised to think about the family he or she will have or might have in the not-so-distant future and to negotiate on behalf of those people.

Comparables and Benchmarks

Probably no other information is perceived to be more valuable in the job negotiation process than what similar employers are offering or what current employees are receiving. It is important to keep in mind that such comparables or benchmarks can affect the perceived attractiveness of the job offer in question, but the negotiator may be unaware of this. For example, people are more likely to accept a lower-paying job that pays other employees the same amount than a higher-paying job that pays other employees even more. People do not want to be "underpaid" and would even give up more absolute money if this meant they were treated like others.[12] Concerns for social comparisons (comps) are more important when people evaluate a single option than when they evaluate two options. Moreover, discrepancies in pay (i.e., social comparison concerns) may take priority over absolute salary amounts in situations in which choosing a job that is favorable on social comparison but unfavorable on actual salary can be "justified," as in the case when an inferior (i.e., dominated) alternative is present.[13] An analysis of how MBA students react to job offers revealed that signing bonuses did not affect acceptance rates; rather, job candidates strongly consider how responsive companies are to their questions and whether recruiters are cordial (rather than derogatory).[14]

POST-OFFER: YOU HAVE THE OFFER, NOW WHAT?

Do Not Immediately Agree to the Offer

Do not start negotiating until you have a firm job offer and a salary figure from the employer. Do not prolong negotiations, however; this approach only frustrates the employer. Instead, give the employer positive reinforcement. Cates suggests something like "This looks great. I need to go over everything one last time before we make this official. I will call you at [a specific time]."[15]

Get the Offer in Writing

If the employer says it is not standard to make written offers, be sure to consult with others who would know this (e.g., the company's human resources division). At the very least, inform them you will write down your understanding of the terms and put it in a letter or memo to them. Keep notes for yourself regarding the points agreed to during each meeting.

---

[12] Bazerman, M. H., Loewenstein, G., & White, S. (1992). Reversals of preference in allocating decisions: Judging an alternative versus choosing among alternatives. *Administrative Science Quarterly, 37,* 220–240; Bazerman, M. H., Schroth, H. A., Shah, P. P., Diekmann, K. A., & Tenbrunsel, A. E. (1994). The inconsistent role of comparison others and procedural justice to hypothetical job descriptions: Implications for job acceptance decisions. *Organizational Behavior and Human Decision Processes, 60,* 326–352; Blount, S., & Bazerman, M. H. (1996). The inconsistent evaluation of comparative payoffs in labor supply and bargaining. *Journal of Economic Behavior and Organizations, 891,* 1–14.

[13] Tenbrunsel, A., & Diekmann, K. (2002). Job-decision inconsistencies involving social comparison information: The role of dominating alternatives. *Journal of Applied Psychology, 87*(6), 1149–1158.

[14] Porter, C., Conlon, D., & Barber, A. (2004). The dynamics of salary negotiations:Effects on applicants' justice perceptions and recruitment decisions. *International Journal of Conflict Management, 15*(3), 273–303.

[15] Cates, "Tips for negotiating a job offer."

Be Enthusiastic and Gracious

Someone has just made you an offer. Thank them and show your appreciation but do not accept immediately. Say, instead, "Let me go home and think about it." Make an appointment to return the following day and state your negotiating position in person.

Assess the Interviewer's Power to Negotiate with You

Before you begin negotiating or contemplating a counteroffer, determine who in the company has the ability to negotiate. Generally, those persons higher up in the organization are the ones who negotiate and the ones who care most about hiring good people. You should be well-versed about the advantages and disadvantages of negotiating with an intermediary, such as a human resources manager (see Chapter 9 on multiple parties). If you sense that things are not going well in the negotiation, try to bring someone else into the loop. However, make this move in a gracious way, so as not to antagonize the person with whom you are dealing.

State Exactly What Needs to Be Done for You to Agree

A powerful negotiating strategy is to let the employer know exactly what it will take for you to agree. This technique is effective because the employer can put aside any fears about the negotiation dragging on forever and being nickel-and-dimed to death. When you make your demands, though, ground them in logic and clear rationale. Requesting something too far out of whack may lose you the job. One man applied for an entry-level job in a company that paid an admittedly low salary for the industry. The salary was made clear to the job applicant in advance. The candidate went through several rounds of interviews and ultimately demanded over double what the employer was willing to pay. He was intransigent about his demands. Of course, he was not offered the position.[16]

Do Not Negotiate If You Are Not or Could Not Be Interested

Suppose that you are the lucky person sitting on four job offers, all from consulting firms (A, B, C, and D). You have done enough research, cost-benefit analysis, and soul searching to determine that, in your mind, firms A and B are superior in all ways to firms C and D. The question is: should you let firms C and D off the hook or string them along so as to potentially improve your power position when negotiating with firms A and B? Our advice is to politely inform firms C and D that you will not be accepting their offers at this time. You still have a wonderful BATNA, and it saves everyone a lot of time.

Exploding Offers

Exploding offers are offers that have a "time bomb" element to them (e.g., "The offer is only good for 24 hours"). The question is how to deal with them. In our experience, companies usually do not rescind exploding offers once they have made them (unless, as a matter of courtesy, it is for family, medical, or emergency reasons). Generally, we advise that job candidates who receive an exploding offer above their BATNA to seriously consider the offer. It certainly cannot hurt to inform other companies that you have an exploding offer and move up the time of the interview, if at all possible.

---

[16] DeZube, D. (2010, November 19). Salary negotiation: Always ask for more, or take the offer? *New York Times*. Nytimes.com

Do Not Try to Create a Bidding War

Bidding wars occur regularly on Wall Street, in professional athletics, and in the business world. We do not advise, however, that job candidates attempt to create bidding wars between companies. Rather, we advise job candidates to signal to potential employers that they have attractive BATNAs, that they do not want to start a bidding war, and that they tell their top-rated company what it would take to get them to work at the company.

Know When to Stop Pushing

According to Cates, it is important to know when to stop negotiating.[17] Cates suggests that negotiators stop when they see one or more of the following signals:

- The other side is not responsive.
- Reciprocal concessions are becoming miniscule.
- After some back and forth the employer says, "Enough!"

Use a Rational Strategy for Choosing Among Job Offers

If you find yourself in the lucky position of having multiple offers, you are then faced with a choice. First, you should recognize this enviable position as an approach-approach conflict. How should you weigh the choices? The simplest way is to use MAUT by constructing a grid listing the choices along a row (e.g., company A, company B) and the relevant attributes along a column underneath (e.g., salary, fringe benefits, travel, vacation, bonus, etc.). Then, fill in the grid with the details of the offer and how they "stack up" compared to the others (on a scale of 1 to 5 or 1 to 10 in your mind). Next, you can simply add the columns to find a "winner." A more sophisticated version of this strategy is to multiply each grid value by its importance before adding columns (with importance defined on a scale of 1 to 5). For example, for most people, salary is highly important (maybe a 5), whereas moving expenses are less important (maybe a 1 or 2). This distinction gives a more fine-grained assessment. (See Appendix 1 for a step-by-step approach to MAUT.)

---

[17] Cates, "Tips for negotiating a job offer."

NAME INDEX

A

Aaron, B., 362
Abbas, M., 34
Abdi, J., 274
Abdullah (king), 252
Abelson, R., 188
Abramowitz, C. V., 352
Abramowitz, S. I., 352
Abt, S., 309
Ackerman, B. A., 304
Ada Howard, E., 262
Adair, W. A., 269, 270, 271
Adair, W. L., 79, 269, 281, 282
Adam, H., 262
Adams, A. A., 74
Adams, S., 56, 58, 59
Adamson, R. E., 197
Adler, N. J., 268
Aik, V., 121
Akerlof, G. A., 14, 130
Akers, M. A., 161
Alba, J. W., 183, 212
Albright, M., 136, 162, 315
Alex, K., 84
Alfred, K. G., 118
Alge, B. J., 326
Allan, N., 14
Allen, H. M., Jr., 247
Allen, T. J., 315
Allison, S. T., 65
Alloway, T., 354
Allred, K. G., 118, 120, 367
Alon, I., 282
Altman, A., 157
Amanatullah, E. T., 97, 99, 118, 163
Ames, D. R., 46, 97, 122
Ancona, D. G., 237
Anders, G., 373
Anderson, C., 28, 168
Anderson, C. M., 307, 320
Anderson, H., 363
Anderson, J. R., 198
Anderson, N. R., 36
Anderson, S. C., 128
Andrade, E. B., 122
Andrews, R. E., 161

Appelt, K. C., 22
Archibald, K., 82
Argote, L., 242
Argyle, M., 144
Ariel, S., 258, 259
Ariely, D., 122
Armstrong, D. J., 317
Arnold, J. A., 2, 144
Aron, A., 249
Aronson, E., 28, 164, 165
Arrow, K. J., 220
Ashmore, R. D., 164
Assange, J., 312
Aubert, V., 28
Austin, W. G., 55, 147, 244, 275
Axelrod, R., 128, 291, 295
Axsom, D., 239

B

Babcock, L., 65, 162
Bachelder, J., 373
Back, K. W., 241
Badenhausen, K., 58
Bailey, J., 145, 151
Bain-Chekal, J., 123
Balakrishnan, P. V. S., 133
Balke, W. M., 73
Ball, G., 308
Ball, J., 108
Ballmer, S., 52
Banaji, M. R., 176
Banner, M ., 7
Bao, Y., 242
Barak, E., 162
Barber, A., 376
Barbour, H., 31
Barboza, D., 318
Bargh, J. A., 143
Baron, J., 62, 65, 66, 272, 330
Baron, R. A., 120
Barron, L., 99
Barron, R. S., 249, 250
Barry, B., 120, 121, 139, 169, 171, 172, 174, 220
Barsness, Z., 263
Bar-Tal, D., 244, 273
Bartlett, D., 303

Bartunek, J., 27
Bashir, O. al-, 32
Battista, J., 51
Bazerman, M. H., 5, 8, 11, 14, 15, 16, 19, 22, 26, 28, 29, 42, 49, 56, 62, 63, 64, 66, 74, 76, 77, 79, 82, 83, 86, 87, 93, 100, 130, 170, 175, 176, 188, 189, 190, 193, 199, 200, 201, 217, 219, 226, 231, 232, 235, 244, 258, 273, 274, 296, 305, 314, 322, 365, 368, 376
Beach, S. R., 135
Beaman, A. L., 167
Beardsley, K. C., 364, 365
Bechtold, D., 256
Beersma, B., 77, 79, 102, 219
Belkin, L. Y., 319, 328
Bell, C. H., 254
Bennett, R., 83, 98
Bennigson, C., 140
Benson, P. L., 164
Ben-Yoav, O., 237
Bereby-Meyer, Y., 14, 193, 201
Berger, J., 274
Berkowitz, L., 54, 56, 120, 217, 278, 320, 358
Berlow, M., 119
Berner, R., 361
Bernieri, F. J., 355
Bernoulli, D., 338, 339
Berry, D. S., 357
Berry, J. W., 282, 283
Berscheid, E., 56, 59
Bettencourt, L., 151
Bettencourt-Meyers, F., 151
Bettenhausen, K., 67
Bezos, J., 236
Bhawuk, D. P. S., 256
Biddle, J. E., 164
Biertempfel, R., 51
Bies, R. J., 140, 145
Bikson, T. K., 324
Billet, M. T., 7
Billings, D. K., 256
bin Laden, O., 114
Biswas, B., 364, 365
Blackwood, L., 237
Blake, A. W., 360
Blanck, P. D., 355
Blank, A. L., 49, 355
Blau, P. M., 56
Bleichrodt, N., 256
Blount, S., 376
Blount-Lyon, S., 225

Blount-White, S., 16
Blumberg, S. J., 239
Bobo, L., 247
Bochner, S., 134
Bodenhausen, G., 168
Boies, D., 215
Boles, T., 42, 51, 359, 360
Bolton, G. E., 221
Bond, M. H., 258
Boon, J., 12
Boras, S., 49, 109
Bornstein, G., 297
Bortel, R., 45
Boswell, W., 61
Bottom, W. P., 21, 22, 23, 26, 141, 142, 217, 219, 226, 227, 231, 232, 287, 293
Boulware, L., 46
Bourgeois, L. J., III, 132
Bowers, R. V., 361
Bowles, H. R., 161
Boyd, J. D., 90
Bradford, D. L., 248
Bradlow, E. T., 139, 141
Bradsher, K., 318
Brady, T., 140
Brandon, E., 374
Braunecker, D., 235
Brazil, D., 297
Brecher, M., 361
Brehm, S. S., 166
Brett, J. M., 30, 79, 80, 83, 98, 101, 102, 103, 107, 108, 109, 110, 112, 113, 114, 224, 225, 241, 253, 255, 257, 258, 263, 265, 268, 269, 270, 271, 274, 279, 280, 282, 284, 302, 304, 307, 318, 320, 362, 369
Brew, F. P., 266
Brewer, M. B., 128, 245, 247, 248, 275, 277, 298, 303, 305
Britton, S., 237
Broder, J. M., 125
Brodt, S., 240, 241, 320, 360
Brower, A. M., 242
Brown, C. E., 353, 354
Brown, J., 69, 177, 309
Brown, P., 222
Brown, R. J., 246, 248
Browning, L., 318
Bryant, F., 188, 235, 368
Bryant, K., 58
Buchan, N. R., 144, 258
Buck, R., 354, 355

Budescu, D. V., 307
Bulkeley, W. M., 216
Bunker, B. B., 128, 130
Burger, J. M., 167
Burkle, R., 224
Burris, E. R., 29, 121, 144
Burt, R. S., 163
Bush, G. W., 114, 138
Buss, J., 150
Butler, D., 359
Buttner, E. H., 139
Byne, J., 29
Byrne, D., 135
Byrnes, N., 153

C

Caccioppo, J. T., 122
Cadsby, C., 237
Cain, D. M., 176
Cairns, D. R., 266
Caldwell, D., 123
Camerer, C. F., 66, 222, 306, 307
Campbell, C., 52
Campbell, D., 144, 275
Campbell, S., 375
Cantor, N., 120, 121
Cantril, H., 275, 367
Caplan, A., 31
Carlsmith, J. M., 351
Carnevale, P. J., 34, 48, 78, 99, 120, 144, 170, 180,
     185, 237, 238, 240, 258, 306, 368
Carney, D. R., 161
Carroll, J. B., 274
Cartwright, D., 54
Carty, D., 100
Caruso, E., 66, 200
Cassella, D. F., 354
Cates, K., 370–371, 373, 375–376, 378
Chaiken, S., 156, 164, 238
Chakravarti, A., 323
Chambers, J. R., 246
Champagne, M. V., 32, 102
Chan, D.K.S., 258
Chanowitz, B., 49
Chao, M., 271
Chapman, J. P., 196
Chapman, L. J., 196
Chassin, L., 194
Chater, N., 210
Chatterjee, K., 221

Chechile, R., 221
Cheldelin, S. I., 163
Chelius, J. R., 368
Chen, C. C., 265
Chen, F. S., 77
Chen, T., 219
Chen, X., 304, 306
Chen, Y., 45, 272
Cheraskin, L., 128
Chi, S-c., 253, 265
Chiu, C., 264, 319
Chiu, C-y., 260, 271
Choi, D. W., 185
Christakopolou, S., 264
Chua, C. H., 279
Chua, R. Y. J., 133, 258
Chua, R. Y. J., 258
Chuan, D. K. S., 258
Chugh, D., 176, 193
Cialdini, R. B., 158, 167, 231, 304
Clare, J., 292
Clark, K., 373, 374
Clark, M., 144, 145, 148
Clark, M. S., 122
Claude, S., 81
Claussen-Schulz, A., 82
Clenney, E. F., 160, 162
Cobbe, P., 51
Cobbledick, G., 363
Cohan, W. D., 140
Cohen, A. R., 248
Cohen, H., 2
Cohen, M. D., 71, 85
Cohen, R., 268
Cohen, S., 32
Cohen, T. R., 172, 305
Colburn, D., 21
Cole, N., 167
Cole, P., 317
Coleman, P. T., 118, 180
Collison, R., 53
Columbus, C., 129, 189
Condor, R., 248
Conlon, D. E., 79, 112, 362, 363, 376
Connolly, C., 71
Coombs, C. H., 334
Cooper, J., 180
Copeland, L., 278
Covey, S., 110, 111
Cowan, C., 153
Cowell, S., 44

Cox, T. H., 258
Crasnick, J., 235
Craver, C., 10
Crawford, V. P., 23
Creighton, M. R., 271
Crenshaw, J. L., 45
Croson, R. T. A., 42, 51, 98, 142, 143, 144, 258, 296, 318, 320, 322, 355, 357, 359, 360
Crotty, S., 77
Csikszentmihalyi, M., 209
Cuddy, A. J. C., 161
Cummings, L. L., 140, 310, 369
Cunningham, M. R., 354
Curhan, J. R., 11, 15, 75, 97, 99, 127, 141, 146, 148, 159, 161, 279
Currall, S., 317
Currey, D. P., 297
Curry, J., 109
Czaja, S. J., 362

D

Daft, R. L., 313
Dagher, V., 188
D'Altorio, T., 72
Daly, J. P., 61
Danan, E., 332
Daniels, M., 169
Daniels, S. E., 141, 142, 293
Danilovic, V., 292
Dardick, H., 303
Darley, J. M., 222, 223
Dasen, P. R., 283
Daubman, K. A., 120
Davenport, J. W., Jr., 134
Davidson, J. E., 184, 213
Davies, J., 188
Davis, B., 16
Dawes, R. M., 144, 258, 305, 334
Dayton, T., 184, 214
Dearen, J., 69
De Bono, E., 182, 212
De Cremer, D., 303
De Dreu, C. K. W., 15, 29, 77, 79, 89, 99, 102, 118, 119, 120, 204, 219, 239
DeFazio, P., 221–222
Degoey, P., 305
DeHarpport, T., 9, 70, 74, 98, 146, 201
Demick, B., 107
Demos, J., 271
DePaulo, B. M., 352, 353, 355, 356, 358, 360
DePaulo, P. J., 360

Dépret, E., 168
Derlega, V. J., 94
DeRue, D. S., 79
Desmaras, M., 281
Detweiler, R., 278
Deutsch, M., 52, 53, 54, 55, 56, 74, 118, 180, 244
DeZube, D., 377
Dickson, E. S., 35, 367
Diehl, M., 225
Diekmann, K. A., 6, 19, 56, 166, 175, 201, 202, 376
Diener, E., 239
Dietz, T., 304
Dillman, T., 180
DiMatteo, M. R., 354, 355
Dimitri, S., 360
Dineen, B. R., 138
Dion, K. K., 164
Dion, K. L., 164, 241
Dolsak, N., 304
Dominguez, A., 260
Donahue, E. M., 162
Donmoyer, R., 52
Donohue, W. A., 101
Doob, A. N., 130
Dorfman, P. W., 256
Douma, B., 177
Dovidio, J. F., 353, 354
Downey, J., 169
Drenth, P. J. D., 256
Dressler, F., 107
Drigotas, S. M., 297
Driver, R., 356
Drolet, A. L., 121, 313, 314, 325
Druckman, D., 28, 36
Dubrovsky, V. J., 319
Duck, S., 144
Dunlap, D. W., 186
Dunn, J. R., 144
Dunning, D., 7
Dunn-Jensen, L., 234
Durso, F. T., 184, 214
Duryea, B., 34
Dworetzky, T., 129, 189
Dworkin, J. B., 368
Dwyer, F. R., 130
Dyer, N., 259
Dykema-Engblade, A., 175

E

Eagly, A. H., 156, 164
Earley, C. P., 45

Earley, P. C., 258, 259, 260
Eatwell, J., 345, 350
Eavey, C. L., 219, 226, 231
Edwards, J., 188, 235, 368
Egido, C., 315
Ehrlinger, J., 7
Eidelson, J. I., 245
Eidelson, R. J., 245
Eisenhardt, K. M., 132
Ekman, P., 355, 356, 357, 358, 359
Elfenbein, H. A., 75, 121, 127
Ellemers, N., 246
Elliott, S., 287
Ellsworth, P. C., 351
Ellyson, S. L., 353, 354
Elsbach, K. D., 140
Emanuel, R., 163
Emshwiller, J. R., 224
Englebart, D., 313
Enzle, M. E., 128
Ephron, D., 244
Epley, N., 66, 200
Epstein, J. A., 353
Erev, I., 307
Ervin, S., 175
Espeland, W., 273
Espinoza, J. A., 260
Espo, D., 114
Etzkowitz, H., 149
Euwema, M., 102
Evans, C. R., 241
Eveland, J. D., 324
Exline, R. V., 354

F

Fader, P., 231
Farber, H. S., 26, 199, 362, 368
Farrell, J., 43
Fast, N. J., 168
Feingold, A., 164
Feldman, R. S., 354
Feller, W., 337
Ferdinand (king), 129, 189
Festinger, L., 241
Fiorina, C., 93, 132–133
Firestone, I. J., 70, 146
Fischer, G. W., 247, 277
Fischhoff, B., 177, 197
Fisher, A., 5
Fisher, R., 2, 15, 20, 74, 81, 102, 108, 109, 110
Fiske, A. P., 148

Fiske, S. T., 168, 238, 248, 319, 352
Fitness, J., 120
Fixx, J. F., 184, 213
Fleck, D., 172
Fleming, J. H., 222, 223
Fletcher, G. J. O., 120
Floyd, J., 165
Flynn, F., 161
Foa, E., 126
Foa, U., 126
Follett, M., 70, 99
Foo, M., 121
Forbus, K. D., 191, 192, 193
Ford, B., 134
Ford, G., 134
Forgas, J. P., 120, 121, 239
Fortune, A., 320
Fost, D., 154
Fouraker, L. E., 48
Fourment, C., 135
Fox, C. R., 217, 338, 342
Fragale, A. R., 155, 156, 354
Frank, M. G., 355, 356
Frantz, C. M., 140
Fraser, S. C., 304
Fredrix, E., 293
Freedman, J. L., 304
French, W. L., 254
Freshman, C., 46
Friedman, H. S., 352, 353, 354, 355
Friedman, L., 285
Friedman, R. A., 27, 237, 253, 265, 317, 320
Friesen, W. V., 355
Froman, L. A., 71, 85
Frommer, D., 154
Fry, W. R., 70, 146
Fu, H-y., 260
Fu, J. Ho-y., 271
Fukuno, M., 259
Fulmer, I. S., 121
Furchgott, R., 14
Fussell, S. R., 222, 234

G

Gabriel, S., 260
Gaertner, L., 245
Galegher, J., 315
Galin, A., 24
Galinsky, A. D., 6, 22, 24, 33, 34, 45, 46, 53, 76, 77, 84, 86, 126, 137, 155, 161, 166, 168, 202

Gamson, W., 217
Garcia, A. J., 266
Gardiner, G. S., 278
Gardner, W. L., 76, 260, 262
Garrett, D., 155
Garza, R. T., 260
Gates, B., 56
Gayer, C. C., 273
Gee, R., 27
Geis, F. L., 359
Gelfand, M. J., 146, 147, 255, 256, 257, 259, 260, 264, 279, 304, 318
Gendler, N., 258
Gentner, D., 2, 5, 9, 191, 192, 193, 200, 201
Gentry, W. A., 315
Gerard, H. B., 248, 274
Gergen, K. J., 60, 130
Gerschlager, C., 355
Getzels, J. W., 207
Geyer, P. D., 61
Giacomantonio, M., 89, 204
Giambusso, D., 51
Gibbons, R., 42, 43, 305
Gibson, K. S., 141, 142, 188, 235, 293, 368
Gick, M. L., 192, 198
Gifford, R. K., 196
Gigone, D., 242
Gilbert, D. T., 239, 248, 319, 352
Gilin, D. A., 44, 76, 77
Gillespie, J. J., 86, 87, 102, 188, 189, 190
Gillespie, T. L., 32
Gilmore, J., 163
Gilovich, T., 24, 25, 81
Gino, F., 175
Girrotto, V., 293
Glader, P., 105
Glentz, B., 167
Glick, S., 98, 142, 143
Glinow, M. A., 282
Goates, N., 320
Goffman, E., 306
Gohring, N., 216
Gold, G., 309
Goldberg, S. B., 30, 102, 107, 108, 109, 110, 112, 113, 114, 241
Goldfarb, L., 215
Goman, C. K., 323
Gonzalez, R., 28, 274
Goodman, P., 372
Goodstein, L., 272
Gorbachev, M., 34, 53, 133, 249

Gore, A., 259
Gottman, J. M., 109
Gouldner, A. W., 136
Govan, C. L., 168
Graetz, K. A., 297
Graham, J. L., 268, 275
Graham, P., 70
Grandey, A., 118
Granovetter, M., 129
Grasz, J., 373
Graziano, W. G., 164
Green, J., 216
Greenberg, J., 59, 60
Greenberg, M., 60, 68
Greenhouse, S., 30
Greziak, J., 94
Griffin, E., 134
Griffin, G., 99
Griggs, L., 278
Grodin, J. R., 362
Grondahl, P., 31, 232
Grosskopf, B., 14, 193
Grover, S. L., 175
Gruenfeld, D. H., 168, 241
Gudykunst, E., 266
Guilford, J. P., 205, 206
Gulliver, M. P., 102
Gun-Gruchy, C., 353
Gunia, B. C., 3
Gunnarsson, S., 53
Gunther, E., 142
Guohong, H., 242
Gupta, V., 256
Guthrie, C., 46

H

Hairfield, J. G., 355
Halberstadt, A. G., 354
Halevy, N., 242
Hall, E. T., 268, 270, 352, 353
Hall, L., 363
Hall, M. R., 268
Hallmark, W., 276, 277
Halperin, E., 273
Halpern, J., 42
Halpert, J. A., 45
Hamermesh, D. S., 164
Hamilton, D. L., 196
Hammock, G., 76
Hammond, K. R., 73

Hand, L., 252
Handlin, L., 219
Hanges, P. J., 256
Hanna, B. A., 128, 168
Hannah, S. T., 144
Hardin, G., 297
Hardin, R., 220
Harinck, F., 29, 169, 204
Harmon, A., 31
Harms, P. D., 242
Harnick, F., 119
Harold, C., 370
Harre, R., 271
Harris, R. J., 65
Harris, V. A., 137
Harrison, G., 4
Harsanyi, J. C., 345, 347, 348, 350
Harvey, J., 146
Harvey, O. J., 133
Haselhuhn, M. P., 139
Hashimoto, R., 259
Hastie, R., 13, 74, 242
Hastorf, A., 275, 367
Hatfield, E., 122
Hatta, T., 319
Hays, R. D., 355
Hayward, T., 6
Heath, L., 188, 235, 368
Heine, S. J., 257
Helft, M., 38, 52, 287
Heltman, K., 354
Hendershot, S., 44
Henderson, M. D., 34, 144, 316, 317
Henley, N. M., 353
Henry, D., 64
Henry, O., 146
Hershey, J. C., 139, 141
Hewstone, M., 67, 244, 248
Hiberd, J., 58
Higgins, E. T., 22, 66, 122, 143, 156, 234, 319
Higgins, M., 26
Hiller, N. T., 219
Hilty, J., 47
Hitler, A., 118
Ho, T. H., 307
Hoch, S. J., 98, 142, 355
Hochschild, A. R., 129
Hoffman, D., 133
Hoffman, M. A., 68
Hofmeister, A., 172

Hofstadter, D. R., 294, 306
Hofstede, G., 256, 266, 267
Hofstede, G. J., 266, 267
Hogg, M. A., 180
Hoh, R., 362
Holcombe, K. M., 259
Hollingshead, A. B., 323
Holloway, J., 227, 231, 232
Holyoak, K. J., 192
Homans, G. C., 56, 58
Hong, K., 367
Hong, Y-y., 264, 271
Honkaniemi, L., 164
Hood, W. R., 133
Hook, L. H., 322
Horn, L., 41
Hornsey, M. J., 237
Horowitz, L. M., 134
House, R. J., 256
Howard-Cooper, S., 150
Hrebec, D., 5, 73
Hsee, C., 360
Hsieh, T., 236, 237
Huber, V. L., 22, 45, 90
Hudson, J., 71
Hughes, C. F., 141
Hui, C. H., 256
Hunt, C., 121
Hussein, S., 138, 315
Hyder, E. B., 78, 82, 83

I

Iacobucci, D., 232, 234
Idson, L., 193
Imai, L., 279
Ingram, P., 133, 258
Insko, C. A., 245, 297, 305
Isabella (queen), 129, 189
Isen, A. M., 120, 121
Issacharoff, S., 65
Iyengar, S. S., 264

J

Jackson, P. W., 207
Jackson, S. E., 317
Janis, I. L., 120
Jankowsko, M., 178
Javidan, M., 256
Jehn, K. A., 133, 366
Jensen, M. C., 232

Jepson, C., 194
Jobs, S., 40–41, 132, 323
Johansen, R., 313
Johar, G. V., 122
Johnson, K., 7
Johnson, L., 134, 227, 252, 308
Johnson, M., 150
Johnson, R., 85
Johnson-Laird, P. N., 181, 210
Jones, E. E., 137, 274
Jones, G., 87
Jones, J., 3
Jones, P., 188
Joyce, M., 65
Juieng, D., 128
Jun, C., 112

K

Kagel, J., 43, 363
Kahn, R. L., 274
Kahneman, D., 19, 21, 24, 66, 181, 193, 194, 195,
    208, 209, 211, 239, 325, 338, 341, 343
Kahwajy, J. L., 132
Kalt, J. P., 367
Kamath, S., 281
Kameda, T., 55
Kane, T., 107
Kaplan, J., 35–36
Kaplan, R., 199
Kaplan, S., 199
Karabenick, S. A., 164
Karambayya, R., 362, 369
Kasich, J., 14
Kass, E., 60
Kastle, K., 252
Katz, H., 362
Kaufman-Gilliland, C. M., 305
Kayani, A. P., 244
Kayser, E., 147
Keating, C. F., 354
Keats, D. M., 256
Kedrosky, P., 1
Keenan, J., 43
Kelley, H. H., 28, 82, 101, 129
Kelly, J. R., 76
Keltner, D. J., 168, 246, 277, 367
Kemelgor, C., 149
Ken-ichi, O., 319
Kern, M. C., 225
Kernan, J. B., 164

Kernan, M., 121
Keros, A. T., 145
Kerr, K., 101
Kerr, N. L., 249, 250, 260, 305
Kerstetter, J., 216
Keysar, B., 222
Kiesler, C. A., 164
Kiesler, S. B., 164, 319, 322, 323, 324, 325, 326
Kilduff, G. J., 75, 127
Kilpatrick, K., 112
Kim, P. H., 24, 47, 121, 155, 156, 201, 202, 232, 366
Kim, S. H., 144, 361
Kim, T. G., 33
Kim, U., 256
Kim, Y., 266
Kim Jong-c.hul, 107
Kim Jong II, 105–106
Kim Jong-un, 106–107
King, R. R., 219
Kipnis, D. M., 136
Kirk, M., 163
Kirkendol, S. E., 360
Kiser, K., 75, 318, 320
Kitayama, S., 258
Kivisilta, P., 164
Klar, Y., 244
Klein, A., 21, 44, 59, 119
Klein, H. J., 326
Knetsch, J. L., 24
Knez, M., 306
Knippenberg, D., 15
Kochan, T. A., 362
Kocieniewski, D., 306
Koestner, R., 356
Kolb, D. M., 27, 237, 238
Kollock, P., 129, 130
Komorita, S. S., 217, 305
Kopelman, S., 116, 301, 304, 307, 323
Kornienko, G., 133
Kotter, J., 60
Koukova, N. T., 160
Kraft, R., 140
Kramer, R. M., 70, 116, 120, 126, 128, 139, 149,
    151, 162, 168, 217, 237, 244, 245, 274, 293,
    303, 320, 325, 368
Krames, L., 354
Krantz, D. H ., 194
Krauss, R. M., 234, 319
Kraut, R. E., 315
Kravitz, L., 47
Kray, L. J., 22, 45, 86, 144, 161, 162, 163, 202

Kreps, D. M., 291
Kressel, K., 362
Kreuz, R. J., 222
Krishnamurthy, S., 287
Krishnan, R., 242
Kriz, M., 304
Kroll, L., 151
Kruger, J., 7, 33
Kruglanski, A. W., 66, 102, 122, 156, 244
Krukowski, A., 58
Ku, G., 76
Kuhlman, D. M., 96
Kumar, R., 120
Kunda, Z., 194
Kunreuther, H., 98, 142, 355
Kurtzberg, T., 70, 121, 137, 145, 234, 318, 319,
    327, 328
Kwak, R. S., 279
Kwon, S., 49, 99

L

Ladha, K., 217
LaFrance, M., 134
LaHood, R., 14
Lambert, A., 168
Lamm, H., 147
Lancaster, H., 47
Landman, S., 273
Landy, D., 164
Lane, J. D., 360
Langer, E., 49, 177
Langfitt, F., 153
Langner, C., 97
Larrick, R. P., 138
Larson, M., 105, 107
Lashinsky, A., 216
Lassek, P. J., 303
Lassiter, G. D., 356, 358
Latané, B., 241
Law, K., 191
Lawee, D., 134
Lawler, E. J., 78, 217
Lax, D. A., 2, 20, 39, 71, 81, 85, 86, 88, 89,
    186, 188
L'Ecuyer, D., 327
Leder, S., 89
Lee, C., 235
Lee, F., 270
Lee, S., 234, 264
Lee, S-I., 271

Lee, W., 338
Lehman, D. R., 257
Leib, J., 99
Leliveld, M. C., 292
Lemonick, M., 259
Lempereur, A., 269, 270
Lengel, R. H., 313
Leonardelli, G. J., 45, 82
Lepper, M. R., 196, 367
Lerner, H. G., 109
Lerner, J., 272, 273
Lerner, M., 197
Lerner, R. M., 164
Le Tareau, A., 104, 365
Leung, K ., 264
Levenson, R. W., 109, 354
Leventhal, H., 54, 60
Levine, J. M., 66, 67, 121, 234, 319
Levine, M., 221
Levine, R., 118
LeVine, R. A., 275
Levinson, S., 222
Lewich, R., 145
Lewicki, R. J., 50–51, 74, 93, 128, 130, 138, 162,
    169, 170, 171, 172, 174, 217, 244, 256
Lewis, D. J., 131
Lewis, M., 353
Lewis, S. A., 98
Lewthwaite, G., 34
Liberman, V., 36, 304
Lichtenstein, S., 177
Liebrand, W. B. G., 65, 101, 231, 305
Light, J., 324
Lightdale, J. R., 242
Lillich, M., 327
Lim, S. G., 32, 102
Lind, E. A., 141, 144, 362
Linder, D., 164, 165
Lindsley, S. L., 283
Lindzey, G., 28, 248, 319, 352
Linville, P. W., 247, 277
Lippman, T. W., 136
Lisco, C., 320
Litcher, C. D., 45
Liu, L. A., 253, 279
Liu, W., 265
Lobel, M., 57
Lobel, S. A., 258
Locke, C. C., 163
Locke, K. D., 134
Lockyer, S., 93

Loewenstein, G. F., 49, 62, 63, 64, 65, 81, 100, 176, 222, 226, 239, 296, 376
Loewenstein, J., 2, 5, 9, 180, 192, 193, 200, 201, 323
Lombardi, W. J., 143
Long, B., 354
Longo, L. C., 164
Loomis, C., 184
Lott, T., 135
Lovallo, D., 19
Luchins, A. S., 181, 211
Lui, L., 303
Lytle, A. L., 101, 103, 108, 109, 114, 253, 263, 268, 269, 270

M

MacDonald, C., 112
Machatka, D. E., 76
MacMillan, D., 1, 134
Maddux, W. W., 76, 77, 137, 262
Madey, S. F., 25
Magliozzi, T., 22
Maher, K., 105
Maiman, R. J., 361
Maisonneuve, J., 135
Major, V., 146, 147
Makhijani, M. G., 164
Makowski, D. G., 55
Malhotra, D., 137, 165
Mallozzi, J. S., 118, 120
Mandel, D. R., 146
Manley, E., 119
Mann, L., 120, 256
Mannix, E. A., 45, 83, 130, 145, 217, 219, 225, 226, 227, 231, 241, 272
Manstead, A. S. R., 118, 119, 354
Manuel, C., 362
Mara, J., 51
March, R. M., 268
Marcus, E. C., 180
Marinucci, C., 93
Maritz, B., 151
Maritz, J., 145
Maritz, L., 145
Maritz, P, 151
Markman, K. D., 202
Markovsky, B., 217
Marks, M., 370
Marlowe, D., 130
Marmo, M., 362

Marshello, A., 96
Martin, J. N., 278
Martin, T. W., 188
Martinez, I., 237
Marwell, G., 59
Matas, C., 134
Mathew, A., 248
Mathewes-Green, F., 276
Matsibekker, C. L. Z., 234
Matsui, F., 118, 120
Matsumoto, D., 282
Matsuzaka, D., 109
Maurizio, A. M., 2
May, K., 220
Mayer, R. E., 208
Mazur, A., 160
McAlister, D., 131
McAlister, L., 231
McBride, D., 215, 232
McCarthy, C., 68
McCartney, P., 4
McClelland, G., 62
McClintock, C. G., 82, 94, 101, 231
McClurg, S., 227
McCourt, F., 104
McCusker, A., 134
McEwen, C. A., 361
McFadden, R. D., 172
McGinn, K. L., 143, 145, 156, 162, 221, 318, 320, 322
McGrath, J. E., 76, 323, 361
McGraw, A. P., 272
McGuire, T., 323, 325
McInnes, D., 82
McKelvey, R. D., 229
McKersie, R. B., 8, 73
McLaughlin-Volpe, T., 249
McLeod, P. L., 258
McSherry, A., 222
Mealey-Lohmann, L., 361
Meckling, W. H., 232
Medina, F. J., 237
Medvec, V. H., 24, 25, 29, 45, 46, 47, 70, 81, 82, 84, 126, 145, 273
Meherabian, A., 315
Mellers, B. A., 62, 65, 66
Melnyk, D., 246
Menon, T., 264
Messick, D. M., 28, 62, 64, 65, 66, 121, 162, 175, 193, 234, 247, 274, 293, 296, 298, 301, 303, 305, 319, 320, 368

Meyer, G. D., 73
Meyers, J., 239
Meyerson, D., 149
Mikula, G., 54
Miles, E. W., 160, 162
Milgate, M., 345, 350
Milgrom, P., 291
Millar, M. G., 164
Miller, D. T., 157, 242
Miller, G. A., 200
Miller, G. J., 217, 219, 226, 227, 231, 232
Miller, L., 135
Miller, N., 247, 249, 250
Mills, J., 144, 145, 148
Minkov, M., 266, 267
Minson, J. A., 77
Mishra, B., 281
Mislin, A., 231, 232
Miyamoto, Y., 258
Mnookin, R. H., 221
Moag, J., 314
Mohammed, S., 219
Montgomery, A. H., 289
Moon, H., 79, 112, 363
Moore, D. A., 11, 32, 33, 81, 121,
    159, 160, 176, 193, 258, 274, 327, 328
Moore, H., 4
Moore, J. S., 164
Moore, M. C., 107, 130
Moran, S., 193, 201, 202
Moreland, R. L., 67, 135, 242
Morgan, P., 240
Morgenstern, O., 333, 336, 346
Moritz, O., 119
Morling, B., 258
Morris, M. W., 97, 99, 118, 121, 133, 137, 138, 258,
    259, 264, 271, 293, 313, 314, 318, 319, 323, 325,
    327, 328, 367, 368
Morris, T., 237
Morrissett, M. G., 365
Mouawad, J., 49
Mubarak, H., 318
Mueller, J. S., 141
Mullen, E., 137
Mullen, M., 244
Munduate, L., 237
Munro, G. D., 6
Munroe, D., 256
Murakami, F., 260
Murnighan, J . K., 32, 42, 51, 67, 86, 102, 141,
    142, 217, 293, 296, 359, 360

Murray, A., 133
Murrow, E. R., 276
Mussweiler, T., 45, 46, 47, 76, 126, 155
Mutzabaugh, B., 186
Myers, F., 223, 333
Myers, J. P., 151

N

Nadler, J. S., 9, 121, 137, 201, 203, 318, 319, 320,
    321, 327, 328
Nalebuff, B., 193
Naquin, C. E., 139, 157, 240, 319, 322, 328
Narenda, D., 38
Narlikar, A., 244
Nash, J., 286, 346, 348–350
Nauta, A., 366
Neal, R., 316
Neale, M. A., 5, 8, 14, 15, 16, 22, 23, 26, 45,
    55, 74, 76, 77, 79, 82, 86, 90, 93, 145,
    146, 148, 151, 159, 168, 200, 225, 232,
    241, 365, 368
Nelson, L. D., 246
Nelson, N., 365
Netanyahu, B., 34, 162
Neuberg, S. L., 238
Newman, D. A., 219
Newman, M. L., 357
Newman, P., 345, 350
Newton, E., 120, 237
Ng, K. Y., 112, 363
Nicholson, N. K., 129
Niedenthal, P. M., 120, 121
Nisbett, R. E., 194
Nishii, L. A., 146, 147
Nishii, L. H., 256, 259, 260
Nobel, O. B., 144
Northcraft, G., 22, 45, 86
Notarius, C. I., 354
Notz, W. W., 362
Nowicki, G. P., 120
Nye, J. L., 242

O

Oaksford, M., 210
Obama, B., 163, 252, 315
O'Brien, A. T., 237
O'Brien, K., 146, 147
O'Connell, V., 282
O'Connor, K. M., 2, 29, 51, 74, 121, 144, 170, 237,
    238, 240

Oetzel, J., 266
Oh, S., 130
Ohbuchi, K.-I., 259
O'Heeron, R. C., 141
Ohtsubo, Y., 55
Oka, T., 260
Okamoto, K., 260
Okhuysen, G., 33, 34, 45
Okumura, T., 45, 258, 265, 269, 270, 271, 272, 274, 280
Olekalns, M., 36, 98, 101, 131, 224, 225, 320
Oliver, R. L., 120
Olson, B. J., 242
Olson, J., 272
Olson-Buchanan, J., 61
Orbell, J. M., 305
Ordeshook, P. C., 221, 229
Ordonez, L., 177
Orr, R. F., 153
Osborn, A. F., 205, 206
Osgood, C. E., 48, 143, 249, 293
Oskamp, S., 15, 276
Ostrom, E., 301, 304
O'Sullivan, M. O, 315, 355, 356
Ouwehand, E., 239
Overbeck, J. R., 161, 168
Oza, S. S., 160

P

Pachtman, A., 266
Paddock, L., 22, 86
Padilla, A., 282
Paese, P. W., 26, 44
Page, M. S., 360
Pagliario, S., 120
Palmade, G., 135
Palmer, L. G., 218, 221, 225
Papandreou, G., 16
Parayitam, S., 242
Parkinson, B., 122
Parks, C. D., 217, 305, 307
Parr, S., 149
Parrott, W. G., 271
Pataki, G., 31
Patton, B., 20, 102, 108, 109, 110
Patton, C., 133
Paulson, G., 322
Peck, D., 11
Peck, S., 16
Pelham, B. W., 274
Pelosi, N., 161

Peng, K., 264
Pennebaker, J. W., 128, 141, 357
Peppers, J., 58
Perkins, A., 137
Perlman, D., 144
Perlmutter, I., 155
Peterman, E., 58
Peterson, B. S., 115
Peterson, E., 239, 240, 244
Peterson, R., 272, 273
Philip, G., 316
Pierce, L., 175
Pierce, R. S., 362
Pietroni, D., 120
Pillutla, M. M., 257, 296, 304, 306
Pinel, E. C., 239
Pinkley, R. L., 55, 156
Pinto, P. R., 368
Pliner, P., 354
Plott, C., 219, 221
Podolny, J. M., 258, 259
Poincaré, H., 203
Poitras, J., 104, 365, 366, 369
Pólya, G., 204
Pommerenke, P., 120, 237
Poortinga, Y. H., 283
Popkin, S. L., 129
Popper, N., 51
Porter, C., 376
Posey, D. C., 307
Posner, J, 115
Postman, D., 171
Postmes, T., 247
Povedano, A., 237
Pradel, D. W., 162
Prentice, D. A., 242
Presson, C. C., 194
Preston, M., 167
Prietula, M. J., 78, 82, 83
Primus, W., 161
Prince, L. M., 354, 355
Pruitt, D. G., 78, 98, 144, 185, 237, 238, 306, 361, 362
Putnam, L. L., 101

Q

Qaddhafi, M., 365
Qian, Y., 7
Quach, H., 85
Queally, J., 51
Quinn, D. M., 364, 365

R

Raia, C. P., 118, 120
Raiffa, H., 27, 28, 30, 32, 34, 35, 39, 42,
    45, 87, 115, 226, 227, 228, 230, 231,
    238, 318, 368
Ramesh, J., 125
Ramirez-Marin, J. Y., 239
Ramon, A., 247
Rangel, C., 306
Rao, A. G., 287
Rapoport, A., 291
Rapson, R. L., 122
Rattermann, M. J., 161
Raven, B. H., 118
Raver, J. L., 146, 147, 260
Rayburn, S., 227
Reagan, R., 31, 34, 53, 133, 223, 249
Realo, A., 257
Reed, E. S., 246
Reid, H., 163
Rein, S., 257
Reingen, P. H., 164, 166
Riceanu, T., 44
Richards, J. M., 357
Richardson, D., 76
Ricketts, L., 150
Ricketts, P., 150
Riggio, R. E., 354
Rime, B., 354
Ritov, I., 202
Rizzuto, T., 219
Roberts, D. C., 274
Roberts, J., 291
Robertson, G., 187
Robinson, R. J., 93, 162, 246, 256, 277, 367
Rockefeller, D., 21
Rodriquez, Alex, 49
Roefs, M., 246
Rogers, H., 136
Rohr, T. J., 153
Rohrbaugh, J., 62
Ropp, S. A., 249
Rose, J. B., 362
Rosencranz-Engelmann, J., 15, 146, 148
Rosenthal, R., 353, 355, 358
Rosenwald, M., 4
Rosette, A. S., 116, 263
Rosner, B., 375
Ross, B. H., 161, 280

Ross, D., 83
Ross, J., 309, 310
Ross, L. D., 15, 36, 56, 146, 148, 159, 196,
    246, 278, 304, 320, 363, 367
Ross, M., 65
Ross, S., 48
Ross, W. H., 362
Rostenkowski, D., 227
Roth, A. E., 32, 43
Rothacker, R., 373
Rothbart, M., 276, 277
Rothko, M., 21
Rothman, W., 318
Ruback, R. B., 128
Rubin, J. Z., 144, 232, 361
Rubin, Robert, 184
Ruderman, M. N., 317
Rupert, J., 366
Russ, L. E., 87
Russell, C. S., 129
Russell, J. A., 115
Rutte, C. G., 65, 247, 303
Rynecki, D., 201

S

Saarni, C., 353
Sagan, S. D., 289
Sager, I., 216
Sally, D. F., 305
Salovey, P., 247, 277
Samuels, S. M., 56, 304
Samuelson, C. D., 303
Samuelson, W. F., 193
Sanchez, F., 51
Sander, F. E. A., 232, 363
Sanders, D. Y., 128
Sandomir, R., 23
Sanna, L. J., 307
Sano, Y., 268
Sarkozy, N., 92
Sattler, L., 201
Saunders, D. G., 197
Saunders, D. M., 169, 171, 172, 174
Savage, L. J., 25
Savitsky, K., 81
Sawyer, J. P., 199
Schaper, D., 15
Schatzki, M., 82
Scheer, M., 182, 211
Schellenbarger, S., 27

Schelling, T., 274, 286, 348
Schenitzki, D. P., 82
Scherer, K., 357
Schkade, D., 239
Schlenker, B. R., 273
Schlesinger, L., 60
Schmitt, D., 59
Schneider, A. K., 98, 163
Schofield, J. W., 248
Schopler, J., 297
Schoumaker, F., 32
Schraneveldt, R. W., 184, 214
Schroth, H. A., 19, 123, 376
Schulte, B., 76
Schurr, P. H., 130
Schwandt, B., 356, 358
Schwartz, S., 256
Schweitzer, M. E., 139, 141, 144, 164, 177, 355, 356, 357, 360
Schwinger, T., 54
Scott, G., 31
Scott, J., 31
Sears, D. O., 247
Sebenius, J. K., 2, 20, 39, 71, 81, 85, 86, 88, 89, 186, 188
Segal, M. W., 135
Segall, M. J., 283
Seiden, V., 24, 47
Seilheimmer, S., 306
Seligman, C., 272
Selten, R., 296
Sentis, K. P., 64, 296
Sepulveda, J., 316
Sethna, B. N., 319
Shafir, E., 25
Shah, P. P., 19, 376
Shalvi, S., 89, 204
Shane, S., 312
Shapiro, D. L., 101, 103, 108, 109, 114, 128, 139, 140, 253, 265, 268, 282
Shapiro, M., 31
Shapiro, R., 178
Shapley, L. S., 338
Shaver, K. G., 137
Shaver, P., 198
Shaw, M. E., 322
Shaw, R., 316
Shear, M., 71
Sheehan, N., 309
Shell, G. R., 2, 95, 325
Shepard, J. D., 184, 214

Sheppard, B. H., 128, 145, 217, 244, 369
Sherif, C. W., 133
Sherif, M., 133, 244
Sherman, D. K., 246
Sherman, S. J., 194
Sherman, W., 106
Shestowsky, D., 318, 365
Shikhirev, P., 269, 270
Shirakashi, S., 260
Shirako, A., 28, 262
Shortt, J. W., 360
Shultz, G. P., 133
Shweder, R. A., 196
Siamwalla, A., 129
Sicoly, F., 65
Siegal, A. M., 309
Siegel, J., 323, 325
Siegel, S., 48
Sigall, H., 164
Signo, M., 76
Silveira, J. M., 204
Silverman, S., 366
Sim, D. L. H., 293
Simeonova, D. I., 262
Simms, E. N., 33
Simon, H., 7
Simone, R., 186
Simons, C., 246, 270
Simons, G., 122
Simpson, J. A., 242
Sinaceur, M., 118, 138
Singh, H., 258, 259
Sinha, N., 281
Sivanathan, N., 168
Sixel, L. M., 100
Size, P. B., 197
Skinner, B. F., 122
Sligte, D., 89, 204
Slovic, P., 177, 338
Smith, H., 68
Smith, P. L., 36, 98, 101, 131
Smith, S., 76
Smith, S. L., 297
Smith, V., 193, 219
Smith, W., 119
Snodgrass, S. E., 353
Snyder, M., 168
Sobel, J., 23
Solnick, S. J., 164
Somers, T., 137
Sommer, L., 339

Sondak, H., 55, 130
Song, F., 237
Sonich, S., 304
Sparks, G. G., 134
Spears, R., 247
Spector, B., 150
Sporer, S., 356, 358
Spranca, M., 272
Sproull, L., 319, 322, 323, 324, 326
Srivastava, J., 160, 264
Stahelski, A. J., 101
Stahl, G. K. K., 279
Stanbury, J. A., 6
Stanley, E. A., 199
Stark, N., 50–51
Starke, F. A., 362
Stasser, G., 242
Staudohar, P. D., 35
Staw, B. M., 309, 310, 369
Stawiski, S., 175
Steblay, N. M., 167
Steil, J. M., 55
Steinel, W., 119, 239
Stephens, B., 105
Stern, J. L., 362
Stern, P. C., 304
Stern, R., 42
Stern, T., 125
Sternberg, R. J., 184, 213
Stewart, R. B., 304
Stillinger, C., 15
Stires, L. K., 137
Stone, B., 1
Stone, J. I., 356, 358
Stoppard, J. M., 353
Stratton, R. P., 208
Strayer, D., 6
Streater, S., 179
Stringer, H., 323
Strodtbeck, F. L., 322
Stroebe, I. W., 67
Stroebe, K., 102
Stroebe, W., 225, 244
Studt, A., 22
Stuhlmacher, A. F., 32, 45, 102, 365
Su, S. K., 138, 368
Suci, G. J., 143
Suedfeld, P., 134
Sullins, E. S., 355
Sullivan, B. A., 29, 51, 121
Sullivan, B. N., 259

Sundvi, L., 164
Svensson, I., 368
Swaab, D. F., 315
Swaab, R. I., 247, 315
Swaim, G. W., 355
Swann, W. B., 274
Swapp, W., 221
Sweeney, J., 325

T

Taibbi, M., 49
Tajfel, H., 245, 275, 277, 305
Takata, T., 257
Tam, A., 258
Tan, H., 121
Tannenbaum, P. H., 143
Taranta, A., 354
Tatlow, D. K., 282
Taylor, D. W., 197
Taylor, M. S., 281
Taylor, S. E., 57, 177, 309
Tedeschi, B., 318
Tenbrunsel, A. E., 19, 28, 29, 166, 175, 201, 202, 258, 273, 274, 376
Ten Velden, F. S., 77, 79
Tetlock, P. E., 237, 238, 272, 273
Thaler, R. H., 24
Thatcher, M., 137
Thibaut, J., 28, 60, 129
Thomas, E., 53
Thompson, K ., 373
Thompson, L., 2, 3, 9, 13, 28, 29, 42, 45, 46, 49, 53, 62, 63, 64, 66, 70, 73, 74, 77, 79, 83, 100, 116, 121, 126, 137, 143, 144, 146, 151, 161, 180, 185, 188, 192, 193, 200, 201, 203, 217, 218, 219, 221, 225, 226, 234, 235, 238, 239, 240, 241, 244, 245, 262, 273, 274, 296, 302, 305, 318, 319, 320, 321, 322, 323, 327, 366, 368
Thornton, B., 197
Thurman, R., 3
Tiedens, L. Z., 118, 354
Tietenberg, T., 304
Tillerson, R., 108
Tindale, R. S., 240
Tindale, S. R., 175
Ting-Toomey, S., 266, 268
Tinsley, C. H., 51, 130, 163, 257, 265, 269, 270, 271, 279, 281
Tipton, C. A., 304
Tomlinson, E. C., 138

Torbenson, E., 114
Tormala, Z. L., 77
Tornow, W. W., 368
Tost, L. P., 29, 273
Toyama, M., 260
Trevino, L. K., 313
Triandis, H. C., 256, 258, 278
Trope, Y., 34
Trump, D., 142
Tsai, J. L., 262
Tuchinsky, M., 240
Turiel, E., 246
Turner, J., 275
Turner, M. E., 217
Turque, B., 311
Tversky, A., 21, 25, 66, 181, 193, 194, 195, 208, 209, 211, 325, 334, 338, 341, 342, 343
Tyler, T. R., 128, 139, 141, 149, 305
Tynan, R. O., 53, 240

U

Uptigrove, T., 33, 34
Ury, W. L., 2, 15, 20, 30, 74, 102, 107, 108, 109, 110, 112, 113, 114, 241
Uzzi, B., 144, 149, 150

V

Valenzuela, A., 264
Valley, K. L., 11, 16, 42, 70, 116, 126, 145, 151, 232, 234, 305, 314
Vallone, R. P., 367
Van Avermaet, E., 64, 65, 94
Van Beest, I, 119, 226, 247, 292
Van Boven, L., 2, 5, 9, 185, 201, 203
van de Kragt, A. J. C., 305
Van Den Bossche, S., 366
van Dijk, E., 119, 226, 292, 303
Van Kleef, G. A., 118, 119, 120, 226
van Lange, P. A. M., 101, 292
Van Rijswijk, W., 246
Van Vianen, A. E. M., 29
Van Vugt, M., 303
Victor, J. N., 219, 231
Visser, K., 292
Volkema, R., 172
von Neumann, J., 333, 336, 346
von Schuschnigg, K., 118
Vorauer, J. D., 81

W

Wade, G., 248
Wade-Benzoni, K. A., 28, 29, 175, 258, 273, 274
Wakeham, J., 137
Waldstein, D., 235
Walker, L., 60
Walker, R., 2
Walker, S., 14–15
Walster, E., 54, 56, 59
Walster, G. W., 56, 59
Walter, L., 6
Walton, R. E., 8, 73
Wang, C. S., 76
Wang, J., 3
Ward, A., 246, 367
Wason, P. C., 181, 210
Watanabe, J. T., 262
Webb, T., 7
Weber, E. U., 304
Weber, J. M., 301, 307
Weber, M., 222
Wegner, D. M ., 122, 360
Wei, J., 139
Weick, K. E., 149
Weigert, A., 131
Weingart, L. R., 49, 78, 82, 83, 98, 99, 101, 224, 225, 270
Weisberg, R. W., 183, 212
Weitz, L. J., 352
Weldon, E., 271
Wellens, A. R., 314
Wenzlaff, R. M., 122
Wernau, J., 29
Wheatley, T. P., 239
Wheeler, L., 198
White, B. J., 133
White, J. B., 53, 76, 77, 121
White, R., 113
White, S. B., 232, 234, 376
Whitehead, A. N., 191
Whitford, A. B., 231, 232
Whorf, B. L., 274
Wickelgren, W. A., 183, 212
Wiethoff, C., 326
Wildschut, T., 245, 305
Wilke, H. A. M., 65, 303, 305
Wilkenfeld, J., 361, 364, 365
Willaby, H. W., 79
Willerman, B., 165

Williams, D., 52
Williams, D. L., 70, 146
Williams, J. A., 248
Williams, K., 241
Willis, R., 60
Wills, T. A., 57, 245
Wilson, E. J., 318
Wilson, J., 51
Wilson, R., 291
Wilson, R. B., 43
Wilson, T. D., 239
Wiltermuth, S., 77
Windschitl, P. D., 33
Winklevoss, C., 38
Winklevoss, T., 38
Winstein, K. J., 216
Winter, D., 97
Wiser, M., 163
Wit, A., 303
Wolf, N., 276
Wolfe, R. J., 156
Wood, A. M., 139
Wood, W., 156, 242
Woodroofe, M., 337
Woodside, A. G., 134
Wooten, C., 58
Worchel, S., 242, 244, 275
Wortinger, B., 144
Wright, B., 23
Wright, S. C., 249
Wyatt, E., 186
Wyer, M. M., 353
Wysocki, B., Jr., 105

X

Xu, H., 127

Y

Yakura, E., 87
Yamaguchi, S., 260
Yap, A. J., 161
Yarro, R., 215
Yates, J. F., 332, 337
Ybarra, O., 247
Ye, J., 282
Yoon, G., 256
Young, E. S., 316
Young, M. J., 178, 260, 264
Yuille, J. C., 360
Yukl, G. A., 48
Yurtserver, G., 172

Z

Zajac, E., 232
Zajonc, R., 134
Zamiska, N., 282
Zander, A., 54
Zanna, M. P., 238, 272
Zechmeister, K., 28
Zemba, Y., 264
Zemke, P. E., 303
Zielenziger, M., 105, 106
Zuckerberg, M., 38, 40–41
Zuckerman, M., 355, 356, 358
Zwick, R., 307

SUBJECT INDEX

A

Abilene paradox, 146–147
Acceptance, 90
Accountability
    in constituent relationships,
        237–238
    in team negotiations, 244
Accountability pressure, 257
Acculturation, 283
Active misrepresentation, 170
Adaptors, 351
Adjudication, 105
Adjustment, 195
Adversarial adjudication, 264
Advisory arbitration, 111
Affiliation bias, 275–276
Agenda, power of, 157
Agents. *See also* Principal-agent
        negotiations
    advantages of, 232
    disadvantages of, 233–235
    role of, 231–232
    selection of, 235
    strategies for working with, 235–236
Agreement bias, 226
Agreements. *See also* BATNA (Best
        Alternative To a Negotiated
        Agreement); Contracts;
        Integrative agreements
    consensus, 221
    friendship and, 146–147
    reneging on, 171
    requirement for, 30–31
Air traffic controllers strike, 30–31
Alignment, issue, 186
Allais Paradox Decision Tree, 341
Allied, 224
Alternatives, power of, 157
Amazon, 236–237
American Airlines, 88
Analogical training, 200–201
Anchoring
    aggressive, 84
    function of, 195
    with multiple-offer strategy, 83–84
Anchor point, 44

Anger
    communication of, 119
    cultural orientation and, 262
    electronic communication and, 319–320
AOL, 33
Apologies, 140
Apple Computer, 3, 157, 292
Approach-approach conflict, 330
Arbitration. *See also* Third-party
        intervention
    advisory, 111
    conventional, 112
    explanation of, 362
    final-offer, 112, 362–363
    traditional, 362
Arbitration hearing, 363
Arbitration-mediation (arb-med),
        363. *See also* Third-party intervention
Arb-med, 112
Aspiration point. *See* Target point
Aspirations, 44–46
Assertiveness, 162–163
Assessment
    of BATNA, 43
    of confidence, 26
    negotiation preparation and self-, 13–26, 37
    resource assessment, 88–89
    of risk, 20–23
    situation, 28–37
Assimilation, 282
Attitudinal structuring, 158
Attractiveness, physical, 163–164
Attribution error, 280
Attributions, 138–139
Autotelic experience, 209–210
Availability heuristic, 193–194

B

Backward induction, 290
Bad apples, 139
Bargaining. *See also* Negotiations
    competitive, 171
    distributive, 224
    integrative, 224
    sequential, 226
    symmetric, 348

Bargaining surplus
  achievement of, 42
  explanation of, 41
  first offers and, 46
Bargaining theory. *See* Nash bargaining theory
Bargaining zone
  agents and, 233, 234
  bargaining surplus and, 41
  explanation of, 39
  first offers in, 46
  negative, 40–41
  negotiator's surplus and, 41–42
  positive, 39, 40, 366
Bartender problem, 184, 214
Base rates, 194–195
BATNA (Best Alternative To a
    Negotiated Agreement)
  assessment of, 43, 155, 372
  commitment to, 16, 310
  function of, 15, 68, 170, 370
  of other party, 27–28, 37
  as power source, 154–155, 266
  premature concession and, 20
  researching other party's, 44
  reservation point and, 16–18, 43
  revealing information about, 43–44, 79, 154, 158,
      177–178, 232, 235–236, 375
  risk and, 21–23
  sacred issues and, 273
  sunk costs and, 19
  time sensitive nature of, 15–16, 32–34
BATNA risk, 22–23
Beatles, 3–4
Behavior monitoring, 302–303
Beirut Massacre (1982), 367
Betting decision, 181, 211
Betweenness axiom, 336
Bias
  affiliation, 275–276
  agreement, 226
  common information, 242
  confirmation, 6–7, 207
  conflict, 367
  dispositionalism and, 264
  egocentric, 64, 239, 359
  equal shares, 225–226
  exit, 319
  flaming, 319–320
  getting to yes, 235
  hindsight, 197
  hostile media, 367
  in-group, 245–246
  out-group homogeneity, 247
  overconfidence, 367–368
  psychological, 175–178
  sinister attribution, 320, 322
Biased punctuation of conflict, 274–275
Bilateral concessions, 48
Black-hat/white-hat (BH/WH) negotiators, 48–49
Blaming-the-victim attributions, 197
Blind justice. *See* Equality rule
Body movements, 351, 359
Boomerang effect. *See* Reactance technique
Boulwarism, 7, 46
Boundary spanners, 163
Bounded ethicality, 176
BP Deepwater Horizon oil disaster, 6–7
Brainstorming
  explanation of, 205–206
  guidelines for, 206
  solitary, 225
Brainwriting, 225
Breach, 138
Bridging, 187
Business
  dynamic nature of, 3
  as social dilemma, 287
Businesspeople, 148–150

C

Canadian National Railway, 90
Capabilities, 86
Card decision, 181, 210
CarWoo, 47
Caucuses, private, 221–222
Causal chunking, 274–275
Causal relationship, 195–196
Causation, unwarranted, 195–196
Central route persuasion tactics
  attitudinal structuring and, 158
  commitment and consistency and, 159
  explanation of, 156
  fairness heuristics and, 159
  framing and, 159
  power of agenda and, 157
  power of alternatives and, 157
  power of contrast and, 158
  power of options and, 157
  time pressure and, 159–160
Certainty effect, 341–342
Chain problem, 182, 212

Change, reluctance for, 8
Charisma, 354–355
Chilling effect, 45
Chocking, 210
Circular logrolling, 218
Circular trade-offs, 218–219
Clarity, importance of, 114, 141
Closure property, 334
Coalitions
  distribution of resources within,
    226–231
  explanation of, 217
  size of, 226
  strategies for effective, 231
  trust and temptation in, 226
Coca, 292–293
Coercion, 276–277
Cognitive conflict. *See* Task conflict
Cognitive consistency, 207
Cohesion, team, 241–242
Collective fences, 298
Collective traps, 298
Collectivism, 256–257. *See also*
    Individualism-collectivism
Commitment
  escalation of, 308–310
  methods to secure, 131–132, 159
  norm of, 304
Common-bond groups, 242
Common-identity groups, 242
Common information bias, 242
Communal norms, 145
Communication
  in constituent relationships, 239
  cooperation and, 305
  deception and, 355–359
  direct vs. indirect, 268–271
  explicit vs. tacit, 36
  face-to-face, 313–316, 318, 326–327
  motivated, 360
  in multiparty negotiations, 221–223
  nonverbal, 315, 351–360
  in principal-agent negotiations, 234
  task-related, 305
  in team negotiations, 241
  trust and, 138
Comparative advertising, 298, 300
Comparison. *See* Social comparison
Comparison with similar others, 57
Competitive advertising, 298–299
Competitive bargaining, ethics and, 171

Competitive negotiators
  effects of, 98–99, 101
  explanation of, 95
  tools for, 97–98
Compound gamble, 335
Compromise, 70, 75
Concave functions, 339–342
Concessions
  bilateral, 48
  ethical issues related to, 171
  explanation of, 47–48
  magnitude of, 48–49
  overcoming aversion to, 85
  premature, 20, 47, 74
  timing of, 49
  unilateral, 48
Conciliation, 276–277
Concreteness, 126
Condorcet paradox, 220
Confidence, 26, 121
Confirmation bias, 6–7, 207
Conflict
  approach-approach, 330
  biased punctuation of, 274–275
  consensus, 28–29
  false or illusory, 73
  interests-based response to, 102
  internal value, 151
  personal, 132–133
  power-based response to, 103
  rights-based response to, 102–103
  scarce resource competition as, 29
  symbolic, 247
  task, 132–133
Conflict bias, 367
Conflict of interest
  in constituent relationships, 238–239
  symbolic conflict vs., 247
Consensus, 67
Consensus agreements, 221
Consensus conflict, 28–29
Consistency, 67, 207
Consistency principle, 159
Consortium, 227
Constituent relationships
  challenges of, 237–239
  explanation of, 236–237
  strategies to improve, 239
Consultation, built-in, 112
Contact, intergroup relations and,
    248–249

Contests, 107
Continental Airlines, 49
Contingency contracts
  advantages of, 189–190
  assessing viability and usefulness of, 190–191
  explanation of, 86–87
  function of, 188–189
Continuity axiom, 336
Contracts
  contingency, 86–87, 188–191
  official vs. unofficial, 34
  psychological, 304
  ratification requirements for, 32
Contractual risk, 23
Contrast, power of, 158
Control, 177, 234
Conventional arbitration, 112
Convergent thinking, 206, 207
Cooling-off periods, 110
Cooperation
  benefits of, 306–307
  cultural orientation and, 258–259
  psychological strategies for, 301, 302, 304–306
  in social dilemmas when parties should not
    collude, 307
  structural strategies for, 301–304
  as unilateral choice, 288–289
Cooperative negotiators
  effects of, 101
  explanation of, 95
  tools for, 97
Cooperative orientation, 75, 98
Cost-benefit analysis, 184
Cost cutting, 187–188
Costs
  sunk, 19, 311
  time-related, 33
Counterfactual reflection, 202
Counterfactual thinking, 24–25
Counteroffers
  considerations for, 48–49
  function of, 47
Creative negotiation agreements
  bridging in, 187
  cost cutting in, 187–188
  expanding the pie in, 186–187
  fractionating problems into solvable parts in,
    185–186
  issue alignment and realignment in, 186
  nonspecific compensation in, 188
  structuring contingencies in, 188–191

Creative negotiation strategies
  analogical training as, 200–201
  brainstorming as, 205–206
  convergent vs. divergent thinking as, 206–207
  counter-factual reflection as, 202
  deductive reasoning as, 207
  feedback as, 201–202
  flow as, 209–210
  fluency, flexibility, and originality as, 205
  incubation as, 202–204
  inductive reasoning as, 207–209
  rational problem-solving model as, 204
Creativity
  explanation of, 180
  threats to, 191–200
Creativity tests, 180–184, 210–214
Credibility, 114
Creeping determinism, 197
Crisis procedures, 112
Cross-cultural negotiations. *See also* Culture/cultural
    differences
  affiliation bias and, 275–276
  biased punctuation of conflict and, 274–275
  conduct of, 266–268
  cooperation and, 258–259
  disproportionalism vs situationalism and, 262–264
  dispute resolution and, 264–265, 270–271
  dividing the pie and, 271–272
  emotion and inner experience and, 260, 262
  ethnocentrism and, 275
  expanding the pie and, 271
  face concerns and, 266
  faulty perceptions of conciliation and coercion
    and, 276–277
  function of, 252–253, 283–284
  information communication and, 269–270
  in-group favoritism and, 260
  naïve realism and, 277–278
  predictors for success in, 278–279
  relationship networks and, 266
  representative choice and, 266
  sacred values and taboo trade-offs and, 272–274
  social loafing and social striving and, 260
  social networks and, 257–258
  strategies for, 279–283
Crossover probability, 343
Cuban Missile Crisis, 73
Culture/cultural differences. *See also* Cross-cultural
    negotiations
  affiliation bias and, 275–276
  biased punctuation of conflict and, 274–275

dimensions of, 255
direct vs. indirect communication, 255, 268–271
dispute resolution and, 264–265, 270–271
egalitarian vs. hierarchy, 255, 265–268
emotion and inner experience and, 260, 262
explanation of, 253–254
face concerns and, 266
faulty perceptions of conciliation and
    coercion and, 276–277
globalization and, 4–5
as iceberg, 254–255
individual vs. collective, 255–265
information communication and, 269–270
in-group favoritism and, 260
maintaining relationships and, 282–283
naïve realism and, 277–278
relationship networks and, 266
representative choice and, 266
respect for, 281
sacred values and taboo trade-offs and, 272–274
social loafing and social striving and, 260
social networks and, 257–258
time perception and, 282
Curse of knowledge, 222
CVS, 187–188

D

Deadlines, 32–33, 159–160
Deception. *See also* Lying
    detection of, 355–359
    as ethical issue, 50–51
    role of motivation and temptation in, 359–360
Decision accountability, 238
Decision making. *See also* Problem solving
    multiattribute, 331–332
    rational models of, 329
    riskless choice and, 330–332
    risky choice and, 332–345
    under uncertainty, 332–334
Decision weights, 342–345
Deductive reasoning, 207
Deep-level transfer, 192
Defection
    cost of, 297
    explanation of, 138
    recovering from, 292–295
    as unilateral choice, 288–289
Defectors, 301
Defensive attributions, 197
Defensive behavior, 141

Delayed liking, 164–165
Deterrence-based trust, 128–129
Different place, different time negotiations,
    317–320, 322
Different time, same place negotiations, 317
Diffusion of responsibility, 238
Diminishing marginal utility, 339
Direct-indirect communication
    dispute resolution and, 270–271
    explanation of, 255, 256,
        268–269
    information for agreements and, 269–270
Dispositional attributions, 138–139
Dispositionalism, 262–264
Dispute resolution
    cultural orientation and, 264–265, 270–271
    interest-based approach to, 102
    power-based approach to, 103
    rights-based approach to, 102–103
Distributive negotiations
    bargaining surplus and, 41
    bargaining zone and, 39–42
    commonly asked questions and, 40–52
    egocentrism and, 62–67
    equity principle and, 58–59
    equity restoration and, 59–60
    fairness and, 53–56, 62–65
    function of, 58
    information for, 78
    negotiator's surplus and, 41–42
    pie-slicing strategies and, 42–50
    principles of, 66–68
    procedural justice and, 60–62
    saving face and, 52–53
    social comparison and, 56–57
Distributive self-efficacy, 121
Distrust, 138–139. *See also* Trust
Divergent thinking, 206–207
Dividing the pie, 271–272
Dominance, 353–354
Dominance detection, 289
Dominance principle, 331–332
Door-in-the-face technique, 167
Downward comparison, 56, 245

E

eBay, 31
Economic Community of West African states
    (ECOWAS), 365
Economic issues, 4

Effectiveness, 67
Egalitarianism, 265
Egalitarianism-hierarchy
    explanation of, 255, 256, 265–266
    face concerns and, 266
    negotiation communication and, 268
    relationship network and, 266
    representative choice and, 266
Egocentric bias, 64, 239, 359
Egocentrism
    development of, 66–67
    explanation of, 6
    fairness issues and, 62–66
80-20 rule, 13
Embedded relationships
    business dealings and, 150
    explanation of, 144–145
    pitfalls in, 150
Emblems, 351
Emotional conflict. *See* Personal conflict
Emotional intelligence (EQ)
    explanation of, 119–120
    negotiated outcomes and, 121
Emotional style questionnaire, 117
Emotional styles, 116
Emotions
    at bargaining table, 122–123
    cultural orientation and, 260, 262
    in embedded relationships, 150–151
    explanation of, 114–115
    expressed vs. felt, 115–116
    genuine vs. strategic, 116, 118
    negative, 118–119
    positive, 120–121
    suppression of, 122
Empathy, 76–77
Endowment effects, 23–24
e-negotiations, 318–320, 322
Enlightened negotiators, 91
Epistemic motivation, 77, 79, 102
Equal-concession negotiation, 75
Equal division principle, 230
Equality, 64–65
Equality principle, 230
Equality rule
    explanation of, 54, 55
    friends and, 147
"Equal shares" bias, 225–226
Equilibrium outcome, 289
Equity
    function of, 58–59

    psychological, 60
    restoration of, 59–60
Equity formula, 58–59
Equity rule, 54, 55, 147–148
Escalation dilemmas, 308–309
Escalation of commitment process, 308–310
Ethical issues
    deception as, 50–51
    lying as, 50–51, 169–171, 175
    negotiating strategies presenting, 171–172
    psychological bias and, 175–178
    sins of omission and commission as, 172, 174
Ethnocentrism, 275
Even splits, 70
Even split technique, 50
Everyman's utility function (EU), 339
Exchange norms, 145
Exit bias, 319
Expanding the pie. *See also* Win-win negotiations
    cultural orientation and, 271, 280
    explanation of, 186–187
Expectations, 85–86
Expected utility principle
    diminishing marginal utility and, 339
    explanation of, 338
    risk-taking and, 340–342
Expected utility theory, 332–334
Expected value principle, 336–338
Explicit negotiations, 286
Expressiveness, 354–355
Extremism, 246
Extremity effect, 342
Eye contact, 351, 359

F

Face, 52–53
Facebook, 38
Face-giving/saving concerns, 52–53, 266
Face threat sensitivity (FTS), 53
Face-to-face negotiations, 314–316, 318, 326–327
Facial expressions, 351, 352, 357–358
Facilitation, 364
Fairness
    egocentric judgments of, 62–67
    equity principle and, 58–59
    equity restoration and, 59–60
    importance of, 53, 159
    norms of, 49
    principles of, 54
    procedural justice and, 60–62

in relationships, 62
  situation-specific rules of, 54–56
  social comparison and, 56–57
  strikes and, 66
  variations in views of, 141
False conflict, 73–74
False consensus effect, 194
Family businesses, 150
Faulty perceptions, 276–277
Feedback
  function of, 201
  separation of, 317
  types of, 201–202
Females. *See* Gender; Women
Final-offer arbitration, 112, 362–363
Fixed-pie perception
  explanation of, 13, 180
  issues related to, 74, 186
Flaming bias, 319–320
Flattery, 137
Flexibility, 205
Flow, 209–210
Flower child negotiators, 91
Fluency, 205
Focal points, 19
Foot-in-the-door technique, 167
Forked-tail effect, 143
Formulation, 365
Fortress story, 198
Forum, 112
Fractionating problems, 185–186
Framing effects, 159, 325
Fraternal twin model, 10
Fraudulent statements, 169. *See also* Lying
Free riders, 301
Friends
  in business with, 150
  negotiating with, 145–148
Friendship
  agreements and, 146–147
  status and, 148
Front-page test, 177
Functional distance, 136
Functional fixedness, 197–198
Fundamental attribution error, 278
Future, focus on, 133–134

G

Gain-frame, 86
Gambler's fallacy, 195

Game playing, 184–185
Game theoretic rationality
  explanation of, 345–346
  Nash bargaining theory and, 346–350
Game theory, 289–291, 296
Gender
  accountability and, 237
  assertiveness and, 162–163
  effect as bargaining table, 161–163
  mediation and, 365
  negotiators and, 99
  nonverbal communication and, 352–353
Gender stereotypes, 161–163
Generalizability, 67
General Motors, 71–72
Gestures, 351
Getting to yes bias, 235
Globalization, 4–5
Goals
  common, 132–133
  superordinate, 304
Goal-setting paradox, 46
Gold chain problem, 183, 212
Golden Rule, 177
Google, 1, 71, 153
Graduated reduction in tension (GRIT) model, 48
Grass-is-greener negotiators, 15
GRIT model, 249, 250, 293
Group negotiations. *See* Multiparty negotiations
Groupon, 1
Guanxi, 257

H

Haggling model, 180, 182–184
Halo effect
  attractiveness and, 164
  explanation of, 143
  team, 240
Hidden table, 27
Hierarchy, 265. *See also* Egalitarianism-hierarchy
Hindsight bias, 197
Horizontal thinking, 239
Hospital problem, 209
Hostile media bias, 367
Human error, 165
Humor, 328

I

IBM, 215, 216, 237
Identification-based trust, 130

Illumination phase of problem solving, 204
Illusion of control, 177
Illusion of superiority, 177
Illusory conflict. *See* False conflict
Illusory correlation, 196
Illustrators, 351, 359
Impossibility theorem, 220
Impression management, 306
Incentives, cooperation and, 302
Incidents in Negotiation
    Questionnaire: SINS II SCALE, 173–174
Incubation
    effects of, 203
    explanation of, 202
Independence of irrelevant alternatives,
    349–350
Indirect communication, 268–269. *See also* Direct-
    indirect communication
Indirect speech acts, 222
Individual decision making
    riskless choice and, 330–332
    risky choice and, 332–345
    under uncertainty, 332–334
Individualism
    explanation of, 256
    power distance and, 266–267
Individualism-collectivism
    cooperation and, 258–259
    dispositionalism vs. situationalism and, 262–264
    dispute resolution preferences and, 264–265
    emotion and inner experience and, 260, 262
    explanation of, 255–257
    in-group favoritism and, 260
    negotiations and, 261–262
    social loafing vs. social striving and, 260
    social networks and, 257–258
Individualistic negotiators
    effects of, 98, 101
    explanation of, 95
Inductive reasoning, 84, 207–209
Inequity, 59–60. *See also* Equity
Inert knowledge problem, 191–193
Information
    about reservation point, 42–44, 50
    cultural orientation and communication of,
      268–270
    for integrative agreements, 77, 78
    multiparty negotiations and management of, 224
    negotiator exchange of, 79, 81
Information pooling, 241
Information procedures, 111

Information technology
    negotiation strategies and, 326–328
    negotiator performance and, 321
    paranoia and, 325–326
    place-time model of social interaction and,
      313–322
    present state of, 4
    rapport and social norms and, 325
    risk taking and, 324–325
    social networks and, 324 (*See also*
      Social networks)
    status and power and, 322–323
    trust and, 322
In-group bias, 245–246
In-group favoritism, 260
Inquisitorial adjudication, 264
Integration, 282
Integrative agreements. *See also*
    Win-win negotiations
    friendship and, 146
    information for, 77, 78, 269–270
    issues in, 81
    pyramid model of, 72–73
    strategic framework for reaching, 88–90
Integrative negotiations. *See also* Win-win
    negotiations
    decision-making model of, 88, 89
    explanation of, 70
    stages in, 90–91
Integrative self-efficacy, 121
Intercultural communication. *See* Cross-cultural
    negotiations
Interest-based approach
    application of, 102–104, 110–111
    cognitive processing and, 110
    effects of, 108
    explanation of, 102, 103
    process intervention and, 109
    strategies to refocus on, 108–112, 114
Interests
    focus on, 102, 103, 110–111
    misrepresentation of, 170
Intergroup negotiations
    challenges of, 244–246
    explanation of, 244
    stereotyping in, 244, 276
    strategies to optimize, 246–249
Internal value conflict, 151
Interpersonal escalation dilemmas, 308–309
Interpersonal spacing, 351
Issues mix, 89

J

Job-offer negotiations
   post-offer, 376–378
   preparation for, 370–373
   steps in actual, 373–376
Justice, procedural, 60–62
Justifiability, pie-slicing and, 66–68

K

Knowledge-based trust, 129–130
Koyoto Protocol, 285

L

Labeling, 110
Law of large numbers, 337
Letter sequence problem, 182, 212
Light-of-day test, 177
Linkage effects, 30
List technique, 166
Logrolling, 85
Lose-lose effect, 73–74
Loss-frame, 86
Loyalists, 64
Lying. *See also* Deception
   about reservation point, 50–51
   conditions for, 175, 176
   cost of, 175
   examination of, 169–170
   monitoring-dependent, 360
   monitoring-independent, 360

M

Majority rule
   explanation of, 219
   voting and, 219–221
Mandatory negotiations, 110
Manipulation, 365
Marginalization, 283
Market pricing, 148
Med-arb, 112
Mediation. *See also* Third-party
   intervention
   cultural orientation and, 264
   function of, 111, 361–363
   gender and, 365
   preferences related to, 365
Mediation-arbitration (med-arb), 363. *See also*
   Third-party intervention

Mental model of negotiations
   cost-benefit analysis as, 184
   explanation of, 2, 180
   game planing as, 184–185
   haggling as, 180
   partnership as, 185
   problem solving as, 185
Mere contact strategy, 248–249
Mere exposure effect, 134–135
Merit-based rule. *See* Equity rule
Message tuning, 234
Microexpressions, 358–359
Microsoft, 157
Millennials, 3
Mimicry, 137–138
Minitrials, 111–112
Mirroring, 137–138
Miscommunication, 138. *See also*
   Communication
Misrepresentation, 154
Misrepresentation, of reservation point,
   50–51
Mixed-motive enterprise, 13
Monolithic parties, 27
Moods, 115, 120
Motivated communication, 360
Motivation
   epistemic, 77, 79, 102
   impact on lying and deception, 359–360
Motivational styles
   assessment of, 95–98
   clashes between, 101
   convergence and, 101–102
   strategic issues concerning, 98–102
   types of, 94–95
Multiattribute utility technique (MAUT),
   331–332
Multiparty negotiations
   analysis of, 216–218
   communication breakdowns and,
     221–223
   dealing with coalitions and, 217
   explanation of, 217
   formulating trade-offs and, 218–219
   key strategies for, 224–226, 250–251
   voting and majority rule and, 219–221
Multiple audience problem, 222–223
Multiple-offer strategy, 82–84
Multistep negotiation procedure, 110
Myopia, 151
Mystery shoppers, 12

N

Naïve realism, 246, 277–278
Nash bargaining theory
  explanation of, 346
  independence of equivalent utility representations
    and, 348–349
  independence or irrelevant alternatives and, 349–350
  Pareto-optimality and, 346–348
  symmetry and, 348
  uniqueness and, 346
Nash product, 350
Nash solution, 346, 348–350
National health care legislation, 71
National Rehabilitation Medicine Research Council
    (NRMR), 227
Necklace problem, 183, 212
Needs-based rule, 54
Negative advertising, 298–299
Negative bargaining zone, 40–41
Negative emotion
  effect of, 118–119
  explanation of, 116
Negative transfer, 198–199
Negotiation dance, 39, 318
Negotiation preparation
  alternative identification and, 20
  BATNA identification and, 15–16
  confidence and, 26
  counterfactual thinking and, 24–25
  endowment effects and, 23–24
  equivalent multi-issue proposal identification
    and, 20
  focal points and, 19
  importance of, 13, 36–37
  issue identification and, 19–20
  reservation points and, 16–19
  risk and, 20–23
  self-assessment and, 13–26, 37
  situation assessment and, 28–37
  sizing up other party and, 26–28, 37
  sunk costs and, 19
  sure thing principle and, 25–26
  target identification and, 14–15, 19
  worksheets for, 37, 79
Negotiations. *See also* Cross-cultural negotiations;
    Distributive negotiations; Win-win negotiations
  avoiding escalation of commitment in, 310–311
  with business people, 148–150
  conventions related to, 35
  cooperative, 286

creativity in, 180, 181, 185–191 (*See also* Creative
    negotiation agreements; Creative negotiation
    strategies; Creativity)
  different place, different time, 317–320, 322
  different time, same place, 317
  embedded relationships and, 150
  equal-concession, 75
  ethical, 50–51, 169–178 (*See also* Ethical issues)
  explanation of, 2–3
  explicit, 286
  face-to-face, 314–316, 318, 326–327
  with friends, 145–148
  intergroup, 244–249
  involving more than one offer in, 35–36
  job offer, 370–378
  legal issues related to, 31–32
  linkage effects of, 30
  location of, 34
  loop-backs to, 111–112
  mandatory, 110
  mental model of, 180, 182–185
  mixed-motive nature of, 42
  multiparty, 216–226
  multiple-offer strategy for, 82–84
  myths about, 8–10
  of necessity, 29
  noncooperative, 286
  one-shot, 28
  of opportunity, 29
  for package deals, 81–82
  precedent in, 36
  principal-agent, 231–236
  prolonged, 90
  public vs. private, 34–35
  questioning during, 77, 79
  relationships in, 143, 150–151
  repetitive, 28
  revealing information during, 79, 81
  same time, different place, 316–317
  side deals in, 71
  single-issue, 70
  skills in, 3–8
  tacit, 286–295, 308–311 (*See also* Social dilemmas;
    Tacit negotiations)
  team, 240–244
  technology-mediated, 326–328 (*See also*
    Information technology)
  third-party intervention in, 35
  as transactions of disputes, 30
Negotiation styles
  emotions and emotional knowledge and, 114–123

interests, rights, and power model of disputing and, 102–114

motivational orientation and, 94–102

overview of, 93–94

Negotiators

authority of, 266

black-hat/white-hat (BH/WH), 48–49

competitive, 95

cooperative, 95

enlightened, 91

flower child, 91

gender and, 99

grass-is-greener, 15

individualistic, 95, 98, 101

major concerns of, 126–127

old-fashioned, 90

overaspiring or positional, 14–15, 20

power differential between, 36

soft, 93

tough, 93

training for, 111

underaspiring, 14

white-hat/black-hat (WH/BH), 48, 49

Networks. *See* Social networks

Neutrality, 368–369

NextEra Energy Resources, 69

Nez Pearce Tribe, 367

Nine dot problem, 183, 212–213

Nonspecific-compensation negotiated agreement, 188

Nonverbal communication

deception and, 355–360

dominance and, 353–354

elements of, 351

explanation of, 315, 351–352

gender and, 352–353

personal charisma and, 354–355

Nonverbal expression, 352–353

Nonverbal reception, 353

Norm of commitment, 304

O

Offers

decision to make final, 52

facts to support, 49

function of counteroffers, 47

making first, 46–47

retraction of, 171, 172

value of, 84

Old-fashioned negotiators, 90

One-shot decision, 289–290

One-shot negotiations, 28

OPEC (Organization of the Petroleum Exporting Countries), 297

Optimizing, 7

Options, 157

Organizations, interdependence within, 3–4

Originality, 205

Oslo Accords (1993), 87

Outcome control, 363–364

Out-group homogeneity bias, 247

Overaspiring negotiators. *See* Positional negotiators

Overconfidence

effect of, 26, 199–200

ethics and, 177

Overconfidence bias, 367–368

P

Package deals, 81–82

Paralinguistic cues, 351

Paranoia, 325–326

Paraphrasing, 110

Pareto-efficient frontier, 346–348

Pareto-optimal frontier, 73, 346–348

Particularism, 126

Parties

BATNA and, 27–28

explanation of, 27

interests and positions of, 27

monolithic, 27

Partnership model, 185

Passive misrepresentation, 170

Pepsi, 292–293

Perceived power, 155–156

Peripheral route persuasion tactics, 160

delayed liking as, 164–165

door-in-the-face technique as, 167

foot-in-the-door technique as, 167

gender as, 161–163

human error and, 165

physical appearance as, 163–164

reactance technique as, 166–167

reciprocity vs. complementarity as, 166

social networks as, 163

social proof as, 166

status as, 160–161

that's not-all technique as, 167

unconscious priming as, 166

Perseverance effect, 196

Personal conflict, 132

Personal escalation dilemmas, 308

Person in a room decision, 181, 211
Perspective taking, 76–77
Persuasion, 156, 168
Persuasion tactics
  central route, 156–160
  explanation of, 156
  peripheral route, 160–167
Physical appearance, 163–164
Physical presence, 135–136
Pie slicer profiles, 64
Pie slicing. *See* Distributive negotiations
Pigpen problem, 184, 213
Pivotal power, 230
Place-time model of social interaction
  different place, different time and, 317–320, 322
  different time, same place and, 317
  explanation of, 313–314, 328
  face-to-face communication and, 315–316
  same time, different place and, 316–317
Positional negotiators, 14–15, 20
Positions, lying about, 170
Positive bargaining zone, 39, 40, 366
Positive emotion
  effect of, 120–121
  explanation of, 116, 120
Possibility effect, 342
Postdispute analysis/feedback, 112
Postsettlement settlement strategy, 87–88
Posture, 351
Potential power, 155
Power
  of agenda, 157
  of alternatives, 157
  analysis of, 155–156
  BATNA as source of, 154–155, 266
  of contrast, 158
  effects on high-power people, 168
  effects on less powerful people, 168
  focus on, 102, 103
  information technology and, 322–323
  network, 163
  nonverbal cues to transmit, 353–354
  of options, 157
  perceived, 155–156
  pivotal, 230
  potential, 155
  realized, 156
  of reciprocity, 101
  verbal and nonverbal skills of, 162
Power-based approach
  application of, 105–107

costs associated with, 113
explanation of, 103
strategies to refocus, 108–112, 114
third-party interventions and, 112
types of, 107
when to use, 113–114
Power distance, 266–267
Power tactics, 156
Pratt Whitney, 81–82
Preferences, 170
Premature concessions, 20, 47, 74
Preparation. *See* Negotiation preparation
Preparation phase of problem solving, 202
Presettlement settlements (PreSS)
  explanation of, 87
  search for, 87–88
Primary status characteristics, 160
Primary table, 238
Priming the pump, 165
Principal-agent negotiations
  advantages of, 232
  disadvantages of, 233–235
  explanation of, 231–232
  strategies for working with, 235–236
Priorities, 170
Prisoner's dilemma
  decision making in, 288–289
  explanation of, 286–288, 297
  psychological analysis of tit-for-tat and, 291–295
  rational analysis in, 289–291
  risk and, 297
Privatization, 303
Probability
  crossover, 343
  estimation of, 208–209
  risk and, 333
Probability weighting function, 342–343
Problem representation, 186
Problem solving. *See also* Decision making
  divergent thinking and, 206–207
  explanation of, 185, 186
  rational model of, 204
  steps in, 202–204
  threats to, 191–200
Procedural justice, 60–62
Process control, 364
Process intervention, 109
Propinquity effect, 135
Proportionality of contributions principle. *See* Equity rule
Prospect theory, 342

Prototypes, 253
Pseudosacred, 274
Pseudostatus characteristics, 160–161
Psychological contracts, 304
Psychological contrast effect, 158
Psychological distancing model, 314
Psychological equity, 60
Psychological strategies, to maximize cooperation,
    301, 302, 304–307
Psychological trust-building strategies
    flattery as, 137
    mere exposure effect as, 135–136
    mimicry and mirroring as, 137–138
    physical presence as, 135–136
    reciprocity as, 136–137
    schmoozing as, 137
    self-disclosure as, 138
    similarity as, 134
Public goods dilemmas, 298–299, 301
Punctuation, 274–275
Punishment, 306
PXP (Plains Exploration and Production Company), 179

Q

QUE (Quality of Communication Experience), 279
Questioning, during negotiation, 77, 79

R

Raiffa's hybrid model, 230
Rapport, 325
Ratification, 32
Rational analysis, 289–291
Rational bargaining theory, 273
Rational emotion, 116
Rationality
    game theoretic, 329, 345–350
    individual, 329–345 (*See also* Individual decision
        making)
    principles of, 273
Rational problem-solving model, 204
Reactance technique, 166–167
Reactive devaluation, 15
Realignment, issue, 186
Realized power, 156
Reasoning
    deductive, 207
    inductive, 84, 207–209
Reciprocal trade-offs, 219
Reciprocity
    complementarity vs., 166

effects of, 109
    power of, 101
Reciprocity principle, 108, 136–137
Reducibility axiom, 335
Reference point
    endowment effects and, 23–24
    explanation of, 21, 159
Regressiveness principle, 343
Regulation, 303
Reinforcement, 101, 121
Rejection, 90
Rejection-then-retreat technique, 167
Relational accommodation, 75
Relational self-construals (RSC), 147
Relationships
    causal, 195–196
    constituent, 236–239
    embedded, 144–145, 150
    fairness in, 62
    focus on long-term, 75
    in negotiating with businesspeople,
        148–150
    in negotiating with friends, 145–148
    role of, 143–144
    trust in, 70, 139
Repetitive negotiations, 28
Representativeness heuristic, 194–195
Reputations, 142–143
Reservation point
    determining your, 16–19
    explanation of, 16
    lying or misrepresenting, 50–51
    manipulation of counterparty's, 52
    revealing information about,
        42–44, 50
    target point vs, 19
Reservation price, 170
Resource assessment, 88–89
Resource conservation dilemmas,
    298, 301
Reverse Golden Rule, 177
Reverse psychology. *See* Reactance
    technique
Richness, 313
Rights, 102–103
Rights-based approach
    application of, 104–105
    costs associated with, 113
    explanation of, 102–103
    strategies to refocus, 108–112, 114
    when to use, 113–114

Risk
   assessment of, 20–23
   attitude toward, 338, 340
   BATNA, 22–23
   contractual, 23
   differences in attitudes toward, 86
   information technology and, 324–325
   probability and, 333
   strategic, 21–22
Risk-aversion
   example of, 100
   explanation of, 21, 159, 338
Riskless choice, 330–332
Risk-taking, 340–342
Risky choice situations
   combination rules and, 345
   decision weights and, 342–345
   expected utility principle and, 338–342
   expected utility theory and, 332–334
   explanation of, 332–334
   utility function and, 334–339
Role modeling, 177
Ruling phase, 363
Ruthless competitors, 64

S

Sacred, 274
Sacred values, 272–274
Saints, 64
Same time, different place mode of communication,
      316–317
Satisfaction, 70
Satisfaction and, pie-slicing and, 68
Satisficing, 7
Scarce resource competition, 29
Schmoozing, 137, 327–328
SCO Group, 215–216
Secondary status characteristics, 160, 161
Second table, constituent relationships and,
      237–238
Secrecy, 360
Secular values, 273
Selective attention, 199
Self-assessment, 13–26, 37
Self-disclosure, 138
Self-efficacy, 121
Self-enhancement, 57
Self-evaluation, accurate, 57
Self-fulfilling prophesy, 161
Self-improvement, 57

Self-reinforcing incompetence, 7–8
Separation, 283
Sequential bargaining, 226
Set effect, 198–199
Shapley model, 230
Short-term memory, 200
Side deals, 71
Similarity-attraction effect, 134
Simplicity, pie-slicing and, 67
Sinister attribution bias, 320, 322
Sins of commission, 172
Sins of omission, 172, 174
Situational attribution, 138–139
Situationalism, 262–264
Social capital, 163
Social comparison
   downward, 245
   explanation of, 56
   goals of, 57
   negotiation breakdown resulting from,
      99–100
   self-interest vs., 56, 57
   types of, 56–57
Social dilemmas. *See also* Tacit negotiations
   business as, 287
   cooperation building in, 301–307
   explanation of, 286, 295, 297
   tragedy of the commons and, 297–298
   types of, 298–301
   ultimatum, 295–296
   volunteer, 295
Social interaction, place-time model of, 313–322,
      328
Social loafing, 260
Social motivations, 94, 95. *See also* Motivational
      styles
Social networks
   in business, 150
   capitalization on, 133
   cultural orientation and, 257–258
   information technology and, 324
   manipulation of, 171
   power or, 163
Social norms, 325
Social proof principle, 166
Social sanctions, 306
Social status, 353
Social striving, 260
Solitary brainstorming, 225
Spontaneous sending, 354–355
Star Wars, 249

Status
information technology and, 322–323
in negotiations, 160–161
types of, 160
Stereotypes
explanation of, 253
gender, 161–163
in intergroup negotiations, 244, 276
Stick problem, 182, 211–212
Sticky ties, 151
Strategic risk, 21–22
Strategic voting, 221
Structural strategies to maximize cooperation,
301–304
Structured contingencies, 188–191
Subadditivity, 343
Subcertainty, 343
Subgame perfect equilibrium, 296
Subjective Value Inventory (SVI), 126–127
Suboptimal outcome, 40
Substantiation, 83
Substitutability axiom, 335
Suckers, 301
Sunk costs, 19, 311
Superiority, illusion of, 177
Superordinate goals, 304
Superrationality, 295
Sure thing principle, 25–26
Surface-level transfer, 192
Surplus
bargaining, 41
negotiator's, 41–42
Susan and Martha problem, 183, 212
Suspicion, 138
Sweetening the deal, 167
Swift trust, 148–149
Syllogisms, 207, 208
Symbolic conflict, 247
Symmetric bargaining, 348

T

Tacit negotiations. *See also* Social dilemmas
commitment escalation and, 308–311
cooperation and defection and, 288–289
explanation of, 286
psychological analysis of tit-for-tat and, 291–295
rational analysis and, 289–291
Target point
explanation of, 14
function of, 44–46
identification of, 14–15
reservation point vs., 19
Task conflict, 132
Team efficacy effect, 240
Team halo effect, 240
Team negotiations
challenges of, 241–242
explanation of, 240–241
strategies to improve, 242–244
Teleconferences, 327
Temporal synchrony bias, 318
Temptation, 359–360
That's-not-all technique, 167
Third-party advice, 177
Third-party intervention
arbitration as, 362–363
challenges of, 365–368
effects of, 35
explanation of, 361
key choice points in, 363–365
maintaining neutrality in, 368–369
mediation-arbitration as, 363
mediation as, 361–362
in power contests, 112
strategies to enhance, 369
Threats, 107
Time horizon, 33–34
Time-related issues
BATNA and, 15–16
for concessions, 49
costs and, 33
cultural perceptions of time, 282
deadlines and, 32–33, 159–160
differences in time preferences, 86
distance and, 317
for integrative agreements, 75–76
time horizon and, 33–34
Tit-for-tat strategy
effectiveness of, 291–295
explanation of, 291
Touching, 351
Tradable environmental allowance (TEA), 303–304
Tradable permits, 303–304
Trade-offs
explanation of, 90
in multiparty negotiation, 218–219
scarce resource conflicts and, 273
Traditional arbitration, 362
Tragedy of the commons, 297–298
Transfer
explanation of, 191–192
rates of, 192–193

Transitivity, 335
Transparency, illusion of, 81
Triangulation, 357
Trust
    affective route to build, 132, 257–258
    cognitive route to build, 132, 257–258
    cultural orientation and, 257–258
    deterrence-based, 128–129
    identification-based, 130
    importance of, 128
    information technology and, 322
    knowledge-based, 129–130
    psychological strategies to build, 134–138
    rational and deliberate mechanisms to build, 131,
        133–134
    repairing broken, 139–142
    swift, 148–149
    threats to, 138–139
Trust relationship grid, 130, 131–132
Tumor problem, 192, 197–198
Tunnel vision, 224

U

Ultimatum dilemma, 295–296
Unanimity rule, 219
Unbundling, 89
Uncertainty
    decision making under, 332
    unemployment and, 4
Unconscious priming, 165
Underaspiring negotiators, 14
Unemployment, uncertainty and, 4
Unilateral concessions, 48
Uniqueness axiom, 346
United Airlines, 49, 104
Unwarranted causation, 195–196
Upward comparison, 56
Utility functions
    axioms of, 334–336
    behavior of, 348–349
    explanation of, 334

V

Valuation, differences in, 85
Value function, 343–345
Venting, 141

Verification phase of problem solving, 204
Videoconferences, 327
Vocal cues, 351
Voice tone, 358, 359
Volunteer dilemma, 295
Voting
    majority rule and, 219–221
    strategic, 221

W

Walgreens, 187–188
Wal-Mart, 83
Water jugs problem, 181–182, 211
Water lilies problem, 184, 213–214
Welfare-based allocation. *See* Needs-based rule
White-hat/black-hat (WH/BH) negotiators, 48, 49
WikiLeaks, 312, 313
Winner's curse, 14, 46
Win-win negotiations
    assessing potential of, 70–72
    effective strategies for, 76–87
    explanation of, 70
    false conflict and, 73–74
    fixed-pie perception and, 74
    ineffective strategies for, 75–76
    integrative agreements and, 72–73,
        88–90
    presettlement settlements and, 87–88
    relationships and, 144
    stages in, 90–91
    training in, 369
Wise counselor, 110
Women. *See also* Gender
    accountability and, 237–238
    at bargaining table, 161–163
    nonverbal communication and, 352–353
Words/phrases, as emotional triggers, 123
World War II, 276–277

Y

Yucaipa, 224

Z

Zappos, 236–237
Zone of possible agreements (ZOPA). *See*
        Bargaining zone